T0073480

Data Communications and Network Technologies

Huawei Technologies Co., Ltd.

Data Communications and Network Technologies

 Springer

Huawei Technologies Co., Ltd.
Hangzhou, China

This work was supported by Huawei Technologies Co., Ltd.

ISBN 978-981-19-3028-7   ISBN 978-981-19-3029-4   (eBook)
https://doi.org/10.1007/978-981-19-3029-4

Jointly published with Posts & Telecom Press, Beijing, China
The print edition is not for sale in China (Mainland). Customers from China (Mainland) please order the
print book from: Posts & Telecom Press.

This Springer imprint is published by the registered company Springer Nature Singapore Pte Ltd.
The registered company address is: 152 Beach Road, #21-01/04 Gateway East, Singapore 189721,
Singapore

Preface

Computer network textbooks are mainly divided into two categories: computer network textbooks for colleges and universities, and network engineer certification textbooks of vendors such as Huawei, H3C, and Cisco.

Computer network textbooks for colleges and universities mainly focus on computer communication protocols and organize contents of each chapter by TCP/IP layers, without specific experiments and operations for these computer network theories. As a basic course, it is reasonable to introduce principles and theories, which are applicable to devices of all network vendors. Students in colleges and universities have zero experience in operating and configuring network devices, and have not even seen them before, so they are not well informed about the various applications on the Internet. Consequently, they will feel learning theoretical network courses relatively abstract and will not realize how these theories can contribute to their future work.

This book uses Huawei network devices to set up computer networks and uses virtual machines to construct learning environments so as to design experiments and cases for computer network theories. It can train network engineers who can both have a deep understanding on the theories of computer data communications and use Huawei routers, switches as well as wired and wireless devices to design and set up campus networks.

Content Organization of This Book

This book contains 18 chapters, and the content of each chapter is briefly described as follows:

Chapters 1 to 4 explain the theoretical basis of communication technologies, including data communications basics, TCP/IP protocol, management of Huawei devices, IP address, and subnetting.

Chapter 5 explains routing basics, including the basic concepts of routing, static routing, route summarization, and default routing.

Chapter 6 introduces dynamic routing, including introduction to dynamic routing, dynamic routing protocol OSPF, and the configuration of OSPF protocol.

Chapter 7 explains how switches work, VLAN and inter-VLAN routing.

Chapter 8 elaborates Spanning Tree Protocol, link aggregation, Smart Link, and Monitor Link technology.

Chapter 9 is an introduction to network security, including the working principles of ACL and AAA.

Chapter 10 illustrates network address translation, including NAT types, implementation of Static NAT, NAPT, Easy IP, and implementation of NAT Server.

Chapter 11 explains Dynamic Host Configuration Protocol, enabling DHCP Server on the router so as to configure IP addresses for the computers in the network.

Chapter 12 describes the enterprise network WLAN, introducing the basic concepts of WLAN, the working principles and configuration implementation of WLAN.

Chapter 13 covers IPv6, including IPv6 addressing, IPv6 address configuration, IPv6 static routing and dynamic routing.

Chapter 14 illustrates WANs, mainly PPP protocol and PPPoE protocol.

Chapter 15 explains the typical networking architectures and case practices of campus networks, including the basic concepts and the case practices of the campus network. Among them, the hands-on practice includes the design of a networking scheme, VLAN design and planning, IP address design and planning, IP address assignment methods, routing design, WLAN design and planning, reliability design, egress NAT design, and security design.

Chapter 16 covers network management and operation and maintenance, including SNMP principles and configuration, and the configuration of Network Time Protocol (NTP) to synchronize network equipment time.

Chapter 17 explains SND and NFV.

Chapter 18 introduces network programming and automation, using Python for network device management.

Resources of this Book

Supporting PPT.

Supporting lab manual.

After-class exercises and answers.

Syllabus and teaching plan.

QQ group and WeChat group for teaching, providing Q&A and required software.

Applicable Readers

This book is a basic data communications textbook, positioned as a computer network textbook for undergraduate colleges and universities. The data communications, knowledge, and network cases in the book are designed for the application of computer network theories, and readers can take the HuaWei Certified ICT Associate (HCIA) certification after learning it.

This book is suitable for students of network engineering and software engineering in colleges and universities; for employees engaged in IT operation and maintenance, network security, software development, and software testing; for graduate students in computer science; and for students and employees who have passed Huawei HCIA.

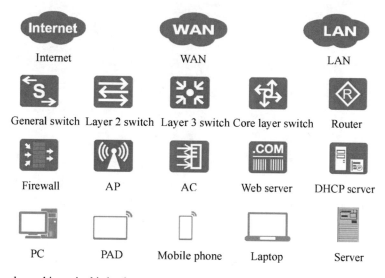

Internet WAN LAN

General switch Layer 2 switch Layer 3 switch Core layer switch Router

Firewall AP AC Web server DHCP server

PC PAD Mobile phone Laptop Server

Commonly used icons in this book

Authors of this Book

This book is organized and compiled by Huawei Technologies Co., Ltd. and is written by Han Ligang. Sun Rui, Mao Jingli, Li Xianzhi, Han Lihui, Wen Jing, Ren Shuo, Wang Yanhua, Ma Qing, Ding Leilei, Li Shengchun, Li Xiaopeng, Wang Yuanchen, Wang Xueguang, Wang Xiaodong, Guo Zhipeng, and Xu Kan have also participated in writing some of the contents.

Hangzhou, China
December 2021

Huawei Technologies Co., Ltd.

Contents

About the Author

Huawei Technologies Co., Ltd. Founded in 1987, Huawei is a leading global provider of information and communications technology (ICT) infrastructure and smart devices. We have approximately 197,000 employees and we operate in over 170 countries and regions, serving more than three billion people around the world.

Huawei's mission is to bring digital to every person, home, and organization for a fully connected, intelligent world. To this end, we will: drive ubiquitous connectivity and promote equal access to networks to lay the foundation for the intelligent world; provide the ultimate computing power to deliver ubiquitous cloud and intelligence; build powerful digital platforms to help all industries and organizations become more agile, efficient, and dynamic; redefine user experience with AI, offering consumers more personalized and intelligent experiences across all scenarios, including home, travel, office, entertainment, and fitness and health.

Chapter 1
Network Fundamentals

This chapter introduces the concept of network and Internet, common network topologies, network types, common networking equipment (routers, switches, firewalls and wireless devices), the design of Layer 2 enterprise LAN and Layer 3 enterprise LAN, and the concept of WAN.

1.1 Overview of Network

1.1.1 Network and Internet

If you want to interconnect two computers, you can connect them directly through a network cable; however, if you want to interconnect three, four or even more computers, then network devices will be needed. As shown in Fig. 1.1, a network is be formed by connecting computers in close proximity to a switch via network cables.

For the communication among multiple networks in different locations, they need to be connected through a router. Routers have WAN ports that can be used for long-distance data transmission and data packets forwarding between different networks. Multiple networks are interconnected by routers to form the Internet, as shown in Fig. 1.2.

The Internet was originally formed by interconnecting the networks of universities and research institutions in the United States, and later more and more companies and government agencies were connected to the network. Gradually, the open network initiated in the United States was no longer limited within the country, and networks in a growing number of countries around the world are connected to this open network through submarine optical cables, satellites and so on, making it the largest global Internet at present, as shown in Fig. 1.3. Planning the network, configuring network devices and choosing the best path for data packets are the main and imperative tasks of network engineers.

© The Author(s) 2023
Huawei Technologies Co., Ltd., *Data Communications and Network Technologies*,
https://doi.org/10.1007/978-981-19-3029-4_1

Fig. 1.1 Network
illustration

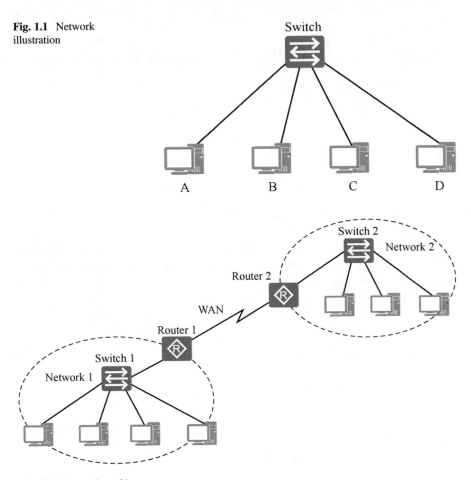

Fig. 1.2 Illustration of internet

1.1.2 Network Topology

Network devices (such as computers, routers, switches, etc.) are connected into
different network topology through transmission media (such as twisted pair and
optical fiber). Each network topology has its own advantages and disadvantages.
According to the topological form, networks can be divided into star network, bus
network, ring network, tree network, full mesh network, partial mesh network and
hybrid network, as shown in Fig. 1.4.

- Star network: al nodes are connected to a central node.

  - Advantages: it is easy to add new nodes to the network. Communication data
    must be relayed through the central node, which makes it easy for network
    monitoring.

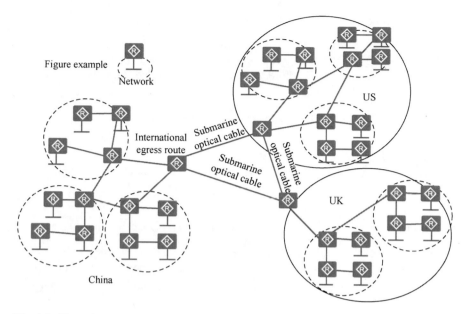

Fig. 1.3 Illustration of the internet

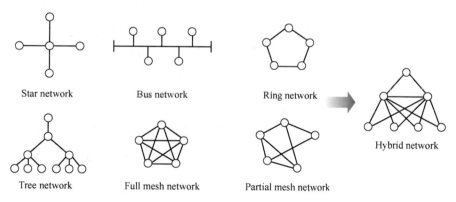

Fig. 1.4 Network topologies

  – Disadvantage: if the central node fails, the communication of the whole
    network will be affected.

• Bus network: all nodes are connected to a bus (e.g., coaxial cable).

  – Advantages: it is easy to install and doesn't require many cables; if a node
    fails, usually the communication of the whole network will not be affected.
  – Disadvantages: if the bus fails, the communication of the whole network will
    be affected; a message sent by one node can be received by all other nodes,
    which leads to low security.

- Ring network: all nodes are connected into a closed ring.
    - Advantages: it doesn't require many cables.
    - Disadvantage: it is troublesome to add new nodes, which requires the original "ring" to be interrupted before new nodes can be added to form a "new ring".

- Tree network: the tree structure is actually a layered star structure.
    - Advantages: it can quickly connect multiple star networks together, and can be layered as needed, which makes it easy for network expansion.
    - Disadvantages: the higher level the nodes are in, the more serious the network problems will be.

- Full mesh network: all nodes are connected to each other through cables.
    - Advantages: high reliability and high communication efficiency.
    - Disadvantages: each node requires a large number of physical ports, as well as a great many interconnecting cables, which is costly and difficult for network expansion.

- Partial mesh network: only the key nodes are interconnected with each other.
    - Advantages: lower cost than full mesh network.
    - Disadvantage: lower reliability than full mesh network.

- Hybrid network: this network topology is formed by combining the star, tree and partial mesh networks mentioned earlier.
    - Advantages: it has the characteristics of a star network, that is it is easy to increase nodes and monitor traffic in the center, as well as the layered characteristics of a tree network, and in the meantime, it is as reliable as a partial mesh network.
    - Disadvantages: redundant equipment and cables are required, which results in high cost.

1.1.3   Network Types

Computer networks can be classified into different types according to the geographic coverage or users.

1. Classification by the network geographical coverage
    According to the network geographical coverage, computer networks can be categorized into Local Area Network (LAN), Wide Area Network (WAN) and Metropolitan Area Network (MAN), which is between a LAN and WAN.

LANs usually cover an area of a few square kilometers, and its main function is to connect several terminal computers in close proximity (e.g., within a household, within a building or several buildings, and within a campus.). Generally, organizations purchase their own equipment to set up LANs. The technologies used in LAN include Ethernet, Wi-Fi, etc.

WANs usually cover a geographical area of tens to thousands of kilometers, and are able to connect multiple cities or countries, or span several continents and meanwhile provide long-distance communication, thus forming an international remote network. For example, an enterprise has two LANs in Beijing and Shanghai, and when these two LANs are connected, a WAN is created. Generally, WAN requires to lease the line of Internet Service Provider (ISP) and pay a certain fee to ISP for bandwidth every year. The bandwidth is related to the fee paid. In the early days, households used Asymmetric Digital Subscriber Line (ADSL) to dial up to access the Internet, so there were different bandwidth standards such as 2 Mbit/s bandwidth, 4 Mbit/s bandwidth and 8 Mbit/s bandwidth, and corresponding charges. The technologies used in WAN include PPP, PPPoE and HDLC. The larger ISPs in China are China Telecom, China Mobile and China Unicom.

A MAN is a larger LAN, which requires higher cost but can provide faster transmission. It improves the transmission media in LAN and expands its coverage to include a university campus or a city. Its main role is to connect hosts, databases and LANs in different locations within the same city. MANs are similar to WANs in terms of the role they play, but they differ in implementation and performance. A MAN is a large-scale LAN, using technologies such as Ethernet (10 Gbit/s, 100 Gbit/s) and World Interoperability for Microwave Access (WiMAX), which is similar to LAN technology.

2. Classification by users of the network

According to their users, computer networks can be classified into public networks and private networks.

A public network refers to a large network funded by a telecom company (state-owned or private). "Public" means that the network is available to anyone who is willing to pay for it as stipulated by the telecom company. The Internet is the largest public network in the world.

A private network is a network built by a department for the special business needs of the organization. This kind of network does not provide services to people outside the organization. For example, military, railway, and electric power systems all have their own private networks.

Both public and private networks are able to handle a variety of services. If they transmit computer data, they are called public computer networks and private computer networks, respectively.

1.2   Networking Equipment

Figure 1.5 shows a typical enterprise computer network, which looks a little complex, but can be seen as a network with a Layer 3 structure, i.e., access layer, aggregation layer and core layer. The only difference is that in order to avoid single point of failure, a high availability architecture with dual aggregation and dual core layers is applied. In addition, firewalls are deployed on the links to the Internet of the egress area, and the Internet is connected via dual links.

The devices in this network are switches, routers, firewalls, wireless devices, etc. The functions of various network devices are introduced in detail below.

1. Switch

   As shown in Fig. 1.6, in a campus network, the switch is generally the closest device to the end user. The network formed by an Ethernet switch is a broadcast domain, that is the broadcast frames sent by one node can be received by the rest of the nodes.

2. Router

   As shown in Fig. 1.7, a router is responsible for forwarding messages in different network segments, selecting a suitable path to deliver the message to the next router or destination based on the destination IP address of the message received, and the last router in the path is responsible for delivering the message to the destination host. Routers isolate broadcast domains, run routing protocols, build routing tables, maintain routing tables, forward IP messages, connect to

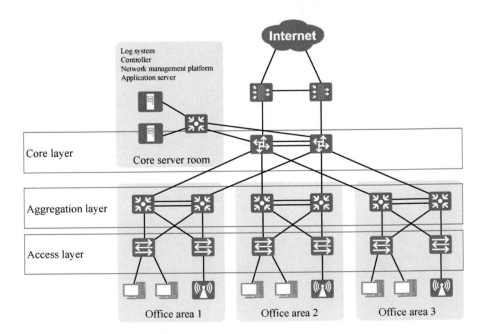

Fig. 1.5 Enterprise computer network

Fig. 1.6 Switch

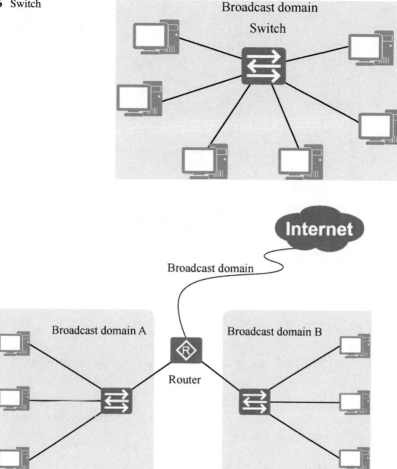

Fig. 1.7 Router

WANs, perform network address translation and are connected to networks formed by switches.

3. Firewall

A firewall is a network security device, as shown in Fig. 1.8, which is used to control secure communication between two networks with varying trust levels (e.g., the internal network of the enterprise and the Internet). It monitors, restricts and modifies the data flow crossing the firewall by formulating and implementing a unified security policy, so as to prevent external users of the network from illegally accessing important information resources inside the network. In other words, it shields the information, structure and operation status inside the network from those outside the network as much as possible, so as to provide security

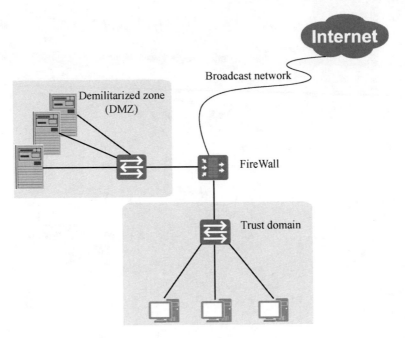

Fig. 1.8 Firewall

protection for the internal network of the enterprise. The main functions of a firewall are as follows.

- Isolation of networks with different security levels.
- Implementation of access control (security policies) between networks of varying security levels.
- User identity authentication.
- Implementation of remote access.
- Implementation of data encryption and virtual private network services.
- Performing network address translation.
- Other security functions.

4. Wireless devices

   Common wireless devices are access points (AP) and access controllers (AC).

   - Access points

     An access point is used for a wireless switch of the wireless network, and is also the core of the wireless network. An access point enables mobile computer users to access the wired network, and is mainly used for broadband home, inside the building and campus. It typically covers a distance ranging from tens of meters to hundreds of meters.

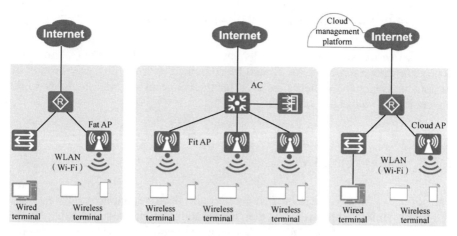

Fig. 1.9 Access points

Access points generally support three working modes, namely, fat AP, fit AP and cloud AP, as shown in Fig. 1.9. According to the demand of network planning, various modes can be chosen flexibly.

Fat AP: it is suitable for home, as it works independently, requires separate configuration, provides single function, and is low-cost.

Fit AP: it is suitable for large and medium-sized enterprises, as it needs to be used in conjunction with ACs, requires the unified management and configuration by AC, and provides rich functions.

Cloud AP: Cloud AP is interconnected with cloud management platform and covers tens of thousands of square meters. With the help of cloud management platform, cloud AP is capable of plug-and-play deployment and cloud-based remote operation and maintenance in small and medium-sized simple networks and large complex networks. The "cloud management platform + Cloud AP" networking model has become the preferred option for enterprises with a multitude of branches, such as retail stores, small and medium enterprises as well as hotels.

- Access controllers

An access controller (AC) is an access point control device of wireless LAN, which is responsible for converging and connecting data from different APs to the Internet, and performing the configuration management of AP devices and control functions such as authentication, management, broadband access and security of wireless users.

Access controllers are generally located in the aggregation layer of the whole network, providing wireless data control services with high capacity, high performance, high reliability, easy installation and easy maintenance. It has multiple advantages, such as flexible networking, green and energy saving.

1.3   Planning and Design of Enterprise Networks

Enterprise networking involves LANs and WANs. The deployment of network devices for the enterprise LAN should be combined with the physical location of computers. Generally, switches are used for the connection within the LAN while routers for the connection of WAN.

1.3.1   Enterprise LANs

The concepts of network and Internet are introduced earlier, but networks that most people are familiar with are those at their homes and in enterprises. Depending on the network size and the physical distribution location of computers, enterprise networks can be designed with a Layer 2 or Layer 3 structure, and are usually designed with a tree or a hybrid network topology. A Layer 2 network has limited networking capability and is usually only a small LAN; and a Layer 3 network can form large networks. The following are two typical scenarios to demonstrate the design of Layer 2 and Layer 3 enterprise networks.

1. Layer 2 LAN

    Here is an enterprise network as an example to introduce the network topology of an enterprise LAN. As shown in Fig. 1.10, first, a switch is deployed in Office 1, Office 2 and Office 3 to connect the computers in the offices. The switches in the offices require many ports so that more computers can be connected to the network. The switches at this level are called access layer switches, which are, at present, typically connected to computer ports with bandwidth of 100 Mbit/s.

    The aggregation layer can be deployed with either a router or a switch. If a switch is deployed there, it is usually a Layer 3 deployment that performs IP message forwarding tasks.

    A switch can be deployed in an enterprise server room to connect servers in the enterprise to switches in each office, so as to converge Internet flow from access layer switches in the offices, and Internet connection is enabled through a router. Switches at this level are called aggregation layer switches. The switch at this level does not need many ports, but the port bandwidth should be higher than that of the access layer switch, otherwise it will be a bottleneck that limits the network speed.

2. Layer 3 LAN

    In enterprises with larger network size, a Layer 3 structure may be adopted for LAN. There are three levels of switches in a Layer 3 LAN: access layer switches, aggregation layer switches and core layer switches. The layered model can be used to help design layered networks that are expandable, reliable, and cost-effective.

    As shown in Fig. 1.11, an enterprise has three branches, each of which has its own office building with its own server room and network. The network center of

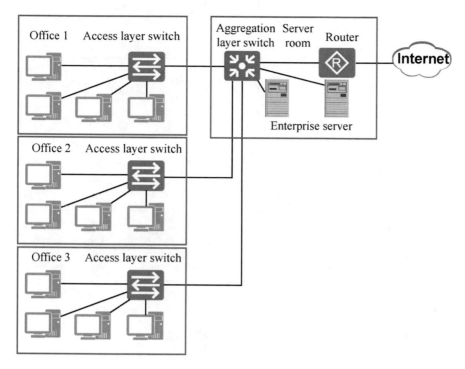

Fig. 1.10 Layer-2 LAN

this enterprise provides Internet access for the three branches, so the aggregation layer switches of each branch have to be connected to the switches in the network center, and the switches at this level are called core layer switches. The enterprise's servers are connected to the core layer switch to provide services to the three branches.

The aggregation and core layers can be deployed with routers or switches. If a switch is deployed, it is usually a Layer 3 deployment that performs IP message forwarding tasks.

1.3.2 Enterprise WANs

In the networking process, in addition to LAN, enterprises may also use WAN. As depicted in Fig. 1.12, the vehicle factory has plants in both Shijiazhuang and Tangshan, and the vehicle factory of CSR in Shijiazhuang and that of CNR in Tangshan have formed their own networks. It can be seen that the vehicle factory has planned the network according to the department (such as vehicle assembling workshop, wood company, transportation company, mechanical and electrical plant in the figure). Basically, each department has a network (network segment), and a core layer switch (equivalent to router) is used to connect the network segment of

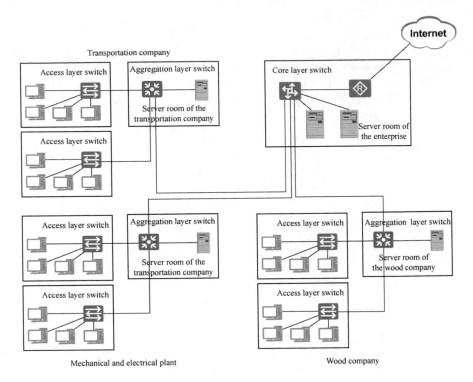

Fig. 1.11 Layer 3 LAN

each department, that is, the enterprise's server is connected to the Layer 3 switch. This is the enterprise's LAN.

At this time, if the CNR vehicle factory in Tangshan needs to access the server of CSR vehicle factory in Shijiazhuang, the networks of the two factories need to be connected. It is unlikely for the vehicle factory to connect the LANs of these two factories by setting up network cables or optical fibers by itself, as this will lead to a sky-high cost for construction and maintenance. Enterprises usually connect the two LANs by leasing the carrier's line, so that they only need to pay the annual fee, thus forming the enterprise WAN.

In general, an enterprise LAN is usually formed by the enterprise by paying for network devices by themselves with a usual bandwidth of 10 Mbit/s, 100 Mbit/s or 1000 Mbit/s, which is maintained by enterprises themselves and covers a small area. An enterprise WAN is usually set up by enterprises by paying for the leased lines of carriers, i.e., they pay for the bandwidth so as to achieve long-distance communication.

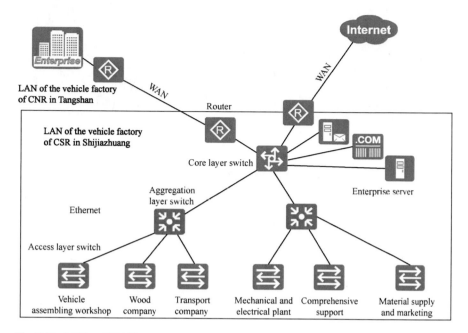

Fig. 1.12 LAN and WAN

1.4 Exercises

1. What is a network? What is the Internet? What is the largest interconnected network at present?
2. List some common network topologies and explain what kind of network topology is usually used for enterprise networking.
3. List some common network devices and state their roles.

Chapter 2
TCP/IP

To enable open communication among computers worldwide, the International Organization for Standardization (ISO) has developed a reference model for network interconnection, that is the Open System Interconnection Reference Model (OSI/RM). This reference model (architecture standard) defines a 7-layer framework for network interconnection, namely the physical layer, data link layer, network layer, transport layer, session layer, presentation layer, and application layer.

The TCP/IPv4 stack is the current industry standard that streamlines the OSI 7-layer model by integrating it into four layers. Based on functions, the TCP/IPv4 stack is a set of protocols that can be categorized into application layer protocols, transport layer protocols, network layer protocols and network interface layer protocols from top to bottom. This chapter introduces these protocols in detail.

2.1 Overview of Protocols

The most important thing in learning about computer networks is to master and understand the protocols used for computer communication. For many people learning computer networks, the protocols used for computer communication are concepts they struggle to understand. For this reason, before talking about the protocols used for computer communication, let's take a look at a lease agreement.

2.1.1 Introduction to Protocols

You are no stranger to agreements, as university students have to sign employment agreements with employers when they leave school to work; and when they start working, they might need to rent a room, so they may have to sign lease agreements with landlords. In the following, we introduce the meaning of the protocol and its

© The Author(s) 2023
Huawei Technologies Co., Ltd., *Data Communications and Network Technologies*,
https://doi.org/10.1007/978-981-19-3029-4_2

content through a lease agreement, and then introduce the protocols used for computer communication.

If the lessor and the lessee do not sign an agreement, but only verbally agree on the amount of rent, when to pay the monthly rent, the amount of the deposit, and who is responsible for repairing the damaged furniture and appliances, over time neither party may remember these agreements. Once the lessor and the lessee do not agree over a certain situation, misunderstandings and conflicts will easily occur.

In order to avoid disputes, the lessor and the lessee need to sign a lease agreement, and write the matter of mutual concern into the agreement. Both sides sign their names upon confirmation and the agreement is done in duplicate, which must be abide by both sides. If the lessor and lessee are inexperienced in signing the lease agreements and are worried about missing some important matters, they can find a recognized and standardized lease agreement template from the Internet. Figure 2.1 is an example of a lease agreement template where the covenants are defined and the lessor and lessee simply need to fill in the specified content on the template.

To simplify the filling process, the lease agreement template also provides a table, as shown in Fig. 2.2. When the lessor and the lessee sign the lease agreement, they only need to fill in the information in the position specified in the table, and the detailed terms and conditions of the agreement are not required to be filled. In the table, the "name of the lessor", "name of the lessee", "ID number", "location of the house" and other information are called fields. These fields can be either fixed length or variable length. In case of variable length, the delimiters between the fields should be defined.

Figure 2.3 is a specific lease agreement filled out based on the table in the lease agreement template, according to which you can know the information such as lessor and lessee, the location of the house, rent, and deposit. The terms of the agreement that both Party A and B should follow do not need to be filled in, but both parties must comply with the matters agreed in the lease agreement template.

Similar to the lease agreement template, the protocols used for computer communications are standardized, that is, common templates with Party A and Party B are formed. In addition to stipulating the conventions that both Party A and Party B need to follow, computer communication protocols also define the format of the messages (messages are the information communicated and exchanged by the application) when Party A and Party B exchange information with each other. It usually includes the format of request messages and response messages. The message format is similar to the format shown in Fig. 2.2.

During data communication, when data packets are analyzed using packet capture tools, the tables specified by the protocol to be filled in by both sides of the communication and the values of each field are similar to the values of each field filled in the lease agreement shown in Fig. 2.3. Figure 2.4 shows the table that needs to be filled in by both sides of the communication as defined by the IPv4 protocol, which is called the IPv4 header. In communications of computers in the network, only the contents of the IPv4 header need to be filled in as specified, then the computers of both communicating parties and the network devices along the way will be able to work according to the IP.

Lease Agreement Template

Party A (Lessor):_____ ID number:_____

Party B (Lessor):_____ ID number:_____

By mutual agreement, Party A leases the house located in _____ to Party B for use.
I. The lease starts from____(month)_____(date)____(year) to ____(month)_____(date)____(year).
II. The rent is ___ Yuan/month; the deposit is _____(Yuan); and the rent is paid on____each month.
III. Water _____ tons, gas _____ cubic meters, electricity _____ KWH.
IV. Covenant

1. Party B should change the door locks in time when they officially move in. Party A bears no responsibility for accidents that occur due to door lock problem. Party B shall be responsible for all losses caused by fire disasters due to careless use or improper use of fire, electrical disasters and other non-natural disasters.
2. Party B has no right to sublet, sublease, resell the house, and the furniture and appliances in the house, and shall not alter the structure of the house without permission. They shall take care of the facilities in the house. If the damage is caused by man-made reasons, it should be repaired, otherwise it shall be compensated at the price. Party B shall take precautions on fire, theft, water leakage and pay attention to the safety of the arrangement and the flower pots on the balcony. If any losses arise, Party B will be held responsible.
3. Party B must pay the rent on time. Otherwise, Party B is in breach of contract and the agreement will be terminated.
4. Party B shall abide by the rules and regulations of the living area and pay the fees for water, electricity, gas, fiber optics, telephone and property management on time. Party B shall pay deposit to Party A. Party B shall pay water, electricity, gas, fiber optic and property management fees when checking out, and Party A shall return the deposit in full if there is no damage to the furniture and appliances in the house and no blockage or leakage in the sewer and toilet.
5. Party A guarantees that there is no property dispute in the house. In case of demolition, Party B shall move out unconditionally, and the deposit paid will be refunded by Party A according to the number of days left.

V. This agreement is in duplicate and shall be effective from the date of signature by both parties.

Party A (lessor):   Party B (Lessee):

                                            _____(month)____(date)_____(year)

32 bytes		
Name of the lessor	ID number	
Name of the lessee	ID number	
Location of the house		
When the lease starts	When the lease ends	
Rent	Deposit	Time to pay the rent each month
Water	Electricity	Gas
8 bytes	8 bytes	16 bytes

Fig. 2.1 Lease agreement template

Fig. 2.2 Table in the lease
agreement template that
needs to be filled in

32 bytes			
Name of the lessor	ID number		
Name of the lessee	ID number		
Location of the house			
When the lease starts		When the lease ends	
Rent	Deposit	Time to pay the rent each month	
Water	Electricity	Gas	
8 bytes	8 bytes	16 bytes	

Fig. 2.3 The detailed lease
agreement

Han Ligang	13230219770605****		
Zhang Jingling	13230219871205****		
12-1-**, Tatan Community, Shijiazhuang, Hebei			
2019-11-01		2020-11-01	
1400	1000	15th of each month	
122	1444	32	

0	4	8		16	19	24	31
Version	Header length	Differentiated services		Total length			
Identification				Flags		Fragment offset	
Time to live		Protocol		Header checksum			
Source IP address							
Destination IP address							
Option field (variable length)						Stuffing	

Fig. 2.4 IPv4 header

2.1.2   Computer Communication Protocols

1. Overview of protocol layering

 The protocols used for computer communication in the Internet today are a set of
 protocols, namely the TCP/IPv4 protocol stack. The TCP/IPv4 protocol stack is a
 communication protocol that is most complete and most widely used at present.
 As shown in Fig. 2.5, each protocol in the TCP/IPv4 stack is independent, and
 each contains a Party A, a Party B, an objective, and terms of agreement. This set
 of protocols can be divided by function into the application layer, transport layer,
 network layer and network interface layer protocols, which collaborate to enable
 the communication between computers in the network.

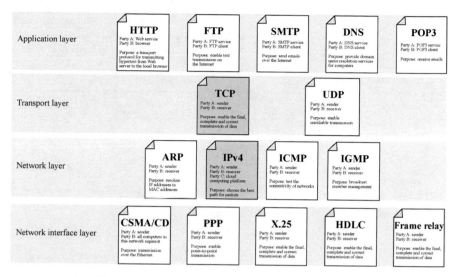

Fig. 2.5 TCP/IPv4 protocol stack

TCP/IPv4 protocol stack can be used for both WAN and LAN. It is the cornerstone of Internet/Intranet, and its charm lies in its ability to enable computers with different hardware structures and operating systems to communicate with each other. As shown in Fig. 2.5, its main protocols are Transmission Control Protocol (TCP) and Internet Protocol (IPv4).

2. The reason for protocol layering

Why do we need this set of protocols for computer communication? How to understand the layering? What is the relationship between the layers? In the following, we use an example of online shopping for illustration.

In the process of online shopping, a shopping protocol need to be formed between the merchant and the customer, and both parties need to follow the procedure specified by the shopping platform for transactions, that is, the merchant provides the products; the customer browses and chooses a product, and pays online; the merchant ships the product; the customer receives the product and confirms receipt, after which the payment is finally transferred to the merchant's account; the customer can return the product if he or she is not satisfied with the product received; the customer who has purchased the product can comment on it. This is the shopping procedure, which can also be considered as the protocol used in online shopping. The Party A and Party B of the shopping agreement are the merchant and the customer, and the shopping agreement stipulates the shopping procedure, i.e., what the merchant can do, what the customer can do, and what is the order of the operation. For example, a merchant cannot ship a product before the payment is made, and a customer cannot comment on a product without making a purchase. Such an "online shopping protocol" is equivalent to an application layer protocol adopted for computer communication. Similarly, each of online restaurant delivery services, accessing

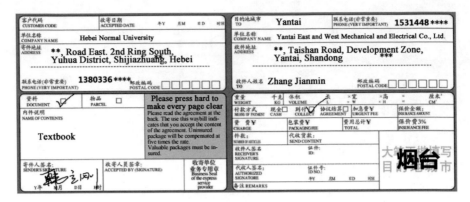

Fig. 2.6 Express waybill

websites, sending and receiving emails, remote login, and other applications requires an application layer protocol.

Therefore, is the shopping protocol (the protocol of this layer) enough for conducting online shopping? As we all know, the purchased products also need to be delivered to the customer's home by express delivery, and if the customer is not satisfied, the product will also need to be returned to the merchant through express delivery. That means online shopping also needs the logistic services provided by delivery companies. Delivery companies such as SF Express, YTO Express, and ZTO Express all offer such function, that is, to provide logistics services for online shopping.

It is worth noting that delivery companies also need a layer of protocol to deliver express packages, namely the express protocol. The express protocol stipulates the procedure and express waybill to be filled in for the express delivery. The customer fills in the information such as recipient and sender in the designated place in accordance with the format of the express waybill. The express waybill specifies the form that needs to be filled out for logistics, and the form specifies the content and location to be filled in. According to the recipient's city, the delivery company sorts the packages, and selects the consignment route, and upon arrival at the target city, the couriers deliver the package to the recipient based on the specific address on the express waybill. As shown in Fig. 2.6, the IP header defined by IP is equivalent to the courier company's express waybill, the purpose of which is to send the data packet to the destination address.

Similar to the delivery company's provision of logistic services for online shopping, there is a "service" relationship between the four layers of protocols included in TCP/IPv4, that is, the lower layer protocols provide services for its upper layer protocols. Specifically, the transport layer provides services for the application layer, the network layer provides services for the transport layer, and the network interface layer provides services for the network layer.

Figure 2.7 depicts the layering of the TCP/IPv4 protocol stack and the functional range of each layer's protocol. Party A and Party B of the application

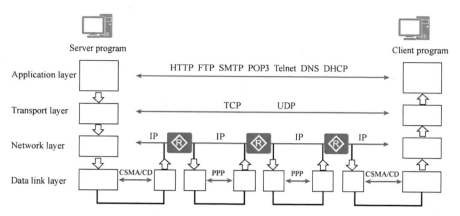

Fig. 2.7 The layering and functional range of protocols

layer protocol are the server program and the client program, which execute the functions of the application. Party A and Party B of the transport layer protocol are located in the two computers of the communication. TCP implements reliable transmission for the application layer protocol, while UDP provides message forwarding service for this protocol. IP in the network layer protocol selects the path for forwarding data packets across network segments. IP is a multi-party protocol that includes the two computers of the communication as well as the routers passed through along the way. The data link layer is responsible for sending the packets of the network layer from one end of the link to the other. Devices on the same link are peer entities for the data link layer protocol, which works on a segment of the link and varies for different types of links. As shown in Fig. 2.7, Ethernet uses the CSMA/CD protocol while a point to point link uses Point to Point Protocol (PPP).

3. Advantages of protocol layering

The following describes the advantages of protocol layering of computer communication.

(a) Each layer is independent of each other. A certain layer does not need to know how its lower layer works, but only the services provided by that layer through the interlayer interface. For the lower layer, the upper layer is the data to be processed, as shown in Fig. 2.8.

(b) Good flexibility. Improvements and changes made in each layer do not affect other layers. For example, IPv4 implements the network layer function, and when it is upgraded to IPv6, it still implements the network layer function, while no change will be made to the TCP and UDP in the transport layer, nor will any change be made to the protocols used in the data link layer. As shown in Fig. 2.9, computers can use TCP/IPv4 and TCP/IPv6 for communication.

(c) The functions of each layer can be implemented using the most appropriate technology. For instance, twisted-pair cable is used to connect the network if

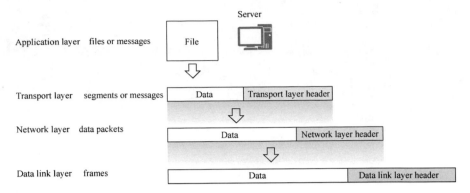

Application layer   files or messages

Transport layer   segments or messages

Network layer   data packets

Data link layer   frames

Fig. 2.8 Relationships between layers

Fig. 2.9 IPv4 and IPv6
have the same function

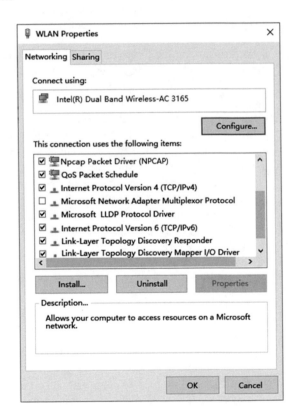

it is suitable for cabling, and wireless coverage is adopted if there are
obstacles.

(d) Promote standardization. Routers implement network layer functions and
switches implement data link layer functions. Network layer standards and
data link layer standards are the reason why routers and switches from

different vendors can be connected to each other for computer communication.

(e) The layering helps to break up complex computer communication problems into multiple simple problems and is conducive to network troubleshooting. For example, the network failures caused by the lack of gateway in the computer belong to the network layer problems, those caused by MAC address conflict are data link layer problems, and the failure to access websites due to the wrong proxy server set by the IE browser belongs to the application layer problems.

2.1.3   Relationship Between OSI 7-Layer Model and the TCP/IPv4 Protocol Stack

The TCP/IPv4 protocol stack introduced earlier is the industry standard for Internet communication. When the Internet first emerged, communication was typically only possible between computer products manufactured by the same manufacturer. This barrier was shattered in the late 1970s when the ISO created the Open Systems Interconnection (OSI) reference model (referred to as the OSI 7-layer model in this book).

The OSI 7-layer model divides the computer communication process into seven layers based on the functions and specifies the functions that each layer performs. This allows vendors of Internet devices as well as software companies to design their own hardware and software with reference to the OSI reference model, and network devices from different vendors can work in collaboration with each other.

The OSI 7-layer model is not a detailed protocol; the TCP/IPv4 stack is. So how to understand the relationship between them? For instance, the International Organization for Standardization defines a reference model for automobiles stipulating that automobiles shall be equipped with a power system, steering system, braking system, and transmission system, which are equivalent to the functions that each layer of the computer communication is intended to implement as defined by the OSI 7-layer model. The automobile manufacturer, such as Audi, develops its own automobiles with reference to this automobile reference model and equips the car with all the functions required by the model, then the Audi automobile at this time is tantamount to the TCP/IPv4 protocol. If some Audi automobiles use gasoline and some use natural gas for their power system, some use 8-cylinder engines and others 10-cylinder engines, then all the functions implemented are the power system functions of the automobile reference model. Similarly, the OSI reference model only defines the functions to be implemented by each layer of computer communication, without specifying how to implement them and the details of the implementation. They can be implemented differently by different protocol stacks.

In the OSI reference model developed by the International Organization for Standardization, the computer communication process is divided into seven layers, which are illustrated below.

1. Application layer: application layer protocols are used to implement the functions of applications, and the standardization of the implementation methods leads to the application layer protocols. Due to the variety of applications in the Internet, such as accessing websites, sending and receiving emails, accessing file servers, there are all kinds of application layer protocols. The application layer protocols shall include what requests (commands) the client can send to the server, what responses the server can return to the client, the message formats used, the interaction order of commands, and so on.

2. Presentation layer: the presentation layer provides a presentation method for the information transmitted by the application layer. If a character file is transmitted by the application layer, it should be converted into data using the character set. If it an image file or an application binary file, it should be converted into data by coding. Whether the data is compressed or whether it is encrypted before transmission is a matter to be solved by the presentation layer. The presentation layer of the sender and of the receiver are the two sides of the protocol. Encryption and decryption, compression and decompression, as well as the encoding and decoding of character files shall all follow the specification of the presentation layer protocol.

3. Session layer: the session layer establishes, maintains and closes a session for the client and server programs of the communication. Establishing a session: for Computer A and B to communicate, a session should be established for them; in the process of establishing a session, there will be authentication, authority identification, etc. Maintaining a session: after the session is established, the both sides of the communication start to transfer data. When the data transfer is completed, the session layer will not necessarily disconnect the communication session immediately, but maintain the session according to the settings of the application and application layer, during which the two sides of the communication are capable of transferring data by the session at any time. Closing a session: when the time specified by the application or application layer runs out, or when A/B reboots or shuts down, or when the session is manually disconnected, the session between A and B will be disconnected.

4. Transport layer: the transport layer mainly provides end to end services for the process of communication between hosts, and handles transmission problems such as datagram errors and wrong datagram orders. The transport layer is a key layer in the computer communication architecture, which can shield the communication details of the lower data layers from the upper layers by using the data forwarding services provided by the network layer, so as to spare the users from considering the details of the work of the physical layer, data link layer and network layer.

5. Network layer: the network layer is responsible for routing selection during the transmission process of data packets from the source network to the destination

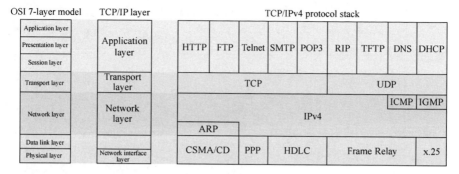

Fig. 2.10 OSI reference model and TCP/IP layering

network. The Internet is a collection of multiple networks, and it is with the help of the routing path selection of the network layer that multiple networks can be connected and information can be shared.

6. Data link layer: The data link layer is responsible for transferring data from one end of the link to the other, the basic unit of transmission being the "frame". It provides error control and flow control services for the network layer.

7. Physical layer: the physical layer is the lowest layer in the OSI reference model, which mainly defines the electrical, mechanical, procedural and functional standards of the system, such as voltage, bandwidth, maximum transmission distance and other similar characteristics. The primary function of the physical layer is to provide physical transmission for the data link layer by using transmission media. The basic unit of physical layer transmission is bitstream, i.e., 0s and 1s, which are also the most basic electrical or optical signals.

The TCP/IPv4 protocol stack merges and streamlines the OSI reference model, as its application layer implements the functions of the application, presentation, and session layers of the OSI reference model, and merges the data link layer and physical layers into a network interface layer, as shown in Fig. 2.10.

2.2 Application Layer Protocols

Computer communication is essentially application communication on a computer, which usually consists of a client program initiating a communication request to a server program, and the server program returning a response to the client program, thus implementing the functions of the application.

There are many applications in the Internet, such as accessing websites, domain name resolution, sending e-mails, receiving e-mails, and transferring files. Each application needs to specify what requests the client program can send to the server, what responses the server program can return to the client, the order in which the client sends requests (commands) to the server, how to handle accidents when they

Application layer protocol

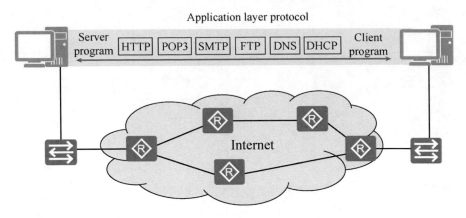

Fig. 2.11 Application layer protocol

occur, what fields are in the messages sending requests and responses, the length of each field, and what the value of each field means. These provisions are the protocols used for application communication, and these protocols are called application layer protocols.

Since it is a protocol, there is a Party A and a Party B. The client program and the server program of the communication are the Party A and Party B of the protocol, which are called peer entities in many books on computer networks, as shown in Fig. 2.11.

The following lists the common application layer protocols in the TCP/IPv4 protocol stack and their uses.

- HyperText Transfer Protocol (HTTP), which is used to access Web services.
- HyperText Transfer Protocol over Secure Socket Layer (HTTPS), which enables the encrypted transmission of HTTP communication.
- Simple Mail Transfer Protocol (SMTP), which is adopted to send e-mails.
- Post Office Protocol version 3 (POP3), which is used to receive e-mails.
- Domain Name System (DNS), which is for domain name resolution.
- File Transfer Protocol (FTP), which is used to upload and download files on the Internet.
- Telnet, which is used to remotely configure network devices, Linux systems, and Windows systems.
- Dynamic Host Configuration Protocol (DHCP), which is adopted to automatically configure IP addresses, subnet masks, gateways, DNS, etc. for computers or other network devices.

The following is a packet capture analysis of the traffic for accessing websites and for file transfers to observe the working process of the application layer protocols (with HTTP and FTP as the examples)., i.e., the interaction process between the client and the server, the requests sent by the client to the server, the responses sent by the server to the client, the format of request messages, and the format of response messages, which help readers understand the application layer protocols.

2.2.1 HTTP Protocol

HTTP is the most widely used application layer protocol in the Internet. By the packet capture analysis of HTTP, this section observes the requests (commands) sent by the client (browser) to the Web server, the responses (status codes) returned by the Web server to the client, as well as the format of the request and response messages. The illustration of HTTP enabling the Web browser to access the Web server is presented in Fig. 2.12.

1. The main contents of HTTP
    In order to make it easier for readers to understand, the following part elaborates HTTP by a lease agreement format (only its main contents are shown).

HTTP

Party A: Web server
Party B: Web browser
HTTP is a transport protocol used to transfer hypertext from a World Wide Web (WWW) server to a local browser. HTTP is an application layer protocol of the TCP/IPv4 protocol stack and is used to transfer HTML files, image files, query results, etc.
HTTP works on top of the client-server architecture. The browser acts as the HTTP client, sending all requests to the HTTP server (i.e., the Web server) through the Uniform Resource Locator (URL) (in this case, the URL entered in the browser). After the Web server receives the request, it sends a response message to the client.
The terms of the protocol are as follows.

(a) Steps of HTTP requests and responses

   (i) The client is connected to the Web server

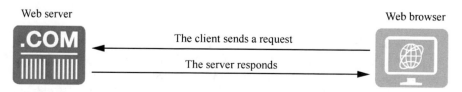

Fig. 2.12 The illustration of HTTP enabling the Web browser to access the Web server

Fig. 2.13 HTTP message
format

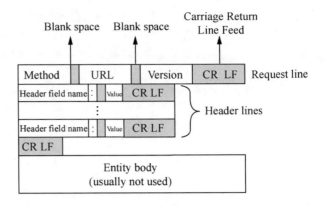

An HTTP client, usually a browser, establishes a TCP socket connection with the HTTP port of the Web server (TCP port 80 is used by
default).

(ii) Send HTTP request

Through a TCP socket, the client sends a text request message to the
Web server. A request message consists of four parts: request line,
request header, blank line and request data.

(iii) The Web server accepts the request and returns an HTTP response

The web server parses the request and locates the requested resource.
The server writes a copy of the resource to a TCP socket, which is read
by the client. A response message consists of four parts: status line,
response header, blank line and response data.

(iv) Release the TCP connection

If the connection mode is "close", the server will actively close the
TCP connection and the client will passively close the connection to
release the TCP connection. If the connection mode is "keepalive", the
connection will be maintained for a period of time, during which the
request can continue to be received.

(v) The client browser parses the HTML content

The client browser first parses the status line to check the status code
indicating whether the request is successful or not. Then each response
header is parsed, and the response header advertise the following HTML
document of certain bytes and its character set. The client browser reads
the response data HTML, formats it according to the HTML syntax, and
displays it in the browser window.

(b) Format of request messages

Since HTTP is text-oriented, each field in the message is some ASCII
codes, and thus the length of each field is not fixed. As shown in Fig. 2.13, an
HTTP request message consists of three parts, namely the request line, the

header line and the entity body. The "CR" and "LF" in the figure represent "carriage return" and "line feed", respectively.

(i) Request line

The request line is used to indicate that it is a request message. The three fields of the line are separated by spaces.

(ii) Header line

This is used to specify some information about the browser, server or message body. The header can have multiple lines or can be left out. In each header line there is the field name of the header and its value, and each line ends with a "carriage return" and a "line feed". At the end of the header line, there is a blank line to separate the header line from the entity body that follows.

(iii) Entity body

This field is generally not used in the request message.

(c) Methods in HTTP request messages

The browser can send the following eight request methods (sometimes called "actions" or "commands") to the Web server to indicate the different ways to operate the resources specified by the Request-URL.

- GET: to request the resource identified by the Request-URL. When a web page is accessed by entering a URL in the browser's address bar, the browser uses the GET method to request the web page from the server.
- POST: to append new data to the resource identified by Request-URL and ask the requested server to accept the data attached to the request. It is often used to submit forms, such as submitting information to the server, posting, and logging in.
- HEAD: to request to get the response message header of the resource identified by Request-URL.
- PUT: to request the server to store a resource and use Request-URL as its identifier.
- DELETE: to request the server to delete the resource identified by Request-URL.
- TRACE: to request the server to return the request information received, mainly for testing or diagnostics.
- CONNECT: it is used for proxy servers.
- OPTIONS: to request to query the performance of the server, or to query options and requirements related to the resource.

The names of the methods are case-sensitive. When the resource targeted by a request does not support the corresponding request method, the server should return the status code 405 (Method Not Allowed); when the server does not recognize or support the corresponding request method, it should return the status code 501 (Not Implemented).

Fig. 2.14 Response
message format

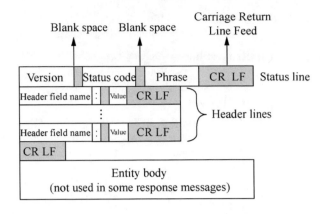

(d) Format of response messages

 After each request message is sent, a response message will be received. The first line of the response message is the status line. As shown in Fig. 2.14, the status line includes three items, namely, the version of HTTP, the status code and a simple phrase explaining the status code.

(e) Status codes of HTTP response messages

 All status codes are three-digit, with a total of 33 types in five categories. The description is as follows.

- lxx indicates the notification information, such as the request is received or it is being processed.
- 2xx indicates success, such as accepted or understood.
- 3xx indicates a redirect, such as further action must be taken to complete the request.
- 4xx indicates a client error, such as the request has incorrect syntax or cannot be completed.
- 5xx indicates a server error, for example, the server fails to complete the request.

 The following three status lines are commonly seen in response messages.

- HTTP/1.1 202 Accepted.
- HTTP/1.1 400 Bad Request.
- HTTP/1.1 404 Not Found.

 In summary, HTTP defines the steps a browser takes to access a Web server, what requests (methods) can be sent to the Web server, the format of HTTP request messages (what fields are there and what they mean), and what responses the Web server can send to the browser (status codes), and the format of HTTP response messages (what fields are there and what they mean).

 Likewise, the following content also have to be defined for other application layer protocols.

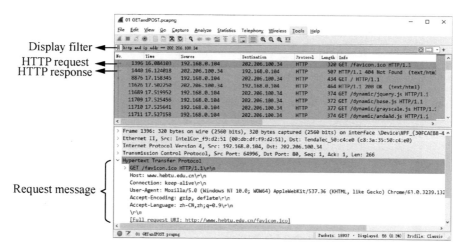

Fig. 2.15 GET method of HTTP request messages

- What requests (methods or commands) the client can send to the server.
- The order in which the client and server commands interact, such as the POP3 protocol, which requires user authentication before receiving e-mails.
- What responses (status codes) the server has, and what each status code means.
- Define the format of each message in the protocol. What fields the message contains, whether the fields are fixed-length or variable-length, and if they are variable-length, what the field delimiters are. These all have to be defined in the protocol.

2. Packet capture analysis of HTTP

A packet capture tool installed in the computer can capture the data packets sent and received by the network interface card, as well as the those of the application communication. This allows you to visualize the interaction between the client and the server, that is, what requests the client sends and what responses the server returns. This is how the application layer protocol works.

As shown in Fig. 2.15, enter "http and ip.addr == 202.206.100.34" at the display filter toolbar, click 🖃 to enable the display filter. At this point, only the http request and response packets are displayed. Select the 1396th packet, then you can see the HTTP request message in the data packet, which you can compare with the format of HTTP request messages introduced earlier, whose request method is GET.

The 1440th data packet is a Web server response packet with a status code of 404. Status code 404 stands for "Not Found".

As shown in Fig. 2.16, the 11626th data packet is an HTTP response packet with a status code of 200, which indicates that the request is successfully

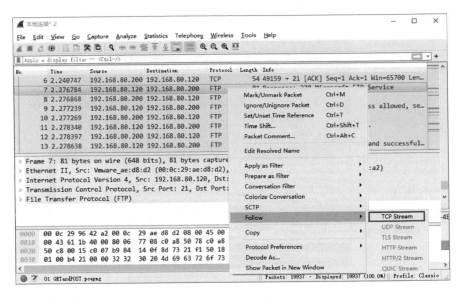

Fig. 2.18 Follow stream

computer; and uploading files is duplicating files from its own computer to the remote host. The following is a packet capture analysis of how FTP works.

By installing Windows Server 2012 R2 server in the virtual machine, installing FTP service, using packet capture tool to analyze the packets of FTP client accessing FTP server in the client (Windows 10), observing the interaction process of FTP client accessing FTP server, you can see the request sent by the client to the server, and the response returned by the server to the client. Setting certain methods to disable FTP on the FTP server enables secure access to the FTP server, such as disabling the deletion of files on the FTP server.

After running the packet capture tool on the FTP client to start capturing data packets, upload a test.txt file, rename it to "abc.txt", and finally delete the abc.txt file on the FTP. The packet capture tool will capture all the commands sent by the FTP client and all the responses returned by the FTP server. As shown in Fig. 2.18, right-click one of the FTP packets, click "Follow Stream" → "TCP Stream", the window in Fig. 2.19 will appear. After collating the data generated from all the interactions of the FTP client accessing the FTP server, you can see the methods in FTP, among which, STOR method can upload test.txt files, CWD method can change the working directory, RNFR method can rename test.txt files, and DELE method can delete abc.txt files. Other FTP methods can also be seen using the packet capture tool, such as methods corresponding to operations of using the FTP client to create folders on FTP server, deleting folders, and downloading files.

In order to prevent the client from performing certain operations, you can set the FTP server to disable some commands in FTP. For example, to prohibit FTP client from deleting files on FTP server, you can set FTP service request filtering and disable DELE method. As shown in Fig. 2.20, click "FTP Request Filtering".

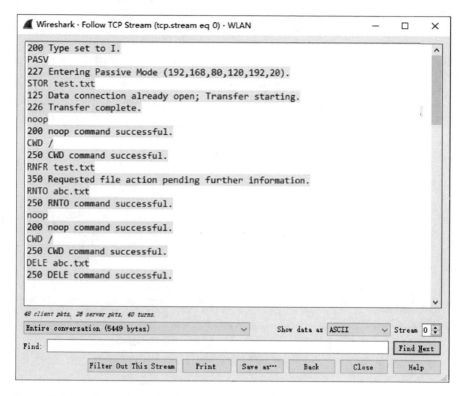

Fig. 2.19 Interaction process of FTP client accessing FTP server

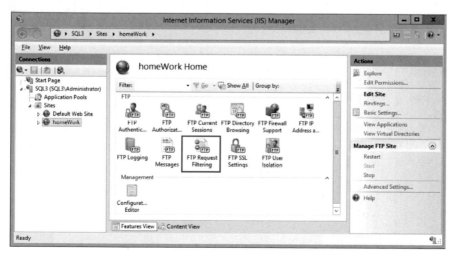

Fig. 2.20 Manage FTP request filtering

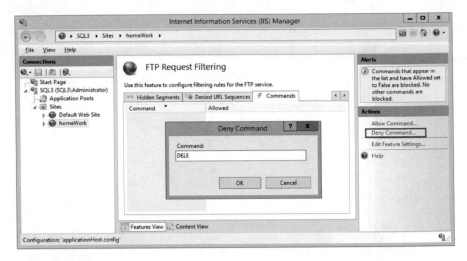

Fig. 2.21   Disable DELE method

Fig. 2.22   Command not allowed

As shown in Fig. 2.21, click the "Commands" tab in the "FTP Request Filtering" interface that appears, click "Deny Command", enter "DELE" in the pop-up "Deny Command" dialog box, and click the "OK" button.

When you delete a file on the FTP server again on Windows 10, the prompt "500 Command not allowed" will appear, as shown in Fig. 2.22.

2.3 Transport Layer Protocols

The transport layer primarily provides end to end communication between applications on two hosts. In the TCP/IPv4 protocol stack, the transport layer contains two protocols, Transmission Control Protocol (TCP) and User Datagram Protocol (UDP).

2.3.1 Application Scenarios of TCP and UDP

TCP and UDP at the transport layer have their own application scenarios. In the following, the application scenarios of each will be described respectively.

1. Application scenarios of TCP

   TCP provides reliable transmission services for application layer protocols. The sender sends data in order, and the receiver receives data in order. TCP is responsible for retransmission and sorting in case of packet loss or disorder. The following are the application scenarios of TCP.

   (a) The client program and the server program need several interactions to achieve the function of the application, such as POP3 for receiving e-mails and SMTP for sending e-mails, as well as FTP for transferring files, which all use TCP at the transport layer.

   (b) When an application transfers a file that requires segmentation, such as accessing a web page through a browser or transferring a file using QQ, TCP is selected at the transport layer for segmentation.

   For example, downloading a 500 MB movie or a 200 MB software from the network requires splitting such a large file into multiple packets for sending, which may take several minutes or tens of minutes. During this period, the sender sends the content as a byte stream and in the meantime put it into the cache while the transport layer segments and numbers the byte stream in the cache, and then sends them in order. This process requires the sender and receiver to establish a connection and negotiate some parameters regarding the communication process (e.g., the maximum number of bytes in a segment). It is important to note that the segments referred to here can be formed into data packets by adding the IP headers at the network layer. If a data packet is lost due to unstable network, the sender must resend the lost packet, otherwise the received file will be incomplete. The TCP protocol is capable of reliable transmission. If the sender sends too fast for the receiver to process, the receiver will also notify the sender to slow down or even stop sending, which is the TCP flow control mechanism. The flow in the Internet is not fixed, and flow peaks may result in network congestion (which is easy to understand, just like traffic jams in the city during rush hour), so that packets that are too late to be forwarded will be dropped by the router. The TCP

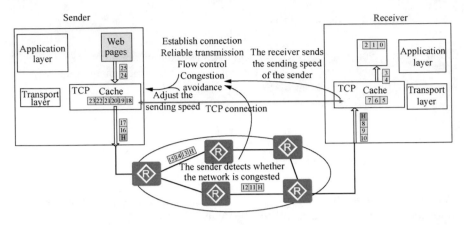

Fig. 2.23 TCP functions

protocol detects network congestion during transmission so as to adjust the sending speed. TCP protocol has a mechanism for congestion avoidance.

As shown in Fig. 2.23, the sending speed of the sender is controlled by two factors: whether the network is congested or not, and the receiving speed of the receiver, whichever speed is lower.

There are some application communications that become inefficient by using the TCP protocol. For example, some applications fulfill their function simply by the client sending a request message to the server and the server returning a response message. Such applications are not efficient if they use TCP, sending three packets to establish a connection and then sending four packets to close the connection. For such applications, UDP is usually used in the transport layer.

2. Application scenarios of UDP

(a) The client program and the server program communicate, and the packets sent by the application do not need segmentation. For example, for domain name resolution, the DNS protocol uses UDP at the transport layer. The client sends a message to the DNS server requesting the resolution of a website's domain name, and the DNS server returns the result of the resolution to the client using a message.

(b) Real-time communication. Examples include using QQ and WeChat for voice chat and video chat. For such applications, the sender and receiver need real-time interaction, i.e., no long delays are allowed. Even if a few sentences are missed due to network congestion, there is no need to use TCP to wait for lost messages, because if the waiting time is too long, it will not be real-time chatting.

(c) Multicast or broadcast communication. For example, in a multimedia room in a school, the content on the teacher's computer screen needs to be received by the students in the classroom with their computers. By installing the multi-media classroom server software on the teacher's computer and the multimedia classroom client software on the students' computers, when the teacher's computer sends messages using a multicast address or broadcast address, all students' computers can receive. One-to-many communications like this use UDP at the transport layer.

Knowing the characteristics and application scenarios of the two protocols at the transport layer, it is easy to determine what protocol a certain application layer protocol uses at the transport layer. Next, let's analyze and determine what protocols are used at the transport layer for QQ file transfers and what protocols are used at the transport layer for QQ chats.

When you transfer files to your friends by QQ, the process of the transfer will last for several minutes or tens of minutes, and the file transfer will not complete by a single packet, so the file to be transferred needs to be segmented. The reliable transmission, flow control, congestion avoidance and other functions that need to be implemented during the transfer process must all be implemented at the transport layer using the TCP protocol.

When using QQ to chat with a friend, normally not much text is entered at one time, and a single packet is enough to send the chat content. After the first sentence is sent, it is not certain when the second one will be sent, that is, the process of sending data is not continuous, so it is not necessary to keep the two communicating computers connected all the time. Therefore, UDP is used at the transport layer to send the QQ chat content.

In summary, it can be seen that depending on the characteristics of the communication, applications can choose different protocols at the transport layer.

2.3.2   Relationship Between Transport Layer Protocols and Application Layer Protocols

There are many application layer protocols, but only two transport layer protocols. So how to use these two transport layer protocols to identify the different application layer protocols?

Usually, a transport layer protocol is used in conjunction with a port number to identify an application layer protocol. At the transport layer, a 16-bit binary system is used to identify a port, and port numbers take a value range of 0 to 65,535, which is sufficient for a computer.

Port numbers can be divided into two categories, namely, port numbers used by servers and those used by clients.

1. Port numbers used by servers.

Fig. 2.24 Well-known port numbers

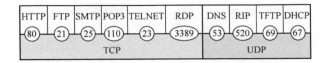

The port numbers used by servers can be divided into two categories, the most important one being well-known port number or system port number, the value of which is from 0 to 1023. The Internet Assigned Numbers Authority (IANA) assigned these port numbers to some of the most important TCP/IP applications of TCP/IP, so that all users know them. Some commonly used well-known port numbers are given below in Fig. 2.24.

Another category is called registered port numbers, with a value range of 1024 to 49,151. These port numbers are for applications that do not have a well-known port number. Such port numbers must be registered with IANA according to the prescribed procedures to prevent duplication. For example, Microsoft's Remote Display Protocol (RDP) uses TCP port 3389, which belongs to registered port numbers.

2. Port numbers used by clients.

When you open a browser to visit a website or log in to QQ and other client software to establish a connection with the server, the computer will assign a temporary port for the client software, which is the client port, with a value range between 49,152 and 65,535. Since these port numbers are dynamically selected only when the client process is running, they are also called temporary (ephemeral) port numbers. These port numbers are reserved for temporary use of the client process selection. When the server process receives a message from the client process, it knows the port number used by the client process and can therefore send the data to the client process. When the communication ends, the client port number that has just been used no longer exists. This port number is then available for other client processes later.

The following is a list of the default protocols and port numbers used by some common application layer protocols.

- HTTP uses TCP port 80 by default.
- FTP uses TCP port 21 by default.
- SMTP uses TCP port 25 by default.
- POP3 uses TCP port 110 by default.
- HTTPS uses TCP port 443 by default.
- DNS uses UDP port 53 by default.
- RDP uses TCP port 3389 by default.
- Telnet uses TCP port 23 by default.
- Windows uses TCP port 445 to access shared resources by default.
- Microsoft SQL database uses TCP port 1433 by default.
- MySQL database uses TCP port 3306 by default.

The above list is the default ports, and the port used by the application layer protocol can also be altered. If the default port is not used, the client needs to

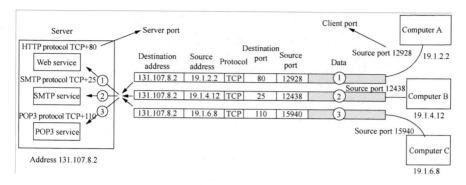

Fig. 2.25 Relationship between ports and services

specify the port used. As shown in Fig. 2.25, the server is running Web service, SMTP service and POP3 service, which use HTTP, SMTP and POP3 to communicate with the client, respectively. Now Computer A, Computer B and Computer C in the network intend to access the server's Web service, SMTP service and POP3 service, respectively, and send three packets ①②③, the destination ports of which are 80, 25 and 110, respectively. After the server receives these three packets, it will submit them to different services according to the destination ports.

In summary: the destination IP address of the data packet is used to locate a certain server in the network, and the destination port is to locate a certain service on the server.

2.3.3 TCP Headers

The following illustrates the format of TCP message headers. The TCP protocol is capable of data segmentation, reliable transmission, flow control, network congestion avoidance, etc. Therefore, the TCP message header has more fields than the UDP message header, and the header length is not fixed. As shown in Fig. 2.26, the first 20 bytes of the header of TCP message segment are fixed, followed by $4N$ bytes as an option to be added as needed (N is an integer). Therefore, the minimum length of a TCP header is 20 bytes.

The meanings of each field in the fixed part of the TCP header are described below.

1. Both source port and the destination port are two bytes, which are written into the source port number and the destination port number, respectively. The transport layer port number is used to identify an application layer protocol.
2. Sequence number is four bytes. The range of sequence number is $[0, 2^{32} - 1]$, a total of 2^{32} (i.e., 4,294,967,296). After the sequence number increases to

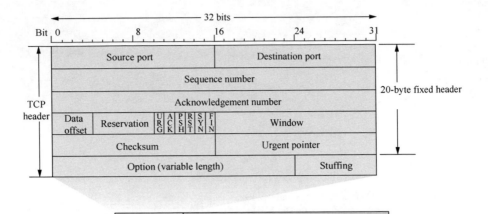

Fig. 2.26 TCP header

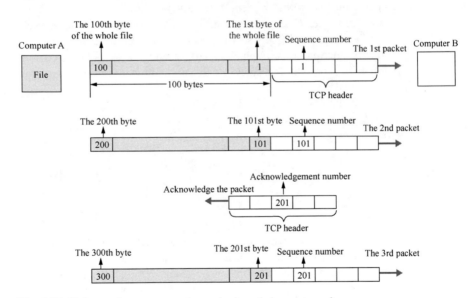

Fig. 2.27 Understand sequence number and acknowledgement number

$2^{32} - 1$, the next number goes back to 0. TCP is byte-stream oriented. Each byte of the byte stream transmitted in a TCP connection is numbered sequentially. The starting number of the entire byte stream to be transferred must be set at the establishment of the connection. The value of sequence number field in the header refers to the sequence number of the first byte of the data sent in this message segment. Figure 2.27 is an example in which Computer A sends a file to Computer B, which is used to illustrate the usage of the sequence number and acknowledgement number. To facilitate the illustration, the other fields of the transport layer are not shown. The value of the sequence number field of the first message segment is 1, and a total of 100 bytes of data is carried. This means that the sequence number of the first byte of the data in this segment is 1 and that of the last byte is 100. The data sequence number of the next message segment should start from 101, that is, the value of the sequence number field of the next message segment should be 101. The name of this field is also called "message segment sequence number".

Computer B will store the received packets into the cache, and sort the bytes in the received packets according to the sequence number, and then the program of Computer B will read the bytes with consecutive numbers from the cache.

3. The acknowledgement number is four bytes and is the sequence number of the first data byte of the next message segment the other party is expected to send.

The TCP protocol is capable of reliable transmission. After the receiver receives several packets, it will send the sender an acknowledgement packet to inform the sender what byte to send for the next packet. As shown in Fig. 2.27, after Computer B receives two packets, it sorts the bytes in the two packets to get the first 200 consecutive bytes. Computer B will send an acknowledgement packet to Computer A, informing Computer A that it should send the 201st byte, and the acknowledgement number of this acknowledgement packet is 201. There is no data division in the acknowledgement packet, only the TCP header.

In a word, we should remember that if the acknowledgement number is N, then all data up to the sequence number of N-1 has been received correctly.

Since the sequence number field is 32 bits long and can number 4 GB (i.e., 4 gigabytes) of data, in general, it ensures that when the sequence number is reused, the data of the old sequence number will have already reached the destination of the network.

4. The data offset occupies four bits, which indicates the distance between where the data of TCP message segment starts and where the TCP message segment starts. This field actually points out the length of the header of TCP message segment. The data offset field is essential because there are option fields in the header that are of indeterminate length. It should be note, however, that the unit of "data offset" is four bytes, and since the largest decimal number that can be represented by a four-bit binary number is 15, the maximum value of data offset is 60 bytes, which is the maximum length of a TCP header, so it means that the option length cannot exceed 40 bytes. If there is only a fixed-length 20-byte header, then the value of data offset is 5, which is 0101 as a four-bit binary number.

5. Reservation takes six bits, reserved for future use, but should be set to 0 for now.

6. URG (URGent). When URG $= 1$, it indicates that the urgent pointer field is valid. It tells the system that there is urgent data in this message segment that should be transmitted as soon as possible (tantamount to high-preference data), rather than in the original sequence. For example, a long program has been sent to run on a remote host, but then some problem is discovered, which requires the program to be terminated, so the user issues an interrupt command (Control + C) via the keyboard. If the urgent data is not used, then these two characters will be

stored at the end of the cache of the receiving TCP. Only after all the data has been processed will these two characters be delivered to the application process of the receiver, which wastes a lot of time.

When URG is set to 1, the sending application process tells the TCP sender that it has urgent data to transmit. The TCP sender then inserts the urgent data at the forefront of the data in this message segment, while the data following the urgent data remains ordinary data. This is used in conjunction with the Urgent Pointer fielder in the header.

7. ACK (ACKnowledgement). The acknowledgement number field is valid only when ACK = 1. When ACK = 0, the acknowledgement number is invalid. TCP stipulates that all transmitted message segments must have ACK set to 1 after the connection is established.

8. PSH (PuSH). In the interactive communication of two application processes, sometimes the application process at one end expects to receive a response from the other end immediately after entering a command. In this case, TCP can use the Push operation, that is, the TCP sender sets PSH to 1 and immediately creates and sends a message segment. When the TCP receiver receives a message segment with PSH = 1, it delivers it to the receiving application process as soon as possible (i.e., "pushes" forward), rather than delivering it after the entire cache is filled. Although the application process can choose to use Push, it is rarely used.

9. RST (ReSeT). When RST = 1, it indicates a serious error in the TCP connection (such as a host crash or other causes), so the connection must be released and then the transport connection will be re-established. Setting RST to 1 can also be used to deny an illegal message segment or refuse to open a connection.

10. SYN (SYNchronization). This is used by TCP to synchronize sequence numbers when a connection is established. When SYN = 1 and ACK = 0, this is a message segment requesting connection. If the other party agrees to establish the connection, then SYN = 1 and ACK = 1 shall be used in the response message segment. Therefore, a SYN of 1 indicates that this is a message of requesting a connection or accepting the connection. The establishment and release of connections will be explained in detail later in the TCP Connection Management section.

11. FIN (FINish, meaning "finished" or "end"). TCP uses this field to release a connection. FIN = 1 indicates that the sender of this message segment has finished transmitting the data and requests to release the transmission connection.

12. The window is two bytes. The window value is an integer between $[0, 2^{16} - 1]$. TCP protocol can control flow, and the window value is used to tell the other party the amount of data (in bytes) the receiver currently allows the sender to send, starting from the acknowledgement number in the header of this message segment. The reason for this limit is that the receiver has limited data cache space. In short, the window value is the basis for the receiver to instruct the sender to set its sending window. The computer that uses TCP protocol to transmit data will adjust the window value at any time according to its own

receiving capability, and the sender will adjust the sending window in time with reference to this value, so as to control the flow.

13. Checksum takes two bytes. The scope of the checksum field includes both the header and the data.

14. Urgent pointer is two bytes. The urgent pointer is meaningful only when URG = 1, and it points out the number of bytes of urgent data in this message segment (the urgent data is followed by ordinary data). Thus, the urgent pointer indicates the position of the end of the urgent data in the message segment. After all the urgent data has been processed, TCP tells the application process to resume normal operation. It is important to note that urgent data can be sent even when the window value is zero.

15. Options are variable in length, up to 40 bytes. When no options are used, the TCP header is 20 bytes. TCP originally specified only one option, that is the Maximum Segment Size (MSS). MSS is the maximum length of the data field in each TCP message segment. The entire TCP message segment consists of the data field and the TCP header equals, so the MSS is not the maximum length of the entire TCP message segment, but rather "the length of the TCP message segment minus the length of the TCP header".

2.3.4   TCP Connection Management

The TCP protocol is a reliable transmission protocol, and computers using TCP communication need to make sure of the presence of the other party before the communication formally starts and determine the parameters for negotiating the communication, such as the size of the receiving window at the receiving end, the maximum message segment length supported, whether selective acknowledgement (SACK) is allowed, and whether timestamps are supported. Once a connection is established, two-way communication is enabled, and the connection must be released when the communication ends.

TCP connections are established using the client/server method. The application process that actively establishes the connection is called the client, while the application process that passively waits for the connection to be established is called the server. The following section describes the establishment and release of TCP connections in detail.

1. The establishment of TCP connection

The process of establishing a TCP connection is elaborated in Fig. 2.28. The client initiates communication with the server, and a TCP session is established between the TCP modules of the client and the server through "three-way handshaking". "Three-way handshaking" means that a total of three TCP packets (which contain no data, but only TCP headers) are exchanged during the establishment of the TCP session, and these three packets are the packets that TCP

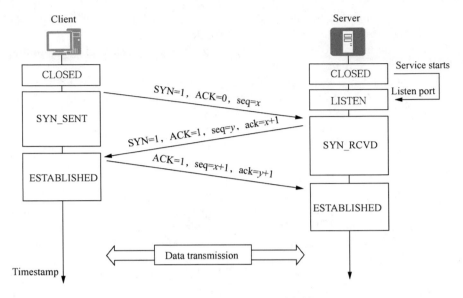

Fig. 2.28   Establish TCP connection through three-way handshaking

protocol uses to establish the connection. It should be noted that at different phases, different states can be observed on the client and server.

When the server starts the service, it will listen to the client's request using one of the TCP ports and wait for the client's connection, and the status will change from CLOSED to LISTEN. The process of the three-way handshaking is introduced in detail below, in which the abbreviations are case-sensitive, for example, upper-case ACK refers to the ACK flag bits, while lower-case ack means the value of the acknowledgement number.

(a) The client application sends a TCP connection request message to tell the other party its status. The SYN flag bit of the TCP header of this message is 1, the ACK flag bit is 0, and the sequence number (seq) is x, which is called the initial sequence number of the client with its value usually being 0. After sending the connection request message, the client is in the SYN_SENT state.

(b) After receiving the TCP connection request from the client, the server sends an acknowledgement message for connection to inform the client about its state. The SYN flag bit of the TCP header of this message is 1, the ACK flag bit is 1, the acknowledgement number (ack) is $x + 1$, and the sequence number (seq) is y (y is the initial sequence number of the server). The server is then in the SYN_RCVD state.

(c) After the client receives the acknowledgement message for connection request, the status changes to ESTABLISHED and then sends another acknowledgement message to the server to confirm the establishment of the session. The SYN flag bit of this message is 0, the ACK flag bit is 1, and the

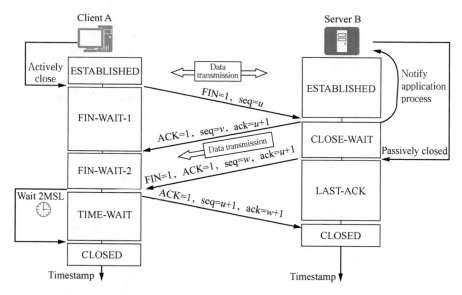

Fig. 2.29 The process of TCP connection release

acknowledgement number (ack) is $y + 1$. The server receives the acknowledgement message, and the status changes to ESTABLISHED.

It is important to note that after the three-way handshaking, in fact, two
TCP sessions are established between the client and the server, one from the
client to the server and the other from the server to the client. Since the client
is the one initiating the communication, it means that the client has information to pass to the server, so the client first sends a SYN segment requesting
the establishment of a TCP session from the client to the server. The purpose
of this session is to control that information is passed from the client to the
server in a correct and reliable manner. After receiving the SYN segment, the
server sends a SYN + ACK segment in response. This SYN + ACK segment
means: The server agrees to the client's request on the one hand, and requests
to establish a TCP session from the server to the client on the other, the
purpose of which is to enable the correct and reliable delivery of information
from the server to the client. After receiving the SYN + ACK segment, the
client responds with an ACK segment, indicating that it agrees to the server's
request. After that, two-way reliable communication is enabled.

2. Release of TCP connection

After TCP communication is completed, the connection shall be released. The
process of releasing a TCP connection is complicated, so we will clarify the
process of releasing a connection by combining the change of status of both
parties. When the data transfer is over, both the sender and the receiver can
release the connection. As shown in Fig. 2.29, both A and B are now in the

ESTABLISHED state, and A's application process first sends a connection release message to its TCP, stops sending data, and actively closes the TCP connection. A sets the FIN of the header of the release message segment to 1, with the sequence number of $seq = u$, which is equal to the sequence number of the last byte of the previously transmitted data plus 1. At this point, A enters the FIN-WAIT-1 state, waiting for the acknowledgement from B. Note that TCP specifies that the FIN message segment consumes a sequence number even if it contains no data.

When B receives the connection release message, it sends an acknowledgement with an acknowledgement number of $ack = u + 1$, and the message's own sequence number is v, which is equal to the sequence number of the last byte of the data that B has previously transmitted plus 1. B then enters the CLOSE-WAIT state, at which point the TCP server process notifies the higher-layer application process, so the connection is released in the direction from A to B. At this point, while the TCP connection is in the Half-Close state, that is A has no more data to send, but if B sends data, A still has to receive it. In other words, the connection in the direction from B to A is not closed. This state may last for some time.

Once A receives the acknowledgment from B, it enters the FIN-WAIT-2 state and waits for B to send a connection release message segment. If B has no data to send to A, its application process will notify TCP to release the connection. Then B must send a connection release message with FIN = 1. Now assume that B's sequence number is w (B may have sent some more data in the half-close state.). Meanwhile, B must also repeat the acknowledgement number $ack = u + 1$ that it has sent the last time. At this point, B enters the LAST-ACK (last-acknowledgment) state and waits for A's acknowledgement.

After receiving the connection release message segment from B, A must send an acknowledgement for this. In the acknowledgment message segment, ACK is set to 1, the acknowledgment number is $ack = w + 1$, and its own sequence number is $seq = u + 1$ (according to the TCP standard, a sequence number is consumed by the previously sent FIN message segment). Then it enters the TIME-WAIT state. Note that the TCP connection has not been released yet. Only after the TIME-WAIT Timer is set for 2MSL will A enter the CLOSED state. The time MSL is called Maximum Segment Lifetime and is recommended by RFC 793 to be set to 2 min. However, this is purely for engineering reasons and MSL = 2 min may be too long for today's networks. Therefore, TCP allows smaller MSL values to be applied for different implementations on a case-by-case basis. Thus, after A enters the TIME-WAIT state, it takes 4 min to enter the CLOSED state before a new connection can start to be established.

2.3.5 Implementation of TCP Reliable Transmission

The TCP protocol implements reliable transmission by using the sliding window protocol and the Automatic Repeat-reQuest (ARQ) protocol. The following

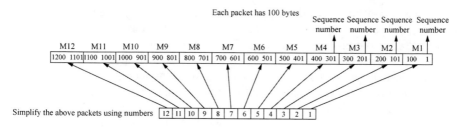

Fig. 2.30 Simplified representation of packets

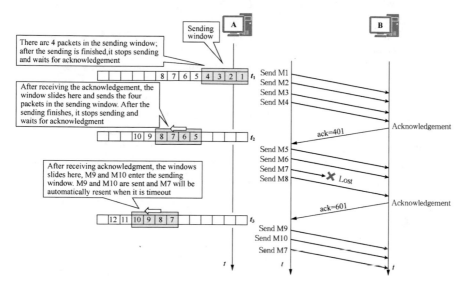

Fig. 2.31 The continuous ARQ protocol and sliding window protocol

describes the working process of the sliding window protocol and the continuous
ARQ protocol.

1. Working process of sliding window protocol

After the TCP protocol establishes a connection, both parties can use the
established connection to send data to each other. For the convenience of
discussion, here we only consider that A sends data while B receives data and
sends an acknowledgement. Therefore, A is called the sender and B the receiver.

The sliding window is byte-stream oriented, and to make it easier for readers to
remember the sequence number of each packet, it is assumed here that each
packet is 100 bytes. To facilitate the drawing, the packets are numbered for a
simplified representation, as shown in Fig. 2.30. But be sure to remember the
sequence number of each packet.

As shown in Fig. 2.31, when establishing a TCP connection, Computer B tells
Computer A that it has a receiving window of 400 bytes, and Computer A sets a
sending window of 400 bytes. If a packet has 100 bytes, then there will be a total

of four packets in the sending window, M1, M2, M3, M4, and Sender A can send these four packets consecutively. A sending time will be recorded for each packet, as shown at the time t_1 in Fig. 2.31. The sending stops when it is finished. The Receiver B receives these four consecutive packets and only needs to send one acknowledgement to A with the acknowledgement number 401, notifying A that it has received all bytes before 400. As shown at the moment t_2 in Fig. 2.31, as Sender A receives an acknowledgement for M4, the sending window slides forward, and M5, M6, M7 and M8 enter the sending window. These four packets can be sent consecutively, and after they are sent, the sending stops and waits for an acknowledgement. This is the sliding window protocol.

2. The working process of continuous ARQ protocol

If M7 is lost during transmission, and Computer B receives M5, M6 and M8 packets, as well as consecutive packets from M1 to M6, it will send an acknowledgement to Computer A. The sequence number of the acknowledgement is 601, notifying Computer A that all bytes before 600 have been received. At the time of t_3 in Fig. 2.31, Computer A receives the acknowledgement and instead of sending M7 immediately, it slides forward the sending window so that M9 and M10 enter the sending window and are sent. When to send M7? M7 will automatically be resent when it is timeout. The timeout is a little longer than a round trip time. If M9 is sent and M7 is timeout, the sending sequence becomes M9, M7 and M10. This is the continuous ARQ protocol.

2.3.6 UDP

UDP is used to process packets in the same way as TCP, and both are located at the transport layer (at the layer above the IP protocol) in the OSI model. UDP at the transport layer is a connectionless transport protocol. It provides a way for applications to send IP packets without establishing a connection.

UDP does not have features such as sequencing of packets sent, retransmission for lost packets, or flow control. In other words, after the message is sent, there is no way to know whether it has arrived securely and completely. UDP exists mainly to identify an application layer protocol by using UDP+port.

2.4 Network Layer Protocols

The network layer is used to process the packets that flow over the network. A packet is the smallest unit of data transmitted over the network, and this layer specifies the path (the so-called transmission line) through which the packet reaches the other computer and delivers the packet to the other party.

2.4.1   Two Versions of Network Layer Protocols

There are two versions of the core protocols of the network layer in the TCP/IP layered model, that is IPv4 and IPv6, which are collectively referred to in this book as IP. IPv6 is an improvement over IPv4, but their functions are the same. The network layer protocol serves the transport layer, responsible for sending segments of the transport layer to the receiver. IP protocol implements the functions of network layer protocols. The sender adds the IP headers to the transport layer segments. The IP header includes the source and target IP addresses, and the segments with the IP headers are called "packets". Routers in the network forward packets based on IP headers.

As shown in Fig. 2.32, there are four protocols in the network layer of the TCP/IPv4 stack: ARP, IPv4, ICMP, and IGMP, among which ARP, ICMP, and IGMP are secondary protocols. TCP and UDP use port numbers to identify application layer protocols, while TCP segments, UDP messages, ICMP messages, and IGMP messages can all be encapsulated in IPv4 packets, differentiated by protocol numbers. It means that IPv4 uses protocol numbers to identify the upper-layer protocols, with TCP's protocol number being 6, UDP's being 17, ICMP's being 1, and IGMP's being 2. Although ICMP and IGMP are both at the network layer, in terms of their relationship, ICMP and IGMP are above the IP protocol, which means that ICMP and IGMP messages are to be encapsulated in IPv4 packets.

ARP is used only in Ethernet to resolve IP addresses to MAC addresses. Only when the MAC address is resolved can the packet be encapsulated into a frame and sent out. Therefore, ARP provides a service for IP. Although ARP belongs to the network layer, in terms of relationship, ARP is under the IP protocol.

Figure 2.33 shows the TCP/IPv6 protocol stack, in which the network layer protocols have changed significantly, but it does not affect the transport layer protocols, nor the data link layer protocols. The network layer of the TCP/IPv6 protocol stack does not have ARP or IGMP protocols, the functions of ICMP protocols have been greatly extended, and the functions of ARP and IGMP protocols are also

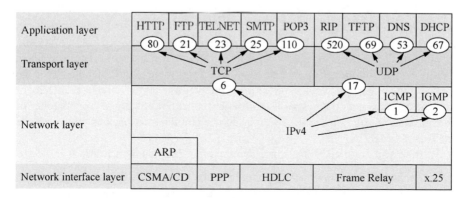

Fig. 2.32 TCP/IPv4 protocol stack

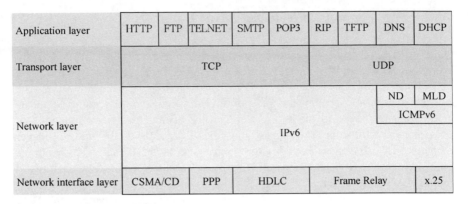

Application layer	HTTP	FTP	TELNET	SMTP	POP3	RIP	TFTP	DNS	DHCP
Transport layer	TCP					UDP			
Network layer	IPv6							ND	MLD
								ICMPv6	
Network interface layer	CSMA/CD		PPP	HDLC		Frame Relay			x.25

Fig. 2.33 TCP/IPv6 protocol stack

embedded in ICMPv6, namely, Neighbor Discovery (ND) and Multicast Listener
Discovery (MLD) protocols, respectively.

IPv6 is covered in detail in later chapters of this book. If not specified in this book,
the default IP protocol refers to IPv4.

2.4.2 IP

The IP (Internet Protocol), also known as the Internet Protocol, is the core of the
TCP/IP protocol that is responsible for communication between networks on the
Internet and defines the rules for transmitting packets from one network to another.

When IP is adopted as the network layer protocol, both sides of the communication are assigned a "unique" IP address to identify themselves. IP addresses can be
written in 32-bit binary form, but to make it easier for people to read and analyze, it is
usually written in dotted decimal form, i.e., four bytes are separated and represented
in decimal form, using dots for separation, such as 192.168.1.1.

When IP protocols work, various routing protocols such as OSPF, IS-IS, BGP,
are needed to help routers build routing tables, so ICMP is required to assist in
network state diagnosis. If the influx of packets on a link exceeds the processing
capacity of the router, the router drops the packets that it has not processed. Since
each packet is individually selected for forwarding, there is no guarantee that the
packets will reach the receiver in order. The IP protocol is only responsible for
forwarding packets to the best of its ability, but it cannot guarantee the reliability of
transmission and may lose packets, nor can it guarantee that packets will reach the
receiver in order.

The encapsulation and forwarding process of IP packets is as follows.

1. When the network layer receives data from the upper layer (such as the transport
   layer) protocols, it encapsulates an IP message header and adds both the source
   and destination IP addresses to that header.

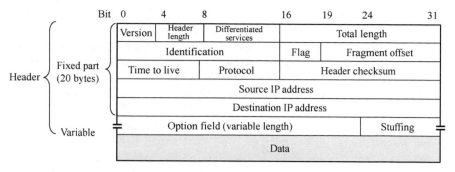

Fig. 2.34 Network layer IP packet header format

2. The network devices (e.g., router) that are passed through along the way will maintain a routing table that guides the forwarding of IP messages, and by reading the destination address of the IP packet, forward the IP messages according to the local routing table.
3. The IP message finally reaches the destination host, which reads the destination IP address to determine whether to receive and continue the next processing.

The IP packet consists of two parts: the header and the data. The IP protocol defines the IP message header, as shown in Fig. 2.34. The first part of the IP message header is a fixed length of 20 bytes, which exists in all IP packets. Following the fixed part of the header are some optional fields whose length is variable.

The following is a detailed explanation of each field in the fixed part of the network layer IP packet header.

1. Version is a four bits value and refers to the version of the IP protocol. There are currently two versions of the IP protocol: IPv4 and IPv6. The version of the IP protocol used by both sides of the communication must be the same. The IP protocol version number that is widely used now is 4 (i.e., IPv4).
2. The header length field is four bits in size, and the maximum decimal value that can be represented is 15. Please note that the unit of the number represented by this field is a 32-bit binary number (i.e., four bytes), so when the header length of IP is 1111 (i.e., 15 in decimal), the header length reaches 60 bytes. When the IP packet's header length is not an integer multiple of four bytes, it must be filled using stuffing fields in the end. Therefore, the data division always starts with an integer multiple of four bytes, which is more convenient when implementing IP protocols. The disadvantage of limiting the header length to 60 bytes is that sometimes it may not be enough. However, such limit is posed in the hope that the user will minimize the cost. The most common header length is 20 bytes (i.e., a header length of 0101), at which point no options are used. It is because of the variable part of the header that a field is needed to specify the header length; if the header is fixed in length, the header length field will no longer be needed.
3. Differentiated Services (DS) is eight bits long. The differentiated services configure the computer to add a flag to the packets of a particular application,

and then configure the routers in the network to give priority to forwarding these packets with flags, so as to guarantee the sufficient bandwidth of this application even the network bandwidth is relatively tight. This is the differentiated services, which ensure the Quality of Service (QoS). This field was called Type of Service in the former standard, but has never actually been used. In 1998, the Internet Engineering Task Force (IETF) renamed this field differentiated services, which only take effect when a differentiated service is used.

4. Total length refers to the total length of the IP packet header and data, which is the length of the packet in bytes. The total length field is 16 bits, so the maximum length of the packet is $2^{16} - 1 = 65,535$ bytes. In fact, the transmission of such a long packet is rarely encountered in reality.

5. The Identification field is 16 bits. IP software maintains a counter in memory, and for each packet generated, the counter is incremented by 1, and this value is assigned to the identification field. However, this "Identification" is not a sequence number. Since IP is a connectionless service, the problem of receiving packets in order does not exist. When a packet must be fragmented because its length exceeds the network's Maximum Transfer Unit (MTU), the same packet is split into multiple fragments sharing the same identifier, that is, the value of the packet's identification field is copied to the identification fields of all packet fragments. The same value of the identification field enables the packet fragments to be correctly reassembled into the original packet after the fragmentation.

6. Flag has three bits, but currently only two bits mean something. The lowest bit in the flag field is recorded as MF (More Fragment). MF = 1 means that there are "more fragments" of packets following, and MF = 0 means that this fragment is the last one of the several packet fragments. The middle bit of the flag field is DF (Don't Fragment). Fragmentation is allowed only when DF = 0.

7. Fragment offset is 13 bits in size. The fragment offset indicates the relative position of a fragment in the original packet when a relatively long packet is fragmented. In other words, it means where the fragment starts relative to the beginning of the user data field. The unit of fragment offsets is eight bytes, which means that the length of each fragment must be an integer multiple of eight bytes (64 bits).

8. The common abbreviation for the Time to Live field is TTL, indicating the lifetime of the packet in the network. This field is set by the source point of the outbound packet. It aims to prevent undeliverable packets from circling in the network indefinitely, such as forwarding from router R1 to R2, then to R3, and then back to R1, thus wasting network resources. TTL is originally designed in seconds. Each time a router is passed, the period of time consumed by the packet at the router is subtracted from TTL. If the packet spends less than 1 s at the router, the TTL value is subtracted by 1. When the TTL value is reduced to zero, the packet is discarded. However, as technology progresses, the time required by the router to process the packet keeps to be reduced, and generally it takes much less time than 1 s, so later the function of the TTL field is changed to "hop limit" (but the name remains the same). The TTL value is subtracted by 1 before the

Protocol name	ICMP	IGMP	IP	TCP	IGP	UDP	IPv6	ESP	OSPF
Protocol field value	1	2	4	6	9	17	41	50	89

Fig. 2.35 Commonly used protocols and corresponding protocol field values

router forwards the packet. If the TTL value is reduced to zero, the packet is discarded and will not be forwarded. Therefore, TTL is now no longer in seconds, but hops, and TTL indicates the maximum number of routers through which a packet can pass in the network. Obviously, the maximum number of routers a packet can pass through in the network is 255. If the initial value of TTL is set to 1, it means that the packet can only be transmitted in this LAN. It is because that as soon as the packet is transmitted to one of the routers on the LAN, before it is forwarded, the TTL value decreases to zero, and will be discarded by this router.

9. Protocol is eight bits in size. The protocol field indicates which protocol is used for the data carried by this packet so that the network layer of the destination host knows which process the data division should be passed to. Some of the commonly used protocols and the corresponding protocol field values are shown in Fig. 2.35.

10. The header checksum is 16 bits in size, and this field only checks the header of the packet and not the data division. This is because every time a packet passes through a router, the router has to recalculate the header checksum (some fields, such as time to live, flags, fragment offsets, may change). The workload of the calculation can be reduced if the data division is not checked.

11. The source IP address is 32 bits long.

12. The target IP address is 32 bits long.

2.4.3 ICMP

ICMP (Internet Control Message Protocol) is a TCP/IPv4 network layer protocol for delivering control messages between IP hosts and routers. Control messages are messages about the network itself, such as the network connectivity, host reachability, and route availability.

ICMP messages are transmitted and encapsulated inside IP packets. ICMP messages are usually adopted by IP layer or higher-layer protocols (TCP or UDP). Some ICMP messages return error messages to the user process.

ICMP request messages can be sent using the ping and tracert commands on Windows, Linux, and network devices to test whether the network is running smoothly or to track the routers that the packets pass through to reach the destination IP address.

As shown below, when the ping command is used to query a website domain name on Windows 10, 4 ICMP request messages are sent and 4 ICMP responses from this address are received, indicating that the network is smooth.

```
C:\Users\hanlg>ping www.huawei.com
Pinging www.huawei.com.lxdns.com [111.11.0.121] with 32 bytes
of data:
Reply from 111.11.0.121: bytes=32 time=10ms TTL=57
Reply from 111.11.0.121: bytes=32 time =11ms TTL=57
Reply from 111.11.0.121: bytes=32 time =10ms TTL=57
Reply from 111.11.0.121: bytes=32 time =11ms TTL=57
Ping statistics for 111.11.0.121:
   Packets: Sent = 4, Received = 4, Lost = 0 (0% loss),
Approximate round trip times in milli-seconds:
   Minimum = 10ms, Maximum = 11ms, Average = 10ms
```

As shown below, when the tracert command is used to trace the routers along the path of the packet, it can be seen that the packet has passed 13 routers along the way, and the 14th is the destination address.

```
C:\Users\hanlg>tracert www.91xueit.com
Tracing route to www.91xueit.com [129.226.71.87]
Over a maxim of 30 hops:
  1    2 ms    1 ms    3 ms phicomm.me [192.168.2.1]
  2    4 ms    6 ms    8 ms 10.220.0.1
  3    5 ms    4 ms    4 ms 111.63.220.13
  4    4 ms    4 ms    5 ms 111.11.64.17
  5   10 ms    4 ms    5 ms 111.24.8.253
  6    9 ms    9 ms    8 ms 111.24.3.161
  7   38 ms   38 ms   59 ms 221.176.24.241
  8   37 ms   38 ms   39 ms 221.176.22.106
  9   53 ms   39 ms   42 ms 221.176.19.198
 10   77 ms   59 ms   48 ms 221.183.55.81
 11   49 ms   63 ms   65 ms 218.189.5.25
 12   61 ms   70 ms   71 ms 218.189.29.122
 13   47 ms   63 ms   46 ms 10.196.94.241
 14   45 ms   55 ms   47 ms 129.226.71.87
```

In the following, packet capture is used to view the format of ICMP messages. As shown in Fig. 2.36, PC1 pings 192.168.8.2, and the ping command generates an ICMP request message to send to the destination address to test whether the network is connected. If the destination computer receives the ICMP request message, it will return an ICMP response message.

The following part describes how to use the packet capture tool to capture ICMP request and response messages on the link, and observes the differences between the two types of messages.

As demonstrated in Fig. 2.37, packets on router links AR1 and AR2 are captured. The figure shows an ICMP request message, which has an ICMP message type field,

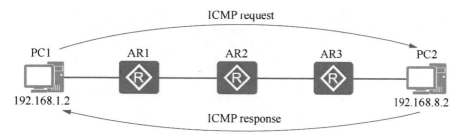

Fig. 2.36 ICMP request and response messages

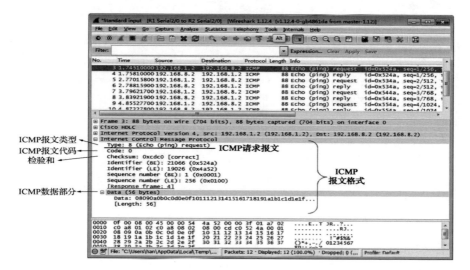

Fig. 2.37 ICMP request message

an ICMP message code field, a checksum field, and an ICMP data division. The value of request message type is 8 and the message code is 0.

Figure 2.38 shows an ICMP response message with a type value of 0 and a message code of 0.

ICMP messages can be divided into three types, each of which uses a code to further specify the different meanings it represents. Table 2.1 lists the common ICMP message types and codes and what they represent.

As can be seen from Table 2.1, there are five types of ICMP error reports, which are introduced in detail below.

1. Destination unreachable. When a router or host does not have a route to the destination address, it discards the packet and sends a destination unreachable message to the source.
2. Source quench. When a router or host discards a packet due to congestion, it sends a source quench message to the source, so that the source understands that it should slow down the sending of packets.

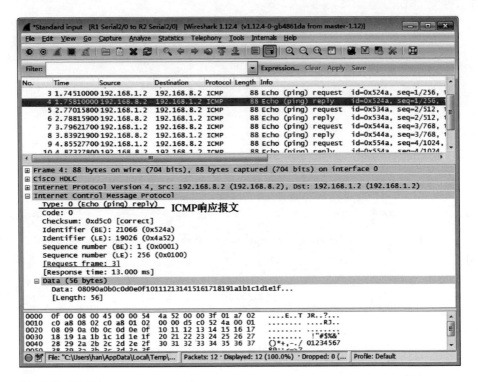

Fig. 2.38 ICMP response message

Table 2.1 ICMP message types and codes and what they represent

Message type	Type value	Code	Description
Request message	8	0	Echo request message
Response message	0	0	Echo response message
Error reporting message	3 (Destination Unreachable)	0	Net unreachable
		1	Host unreachable
		2	Protocol unreachable
		3	Port unreachable
		4	Fragmentation is needed, but don't-fragment bit set
		13	Communication administratively prohibited by filtering
	4 (Source Quench)	0	Source is closed
	5 (Redirect)	0	Redirect for network
		1	Redirect for host
	11 (Time Exceeded)	0	Time to live equals 0 during transit
	12 (Parameter Problem)	0	IP header bad
		1	Required option missing

3. Redirect. The router sends a redirect message to the host to let it know that the packet should be sent to a different router next time (which might be a better routing).
4. Time exceeded. When a router receives a packet with a time to live of zero, in addition to discarding the packet, it sends a time exceeded message to the source. When the destination fails to receive all the packet fragments of a packet within a pre-defined time, it discards all the received packet fragments and sends a time exceeded message to the source.
5. Parameter problem. When the router or the destination host receives a packet with incorrect field values in its header, it discards the packet and sends a parameter problem message to the source.

2.4.4 ARP

Address Resolution Protocol (ARP) is an indispensable protocol of IPv4. Its main function is to resolve IP addresses into MAC addresses, maintain a cache of the mapping relation between IP addresses and MAC addresses, i.e., the ARP table entries, as well as detect duplicate IP addresses within a network segment.

1. Ethernet and MAC addresses

   To better illustrate the problem, before explaining ARP, we will first introduce the Ethernet and MAC addresses.

   (a) Ethernet. Ethernet is a broadcast data link layer protocol that supports multipoint access. A network formed by a switch is a typical Ethernet, and the computer's network interface card follows the Ethernet standard. In Ethernet, the network interface card and network device interface (such as router interfaces and virtual interfaces of Layer 3 switches) of each computer have a MAC address.

   The MAC address is also called the physical address, or hardware address, and is burned into the flash memory chip of the Network Interface Card (NC) by the manufacturer of the network device. MAC addresses are represented in the computer in 48-bit binary form. Computer communication over Ethernet must specify the destination MAC address and the source MAC address.

   In order to view the MAC address of a computer's network interface card on Windows, you only need to type "ipconfig /all", as shown below. In Windows, it is called "physical address". Here is the MAC address in hexadecimal.

```
C:\Users\hanlg>ipconfig /all
Windows IP Configuration
  Connection-specific DNS Suffix . .   : lan
  Description. . . . . . . . . . . .   : Intel(R) Dual Band Wireless-
AC 3165
```

```
    Physical Address. . . . . . . . . . : 00-DB-DF-F9-D2-51
    DHCP Enabled . . . . . . . . . . . : Yes
    Autoconfiguration Enabled. . . . . . : Yes
   Link-local IPv6 Address. . . . . . : fe80::65d6:9e31:63a0:9dd1%
11 (Preferred)
    IPv4 Address . . . . . . . . . . . : 192.168.2.161(Preferred)
    Subnet Mask  . . . . . . . . . . . : 255.255.255.0
    Lease Obtained . . . . . . . . . : August-03-20 15:46:18
    Lease Expires  . . . . . . . . . : August-04-20 16:43:43
    Default Gateway. . . . . . . . . . : 192.168.2.1
```

Network devices generally have an ARP Cache. The ARP cache is used to store the association information of IP addresses and MAC addresses.

Before the data is sent, the device will look for the ARP cache table first. If the ARP table entry of the other device exists in the cache table, the MAC address in that table entry will be directly used to encapsulate the frame and then send the frame. If the corresponding information does not exist in the cache table, it is obtained by sending an ARP Request message.

The mapping relation between IP address and MAC address is stored in the ARP cache table for a period of time. During the validity period (default: 180 s), the device can directly look up the target MAC address from this table for data encapsulation without ARP query. After this validity period, the ARP table entry will be automatically deleted.

If the target IP address is located in another network, the source device will look up the MAC address of the gateway (router interface in this network) in the ARP cache table and then send the data to the gateway. After receiving the packet, the router selects a forwarding path for the packet.

2. Working process of ARP

The working process of ARP is shown in Fig. 2.39. Computer A sends an ARP request message requesting to resolve the target MAC address of 192.168.1.20. Since Computer A does not know the target MAC address of 192.168.1.20, the request writes the target MAC address as a broadcast address, that is, FF-FF-FF-FF-FF-FF. Then the switch forwards the request to all ports once it receives the request.

When all hosts receive this ARP request message, they check whether its target IP address field matches their own IP address. If not, the host will not respond to the ARP request message. And if it matches, the host will record the sender's MAC address and IP address information in the ARP request message into its own ARP cache table, and then respond via an ARP reply message, as shown in Fig. 2.40. The target MAC address of ARP Response frame is the MAC address of Computer A.

3. Communication within the same network segment and cross-segment communication

As shown in Fig. 2.41, there are two Ethernet networks and a point to point link in the network. The addresses of the computer and router interfaces are

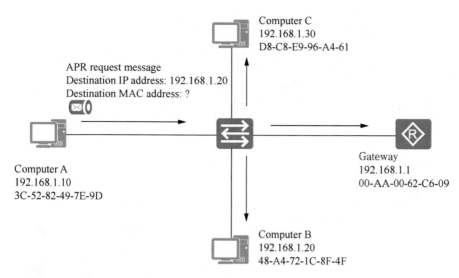

Fig. 2.39   ARP request using broadcast frames

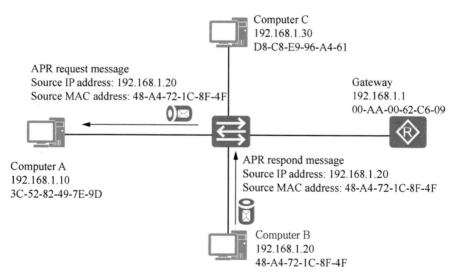

Fig. 2.40   ARP response using unicast frames

shown in the figure. The MA, MB...MF in the figure represent the MAC addresses of the corresponding interfaces. Computer A communicates with Computer B on the same network segment. Computer A sends an ARP broadcast frame to resolve the MAC address of the target IP address, and later the frames for communication encapsulate the target IP address and MAC address.

When Computer A communicates with Computer F on a different network segment, Computer A needs to resolve the MAC address of the gateway. The

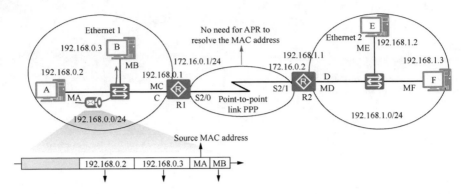

Fig. 2.41 The computer on the same network segment sends an ARP broadcast frame to resolve the MAC address of the target IP address

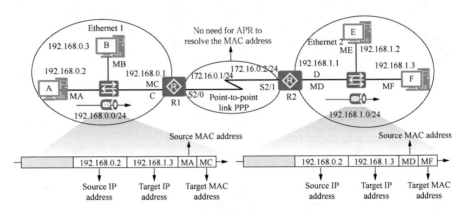

Fig. 2.42 The computer for cross-segment communication sends ARP broadcast frame to resolve the MAC address of the gateway

frame sent from Computer A to Computer F is as in Fig. 2.42. Pay attention to the IP address and MAC address of the packet encapsulated in the two Ethernet networks. The source and target IP addresses of the packet remain unchanged during the transmission. For the packet to be sent from Computer A to Computer F, it needs to forward the MAC address of interface C of router R1, so the source MAC address of the packet encapsulated in Ethernet 1 is MA, while the target MAC address is MC. When the packet arrives at router R2, it has to be sent to Computer F from interface D of R2. The packet has to re-encapsulate the data link layer with the source MAC address as MD and the target MAC address as MF.

In terms of encapsulating frames for cross-segment communication, the target IP address of the packet determines its destination, and the target MAC address of the frame determines the next hop interface of the packet. ARP can only resolve the MAC address of the same network segment. For packets from computers in other network segments, the source MAC address is that of the router interface. In

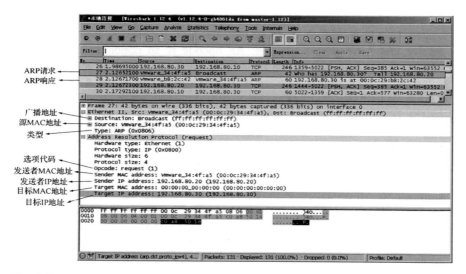

Fig. 2.43 ARP request frame

this example, Computer F does not know the MAC address of Computer A. The source MAC address of the packet from Computer A that Computer F sees is the MAC address of interface D of router R2.

Note	ARP is only used in Ethernet. Point to point links commonly use PPP at the data link layer. The frame format defined by PPP has no MAC address field, so there is no need to use ARP to resolve the MAC address.

After the MAC address is resolved by ARP, the Ethernet interface will cache the resolved MAC address. You can run "arp -a" on Windows system to view the ARP table entries. "Dynamic" in type column indicates the entry is obtained by ARP resolution and will be cleared from the cache if it is not used for a period of time.

```
C:\Users\hanlg>arp -a
Interface: 192.168.2.161 --- 0xb
  Internet Address      Physical Address      Type
  192.168.2.1        d8-c8-e9-96-a4-61      dynamic
  192.168.2.255      ff-ff-ff-ff-ff-ff       static
  224.0.0.22         01-00-5e-00-00-16       static
  224.0.0.251        01-00-5e-00-00-fb       static
  224.0.0.252        01-00-5e-00-00-fc       static
  255.255.255.255    ff-ff-ff-ff-ff-ff       static
```

4. Packet capture analysis of ARP frames

Figure 2.43 shows an ARP request packet captured by the packet capture tool. The 27th frame is the ARP request packet sent by computer 192.168.80.20 to

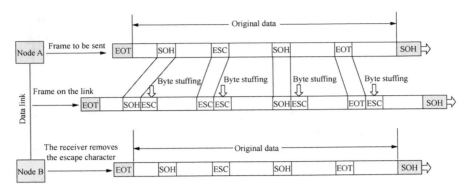

Fig. 2.46 Solve the problem of transparent transmission by byte stuffing

appear in the data division of the frame, an escape character shall be inserted. The receiver will remove the escape character once it encounters one upon receipt and treat the characters after the escape character as data, that is, transparent transmission. As shown in Fig. 2.46, a data link layer protocol has SOH as the start frame delimiter, EOT as the end frame delimiter, and ESC as the escape character. Node A sends a data frame to Node B, and before sending it to the data link, the code of the escape character ESC is inserted at the position before characters SOH, ESC and EOT in the data, and this process is called byte stuffing. After receiving it, Node B removes the stuffing escape character, and treats the character after the escape character as data.

The sender Node A inserts escape characters in the original data at the necessary position before sending the frame, and the receiver Node B removes the escape characters after receiving the frame to get the original data. The escape characters are inserted in the frame to allow the original data to be sent to Node B as it is, and this process is called "transparent transmission".

3. Error check.

Communication links in reality are not ideal. This means that errors may occur when bits are transmitted. A 1 can become a 0 or a 0 can become a 1, which is called a bit error. Bit error is a type of transmission error. The ratio of bit error to the total number of bits transmitted over a period of time is called the bit error rate (BER). For example, a BER of 10^{-10} means that on average, one bit error occurs for every 10^{10} bits transmitted. The BER is closely related to the signal-to-noise ratio (SNR). Improving the SNR can lower BER. However, in reality, the communication link is not ideal and it is not possible to reduce the BER to zero. Therefore, to ensure the reliability of data transmission, various error check measures must be applied when transmitting data in computer networks. Currently, the error check technology widely used in the data link layer is Cyclic Redundancy Check (CRC).

To enable the receiver to determine whether there is an error during the transmission of the frame, it is necessary to include information for error check in the transmitted frame, which is called Frame Check Sequence (FCS). As

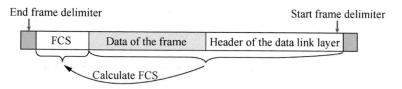

Fig. 2.47 Frame check sequence

shown in Fig. 2.47, the FCS is calculated using the data division of the frame and
the header of the data link layer, and the FCS is placed at the end of the frame.
After receiving the frame, the receiver uses the data division and the header of the
data link layer to calculate the FCS, and compares the two calculation results to
see if they are the same. If they are the same, it is assumed that there is no error
during the transmission; and if there is an error, the receiver discards the frame.

2.6 Exercises

1. Which layer of the TCP/IPv4 protocol stack is used for reliable transmission of
   computer communications? ( )

   A. Physical layer
   B. Application layer
   C. Transport layer
   D. Network layer

2. As IPv4 is upgraded to IPv6, which layer of the TCP/IPv4 protocol stack has
   been changed? ( )

   A. Data link layer
   B. Network layer
   C. Application layer
   D. Physical layer

3. What can ARP do? ( )

   A. Resolve computers' MAC addresses to IP addresses
   B. Domain name resolution
   C. Reliable transmission
   D. Resolve IP addresses into MAC addresses

4. What is the range of TCP and UDP port numbers? ( )

   A. 0–256
   B. 0–1023

C. 0–65,535
D. 1024–65,535

5. Which of the following network protocols uses TCP port 25 by default? ( )

   A. HTTP
   B. Telnet
   C. SMTP
   D. POP3

6. In Windows system, the command used to check the listening ports is ( ).

   A. ipconfig /all
   B. netstat –an
   C. ping
   D. telnet

7. In Windows, the ping command uses the ( ) protocol.

   A. HTTP
   B. IGMP
   C. TCP
   D. ICMP

8. Which of the following statements about the functions of the network layer in the OSI reference model is correct ( )?

   A. It is the layer closest to the user in the OSI reference model and provides network services for applications
   B. It transfers bitstreams between devices, specifying levels, speeds, and cable pins
   C. It provides connection-oriented or non-connection-oriented data transfer and error check before retransmission
   D. It provides logical addresses for routers to determine paths

9. OSI reference model from the upper to lower layers are ( ).

   A. Application layer, session layer, presentation layer, transport layer, network layer, data link layer, physical layer
   B. Application layer, transport layer, network layer, data link layer, physical layer
   C. Application layer, presentation layer, session layer, transport layer, network layer, data link layer, physical layer
   D. Application layer, presentation layer, session layer, network layer, transport layer, data link layer, physical layer

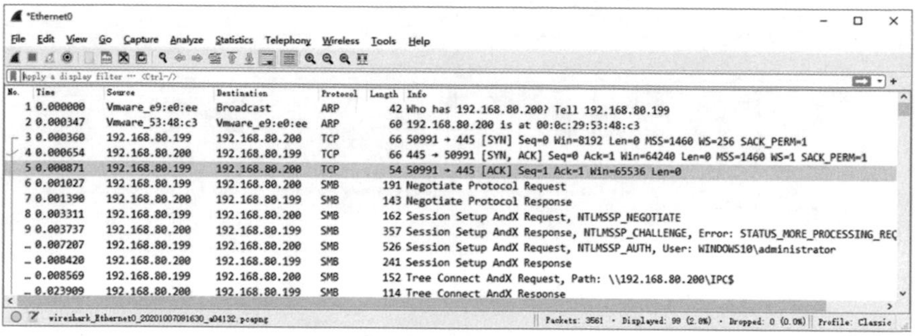

Fig. 2.48 Captured packet

10. (Multi-selection) A network administrator uses the ping command to test the connectivity of a network. In this process, which of the following protocols may be used? ( )

   A. ARP
   B. TCP
   C. ICMP
   D. IP

11. Figure 2.48 shows a packet of accessing a shared folder on a file server (the server) captured on a Windows system (the client). Please answer the following questions based on the content displayed in the figure.

   A. What are the IP address and MAC address of the file server?
   B. Which three packets are used to establish a TCP connection? How many bytes does the receiving window have when the server establishes a TCP connection?
   C. Which layer does the Server Message Block (SMB) protocol belong to? Does the SMB protocol use the TCP or UDP protocol at the transport layer? And what is the port?

12. Based on the contents of the seventh packet transport layer shown in Fig. 2.49, write the value of the "Sequence number" of the seventh packet transport layer, as well as the values of "Source Port" and "Destination Port".

13. Figure 2.50 shows the packets captured by the packet capture tool. A computer is infected with a "virus" and sends ARP broadcast frames on the Internet. Observe the packets in the figure and find out which computer is sending the ARP broadcast frames.

14. What is the TCP/IP protocol layered by? Write down the functions that each protocol layer implements.

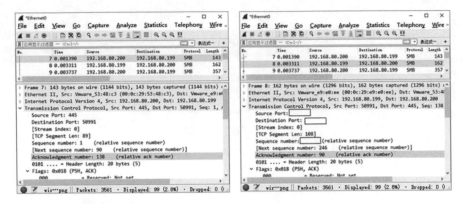

Fig. 2.49 Packet transport layer header

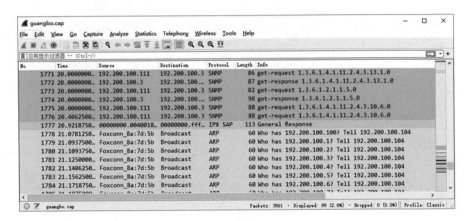

Fig. 2.50 ARP broadcast

15. List a few common application layer protocols.
16. What contents should the application layer protocols define?
17. Write down two transport layer protocols and their application scenarios.
18. Write down four network layer protocols and the functions of each protocol.

Chapter 3
VRP Fundamentals

One needs to be familiar with Huawei network devices, such as routers, switches and firewalls, so as to configure them. Huawei has developed a general operating system for these network devices, which undoubtedly reduces the learning cost for IT practitioners. Versatile Routing Platform (VRP) is a general network operating system for Huawei network devices.

VRP provides users with a Command-Line Interface (CLI), and users are required to master how to use the command line in order to manage network devices.

When configuring Huawei network devices for the first time, you usually log in through the Console port. After the network is configured, you can log in to the network devices through Telnet, SSH, or Web to configure the device. The general configuration of the network devices includes changing the device name, setting the device clock, configuring the IP address for the network device interface, and setting the login password.

The configuration of the device will take effect immediately after completion. At this point, the current configuration can be viewed by the display current-configuration command and can be saved by the display saved-configuration command. In addition, the configuration file to be loaded at the next boot can also be changed.

VRP manages all files (including configuration files, system files, License files and patch files of the device) and directories on the device through the file system. The VRP file system is mainly used to create, delete, modify, copy and display files and directories on the device.

3.1 Introduction to VRP

VRP is a general network operating system of which Huawei Technologies Co., Ltd. has completely independent intellectual property rights. It can run on a full range of communication products from low-end to high-end, such as routers and switches. It

© The Author(s) 2023
Huawei Technologies Co., Ltd., *Data Communications and Network Technologies*,
https://doi.org/10.1007/978-981-19-3029-4_3

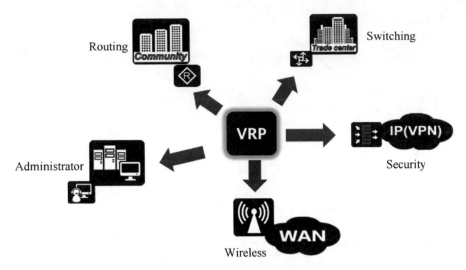

Fig. 3.1 VRP application solutions

is similar to Microsoft's Windows operating system and Apple's iOS operating system. At present, Huawei devices are almost ubiquitous in network devices around the world, so it is especially important for network communication technicians to learn about the knowledge of VRP.

VRP can run on a variety of hardware platforms, including routers, LAN switches, ATM switches, dial-up access servers, IP telephony gateways, carrier-grade integrated service access platforms, intelligent service selection gateways and dedicated hardware firewalls. VRP has a consistent network interface, user interface and management interface, providing users with flexible and rich application solutions, as shown in Fig. 3.1.

With TCP/IP protocol stack as the core, VRP implements various data link layer, network layer and application layer protocols, integrates data communication functions such as routing and switching technology, QoS technology, security technology and IP voice technology in the operating system, and provides excellent data forwarding function for network devices based on IP forwarding engine technology.

3.2 VRP Command Lines

The commands in the VRP command line consist of keywords and parameters, and the total number of commands mounts to thousands. In order to realize the layered management of these commands, the VRP system registers them under different views according to the types of their functions. VRP command levels are divided into level 0 (visit), level 1 (monitoring), level 2 (configuration) and level

3 (management), while users logging into network devices are divided into levels from 0 to 15. Users of different levels can execute commands of different levels.

3.2.1 Basic Concepts of the Command Line

1. Command lines

   The function configuration and service deployment of Huawei network devices are done through VRP command lines. A command line is a string with a certain format and functions registered inside the device. A command line consists of keywords and parameters. Keywords are a set of words or phrases related to the function of the command line. A command line can be uniquely identified by keywords, and keywords of command lines are in bold font in this book. Parameters are words or numbers specified to improve the format of the command line or to indicate the object of the command, including data types such as integers, strings and enumerated values. For example, in the command line ping *ip-address* for testing inter-device connectivity, ping is the keyword of the command line and *ip-address* is the parameter (its value is an IP address).

   A newly purchased Huawei network device is initially configured to be empty. If you want it to have functions such as file transfer and network interoperability, you need to enter the command line interface of the device and configure it using corresponding commands.

2. Command line interface

   The command line interface is the interface for text-based command interaction between the user and the device, just like the Disk Operation System (DOS) window in the Windows operating system. The VRP command line interface is shown in Fig. 3.2.

3. Command line view

   The command line interface is divided into several command line views. When using a command line, you need to first enter the view where the command line is located. Commonly used command line views are the user view, system view and interface view, which are inter-related but have certain differences.

   As shown in Fig. 3.3, after logging in to a Huawei device, you will first enter the user view <R1>, and in the prompt "<R1>", "<>" indicates the user view and "R1" is the host name of the device. In the user view, users can learn about the basic information of the device and query its status, but they cannot perform configurations related to service functions. If you need to configure the service functions of the device, you need to enter the system view.

   By entering "system-view", you can enter the system view [R1], and configure the system parameters. At this point, the prompt uses the square bracket "[ ]". You can use most of the basic configuration commands and configure some global parameters of the router in system view, such as the router host name.

   From the system view, you can enter the interface view, protocol view, AAA view and other views. To configure parameters such as interface parameters,

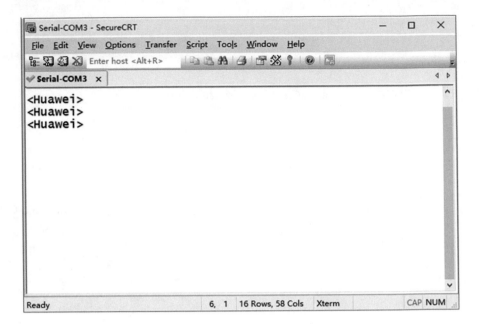

Fig. 3.2   VRP command line interface

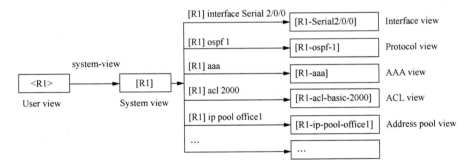

Fig. 3.3   The command line views

routing protocol parameters and IP address pool parameters, you have to enter their respective views. By entering different views, you can use the commands in that view. If you want to enter other views, you must first enter the system view.

By entering "quit", you can return to the view of the previous level. By entering "return", you can return directly to the user view. By pressing the "Ctrl+Z", you can return to the user view. When you enter different views, the prompt content will change accordingly. For example, when you enter the interface view, the host name is appended with the information on interface type and interface number. In the interface view, you can complete the configuration operation of the corresponding interface, such as configuring the IP address of the interface. The exemplary code is as follows.

Table 3.1 Correspondence between user privilege levels and command levels

0	0	Network diagnostic commands (ping, tracert), commands to access other devices from this device (telnet), etc.
1	0, 1	System maintenance commands, such as display. However, not all display commands are monitoring level, for example, display current-configuration and display saved-configuration are management level commands
2	0, 1, 2	Service configuration commands, including routing, commands for each network level, etc.
3– 15	0, 1, 2, 3	Commands related to basic system operation, such as file system, FTP downloads, the configuration file switch command, the user management command, the command level setting command, the system internal parameter setting command., as well as the debugging command for fault diagnosis

```
[R1] interface GigabitEthernet 0/0/0
[R1-GigabitEthernet0/0/0] ip address 192.168.10.111 24
```

The VRP system has classified commands and users, with each command having a corresponding level, and each user its own privilege level. The user privilege level corresponds with the command level in a certain way. After logging in, users with certain privilege levels can only execute commands equal to or lower than their own levels.

4. Command levels and user privilege levels

VRP commands are divided into four levels, i.e., level 0 (visit), level 1 (monitoring), level 2 (configuration) and level 3 (management). Network diagnostic commands belong to the visit level commands, and are used to test whether the network is connected or not. Monitoring level commands are used to view the network status and basic information of the device. Configuration level commands are required for service configuration of the device. For some special functions, such as uploading or downloading configuration files, management level commands are needed.

User privileges are divided into 16 levels from 0 to 15. By default, level 3 users can operate all commands of the VRP system, which means that users of levels 4 to 15 have the same privilege as level 3 users by default. User privileges of levels 4 to 15 are generally used in conjunction with the functions to upgrade command levels. For example, when there are many device administrators, their privilege levels should be further categorized, and then you can elevate the user privilege corresponding to a key command, such as to level 15, so that the default level 3 administrator can no longer use the key command.

The correspondence between user level and command level is shown in Table 3.1.

3.2.2 How to Use Command Lines

1. Enter the command view

After entering the VRP system, the first view the user enters is the user view. If "<Huawei>" appears as shown below, with the cursor flashing to the right of ">", the user has successfully entered the user view.

```
<Huawei>
```

Once you enter the user view, you can use commands to understand the basic information of the device and view the device status, etc. If you need to configure interface GigabitEthernet1/0/0, you need to enter the system view first using the system-view command, and then use the interface *interface-type interface-number* command to enter the corresponding interface view.

```
<Huawei>system-view      -- Enter the system view
[Huawei]
[Huawei] interface gigabitethernet 1/0/0   --Enter the interface view
[Huawei-GigabitEthernet1/0/0]
```

2. Exit command view

The function of the quit command is to exit from any view to the view of the previous level. For example, the interface view is entered from the system view, so the system view is the view of the previous level of interface view.

```
[Huawei-GigabitEthernet1/0/0] quit        --Exit to system view
[Huawei]
```

If you wish to continue exiting to the user view, you can execute the quit command for another time.

```
[Huawei] quit        --Exit to user view
<Huawei>
```

Some command views are in such a high level that you need to execute the quit command several times in order to exit from the current view to the user view. In this case, you can use the return command to directly exit from the current view to the user view.

```
[Huawei-GigabitEthernet 1/0/0] return        -- Exit to user view
<Huawei>
```

In addition, in any view, pressing "Ctrl+Z" can have the same effect as using the return command.

3. Command line input

The VRP system provides rich command line input methods, supporting multi-line input. The maximum length of each command is 510 characters. The command keywords are not case-sensitive. And incomplete keyword input is supported. Table 3.2 lists the functions of some commonly used function keys in the command line input process.

Table 3.2 Functions of function keys

Function keys	Functions
BackSpace	Delete the previous character at the cursor position, the cursor moves to the left and it stops if it has reached the start of the command
Left cursor key ← or "Ctrl+B"	The cursor moves one character to the left and it stops if it has reached the start of the command
Right cursor key → or "Ctrl+F"	The cursor moves one character to the right and it stops if it has reached the end of the command
Delete	Delete a character at the cursor position; the cursor position remains unmoved, and the character behind the cursor moves one character to the left, and it stops if it has reached the end of the command
Up cursor key ↑ or "Ctrl+P"	Display the previous history command. If you need to display an earlier history command, the function key can be repeatedly used
Lower cursor key ↓ or "Ctrl+N"	Display the next history command, and the function key can be repeatedly used

4. Incomplete keyword input

In order to improve the efficiency and accuracy of command line input, the VRP system supports incomplete keyword input, that is, in the current view, you do not need to enter complete keywords if the entered characters can match a unique keyword. For example, in the case of entering the "display current-configuration" command, the user can enter "d cu", "di cu", "di cu" or "dis cu", but not something like "d c" or "dis c". This is because there are multiple commands in the system starting with "d c" and "dis c", such as "display cpu-defend", "display clock" and "display current-configuration".

5. Online help

Online help is a real-time help function provided by the VRP system. When entering command lines, users can enter a question mark (?) at any time to obtain online help. You can choose to obtain full help or partial help.

(a) Example of full help.

If we want to check the current configuration of the device, but do not know what to do next after entering the user view, we can enter "?" to obtain the following help information.

```
<Huawei>?
User view commands:
  arp-ping          ARP-ping
  autosave           <Group> autosave command group
  backup           Backup information
  ......
  dialer          Dialer
  dir            List files on a filesystem
  display           Display information
  factory-configuration Factory configuration
---- More ----
```

You can see "display" in the keyword displayed, which is interpreted as "Display information". It is natural to think that to view the current configuration of the device, the keyword "display" will probably be used. So, after pressing any letter key to exit help, enter "display" and a question mark "?" separated by a space. Then the following help information will be obtained.

```
<Huawei>display ?
 Cellular            Cellular interface
 aaa                 AAA
 access-user         User access
 accounting-scheme   Accounting scheme
 ......
 cpu-usage             Cpu usage information
 current-configuration   Current configuration
 cwmp                  CPE WAN Management Protocol
---- More ----
```

From the information, we find "current-configuration". Through simple analysis and reasoning, we know that the command we should enter to view the current configuration of the device is "display current-configuration".

(b) Example of partial help.

Usually, we would not be completely ignorant of the command line we need to enter, and instead we know part of the command line keywords. Suppose we want to enter the command "display current-configuration". However, we do not remember the full command format, but only that the keyword "display" starts with "dis", and current-configuration starts with the letter "c". At this point, we can use the partial help function to determine the complete command.

After entering "dis", enter the question mark "?".

```
<Huawei>dis?
display Display information
```

The echo message shows that the only keyword starting with "dis" is display, and based on the principle of incomplete keyword input, the keyword display can be uniquely determined by using "dis". So, after entering "dis", you can type a space, then "c", and finally "?" to get help information for the next keyword.

```
<Huawei>dis c?
 <0-0>            Slot number
 Cellular         Cellular interface
 calibrate        Global calibrate
 capwap           CAPWAP
 channel           Informational channel status and configuration
          information
 clock            Clock status and configuration information
 config           System config
```

Table 3.3 Common VRP system-defined shortcut (combination) keys

Shortcut (combination) keys	Functions
Ctrl+A	Move the cursor to the beginning of the current line
Ctrl+E	Move the cursor to the end of the current line
ESC+N	Move the cursor downward a line
ESC+P	Move the cursor upward a line
Ctrl+C	Stops performing current functions
Ctrl+Z	Returns to the user view, which is equivalent to the return command
Tab	Partial help function; enter incomplete keywords and press "Tab", and then the system automatically completes the keywords

```
controller        Specify controller
cpos              CPOS controller
cpu-defend        Configure CPU defend policy
cpu-usage         Cpu usage information
current-configuration Current configuration
cwmp              CPE WAN Management Protocol
```

The information shows that after the keyword "display", there are only a few dozen keywords starting with "c", from which "current-configuration" can be easily identified. At this point, we can use such memory fragments as "dis" and "c" to obtain the complete command "display current-configuration".

6. Shortcut keys

shortcut keys can further improve the efficiency of command line input. VRP system has defined some shortcut keys, which are called system-defined shortcut keys. System-defined shortcut keys have fixed functions and cannot be redefined by the user. Common VRP system-defined shortcut (combination) keys are shown in Table 3.3.

The VRP system also allows the user to customize some shortcut keys, but customized shortcut keys may be confused with some operation commands, so it is generally suggested not to customize shortcut keys.

7. Use the undo command line

The undo command is to add the keyword "undo" in front of the command. It is used to restore the default situation, disable a function or delete a configuration. The following is a reference example.

Use the undo command to restore the default situation.

```
<Huawei>system-view
[Huawei] sysname Server
[Server] undo sysname
[Huawei]
```

Use the undo command to disable a function.

```
<Huawei>system-view
[Huawei] ftp server enable
[Huawei] undo ftp server
```

Use the undo command to delete a configuration.

```
[Huawei] interface g0/0/1
[Huawei-GigabitEthernet0/0/1] ip address 192.168.1.1 24
[Huawei-GigabitEthernet0/0/1] undo ip address
```

3.3   Login to Network Devices

Configuring a Huawei network device can be done using the Console (control) port, Telnet (remote login system), SSH (Secure Shell), or Web methods. This section introduces the various ways to configure the user interface and log in to the device.

3.3.1   Configure the User Interface

1. Concept of user interface
   Different users have different user interfaces in the process of information interaction with the device. A user who logs in to the device using the Console port has a user interface that corresponds to the physical Console port of the device. A user who logs into the device using Telnet has a user interface that corresponds to the Virtual Type Terminal (VTY) port of the device. The total number of VTY ports supported may vary from device to device.

   If you want to control the login of different users, you need to first enter the corresponding user interface view and configure it accordingly (e.g., specify user privilege level, set user name and password, etc.). For example, assuming that the user logging in via the Console port has a privilege level of 3, then the corresponding operation is as follows.

```
<Huawei>system-view
[Huawei] user-interface console 0          --Enter Console port user
interface view
[Huawei-ui-console0] user privilege level 3     --Set privilege
level of user logging in through Console port as 3
```

   If multiple users have logged into the device, such as two administrators using Telnet to configure the same network device at the same time, each user will have their own user interface. So how does the device recognize these different user interfaces? The following section will focus on this issue.

2. The numbers of user interface

When a user logs in to the device, according to how the user logs in, the system will automatically assign the user with the smallest number of the corresponding type of user interface that is currently available. There are two types of user interface numbers, namely relative number and absolute number.

(a) Relative numbers.

The form of a relative number is: user interface type + sequence number. Generally, a device has only 1 Console port (plug-in devices may have multiple Console ports with each main control board providing one Console port), and there are generally 15 user interfaces of VTY type (by default, five of them are turned on). Therefore, the relative number is presented in the following form.

Relative number of console user interface: CON 0.

Relative number of VTY user interface: the first one is VTY 0, the second one is VTY 1, and so on.

(b) Absolute numbers.

An absolute number is just a numerical value to uniquely specify a user interface. An absolute number has a one-to-one relationship with the relative number: the relative number of console user interface is CON 0, and the corresponding absolute number is 0; the relative numbers of VTY user interface are VTY 0 to VTY 14, and the corresponding absolute numbers are 129 to 143.

The information on user interfaces currently supported by the device can be viewed by using the display user-interface command. As shown below, we can see that there is one user of privilege level 3 connected to CON 0, and one user of privilege level 2 connected to VTY 0 through the virtual port. Auth means authentication mode, P stands for Password (only password needs to be entered), and A stands for AAA authentication (user name and password need to be entered).

```
<Huawei>display user-interface
  Idx  Type    Tx/Rx    Modem Privi ActualPrivi  Auth Int
 + 0   CON 0   9600       -     15      15          P    -
 + 129 VTY 0              -      2       2          A    -
   130 VTY 1             -      2       -          A    -
   131 VTY 2             -      2       -          A    -
   132 VTY 3             -      0       -          P    -
   133 VTY 4             -      0       -          P    -
   145 VTY 16            -      0       -          P    -
   146 VTY 17            -      0       -          P    -
   147 VTY 18            -      0       -          P    -
   148 VTY 19            -      0       -          P    -
   149 VTY 20            -      0       -          P    -
   150 Web 0   9600       -     15      -          A    -
```

```
151  Web 1   9600      -      15      -         A   -
152  Web 2   9600      -      15      -         A   -
153  Web 3   9600      -      15      -         A   -
154  Web 4   9600      -      15      -         A   -
155  XML 0   9600      -      0       -         A   -
156  XML 1   9600      -      0       -         A   -
157  XML 2   9600      -      0       -         A   -
UI(s) not in async mode -or- with no hardware support:
1-128
 +   : Current UI is active.
 F   : Current UI is active and work in async mode.
 Idx : Absolute index of UIs.
 Type : Type and relative index of UIs.
 Privi: The privilege of UIs.
 ActualPrivi: The actual privilege of user-interface.
 Auth : The authentication mode of UIs.
   A: Authenticate use AAA.
   N: Current UI need not authentication.
   P: Authenticate use current UI's password.
 Int : The physical location of UIs.
```

In the echo message, the first column Idx indicates the absolute numbers and the second column Type represents the relative numbers.

3. User authentication

Each user logs in to a device with a user interface corresponding to it. So, how to make sure that only legitimate users can log into the device? The answer is through the user authentication mechanism. There are three types of user authentication modes supported by the device: Password authentication, AAA authentication and None authentication.

(a) Password authentication.

Password authentication only requires entering the password, and once the password authentication is passed, you can login to the device. By default, the device uses the password authentication mode. When using this method, you cannot login to the device without configuring the password.

(b) AAA authentication.

AAA authentication requires entering the username and password, and only when the correct username and its corresponding password are entered can you login to the device. Since both user name and password need to be verified, AAA authentication is more secure than password authentication. Meanwhile, the method can distinguish different users, and different users can be set with different privilege levels without interfering with each other. Therefore, when using Telnet to login, AAA authentication is generally used.

(c) None authentication.

None authentication enables the user to directly login to the device without entering the username and password, that is, no authentication is required. For security reasons, this authentication mode is not recommended.

The user authentication mechanism ensures the legitimacy of user login. By default, users who login via Telnet have a privilege level of 0 after they login.

4. User privilege levels

The meaning of user privilege level and its correlation with command level have been described earlier. The user privilege level is also called user level. By default, a user with a user level of 3 or above can operate all commands of the device. The level of a certain user can be configured by executing the user privilege level *level* command under the corresponding user interface view, where *level* is the specified user level.

3.3.2 Login to the Device via the Console Port

We configure the console user interface in the following, using the password authentication mode, and setting the login password.

During the initial configuration of the router, the console cable can be used to connect the console port of the switch (or router) to the cluster communication port (COM) of the computer so that local debugging and maintenance can be enabled. The console port is a RJ45 port conforming to the RS232 serial port standard. Most desktop computers today provide a COM port that can be connected to the console port, as shown in Fig. 3.4. Laptops generally do not provide a COM port and require the use of a USB to RS232 port converter.

Open the "Computer Management" interface, as shown in Fig. 3.5, and click "Device Manager"; after installing the driver, you can see that the USB port acts as a COM3 port.

Install SecureCRT on Windows [SecureCRT is a terminal emulation program that supports SSH (SSH1 and SSH2), and in short, it is a software to login to UNIX, Linux server hosts and Huawei network devices on Windows]. Open SecureCRT software, as shown in Fig. 3.6, select "Serial" for SecureCRT protocol, and click

Fig. 3.4 Configure a router

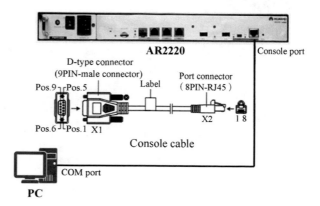

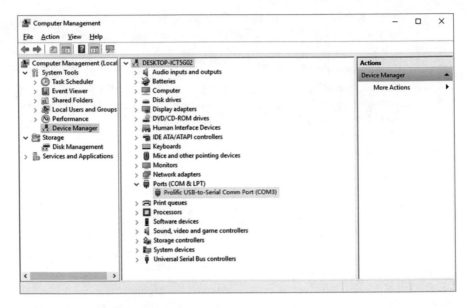

Fig. 3.5 View the COM3 port that the USB port acts as

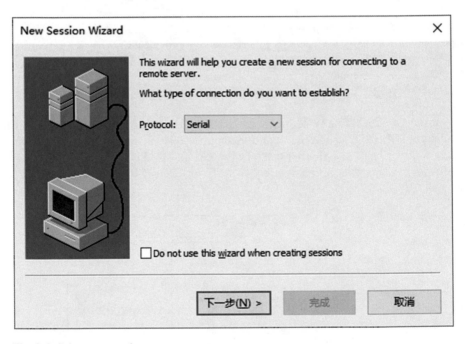

Fig. 3.6 Select a protocol

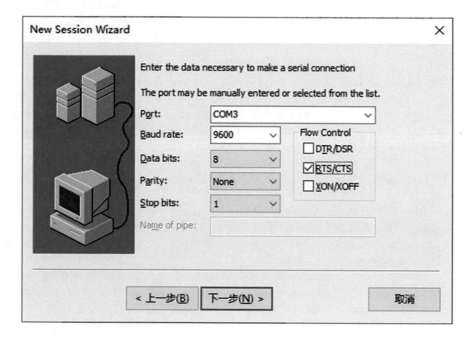

Fig. 3.7 Select "COM3" port

"Next". In the port selection interface displayed, as shown in Fig. 3.7, according to the port simulated by the USB device, select "COM3" here, and refer to Fig. 3.7 for other settings, and then click "Next".

The console user interface corresponds to users logging in directly through the console port, usually using Password authentication. Users logging in through the console port are generally network administrators that require the user privileges of the highest level.

1. Enter the console user interface.

    The command used to enter the console user interface is user-interface console *interface-number*. The *interface-number* indicates the relative number of the console user interface and takes the value of 0.

```
[Huawei]user-interface console 0
```

2. Configure the user interface.

    In console user interface view, configure the authentication mode as password authentication, and set the password as huawei, and the password is saved in the configuration file in cipher text.

    The command to configure the user authentication mode of the user interface is authentication-mode {aaa l password}.

```
[Huawei-ui-console0] authentication-mode ?
  aaa     AAA authentication
  password Authentication through the password of a user terminal
interface
[Huawei-ui-console0] authentication-mode password
Please configure the login password (maximum length 16) :huawei
```

If you intend to reset the password, you can enter the following command to set the password to huawei.com. The keyword cipher indicates that the configured password will be stored in the configuration file in cipher text.

```
[Huawei-ui-console0] set authentication password cipher huawei.com
```

After the configuration is complete, the configuration information will be saved in the device's memory and can be viewed using the display current-configuration command. If the information is not saved, it will be lost when the device is powered on or rebooted.

Enter "display current-configuration section user-interface" to display the user-interface settings in the current configuration. If you only enter "display current-configuration", all settings will be displayed.

```
<Huawei>display current-configuration section user-interface
[V200R003C00]
#
user-interface con 0
 authentication-mode password
set authentication password cipher %$%${PA|GW3~G'2AJ%@K{;MA,$/:\,
wmOC*yI7U_x!,w
    kv].$/=,%$%$
user-interface vty 0 4
user-interface vty 16 20
#
return
```

3.3.3   Login to the Device via Telnet

The VTY user interface corresponds to the user logging in using Telnet. Considering that Telnet is a remote login method, it is prone to security risks, so AAA authentication is used to authenticate users. Generally, during the commissioning phase of the device, a lot of people need to login to the device and service configuration is required, so the maximum number of VTY user interfaces is usually configured to 15, which allows up to 15 users to login to the device via Telnet at the same time. Also, the user level should be set to level 2, that is the configuration level, so that normal service configuration can be performed. The following configures the number of VTY interfaces, setting the user level of VTY user interface to level 2 and the authentication mode to AAA authentication.

1. Configure the maximum number of VTY user interfaces to 15.

    The command used to configure the maximum number of VTY user interfaces is user-interface maximum-vty *number*. If you want to configure the maximum number of VTY user interfaces to 15, then the value of number should be 15.

    ```
    [Huawei]user-interface maximum-vty 15
    ```

2. Enter the VTY user interface view.

    Enter the user-interface vty *first-ui-number [last-ui-number]* command to enter the VTY user interface view, where *first-ui-number* and *last-ui-number* are the relative numbers of the VTY user interfaces, and the square brackets "[ ]" means that the parameter is optional. Suppose now you need to configure all the 15 VTY user interfaces. Then the value of *first-ui-number* should be 0, and that of *last-ui-number* should be 14.

    ```
    [Huawei]user-interface vty 0 14
    ```

    Enter the VTY user interface view.

    ```
    [Huawei-ui-vty0-14]
    ```

3. Configure the user level of VTY user interface as level 2.

    The command to configure the user level is user privilege level *level*. Since now you need to configure the user level as level 2, the value of level should be 2.

    ```
    [Huawei-ui-vty0-14]user privilege level 2
    ```

4. Configure the user authentication mode of VTY user interface as AAA authentication.

    The command to configure the user authentication mode is authentication-mode {aaa l password}, where the braces "{ }" indicate that you can choose either one of the parameters.

    ```
    [Huawei-ui-vty0-14]authentication-mode aaa
    ```

5. Configure the user name and password for AAA authentication mode.

    First exit VTY user interface view and execute the aaa command to enter AAA view. Then execute the local-user *user-name* password *cipher password* command to configure the username and password. The *user-name* represents user name, *password* represents password, and the keyword cipher means the configured password will be saved in cipher text in the configuration file. Finally, execute the local-user *user-name* service-type telnet command to define the access type of these users as Telnet.

Fig. 3.8 Telnet secondary
connection

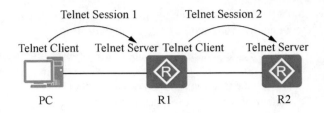

```
[Huawei-ui-vty0-14]quit
[Huawei]aaa
[Huawei-aaa]local-user admin password cipher admin@123
[Huawei-aaa]local-user admin service-type telnet
[Huawei-aaa]quit
```

After the configuration is completed, when a user logs in to the device via Telnet, the device will automatically assign the available VTY user interface with the smallest number to the user, and the username (admin) and password (admin@123) configured above need to be entered before entering the command line interface.

The Telnet protocol is one of the application layer protocols of TCP/IP protocol stack. Telnet works in a "server/client" mode, providing a way to remotely login from one device (Telnet client) to another (Telnet server). A TCP connection is required between the Telnet server and the Telnet client, and the default port number for the Telnet server is 23.

The VRP system supports both the Telnet server and Telnet client functions. With the VRP system, users can also first login to a device, and use this device as a Telnet client to remotely login to other devices on the network via Telnet, thus allowing more flexible maintenance and operations of the network. As shown in Fig. 3.8, router R1 is both a Telnet server for PC and a Telnet client for router R2.

In Windows, open the command line tool, make sure the network between Windows and the router is unobstructed. By entering "telnet *ip-address*", and then the account and password, you can remotely login to the router for config-uration. As shown in Fig. 3.9, telnet 192.168.10.111 enters the account and password to successfully login to <Huawei>, then telnet 172.16.1.2 enters the password to successfully login to router <R2>. Then exit Telnet and enter "quit".

3.3.4   Login to the Device via SSH

SSH is abbreviated for Secure Shell and was developed by the IETF network group. SSH is a protocol specifically designed to provide security for remote login sessions. Using SSH protocol can effectively prevent information leakage during remote management.

When using Telnet to login to the router, the account and password are transmit-ted in plain text over the network so it is not secure. Using SSH to login to the router over the network is more secure than Telnet.

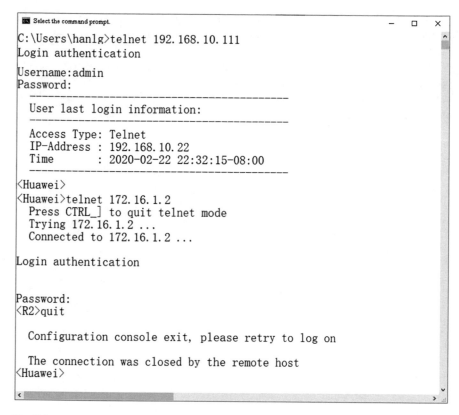

Fig. 3.9 Login to the router via Telnet on Windows

From the client's perspective, SSH provides two levels of security authentication.

The first level is password-based security authentication. As long as you know your own account and password, you can login to the remote host. All data transmitted is encrypted, but there is no guarantee that the server you are connecting to is the one you want to connect to. It is possible that some other servers may be impersonating the real server, i.e., it is subject to the "man-in-the-middle" attack.

The second level is key-based security authentication. You need the keys, that is, you have to create a key pair for yourself and put the public key on the server you need to access. If you want to connect to an SSH server, the client software will send a request to the server for security authentication with your key. After receiving the request, the server first looks for your public key in your home directory on that server, and then compares it to the public key you have sent over. If the two keys match, the server a "challenge" encrypted with the public key and sends it to the client software. Once the client software receives the "challenge", it can decrypt it with your private key and send it to the server.

In this way, the user must know his own key passphrase. However, in contrast to the first level, the second level does not require the transmission of the passphrase over the network.

The following operation will change the login type of the admin user created above to SSH. Set the authentication mode of SSH user admin to password authentication, turn on the SSH authentication service of the router, generate the local authentication key, and configure the VTY to use the SSH protocol.

```
[Huawei-aaa]local-user admin service-type ?
 8021x   802.1x user
 bind    Bind authentication user
 ftp     FTP user
 http    Http user
 ppp     PPP user
 ssh     SSH user
 sslvpn  Sslvpn user
 telnet  Telnet user
 terminal Terminal user
 web     Web authentication user
 x25-pad X25-pad user
[Huawei-aaa]local-user admin service-type ssh    --The default admin
authentication is SSH
[Huawei-aaa]quit


[Huawei]ssh user admin authentication-type password   --The SSH user
admin authentication service is password authentication
[Huawei]stelnet server enable              --Enable SSH authentication
service


[Huawei]rsa local-key-pair create               -- Generate local
authentication key
The key name will be: Host
% RSA keys defined for Host already exist.
Confirm to replace them? (y/n) [n] :y
The range of public key size is (512 ~ 2048).
NOTES: If the key modulus is greater than 512,
     It will take a few minutes.
Input the bits in the modulus [default = 512] :
Generating keys...
.........++++++++++++
.....++++++++++++
.........++++++++
.......++++++++


[Huawei]user-interface vty 0 14
[Huawei-ui-vty0-14]authentication-mode aaa  --Set virtual terminal
authentication mode to AAA
[Huawei-ui-vty0-14]protocol inbound ssh     --Enable SSH
[Huawei-ui-vty0-14]quit
```

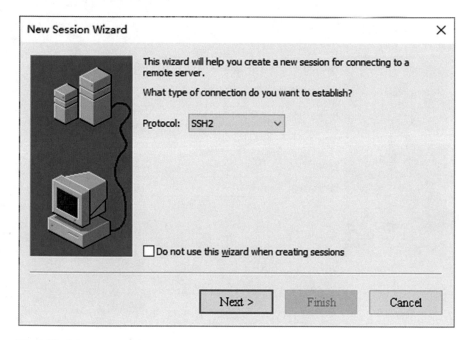

Fig. 3.10 Select a protocol

Open SecureCRT and create a new connection as shown in Fig. 3.10. Select SSH2 as the protocol to use for the connection, and click "Next". As shown in Fig. 3.11, enter the hostname, port and username of the router, and click "Next".

When you click the created connection, a dialog box will appear, as shown in Fig. 3.12. Enter the password for the account and click "OK". You will enter the user view after successfully logging in, as shown in Fig. 3.13.

3.3.5   Login to the Device via Web

Some Huawei network devices can also be logged in through the Web. The Web login process is configured as follows.

1. Login to the device via the console port.
2. Configure the management IP address of the device.

```
<Huawei> system-view
[Huawei] interface gigabitethernet 0/0/0
[Huawei-GigabitEthernet0/0/0] ip address 10.1.1.1 24
[Huawei-GigabitEthernet0/0/0] quit
```

3. Configure the Web user.

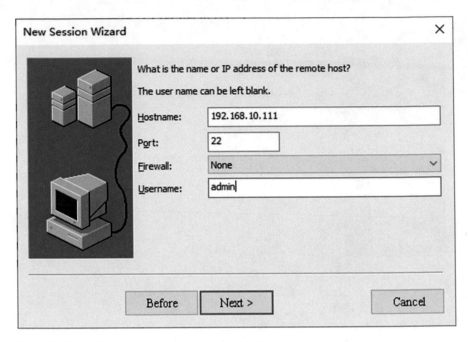

Fig. 3.11 Enter the hostname, port and username of the router

Fig. 3.12 Enter the username and password

```
[Huawei] aaa
[Huawei-aaa] local-user admin password cipher huawei
[Huawei-aaa] local-user admin privilege level 15
[Huawei-aaa] local-user admin service-type http
[Huawei-aaa] quit
```

4. Configure Web network management and use the Web network management function of the device.

```
[Huawei] http server enable
 This operation will take several minutes, please
wait............................
```

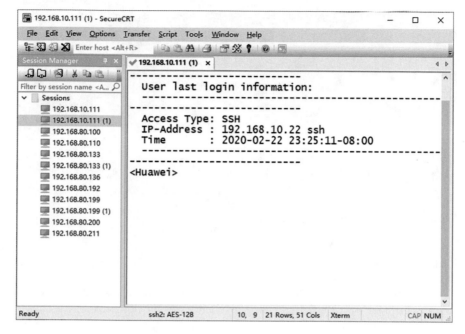

Fig. 3.13 Login to the router via SSH

```
Info: Succeeded in starting the HTTP server
[Huawei] quit
```

5. Login to the device via the Web Network Management interface.

Enter "https://10.1.1.1" in the address bar of the browser and hit the Enter key to enter the Web Network Management interface to login to the device, as shown in Fig. 3.14.

3.4   Basic Configurations of Network Devices

The following introduces some basic configurations of Huawei network devices, including configuring the device name, device clock, and device IP address.

3.4.1   Configure the Device Name

Normally more than one device will be deployed on the network, and these devices needs unified management from the administrator. When commissioning a device,

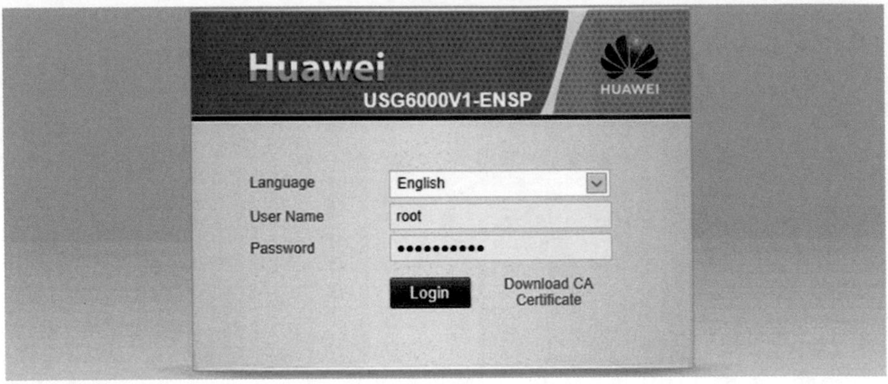

Fig. 3.14 Login interface

the primary task is to configure the device name, which is used to uniquely identify a device.

The command line interface contains the name of the device in pointed brackets "< >" or square brackets "[ ]", which is also known as the hostname of the device. The default device name is "Huawei". To better distinguish between different devices, it is often necessary to change the device name. We can change the device name by using the *sysname hostname* command, where sysname is the keyword of the command line and *hostname* is the parameter that indicates the device name you wish to set to.

For example, by the following operation, you can set the device name to Huawei-AR-01.

```
<Huawei>?                    --View the commands that can be executed in the
user view
 <Huawei>system-view    --Enter the system view
 [Huawei]sysname Huawei-AR-01                       --Change the router name to
Huawei-AR-01
 [Huawei-AR-01]
```

3.4.2   Configure the Device Clock

To ensure coordinated work with other devices, the system clock needs to be set accurately. System clock = Universal Time Coordinated (UTC) + the time offset between the current time zone and UTC. Generally, there is a built-in UTC and time offest configuration on the device.

The Huawei devices use UTC by default in factory, but no time zone is configured, so before configuring the device system clock, you need to know the time zone where the device is located.

The command line to set the time zone is clock timezone *time-zone-name* {add |
minus} *offset*, where *time-zone-name* is the name of the user-defined time zone,
which is used to identify the configured time zone. According to the offset direction,
select "add" for positive offset (UTC time adds offset to get the local time) and
"minus" for negative offset (UTC time minuses offset to get the local time). The
offset is the offset time. Assuming the device is located in Beijing time zone, then the
corresponding configuration is as follows. (Note: Setting the time zone and time is
done in user mode.)

```
<Huawei>clock timezone BJ add 8:00
```

After setting the time zone, you can set the current date and time of the device.
Huawei device only supports 24-h system, and the command line used is clock
datetime *HH:MM:SSYYYY-MM-DD*, where *HH:MM:SS* is the time configured and
YYYY-MM-DD the date configured. Suppose the current date is October 19, 2020,
and the time is 16:37:00, then the corresponding configuration is as follows.

```
<Huawei>clock datetime 16:37:00 2020-10-19
```

Enter "display clock" to display the time zone, date and time of the current device.

```
<Huawei>display clock
2020-10-19 16:37:07
Monday
Time Zone(BJ) : UTC+08:00
```

3.4.3   Configure the Device IP Address

To run IP services on an interface, you must configure an IP address for it. An
interface generally requires only one IP address, and if the it is configured with a new
one, then the new IP address replaces the original one.

The command to configure an interface IP address is ip address *ip-address* {*mask*
| *mask-length*}, where ip address is the command keyword and *ip-address* is the IP
address you wish to set to. The *mask* indicates the subnet mask in dotted decimal
mode, and *mask-length* represents the subnet mask in length mode, that is, the
number of the binary number 1 in the mask.

Assuming that the IP address assigned to the Huawei's interface Ethernet 0/0/0 is
192.168.1.1 and the subnet mask is 255.255.255.0, then the corresponding configuration is as follows.

```
[Huawei] interface Ethernet 0/0/0              --Enter the interface view
 [Huawei-Ethernet0/0/0]ip address 192.168.1.1 255.255.255.0    --Add
the IP address and subnet mask
 [Huawei-Ethernet0/0/0]undo shutdown                   --Enable the
```

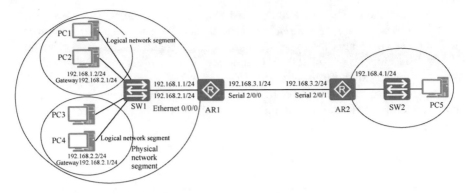

Fig. 3.15 Physical network segments and logical network segments

```
interface
  [Huawei-Ethernet0/0/0] ip address 192.168.2.1 24 ?
   sub  Indicate a subordinate address
   <cr> Please press ENTER to execute command
  [Huawei-Ethernet0/0/0] ip address 192.168.2.1 24 sub        -- Add a
second address to the interface (the second address and the first address
must be on different network segments)
  [Huawei-Ethernet0/0/0] display this              --Display the interface
configuration
  [V200R003C00]
  #
  interface Ethernet0/0/0
   ip address 192.168.1.1 255.255.255.0
   ip address 192.168.2.1 255.255.255.0 sub
  #
  return
  [Huawei-Ethernet0/0/0] quit                      --Exit interface
configuration mode
```

Usually, a router interface only needs to be configured with one IP address, but sometimes it needs to be configured with multiple addresses. As shown in Fig. 3.15, four computers are connected on switch SW1, which are not separated by routers and belong to the same physical network segment, but PC1 and PC2 are assigned with the address of network segment 192.168.1.0/24, while PC3 and PC4 are assigned with the address of network segment 192.168.2.0/24. PC1 and PC2 belong to the same logical network segment, while PC3 and PC4 belong to the same logical network segment. The computers in these two logical network segments need to be forwarded by the router for communication, which requires interface Ethernet0/0/0 of router AR1 to be configured with two IP addresses to act as the gateway for the computers in these two logical segments.

Note	The shutdown command is used to shut down the interface, and the undo shutdown command is used to enable the interface. The device port state itself is already enabled so it is not necessary to use this command.

Enter "display ip interface brief" to display summary information about the IP address of the interface.

```
<Huawei>display ip interface brief
*down: administratively down
^down: standby
(l): loopback
(s): spoofing
The number of interface that is UP in Physical is 3
The number of interface that is DOWN in Physical is 1
The number of interface that is UP in Protocol is 3
The number of interface that is DOWN in Protocol is 1

Interface              IP Address/Mask      Physical    Protocol
Ethernet0/0/0             192.168.1.1/24        up         up
Ethernet0/0/8             unassigned           down       down
NULL0              unassigned          up        up(s)
Vlanif1                  192.168.10.1/24        up         up
```

As you can see from the above output, the Physical layer of interface Ethernet0/0/0 is enabled (up), and the Protocol layer is also enabled.

Enter "undo ip address" to delete the IP address configured for the interface.

```
[Huawei-Ethernet0/0/0]undo ip address
```

A loopback interface is a logical interface that can be used to virtualize a network or an IP host. Loopback can also be used as management interfaces for its stability and reliability.

When configuring an IP address for a physical interface, you need to pay attention to the physical status of the interface. By default, the interface state of Huawei routers and switches is up. If the interface has been manually shut down, you should use "undo shutdown" to enable the interface after configuring the IP address.

3.5   Introduction to Configuration Files

The configuration of a Huawei network device takes immediate effect after it is changed, which is called the current configuration and is saved in memory. If the device is restarted due to power failure or shutdown, the configuration saved in memory will be lost. If you want the current configuration to remain effective after the device is restarted, you need to save the configuration to the root directory of external memory. In the following part, the book explains the configuration files in Huawei network devices and how to manage these files.

3.5.1   Configuration Files of Huawei Network Devices

This section introduces the configurations and configuration files of Huawei routers, involving three concepts: current configuration, configuration file, and configuration file at the next startup.

1. Current configuration.

    The configuration in the device memory is the current configuration. Change the current configuration is to enter the system view and change the configuration of the router. When the device is powered off or rebooted, all information in the memory (including configuration information) disappears.

2. Configuration file.

    The file containing the device configuration information is called the configuration file, which is stored in the device's external memory (note that it is not stored in memory), and its file name is generally in the format of "*.cfg" or "*. zip". The user can save the current configuration in the configuration file. When the device is rebooted, the contents in the configuration file can be reloaded into the memory and become the new current configuration. In addition to the role of saving configuration information, the configuration file can also facilitate maintenance personnel to view, backup, and port configuration information for other devices. By default, when saving the current configuration, the device will save the configuration information to a configuration file named "vrpcfg.zip" and save it in the root directory of the device's external memory.

3. Configuration file for the next startup.

    When saving the configuration, you can specify the name of the configuration file, that is, there can be more than one configuration file saved, and you can specify which configuration file will be loaded at the next startup. By default, the name of the configuration file to be loaded at next startup is "vrpcfg.zip".

3.5.2   Save the Current Configuration

There are two ways to save the current configuration: manual save and autosave.

1. Manual save.

    Users can use the save [*configuration-file*] command to manually save the current configuration to the configuration file at any time. The parameter *configuration-file* is the specified configuration file name, whose format must be "*.cfg" or "*.zip". If no configuration file name is specified, the configuration file will be named "vrpcfg.zip" by default.

For example, if you need to save the current configuration to a configuration file named "vrpcfg.zip", you can do the following.

In the user view, use the save command, and then enter "y" to confirm to save the router's configuration. If you do not specify the configuration file name to be saved, it will be named "vrpcfg.zip". Enter "dir" to display all the files and folders in the flash root directory, and you can see the configuration file there. The flash in the router is equivalent to the hard disk in the computer, which can store files and the configuration saved.

```
<R1>save
The current configuration will be written to the device.
Are you sure to continue? (y/n)[n]:y                    --Enter y
It will take several minutes to save configuration file, please
wait.......
Configuration file had been saved successfully
Note: The configuration file will take effect after being activated
```

If there is further need to save the current configuration to a configuration file named "backup.zip" as a backup of vrpcfg.zip, you can do the following.

```
<Huawei>save backup.zip
Are you sure to save the configuration to backup.zip? (y/n)[n]:y
It will take several minutes to save configuration file, please
wait......
Configuration file had been saved successfully
Note: The configuration file will take effect after being activated
```

2. Autosave.

Configuration autosave function can effectively reduce the risk of configuration loss caused by the user forgetting to save the configuration. Autosave is divided into two ways: autosave interval and autosave time.

In the autosave internal mode, the device will automatically save the configuration according to the saving interval set by the user. Regardless of whether the current configuration of the device has changed compared to the configuration file, the device will automatically save. In the autosave time mode, the user sets a time value and the device will automatically save at the specific time once a day. By default, the autosave feature of the device is off and needs to be turned on by the user before it can be used.

How to set the autosave internal method: first, execute the autosave interval on command to enable the autosave interval function of the device, and then execute the autosave interval *time* command to set the autosave interval. The *time* is the specified time interval in minutes, and the default value is 1440 min (24 h).

How to set autosave time: first, execute the autosave time on command to enable the autosave time function of the device, then execute the autosave time *time-value* command to set the specific time for autosave. The *time-value* is the specified time in the format of hh:mm:ss, and the default value is 1440 min.

You can turn on autosave interval using the following command and set the autosave interval to 120 min.

```
<R1>autosave interval on    --Enable autosave interval
  System autosave interval switch: on
  Autosave interval: 1440 minutes   --Save every 1440 minutes by
default
  Autosave type: configuration file
```

```
System autosave modified configuration switch: on  -- If the
configuration is changed, it will be saved automatically every 30 minutes
  Autosave interval: 30 minutes
  Autosave type: configuration file
```

```
<R1>autosave interval 120                    -- Set autosave interval to
120 minutes
  System autosave interval switch: on
  Autosave interval: 120 minutes
  Autosave type: configuration file
```

Autosave interval and autosave time cannot be enabled at the same time. Turn off autosave interval, then turn on autosave time, and change the autosave time to 12:00 at noon.

```
<R1>autosave interval off              --Disable autosave interval
<R1>autosave time on                   --Enable autosave time
  System autosave time switch: on
  Autosave time: 08:00:00              --Autosave at 8 every day by
default
  Autosave type: configuration file
<R1>autosave time ?                 --Parameters that can be entered
after viewing time
  ENUM<on,off>   Set the switch of saving configuration data
automatically by
          absolute time
  TIME<hh:mm:ss> Set the time for saving configuration data
automatically
<R1>autosave time 12:00:00               --Set the time for saving to
12
  System autosave time switch: on
  Autosave time: 12:00:00
  Autosave type: configuration file
```

By default, the device saves the current configuration to the file "vrpcfg.zip". If the user specifies another configuration file as the configuration file for the next startup, the device will save the current configuration to the newly specified configuration file for the next startup.

3.5.3 Set the Configuration File for the Next Startup

You can set any "*.cfg" or "*.zip" file in the root directory of the device's external memory (e.g., flash:/) as the configuration file for the device's next startup. You can set the configuration file for the next startup of the device by using the startup saved-configuration *configuration-file* command, where *configuration-file* is the specified configuration file name. If the configuration file is not available in the root directory of the device's external memory, the system will prompt that the setting has failed.

For example, if you need to specify the saved backup.zip file as the configuration file for the next startup, you can do the following.

```
<R1>startup saved-configuration backup.zip          --Specify the
configuration file to be loaded at the next startup
 This operation will take several minutes, please wait.....
 Info: Succeeded in setting the file for booting system
<R1>display startup               --Display the configuration file to be
loaded at the next startup
 MainBoard:
  Startup system software:            null
  Next startup system software:         null
  Backup system software for next startup:  null
  Startup saved-configuration file:      flash:/vrpcfg.zip
  Next startup saved-configuration file:   flash:/backup.zip    --
Configuration file to be loaded at the next startup
```

After setting the configuration file for the next startup, if the current configuration is saved again, the current configuration will be saved to the configuration file set for the next startup by default, thus overwriting the original content of the configuration file for the next startup. Autosave interval configuration and autosave time configuration will also save the configuration to the specified configuration file for the next startup.

3.5.4 View Configuration Results

The display startup command is used to view the system software, backup system software, configuration file, license file, patch file, and voice file related to the current and next startup of the device. It is illustrated as follows.

```
<Huawei>display startup
 MainBoard:
  Startup system software:            null
  Next startup system software:         null
  Backup system software for next startup:  null
  Startup saved-configuration file:      flash:/vrpcfg.zip
  Next startup saved-configuration file:   flash:/vrpcfg.zip
```

```
Startup license file:                null
Next startup license file:             null
Startup patch package:               null
Next startup patch package:             null
Startup voice-files:                 null
Next startup voice-files:              null
```

- "Startup system software" indicates the VRP file used for the current system startup.
- "Next startup system software" means the VRP file to be used for the next system startup.
- "Startup saved-configuration file" indicates the configuration file used for the current system startup.
- "Next startup saved-configuration file" represents the configuration file used for the next system startup.

When the device starts, the configuration file is loaded from the storage device and initialized. If there is no configuration file in the storage device, the device will be initialized using the default parameters.

The following commands can be used to view the configuration parameters that are currently in effect for the router.

```
<Huawei>display current-configuration
```

The following commands can be used to display the saved configuration parameters.

```
<Huawei>display saved-configuration
```

If you do not save, the configuration parameters that are currently in effect may be different from the configuration parameters saved. If no further configuration is done after saving, they are the same.

3.5.5 File Management

VRP manages all files (including device configuration files, system files, license files, patch files) and directories on the device through the file system. VRP file system is mainly used to create, delete, modify, copy and display files and directories, which are stored in the external memory of the device. The external memory supported by Huawei routers is generally Flash and SD card, and that supported by switches is generally Flash and CF card.

There are various types of files in the external memory of the device. In addition to the configuration files mentioned earlier, there are also system software files, license files, patch files and so on. Among these files, the system software file is of particular importance because it is in fact the device's VRP operating system itself. The system software file has the extension ".cc" and must be stored in the root directory of the external memory. When the device starts up, the contents of the system software file are loaded into memory and run.

In the following example, a backup configuration file is used to show the file management process.

1. View files.

View the files in the current path and confirm the name and size of the configuration file to be backed up. The dir [/all] [filename | directory] command can be used to view the files in the current path, where "all" means to view all the files and directories in the current path, including the files that have been deleted to the recycle bin, *filename* indicates the name of the file to be viewed, and *directory* represents the path of the directory to be viewed.

The default external memory of the router is Flash. By executing the following commands, you can view the files and directories in the root directory of the Flash memory of router R1.

```
<R1>dir    --List current directory files and folders
Directory of flash:/
  Idx Attr   Size(Byte)  Date       Time(LMT)      FileName
   0 drw-       -    May    01 2018 02:51:18   dhcp     --d means this is a
folder
   1 -rw-    121,802   May      26 2014 09:20:58     portalpage.zip
   2 -rw-      2,263   May      01 2018 08:13:21     statemach.efs
   3 -rw-    828,482   May      26 2014 09:20:58     sslvpn.zip
   4 -rw-        408   May    01 2018 07:27:28   private-data.txt
   5 -rw-        897   May    01 2018 08:18:00   backup.zip
   6 -rw-        872   May    01 2018 07:27:28   vrpcfg.zip

1,090,732 KB total (784,452 KB free)
```

In the echo message, you can see an 872-byte configuration file named "vrpcfg.zip". Assume it is the configuration file we need to backup.

2. Create a new directory.

The command to create a directory is mkdir *directory*, where *directory* means the directory to be created. Create a directory named backup in the root directory of Flash.

```
<R1>mkdir /backup     --Create a folder
Info: Create directory flash:/backup......Done
```

3. Copy and rename the file.

The command to copy the file is copy source-filenames *destination-filename*, where *source-filename* indicates the path of the copied file and the source filename, and *destination-filename* indicates the path of the destination file and the destination filename. Copy the configuration file vrpcfg.zip that needs to be backed up to the new directory and rename it to cfgbak.zip.

```
<R1>copy vrpcfg.zip flash:/backup/cfgbak.zip        --Copy vrpcfg.zip
to backup folder
    Copy flash:/vrpcfg.zip to flash:/backup/cfgbak.zip? (y/n) [n] :y
    100% complete
    Info: Copied file flash:/vrpcfg.zip to flash:/backup/cfgbak.zip...
Done
```

4. View the files after backup.

The cd directory command is used to modify the current working path. We can perform the following actions to see if the file backup is successful.

```
    <R1>dir flash:/backup/     --List the contents in Flash:/backup
    Directory of flash:/backup/
     Idx Attr   Size(Byte) Date      Time(LMT) FileName
       0 -rw-        872 May 01 2018 08:58:49  cfgbak.zip
```

The echo message shows that there is already a cfgbak.zip file in the backup directory, so the backup process of the configuration file vrpcfg.zip has been successfully completed.

5. Delete the file.

When there is not enough space available in the device's external memory, we will probably need to delete some of the trash files. The command to delete a file is delete [/unreserved] [/force] *filename*, where /unreserved means to completely delete a specified file and the deleted file will not be recovered, /force means to directly delete the file without confirmation, and *filename* represents the name of the file to be deleted.

If you do not use /unreserved, the files deleted by using the delete command will be saved to the recycle bin, and the files in the recycle bin can be restored with the undelete command. Note that files saved to the recycle bin will still occupy memory space. Using the reset recycle-bin command will completely delete all files in the recycle bin, and these files will be permanently deleted and cannot be restored.

The following are the operations to delete files, view deleted files, and clear files in the recycle bin.

```
    <R1>delete backup.zip             --Delete the file
    Delete flash:/backup.zip? (y/n) [n] :y
    Info: Deleting file flash:/backup.zip...succeed.
    <R1>dir /all          --The parameter all is used to display all files,
```

including files in the recycle bin
  Directory of flash:/
    Idx Attr   Size(Byte)   Date   Time(LMT)   FileName
     0 drw-   -   May   01 2018 02:51:18 dhcp
     1 -rw-   121,802   May   26 2014 09:20:58 portalpage.zip
     2 drw-   -   May   01 2018 08:58:49 backup
     3 -rw-   2,263   May   01 2018 08:13:21 statemach.efs
     4 -rw-   828,482   May   26 2014 09:20:58 sslvpn.zip
     5 -rw-   408   May   01 2018 07:27:28 private-data.txt
     6 -rw-   872   May   01 2018 07:27:28 vrpcfg.zip
     7 -rw-   897   May   01 2018 09:11:32 [backup.zip]   --Files in
  recycle-bin

1,090,732 KB total (784,440 KB free)
<R1>reset recycle-bin   --Clear the recycle bin
Squeeze flash:/backup.zip? (y/n) [n] :y
Clear file from flash will take a long time if needed...Done.
%Cleared file flash:/backup.zip.

Use the move command to move a file.

<R1>move backup.zip flash:/backup/backup1.zip

Enter the backup directory.

<R1>cd backup/

Use the pwd command to display current directory.

<R1>pwd
flash:/backup

You can use the move command in the same directory to rename a file.

<R1>move backup1.zip backup2.zip

3.6 Exercises

1. Which of the following commands is used to change the name of the router? ( )

   A. < Huawei > sysname R1
   B. [Huawei]sysname R1

15. (Multi-selection) At present, the company has a network administrator, and AR2200 in the company network can be managed remotely by entering the password directly through Telent. After the arrival of two new administrators, the company wants to assign all the administrators their respective usernames and passwords, as well as different privilege levels. So how should this be done? ( )

    A. Configure three usernames and their corresponding passwords in the AAA view
    B. The user authentication mode configured by Telent must be AAA mode
    C. When configuring each administrator's account, different privilege levels need to be configured
    D. Each administrator uses a different public IP address of the device when running Telent commands

16. (Multi-selection) VRP supports the configuration of the router in which ways? ( )

    A. Configuring the router via console port
    B. Configuring the router via Telent
    C. Configuring the router via mini USB port
    D. Configuring the router via FTP

17. After the carrier successfully Telnetted to the router, the interface IP address cannot be configured using the configuration command. This is probably because ( ).

    A. The Telnet terminal software of the operating user does not allow the user to configure the IP address of the device's interface
    B. The authentication mode of the Telnet user is not set correctly
    C. The Telnet user's level is not set correctly
    D. The SNMP parameter is not set correctly

18. Which of the following descriptions of display information is correct ( ).

```
[R1] display interface g0/0/0
 GigabitEthernet0/0/0 current state:Administratively DOWN Line
protocol current state: DOWN
```

A. The interface Gigabit Ethernet 0/0/0 is connected to a wrong cable
B. The interface Gigabit Ethernet 0/0/0 is not configured with an IP address
C. The interface Gigabit Ethernet 0/0/0 is not enabled with a dynamic routing protocol
D. The interface Gigabit Ethernet 0/0/0 is manually disabled by the administrator

Chapter 4
IP Addresses and Subnetting

Learning about IP addresses and subnetting requires mastering binary and decimal conversions; in order to quickly determine whether an address is available and which network segments can be merged, you also need to master some of the laws of binary numbers.

There are two major versions of IP addresses: IPv4 and IPv6. IP addresses in this chapter specifically refer to IPv4, which is a 32-bit binary number and is divided into a network part and a host part. The subnet mask is used to determine which bits are the network part and which bits are the host part. A gateway functions as a network segment's exit to other network segments and is the interface address of the Layer 3 device connected to that network segment.

IP addresses can be divided into five classes, namely Class A, B, C, D, and E.

IP addresses can be further categorized into public addresses and private addresses. Public addresses are planned and assigned globally and cannot overlap with each other. Private addresses are used within the campus network. Network address translation (NAT) is required to access the public network using private addresses.

All public IPv4 addresses have already been assigned, so in order to make full use of public IP addresses and avoid waste, a large network segment can be divided into multiple subnets, and appropriate subnets can be assigned according to the number of computers. Both fixed length subnetting or variable length subnet division are available.

Contrary to subnetting, if there are too many computers in a network segment and a lot of network segments need to be assigned addresses, multiple consecutive network segments can be merged into a large one by reducing the number of 1s in the subnet mask.

© The Author(s) 2023
Huawei Technologies Co., Ltd., *Data Communications and Network Technologies*,
https://doi.org/10.1007/978-981-19-3029-4_4

4.1   Preliminary Knowledge

All IP addresses of computers and network device interfaces in the network are 32-bit binary numbers. The process of learning IP addresses and subnetting later requires converting binary numbers to decimal numbers and also decimal numbers to binary numbers. Therefore, before learning IP address and subnetting, the readers should first learn about the knowledge of binary system, and are required to familiarize themselves with the relationship between binary and decimal numbers as described below.

4.1.1   Binary System and Decimal System

In learning subnetting, when readers see subnet mask in decimal, they are required to quickly determine how many 1s there will be when the subnet mask is written in binary; and when they see a subnet mask in binary, they shall also proficiently write the corresponding subnet mask in decimal.

Binary system is a numeral system widely used in computer technology. Binary data is a number represented by two digits, 0 and 1. It is a base-2 numeral system where $1 + 1 = 0$ (with a carry to the adjacent left bit) and $0 - 1 = 1$ (borrow 1 from the adjacent bit to the left). Almost all numeral systems used in current computer systems are a binary system.

Readers are suggested to remember the following list of binary and decimal correlation. In fact, there is no need for rote learning, as there are rules to follow. As follows, when the 1 in binary shifts one bit to the left, the corresponding decimal is multiplied by 2.

Binary number	Decimal number
1	1
10	2
100	4
1000	8
10 000	16
10 0000	32
100 0000	64
1000 0000	128

You should also remember the correlation between binary and decimal numbers listed below. The requirement is that: when one of the decimal numbers below is given, the reader can immediately write the corresponding binary number; and when one of the binary numbers below is given, the reader can immediately write the corresponding decimal number.

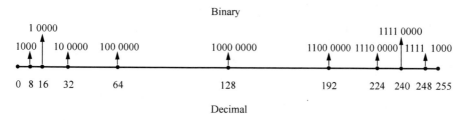

Fig. 4.1 Correlation between binary numbers and decimal numbers

Binary number	Decimal number	
1000 0000	128	
1100 0000	192	It shall be remembered like this: 1000 0000 + 100 0000, that is 128 + 64 = 192.
1110 0000	224	It shall be remembered like this: 1000 0000 + 100 0000 + 10 0000, that is, 128 + 64 + 32 = 224.
1111 0000	240	It shall be remembered like this: 128 + 64 + 32 + 16 = 240.
1111 1000	248	It shall be remembered like this: 128 + 64 + 32 + 16 + 8 = 248.
1111 1100	252	It shall be remembered like this: 128 + 64 + 32 + 16 + 8 + 4 = 252.
1111 1110	254	It shall be remembered like this: 128 + 64 + 32 + 16 + 8 + 4 + 2 = 254.
1111 1111	255	It shall be remembered like this: 128 + 64 + 32 + 16 + 8 + 4 + 2 + 1 = 255.

It can be seen that when the eight-digit binary number is consisted of all 1s, it is 255 in decimal.

In case you forget the above correlation, you can remember it by its rule. As shown in Fig. 4.1, by remembering a few key points on the number axis, you can immediately figure out the correlation. Draw a line, and the left end represents the binary number 0000 0000, while the right end represents the binary number 1111 1111. You can see that there are a total of 256 numbers from 0 to 255, the middle of which is 128. 128 corresponds to the binary number 1000 0000, which is a demarcation point. For numbers before 128, the leftmost digit of their corresponding binary number is 0, while for numbers after 128, the leftmost digit of their corresponding binary number is 1.

The number in the middle of 128 to 255 is 192, and the corresponding binary number is 1100 0000, which means that starting from 192, the leftmost two bits of the binary number of the number are 1.

The number in the middle of 192 to 255 is 224, and the corresponding binary number is 1110 0000, which means that starting from 22, the leftmost three bits of the binary number of the number are 1.

In this way it is easy to find that the number in the middle of 0 to 128 is 64, and the corresponding binary number is 100 0000. The number in the middle of 0 to 64 is 32, and the corresponding binary number is 10 0000.

In this way, even if you forget the above correlation, you can quickly find the correlation between binary and decimal numbers by drawing a number axis and following the above method.

4.1.2   Rules for Converting Decimal Numbers to Binary Numbers

When learning to merge network segments later, you need to determine whether the given subnets can be merged into a single network segment, a process that requires the readers to be able to converting a decimal number into a binary number and write the last few digits of the converted binary number. The correlation between decimal and binary numbers is shown in Table 4.1.

By using the correlation between decimal and binary numbers in Table 4.1, the following rules can be found.

1. If a number can be divided by 2, when it is written in binary, its last digit is 0. If the remainder is 1, then the last digit is 1.
2. If a number can be divided by 4, when it is written in binary, its last two digits are 00. If the remainder is 2, then 2 is written in binary form, so the last two digits are 10.
3. If a number can be divided by 8, when it is written in binary, its last three digits are 000. If the remainder is 5, then 5 is written in binary form, so the last three digits are 100.
4. If a number can be divided by 16, when it is written in binary, its last four digits are 0000. If the remainder is 6, then 6 is written in binary form, so the last four digits are 0110.

Based on the above rules, it can be seen that when converting a decimal number into a binary number, for the last n digits of the binary number, it can be determined by dividing the number by 2^n and writing the remainder as an n-digit binary number.

Based on the previous rules, convert decimal number 242 to a binary number and write the last four digits of the binary number.

Table 4.1 Correlation between decimal and binary numbers

Decimal number	Binary number	Decimal number	Binary number
0	0	11	1011
1	1	12	1100
2	10	13	1101
3	11	14	1110
4	100	15	1111
5	101	16	10000
6	110	17	10001

$2^4 = 16$, and the remainder of 242 divided by 16 is 2. When the remainder is written as a four-digit binary number, it becomes 0010, which means that when the decimal number 242 is converted into a binary number, the last four digits of the converted binary number is 0010.

4.2   Detailed Explanation of IP Addresses

An IP address is a 32-bit binary address assigned to each host connected to the Internet. IP addresses are used to locate computers and network devices on a network.

4.2.1   MAC Addresses and IP Addresses

Since a computer's network interface card has a physical address (MAC address), why does it still need an IP address?

As shown in Fig. 4.2, there are three network segments in the network. One switch corresponds to one network segment, and two routers are used to connect these three network segments. MA, MB, MC, MD, ME, MF, and M1, M2, M3 and M4 in Fig. 4.2 represent the MAC addresses of the computer and router interfaces, respectively.

If Computer A wants to send a packet to Computer F, it must add a source IP address (10.0.0.2) and a destination IP address (12.0.0.2) to the packet at the network layer.

For that packet to reach Computer F, it has to be forwarded by Router 1. So how can the packet be encapsulated in order for Switch 1 to forward it to Router 1? The answer is that the MAC address needs to be added at the data link layer with the source MAC address of MA and the target MAC address of M1.

Router 1 receives the packet and needs to forward it to Router 2, which requires re-encapsulating the packet into a frame with a target MAC address of M3 and a source MAC address of M2.

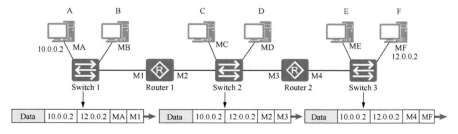

Fig. 4.2 The role of MAC addresses and IP addresses

The packet arrives at Router 2 and needs to be re-encapsulated with a target MAC address of MF and a source MAC address of M4. Switch 3 forwards the frame to Computer F.

As can be seen from Fig. 4.2, the destination IP address of the packet determines which computer the packet eventually arrives at, while the destination MAC address determines which device the next hop of the packet, which is not necessarily the destination.

If the global computer network were one large Ethernet network, then IP addresses would no longer be needed for communication, and only MAC addresses would be enough. Imagine what that would be like. When one computer sends a broadcast frame, all computers around the world can receive it, and if they all have to process it, the bandwidth of the entire network will be exhausted by the broadcast frame. Therefore, a Layer 3 device (a router or Layer 3 switch) must also be used to isolate the Ethernet broadcasts. By default, routers do not forward broadcast frames, and they only forward packets between different networks.

4.2.2   Composition of IP Addresses and Gateways

Before explaining the composition of IP addresses, let's introduce telephone numbers that everyone knows to understand the composition of IP addresses by telephone numbers.

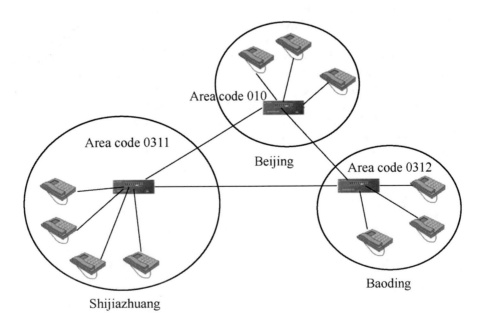

Fig. 4.3 Area codes

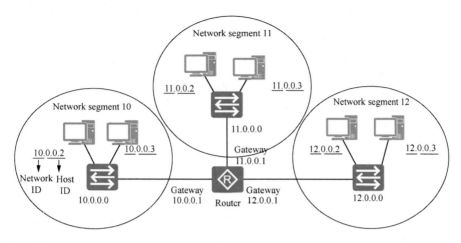

Fig. 4.4 Network IDs, host IDs and gateways

A telephone number consists of an area code and a local number. As shown in Fig. 4.3, the area code is 0311 for Shijiazhuang, 010 for Beijing, and 0312 for Baoding. Telephone numbers in the same area have the same area code, and there is no need to dial the area code for local calls, which is only needed for long-distance calls.

Similar as a phone number, an IP address of a computer also consists of two parts: one part is the network ID; and the other is the host ID. As shown in Fig. 4.4, computers in the same network segment have the same network part. Routers connect different network segments and are responsible for forwarding data between them; and switches connect computers on the same network segment.

In addition to configuring IP addresses and subnet masks for computers, you also have to configure gateways for them. A gateway is an exit for the computer to send packets to computers in other network segments, which is the address of the router (or Layer 3 device) interface. In order to avoid address conflicts with computers in the network, the gateway usually uses the first available address or the last available address of the network segment, and the subnet mask is also required to configure the IP address for the router interface.

Before a computer communicates with other computers, it must first determine whether the destination IP address and its own IP address are in the same network segment. If they are in the same network segment, the destination MAC address of the frame is the MAC address of the destination host; if not, the destination MAC address of the frame is the MAC address of the gateway.

4.2.3   Format of IP Addresses

According to the TCP/IPv4 protocol stack, an IP address is represented by a 32-bit binary number, that is, 32 bits, which is four bytes when converted into bytes. For example, an IP address in binary is "10101100000100000001111000111000", which is too long for people to process. To make it easier to use, such a long address is divided into four parts, each part eight bits long in binary, separated by the symbol ".". The four-part binary IP address 10101100.00010000. 00011110.00111000 is often written in decimal, so the IP address can be represented as "172.16.30.56". This notation of IP addresses is called "dotted decimal notation", which is obviously easier to remember than the combination of 1s and 0s.

The dotted decimal notation of IP addresses simplifies writing and memorization, so it is generally used when configuring IP addresses for computers, as shown in

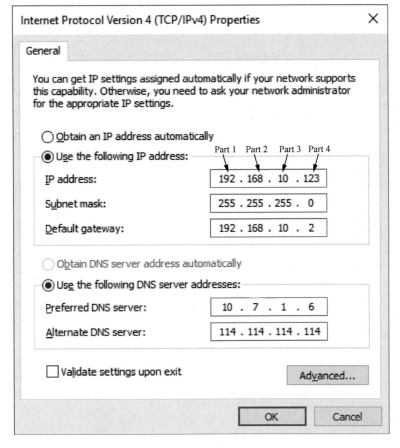

Fig. 4.5 The dotted decimal notation

Fig. 4.5. In this book, these four parts of the IP address are numbered to facilitate description, which are called part 1, part 2, part 3 and part 4 from left to right.

The eight-bit binary number 11111111 is 255 when converted to a decimal number, so the maximum number of each part represented by the dotted decimal notation cannot exceed 255. After configuring the IP address for the computer, you also need to configure the subnet mask and gateway.

4.2.4 Subnet Masks of IP Addresses

A subnet mask, also known as a network mask, is used to specify which bits of an IP address are the network part and which are the host part. The subnet mask has only one function, which is to divide a certain IP address into network part and host part.

There are two ways to represent the subnet mask, which are described below.

1. By the dotted decimal notation with the same format as the IP address, such as 255.0.0.0 or 255.255.255.128.
2. By adding the symbol "/" and numbers from 1 to 32 to the end of the IP address. The numbers 1 to 32 indicate the length of the network ID bits in the subnet mask, for example, the subnet mask 192.168.1.1/24 can also be expressed as 255.255.255.0, and the subnet mask 192.168.1.1/16 can be expressed as 255.255.0.0.

As shown in Fig. 4.6, the IP address of the computer is 131.107.41.6, the subnet mask is 255.255.255.0, and the computer is in the network segment 131.107.41.0/24. If the host part becomes all 0s, it is the network segment in which the host is located. When this computer communicates with a remote computer, as long as the first three parts of the remote computer's IP address are 131.107.41, the two computers are considered to be in the same network segment. For example, this computer is in the same network segment as the computer with IP address 131.107.41.123, but not in the same network segment as the computer with IP address 131.107.42.123, because they do not share the same network part.

As shown in Fig. 4.7, the IP address of the computer is 131.107.41.6, the subnet mask is 255.255.0.0, and the computer is in the network segment 131.107.0.0/16. When it communicates with a remote computer, as long as the first two parts of the IP address of the remote computer are 131.107, the two computers are considered to be in the same network segment. For example, the computer is in the same network segment as the computer with IP address 131.107.42.123, but not in the same network segment as the computer with IP address 131.108.42.123, because they do not share the same network part.

As shown in Fig. 4.8, the IP address of the computer is 131.107.41.6, the subnet mask is 255.0.0.0, and the computer is in network segment 131.0.0.0/8. When this computer communicates with a remote computer, as long as the first part of the remote computer's IP address is 131, the two computers are considered to be in the same network segment. For example, the computer is in the same network segment

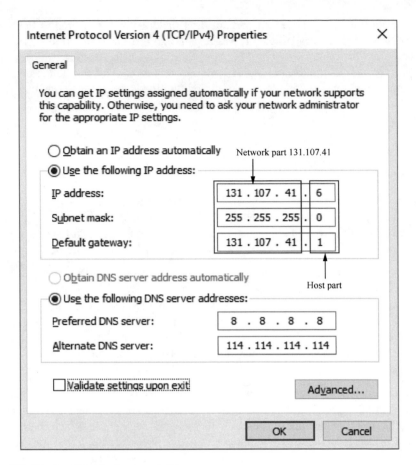

Fig. 4.6 The function of subnet mask (1)

as the computer with IP address 131.108.42.123, but not in the same network segment as the computer with IP address 132.108.42.123, because they do not share the same network part.

So how does a computer use a subnet mask to calculate which network segment it is on?

As shown in Fig. 4.9, a computer's IP address is configured as 131.107.41.6 and its subnet mask is 255.255.255.0. Write both its IP address and subnet mask in binary, and perform the "AND" operation on the corresponding binary bits of these two binary numbers, and it will get 1 only if both digits are 1, otherwise it will get 0. In other words, after the "AND" operation, 1 and 1 arrives at 1, while 0 and 1, 1 and 0, 0 and 0 arrives at 0. Therefore, after the IP address and subnet mask finish the "AND" operation, the host part will be zero regardless of the value, and the network part will remain unchanged, so that the computer is in the network segment 131.107.41.0/24.

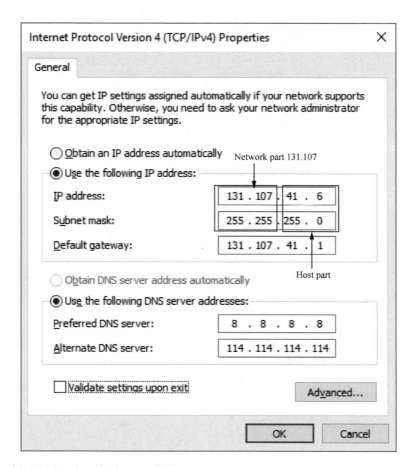

Fig. 4.7 The function of subnet mask (2)

Subnet masks are very important, and will lead to computer communication failure if incorrectly configured. When a computer communicates with other computers, it first determines whether it is in the same network segment as the destination address. First, an AND operation is performed on its subnet mask and IP address to learn about its network segment, then an operation is performed on its subnet mask and the destination address to see if the network part observed is the same as the network segment it is in. If the part address is not the same, they are not in the same network segment, so the MAC address of the gateway is used as the destination MAC address when encapsulating the frame and the switch forwards the frame to the router interface; if it is the same, the MAC address of the destination IP address is used to encapsulate the frame, and the frame is directly sent to the destination IP address.

As shown in Fig. 4.10, the router is connected to two network segments "131.107.41.0 255.255.255.0" and "131.107.42.0 255.255.255.0", and the computers in the same segment have the same subnet mask. The gateway of the computer

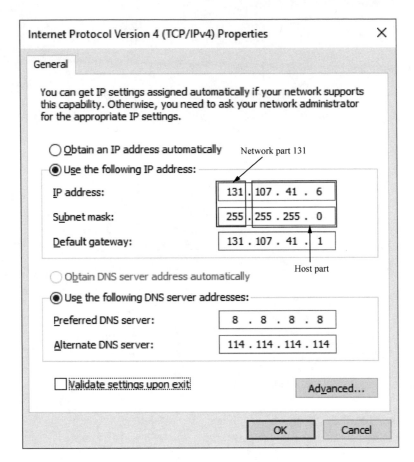

Fig. 4.8 The function of subnet mask (3)

IP address	131	107	41	6
Binary IP address	1 0 0 0 0 0 1 1	0 1 1 0 1 0 1 1	0 0 1 0 1 0 0 1	0 0 0 0 0 1 1 0
	AND	AND		
Subnet mask	255	255	255	0
Binary subnet mask	1 1 1 1 1 1 1 1	1 1 1 1 1 1 1 1	1 1 1 1 1 1 1 1	0 0 0 0 0 0 0 0
"AND" operation of the address and the subnet mask				
Network number	131	107	41	0
Binary network number	1 0 0 0 0 0 1 1	0 1 1 0 1 0 1 1	0 0 1 0 1 0 0 1	0 0 0 0 0 0 0 0

Fig. 4.9 The function of subnet mask (4)

is the exit to the other network segment, which is the router interface address. The address used for the router interface can be any address in the network segment, but usually the first available address or the last available address in the segment is used, in order to avoid conflicts with other computer addresses in the network as much as possible.

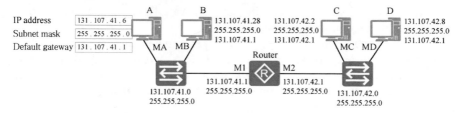

Fig. 4.10   The function of subnet masks and gateways

Fig. 4.11   Different subnet mask settings (1)

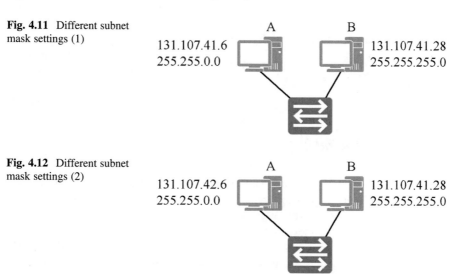

Fig. 4.12   Different subnet mask settings (2)

If a computer is not configured with a gateway, it will not know which is the router interface in cross-network segment communication and will not know which device is the target for the next hop. Therefore, for a computer to communicate across network segments, a gateway must be specified.

As shown in Fig. 4.11, Computer A and Computer B, which are connected to the switch, have different subnet mask settings, and neither of them has set a gateway. Think about it. Is Computer A able to communicate with Computer B? Note: only when the packets can be sent and returned will the network be considered connected.

Answer: Computer A performs an "AND" operation with its own subnet mask to learn that it is in network segment 131.107.0.0/16, and the destination address 131.107.41.28 also belongs to network segment 131.107.0.0/16. Computer A sends a packet directly to Computer B, and Computer B returns a packet to Computer A. Computer B is in network segment 131.107.41.0/24, and the destination address 131.107.41.6 also belongs to network segment 131.107.41.0/24, so Computer B is also able to send the packet directly to Computer A. Therefore, Computer A is able to communicate with Computer B.

As shown in Fig. 4.12, Computer A and Computer B, which are connected to the switch, have different subnet mask settings, and their IP addresses are as shown in the figure. Neither Computer A nor B has set a gateway. Think about it. Is Computer A able to communicate with Computer B?

Answer: Computer A performs an "AND" operation with its own subnet mask to learn that it is in network segment 131.107.0.0/16, and the destination address 131.107.41.28 also belongs to network segment 131.107.0.0/16. Computer A sends the packet directly to Computer B. When Computer B returns a packet to Computer A, it calculates which network segment it is in using its own subnet mask, and learns that it is in network segment 131.107.41.0/24. Since the destination address 131.107.41.6 does not belong to network segment 131.107.41.0/24, Computer B thinks that it is not in the same network segment as Computer A, so it needs to send the packet to the gateway. Because no gateway is set, it is not possible for Computer B to send packets to Computer A. Therefore, Computer A can send packets to Computer B, but Computer B cannot return packets, thus the network is not working.

4.2.5 Classification of IP Addresses

When the Internet was first designed, the Internet Council defined five types of IP addresses to suit networks of different capacities. IPv4 addresses are 32-bit binary numbers divided into network IDs and host IDs. As for which bits are network IDs and which are host IDs, they are initially identified using the first part of the IP addresses. This means that as soon as you see the first part of the IP address, you should know its subnet mask. In this way, IP addresses are divided into five classes: Class A, Class B, Class C, Class D and Class E.

1. Class A

As shown in Fig. 4.13, an IP address is a Class A address if its first bit is 0. The network ID is all 0s, so it cannot be used, and 127 is used as a reserved network segment, so the first part of the Class A address takes a value from 1 to 126.

The default subnet mask for Class A networks is 255.0.0.0. The second to fourth parts is the host ID, and each part takes the value from 0 to 255, a total of 256 values. If you have learned permutation, you will know that the number of hosts in a Class A network is $256 \times 256 \times 256 = 1,67,77,216$, the range of values being 0 to 1,67,77,215 with 0 also counted as a number. The number needs to be subtracted by 2 for available addresses, because the address whose host ID is all

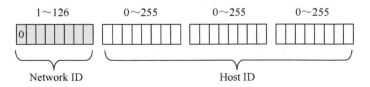

Fig. 4.13 Network ID and host ID of Class A address

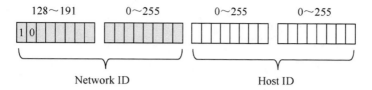

Fig. 4.14 Network ID and host ID of Class B address

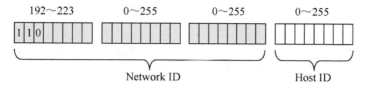

Fig. 4.15 Network ID and host ID of Class C address

0s is a network address and cannot be used by computers, while the address whose host ID is all 1s is a broadcast address and also cannot be used by computers. Therefore, the number of available addresses is 16777214. If you send a packet to an address with a host ID of all 1s, the computer generates a broadcast frame and sends it to all computers in the network segment.

2. Class B

As shown in Fig. 4.14, an IP address is a Class B address if its first two bits are 10. The value of the first part of Class B addresses ranges from 128 to 191.

The default subnet mask for Class B networks is 255.255.0.0. The third and fourth parts are the host ID, and the maximum number of hosts that can be accommodated in each Class B network is $256 \times 256 = 65,536$, with a value range of 0 to 65,535. The number of available addresses is 65,534 by removing the addresses with host ID of all 0s and all 1s.

3. Class C

As shown in Fig. 4.15, an IP address is a Class C address if its first three bits are 110. The first part of the Class C address takes the value from 192 to 223.

The default subnet mask for a Class C network is 255.255.255.0. The fourth part is the host ID. Each Class C network has 256 address, taking values from 0 to 255. Removing the addresses with host IDs of all 0s and all 1s, the number of available addresses is 254.

You can use $2^n - 2$ to calculate the available addresses for a network segment, where n is the number of host bits.

4. Class D

As shown in Fig. 4.16, an IP address is a Class D address if its first four bits are 1110. The values for the first part of a Class D address ranges from 224 to 239. A Class D address is a multicast address. A multicast address does not have a subnet mask, and can only be used as the destination address. We hope that the readers can remember the range of multicast addresses because in addition to broadcasts, some viruses may also send multicast packets in the network, and when using

Fig. 4.16 Class D address

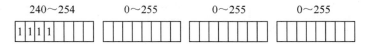

Fig. 4.17 Class E address

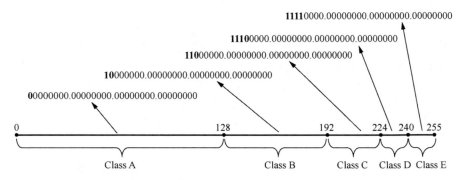

Fig. 4.18 A chart to help remember IP address classification

packet capture tools to troubleshoot the network, you must be able to determine whether the captured packets are multicast or broadcast packets.

5. Class E

As shown in Fig. 4.17, an IP address is a Class E address if its first four bits are 1111. Class E addresses do not distinguish between network ID and host ID. Its first part takes a value range from 240 to 254 and is reserved for future use. Class D and E addresses are not discussed in this book.

In order to conveniently remember the demarcation points of Class A, Class B, Class C, Class D, and Class E addresses, observe Fig. 4.18 and draw the first part of IP addresses as a numeric axis with values from 0 to 255, and the value ranges of Class A, B, C, D, E addresses are clear.

4.2.6 Special IP Addresses

Some IP addresses are reserved for certain purposes, and network administrators cannot assign these addresses to computers. The following lists these addresses that are excluded and explains the reason why they should be reserved.

- Addresses with host IDs of all 0s are network addresses, such as "192.168.10.0 255.255.255.0", which refers to network segment 192.168.10.0/24.

- Addresses with host IDs of all 1 address are broadcast addresses, which specifically refer to all hosts in the network segment. If a computer sends a packet using the IP address with a host ID of all 1s and the data link layer address with the broadcast address FF-FF-FF-FF-FF-FF, the computer name resolution of the same network segment will need to send a broadcast packet for name resolution. For instance, if a computer, whose IP address is 192.168.10.10 and subnet mask is 255.255.255.0, sends a broadcast packet, e.g., the destination IP address is 192.168.10.255, and the frame's destination MAC address is FF-FF-FF-FF-FF-FF, then all computers in the segment can receive it.
- 127.0.0.1 is the loopback address, which refers to the local address and is generally used for testing. The loopback address (127.0.0.1) is the IP address inside the host IP stack, mainly used for network software testing and inter-process communication of the local machine. For whatever program, once the data is sent using the loopback address, the protocol software immediately returns the data without any network transmission. Any computer can use this address to access its own shared resources or websites. If you can ping this address, it means that the computer's TCP/IPv4 stack is working properly. Even if the computer does not have a network interface card, ping 127.0.0.1 shall still work.
- 169.254.0.0: 169.254.0.0 to 169.254.255.255 are actually automatic private IP addresses. In operating systems before Windows 2000, if a computer could not obtain an IP address, it was automatically configured as "IP address: 0.0.0.0" and "subnet mask: 0.0.0.0", so it could not communicate with other computers. For Windows 2000 and later operating systems, it is automatically configured as "IP address: 169.254.x. x" and "subnet mask: 255.255.0.0" when it cannot obtain an IP address. In this way, all computers that fail to obtain an IP address can communicate with each other, as shown in Figs. 4.19 and 4.20.
- 0.0.0.0: If the IP address of the computer conflicts with the addresses of other computers in the network, by using the ipconfig command, you can see the IP address is 0.0.0.0, and the subnet mask is also 0.0.0.0, as shown in Fig. 4.21.

4.3   Public Addresses and Private Addresses

Computers on the Internet use IP addresses that are globally planned, which are called public addresses. Private addresses are usually used and reserved on intranets such as businesses and schools.

4.3.1   Public Addresses

There are millions of hosts on the Internet, all of which need to use IP addresses for communication, so it is required that IP address blocks used by ISPs at all levels in each country accessing the Internet must not overlap, and an organization is required

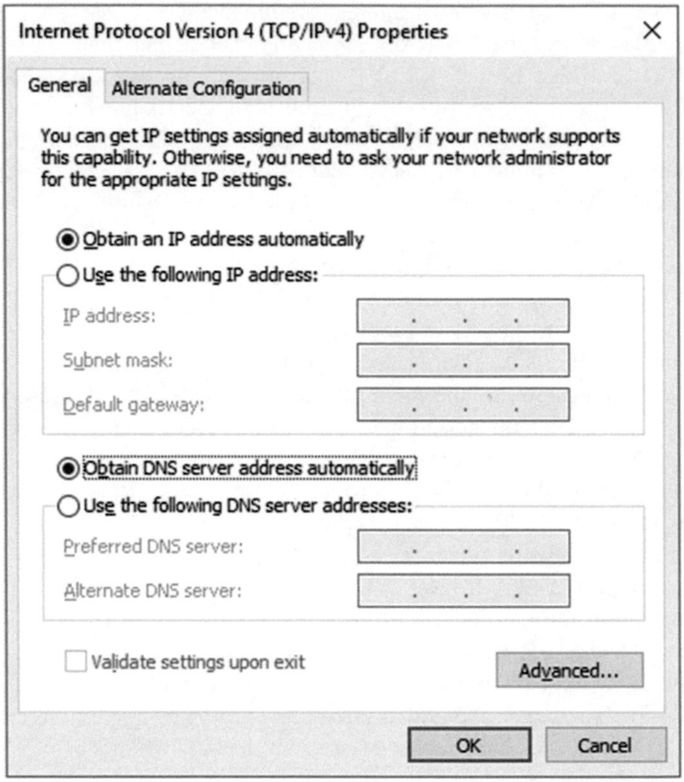

Fig. 4.19 Obtain address automatically

for unified address planning and assignment for the Internet. These globally unique addresses that are uniformly planned and assigned are called public addresses.

Internet Network Information Center (InterNIC) is responsible for the assignment and management of public addresses. The ISPs at all levels need to apply to InterNIC for public addresses, which are issued by InterNIC in a unified manner, so as to ensure that the address blocks do not conflict.

It is because IP addresses are under unified planning and assignment, as long as the IP address is known, it is easy to find out which ISP in which city the address belongs to. If a website is attacked from a certain address, the city where the attacker is located and the carrier it belongs to can be known by the following way.

As shown in Fig. 4.22, if you type in an IP address on Baidu, you can find out the carrier and location of this IP address.

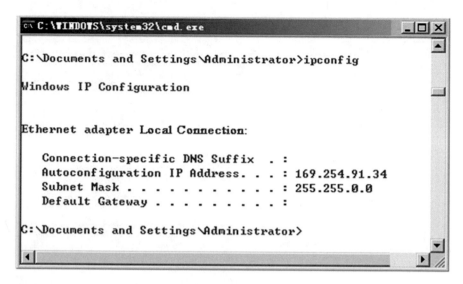

Fig. 4.20 IP address automatically configured by Windows

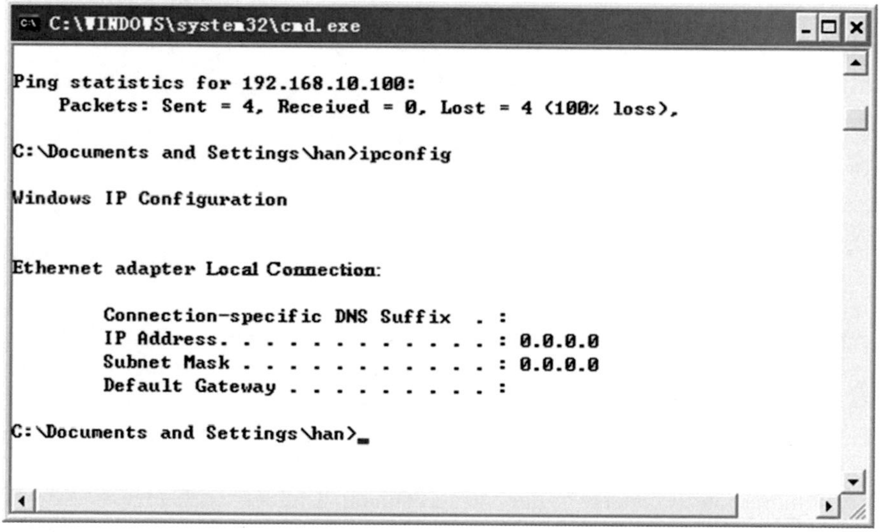

Fig. 4.21 Address conflict

4.3.2   Private Addresses

Private IP addresses are created simultaneously with the IP addressing scheme. These addresses can be used for private networks and are not available on the Internet, nor do routers on the Internet have routes to private addresses. These private addresses are not accessible on the Internet, and in this respect, computers

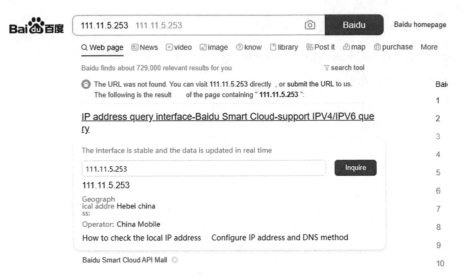

Fig. 4.22   View the carrier and location of the IP address

using private addresses are more secure and can also effectively save public IP addresses.

Intranets of different enterprises or schools can use the same private address. Reserved private IP addresses are listed below.

- Class A: 10.0.0.0 255.0.0.0, only one Class A network is reserved.
- Class B: 172.16.0.0 255.255.0.0 to 172.31.0.0 255.255.0.0, a total of 16 Class B networks are reserved.
- Class C: 192.168.0.0 255.255.255.0 to 192.168.255.255.0 255.255.255.0, a total of 256 Class C networks are reserved.

You can choose which class of private address to use depending on the number of computers in the enterprise or school intranet and the size of the network. If the company currently has seven departments, each with no more than 200 computers, you can consider using the reserved Class C private addresses. If the network is large in scale, for example, when planning a network for Shijiazhuang Municipal Education Commission to connect Shijiazhuang Municipal Education Commission with hundreds of primary and secondary schools in the Shijiazhuang area, the reserved Class A private address shall be selected. It is suggested to use network address 10.0.0.0 and a subnet mask with "/24", which can provide 65,536 subnets, and each network is allowed to have 254 hosts, leaving the school with a large number of addresses to choose from.

4.4 Subnetting

4.4.1 Why Is Subnetting Needed

The protocol used on the Internet today is the TCP/IPv4 protocol stack. IPv4 addresses are 32-bit binary numbers. If they could all be assigned to computers, there would a total of $2^{32} = 4,294,967,296$ (about 4 billion) available addresses. With the removal of Class D and Class E addresses, and the reserved private addresses, the public addresses that can be used on the Internet are becoming more and more limited. Besides, everyone needs to use more than one address, as now both smartphones and smart appliances need IP addresses to access the Internet. By now there are no more available IPv4 public addresses to be assigned to new networks.

In the stage of coexistence of IPv4 and IPv6 when IPv6 is not yet fully used in the Internet, IPv4 public address resources are getting increasingly scarce, so the subnetting technology mentioned in this chapter is required to make full use of IP addresses and reduce address waste.

As shown in Fig. 4.23, according to the traditional classification of IP addresses, there are 200 computers in a network segment, and a Class C network "212.2.3.0 255.255.255.0" is assigned, with the available addresses ranging from 212.2.3.1 to 212.2.3.254. Although not all of these addresses are used, this situation is not considered a waste. Usually, some extra IP addresses are reserved during the network planning, so that there will still be IP addresses to assign if new computers are connected.

If there are 400 computers in a network and a Class C network is assigned, then the addresses are insufficient. If a Class B network "131.107.0.0 255.255.0.0" is assigned, the addresses available for the Class B network range from 131.107.0.1 to 131.107. 255.254, a total of 65,534 available addresses, which results in a huge waste. Therefore, subnetting is needed to break the address blocks limited by the classification of IP addresses, so that the number of IP addresses and the number of computers in the network can be better matched.

Subnetting means to borrow host bits from existing network segments as subnet bits and making multiple subnets. The tasks of subnetting include the following two.

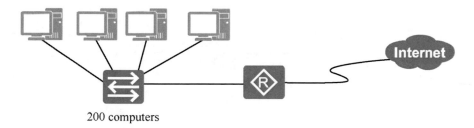

200 computers

Fig. 4.23 Address waste

- Determine the length of the subnet mask.
- Determine the first and the last available IP address in the subnet.

There are FLSM (fixed length subnet masks) subnetting and VLSM (variable length subnet masks) subnetting, and fixed subnetting is first introduced in the following part.

4.4.2   FLSM Subnetting

FLSM subnetting is to equally divide a network segment into multiple segments, that is, into multiple equal-size subnets.

1. Equally divide the network into two subnets.
   The following is an example of a Class C network divided into two subnets to explain the process of subnetting.
   As shown in Fig. 4.24, a company has two departments, with 100 computers in each department, and is connected to the Internet through the router. These 200 computers are assigned a Class C network 192.168.0.0, the subnet mask of the network segment is 255.255.255.0, and the router interface uses the first available IP address of this segment, 192.168.0.1.
   For security reasons, it is planned is to divide the computers in these two departments into two network segments, separated by a router. The number of computers has not increased, which is still 200, so a Class C IP address is sufficient. Now "192.168.0.0 255.255.255.0", the Class C network, is divided into two subnets.
   As shown in Fig. 4.25, the fourth part of the IP address is written in binary, and the subnet mask is represented using two ways: binary and decimal numbers. The subnet mask is shifted one bit to the right (that is, the number of 1s in the subnet mask is increased by one) so that the first bit of the host ID of the Class C address becomes a network bit. If this bit is 0, it is Subnet A, and if this bit is 1, it is Subnet B.

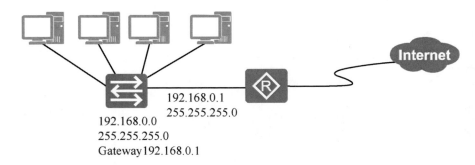

Fig. 4.24 The situation of a network segment

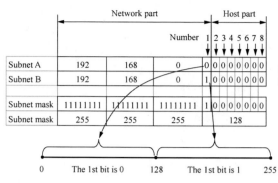

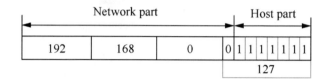

Fig. 4.25 Equally divide the network into two subnets

Fig. 4.26 Network part and host part

As shown in Fig. 4.25, for the fourth part of the IP address, if its value is between 0 and 127, its first bit is 0; and if its value is between 128 and 255, its first bit is 1. Divide it into two subnets, A and B, with 128 as the demarcation point. Now the number of 1s in the subnet mask becomes 25, which is 255.255.255.128 when written in decimal. The subnet mask is shifted by one bit to the right (i.e., the number of 1s in the subnet mask increases by 1), and two subnets are made.

Both Subnet A and Subnet B have a subnet mask of 255.255.255.128.

Subnet A can use addresses from 192.168.0.1 to 192.168.0.126. Since the host bits of IP address 192.168.0.0 are all 0s, it is the network address of the network segment, so it cannot be assigned to the computer for use. As shown in Fig. 4.26, Since the host bits of IP address 192.168.0.127 are all 1s, it is the broadcast address of this network segment, so it also cannot be assigned to the computer.

Subnet B can use addresses from 192.168.0.129 to 192.168.0.254. IP address 192.168.0.128 is the network address, so it cannot be assigned to computers for use, while IP address 192.168.0.255 is the broadcast address, and also cannot be assigned to computers.

The address planning after the network is divided into two subnets is as shown in Fig. 4.27.

2. Equally divide the network into four subnets.

Assume the company has four departments, with 50 computers in each department, and now it uses the Class C network 192.168.0.0/24. From security considerations, it is planned to allocate computers of each department to different network segments, which requires the Class C network "192.168.0.0 255.255.255.0" to be divided into four subnets. Then how to divide it into four subnets?

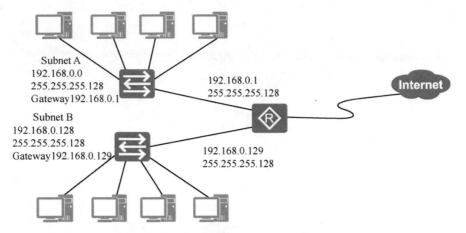

Fig. 4.27 The address planning after subnetting

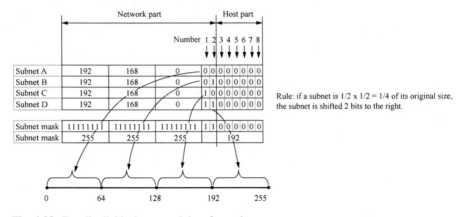

Fig. 4.28 Equally divide the network into four subnets

As shown in Fig. 4.28, write the fourth part of the IP address of the network segment "192.168.0.0 255.255.255.0" in binary. If the network is to be divided into four subnets, you need to move the subnet mask two bits to the right, so that the first and second bits become network bits, and the network can be divided into four subnets. If the first two bits are 00, then it is Subnet A; if the first two bits are 01, then it is Subnet B; if the first two bits are 10, then it is Subnet C; if the first two bits are 11, then it is Subnet D.

The subnet masks for Subnet A, B, C, and D are all 255.255.255.192.

The addresses available for Subnet A are 192.168.0.1 to 192.168.0.62.

The addresses available for Subnet B are 192.168.0.65 to 192.168.0.126.

The addresses available for Subnet C are 192.168.0.129 to 192.168.0.190.

The addresses available for Subnet D are 192.168.0.193 to 192.168.0.254.

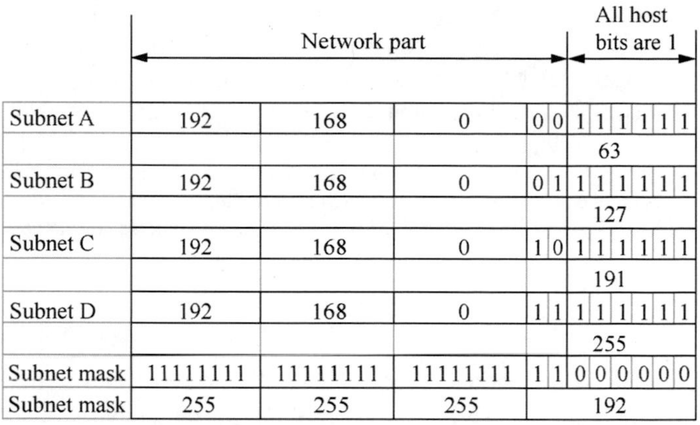

	Network part			All host bits are 1							
Subnet A	192	168	0	0	0	1	1	1	1	1	1
				63							
Subnet B	192	168	0	0	1	1	1	1	1	1	1
				127							
Subnet C	192	168	0	1	0	1	1	1	1	1	1
				191							
Subnet D	192	168	0	1	1	1	1	1	1	1	1
				255							
Subnet mask	11111111	11111111	11111111	1	1	0	0	0	0	0	0
Subnet mask	255	255	255	192							

Fig. 4.29 Network part and host part

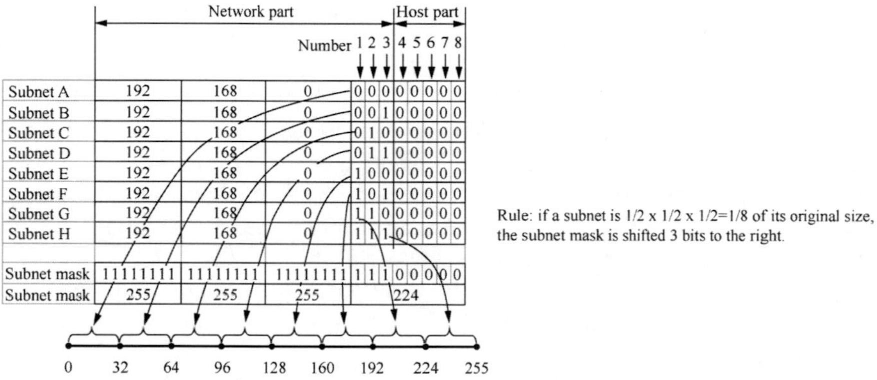

Fig. 4.30 Equally divide the network into eight subnets

Note	As shown in Fig. 4.29, the last address of each subnet is the broadcast address of this subnet and cannot be assigned to a computer for use, for example, 63 of Subnet A, 127 of Subnet B, 191 of Subnet C, and 255 of Subnet D.

3. Equally divide the network into eight subnets.

   If you want to equally divide a Class C network into eight subnets, as shown in Fig. 4.30, the subnet mask needs to be shifted three bits to the right for the eight subnets, and the first, second and third bits become network bits.

   The subnet mask is the same for each subnet and is 255.255.255.224.

   The addresses available for Subnet A are 192.168.0.1 to 192.168.0.30.

   The addresses available for Subnet B are 192.168.0.33 to 192.168.0.62.

   The addresses available for Subnet C are 192.168.0.65 to 192.168.0.94.

   The addresses available for Subnet D are 192.168.0.97 to 192.168.0.126.

The addresses available for Subnet E are 192.168.0.129 to 192.168.0.158.
The addresses available for Subnet F are 192.168.0.161 to 192.168.0.190.
The addresses available for Subnet G are 192.168.0.193 to 192.168.0.222.
The addresses available for Subnet H are 192.168.0.225 to 192.168.0.254.

Note	Addresses whose host bits are all 0s and all 1s should be left out, and the remaining addresses are the host IP addresses that each subnet can use. As shown in Fig. 4.30, 31, 63, 95, 127, 159, 191, 223, and 255 are the broadcast addresses of the corresponding subnets. Each subnet is the $\frac{1}{2} \times \frac{1}{2} \times \frac{1}{2}$ of the original size, that is, three $\frac{1}{2}$, so the subnet mask is shifted three bits to the right.

Summary: if a subnet address block is $\left(\frac{1}{2}\right)^n$ the size of the original network segment, the subnet mask is shifted n bits to the right on the basis of the original network segment.

4.4.3   Examples of FLSM Subnetting

The previous section explains the FLSM subnetting using a Class C network, and the summarized rule is also applicable to the subnetting of Class B networks. However, it is easy to make mistakes if you are not familiar with the rule, so when subdividing a network, it is best to write the host bits in binary form and determine the subnet mask as well as the first and last address that each subnet can use.

As shown in Fig. 4.31, network "131.107.0.0 255.255.0.0" is equally divided into two subnets. The network can be divided into two subnets by moving the subnet mask one bit to the right.

The subnet masks of the two equal-size subnets are both 255.255.128.0.

First determine the first and the last available address of Subnet A. When you are not familiar with it, it is better to write the host part in binary as it is shown in Fig. 4.32. The host bits cannot be all 0s or all 1s. And then write the first and the last available address according to the binary number.

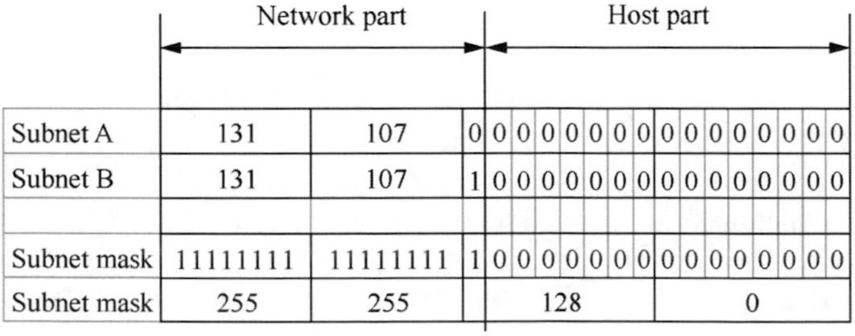

	Network part		Host part	
Subnet A	131	107	0 0 0 0 0 0 0 0 0 0 0 0 0 0 0 0	
Subnet B	131	107	1 0 0 0 0 0 0 0 0 0 0 0 0 0 0 0	
Subnet mask	11111111	11111111	1 0 0 0 0 0 0 0 0 0 0 0 0 0 0 0	
Subnet mask	255	255	128	0

Fig. 4.31 Subnetting of Class B network

	Network part		Host part	
	131	107	0 0 0 0 0 0 0 0	0 0 0 0 0 0 0 1
The first available address of Subnet A	131	107	0	1
	131	107	0 1 1 1 1 1 1 1	1 1 1 1 1 1 1 0
The last available address of Subnet A	131	107	127	254

Fig. 4.32 Address range of Subnet A

	Network part		Host part	
	131	107	1 0 0 0 0 0 0 0	0 0 0 0 0 0 0 1
The first available address of Subnet B	131	107	128	1
	131	107	1 1 1 1 1 1 1 1	1 1 1 1 1 1 1 0
The last available address of Subnet B	131	107	255	254

Fig. 4.33 Address range of Subnet B

The first available address of Subnet A is 131.107.0.1 and the last is 131.107.127.254. Think about it. Can the address 131.107.0.255 of Subnet A be assigned to a computer for use? Writing the host bits in binary shows that not all host bits are 1 so it can be used by the computer.

As shown in Fig. 4.33, the first available address of Subnet B is 131.107.128.1, and the last is 131.107.255.254.

Although this method takes many steps, it can prevent making mistakes. When you have familiarized yourself with it, you can directly write the first and last address of the subnet.

4.4.4 VLSM Subnetting

The above mentioned subnetting is to equally divide a network segment into multiple subnets. If the number of computers in each subnet is not the same, it is necessary to divide the network segment into subnets with different address spaces, which is VLSM subnetting. The following is an example for VLSM subnetting.

As shown in Fig. 4.34, there is a Class C network "192.168.0.0 255.255.255.0" that needs to be divided into five network segments in order to meet the following network requirements: The network has three switches, each connected to 20 computers, 50 computers and 100 computers, respectively; the connection interfaces between routers also need addresses, and although there are only two addresses, they also need to occupy a network segment, so that there are a total of five network segments in the network.

Each subnet is $\frac{1}{2} \times \frac{1}{2} \times \frac{1}{2} \times \frac{1}{2} \times \frac{1}{2} \times \frac{1}{2}$ the size of the original network, that is, $\left(\frac{1}{2}\right)^6$, and the subnet mask is moved six bits to the right. 111111111.11111111.111111111.11111100 is 255.255.255.252 (or "/30") when written in decimal.

The final result of subnetting is shown in Fig. 4.36. After careful planning, in addition to satisfying the address requirements of five network segments are satisfied, there are two address blocks remained, i.e., address blocks 8 to 16 and address blocks 16 to 32 are not used.

FLSM and VLSM subnetting shatter the concept of IP address "classes", so that Internet service providers (ISPs) can flexibly divide large address blocks into appropriate small ones (subnets) for customers to prevent the waste of a large number of IP addresses. At the same time, the subnet mask also elevates the byte limit, and this kind of subnet mask is called Variable Length Subnet Masking (VLSM). The variable length subnet masking is usually expressed in the form of "/n", such as 131.107.23.32/25, 192.168.0.178/26, and the number after the slash (/) indicates the length of the network identification bits in the subnet mask.

4.5 Merge Subnets

The subnetting described earlier treats the host bits of a network as network bits to divide the network into multiple subnets. In addition, it is also possible to merge multiple networks (subnets) into one large network (subnet) by treating the network bits of multiple networks (subnets) as host bits.

4.5.1 Merge Network Segments

As shown in Fig. 4.39, an enterprise has a network segment with 200 computers; after using network segment "192.168.0.0 255.255.255.0", the number of computers has increased to 400.

The size of the network can be expanded by adding a switch to the network. At this time, if a Class C IP address is not enough, you can add another Class C address "192.168.1.0 255.255.255.0". These computers are in the same network segment at the physical level, but the IP addresses are not in the same network segment, that is, they are logically not in the same network segment. If you want these computers to be able to communicate with each other, you can add the addresses of these two Class C networks to the router's interface as gateways to these two network segments.

In this case, for the communication between Computer A and Computer B, packets have to be forwarded by a router so that the two subnets can communicate. These computers are physically in one network segment, but the packets still need to

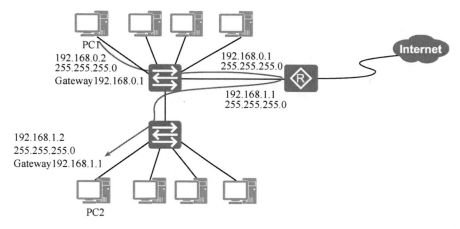

Fig. 4.39   Addresses of two network segments

	Network part		Host part	
192.168.0.0	192	168	0 0 0 0 0 0 0 0	0 0 0 0 0 0 0 0
192.168.1.0	192	168	0 0 0 0 0 0 0 1	0 0 0 0 0 0 0 0
Subnet mask	11111111	11111111	1 1 1 1 1 1 1 0	0 0 0 0 0 0 0 0
Subnet mask	255	255	254	0

Fig. 4.40   Merge two subnets

be forwarded by a router, which is obviously inefficient. Is there a better way to make these two Class C networks of computers think that they are in the same network segment? This requires merging the two Class C networks 192.168.0.0/24 and 192.168.1.0/24.

As shown in Fig. 4.40, after writing the third and fourth parts of the IP addresses of the two network segments in binary, you can see the subnet mask is moved one bit to the left (the number of 1s in the subnet mask is reduced by 1), so the network parts of the two network segments become the same, and the two network segments are in the same network segment.

The merged network segment is 192.168.0.0/23, and the subnet mask is 255.255.254.0 when written in decimal. The available addresses are from 192.168.0.1 to 192.168.1.254, and the IP addresses of computers in the network and the address configuration of the router interface is shown in Fig. 4.41.

After the merger, IP address 192.168.0.255/23 can be given to the computer for use. The host bits of the address seem to be all 1s, and the address cannot be used by the computer, but after converting the third and fourth parts of the IP address into binary numbers, you can see that the host bits are not all 1s, as shown in Fig. 4.42.

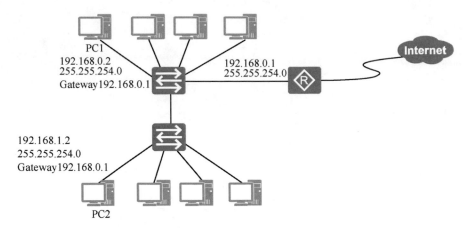

Fig. 4.41 The address assignment after the merge

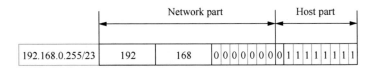

Fig. 4.42 Method to determine whether it is a broadcast address

Rule: by shifting the subnet mask one bit to the left, you can merge two consecutive network segments. However, not all consecutive segments can be merged. The following will introduce the rules of merging network segments.

4.5.2   Rules of Merging Network Segments

As mentioned earlier, when the subnet mask is moved one bit to the left, two consecutive network segments can be merged, but not any two consecutive segments can be merged into a network segment by this method.

For example, 192.168.1.0/24 and 192.168.2.0/24 cannot be merged into one network segment by moving the subnet mask one bit to the left. After writing the third and fourth parts of these two network segments into binary, you can see that, as shown in Fig. 4.43, though the subnet mask is moved one bit to the left, the network parts of the two network segments are still different, indicating that the two segments cannot be merged into one network segment.

To merge them into one network segment, the subnet mask should be moved two bits to the left, but if that is done, you are actually merging four network segments, as shown in Fig. 4.44.

The following explains which consecutive network segments (subnets) can be merged, i.e., the rules of merging network segments.

	Network part		Host part
192.168.1.0	192	168	0 0 0 0 0 0 0 1 | 0 0 0 0 0 0 0 0
192.168.2.0	192	168	0 0 0 0 0 0 1 0 | 0 0 0 0 0 0 0 0
Subnet mask	11111111	11111111	1 1 1 1 1 1 1 0 | 0 0 0 0 0 0 0 0
Subnet mask	255	255	254 | 0

Fig. 4.43 The rule of merging network segments (1)

	Network part		Host part
192.168.0.0	192	168	0 0 0 0 0 0 0 0 0 0 0 0 0 0 0 0
192.168.1.0	192	168	0 0 0 0 0 0 0 1 0 0 0 0 0 0 0 0
192.168.2.0	192	168	0 0 0 0 0 0 1 0 0 0 0 0 0 0 0 0
192.168.3.0	192	168	0 0 0 0 0 0 1 1 0 0 0 0 0 0 0 0
Subnet mask	11111111	11111111	1 1 1 1 1 1 0 0 0 0 0 0 0 0 0 0
Subnet mask	255	255	252 | 0

Fig. 4.44 The rule of merging network segments (2)

	Network part		Host part
192.168.0.0/24	192	168	0 0 0 0 0 0 0 0 | 0 0 0 0 0 0 0 0
192.168.1.0/24	192	168	0 0 0 0 0 0 0 1 | 0 0 0 0 0 0 0 0

Fig. 4.45 Merge 192.168.0.0/24 and 192.168.1.0/24

	Network part		Host part
192.168.2.0/24	192	168	0 0 0 0 0 0 1 0 | 0 0 0 0 0 0 0 0
192.168.3.0/24	192	168	0 0 0 0 0 0 1 1 | 0 0 0 0 0 0 0 0

Fig. 4.46 Merge 192.168.2.0/24 and 192.168.3.0/24

1. Determine whether two subnets can be merged.

   As shown in Fig. 4.45, 192.168.0.0/24 and 192.168.1.0/24 can be merged into a network segment 192.168.0.0/23 by moving their subnet masks one bit to the left.

			Network part								Host part							
192.168.0.0	192	168	0	0	0	0	0	0	0	0	0	0	0	0	0	0
192.168.1.0	192	168	0	0	0	0	0	0	0	1	0	0	0	0	0	0
192.168.2.0	192	168	0	0	0	0	0	0	1	0	0	0	0	0	0	0
192.168.3.0	192	168	0	0	0	0	0	0	1	1	0	0	0	0	0	0

| Subnet mask | 11111111 | 11111111 | 1 | 1 | 1 | 1 | 1 | 1 | 0 | 0 | 0 | 0 | 0 | 0 | 0 | 0 |
| Subnet mask | 255 | 255 | 252 | | | | | | | | 0 | | | | | | |

Fig. 4.47 Merge four network segments 1

As shown in Fig. 4.46, 192.168.2.0/24 and 192.168.3.0/24 can be merged into a network segment 192.168.2.0/23 by moving their subnet masks one bit to the left.

Rule: when merging two consecutive network segments, if the last bit of the network number of the first segment is 0 when written in binary form, the two segments can be merged. According to the rule described in 4.1.2, as long as a number is divisible by 2, the last bit must be 0 when written in binary form.

Conclusion: to determine whether two consecutive network segments can be merged, as long as the network number of the first segment is divisible by 2, the two network segments can be merged by shifting their subnet mask one bit to the left.

Can 131.107.31.0/24 and 131.107.32.0/24 be merged by shifting the subnet mask one bit to the left?

Can 131.107.142.0/24 and 131.107.143.0/24 be merged by shifting the subnet mask one bit to the left?

According to the above conclusion, when 31 is divided by 2, the remainder is 1, so 131.107.31.0/24 and 131.107.32.0/24 cannot be merged into one network segment by shifting the subnet mask one bit to the left. When 142 is divided by 2, the remainder is 0, so 131.107.142.0/24 and 131.107.143.0/24 can be merged into one network segment by shifting the subnet mask one bit to the left.

2. Determine whether four network segments can be merged

As shown in Fig. 4.47, in order to merge four network segments, 192.168.0.0/24, 192.168.1.0/24, 192.168.2.0/24, and 192.168.3.0/24, the subnet mask needs to be shifted two bits to the left.

You can see that to merge the four network segments 192.168.4.0/24, 192.168.5.0/24, 192.168.6.0/24, and 192.168.7.0/24, the subnet masks need to be moved two bits to the left, as shown in Fig. 4.48.

Rule: for four consecutive segments, as long as the last two bits of the network number of the first network segment are 00 when written in binary form, these four segments can be merged. According to the law of binary numbers in 4.1.2, as long as a number is divisible by 4, its last two bits must be 00 when written in binary form.

			Network part													Host part							
192.168.4.0/24	192	168	0	0	0	0	0	1	0	0	0	0	0	0	0	0	0	0
192.168.5.0/24	192	168	0	0	0	0	0	1	0	1	0	0	0	0	0	0	0	0
192.168.6.0/24	192	168	0	0	0	0	0	1	1	0	0	0	0	0	0	0	0	0
192.168.7.0/24	192	168	0	0	0	0	0	1	1	1	0	0	0	0	0	0	0	0

Subnet mask	11111111	11111111	1	1	1	1	1	1	0	0	0	0	0	0	0	0	0	0
Subnet mask	255	255	252									0							

Fig. 4.48 Merge four network segments 2

Fig. 4.49 Determine which subnet the address belongs to (1)

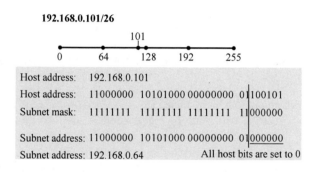

192.168.0.101/26

Host address: 192.168.0.101

Host address: 11000000 10101000 00000000 01100101

Subnet mask: 11111111 11111111 11111111 11000000

Subnet address: 11000000 10101000 00000000 01000000

Subnet address: 192.168.0.64   All host bits are set to 0

Conclusion: to determine whether four consecutive network segments can be merged, as long as the network number of the first network segment is divisible by 4, the four segments can be merged by shifting the subnet mask two bits to the left.

Think about how to determine whether eight consecutive segments can be merged.

4.6 Determine Which Network Segment an IP Address Belongs

In the following, we will introduce how to determine which network segment an IP address belongs based on the IP address and subnet mask given. When all host bits are 0, it is the network segment which the IP address belongs to.

Determine which subnet 192.168.0.101/26 belongs to. This is a Class C address, whose subnet mask is 24 bits by default and is now 26 bits. The subnet mask is moved two bits to the right, so according to the above summarized rule, each subnet is $\frac{1}{2} \times \frac{1}{2}$ the size of the original, that is, this Class C network is equally divided into four subnets. As shown in Fig. 4.49, 101 is located between 64 and 128, and after all host bits are set to 0, it is 64. Therefore, the address belongs to subnet 192.168.0.64/26.

Fig. 4.50 Determine which subnet the address belongs to (2)

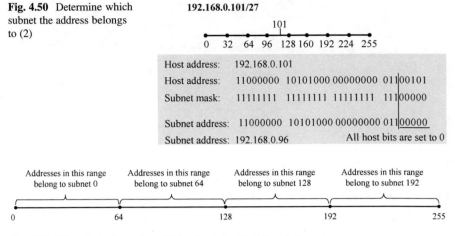

192.168.0.101/27

101

0   32   64   96   128 160 192 224   255

Host address: 192.168.0.101

Host address: 11000000 10101000 00000000 01100101

Subnet mask: 11111111   11111111 11111111   11100000

Subnet address: 11000000 10101000 00000000 01100000

Subnet address: 192.168.0.96   All host bits are set to 0

Addresses in this range   Addresses in this range   Addresses in this range   Addresses in this range
belong to subnet 0   belong to subnet 64   belong to subnet 128   belong to subnet 192

0   64   128   192   255

Fig. 4.51 The rule to determine which subnet the IP address belongs to

Determine which subnet 192.168.0.101/27 belongs to. The is a Class C address whose subnet mask is 24 bits by default and is now 27 bits. The subnet mask is moved three bits to the right, so according to the above summarized rule, each subnet is $\frac{1}{2} \times \frac{1}{2} \times \frac{1}{2}$ the size of the original, that is, this Class C network is equally divided into eight subnets. As shown in Fig. 4.50, 101 is located between 96 and 128, and after all host bits are set to 0, it is 96. Therefore, the address belongs to subnet 192.168.0.96/27.

Summary: all IP addresses 192.168.0.0 to 192.168.0.63 belong to subnet 192.168.0.0/26; all IP addresses from 192.168.0.64 to 192.168.0.127 belong to the 192.168.0.64/26 subnet; all IP addresses from 192.168.0.128 ~ 192.168.0.191 belong to the subnet 192.168.0.128/26; and all IP addresses from 192.168.0.192 to 192.168.0.255 belong to the subnet 192.168.0.192/26, as shown in Fig. 4.51.

4.7   Exercises

1. (Multi-selection) Which of the following addresses belong to network segment 113.64.4.0/22. ( )

   A. 113.64.8.32
   B. 113.64.7.64
   C. 113.64.6.255
   D. 113.64.5.255
   E. 113.64.3.128
   F. 113.64.12.128

2. (Multi-selection) Which of the following subnets are included in network segment 172.31.80.0/20. ( )

   A. 172.31.17.4/30
   B. 172.31.51.16/30
   C. 172.31.64.0/18
   D. 172.31.80.0/22
   E. 172.31.92.0/22
   F. 172.31.192.0/18

3. A company designs a network that requires 300 subnets, each with a maximum of 50 hosts. To subdivide a Class B network, which of the following subnet masks can be used ( ).

   A. 255.255.255.0
   B. 255.255.255.128
   C. 255.255.255.224
   D. 255.255.255.192

4. (Multi-selection) The network segment 172.25.0.0/16 is divided into eight equal-length subnets, and which of the following addresses belong to the third subnet. ( )

   A. 172.23.78.243
   B. 172.25.98.16
   C. 172.23.72.0
   D. 172.25.94.255
   E. 172.25.96.17
   F. 172.23.100.16

5. (Multi-selection) According to Fig. 4.52, which of the following network segments can be assigned to Network A and Link A. ( )

   A. Network A: 172.16.3.48/26
   B. Network A: 172.16.3.128/25
   C. Network A: 172.16.3.192/26
   D. Link A: 172.16.3.0/30
   E. Link A: 172.16.3.40/30
   F. Link A: 172.16.3.112/30

6. The network part of the IP address is used to identify ( ).

   A. Router
   B. Host

Fig. 4.52 Network topology

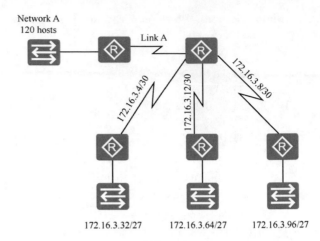

C. Network interface card

D. Network segment

7. Which of the following networks belongs to a private address ( ).

A. 192.178.32.0/24

B. 128.168.32.0/24

C. 172.13.32.0/24

D. 192.168.32.0/24

8. The maximum number of addresses available in network 122.21.136.0/22 is ( ).

A. 102

B. 1023

C. 1022

D. 1000

9. The host address 192.15.2.160 is located in the network ( ).

A. 192.15.2.64/26

B. 192.15.2.128/26

C. 192.15.2.96/26

D. 192.15.2.192/26

10. A company's network address is 192.168.1.0/24, which is to be divided into five subnets, each with a maximum of 20 hosts. So the applicable subnet mask is ( ).

A. 255.255.255.192

B. 255.255.255.240

    C. 255.255.255.224
    D. 255.255.255.248

11. The IP address of a port is 202.16.7.131/26, then the broadcast address of the network where the IP address is located is ( ).

    A. 202.16.7.255
    B. 202.16.7.129
    C. 202.16.7.191
    D. 202.16.7.252

12. In IPv4, multicast addresses are ( ) addresses.

    A. Class A
    B. Class B
    C. Class C
    D. Class D

13. A host has an IP address of 180.80.77.55 and a subnet mask of 255.255.252.0. The host sends a broadcast packet to its subnet, and the destination address can be ( ).

    A. 180.80.76.0
    B. 180.80.76.255
    C. 180.80.77.255
    D. 180.80.79.255

14. The IP address space of a network is 192.168.5.0/24, if FLSM subnetting is used, and the subnet mask is 255.255.255.248, then the number of subnets divided, the maximum number of addresses that can be assigned in each subnet are ( ).

    A. 32, 8
    B. 32, 6
    C. 8, 32
    D. 8, 30

15. Network segment 192.168.10.0/24 is divided into three subnets, and the number of computers in each segment is shown in Fig. 4.53. Write down first and last addresses that can be used by computers in each segment and their subnet masks.

	First available address	Last available address	Subnet mask
Segment A	_____	_____	_____
Segment B	_____	_____	_____
Segment C	_____	_____	_____

Fig. 4.53 Subnetting

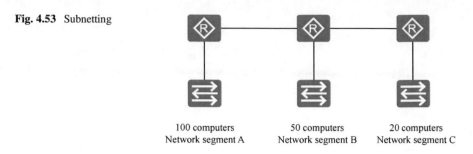

100 computers   50 computers   20 computers
Network segment A   Network segment B   Network segment C

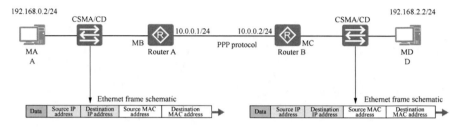

Fig. 4.54 Illustration of the communication between Computer A and Computer D

16. Computer A sends a packet to Computer D over two Ethernet frames as shown in Fig. 4.54. Write down the source and destination IP addresses as well as the source and destination MAC addresses of the packets.

17. There are four "/24" address blocks as follows. Write down the maximum possible aggregation: _____.

    212.56.132.0/24   212.56.133.0/24   212.56.134.0/24
    212.56.135.0/24

18. As shown in Fig. 4.55, the IP addresses, subnet masks, and gateway settings of Computer A and Computer B are indicated, and the router is connected to two network segments and the Internet. Determine whether Computer A and Computer B in the network can communicate, and whether Computer A and Computer B can access the Web server in the Internet.

19. Based on the network topology and the number of hosts in the network shown in Fig. 4.56, move the IP addresses on the left to appropriate positions.

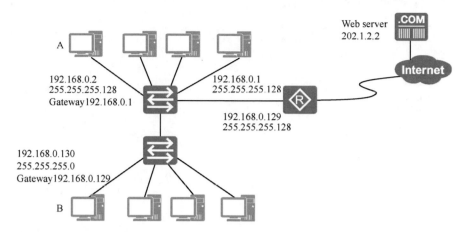

Fig. 4.55   Network topology

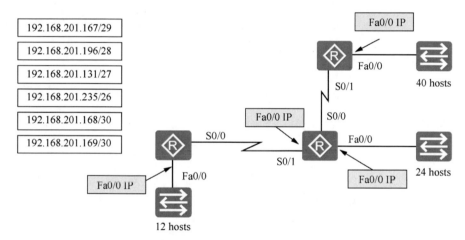

Fig. 4.56   Network planning

Chapter 5
IP Routing Fundamentals

For an unobstructed network, the routers in the network need to know how to forward packets to each network segment. Routers forward packets based on a routing table, which can be constructed through directly connected networks, static routing, and dynamic routing.

Static routing is to manually add a routing entry to the router. By configuring static routing, floating static routes can be enabled, which means that the router will automatically choose an alternate path when the optimal path is not available.

IP addresses, if planned properly, can implement route summarization on the area border router. Route summarization simplifies the routing table and improves the speed of table lookup.

Default routing is a special kind of static routing, which means a router makes its choice when there is no route in the routing table that matches the destination address of a packet. If there is no default routing, packets whose destination address does not have a matching route in the routing table will be discarded. Having a gateway set up on a Windows system is tantamount to adding a default route to the Windows system.

5.1 Basic Concepts of Route

5.1.1 What Is a Route

In network communication, the term "Route" is a network layer term that refers to the path a packet takes from a network device to the destination. A router (or Layer 3 device) in a network is responsible for selecting the forwarding path for packets. As shown in Fig. 5.1, a router has a routing table, which consists of a number of routing messages. In the routing table, a piece of routing information is also called a routing entry, and the router selects the forwarding path for the packets according to

© The Author(s) 2023
Huawei Technologies Co., Ltd., *Data Communications and Network Technologies*,
https://doi.org/10.1007/978-981-19-3029-4_5

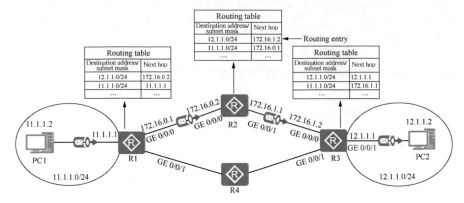

Fig. 5.1 IP routing

the routing table. Routing tables exist only in end computers and routers (and Layer 3 devices); they do not exist in Layer 2 switches.

As shown in Fig. 5.1, PC1 sends PC2 a packet with a source IP address of 11.1.1.2 and a destination IP address of 12.1.1.2. Router R1 receives the packet and checks the routing table and finds a route to network segment 12.1.1.0/24, and the next hop is to 172.16.0.2, so the packet is sent from interface GE 0/0/0 of router R1 to router R2; after receiving it, router R2 checks the routing table, and finds that there is a route to network segment 12.1.1.0/24, and the next hop is to 172.16.1.2, so the packet is sent from interface GE 0/0/1 of router R2 to router R3; after receiving the packet, router R3 checks the routing table and finds a route to network segment 12.1.1.0/24, and the next hop is 12.1.1.1, which is the address of interface GE 0/0/1 of router R3, so the packet is sent out from GE 0/0/1 and finally arrives at PC2. When PC2 sends a packet to PC1, it also needs the routers along the way to query the routing table so as to determine the forwarding path.

It should be noted that if the next hop IP address of a routing entry is the IP address of the outgoing interface, it means that the interface is directly connected to the destination network indicated by the routing entry. It is also important to note that the host interface corresponding to the next hop IP address must be on the same Layer 2 network (Layer 2 broadcast domain) as the outgoing interface.

Here is a routing table of an actual router. By entering "display ip routing-table", you can see the routing table.

```
[AR1] display ip routing-table
Route Flags: R - relay, D - download to fib

------------------------------------------------------------------
-------------
Routing Tables: Public
       Destinations : 14    Routes : 14
```

```
Destination/Mask  Proto    Pre Cost    Flags   NextHop       Interface
  ......
  172.16.0.0/24  Direct   0    0       D    172.16.0.1     Serial2/0/0
  172.16.0.2/32  Direct   0    0       D    172.16.0.2     Serial2/0/0
  172.16.1.0/24  OSPF    10    96      D    172.16.0.2     Serial2/0/0
  192.168.0.0/24 Direct   0    0       D    192.168.0.1    Vlanif1
  192.168.1.0/24 OSPF    10    97      D    172.16.0.2     Serial2/0/0
  192.168.10.0/24 Static 60    0       RD   172.16.0.2     Serial2/0/0
  ......
```

As you can see, the routing table has 14 destinations and 14 routes.

Each field of the routing entry is explained below.

- Destination/Mask represents the destination and subnet mask.
- Proto, short for Protocol, indicates the protocol through which the routing entry is generated. "Direct" means a directly connected network segment, a route that is automatically discovered. OSPF specifies that the routing entry is a dynamic route constructed via the OSPF protocol, and "Static" indicates that the routing entry is a manually configured static route.
- Pre is short for Preference, and is used to reflect the preference of the source of routing information.
- The cost of a route is one of its imperative attributes. The router selects the optimal forwarding path for the packet, which is also the path with low cost.
- Flags means route flags, R means the route is an iterative route, and D means the route is delivered to the FIB table.
- NextHop represents the next hop, i.e., which is the next closest router a packet can go through to get to the destination, so that the router can determine which exit the packet should be sent out from.
- Interface indicates the next hop exit to arrive at the destination network segment.

5.1.2   Sources of Routing Information

A routing table contains a number of routing information, which is generated in three ways: direct routing, static routing, and dynamic routing.

1. Direct routes

We call the routing information automatically discovered by the device a direct route. After the network device starts up, when the router interface status is UP, the router can automatically discover routes to the network directly connected to its own interface.

As shown in Fig. 5.2, when the status of interface GE 0/0/1 of router R1 is UP, R1 can infer that the network address of the network where GE 0/0/1 interface is located is 11.1.1.1/24 based on the IP address of interface GE 0/0/1 is 11.1.1.1/24. Then, R1 will fill 11.1.1.0/24 into its routing table as a routing entry. The destination/mask of this route is 11.1.1.0/24, the outgoing interface is GE 0/0/1,

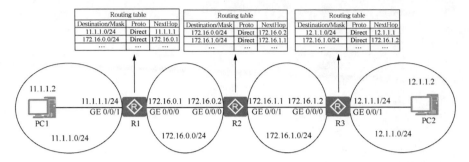

Fig. 5.2 Direct routes

and the next hop IP address is the same as the IP address of the outgoing interface, that is 11.1.1.1. Since this is a direct route, its protocol attribute is direct. In addition, the value of cost is always 0 for a direct route.

Similarly, router R1 will automatically discover another direct route with a destination/mask of 172.16.0.0/24, an outgoing interface of GE 0/0/0, a next hop address of 172.16.0.1, a protocol attribute of direct, and a cost of 0.

You can see that as soon as R1, R2 and R3 in the network are turned on and the ports are up, the network segments connected to these interfaces will appear in the routing table.

2. Static routes

For computers in the network to be able to access any network segment in the network, the routers in the network must have routes to all the network segments. For segments that are directly connected to the router, the router can automatically discover them and add them to the routing table. For those that are not directly connected, the administrator needs to manually add them to the routing table. The manually configured routing information of the router is called static route and is suitable for smaller networks or relatively stable networks.

As shown in Fig. 5.3, there are four network segments in the network, and each router is directly connected to two network segments. For the segments that are not directly connected, static routes need to be manually added, that is, two static routes need to be added to each router. Pay attention to the next hop of the static route. When the route to the network segment 12.1.1.0/24 is added to R1, the next hop is the interface address 172.16.0.2 of R2 that is directly connected to R1, rather than 172.16.1.2 of interface GE 0/0/0 of R3. Note that many beginners are prone to misunderstand "next hop".

3. Dynamic routes

The routing information obtained by a router using dynamic routing protocols (such as RIP, OSPF, etc.) is called a dynamic route. A dynamic route is suitable for larger networks and can automatically select the optimal path according to changes in the network.

If the network is small, we can "tell" the network devices the routes to those non-directly connected networks by manual configuration. However, if there are

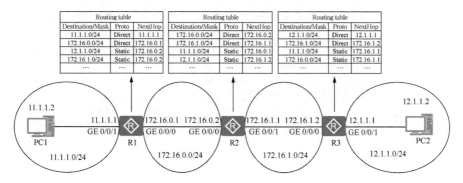

Fig. 5.3 Configure static routes

a great many non-directly connected networks, manual configuration inevitable requires massive labor work, which is often undesirable, if not impossible, in reality. In addition, manually configured static routes have an obvious drawback, that is, they are not adaptive. In the case of erroneous or ineffective static routes caused by a network failure or network structure change, these static routes must be manually modified, which in reality is also often undesirable or impossible.

In fact, network devices can also obtain routing information by running routing protocols. The terms "routing protocol" and "dynamic routing protocol" are actually the same thing. The routes that a network device obtains by running a routing protocol are called dynamic routes. If a new network segment is added to the network, a network segment is deleted, or the network segment of an interface or the network topology is changed (a link is broken or added to the network), the routing protocol can update the routing information in the routing table.

It is important to note that a router can simultaneously run multiple routing protocols. As illustrated in Fig. 5.4, router R2 runs both the RIP routing protocol and OSPF routing protocol. At this point, the router will create and maintain an IP routing table, as well as a RIP routing table and an OSPF routing table. The RIP

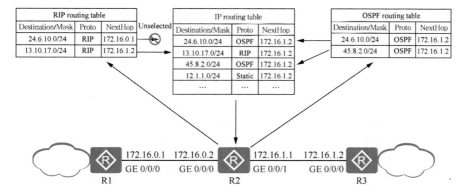

Fig. 5.4 Dynamic route preference

routing table is dedicated to all routes discovered by the RIP protocol, while the OSPF routing table is to all routes discovered by the OSPF protocol.

The routing entries in both the RIP routing table and the OSPF routing table are added to the IP routing table, and if both the RIP and the OSPF routing table have routing entries to a particular network segment, routing protocol preferences shall be compared. In Fig. 5.4, Router R2 has routing information for the network segment 24.6.10.0/24 in both the RIP routing table and the OSPF routing table. Since the OSPF protocol has a higher preference than the RIP protocol, the routing entry 24.6.10.0/24 in the OSPF routing table is added to the IP routing table. And the router eventually refers to the IP routing table to forward IP messages.

5.1.3   Route Preferences

Suppose a Huawei AR router runs both routing protocols, RIP and OSPF, and RIP discovers a route to the destination/mask z/y, and OSPF also discovers a route to the destination/mask z/y. In addition, we also manually configured a route to the destination/mask z/y. In other words, the device simultaneously obtains three different routes to the same destination/mask, so which route will the device actually use to forward the IP message? Or which of these three routes will be added to the IP routing table?

In fact, we specify different preferences for routes from different sources, and stipulate that the smaller the value of the preference, the higher the preference of the route. In this way, when there are multiple routes with the same destination/mask but different sources, the route with the highest preference becomes the optimal route and is added to the IP routing table, while the other routes remain inactive and are not displayed in the IP routing table.

The route preference on a device generally has a default value. Devices of different vendors have different rules for the default value of route preference. The default values of some of the route preferences of Huawei AR routers are specified in Table 5.1. These are the default preferences. Preferences can be changed, for example, when adding a static route, you can specify the preference of that route. The value range of preferences is from 0 to 255.

5.1.4   Route Cost

Route cost is a very important property of a route. The cost of a route is the value that needs to be paid to reach the destination/mask of this route. When a routing protocol finds multiple routes to reach the same destination/mask, it will select the route with the lowest cost, i.e., only the route with the lowest cost will be added to the routing table of this protocol.

Table 5.1 Route preferences

Sources of routes	Default preference
Direct route	0
OSPF	10
IS-IS	15
Static route	60
RIP	100
BGP	255

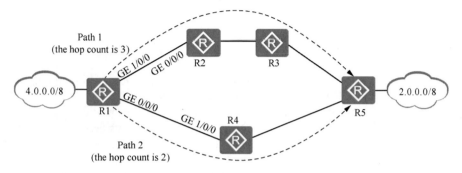

Fig. 5.5 RIP protocol uses "hop count" as the cost of the route

The specific definition of cost varies from one routing protocol to another. For example, RIP protocol can only use "hop count" as the cost. By hop count, we mean the number of routers that need to be passed to reach the destination/mask. As shown in Fig. 5.5, all the routers in the network run RIP protocol. Router R1 finds two routes to the network segment 2.0.0.0/8 via RIP protocol: the first route exits at GE 1/0/0 of R1, with the next hop being the address of interface GE 0/0/0 of R2, and a cost (hop count) of 3 (router R1 needs to go through three routers, R2, R3, R5, to reach the network segment 2.0.0.0/8); the second route exits at GE 0/0/0 of R1, with the next hop being the address of interface GE 1/0/0 of R4, and a cost (hop count) of 2 (router R1 needs to go through two routers, R4 and R5 to reach network segment 2.0.0.0/8). Obviously, the cost of Path 2 is less than that of Path 1, so the second route is the optimal route and will be added to the RIP routing table of router R1.

When the same routing protocol finds multiple routes that reach the same destination/mask and the costs of these routes are equal, what should we do? As shown in Fig. 5.6, assume that R1, R2, R3 and R4 are all running RIP routing protocol. By running RIP protocol, R1 will find two routes to 2.0.0.0/8: the first route exits at GE 1/0/0 of R1 and the next hop is the address of interface GE 0/0/0 of R2; the second route exits at GE 0/0/0 of R1 and the next hop is the address of interface GE 1/0/0 of R4. The costs (hop counts) of Path 1 and Path 2 are equal, so they are called equal-cost routes. In this case, both routes are added to the RIP routing table of R1. If these two routes in the RIP routing table can be preferentially added into the IP routing table, then when R1 forwards traffic to 2.0.0.0/8, some of the traffic will be

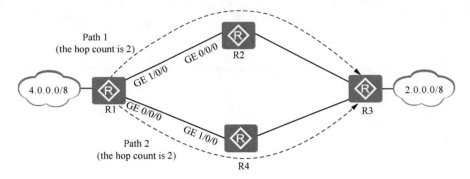

Fig. 5.6 Equal-cost routes

forwarded according to the first route and the other will be forwarded according to the second route, a situation also known as load balance.

In particular, it is important to emphasize that the comparison of costs is meaningful only within the same routing protocol and the route costs between different routing protocols are not comparable and there is no conversion relationship because the specific definition of cost varies for different routing protocols.

If a router is running multiple routing protocols at the same time, and one or more routes are discovered by each routing protocol for the same destination/mask (which assumed to be z/y), each routing protocol determines the optimal route among the several routes it has discovered based on the comparison of the costs, and puts the optimal route into the routing table of this protocol. Then, the optimal routes determined by different routing protocols are compared with each other in terms of route preference, and the route with the highest preference is added to the IP routing table of that router as the route to z/y. Note that if there are also direct routes or static routes to z/y on the router, then these direct routes and static routes shall also be taken into consideration when comparing preferences. The route with the highest preference is eventually added to the IP routing table as the route to z/y.

5.1.5   Conditions for an Unobstructed Network

The condition for an unobstructed computer network is that packets can be sent and returned. This is easy to understand, but it is the theoretical basis for troubleshooting the network.

As shown in Fig. 5.7, for Computer A in the network to communicate with Computer B, all routers along the way must have a route to the destination network 192.168.1.0/24, and for Computer B to return a packet to Computer A, all routers along the way must have a route to reach network 192.168.0.0/24.

Based on the above principles, network troubleshooting becomes simple. If the network is not working, you have to check whether the computer is configured with

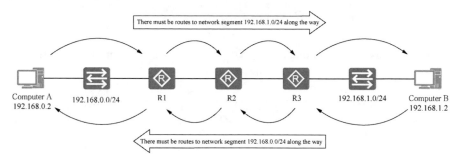

Fig. 5.7 Conditions for an unobstructed network

the correct IP address, subnet mask, and gateway, then check the routing table on each router along the way to see if there is a route to the destination network, and then check the routing table on each router along the way see if there are routes for packets to return.

5.2   Static Routing

5.2.1   Basic Concepts of Static Routing

Static routing is a form of routing that occurs when the routing entry is manually configured rather than dynamically decided. Unlike dynamic routing, static routing is fixed and does not change, even if the network conditions have changed. Generally speaking, static routes are added to the routing table by the network administrator one by one.

One advantage of using static routing is that the network is secure and highly confidential. Dynamic routing requires frequent exchange of respective routing tables between routers, and analysis of a routing table reveals information such as network topology and network addresses, so networks can use static routing for security. Static routing does not generate update traffic and does not consume network bandwidth.

Static routing is generally not suitable for large and complex network environments. On the one hand, it is difficult for network administrators to have a comprehensive understanding of the entire network topology; and on the other hand, when the network topology and link state change, the static routing information in the routers needs to be adjusted on a large scale, which is an extremely difficult and complex task. In addition, when the network changes or the network fails, the route cannot be re-routed, which may lead to the route failures.

5.2.2 Notes on Static Routing Configuration

To enable network-wide communication, that is, any two nodes in the network can communicate with each other, it is required that all routers in the network must have routes to all network segments in their routing tables. For routers, network segments that are directly connected to the interface are automatically added to the routing table, while routes to those non-directly connected network segments need to be manually added by the administrator.

The network topology in Fig. 5.8 has four network segments, A, B, C, and D. The IP addresses of the computers and router interfaces have been marked in the figure. How can the three routers AR1, AR2, and AR3 in the network add routes to make the whole network connected?

Router AR1 is directly connected to two network segments A and B, and is not directly connected to network segments C and D, so the routes to network segments C and D shall be added.

Router AR2 is directly connected to two network segments B and C, and is not directly connected to network segments A and D, so the routes to network segments A and D shall be added.

Router AR3 is directly connected to two network segments C and D, and is not directly connected to network segments A and B, so the routes to network segments A and B shall be added.

To configure static routing on the router, you need to enter system view, and then execute the command *ip route-static ip-address {mask | mask-length} {nexthop-address | interface-type interface-number [nexthop-address]}* [**preference** *preference*], where *ip-address {mask | mask-length}* denotes the destination/mask, *nexthop-address* represents the next hop IP address, *interface-type interface-number* is the outgoing interface, and *preference* denotes the route preference.

Here we must correctly understand the "next hop". As shown in Fig. 5.8, when adding a route to the network segment 192.168.1.0/24 to router AR1, the next hop is the IP of the adjacent device interface, i.e., the address of interface Serial 2/0/1 of router AR2, rather than the address of interface Serial 2/0/1 of router R3.

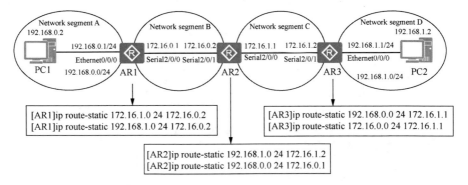

Fig. 5.8 Commands for adding static routes

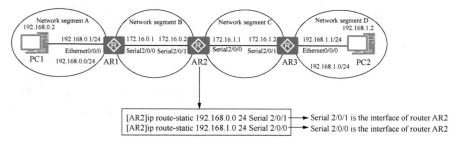

Fig. 5.9 Configure exit information for point to point link routing

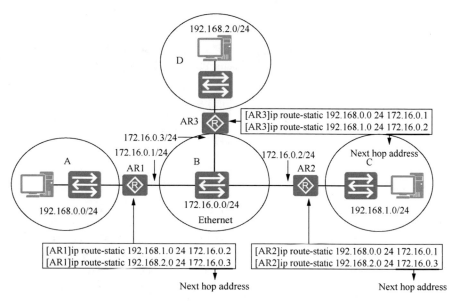

Fig. 5.10 It is suggested to add the next hop address for Ethernet interface

If the packets go through a point to point link to get to the destination network, there is another format for adding a static route, with the destination address and mask followed by the configured exit information. For example, you can add a route to network segment 192.168.1.0/24 on router AR2 as shown in Fig. 5.9. Note that Serial 2/0/0 at the end is the interface of router AR2, which tells router AR2 that the packets to the network segment 192.168.1.0/24 are sent out from interface Serial 2/0/0.

As shown in Fig. 5.10, if the routers are connected to each other by Ethernet, it is better to write the next hop address instead of the router's exit when adding a route. Think about it: why is that?

Multiple computers or routers can be connected in the Ethernet, and if you add a route without writing the next hop address, you cannot tell which interface should receive the packet at the next hop. A point to point link does not have this problem. One end sends and the other receives, so no data link layer address is used at all.

The router only cares about how packets are forwarded to a certain network segment, so when adding a route to a router, it must be a route to a network segment (subnet), rather than a route to a specific address. When adding a route to a network segment, you have to make sure that the host bits of the IP address are all 0s. For example, the following route is added incorrectly, because 172.16.1.2 24 is not a network, but an IP address in the network 172.16.1.0 24.

```
[AR1]ip route-static 172.16.1.2 24 172.16.0.2
 Info: The destination address and mask of the configured static
route mismatched , and the static route 172.16.1.0/24 was generated.
-Wrong address and subnet mask
```

If you want to add a route to a specific IP address (host route), the subnet mask should be written as four 255, which means that all 32 bits of the IP address are network bits.

```
[AR1]ip route-static 172.16.1.2 32 172.16.0.2       --Add a route to
network segment 172.16.1.2/32
```

5.2.3   Examples of Configuring Static Routing

This section describes the configuration of static routes through a case study.

As shown in Fig. 5.11, set the IP addresses of the computers and router interfaces in the network, and the gateways also need to be set for both PC1 and PC2. As you can see, there are four network segments in this network. Now you need to add routes to the router to enable an unobstructed network access of these four network segments.

Once the IP address and subnet mask are configured for the router interface, the routing table of the router has routes to the directly connected network segments and there is no need to add routes to those segments. You need to check the routing table of the router before adding a static route.

On router AR1, by going to the system view and entering "display ip routing-table", you can see the routes to the two directly connected segments.

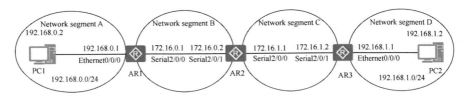

Fig. 5.11 Static routing network topology

```
[AR1]display ip routing-table
Route Flags: R - relay, D - download to fib
------------------------------------------------------------------
--------------
Routing Tables: Public
        Destinations : 11        Routes : 11
Destination/Mask    Proto   Pre  Cost    Flags NextHop     Interface
     127.0.0.0/8  Direct  0    0       D   127.0.0.1    InLoopBack0
     127.0.0.1/32  Direct  0    0       D   127.0.0.1    InLoopBack0
127.255.255.255/32  Direct  0    0       D   127.0.0.1    InLoopBack0
   172.16.0.0/24 Direct 0    0      D  172.16.0.1  Serial2/0/0   --
Route to a directly connected network segment
   172.16.0.1/32  Direct  0    0       D   127.0.0.1    Serial2/0/0
   172.16.0.2/32  Direct  0    0       D   172.16.0.2   Serial2/0/0
  172.16.0.255/32  Direct  0    0       D   127.0.0.1    Serial2/0/0
  192.168.0.0/24 Direct 0    0      D  192.168.0.1 Vlanif1      ---
Route to a directly connected network segment
   192.168.0.1/32  Direct  0    0       D   127.0.0.1    Vlanif1
 192.168.0.255/32  Direct  0    0       D   127.0.0.1    Vlanif1
255.255.255.255/32  Direct  0    0       D   127.0.0.1    InLoopBack0
```

You can see that there are already route entries in the routing table to the two directly connected network segments.

Add static routes to AR1, AR2, and AR3.

1. Add routes to network segments 172.16.1.0/24 and 192.168.1.0/24 to router AR1 to display the added static routes.

```
[AR1]ip route-static 172.16.1.0 24 172.16.0.2        --Add a static
route and next hop address
[AR1]ip route-static 192.168.1.0 255.255.255.0 Serial 2/0/0    --
Add a static route and egress
[AR1]display ip routing-table                        --Display routing
table
[AR1]display ip routing-table protocol static        --Display only
static routing table
Route Flags: R - relay, D - download to fib
------------------------------------------------------------------
------------
Public routing table : Static
      Destinations : 2        Routes : 2        Configured Routes : 2
Static routing table status : <Active>
      Destinations : 2        Routes : 2
Destination/Mask    Proto   Pre  Cost        Flags   NextHop
Interface
  172.16.1.0/24  Static  60   0        RD  172.16.0.2     Serial2/0/0
  192.168.1.0/24  Static  60   0        D   172.16.0.1     Serial2/0/0
Static routing table status : <Inactive>
      Destinations : 0        Routes : 0
```

2. Add routes to network segments 192.168.0.0/24 and 192.168.1.0/24 to router
   AR2.

   ```
   [AR2]ip route-static 192.168.0.0 24 172.16.0.1
   [AR2]ip route-static 192.168.1.0 24 172.16.1.2
   ```

3. Add routes to network segments 192.168.0.0/24 and 172.16.0.0/24 to router
   AR3.

   ```
   [AR3]ip route-static 192.168.0.0 24 172.16.1.1
   [AR3]ip route-static 172.16.0.0 24 172.16.1.1
   ```

   Delete route to network segment 192.168.1.0/24 on Router AR2.

   ```
   [AR2]undo ip route-static 192.168.1.0 24      --Delete a route to a
   network segment, and there is no need to specify next hop address
   ```

   PC1 pings PC2, then it shows "Request timeout!", but in fact the destination host
is unreachable.
   Not all "Request timeout" are caused by the router's routing table. There may be
other reasons for "Request timeout", such as the destination computer being enabled
with a firewall or shutdown.

5.2.4   Floating Static Routes

A floating static route, also known as a backup route, consists of two or more links.
When there are multiple paths to a network, the primary and backup paths can be
specified by setting different preferences for the static routes. When the primary path
is not available, a static route that takes an alternate path is added to the routing table,
and packets are forwarded to the destination network through the alternate path,
which is the floating static route.
   As shown in Fig. 5.12, the optimal path from network segment A to network
segment B is AR1 → AR3, and when the optimal path is not available, you can take
the alternate path AR1 → AR2 → AR3. That is when the floating static route needs
to be configured. When adding a static route, the preference can be specified, and the

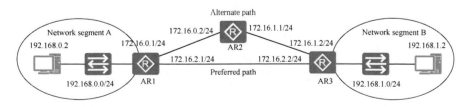

Fig. 5.12 Alternate path

values of this parameter range from 1 to 255. The larger the value, the lower the preference, and the directly connected network takes the preference of 0, while the default preference of the static route is 60.

Add two static routes to network segment 192.168.1.0/24 to AR1, using the default preference for the primary path and setting the static route preference to 100 for the alternate path.

```
[AR1]ip route-static 192.168.1.0 24 172.16.2.2      --Default
preference is 60
[AR1]ip route-static 192.168.1.0 24 172.16.2.2 preference ?
INTEGER<1-255> Preference value range
[AR1]ip route-static 192.168.1.0 24 172.16.0.2 preference 100
```

Add two static routes to network segment 192.168.0.0/24 to AR3, using the default preference for the primary path and setting the static route preference to 100 for the alternate path.

```
[AR3]ip route-static 192.168.0.0 24 172.16.2.1
[AR3]ip route-static 192.168.0.0 24 172.16.1.1 preference 100
```

Add a static route to the network segments 192.168.0.0/24 and 192.168.1.0/24 on AR2.

```
[AR2]ip route-static 192.168.0.0 24 172.16.0.1
[AR2]ip route-static 192.168.1.0 24 172.16.1.2
```

When you look at the routing table on AR1, you can see the route for the primary path while the static route for the alternate path is not added to the routing table.

```
[AR1]display ip routing-table
Route Flags: R - relay, D - download to fib
-------------------------------------------------------------------
--------------
Routing Tables: Public
       Destinations : 14     Routes : 14
  Destination/Mask    Proto  Pre Cost  Flags   NextHop       Interface
  ......
  192.168.0.0/24      Direct 0   0      D       192.168.0.1   Vlanif1
  192.168.0.1/32      Direct 0   0      D       127.0.0.1     Vlanif1
  192.168.0.255/32    Direct 0   0      D       127.0.0.1     Vlanif1
  192.168.1.0/24      Static 60  0      RD      172.16.2.2
GigabitEthernet0/0/1
  255.255.255.255/32  Direct 0   0      D       127.0.0.1     InLoopBack0
```

By viewing all static routes, the route for the primary path and the static route for the alternate path will be displayed. "Active" means the route is added to the IP routing table, while "Inactive" means it is not added to the table.

```
<AR1>display ip routing-table protocol static
Route Flags: R - relay, D - download to fib
---------------------------------------------------------------
--------------
 Public routing table : Static
      Destinations : 1     Routes : 2      Configured Routes : 2
 Static routing table status : <Active>
         Destinations : 1     Routes : 1
 Destination/Mask  Proto  Pre  Cost    Flags NextHop      Interface
    192.168.1.0/24 Static 60 0     RD 172.16.2.2   GigabitEthernet0/0/
1
  Static routing table status : <Inactive>
         Destinations : 1     Routes : 1
 Destination/Mask  Proto  Pre  Cost    Flags NextHop      Interface
    192.168.1.0/24 Static 100 0    R 172.16.0.2   GigabitEthernet0/0/
0
```

Shut down the interface of the primary path on AR1, and check the routing table again, then you can see that the static route of the alternate path is in effect.

```
[AR1] interface GigabitEthernet 0/0/1
[AR1-GigabitEthernet0/0/1] shutdown
<AR1>display ip routing-table
Route Flags: R - relay, D - download to fib

---------------------------------------------------------------
-------------
 ......
 Destination/Mask  Proto  Pre  Cost    Flags NextHop      Interface
    192.168.0.255/32 Direct 0    0     D    127.0.0.1   Vlanif1
    192.168.1.0/24  Static 100 0    RD  172.16.0.2  GigabitEthernet0/
0/0
```

5.3   Route Summarization

The Internet is the largest interconnected network in the world, and if the routers on the Internet add all network segments around the world to the routing table, it will become a massive routing table. For each packet forwarded by a router, the routing table has to be checked to select a forwarding exit for that packet, so a huge routing table will inevitably increase the processing time delay.

If network segments with consecutive addresses are assigned to networks in physically continuous locations, you can combine remote network segments into a single route at the routing border, which is called route summarization. Route summarization can significantly reduce routing table entries on a router.

5.3.1 Simplify Routing Tables with Route Summarization

The following example shows how to implement route summarization.

As shown in Fig. 5.13, networks in Beijing can be considered as networks in physically continuous locations. Assign consecutive network segments for the networks in Beijing, that is, all network segments from 192.168.0.0/24, 192.168.1.0/24, 192.168.2.0/24, 192.168.3.0/24, 192.168.4.0/24 to 192.168.255.0/24.

Networks in Shijiazhuang can also be considered to be in physically continuous locations. Assign consecutive network segments for the networks in Shijiazhuang, that is, all network segments from 172.16.0.0/24, 172.16.1.0/24, 172.16.2.0/24, 172.16.3.0/24, 172.16.4.0/24 to 172.16.255.0/24.

Add routes to all network segments in Shijiazhuang to the router in Beijing. If you add a route for each network segment, 256 routes are needed in total. When adding routes to all network segments in Shijiazhuang to the router in Beijing, if you add a route for each network segment, likewise, 256 routes are needed in total.

Subnets 172.16.0.0/24, 172.16.1.0/24, 172.16.2.0/24 to 172.16.255.0/24 in Shijiazhuang belong to network segment 172.16.0.0/16, which includes all network segments starting with 172.16. Therefore, for the router in Beijing, the network of Shijiazhuang is a network segment of 172.16.0.0/26, and it will suffice by adding a route to network segment 172.16.0.0/16 to the router in Beijing.

Network segments in Beijing from 192.168.0.0/24, 192.168.1.0/24, 192.168.2.0/24, 192.168.3.0/24, 192.168.4.0/24 to 192.168.255.0/24 can also be combined into a network segment 192.168.0.0/16 (at this point, you must recall how to merge network segments discussed in the chapter about IP address and subnetting, that is, by moving the subnet mask eight bits to the left to merge 256 Class C networks),

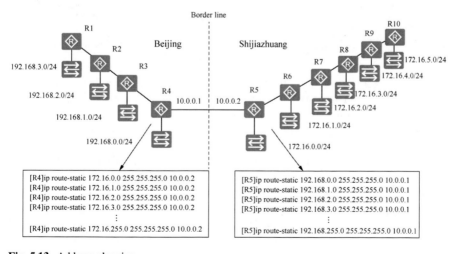

Fig. 5.13 Address planning

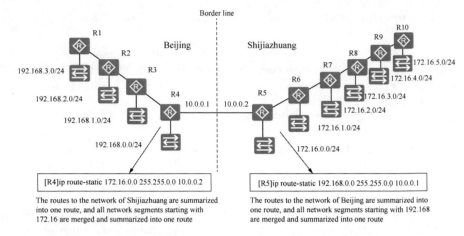

Fig. 5.14 Route summarization can be performed after address planning

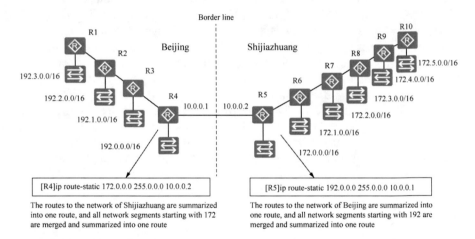

Fig. 5.15 Route summarization

which includes all network segments starting with 192.168. Therefore, it will suffice by adding a route to network segment 192.168.0.0/16 to the router in Beijing.

After summarization, for all routers in Beijing, only one route to the network of Shijiazhuang needs to be added, and for all routers in Shijiazhuang only one route to the network of Beijing needs to be added, so the routing table is significantly streamlined. Figure 5.14 draws only the routes added to R4 and R5. Furthermore, one route to the network of Shijiazhuang also needs to be added to R1, R2, and R3, while one route to the network of Beijing needs to be added to R6, R7, R8, R9 and R10.

Furthermore, as shown in Fig. 5.15, if the network of Shijiazhuang uses network segments from 172.0.0.0/16, 172.1.0.0/26, 172.2.0.0/16 to 172.255.0.0/16, that is, all segments starting with 172 are in Shijiazhuang, then these segments can be merged into one network segment 172.0.0.0/8, and only one route needs to be added to the router in Beijing. If the network of Beijing uses network segments from 192.0.0.0/16, 192.1.0.0/16, 192.2.0.0/16 to 192.255.0.0/26, that is, all network segment starting with 192 is in Beijing, then these segments can be merged into one network segment 192.0.0.0/8, and only one route needs to be added to the router in Shijiazhuang.

The rule is clear, that is, when adding routes, the fewer the network bits (the fewer the number of 1s in the subnet mask), the more the network segments can be summarized using the route summarization.

5.3.2 Longest Prefix Match

The longest prefix match (LPM) is a routing lookup mechanism used by default by almost all routers in the industry today.

Each entry in the routing table of a router specifies a network, and if these network addresses overlap, a destination address may match with multiple entries. When a router receives an IP packet, it compares the packet's destination IP address with all the routing entries in the local routing table bit by bit until it finds the entry with the longest match. This is the longest prefix match mechanism. It is called this because it is also the entry where the largest number of leading address bits of the destination address match those in the table entry.

In the following, the application case of longest prefix match is explained.

As shown in Fig. 5.16, a network in Beijing uses network segment 172.16.10.0/24, and later a network in Shijiazhuang is connected to the network in Beijing and according to the network planning, Shijiazhuang uses network segments starting with 172.16. In this case, can the router in Beijing still summarize the routes to the networks in Shijiazhuang into a single route? In this case, the router in Beijing can still summarize the routes to the networks in Shijiazhuang into a single route, but a

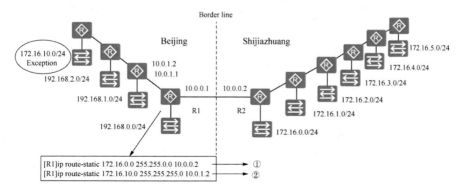

Fig. 5.16 Route summarization exception

separate route needs to be added for the exception network segment, as shown in Fig. 5.16.

If router R1 receives a packet with a destination address of 172.16.10.2, which route should be used for path selection?

Since the destination address of this packet matches both route ① and route ②, the router will use the most precisely matched route ② to forward the packet. This is called longest prefix match.

In another example, the following four routes is added to the router.

```
[R1]ip route-static 172.0.0.0  255.0.0.0  10.0.0.2        --
Route 1
[R1]ip route-static 172.16.0.0 255.255.0.0 10.0.1.2       --
Route 2
[R1]ip route-static 172.16.10.0 255.255.255.0 10.0.3.2    --
Route 3
[R1]ip route-static 172.16.10.10 255.255.255.255 10.0.4.2
--Route 4
```

When receiving a packet with a destination address of 172.16.10.10, router R1 forwards the packet using Route 4. When receiving a packet with a destination address of 172.16.10.12, router R1 forwards the packet using Route 3. And when receiving a packet with a destination of 172.18.17.12, router R1 forwards the packet using Route 1. These are the routes selected according to the longest prefix match.

A routing table often contains a default route. This route has the shortest prefix match when all table entries do not match. The application of the default route will be explained later.

5.3.3 Classless Inter-Domain Routing

To make it easy for readers to understand, the routing summarization introduced above merges 256 network segments by shifting the subnet mask 8 bits to the left. Classless inter-domain routing (CIDR) uses 13 to 27 bits variable network IDs instead of the fixed 8-, 16-, and 24-bit network IDs used for Class A, B, and C networks. This allows the subnet mask to be shifted one bit to the left to merge two network segments, two bits to the left to merge four network segments, three bits to the left to merge eight network segments, and n bits to the left to merge 2^n network segments.

The following is an example of how CIDR can flexibly and accurately merge consecutive subnets.

As shown in Fig. 5.17, there are four consecutive Class C networks in Area A. By shifting the subnet mask two bits to the left, these four Class C networks can be merged into network segment 192.168.16.0/22. There are two consecutive subnets in Area B. By shifting the subnet mask one bit to the left, these two network segments can be merged into network segment 10.7.78.0/23.

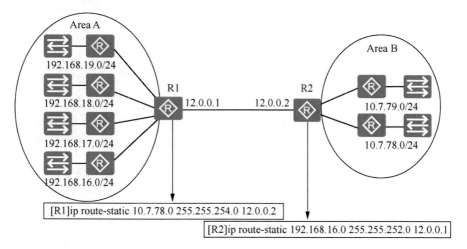

Fig. 5.17 Simplify routing table using CIDR

To improve the learning effect, readers are suggested to study this section in conjunction with Chap. 4, "IP Addresses and Subnetting".

5.4   Default Routing

5.4.1   Overview of Default Routing

A default route is a special kind of static route that is selected by a router when there is no route in the routing table that matches the destination address of a packet. If there is no default route, then packets whose destination address does not have a matching route in the routing table will be discarded. Default routes are useful in some cases, such as in routers connected to end networks, where using a default route will significantly simplify the router's routing table, thus reducing the workload of administrators, and improving network performance.

5.4.2   The Writing of Default Routing

Before we talk about default routing, let's take at a look at how the largest network segment in the world is represented in a router. Add the following three routes to the router.

```
 [R1]ip route-static 172.0.0.0  255.0.0.0  10.0.0.2            --Route
1
  [R1]ip route-static 172.16.0.0  255.255.0.0  10.0.1.2          --
```

```
Route 2
 [R1]ip route-static 172.16.10.0  255.255.255.0  10.0.3.2              --
Route 3
```

As you can see from the three routes above, the shorter the subnet mask (the fewer the number of 1s when the subnet mask is written in binary), and the more the host bits, the larger the number of addresses in the network segment.

If you want a network segment to include all IP addresses, the subnet mask needs to be as short as possible, that is 0. The subnet mask becomes 0.0.0.0, which means that the 32-bit binary IP address for that network segment is all host bits, and all addresses belong to that network segment. Therefore, a network segment whose subnet mask is 0.0.0.0 includes all IPv4 addresses in the world, which means it is the largest network segment in the world. It can also be written as 0.0.0.0/0.

The route added to the network segment "0.0.0.0 0.0.0.0" to the router is the default route.

```
 [R1]ip route-static 0.0.0.0 0.0.0.0 10.0.0.2                    --Route 4
```

Any destination address matching the default route, which, according to the "longest prefix match" algorithm mentioned earlier, is the last route to match if the router does not find a more accurate match for the packet.

The following part introduces some classic application scenarios for default routes.

5.4.3   Simplify Routing Tables with Default Routing

This case is an application scenario of default routing.

A company intranet has four routers A, B, C, and D, and six network segments 10.1.0.0/24, 10.2.0.0/24, 10.3.0.0/24, 10.4.0.0/24, 10.5.0.0/24, and 10.6.0.0/24. The network topology and address planning are illustrated in Fig. 5.18. Now it is required to add routes in these four routers so that the six network segments of the intranet can communicate with each other and also access the Internet.

Routers B and D are the end routers of the network, and are directly connected to two network segments. Packets have to be forwarded to Router C for them to reach other networks. Only one default route needs to be added to these two routers.

For Router C, which is directly connected to three network segments, the routes to 10.1.0.0/24 and 10.4.0.0/24 need to be added separately, while all packets to the Internet network segment 10.6.0.0/24 need to be forwarded to Router A, so adding a default route will suffice.

For Router A, which is directly connected to three network segments, separate routes need to be added for the intranets that are not directly connected, while a single default route is enough as the route to all network segments on the Internet.

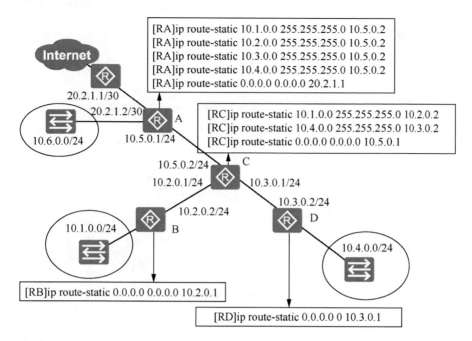

Fig. 5.18 Simplify routing tables by default route

Observe Fig. 5.18: can the routing table in Router A be further simplified? The network segments used by the enterprise intranet can be merged into network segment 10.0.0.0/8. Therefore, the routes to the intranet segments can be summarized into one in Router A, as shown in Fig. 5.19. Think about it: can the routing table in Router C be further simplified?

5.4.4 Simplify Routing Tables with Route Summarization

The Internet is the largest interconnected network and the network with the largest number of network segments in the world. For computers throughout the Internet to communicate with each other, the routing tables of routers on the Internet must be properly configured. If the public IP addresses are properly planned, the routing tables of the routers on the Internet can be greatly simplified using default routes and route summarization.

The following are examples of IP address planning on the Internet and how routers at all levels of the network can use default routes and route summarization to simplify routing tables. For the sake of illustration, only three countries are drawn here (Fig. 5.20).

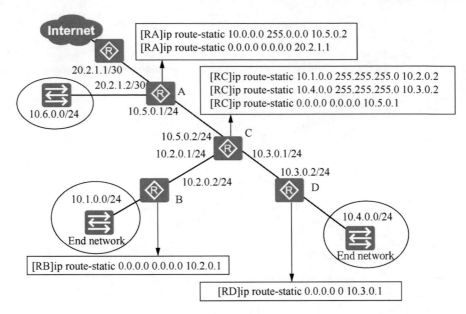

Fig. 5.19 Route summarization of routers and simplify routing table by default routing

National-level network planning: China uses network segment 40.0.0.0/8, the UK uses network segment 30.0.0.0/8, and the US uses network segment 20.0.0.0/8, with each country assigned a large network segment to facilitate route summarization.

Provincial IP address planning in China: Hebei Province uses network segment 40.2.0.0/16, Henan Province uses network segment 40.1.0.0/16, and other provinces use network segments from 40.3.0.0/16, 40.4.0.0/16 to 40.255.0.0/16.

IP address planning in Hebei Province: Shijiazhuang area uses network segment 40.2.1.0/2, Qinhuangdao area uses network segment 40.2.2.0/24, and Baoding area uses network segment 40.2.3.0/24 network segment.

Routes are added as shown in Fig. 5.21. Routers A, D, and E are international exit routers for China, the UK, and the US, respectively. For routers at this level, you only need to add a route "40.0.0.0 255.0.0.0" to China, a route "20.0.0.0 255.0.0" to the US, and a route "30.0.0.0 255.0.0.0" to the UK. The routing table of routers at this level is streamlined because the IP addresses are well planned so that the networks in a country can be summarized into a single route.

For the international exit Router A in China, in addition to adding routes to the US and the UK, you also need to add routes to Henan Province, Hebei Province and other provinces. Since the IP addresses of each province are also well planned, the network of each province can be summarized into a single route, so the routing tables of the routers at this level are also simplified.

How does Router C in Hebei Province add its routes? For Router C, apart from being sent to the networks in Shijiazhuang, Qinhuangdao and Baoding areas, packets are either sent out of the province or out of the country, so they need to be forwarded to Router A. Routes to the networks in Shijiazhuang, Qinhuangdao and

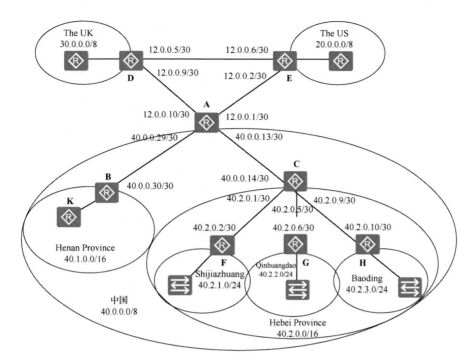

Fig. 5.20 Internet address planning illustration

Baoding areas are to be added in the provincial Router C, and routes to other networks use a default route to Router A. routers at this level can also use default routes to simplify the routing table.

For Routers II, G, and F at the network end, adding a default route to the provincial Router C is enough.

In summary: if the network address planning is rational, routers on the backbone network can use route summarization to streamline the routing table, while routers at the network end can use default routing to streamline the routing table.

5.4.5   Routing on a Ring Network Caused by Default Routing

As shown in Fig. 5.22, Routers RA, RB, RC, RD, RE, and RF in the network are connected into a ring. To enable the smooth connection of the whole network, you only need to add a default route in each router to the address of the next router, which is configured as shown in Fig. 5.22. By configuring the routes in this way, packets in the network will pass clockwise along the loop.

The following takes the communication between Computer A and B in the network as an example. As shown in Fig. 5.23, the packet from Computer A to B passes through routers RF → RA→RB → RC → RD → RE, and the packet from

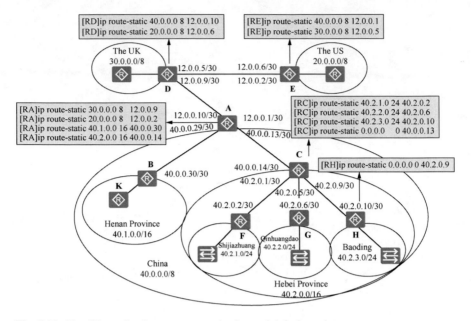

Fig. 5.21 Simplify routing by route summarization and default routing

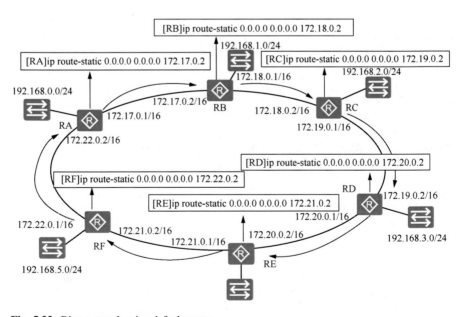

Fig. 5.22 Ring network using default routes

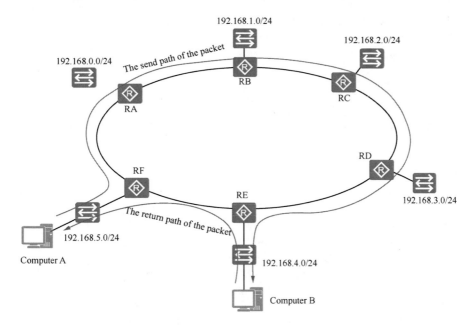

Fig. 5.23   Packet round trip path

Computer B to A passes through routers RE → RF. As you can see, the path of the packet to the destination address and the return path are not necessarily the same, and the routing table is the sole one to decide which path the packet takes.

There is no network segment 40.0.0.0/8 in the ring network. What happens if Computer A pings the address 40.0.0.2?

If Computer A pings the address 40.0.0.2, all routers will forward the packet to the next router by the default route. The packet will keep being forwarded clockwise in this ring network and will never reach the destination network, consuming network bandwidth all the time, which creates a routing loop. Fortunately, the network layer header of the packet has a field to specify the packet's time to live (TTL), which is a numerical value that limits the time an IP packet can exist in a computer network. The maximum value of TTL is 255, and the recommended value is 64.

Although TTL literally means how long the packet can live, in reality, it is the number of routers an IP packet can pass through in a computer network. The TTL field is set by the sender of the IP packet, and the router modifies the value of the TTL field for each router the IP packet passes along its entire forwarding path from the source address to the destination address. This is done by subtracting 1 from the TTL value and then forwarding the IP packet. If the TTL decreases to 0 before the IP packet reaches the destination, the router will discard the received IP packet with TTL = 0 and send a message "ICMP time exceeded" to the sender of the IP packet.

The above-mentioned situation of packets continuing to be forwarded clockwise in the ring network is caused by the ring network's use of default routes. Even if it is

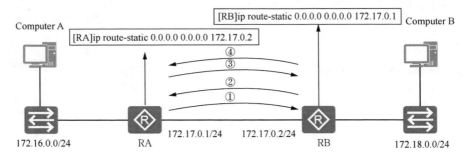

Fig. 5.24 Problems arising from default routing

not a ring network, using default routes may cause packets to be forwarded back and forth on the link until the its TTL is reduced to 0.

As shown in Fig. 5.24, there are three network segments and two routers in the network. Add a default route to Router RA with the next hop to Router RB. Add a default route to Router RB as well, with the next hop to Router RA, thus enabling the network to flow smoothly between these three network segments.

There is no network segment 40.0.0.0/8 in this network. If Computer A pings the address 40.0.0.2, the packet will be forwarded to RA. RA forwards the packet to RB according to the default route. RB then forwards it to RA using the default route, and RA forwards it back to RB. The process continues until the TTL of the packet is reduced to 0, and the router discards the packet and sends a message "ICMP time exceeded" to the sender.

5.4.6 *Default Routes and Gateways on Hosts*

The previous sections introduce adding static routes to the router, but in fact hosts (Windows systems and Linux systems) also have routing tables. The routing table on the Windows system can be displayed by executing the route print command, and the same effect can be achieved by executing the netstat -r command.

As shown in Fig. 5.25, configuring a gateway to a computer means adding a default route to it, and a gateway is usually the address of the router interface on this network segment. If the gateway is not configured, the computer will not be able to communicate across the network segment as it will have no idea which is the next hop interface in order to get to the other network segments. If the computer's local connection is not configured with a gateway, using the route add command to add a default route will work. As shown in Fig. 5.26, by removing the gateway from the local connection, and executing "netstat-r" at the command prompt to display the routing table, you can see that there is no default route.

Execute "route /?" at the command prompt. You can see the help information of this command.

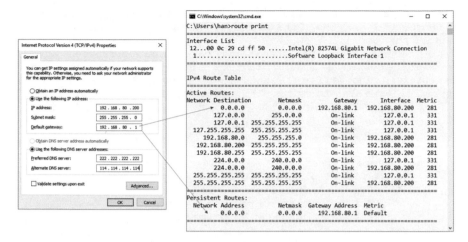

Fig. 5.25 A gateway equals a default route.

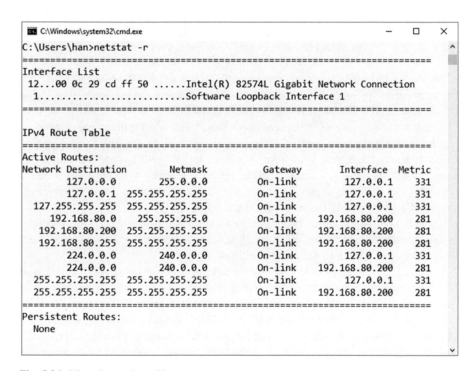

Fig. 5.26 View the routing table

```
C:\Users\win7>route /?
Manipulates network routing tables.
UTE [-f] [-p] [-4|-6] command [destination]
        [MASK netmask]  [gateway]  [METRIC metric]  [IF interface]
```

```
 -f     Clears the routing tables of all gateway entries. If this is used
in conjunction with one of the commands, the tables are cleared prior to
running the command.
 -p     When used with the ADD command, makes a route persistent across
boots of the system. By default, routes are not preserved when the system
is restarted. Ignored for all other commands, which always affect the
appropriate persistent routes. This option is not supported in Windows
95..
 -4        Forces IPv4.
 -6        Forces IPv6.


 command   One of these:
           PRINT      Prints a route
           ADD        Adds a route
           DELETE     Deletes a route
           CHANGE     Modifies an existing route
 destination    Specifies the host.
 MASK           Specifies that the next parameter is the 'netmask' value.
 netmask        Specifies a subnet mask value for this route entry. If not
specified, it defaults to 255.255.255.255.
 gateway        Specifies gateway.
 interface      the interface number for the specified route.
 METRIC         Specifies the metric, ie. cost for the destination.
```

As shown in Fig. 5.27, enter "route add 0.0.0.0 mask 0.0.0.0 192.168.80.1 -p". The parameter "-p" represents the addition of a permanent default route, that is, the default route still exists after the computer is restarted.

Think about it: under what circumstances would you add a route to the computer?

Here is an application scenario. As shown in Fig. 5.28, a company has deployed a Web server in a telecom server room. This Web server needs to access the database server, which is deployed on a separate network segment (intranet) for security purposes. The company deploys another router and a switch in the telecom server room and deploys the database server on the intranet.

There is no route added to the enterprise router and no route to the intranet to the telecom router (the key is that the network administrator in the telecom server room disagrees to add a route to the intranet either).

In this case, you need to add a default route to the Internet on the Web server, and then a route to the intranet, as shown in Fig. 5.29.

In this case, you shall never add two default routes on the Web server, one to 132.108.10.1 and the other to 132.108.10.254, or add two default gateways to the local connection. If you add two default routes, it is tantamount to having two equal-cost paths to the Internet, so that half of the traffic to the Internet will be sent to and dropped by the enterprise router.

If you want to delete the route to network segment "172.16.0.0 255.255.255.0", you can execute the following command.

```
route delete 172.16.0.0 mask 255.255.255.0
```

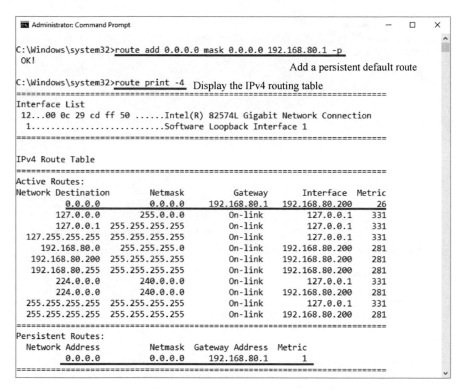

Fig. 5.27 Add a default route

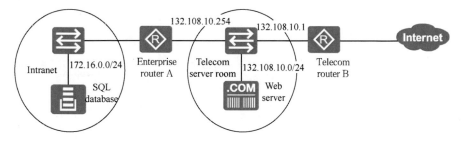

Fig. 5.28 A static route needs to be added.

5.5 Exercises

1. The configuration command for static routing of a Huawei router is ( ).

    A. ip route-static
    B. ip route
    C. route-static ip
    D. route ip

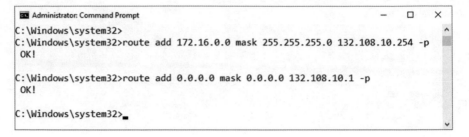

Fig. 5.29 Add a static route and a default route

2. Suppose there are four routes: 170.18.129.0/24, 170.18.130.0/24, 170.18.132.0/24 and 170.18.133.0/24. If you perform route summarization, the address that can cover these four routes is ( ).

   A. 170.18.128.0/21
   B. 170.18.128.0/22
   C. 170.18.130.0/22
   D. 170.18.132.0/23

3. Suppose there are two routes: 21.1.193.0/24 and 21.1.194.0/24. If you perform route summarization, the address that can cover these two routes is ( ).

   A. 21.1.200.0/22
   B. 21.1.192.0/23
   C. 21.1.192.0/22
   D. 21.1.224.0/20

4. The router receives an IP packet whose destination address is 202.31.17.4, and the subnet matching this address is ( ).

   A. 202.31.0.0/21
   B. 202.31.16.0/20
   C. 202.31.8.0/22
   D. 202.31.20.0/22

5. Suppose there are two subnets: 210.103.133.0/24 and 210.103.130.0/24. If you perform route summarization, the network address you get is ( ).

   A. 210.103.128.0/21
   B. 210.103.128.0/22
   C. 210.103.130.0/22
   D. 210.103.132.0/20

6. Setting a default route in the routing table, the destination address and subnet mask should be ( ).

   A. 127.0.0.0 255.0.0.0
   B. 127.0.0.1 0.0.0.0
   C. 1.0.0.0 255.255.255.255
   D. 0.0.0.0 0.0.0.0

7. The network address you get after the route summarization of networks 122.21.136.0/24 and 122.21.143.0/24 is ( ).

   A. 122.21.136.0/22
   B. 122.21.136.0/21
   C. 122.21.143.0/22
   D. 122.21.128.0/24

8. The router receives a packet whose destination address is 195.26.17.4. This address belongs to the subnet ( ).

   A. 195.26.0.0/21
   B. 195.26.16.0/20
   C. 195.26.8.0/22
   D. 195.26.20.0/22

9. As shown in Fig. 5.30, the network segments connected to router R1 are summarized into a route 192.1.144.0/20 on router R2. Which packet will be forwarded to R1 by router R2 using this summarized route?

   A. 192.1.159.2
   B. 192.1.160.11
   C. 192.1.138.41
   D. 192.1.1.144

Fig. 5.30 Example network (1)

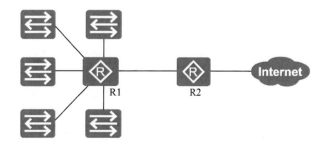

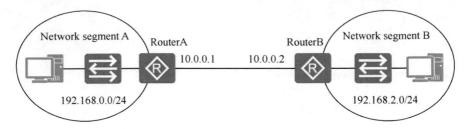

Fig. 5.31 Example network (2)

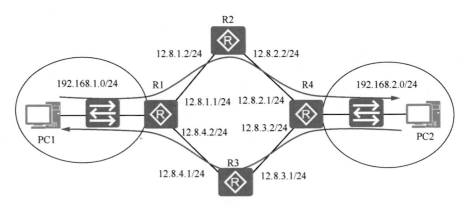

Fig. 5.32 Example network (3)

10. As shown in Fig. 5.31, you need to add routing tables to router A and router B to allow network segments A and B to access each other. Please fill in the corresponding content on the following horizontal lines.

    [RouterA]ip   route-static   _____

    _____   _____

       [RouterB]ip   route-static   _____

    _____   _____

11. As shown in Fig. 5.32, packets from network segment 192.168.1.0/24 to 192.168.2.0/24 are required to pass through R1 → R2 → R4; packets from network segment 192.168.2.0/24 to 192.168.1.0/24 are required to pass through R4 → R3 → R1. Now you need to add static routes to these four routers so that the network segments 192.168.1.0/24 and 192.168.2.0/24 can communicate with each other. Please fill in the appropriate content on the following horizontal line.

    [R1]ip   route-static_____   _____

    _____

       [R2] ip route-static_____   _____

    _____

       [R3] ip route-static_____   _____

    _____

Fig. 5.33 Match the
destination IP addresses and
next hop addresses

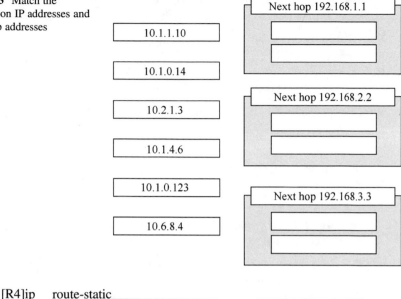

```
[R4]ip    route-static_____                    _____
_____
```

12. As shown in Fig. 5.33, execute the following commands on the router to add
    static routes

    ```
    [R1] ip route-static 0.0.0.0 0 192.168.1.1
    [R1] ip route-static 10.1.0.0 255.255.0.0 192.168.3.3
    [R1] ip route-static 10.1.0.0 255.255.255.0 192.168.2.2
    ```

    Match the destination IP addresses on the left side of Fig. 5.33 and the next
    hop addresses of the router on the right side.

13. Which of the following static route configuration is correct ( )?

    A. [R1]ip route-static 129.1.4.0 16 serial 0
    B. [R1]ip route-static 10.0.0.2 16 129.1.0.0
    C. [R1]ip route-static 129.1.0.0 16 10.0.0.2
    D. [R1]ip route-static 129.1.2.0 255.255.0.0 10.0.0.2

14. There is a TTL field in an IP message header, and which of the following
    statements about this field is correct ( )?

    A. The length of the field is seven bits
    B. The field is used for packet fragmentation
    C. The field is used for packet anti-loop
    D. The field is used to indicate the preference of the packet

15. When a router forwards a packet, if no corresponding detailed route is matched and there is no default route, it will directly discard the packet. Is this statement correct? ( )

    A. Correct
    B. Incorrect

16. Which of the following is not included in the routing table? ( )

    A. Source address
    B. Next hop
    C. Destination network
    D. Routing cost

17. Which of the following statements about static routing preference in Huawei devices is incorrect ( ).

    A. The value range of static route preference is between 0 to 65535
    B. The default value of static route preference is 60
    C. The preference of the static route can be specified
    D. The preference of 255 for a static route means that the route is not available

18. Which of the following statements about the TTL field in the IP message header is correct ( )?

    A. TTL defines the number of packets that the source host can send
    B. TTL defines the time interval between packets sent by the source host
    C. The TTL value is subtracted by 1 for each router an IP message passes through
    D. The TTL value of an IP message is increased by 1 for each router an IP message passes through

19. For the ip route-static 10.0.12.0 255.255.255.0 192.168.11 command, which of the following descriptions is correct ( )?

    A. This command configures a route to network 192.168.1.1
    B. This command configures a route to network 10.0.12.0/24
    C. The route has a preference of 100
    D. If the router learns a route to the same network as this route via another protocol, the router will give preference to this route

20. A router is known to have the following two entries in its routing table.

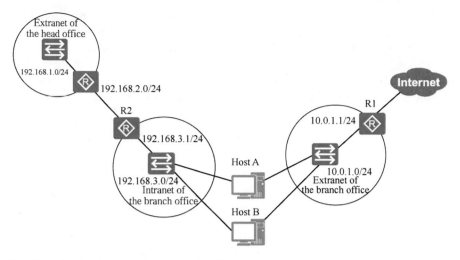

Fig. 5.34 Head office network and branch office network

```
Destination/Mask    Proto    Pre    Cost    NextHop    Interface
   9.0.0.0/8        OSPF     10      50      1.1.1.1    Serial0
   9.1.0.0/16       RIP     100       5      2.2.2.2    Ethernet0
```

If this router wants to forward a message whose destination address is 9.1.4.5, which of the following statements is correct ( )?

A. The first entry is chosen as the best match because OSPF protocol has a higher preference
B. The second entry is chosen as the best match because RIP protocol a has lower cost
C. The second entry is chosen as the best match because the exit is Ethternet 0, which is faster than Serial 0
D. The second entry is chosen as the best match because it is a more accurate match for destination address 9.1.4.5

21. Which of the following programs or commands can be used to probe the path taken by a data message from the source node to the destination node? ( )

A. route
B. netstat
C. tracert
D. send

22. As shown in Fig. 5.34, the intranet of a branch office is connected to the network of the head office. In order to access the Internet, the branch office also set up a branch office extranet. The address planning of the intranet and extranet of the

branch is shown in Fig. 5.34. The computers in the branch office have two network cables, which are connected to the extranet of the branch office when accessing the Internet and to the intranet of the branch office when accessing the network of the head office. Now you need to plan the network of the branch office. How can the computers in the branch office access both the Internet and the network of the head office without switching networks?

Chapter 6
Dynamic Routing

Static routing cannot make automatic adjustment as the network changes. Meanwhile, in large-scale networks, manually managing routing tables of routers is a daunting task prone to mistakes. Therefore, dynamic routing was created.

In dynamic routing, administrators no longer need to manually maintain the routing tables of routers, but simply run a dynamic routing protocol on each router. Dynamic routing protocols generate and maintain routing tables through the exchange of routing information. When the network topology changes, dynamic routing protocols can automatically update the routing table and determine the optimal path for data transmission.

There are numerous dynamic routing protocols, such as Routing Information Protocol (RIP), Open Shortest Path First (OSPF), Intermediate System to OSPF (Open Shortest Path First), IS-IS (Intermediate System to Intermediate System) and BGP (Border Gateway Protocol). Among them, OSPF has a wide range of application scenarios and is based on link state algorithm.

In this chapter, we first introduce the shortest path first algorithm, then explain the features of OSPF protocol, its working process, message types, related terms, network types supported, designated router (DR), backup designated router (BDR), three tables of OSPF and OSPF area, and finally illustrate the single-area configuration and multi-area configuration of OSPF protocol.

6.1 Classification of Dynamic Routing Protocols

Dynamic routing protocols are capable of building routing tables, maintaining routing information, and selecting the optimal path. They can automatically adapt to changes in network state and maintain routing information without the involvement of network administrators. Due to the need to exchange routing information, dynamic routing protocols consume network bandwidth and system resources, so they are less secure than static routing. Dynamic routing protocols are suitable for

© The Author(s) 2023
Huawei Technologies Co., Ltd., *Data Communications and Network Technologies*,
https://doi.org/10.1007/978-981-19-3029-4_6

complex network environments with redundant connections. In dynamic routing protocols, whether the destination network is reachable depends on the network state.

1. Classification by working mechanism and algorithm

    Dynamic routing protocols can be classified into distance vector routing protocols and link state routing protocols according to their working mechanisms and algorithms.

    (a) Distance vector routing protocols.

        Distance vector routing protocols use distance vector (DV) algorithm. Each router using distance vector algorithm periodically exchanges the entire routing table with its directly connected neighbors. After the network topology is changed, routers exchange update packets at regular intervals to obtain information about the changes in the network and thus update the routing table.

        The metric of the distance vector routing protocol has low confidence. Distance vector routing protocols use only the number of hops as the basis for selecting the best path, without taking into consideration factors such as the bandwidth and latency of the links between routers. This results in packets being delivered on a link that seems to have a few hop counts but is actually subject to a narrow bandwidth and long latency. The information exchange is achieved by periodically broadcasting the entire routing table. In slightly larger networks, the routing table exchanged between routers can be massive, which generates a lot of traffic, resulting in slow convergence.

        Distance vector routing protocols include RIP, BGP, etc.

    (b) Link state routing protocols.

        Link state routing protocols use link state (LS) algorithm. Instead of simply learning routes from neighboring routers, routers performing this algorithm divide routers into areas, collect link state information from all routers in the area, and generate network topology based on the link state information, after which each router calculates routes to each network based on the topology.

        Link-state routing protocols include OSPF, IS-IS, etc.

2. Classification by working area

    By working area, dynamic routing protocols can be classified into interior gateway protocols and exterior gateway protocols.

    Large ISP networks may have thousands of routers in their networks, while smaller ones usually have only a dozen routers. Each ISP manages its own intranet, which is called an autonomous system (AS). An AS is a group of networks that exchange routing information with each other through a unified routing protocol. Its connections to other ISPs are called interior connection. Therefore, the Internet can also be seen as an interconnection of domains. The domain mentioned here is an autonomous system.

(a) Interior gateway protocols.

Interior Gateway Protocol (IGP) is a routing protocol responsible for routing within an autonomous system. It is responsible for ensuring that each router in a domain follows the same way of representing routing information and the same rules for publishing and processing information. It is mainly used for discovering and calculating routes.

Interior gateway protocols include RIP, OSPF, IS-IS, etc.

(b) Exterior gateway protocols

Exterior Gateway Protocol (EGP) is responsible for the interaction of routing information and reachable information between autonomous systems or between domains. It is mainly used for delivering routes.

Exterior gateway protocols include EGP and BGP. EGP protocol is an early exterior gateway protocol (here EGP is a kind of exterior gateway protocol), which is only used as a standard exterior gateway protocol and is not widely used because it is inefficient. BGP protocol, especially BGP-4, provides a new set of mechanisms to support classless inter-domain routing. BGP-4 also introduces mechanisms to support route aggregation, including aggregation of AS paths, and these changes provide support for supernet solutions.

6.2 Overview of OSPF Protocol

OSPF protocol uses the shortest path first algorithm to calculate the shortest path to each network segment via the link state database. This section will explain the shortest path first algorithm with the help of practical examples, and introduce the advantages of OSPF protocol, its working process, message types, related terms, network types supported, roles of DR and BDR, three tables and OSPF areas.

6.2.1 Introduction to OSPF Protocol

OSPF protocol is a typical link state routing protocol. Routers running OSPF protocol (OSPF routers) interact with each other with link state information instead of directly interacting routes. OSPF routers collect the link state information in the network and store it in the Link State DataBase (LSDB). Routers in the network have the same link state database, that is, the same network topology. Each OSPF router uses the short path first (SPF) algorithm to calculate the shortest path to each network segment and loads the routes formed by these shortest paths into the routing table.

The main advantages of OSPF protocol are as follows.

1. OSPF supports variable length subnet masks (VLSM) and manual route summarization.

2. OSPF protocol can prevent routing loops. Each router uses the shortest path first algorithm through the link state database so that no loops will be generated.
3. OSPF converges quickly and can pass the routing changes throughout the autonomous system in the shortest possible time.
4. OSPF is suitable for large scale networks. The OSPF protocol has no limit on the number of hop counts of the route. Its concept of area division and multi-area design allows OSPF to support large scale networks.
5. Cost is used as the metric. When the OSPF protocol is designed, the impact of link bandwidth on the routing metric is taken into consideration. OSPF protocol uses the cost as a criterion, and the link cost is inversely associated with link bandwidth, that is, the higher the bandwidth, the lower the cost, so that OSPF routing is mainly based on bandwidth.

6.2.2 Routing Tables Generated from the Shortest Path

Routers running OSPF protocol can generate a complete network topology based on the link state database, and all routers have the same network topology. In Fig. 6.1, the network segments connected by the routers and the cost calculated from the bandwidth on each link are marked. To facilitate our calculations, the costs marked are relatively small. To simply the illustration, network segments occupied by the connections between routers are not drawn here and are not involved in the following discussion.

Each router uses the shortest path first algorithm to compute a loop-free tree of shortest path with itself as a root. The process of the shortest path first algorithm is not elaborated here, and only the results are shown. Fig. 6.2 displays the shortest

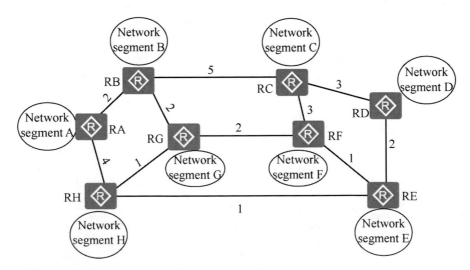

Fig. 6.1 Network topology generated from the link state database

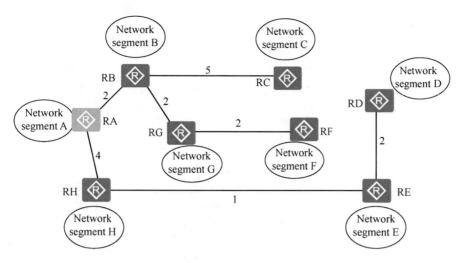

Fig. 6.2 Shortest path tree of Router RA

path tree of Router RA, i.e., the loop-free path with the lowest cumulative cost to other network segments.

The minimum cumulative cost from Router RA to other network segments is easily known from Fig. 6.2, as follows.

To network segment B: RA→RB, with a cumulative cost of 2.

To network segment C: RA→RB → RC, with a cumulative cost of 7.

To network segment D: RA→RH → RE → RD, with a cumulative cost of 7.

To network segment E: RA→RH → RE, with a cumulative cost of 5.

To network segment F: RA→RB → RG → RF, with a cumulative cost of 6.

To network segment G: RA→RB → RG, with a cumulative cost of 4.

To network segment H: RA→RH, with a cumulative cost of 4.

Figure 6.3 shows the shortest path tree of Router RH, i.e., the loop-free path with the lowest cumulative cost to other network segments.

In order to quickly select a forwarding path for packets, each router also generates routes to each network segment based on the calculated shortest path tree. Figure 6.4 shows the routing table generated by Router RA based on the shortest path tree.

6.2.3   Related Terms of OSPF Protocol

1. Router-ID.

   Routers running the OSPF protocol in the network are required to have a unique identifier, which is the Router-ID. The Router-ID cannot be duplicated in the network, otherwise the link state received by the router cannot determine the identity of the sender. The link states sent by OSPF routers all carry their own

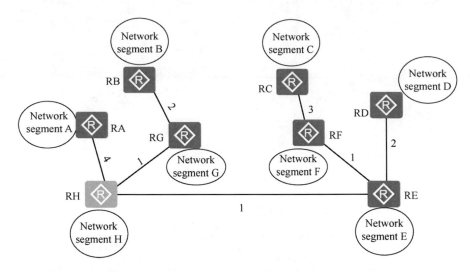

Fig. 6.3 Shortest path tree of Router RH

Destination	Cumulative cost	Next hop
Network segment A	0	RA
Network segment B	2	RB
Network segment C	7	RB
Network segment D	7	RH
Network segment E	5	RH
Network segment F	6	RB
Network segment G	4	RB
Network segment H	4	RH

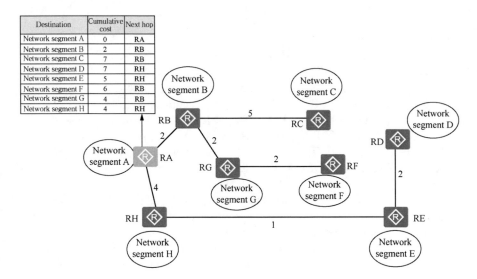

Fig. 6.4 Generate a routing table

Router-ID. The Router-ID is represented in the form of an IP address. There are three methods to determine the Router-ID.

- Manually specify the Router-ID.
- The IP address of the largest active loopback interface of the router, that is, the IP address with the largest number, for example, a Class C address takes precedence over a Class B address. The IP address of an inactive interface cannot be used as the Router-ID.

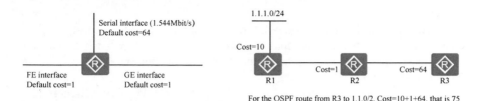

Fig. 6.5   Interface cost and cumulative cost

- If there is no active loopback interface, the largest IP address of the active physical interface is selected.

  In practical projects, Router-ID is usually assigned to the device by manual configuration. It is commonly done by configuring the Router-ID to match the IP address of an interface (usually the loopback interface) of the device.

2. Metric.

OSPF uses cost as a metric for routing. Each OSPF-activated interface maintains an interface cost. The default interface cost value= $\frac{100 \text{ Mbit/s}}{\text{Interface bandwith}}$, where, 100 Mbit/s is the default reference value specified by OSPF, which is adjustable.

As can be seen from the formula, OSPF protocol selects the optimal path based on bandwidth, that is, the higher the bandwidth, the lower the calculated cost. The optimal path is the one with the lowest cumulative cost of the links reaching the destination network.

For example, for an interface with a bandwidth of 10 Mbit/s, to calculate the cost, 10 Mbit is converted to 10000000 bit, and then 100000000 is divided by that bandwidth. The result is 100000000/10000000 = 10, so for a 10 Mbit/s interface, OSPF considers the interface to have a metric of 10. It should be noted that in the calculation, the unit of bandwidth is bit/s instead of kbit/s. For example, for an interface with a bandwidth of 100 Mbit/s, the cost is 100000000/100000000 = 1. The cost must be an integer, so even for an interface with a bandwidth of 1000 Mbit/s (1 Gbit/s), its cost is the same as that of the 100 Mbit/s interface, that is 1. If the router has to go through two interfaces to reach the destination network, then obviously, the costs of the two interfaces have to be accumulated to be the metric for reaching the destination network. Therefore, when the OSPF router calculates the metric for reaching the destination network, it must add up the costs of all the interfaces along the way, and in this process, only the outgoing interfaces are calculated and not the ingoing interfaces. Figure 6.5 illustrates the interface costs and cumulative costs.

OSPF automatically calculates the cost of the interface, however, it is also possible to manually specify the cost for the interface, and the manually specified one takes precedence over the automatically calculated one.

3. Link.

A link is an interface of a router, which refers to the interface running under the OSPF process in this case.

4. Link state.

The link state is the descriptive information of the OSPF interface, such as the interface's IP address, subnet mask, network type, cost, etc. What is exchanged between OSPF routers is not the routing table, but the link state.

5. Neighbor.

Routers on the same network segment can become neighbors. Routers discover neighbors through the Hello messages, which are sent at regular intervals by each interface using IP multicast. Once a router finds itself in the Hello message of its neighboring routers, they become neighbors, and such relationship requires the confirmation from both sides of the communication.

6. Neighbor state.

After the neighboring routers exchange database description, link state request, link state update, and link state acknowledgement messages, the link state databases of the devices at both ends are identical and enter the neighbor state.

6.2.4 OSPF Working Process

A router running the OSPF protocol has three tables, namely, neighbor table, link state table (link state database) and routing table. The following elaborates the working process of OSPF protocol by introducing the process of generating these three tables and analyzing what changes occur in the router during the process.

1. Establish a neighbor table.

A router in an OSPF area first establishes a neighbor relationship with its neighboring routers. When a router starts working, it sends a Hello packet every 10 s, by which it learns which neighboring routers are working and the "cost" of sending data to them, thus generating a "neighbor table".

If a router does not receive a Hello packet from a neighboring router for 40 s, it assumes that the neighboring router is unreachable and the router immediately modifies the link state database and recalculates the routing table.

Figure 6.6 illustrates the process of routers R1 and R2 establishing a neighbor table by Hello packets. At first, the OSPF state of router R1 interface is "down state", and after router R1 sends a Hello packet, the state changes to "init state". When it receives a Hello packet from router R2 and sees its own Router-ID in the neighbor table responded by other routers, a neighbor relationship is established and the state is changed to "two-way state".

2. Establish a link state table.

As shown in Fig. 6.6, after establishing the neighbor table, neighboring routers have to exchange link states to establish a link state table. In establishing the link state table, routers have to go through exchange state, loading state, and full state.

Exchange state: OSPF lets each router exchange the link state summary (description) information already in the database with neighboring routers using

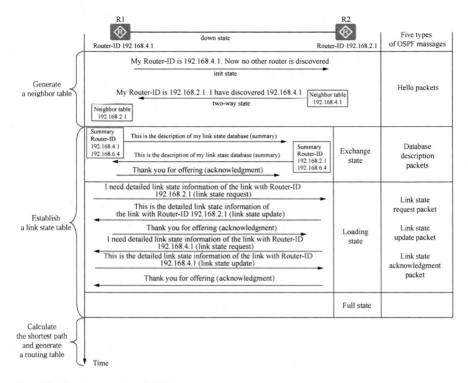

Fig. 6.6 Working process of OSPF protocol

the database description packets. The summary information sent contains all the routers (Router-IDs) in its own link state table.

Loading state: after exchanging database description packets with neighboring routers, the router then uses link-state request packets to request the other side for the detailed information about the link state of certain routers that it lacks. Through this series of packet exchanges, a network-wide synchronized LSDB is established.

Full state: the synchronization of link state database among neighbors is completed, so that all routers in the network have the same link state database and master the full network topology.

3. Generate a routing table.

Based on the link state database, each router uses the shortest path first (SPF) algorithm to calculate a loop-free "tree" of shortest path with itself as a root, thus generating route entries to reach the destination network.

6.2.5   OSPF Message Types

There are five OSPF message types in total, and Fig. 6.6 identifies the message types used in each phase of the OSPF operation.

Type 1: Hello packets, which are used to discover and maintain neighbors.

Type 2: Database Description (DD) packets, which are used to send summary information to neighbors about all link state entries in their own link state database. The summary information is about all routers (Router-IDs) in the link state table.

Type 3: Link State Request (LSR) packets, which are used to request detailed information from the other party about the missing link state information of a router.

Type 4: Link State Update (LSU) packets, which are used to send detailed link state information. Routers use such packets to inform neighboring routers of their link state. In OSPF, only LSU needs to display an acknowledgement.

Type 5: Link State Acknowledgement (LSAck) packets, which are used to acknowledge the LSU.

6.2.6   Network Types Defined by OSPF

Before explaining the designated router (DR) and backup designated router (BDR), it is necessary to understand the OSPF network types.

The OSPF network type is an imperative interface variable that affects the operation of OSPF on the interface, for example, what method is used to send OSPF protocol messages, and whether the designated router and backup designated router need to be elected. The default OSPF network type for an interface depends on the data link layer encapsulation used by the interface.

OSPF defines four network types, namely, point to point (P2P) network, broadcast multi-access (BMA) network, non-broadcast multiple access (NBMA) network, and point to multiple point (P2MP) network.

In general, the network type of the OSPF interfaces at both ends of the link must be the same, otherwise the neighbor relationship cannot be established between the two. The OSPF network type can be manually modified on the interface via commands to suit different network scenarios. For example, a BMA network can be modified to a P2P network.

```
[R1-GigabitEthernet0/0/0] ospf network-type ?
broadcast  Specify OSPF broadcast network
nbma       Specify OSPF NBMA network
p2mp       Specify OSPF point-to-multipoint network
p2p        Specify OSPF point-to-point network
```

P2P refers to an environment where only two network devices can be connected to a link, as shown in Fig. 6.7a. A typical example is a PPP link. When an interface is

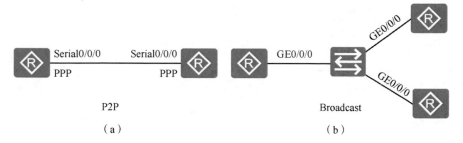

Fig. 6.7 P2P and broadcast networks

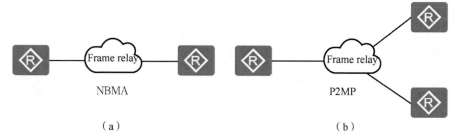

Fig. 6.8 NBMA and P2MP

encapsulated using PPP, the default network type used by OSPF on that interface is P2P.

BMA, also known as Broadcast, refers to a broadcast-enabled environment that allows multiple devices to access, as shown in Fig. 6.7b. A typical example is Ethernet. When an interface is encapsulated using Ethernet, the default network type used by OSPF on that interface is BMA.

NBMA refers to a broadcast-disabled environment that allows multiple network devices to access, as shown in Fig. 6.8a. A typical example is frame relay (FR) networks.

P2MP is equivalent to a network obtained by bundling one end of multiple P2P links, as shown in Fig. 6.8b. By default, no link layer protocol is considered a P2MP network. This network type must be configured by changing the other network types into it. It is commonly done by changing a non-fully connected NBMA to a point-to-multipoint network.

6.2.7   DR and BDR

There are two types of multi-access (MA) networks: broadcast multi-access (BMA) and non-broadcast multi-access (NBMA). Ethernet is a typical type of broadcast multi-access network.

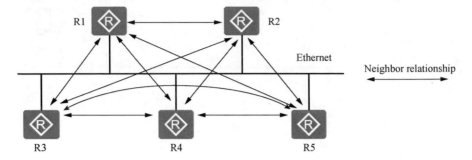

Fig. 6.9 Multi-access network neighbor relationship

In an MA network, if each OSPF router establishes OSPF neighbor relationship with all other routers, there will be too many OSPF neighbor relationships in the network, as shown in Fig. 6.9, which will increase the burden on the devices and the number of OSPF messages flooded in the network. When the topology changes, the LSA flooding in the network may cause waste of bandwidth and loss of equipment resources.

To optimize the OSPF neighbor relationship in MA networks, OSPF specifies three OSPF router identities: designated router (DR), backup designated router (BDR), and DRother router. The OSPF protocol allows only DR and BDR to establish neighbor relationship with DRother, and no neighbor relationship is established between DRother routers, so both parties are stalled in the "two-way" state.

The BDR will monitor the state of DR and take over the role of the current DR in case of its failure.

DR and BDR election rules: DR and BDR are elected by all routers in the same network segment according to the router preference and Router-ID through Hello messages. Only routers with preference greater than 0 are eligible for the election. To conduct DR/BDR election, each router writes the DR it elects in the Hello message and sends it to the router running OSPF protocol on the network segment. When two routers in the same network segment declare themselves as the DR at the same time, the router with higher preference wins. If the preferences are equal, the one with larger Router-ID wins. If a router has a preference of 0, it will not be elected as DR or BDR.

It should be noted that the DR is elected only on broadcast or NBMA interfaces, not on point to point or point to multipoint interfaces. DR is a concept in a particular network segment and is specific to a router's interface. A router may be a DR on one interface and a BDR or a DRother on another interface. The preference of a router can affect an election process, but when a DR/BDR has been elected, even if a router with a higher preference becomes active, it will not replace the DR/BDR already elected in that network segment as the new DR/BDR. A DR is not necessarily the router interface with the highest router preference; and similarly, the BDR is not necessarily the router interface with the next highest router preference.

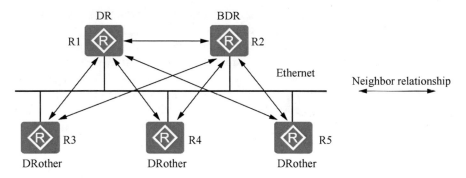

Fig. 6.10 Neighbor relationship

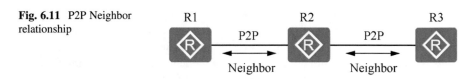

Fig. 6.11 P2P Neighbor relationship

This design means to make the DR or BDR the center of information exchange, as shown in Fig. 6.10, instead of enabling every router to exchange updated information with other routers on that network segment in pairs. Routers first exchange update information with the DR and BDR, and then the DR forwards these updates to the other routers on that network segment.

From Fig. 6.10, we can see that neighbors do not necessarily share a neighbor relationship. R3 has four neighbors, but only forms neighbor relationships with R1 and R2. Routers in point to point networks always form neighbor relationships with their neighbors, as shown in Fig. 6.11. If two routers are directly connected via Ethernet interfaces, you can manually designate the Ethernet interfaces of these two routers as P2P interfaces so that there will be no DR and BDR election.

6.2.8 Three Tables of OSPF

OSPF has three important tables: the OSPF neighbor table, LSDB table, and OSPF routing table.

OSPF requires neighbor relationships to be established before link state information can be passed. The neighbor relationship is established by exchanging Hello messages. OSPF neighbor table shows the neighbor states between OSPF routers, and the neighbor table can be viewed by the display ospf peer command.

Routers running the link state routing protocol flood the network with link state information. In OSPF, this information is called LSA, and the LSDB stores the LSA information it generated by itself and received from its neighbors, so the LSDB can be seen as the router's complete understanding of the network. The command to view the LSDB of a device on a Huawei device is display ospf lsdb.

Based on the data in the LSDB, OSPF runs the SPF algorithm and obtains a loop-free tree of shortest path with itself as a root. Based on this tree, OSPF is able to discover the optimal path to each segment in the network to get routing information and load it into the OSPF routing table. Of course, whether these routes in the OSPF routing table will eventually be loaded to the global routing table is subject to further processes such as comparing route preferences. The command to view the OSPF routing table of the device on a Huawei device is display ospf routing.

6.2.9   OSPF Areas

To enable OSPF to be used in very large-scale networks, OSPF subdivides an autonomous system into a number of smaller ones called areas. The advantage of areas is that the scope of the flooding method for exchanging link state information can be controlled within an area instead of the entire autonomous system, which reduces the amount of traffic throughout the network, decreases the size of the LSDB, improves the scalability of the network, and enables fast convergence. Routers within an area only need to know the complete network topology of this area and not the network topology of other areas. To enable an area to communicate with other areas, OSPF uses a hierarchical division of areas.

When a network contains multiple areas, the OSPF protocol has a special rule that one of the areas must be Area 0, which is commonly called a backbone area. A desirable way to design an OSPF network is to start with the backbone area and then expand to other areas. The backbone area is at the center of all other areas, i.e., all areas must be physically or logically connected to the backbone area. The reason for this design is because the OSPF protocol has to bring routing information from all areas into the backbone area, and then distribute such information from the backbone area to non-backbone areas.

Figure 6.12 illustrates an autonomous system with three areas. Each area has a 32-bit area identifier (expressed in dotted decimal). The size of an area should not be too large, and it is suggested to keep the number of routers in the area under 200.

As shown in Fig. 6.12, multi-area division is used in combination with IP address planning to ensure a contiguous address space of an area so that the network in the area can be summarized into a single route on the area boundary router and advertised to other areas.

As shown in Fig. 6.12, the upper layer area is called the backbone area, whose identifier is specified as 0.0.0.0. The role of the backbone area is to connect other lower layer areas. The information sent from other areas will go through route summarization by area border routers (ABRs). Router R4 and R5 are both area border routers. Obviously, each area should have at least one area border router. A router within the backbone area is called a backbone router, such as R1, R2, R3, R4, and R5. Backbone routers can also be area border routers, such as R4 and R5. There

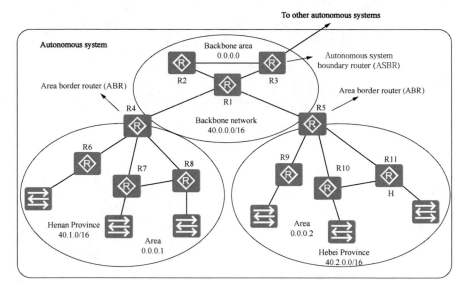

Fig. 6.12   Autonomous system and OSPF areas

is also a router within the backbone area (R3 in Fig. 6.12) that is dedicated to exchanging routing information with other autonomous systems. Such a router is called an autonomous system boundary router (ASBR).

It should be noted that ABR is connected to the backbone area and non-backbone area, and ASBR is connected other ASs.

6.3   Configuration of OSPF Protocol

Small and medium enterprise have small networks and a limited number of routing devices, so they can consider putting all devices in the same OSPF area. Large enterprises have large-scale networks, with a lot of router devices and a distinct network hierarchy, so it is recommended to use OSPF multi-area method.

6.3.1   Single-Area Configuration of OSPF Protocol

When referring to Fig. 6.13 to set up the network environment, routers and computers in the network are connected and configured with interface IP addresses according to the topology in the figure. The following operation configures these routers to run the OSPF protocol, and configures them to be in a single area. Although there is only one area, that area can only be the backbone area, with the area number of 0.0.0.0, which can also be written as 0.

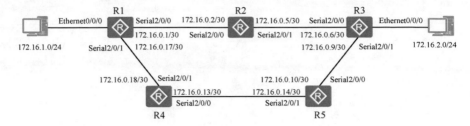

Fig. 6.13 Configure network topology for OSPF protocol

After entering the OSPF view, you need to specify the interfaces running OSPF protocol and the areas where these interfaces are located according to the network planning. First, you need to execute the area *area-id* command in the OSPF view. The command is used to create an area and enter the area view. Then, in the area view, execute the network *address wildcard-mask* command, which is used to specify the area interfaces running the OSPF.

The configuration on router R1 is as follows.

```
[R1]display router id                    --Display current router ID
RouterID:172.16.1.1
[R1]ospf 1 router-id 1.1.1.1             --Enable ospf 1 process and
specify Router-ID used
 [R1-ospf-1]area 0.0.0.0                      --Enter area 0.0.0.0
 [R1-ospf-1-area-0.0.0.0]network 172.16.0.0 0.0.255.255  --Specify
the interface working in Area 0
 [R1-ospf-1-area-0.0.0.0]quit
```

Relevant explanations are as follows.

1. The [R1]ospf 1 router-id 1.1.1.1 command enables the OSPF process on the router. The number "1" after "ospf" is the number assigned to the process. The range of the number is between 1 to 65,535.
2. If Router-ID is not specified when OSPF protocol is enabled, the Router-ID specified by the router-id command is used. The following command is used to specify the Router-ID.

```
[R1]router-id 1.1.1.1
```

3. [R1-ospf-1]area 0.0.0.0: this is a field used to indicate the area in the OSPF protocol packet, accounting for four bytes, which is exactly the space occupied by an IPv4 address. Therefore, when configuring it, you can directly write the number, or you can use dotted decimal to indicate the area of the specified ospf 1 process. Area 0 can be written as 0.0.0.0, and Area 1 can be written as 0.0.0.1.
4. The command to declare the network segment of OSPF is network + IP + wildcard-mask, which filters a set of IP addresses by IP and wildcard-mask so

as to locate the range of interfaces that need to be enabled with OSPF (interfaces with IP addresses in this range will be enabled with OSPF).

Wildcard masks are used to limit the number of host bits, i.e., the number of host bits is represented by a consecutive "1" from right to left, which cannot be interrupted by 0.

If you enter "[R1-ospf-1-area-0.0.0.0] network 172.16.0.0 0.0.255.255" when configuring OSPF, it means that the IP address set contains 172.16.0.0 to 172.16.255.255. This address set contains all interfaces of router R1.

If you want to write the wildcard mask after "network" for the network segment where each interface is located, you have to write three entries, which makes the address set identified more accurate. If different interfaces are in different areas, each of them should be specifically configured. In this example, three entries should be written for router R1 if "network" is written for the network segment where each interface is located, as shown below.

```
[R1-ospf-1-area-0.0.0.0]network 172.16.1.0 0.0.0.255
[R1-ospf-1-area-0.0.0.0]network 172.16.0.0 0.0.0.3
[R1-ospf-1-area-0.0.0.0]network 172.16.0.16 0.0.0.3
```

The configuration on router R2 is as follows.

```
[R2]ospf 1 router-id 2.2.2.2
[R2-ospf-1]area 0
[R2-ospf-1-area-0.0.0.0]network 172.16.0.0 0.0.255.255  --Specify
the interface working in Area 0
[R2-ospf-1-area-0.0.0.0]quit
```

The configuration on router R3 is as follows.

```
[R3]ospf 1 router-id 3.3.3.3
[R3-ospf-1]area 0
[R3-ospf-1-area-0.0.0.0]network 172.16.0.6 0.0.0.0    --Followed by
the interface address, and the wildcard mask is 0.0.0.0
[R3-ospf-1-area-0.0.0.0]network 172.16.0.9 0.0.0.0
[R3-ospf-1-area-0.0.0.0]network 172.16.2.1 0.0.0.0
```

You can also write the address of the interface after "network", and the wildcard mask should be written as 0.0.0.0. In this way, once the IP address of the interface is changed, you have to reconfigure the interface covered by OSPF.

The configuration on router R4 is as follows.

```
[R4]ospf 1 router-id 4.4.4.4
[R4-ospf-1]area 0
[R4-ospf-1-area-0.0.0.0]network 172.16.0.16 0.0.0.3
[R4-ospf-1-area-0.0.0.0]network 172.16.0.12 0.0.0.3
[R4-ospf-1-area-0.0.0.0]quit
```

The configuration on router R5 is as follows.

```
[R5-ospf-1]area 0
[R5-ospf-1-area-0.0.0.0]network 0.0.0.0 255.255.255.255   --This
writing covers all addresses
```

Display the interfaces running the OSPF protocol on R1.

```
[R1]display ospf interface
OSPF Process 1 with Router ID 1.1.1.1
Interfaces
Area: 0.0.0.0        (MPLS TE not enabled)
 IP Address    Type      State  Cost  Pri  DR        BDR
 172.16.1.1    Broadcast  Waiting 1    1    0.0.0.0    0.0.0.0
 172.16.0.1    P2P       P-2-P  48    1    0.0.0.0    0.0.0.0
 172.16.0.17   P2P       P-2-P  48    1    0.0.0.0    0.0.0.0
```

Routers running OSPF are divided into roles such as autonomous system boundary router, and area border router. Routers of different roles generate different types of LSAs. There are five types of LSAs.

Type 1 LSAs is called router-LSA and is generated by all routers. A router within an area generates one LSA1 for that area. In other words, if a device is connected to multiple areas, it generates one LSA for each area. Type 1 LSAs are sent as floods, and the boundary of the flood is the ABR.

Type 2 LSA is called network-LSA and is generated by the DR in the area. In each MA network the DR generates a LSA2 for that network, and no Type 2 LSAs are generated in P2P networks.

Type 3 LSA is called network-summary-LSA and is generated by ABR only. Since ABR is connected to multiple areas, it will receive LSA1 and LSA2 from different regions at the same time, and ABR converts these LSAs into LSA3 for delivery in areas after calculation.

Type 4 LSA is called autonomous system boundary summary LSA (ASBR-Summary-LSA), and it will not be introduced in detail here.

Type 5 LSA is called AS-External-LSA, and it is not explained here.

By entering "display ospf lsdb router x.x.x.x", you can view the Type 1 LSAs generated by routers with Router-ID "x.x.x.x". Type 1 LSAs "introduce themselves" in the areas they are connected to: which of my links are OSPF enabled; with whom I have established OSPF neighbor relationship; how I am connected to my neighbors; and what the network segment is between me and my neighbors.

```
[R1]display ospf lsdb router 1.1.1.1
    OSPF Process 1 with Router ID 1.1.1.1
            Area: 0.0.0.0
        Link State Database
 Type    : Router            --The type is router
 Ls id   : 1.1.1.1
 Adv rtr : 1.1.1.1
```

```
Ls age   : 72
Len     : 84
Options  : E
seq#    : 80000004
chksum   : 0x83e1
Link count : 5
 * Link ID : 172.16.1.0          --Connect network segment 172.16.1.0/
24, and the cost is 1
    Data  : 255.255.255.0
    Link Type : StubNet
    Metric : 1
    Priority : Low
 * Link ID : 2.2.2.2      --Point-to-point connection with router whose
router-id is 2.2.2.2, and the cost is 48
    Data  : 172.16.0.1
    Link Type : P-2-P
    Metric : 48
 * Link ID : 172.16.0.0      -- Connect network segment 172.16.1.0/24,
and the cost is 48
    Data  : 255.255.255.252
    Link Type : StubNet
    Metric : 48
    Priority : Low
 * Link ID : 4.4.4.4       -- Point to point connection with router whose
router-id is 4.4.4.4, and the cost is 48
    Data  : 172.16.0.17
    Link Type : P-2-P
    Metric : 48
 * Link ID : 172.16.0.16     -- Connect network segment 172.16.0.16/30,
and the cost is 48
    Data  : 255.255.255.252
    Link Type : StubNet
    Metric : 48
    Priority : Low
```

6.3.2   Multi-area Configuration of OSPF Protocol

Referring to Fig. 6.14 to build the network environment, the routers in the network are connected according to the topology in the figure, and the interface IP addresses are configured according to the planned network segment. The routers in the network are divided into three areas, as the network in Area 0 is assigned the address block 40.0.0.0/16, the network in Area 1 40.1.0.0/16, and the network in Area 2 40.2.0.0/16. The routers in these three areas are configured to run the OSPF protocol to build routing tables and perform route summarization at the area border routers.

As you can see in Fig. 6.14, OSPF areas and IP address planning are related, and it is best to have consecutive addresses in an area, which makes it convenient for route summarization at the area borders.

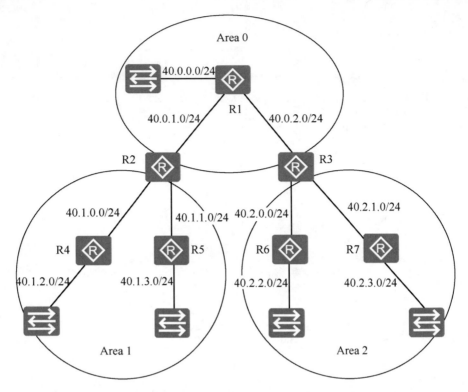

Fig. 6.14 Multi-area OSPF network topology

The following is the configuration on router R1, the backbone area router.

```
<R1>system
  [R1]ospf 1 router-id 1.1.1.1                    --Enable ospf 1 process and
specify the router-ID used
  [R1-ospf-1]area 0.0.0.0                         --Create area and enter area
0.0.0.0
  [R1-ospf-1-area-0.0.0.0]network 40.0.0.0 0.0.255.255   --Specify the
address range working in Area 0
  [R1-ospf-1-area-0.0.0.0]quit
```

The following is the configuration on router R2, an area border router, to specify the interfaces working in Area 0 and Area 1.

```
  [R2]ospf 1 router-id 2.2.2.2
  [R2-ospf-1]area 0
  [R2-ospf-1-area-0.0.0.0]network 40.0.0.0 0.0.255.255      -- Specify
the interface working in Area 0
  [R2-ospf-1-area-0.0.0.0]quit
  [R2-ospf-1]area 0.0.0.1
  [R2-ospf-1-area-0.0.0.1]network 40.1.0.0 0.0.255.255      -- Specify
```

```
the interface working in Area 1
  [R2-ospf-1-area-0.0.0.1]quit
  [R2-ospf-1]display this                    --Follow OSPF 1 configuration
  [V200R003C00]
  #
  ospf 1 router-id 2.2.2.2
   area 0.0.0.0
   network 40.0.0.0 0.0.255.255
   area 0.0.0.1
   network 40.1.0.0 0.0.255.255
  #
  return
```

The following is the configuration on router R3.

```
  [R3]ospf 1 router-id 3.3.3.3
  [R3-ospf-1]area 0.0.0.0
  [R3-ospf-1-area-0.0.0.0]network 40.0.0.0 0.0.255.255
  [R3-ospf-1-area-0.0.0.0]quit
  [R3-ospf-1]area 0.0.0.2
  [R3-ospf-1-area-0.0.0.2]network 40.2.0.1 0.0.0.0  --Write the
interface address, and the wildcard-mask is 0.0.0.0
  [R3-ospf-1-area-0.0.0.2]network 40.2.1.1 0.0.0.0  --Write the
interface address, and the wildcard-mask is 0.0.0.0
  [R3-ospf-1-area-0.0.0.2]quit
```

The following is the configuration on router R4.

```
  [R4]ospf 1 router-id 4.4.4.4
  [R4-ospf-1]area 1
  [R4-ospf-1-area-0.0.0.1]net
  [R4-ospf-1-area-0.0.0.1]network 40.1.0.0 0.0.255.255
  [R4-ospf-1-area-0.0.0.1]quit
```

The following is the configuration on router R5.

```
  [R5]ospf 1 router-id 5.5.5.5
  [R5-ospf-1]area 1
  [R5-ospf-1-area-0.0.0.1]network 40.1.0.0 0.0.255.255
  [R5-ospf-1-area-0.0.0.1]quit
```

The following is the configuration on router R6.

```
  [R6]ospf 1 router-id 6.6.6.6
  [R6-ospf-1]area 2
  [R6-ospf-1-area-0.0.0.2]network 40.2.0.0 0.0.255.255
  [R6-ospf-1-area-0.0.0.2]quit
```

The following is the configuration on router R7.

```
[R7] ospf 1 router-id 7.7.7.7
[R7-ospf-1] area 2
[R7-ospf-1-area-0.0.0.2] network 40.2.0.0 0.0.255.255
[R7-ospf-1-area-0.0.0.2] quit
```

6.3.3   View the Three Tables of the OSPF Protocol

A router running the OSPF protocol has three tables: the neighbor table, link state table, and routing table. These three tables are displayed below.

1. Check the neighbor table of router R1. By entering "display ospf peer" in system view, you can view the information of neighboring routers, and by entering "display ospf peer brief", the brief of neighboring routers is displayed.

```
<R1>display ospf peer brief          --Display the brief of
neighboring router
        OSPF Process 1 with Router ID 1.1.1.1
          Peer Statistic Information
     ---------------------------------------------------------------
     ---------------
    Area Id      Interface          Neighbor id    State
    0.0.0.0      Serial2/0/0          2.2.2.2       Full
    0.0.0.0      Serial2/0/1          3.3.3.3       Full


     --------------------------------------------------------------
     -------------
    <R1>display ospf peer              --Display detailed information of
neighboring routers
```

   When the router and its neighbors are in the full state, the link state databases of all routers are synchronized.
2. Display the link state table. The display ospf lsdb command is used to display how many routers in the link state table have advertised their link state. The router that has advertised the link state is AdvRouter.

```
<R1>display ospf lsdb
        OSPF Process 1 with Router ID 1.1.1.1
          Link State Database
              Area: 0.0.0.0
    Type    LinkState ID  AdvRouter      Age Len  Sequence  Metric
    Router  2.2.2.2       2.2.2.2       1260 48   80000011   48
    Router  1.1.1.1       1.1.1.1       1218 84   80000013   1
    Router  3.3.3.3       3.3.3.3       1253 48   80000010   48
    Sum-Net 40.1.3.0      2.2.2.2        301 28   80000001   49
    Sum-Net 40.1.2.0      2.2.2.2        221 28   80000001   49
    Sum-Net 40.1.1.0      2.2.2.2        932 28   80000001   48
    Sum-Net 40.1.0.255    2.2.2.2        932 28   80000001   48
    Sum-Net 40.2.3.0      3.3.3.3        856 28   80000001   49
```

```
Sum-Net  40.2.2.0      3.3.3.3      856 28  80000001   49
Sum-Net  40.2.1.0      3.3.3.3      856 28  80000001   48
Sum-Net  40.2.0.255    3.3.3.3      856 28  80000001   48
```

From the above output, we can see that subnet information for Area 1 and Area 2 appears in the link state database of the backbone area router R1. This subnet information is advertised to the backbone area by the area border router. If route summarization is configured on the area border router, Area 1 and Area 2 are summarized into one link state.

OSPF calculates the shortest path based on the link state database. The link state database records which routers are running OSPF, how many subnets each router is connected to, which neighbors each router has, and over what link (point to point link or Ethernet link) they are connected.

3. Enter "display ip routing-table" to view the routing table. Proto is the route learned through the OSPF protocol, and its OSPF protocol preference (i.e., Pre) is 10, and the cost is the cumulative cost to reach the destination network segment calculated using bandwidth.

```
<R1>display ip routing-table protocol ospf        --View OSPF route
Route Flags: R - relay, D - download to fib
----------------------------------------------------------------
-----------------
Public routing table : OSPF
        Destinations : 8     Routes : 8
OSPF routing table status : <Active>
        Destinations : 8     Routes : 8
Destination/Mask Proto Pre Cost   Flags   NextHop      Interface
    40.1.0.0/24 OSPF  10  96       D     40.0.1.2    Serial2/0/0
    40.1.1.0/24 OSPF  10  96       D     40.0.1.2    Serial2/0/0
    40.1.2.0/24 OSPF  10  97       D     40.0.1.2    Serial2/0/0
    40.1.3.0/24 OSPF  10  97       D     40.0.1.2    Serial2/0/0
    40.2.0.0/24 OSPF  10  96       D     40.0.2.2    Serial2/0/1
    40.2.1.0/24 OSPF  10  96       D     40.0.2.2    Serial2/0/1
    40.2.2.0/24 OSPF  10  97       D     40.0.2.2    Serial2/0/1
    40.2.3.0/24 OSPF  10  97       D     40.0.2.2    Serial2/0/1
OSPF routing table status : <Inactive>
        Destinations : 0        Routes : 0
```

When entering "display ospf routing", only the routes generated by the OSPF protocol are displayed, and you can see the ID of the advertiser, that is AdvRouter. As you can see from the output below, the default cost is 1 for directly connected Ethernet interfaces and 48 for directly connected serial interfaces.

```
<R1>display ospf routing
    OSPF Process 1 with Router ID 1.1.1.1
      Routing Tables
Routing for Network
Destination Cost Type      NextHop  AdvRouter    Area
```

```
   40.0.0.0/24 1   Stub      40.0.0.1  1.1.1.1   0.0.0.0  --Default cost
of the directly connected Ethernet interface
   40.0.1.0/24 48  Stub      40.0.1.1  1.1.1.1   0.0.0.0  --Default cost
of the directly connected serial interface
   40.0.2.0/24 48  Stub      40.0.2.1  1.1.1.1   0.0.0.0
   40.1.0.0/24 96  Inter-area  40.0.1.2  2.2.2.2  0.0.0.0
   40.1.1.0/24 96  Inter-area  40.0.1.2  2.2.2.2  0.0.0.0
   40.1.2.0/24 97  Inter-area  40.0.1.2  2.2.2.2  0.0.0.0
   40.1.3.0/24 97  Inter-area  40.0.1.2  2.2.2.2  0.0.0.0
   40.2.0.0/24 96  Inter-area  40.0.2.2  3.3.3.3  0.0.0.0
   40.2.1.0/24 96  Inter-area  40.0.2.2  3.3.3.3  0.0.0.0
   40.2.2.0/24 97  Inter-area  40.0.2.2  3.3.3.3  0.0.0.0
   40.2.3.0/24 97  Inter-area  40.0.2.2  3.3.3.3  0.0.0.0
Total Nets: 11
Intra Area: 3 Inter Area: 8 ASE: 0 NSSA: 0
```

6.3.4   Route Summarization on the Area Border Router

1. Perform summarization on the area border router R2. Summarize Area 1 as "40.1.0.0 255.255.0.0" and specify the cost as 10; summarize Area 0 as "40.0.0.0 255.255.0.0" and specify the cost as 10.

```
[R2] ospf 1
[R2-ospf-1] area 1
[R2-ospf-1-area-0.0.0.1] abr-summary 40.1.0.0 255.255.0.0 cost 10
[R2-ospf-1-area-0.0.0.1] quit
[R2-ospf-1] area 0
[R2-ospf-1-area-0.0.0.0] abr-summary 40.0.0.0 255.255.0.0 cost 10
[R2-ospf-1-area-0.0.0.0] quit
```

2. Perform summarization on the area border router R3. Summarize Area 2 as "40.2.0.0 255.255.0.0" and specify the cost as 20; summarize Area 0 as "40.0.0.0 255.255.0.0" and specify the cost as 10.

```
[R3] ospf 1
[R3-ospf-1] area 0
[R3-ospf-1-area-0.0.0.0] abr-summary 40.0.0.0 255.255.0.0 cost 10
[R3-ospf-1-area-0.0.0.0] quit
[R3-ospf-1] area 2
[R3-ospf-1-area-0.0.0.2] abr-summary 40.2.0.0 255.255.0.0 cost 20
[R3-ospf-1-area-0.0.0.2] quit
[R3-ospf-1] quit
```

3. After configuring summarization on the area border router, by checking the OSPF link state on R1, you can see that there is only one record about Area 1 and Area 2 in R1's link state database.

```
<R1>display ospf lsdb
        OSPF Process 1 with Router ID 1.1.1.1
           Link State Database
                 Area: 0.0.0.0
    Type     LinkState ID    AdvRouter      Age  Len  Sequence  Metric
    Router   2.2.2.2         2.2.2.2        1732  48  80000011   48
    Router   1.1.1.1         1.1.1.1        1690  84  80000013    1
    Router   3.3.3.3         3.3.3.3        1725  48  80000010   48
    Sum-Net  40.1.0.0        2.2.2.2          99  28  80000001   10
    Sum-Net  40.2.0.0        3.3.3.3          26  28  80000001   20
```

4. Display the routes generated by the OSPF protocol on R1. You can see that Area 1 and Area 2 are summarized into one route with a cost of 58 and 68 respectively, which is related to the cost specified during summarization.

```
<R1>display ospf routing
       OSPF Process 1 with Router ID 1.1.1.1
          Routing Tables
    Routing for Network
    Destination    Cost Type      NextHop       AdvRouter       Area
    40.0.0.0/24    1    Stub      40.0.0.1      1.1.1.1        0.0.0.0
    40.0.1.0/24    48   Stub      40.0.1.1      1.1.1.1        0.0.0.0
    40.0.2.0/24    48   Stub      40.0.2.1      1.1.1.1        0.0.0.0
    40.1.0.0/16    58   Inter-area  40.0.1.2    2.2.2.2        0.0.0.0
    40.2.0.0/16    68   Inter-area  40.0.2.2    3.3.3.3        0.0.0.0
    Total Nets: 5
    Intra Area: 3 Inter Area: 2 ASE: 0 NSSA: 0
```

6.4   Exercises

1. Which of the following descriptions of the OSPF protocol is the most accurate one ( )?

   A. OSPF protocol calculates the optimal route based on the link state method
   B. OSPF protocol is an exterior gateway protocol used between autonomous systems
   C. OSPF protocol cannot dynamically change the route according to the network communication
   D. OSPF protocol is only suitable for small networks

2. Which of the following descriptions of the OSPF protocol is incorrect ( )?

   A. OSPF is a link-state protocol
   B. OSPF uses link-state advertisements to spread routing information
   C. In a OSPF network, Area 1 is used to represent the backbone network segment
   D. Multiple routing processes can be configured in OSPF routers

3. OSPF supports multiple processes, if you don't specify the process number, the default process number used is ( ).

   A. 0
   B. 1
   C. 10
   D. 100

4. Router AR2200 learns the route entries to the same network via OSPF and RIPv2 at the same time; the cost value of the route learned through OSPF is 4882, and the hop count of the route learned through RIPv2 is 4, then the router will have ( ) in its routing table.

   A. RIPv2 route
   B. OSPF and RIPv2 routes
   C. OSPF route
   D. Neither of them

5. As shown in Fig. 6.15, OSPF protocol is configured for the routers in the network, and the following configurations are performed on routers A and B.

   ```
   [A] ospf 1 router-id 1.1.1.1
   [A-ospf-1] area 0.0.0.0
   [A-ospf-1-area-0.0.0.0] network 172.16.0.0 0.0.255.255
   [A-ospf-1-area-0.0.0.0] network 192.168.0.0 0.0.0.255
   [B] ospf 1 router-id 1.1.1.2
   [B-ospf-1] area 0.0.0.0
   [B-ospf-1-area-0.0.0.0] network 192.168.0.0 0.0.255.255
   ```

   Which of the following statements is incorrect? ( )

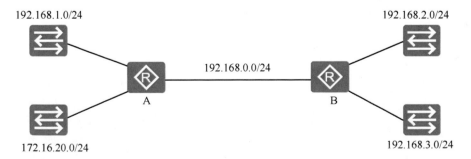

Fig. 6.15 Network topology

    A. Router B can learn the route to network segment 172.16.0.0/24 through the OSPF protocol

    B. Router B can learn the route to network segment 192.168.1.0/24 through the OSPF protocol

    C. Router A can learn the route to network segment 192.168.2.0/24 through the OSPF protocol

    D. Router A can learn the route to network segment 192.168.3.0/24 through the OSPF protocol

6. (Multi-selection) To configure OSPF on a router, the configurations must be done manually are ( ).

    A. Configure Router-ID
    B. Open OSPF process
    C. Create OSPF areas
    D. Specify the network segments contained in each area

7. On the VRP platform, the default protocol preferences of direct routes, static routes, RIP, and OSPF, in descending order, are ( ).

    A. Direct routes, static routes, RIP, OSPF
    B. Direct routes, OSPF, static routes, RIP
    C. Direct routes, OSPF, RIP, static routes
    D. Direct routes, RIP, static routes, OSPF

8. The administrator configures OSPF on a router, but no loopback interface is configured on that router. Which of the following descriptions of Router-ID is correct ( )?

    A. The minimum IP address of the physical interface of the router will become the Router-ID

    B. The maximum IP address of the physical interface of the router will become the Router-ID

    C. The IP address of the router's management interface will become the Router-ID

    D. The preference of the router will become the Router-ID

9. Which of the following descriptions of Router-ID in OSPF is correct ( )?

    A. Router-ID must be the same in the same area, while that in different areas can be different

    B. Router-ID must be the IP address of a router interface
    C. Router-ID must be specified by manual configuration
    D. The prerequisite for the OSPF protocol to work properly is that the router has a Router-ID

10. A router learns a route to the same destination address through RIP, OSPF, and static routing. By default, the VRP will eventually select the route learned through which protocol? ( )

    A. RIP
    B. OSPF
    C. RIP
    D. Static routing

11. (Multi-selection) Assume the configuration is like below.

```
[R1]ospf
[R1-ospf-1]area 1
[R1-ospf-1-area-0.0.0.1]network 10.0.12.0 0.0.0.255
```

    The administrator has configured OSPF on router R1, but R1 cannot learn routes from other routers, so the possible reasons are ( ).

    A. The area ID configured on this router is different from the area ID of its neighboring router
    B. This router is not configured for authentication, but the neighboring routers are configured for authentication
    C. This router is not configured with OSPF process number when it is configured
    D. This router is configured with OSPF without advertising the neighbor's network

Chapter 7
Ethernet Switching Technologies

Most current campus networks use switches for networking. Using a switch to build a network makes network management flexible, allowing you to create virtual local area networks (VLAN) based on departmental, management, and security requirements, and assign computers in the same department or with the same management and security requirements to different VLANs.

This chapter will explain Ethernet knowledge such as the evolution of Ethernet, Ethernet frame format, MAC addresses, the process of building MAC address tables by switches, creation and management of VLANs, and implementation of inter-VLAN routing.

7.1 Ethernet Switching Fundamentals

7.1.1 Evolution of Ethernet

LANs originally used coaxial cables for networking and adopted a bus topology, where a coaxial cable was a link, as shown in Fig. 7.1. A link connects multiple network devices (network interface cards) through a T-shaped port, and two computers on the link can communicate. For example, if Computer A sends a frame to Computer B, the coaxial cable will transmit the digital signal carrying the frame to all terminals, and all computers on the link will receive it (which is called a broadcast channel). To achieve point to point communication in such a broadcast channel, it is necessary to add source and destination addresses to the frames sent, which requires that the network interface card of each computer in the network has a unique physical address, i.e., a MAC address. When the destination MAC address of the frame is the same as the MAC address of the computer's network interface card, the network interface card receives the frame, and discards frames that are for it.

© The Author(s) 2023
Huawei Technologies Co., Ltd., *Data Communications and Network Technologies*,
https://doi.org/10.1007/978-981-19-3029-4_7

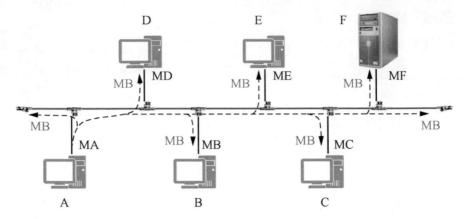

Fig. 7.1 Bus Ethernet

Fig. 7.2 Star broadcast channel

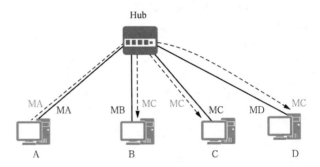

An MAC address consists of 48 binary bits and is globally unique. In Fig. 7.1, MA, MB, and MC are used to indicate the MAC addresses of Computer A, B, and C, respectively.

Multiple computers on the bus send data at the same time, which can cause signal superposition so that the receiver fails to recognize the signal. Therefore, computer communication should avoid conflicts. Before sending data, the computer fist listens if the channel is idle. If it is, then the computer will immediately send the data; if the channel is busy, the computer waits until the information transmission in the channel is completed to send the data. After the data transmission starts, the computer also detects whether there is a collision with the signals sent by other computers on the line. If there is a collision, these computers will wait for a random period of time before sending the data again. This mechanism is called Carrier Sense Multiple Access with Collision Detection (CSMA/CD), which is the data link layer protocol used for broadcast channels.

In addition to bus topography, broadcast channels can also be connected to a star topology using hub devices. As shown in Fig. 7.2, the digital signal sent from Computer A to Computer C is sent to all ports by the hub (which is the same as the bus topology) and is received by the network interface cards of Computer B, C

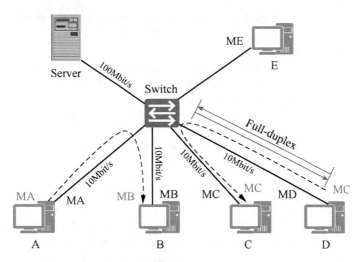

Fig. 7.3 Advantages of switch networking

and D in the network. The frame has the same destination MAC address as Computer C's network interface card, so only Computer C receives this frame. To avoid collision, Computer B and Computer D would not be able to send frames at the same time, so the computers connected to the hub would also have to use the CSMA/CD protocol for communication.

For the LAN formed by using coaxial cable and hub, the computers on the link share the bandwidth, and the more computers there are, the less bandwidth is averaged to each computer. Later, switches replace coaxial cables and hubs. Switches have MAC address table and can forward frames according to their destination MAC address instead of forwarding them to all ports, which avoids collisions.

Now most of the enterprise LANs are formed using switches, as switches are able to build MAC address tables and forward frames based on MAC address tables. Figure 7.3 shows the advantages of switch networking.

The following are the features of using switch networking compared with hub networking.

1. Port exclusive bandwidth.

   Each port of the switch has exclusive bandwidth. 10 Mbit/s switch has 10 Mbit/s bandwidth per port, and for 24-port 10 Mbit/s switch, its overall switching capacity is 240 Mbit/s, which is different from hubs.
2. Security.

   Networks formed using switches are safer than the those formed using hubs. For example, for the frames sent from Computer A to Computer B, and from Computer D to Computer C, the switch only forwards them to the destination port according to the MAC address table, and Computer E in the figure cannot receive digital signals from the communication of other computers at all. And even if the

packet capture tool is installed, it cannot capture packets from the communication of other computers.
3. Full-duplex communication.

   The switch port is directly connected to the computer, and the link between the computer and the switch can adopt full-duplex communication, that is, you can send and receive at the same time.
4. Full-duplex communication no longer uses CSMA/CD protocol.

   The switch port is directly connected to the computer, and if full-duplex communication is adopted, the data link layer no longer needs to use the CSMA/CD protocol, but we still call the network formed by the switch Ethernet, because the frame format is the same as Ethernet.
5. The port can work using different rates.

   The switch uses store-and-forward, which means that each port of the switch can store frames and use different rates when forwarding them from other ports. Usually, the port connected to the server and that connected to the switch have a higher bandwidth than the port connected to a normal computer.
6. Forward broadcast frames.

   Broadcast frames are forwarded to all ports except the sending port. The destination MAC address of a broadcast frame is all 1s when written in the 48-bit binary form, i.e., the destination MAC address is FF-FF-FF-FF-FF-FF. For example, ARP in Ethernet resolves the MAC address of a known IP address in this network segment through the broadcast frame sent. Some viruses also send broadcast frames in the network, so that the switch is occupied in forwarding these broadcast frames and the normal communication of computers in the network is affected, resulting in network congestion. Therefore, an Ethernet formed with a switch is a broadcast domain. Routers are responsible for forwarding packets on different network segments, and broadcast packets cannot cross routers, so it is said that routers isolate broadcasts.

   As shown in Fig. 7.4, the router is connected to two switches, which are connected to computers and hubs, and the router isolates the broadcast. The broadcast domain and collision domain are marked in the figure.

7.1.2   MAC Addresses

In February 1980, the Institute of Electrical and Electronics Engineers (IEEE) held a meeting, and a huge technical standardization project called IEEE Project 802 is launched in the meeting. "80" in 802 refers to 1980, and "2" means February.

The IEEE Project 802 aims to develop a series of standards for local area networks (LANs). Ethernet standard (IEEE 802.3), token ring network standard (IEEE 802.5), token bus network standard (IEEE 802.4), and other LAN standards are the results of the IEEE Project 802. We collectively refer to the various standards developed by the IEEE 802 project as IEEE 802 standards.

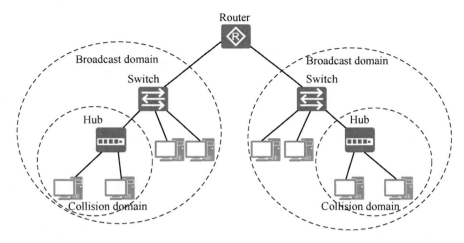

Fig. 7.4 Broadcast domain and collision domain

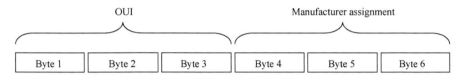

Fig. 7.5 BIA address format

MAC address is defined and standardized in the IEEE 802 standard. Any network interface card (such as Ethernet interface card and token ring network interface card) that complies with the IEEE 802 standard must have a MAC address.

As every person has an ID number to identify himself or herself, each network interface card also has a number to identify itself, which is the 48-bit (six-byte) MAC address. Different network interface cards have different MAC addresses. In other words, the MAC address of a network is unique in the whole world, and the router port connected to an Ethernet network also has a MAC address, just like a computer network interface card.

Before a manufacturer can produce and manufacture a network interface card, it must first register with IEEE to obtain a 24-bit (three-byte) vendor code, also known as Organizationally Unique Identifier (OUI). In the process of manufacturing network interface cards, the manufacturer will burn a 48-bit burned-in address (BIA) in the Read Only Memory (ROM) of each network interface card. The first three bytes of the BIA address is the manufacturer's OUI, and the last three bytes are determined by the manufacturer. But for different network interface cards, the last three bytes of their BIA addresses shall be different. The BIA address burned into the network interface card cannot be changed, and can only be read and used. Figure 7.5 shows the format of the BIA address.

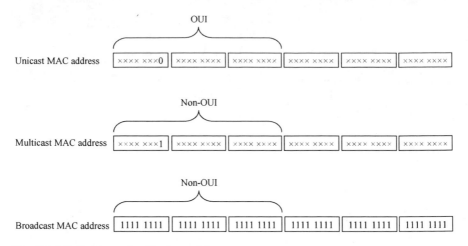

Fig. 7.6 MAC address classification and format

BIA address is a kind of MAC address, or, more precisely, it is a kind of unicast MAC address. There are three kinds of MAC addresses, namely unicast MAC address, multicast MAC address, and broadcast MAC address, as shown in Fig. 7.6.

1. Unicast MAC address is the MAC address whose eighth bit of the first byte is 0.
2. Multicast MAC address is the MAC address whose eighth bit of the first byte is 1.
3. A broadcast MAC address is a MAC address whose every bit is 1.

A unicast MAC address (such as a BIA address) identifies a specific network interface card, a multicast MAC address identifies a group of network interface cards, and a broadcast MAC address is a special case of multicast MAC address that identifies all network interface cards.

From Fig. 7.6, we can find that it is not true that the first three bytes of any MAC address are OUI. Only the first three bytes of unicast MAC addresses are OUI, while those of multicast or broadcast MAC addresses are not OUI.

A MAC address has 48 bits, which is often represented by hexadecimal numbers for the purpose of convenience. Each two hexadecimal digits are one group (i.e., one byte), with a total of six groups, connected by short lines in between. You can also use a total of three groups of four hexadecimal digits (i.e., two bytes), which are connected by short lines. Figure 7.7 is an example of these two representations.

7.1.3 Ethernet Frame Format

The frames used by Ethernet technology are called Ethernet frames. There are two standards for the Ethernet frame format: one is defined by IEEE 802.3, which is called IEEE 802.3 format; the other is jointly defined by three companies, Digital Equipment Corporation (DEC), Intel, and Xerox, and is called Ethernet II format,

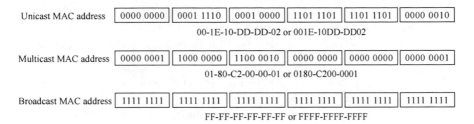

Fig. 7.7 MAC address representation

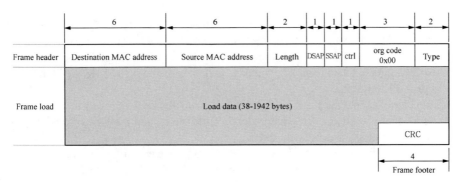

Fig. 7.8 IEEE 802.3 format

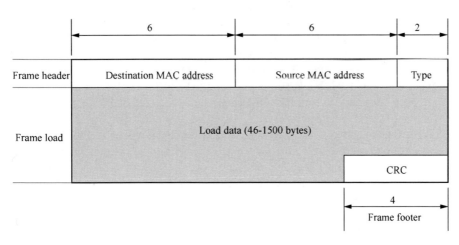

Fig. 7.9 Ethernet II format

also known as DIX format. The two Ethernet frame formats are shown in Figs. 7.8 and 7.9. Although there are some differences between the two formats, they can both be applied to Ethernet. Current network devices are compatible with both formats, but Ethernet II frames are more widely used. Generally, IEEE 802.3 format is only used for Ethernet frames that carry special protocol information, while Ethernet II format is used for the majority of Ethernet frames.

The following is a brief description of each field in an Ethernet frame of Ethernet II format.

1. Destination MAC address: this field has six bytes and is used to indicate the receiver (destination) of the frame. The destination MAC address can be a unicast MAC address, a multicast MAC address, or a broadcast MAC address.
2. Source MAC address: this field has six bytes and is used to indicate the sender (origin) of the frame. The source MAC address can only be a unicast MAC address.
3. Type: this field has two bytes and is used to specify the type of load data. For example, if the value of this field is 0x0800, the load data is an IPv4 packet; if the value of this field is 0x86dd, the load data is an IPv6 packet; if the value is 0x0806, the load data is an ARP packet; and if the value is 0x8848, the load data is an MPLS message; etc.
4. Load data: the length of this field is variable, with the shortest being 46 bytes, and the longest 1500 bytes. It is the payload of the frame, and the type of the load is indicated by the previous type field.
5. CRC field: this field has four bytes. CRC is abbreviated for Cyclic Redundancy Check, which is used to check the frame for errors. The detailed description of its working mechanism is beyond the knowledge scope of this book, so it is omitted here.

The functions and roles of the destination MAC address field, source MAC address field, type field, load data field, and CRC field in Ethernet frames of IEEE 802.3 format are the same as those of Ethernet II format, so they are not repeated here. The descriptions of several other fields (length field, DSAP field, etc.) are beyond the knowledge scope of this book, so they are omitted here.

The network interface card has a filtering feature and the adapter first checks the destination address of the Ethernet frame using hardware for every Ethernet frame it receives from the network. If it is a frame sent to this site, it will be accepted for other processing. Otherwise, the frame will be discarded and no further processing is performed. In this way, CPU and memory resources of the host will not be wasted. It should be noted that, depending on the type of destination MAC address, Ethernet frames can be divided into the following three different types.

1. Unicast Ethernet frames (or unicast frames for short): a frame whose destination MAC address is a unicast MAC address.
2. Multicast Ethernet frames (or multicast frames for short): a frame whose destination MAC address is a multicast MAC address.
3. Broadcast Ethernet frame (or broadcast frame for short): a frame whose destination MAC address is a broadcast MAC address.

7.2   Ethernet Switches

7.2.1   MAC Address Table of Switches

A switch maintains a MAC address table, on the basis of which the switch forwards unicast frames. The switch's MAC address table is also called the MAC address mapping table, and each entry in it is also called an address table entry, which reflects the mapping of MAC addresses to ports.

As shown in Fig. 7.10, by using two switches and five computers to form a network, and pinging the IP addresses of PC2, PC3, PC4 and PC5 on PC1, the switch is able to build a complete MAC address table. By entering "display mac-address" on SW2, you can view the MAC address table, and that interface GE0/0/1 corresponds to the MAC addresses of PC1 and PC2, so you can conclude that the interface GE0/0/1 of switch SW2 correspondingly is connected to SW1. 300 s later, enter "display mac-address" on SW2 again to view the MAC address table, and you can see that the entries in the MAC address table are automatically cleared.

```
<SW2>display mac-address
MAC address table of slot 0:
-----------------------------------------------------------------
MAC Address   VLAN/   PEVLAN CEVLAN Port     Type    LSP/LSR-ID
              VSI/SI                                 MAC-Tunnel
-----------------------------------------------------------------
5489-9853-3b60 1       -      -     GE0/0/1  dynamic 0/-
5489-9851-0fbe 1       -      -     Eth0/0/1 dynamic 0/-
5489-98a6-7d20 1       -      -     Eth0/0/2 dynamic 0/-
5489-985e-16b9 1       -      -     Eth0/0/3 dynamic 0/-
5489-986a-20ec 1       -      -     GE0/0/1  dynamic 0/-


-----------------------------------------------------------------
Total matching items on slot 0 displayed = 5
```

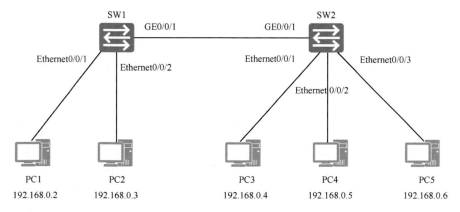

Fig. 7.10 View MAC address table

From the above output, we can see that the Type is dynamic, which means the entry is dynamically built and will be automatically deleted after the aging time expires. Enter "display mac-address aging-time" to view the MAC address table aging time.

```
[SW2]display mac-address aging-time
   Aging time: 300 seconds
```

In reality, the MAC address table of a low-end switch can typically store up to a few thousand address table entries. The MAC address of a middle-end switch can usually store up to tens of thousands of address table entries. And the MAC address table of a high-end switch can normally store up to hundreds of thousands address table entries.

In reality, the location of a switch or computer in a network may change. If the location of the switch or computer does change, some of the original address table entries in the MAC address table of the switch will likely misrepresent the current mapping of MAC addresses to ports. In addition, if there are too many address table entries in the MAC address table, each time it will take an extremely long time for the switch to look up the table (in order for the switch to decide which forwarding operation to perform on a unicast frame, it needs to go through the MAC address table to look up the destination MAC address of that unicast frame). In other words, the forwarding speed of the switch will be affected to some extent. In view of the above two main reasons, an aging mechanism has been designed for the MAC address table.

The default aging time is 300 s, which means that an entry in the MAC address table is removed from the table if it is not used within 300 s. The aging time can also be configured using command. The shorter the aging time, the faster the MAC address table can learn new MAC address and entries corresponding to the port after the computer location or switch location is changed. If the computer and network locations do not change much and the aging time is short, the corresponding entries for MAC addresses and ports are quickly deleted and the switch floods when there are frames to that MAC address.

7.2.2   Three Forwarding Operations of Switches

The switch forwards every frame that enters its port through the transmission media, and the basic role of the switch is to forward frames.

As illustrated in Fig. 7.11, there are three types of switch forwarding operations for frames entering a port from the transmission media: flooding, forwarding and discarding.

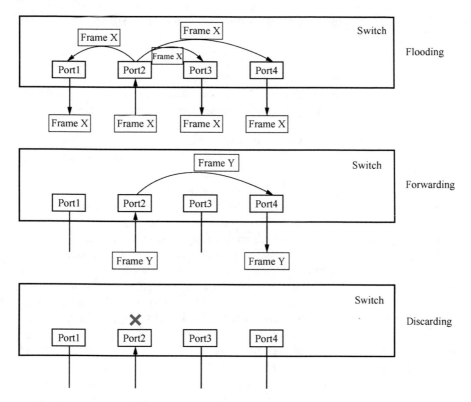

Fig. 7.11 Three frame forwarding actions of the switch

1. Flooding: the switch forwards a frame entering from one port to all other ports (note that "all other ports" means all ports except the one from which the frame enters the switch). Flooding is a point-to-multipoint forwarding. For example, flooding occurs when unknown unicast frames, broadcast frames, and multicast frames are received.
2. Forwarding: the switch uses another port to forward the frame entering from one port (note that the "another port" cannot be the port from which the frame enters the switch). This is a point to point forwarding.
3. Discarding: the switch discards the frame entering from a port. Discarding is actually not a forwarding operation.

   The arrows in Fig. 7.11 indicate the trajectory of the frame's movement. The three types of forwarding operations, flooding, forwarding, and discarding, are often referred to as forwarding in general (i.e., forwarding in the general sense). Therefore, when readers encounter the term "forwarding", they need to clarify whether it refers to forwarding in the general sense or specifically to point to point forwarding, depending on the context.

7.2.3   MAC Address Table Building Process of a Single Switch

A switch forwards frames based on the MAC address table, which is a table corresponding to the port number and MAC address, and the switch automatically builds the MAC address table during computer communication, which is called "self-learning".

As shown in Fig. 7.12, the switch has four ports, and the number after the port is the port number (Port No.), which is 1, 2, 3, and 4. Each port connects a computer, which is PC1, PC2, PC3, and PC4, and the corresponding MAC addresses are MAC1, MAC2, MAC3, and MAC4. In the beginning, the MAC address table is empty, which means that the switch also has no idea which MAC addresses correspond to the interfaces before the computers communicate.

As soon as a computer on the switch sends a frame, the switch is able to construct a MAC address table based on the source MAC address of the frame. Later, it forwards the frames based on the MAC address table.

As shown in Fig. 7.13, for example, PC1 sends a Frame X to PC3, whose source MAC address is MAC1 and destination MAC address is MAC3. The switch fails to find the port corresponding to the MAC3 address in the MAC address table, and the frame is flooded to all ports. The network interface cards of PC2 and PC4 will ignore the frame. Port1 receives the frame with a source MAC address of MAC1 and will add a mapping entry of MAC1 and Port1 to the MAC address table.

As shown in Fig. 7.14, PC4 sends PC1 a Frame Y with the destination MAC address of MAC1 and the source MAC address of MAC4. After receiving the frame,

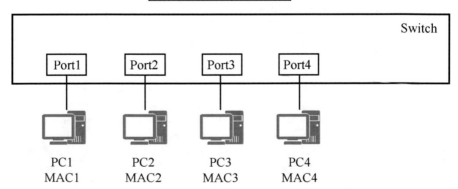

Fig. 7.12 The MAC address table building process of a switch

MAC address	Port No.
MAC1	1

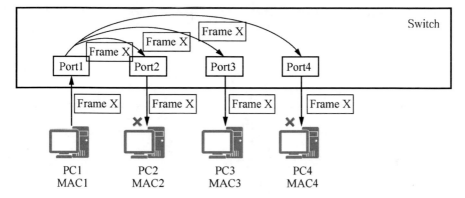

Fig. 7.13 Flooding

MAC address	Port No.
MAC1	1
MAC4	4

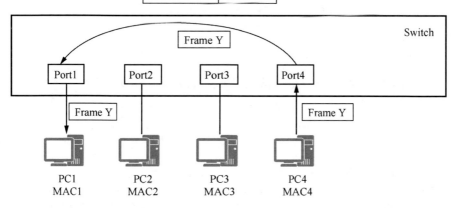

Fig. 7.14 Forwarding according to the MAC address table

the switch checks the MAC address table and finds that MAC1 corresponds to Port1, so the switch forwards the frame to Port1 and, at the same time, adds a mapping entry of MAC4 and Port4 to the MAC address table.

MAC address	Port No.
MAC1	1
MAC4	4
MAC3	3

Frame W: the destination MAC address is FF-FF-FF-FF-FF-FF, and the source MAC address is MAC3

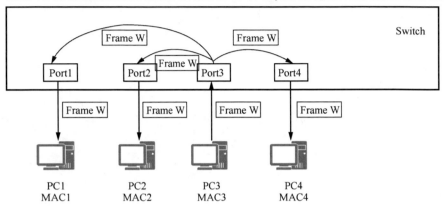

Fig. 7.15 PC3 sends a broadcast frame

If a computer sends a frame that needs to be received by all computers in the network, a broadcast frame is needed. The destination MAC address of the broadcast frame is FF-FF-FF-FF-FF-FF. As shown in Fig. 7.15, PC3 sends a broadcast frame, Frame W, and the switch will not check the MAC address table after receiving the broadcast frame, but directly floods Frame W, while adding a mapping entry of MAC3 and Port3 in the MAC address table.

7.2.4 MAC Address Table Building Process of Multiple Switches

As shown in Fig. 7.16, three switches are connected to four computers through twisted-pair cables, forming a relatively complex network. Assume that the MAC address tables of the switches are all empty at this moment. Some examples are presented in the following part to illustrate the process of frame forwarding in this network. Since the forwarding principles of the switches have been described in detail in the previous section, the following description is relatively concise.

As shown in Fig. 7.17, now assume that PC1 needs to send a unicast frame X to PC3, with a source MAC address of MAC1 and destination MAC address of MAC3. The MAC address tables of all three switches are empty. The switch does not find the

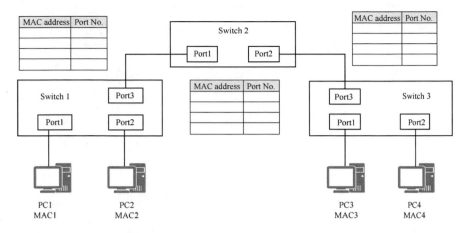

Fig. 7.16 Multi-switch networking

port corresponding to the MAC3 address in the MAC address table, and the frame is flooded to all ports.

The following steps describe the entire process of how Frame X arrives at PC3 from PC1.

1. After receiving Frame X, Switch 1 cannot find the port corresponding to the destination MAC address in the MAC address table, so it floods the frame to all ports and adds a corresponding entry of MAC1 and Port1 to the MAC address table.
2. Switch 2 floods Frame X received by Port1, and Frame X reaches Port1 of Switch 3 through Port2 of Switch 2. Switch 2 writes the correspondence between MAC1 and Port1 in its own MAC address table.
3. Switch 3 floods Frame X received by Port3, and Switch 3 writes the correspondence between MAC1 and Port3 in its own MAC address table.

At this point, the network state is as shown in Fig. 7.17. Frame X has successfully arrived from source host PC1 to destination host PC3, and although non-destination hosts PC2 and PC4 also receive Frame X, they both directly discard it.

In the network state shown in Fig. 7.18, assume that PC4 needs to send PC1 a unicast frame Y with a destination MAC address of MAC1 and a source MAC address of MAC4.

The following steps describe the entire process of how Frame Y arrives at PC1 from PC4.

1. After Port3 of Switch 3 receives Frame Y, it checks the MAC address table and finds that the port corresponding to MAC1 is Port3. Then it forwards the frame to Port3, and at the same time adds the corresponding entries of MAC4 and Port2 to the MAC address table.
2. After Port2 of Switch 2 receives Frame Y, it checks the MAC address table and finds that the port corresponding to MAC1 is Port1. Then it forwards the frame to

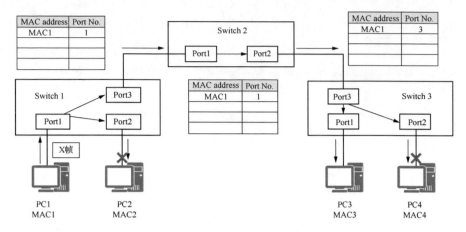

Fig. 7.17 PC1 sends a unicast frame to PC3

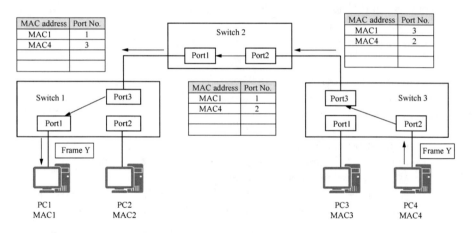

Fig. 7.18 PC4 sends a unicast frame to PC1

Port1, and at the same time adds the corresponding entries of MAC4 and Port2 to the MAC address table.

3. After Port3 of Switch 1 receives Frame Y, it checks the MAC address table and finds that the port corresponding to MAC1 is Port1. Then it forwards the frame to Port1, and at the same time adds the corresponding entries of MAC4 and Port3 to the MAC address table.

As shown in Fig. 7.19, carefully observe the MAC address tables on Switch 1 and Switch 2. In this case, PC2 sends a unicast frame Z to PC1. Switch 1 does not find the forwarding port corresponding to MAC1 in the MAC address table, and Frame Z is flooded to all ports. After Port1 of Switch 2 receives the frame, it checks the MAC

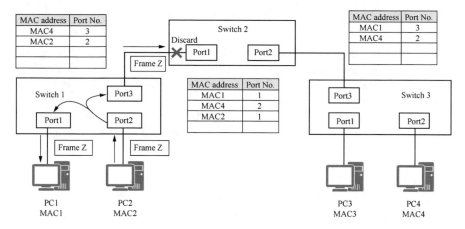

Fig. 7.19 PC2 sends a unicast frame to PC1

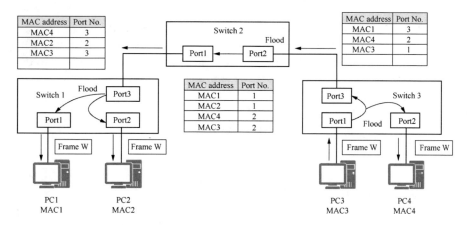

Fig. 7.20 PC3 sends a broadcast frame

address table and finds that the port corresponding to the frame is Port1, so the frame does not need to be forwarded and is discarded.

In the example here, a computer sends a broadcast frame. As shown in Fig. 7.20, PC3 sends a broadcast frame W with a destination MAC address of FF-FF-FF-FF-FF-FF and a source MAC address of MAC3. Port1 of Switch 3 receives the frame and floods it, while adding the corresponding entries of MAC3 and Port1 to the MAC address table. Port2 of Switch 2 receives the broadcast frame and floods it, adding the corresponding entries of MAC3 and Port2 to the MAC address table. Port3 of Switch 1 receives the broadcast frame and floods it, adding the corresponding entries of MAC3 and Port3 in the MAC address table. Computers PC1, PC2, and PC4 in the network can all receive the broadcast frame, so the network formed with the switch is a broadcast domain.

7.2.5   Typical Campus Network Architecture

Figure 7.21 shows a typical campus network architecture. In addition to the access layer, aggregation layer and core layer, in this network architecture, two routers connecting the Internet are also treated as a separate layer, that is, an "exit layer". For network security, firewalls are deployed in the core layer. In order to achieve architectural security (to avoid single point of failure of key devices), dual aggregation layer switches and dual core layer switches are deployed at the aggregation layer and core layer, respectively, and two routers are also deployed at the exit layer, with dual links to the Internet.

7.3   VLANs

7.3.1   Concept and Meaning of VLAN

A virtual local area network (VLAN) is a set of logical devices and users that are not restricted by physical location, so that administrators can logically divide different users in the same physical LAN into different broadcast domains according to the actual application requirements. Each VLAN contains a group of computers or

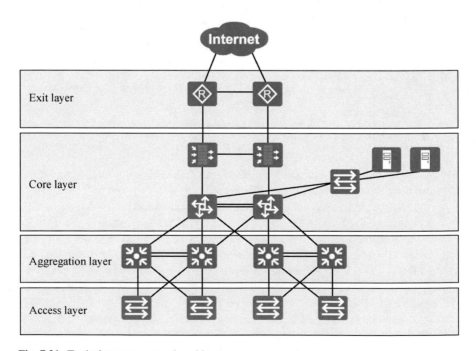

Fig. 7.21 Typical campus network architecture

servers with the same requirements, and communicate with each other as if they are in the same network segment. This is why it is called a virtual local area network. VLANs work at Layer 2 and Layer 3 of the OSI reference model, and a VLAN is a broadcast domain. The communication between VLANs needs to be done through Layer 3 devices (routers or Layer 3 switches).

As shown in Fig. 7.22, a company deploys switches on the first, second and third floors of its office building, and all three switches are access layer switches, which are connected by aggregation layer switches. The company's sales department, R&D department and finance department have computers on each floor. For security and the control of network broadcasts, a VLAN can be created for each department. The different VLANs on the switches are identified using numbers, and VLAN1 can be assigned for computers in the sales department, VlAN 2 for those in the R&D Department, and VLAN 3 for those in the finance department.

VLANs have the following advantages.

1. Control of broadcast range.

   A VLAN is a broadcast domain. Broadcast frames sent by computers in a VLAN will not spread to other VLANs, thus reducing the impact range of broadcasts.
2. Security.

   Different VLANs can be created according to security requirements and computers with the same security requirements can be put into the same VLAN. For instance, computers with sensitive data are isolated from other

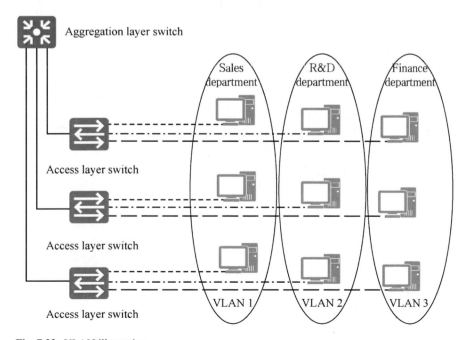

Fig. 7.22 VLAN illustration

computers in the network, thus reducing the possibility of leaking confidential information. Computers in different VLANs are isolated from each other at the data link layer, i.e., users in one VLAN cannot directly communicate with users in other VLANs. For different VLANs to communicate, they need to go through Layer 3 devices such as routers or Layer 3 switches, and control the traffic on Layer 3 devices.

3. Improvement of performance.

Dividing the Layer 2 flat network into multiple logical workgroups (broadcast domains) can reduce unnecessary traffic on the network and improve performance.

4. Improvement of IT staff productivity.

VLANs bring convenience to network management because users with similar network requirements will share the same VLAN.

7.3.2 Multiple VLANs on a Single Switch

All ports of the switch belong to VLAN 1 by default, and VLAN 1 is the default VLAN that cannot be deleted. As shown in Fig. 7.23, all ports of Switch S1 are in VLAN 1. A frame entering the switch port is automatically tagged with the VLAN to which the port belongs, and the VLAN tag is removed when the frame exits the switch port. In Fig. 7.23, Computer A sends a frame to Computer D. The frame enters Port F0, and is tagged with a VLAN 1 tag, then it exits Port F3, at which point the VLAN 1 tag is removed. This process is transparent to the communicating computers A and D. If Computer A sends a broadcast frame, the frame is tagged with a VLAN 1 tag and forwarded to all ports of VLAN 1.

Suppose Switch S1 connects computers in two departments. A, B, C and D are computers in the sales department, and E, F, G and H are computers in the R&D department. For security reasons, the computers in the sales department are assigned to VLAN 1 and the computers in the R&D department are assigned to VLAN 2. As shown in Fig. 7.24, Computer E sends a frame to Computer H through Port F8, and it

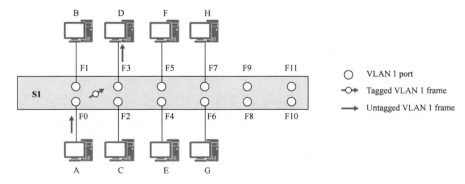

Fig. 7.23 Switch port belongs to VLAN 1 by default

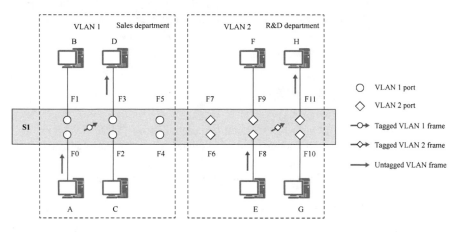

Fig. 7.24 Same VLAN communication process of the switch

is tagged with VLAN 2 tag, and when the frame exits Port F11, the VLAN 2 tag is removed. The frames sent and received by the computer has no VLAN tag.

Switch S1 is divided into two VLANs, which is tantamount to logically dividing this switch into two separate switches S1-VLAN 1 and S1-VLAN 2, as shown in Fig. 7.25. As you can see from Fig. 7.25, commination between computers in different VLANs is impossible even if their IP addresses are set as one network segment. To achieve inter-VLAN communication, the frame must be forwarded by a router (Layer 3 device), which requires different VLANs to be assigned IP addresses of different network segments. The network segment assigned to S1-VLAN 1 in Fig. 7.25 is 192.168.1.0/24, and that assigned to S1-VLAN 2 is 192.168.2.0/24. In Fig. 7.25, a router is added to demonstrate the inter-VLAN communication process. Port F0 of the router is connected to Port F5 of S1-VLAN 1, while Port F1 is connected to Por F7 of S1-VLAN 2. Figure 7.25 shows how Computer C sends a

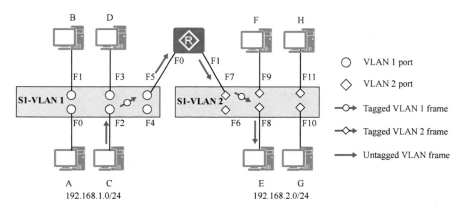

Fig. 7.25 VLAN equivalence diagram

packet to Computer E, frames entering and exiting the switch port, and the change in VLAN tags.

7.3.3   VLANs Across Switches

As mentioned earlier, multiple VLANs can be created on one switch. When sometimes computers in the same department are connected to different switches, they should also be classified into the same VLAN, which is the VLAN across switches.

As shown in Fig. 7.26, there are two switches S1 and S2 in the network, computers A, B, C and D belong to the sales department, and computers E, F, G and H belong to the R&D department. VLANs are divided by department, with VLAN 1 for the sales department and VLAN 2 for the R&D department. In order to enable the communication between VLAN 1 of S1 and VLAN 1 of S2, the VLAN 1 ports of the two switches are connected so that computers A, B, C, and D belong to the same VLAN and VLAN 1 spans across the two switches. Similarly, the VLAN 2 ports on both switches are connected, so VLAN 2 also spans across both switches. Pay attention to how VLAN tags of the frames change when Computer D communicates with Computer C.

Figure 7.26 makes it easy to understand how VLANs across switches are implemented. The figure shows two VLANs across switches, each using a separate network cable for connection. Multiple VLANs across switches can also share the same network cable, which is called a trunk link, and the switch port connected to the trunk link is called a trunk port, as shown in Fig. 7.27.

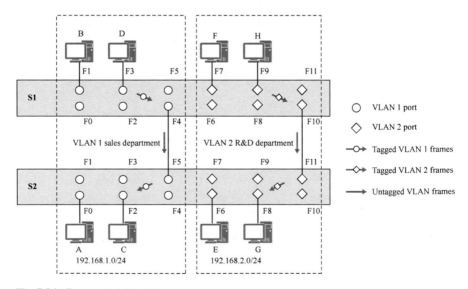

Fig. 7.26 Cross-switch VLAN

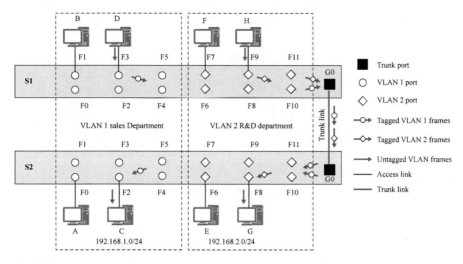

Fig. 7.27 Trunk link frames with VLAN tags

In the network shown in Fig. 7.27, the link where a computer connects to a switch is called an access link. The link between switches that allow multiple VLAN frames to pass is called a trunk link. Frames on an access link are untagged frames, and frames on a Trunk link can be tagged frames. The VLAN information is not lost when frames are passed over the trunk. For example, if Computer B sends a broadcast frame that travels over the trunk link to Switch S2, the latter knows that the broadcast frame came from VLAN 1 and forwards the frame to all ports of VLAN 1.

The ports on the switch are divided into access ports, trunk ports, and hybrid ports. Access ports can only belong to one VLAN and are generally used to connect computer ports; Trunk ports can allow frames from multiple VLANs to pass through, and frames in and out of the port can be tagged with VLANs; Hybrid ports are introduced in detail in the next section.

As shown in Fig. 7.28, there two switches and 3 VLANs/ Think about it. Can a broadcast frame sent by Computer A in VLAN 1 be sent to VLAN 2 and VLAN 3?

As seen in Fig. 7.28, the broadcast frame from Computer A is sent out of Port F2 without VLAN tags. After the frame enters Port F3 of S2 and is tagged with VLAN 2 tag, S2 forwards it to all VLAN 2 ports, and Computer B is able to receive the frame. The frame is sent from Port F5 of S2 and its VLAN 2 tag is removed. Then Port F6 of S1 receives the frame and forwards it to all VLAN 3 ports after the VLAN 3 tag is added, and Computer C can receive the frame.

From the above analysis, it is clear that for switches that create VLANs, it is better not to use access ports for the connection between switches. If the connection is wrong, it will cause inexplicable network failure. Originally, VLANs isolate broadcast frames, and this connection enables broadcast frames to spread to all 3 VLANs.

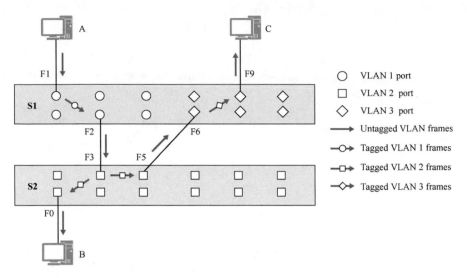

Fig. 7.28 Do not use access port to connect switches

7.3.4 Link Types and Port Types

A VLAN frame may have a tag (called a tagged VLAN frame, or simply a tagged frame), or may not have a tag (called an untagged VLAN frame, or simply an untagged frame). When talking about VLAN technology, if a frame is classified by the switch to VLAN i ($i = 1,2, 3, ...,4094$), we refer to this frame as simply a VLAN i frame. For a VLAN i frame with a tag, i is actually the value of the VLAN ID field in the tag of that frame. Note that for tagged VLAN frames, the switch can obviously determine which VLAN it belongs to from the VID value in its tag; and for untagged VLAN frames (such as those from end computers), the switch needs to determine or classify which VLAN it belongs to according to some principles (such as the port through which the frame enters the switch).

In a VLAN-enabled switch network, we call the link directly connected the switch to the end computer an access link, and the ports on the switch side of the access link access ports. At the same time, we call the link directly connected between the switches a trunk link, and the ports on both sides of the trunk link trunk ports. Frames moving on an access link can (or should) only be untagged frames, and these frames can only belong to a specific VLAN; frames moving on a trunk link can be tagged frames, and these frames can belong to different VLANs. An access port can only belong to a specific VLAN and can only allow frames belonging to that specific VLAN to pass through; a trunk port can belong to multiple VLANs at the same time and allow frames belonging to different VLANs to pass through, as shown in Fig. 7.27.

In the actual implementation of VLAN technology, another type of port, that is hybrid port, is often defined and configured. Both the port on the switch connected to the end computer and the port on the switch connected to other switches can be configured as a hybrid port.

Each switch port (access, trunk, hybrid port) should be configured with a PVID (Port VLAN ID), and untagged frames arriving at this port will always be classified by the switch to the VLAN specified by the PVID. For example, if the PVID of a port is configured as 5, then all untagged frames arriving at this port will be identified as VLAN 5 frames. The value of PVID is 1 by default.

To summarize, frames moving on a link (path) may be either tagged frames or untagged frames. However, frames moving between different ports within a switch must be tagged frames.

Next, we illustrate in detail the rules for processing and forwarding frames on the access, trunk, and hybrid ports.

1. Access ports.

   When the access port receives an untagged frame from a link (path), the switch adds a tag with PVID as the VID to the frame and then forwards (floods, point to point forwards, and discards) the resulting tagged frame.

   When the access port receives a tagged frame from a link (path), the switch checks whether the VID in the tag of this frame is the same as the PVID. If it is, the tagged frame is forwarded (flooded, point to point forwarded, discarded); if not, the tagged frame is directly discarded.

   When a tagged frame arrives at an access port from another port of this switch, the switch checks whether the VID in the tag of the frame is the same as the PVID. If it is, the tag of this tagged frame is stripped and the resulting untagged frame is sent out from the link (path); if not, the tagged frame is directly discarded.

2. Trunk ports

   For each trunk port, in addition to the PVID, it must also be configured with a list of VLAN IDs allowed to pass through.

   When a Trunk port receives an untagged frame from a link (path), the switch adds a tag with PVID as the VID to the frame and then checks if the PVID is in the list of VLAN IDs allowed to pass through. If it is, the resulting tagged frame is forwarded (flooded, point to point forwarded, discarded); if not, the resulting tagged frame is directly discarded.

   When a trunk port receives a tagged frame from a link (path), the switch checks whether the VID in the tag of the frame is in the list of VLAN IDs allowed to pass through. If it is, the tagged frame is forwarded (flooded, point to point forwarded, discarded): if not, the tagged frame is directly discarded.

   When a tagged frame arrives at a trunk port from another port of this switch, if the VID in the tag of this frame is not in the list of VLAN IDs allowed to pass through, the tagged frame is directly discarded.

   When a tagged frame arrives at a trunk port from another port of this switch, if the VID in the tag of the frame is in the list of VLAN IDs allowed to pass through and the VID is the same as the PVID, the switch strips the tag of the tagged frame and sends the resulting untagged frame out of the link (path).

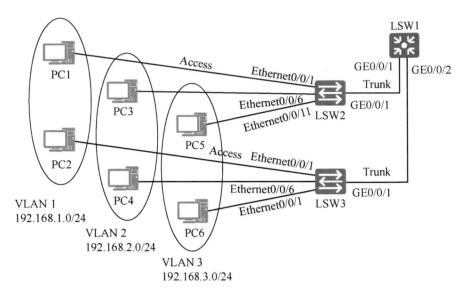

Fig. 7.29 Cross-switch VLAN

in VLAN 1 in network segment 192.168.2.0/24, PC3 and PC4 are in VLAN 2 in network segment 192.168.2.0/24, and PC5 and PC6 are in VLAN 3 in network segment 192.168.3.0/24.

We need to complete the following functions.

1. Create VLAN 1, VLAN 2 and VLAN 3 for each switch; VLAN 1 is the default VLAN and does not need to be created.
2. Assign the access layer switch ports Ethernet0/0/1 to Ethernet0/0/5 to VLAN 1.
3. Assign the access layer switch ports Ethernet0/0/6 to Ethernet0/0/10 to VLAN 2.
4. Assign the access layer switch ports Ethernet0/0/11 to Ethernet0/0/15 to VLAN 3.
5. Set the ports connecting to computers as access ports.
6. Set the ports connecting between switches as trunk ports to allow frames from VLAN 1, VLAN 2 and VLAN 3 to pass through.
7. Capture and analyze tagged VLAN frames on trunk link.

It is important to remember here that ports connecting computers should be set as access ports and the ports connecting between switches should be set as trunk ports. You can also remember it in this way. If the port needs frames from multiple VLANs to pass through, it needs to be set as a trunk port. It should also be noted that the PVID of these trunk ports of the switch should be the same. The aggregation layer switches need to create VLAN 2 and VLAN 3 even though there are no computers connected to VLAN 2 and VLAN 3, which means that these three switches in the network should have the same VLAN.

Create VLANs on Switch LSW2.

```
[LSW2]vlan ?
 INTEGER<1-4094>  VLAN ID               --The number of VLANs supported,
and the maximum is 4094
  batch              Batch process      --Create VLANs in batch
 [LSW2]vlan 2                           --Create VLAN 2
 [LSW2-vlan2]quit
 [LSW2]vlan 3                           --Create VLAN 3
 [LSW2-vlan3]quit
 [LSW2]display vlan summary             --Display VLAN summary
 static vlan:
 Total 3 static vlan.                   --3 VLANs in total
  1 to 3
 dynamic vlan:
 Total 0 dynamic vlan.
 reserved vlan:
 Total 0 reserved vlan.
 [LSW2]
```

Note: VLAN 1 is the default VLAN and does not need to be created.
The following command creates VLAN 4, VLAN 5 and VLAN 6 in batch.

```
[LSW2]vlan batch 4 5 6
```

The following command creates VLAN 10 to VLAN 20 (11 VLANs in total) in batch.

```
vlan batch 10 to 20
```

Delete VLAN 4, VLAN 5 and VLAN 6 in batch.

```
[LSW2]undo vlan batch 4 5 6
```

Since the ports are to be configured in batch, it is necessary to create port groups for batch configuration. The following operation creates the port group vlan1port, sets the ports Ethernet0/0/1 to Ethernet0/0/5 as access ports, and assigns them to VLAN 1.

```
[LSW2]port-group vlan1port
[LSW2-port-group-vlan1port]group-member Ethernet0/0/1 to
Ethernet0/0/5
[LSW2-port-group-vlan1port]port link-type ?          --View port
type supported
  access        Access port
  dot1q-tunnel  QinQ port
  hybrid        Hybrid port
  trunk         Trunk port
[LSW2-port-group-vlan1port]port link-type access     --Set the port
to access port
[LSW2-port-group-vlan1port]port default vlan 1         --Assign the
```

port group to VLAN 1, this command may not be executed
```
[LSW2-port-group-vlan1port]quit
```

Create port group vlan2port for VLAN 2, set the ports Ethernet0/0/6 to Ethernet0/0/10 as access ports, and assign them to VLAN 2.

```
[LSW2]port-group vlan2port
[LSW2-port-group-vlan2port]group-member Ethernet0/0/6 to
Ethernet0/0/10
[LSW2-port-group-vlan2port]port link-type access
[LSW2-port-group-vlan2port]port default vlan 2    --Assign the port
group to VLAN 2. After executing this command, PVID of these ports is
changed to 2
[LSW2-port-group-vlan2port]quit
```

Create port group vlan3port for VLAN 3, set the ports Ethernet0/0/11 to Ethernet0/0/15 as access ports, and assign them to VLAN 3.

```
[LSW2]port-group vlan3port
[LSW2-port-group-vlan3port]group-member Ethernet0/0/11 to
Ethernet0/0/15
[LSW2-port-group-vlan3port]port link-type access
[LSW2-port-group-vlan3port]port default vlan 3   -- Assign the port
group to VLAN 3. After executing this command, PVID of these ports is
changed to 3
[LSW2-port-group-vlan3port]quit
```

Configure port GigabitEthernet0/0/1 as a trunk port to allow frames of VLAN 1, VLAN 2 and VLAN 3 to pass through.

```
[LSW2]interface GigabitEthernet0/0/1
[LSW2-GigabitEthernet0/0/1]port link-type trunk
[LSW2-GigabitEthernet0/0/1]port trunk allow-pass vlan ?
 INTEGER<1-4094>  VLAN ID
all          All                        --Allow all VLAN frames
to pass through
[LSW2-GigabitEthernet0/0/1]port trunk allow-pass vlan 1 2 3      --
Allow designated frames to pass through
```

Note: ① the default PVID of all ports is VLAN 1. Execute the following command to change the PVID of the trunk port to VLAN 2.

```
[LSW2-GigabitEthernet0/0/1]port trunk pvid vlan 2
```

② For an access port, the VLAN to which the port belongs is the PVID of the port. Enter the following command to view the PVID of the port.

```
[LSW2]display interface Ethernet0/0/1
Ethernet0/0/1 current state : UP
Line protocol current state : UP
Description:
Switch Port, PVID : 2 , TPID : 8100(Hex), The Maximum Frame Length is
9216
IP Sending Frames' Format is PKTFMT_ETHNT_2, Hardware address is 4c1f-
cc8d-71bf
```

Display the VLAN settings, and you can see that port GE0/0/1 belongs to VLAN 1, VLAN 2 and VLAN 3 at the same time.

```
[LSW2]display vlan
The total number of vlans is : 3                    --The number of VLANs
---------------------------------------------------------------
U: Up;    D: Down;   TG: Tagged;    UT: Untagged;    --TG: tagged VLAN
frame. UT: untagged VLAN frame
MP: Vlan-mapping;        ST: Vlan-stacking;
#: ProtocolTransparent-vlan;    *: Management-vlan;
---------------------------------------------------------------
VID  Type    Ports
---------------------------------------------------------------
1    common  UT:Eth0/0/1(U)    Eth0/0/2(D)    Eth0/0/3(D)    Eth0/0/
4(D)
             Eth0/0/5(D)    Eth0/0/16(D)    Eth0/0/17(D)    Eth0/0/18(D)
             Eth0/0/19(D)   Eth0/0/20(D)    Eth0/0/21(D)    Eth0/0/22(D)
             GE0/0/1(U)     GE0/0/2(D) --The PVID of GE0/0/1 is VLAN 1, and
VLAN 1 frames usually pass through without a VLAN tag
2    common  UT:Eth0/0/6(U)    Eth0/0/7(D)    Eth0/0/8(D)    Eth0/0/
9(D)
             Eth0/0/10(D)
        TG:GE0/0/1(U)           --TG means that VLAN 2 frames usually pass
through with VLAN tags
3    common  UT:Eth0/0/11(U)    Eth0/0/12(D)    Eth0/0/13(D)    Eth0/
0/14(D)
             Eth0/0/15(D)
        TG:GE0/0/1(U)           --TG means VLAN 3 frames usually pass
through with VLAN tags
 ......
```

Configure LSW3 by referring to the configuration of LSW2; create VLANs and specify the port types.

On the aggregation layer switch LSW1, create VLAN 2 and VLAN 3, set the two port types to trunk, and allow frames of VLAN 1, VLAN 2, and VLAN 3 to pass through.

```
[LSW1]vlan batch  2 3                    --Create VLAN 2 and VLAN 3 in batch
[LSW1]interface GigabitEthernet 0/0/1
[LSW1-GigabitEthernet0/0/1]port link-type trunk
[LSW1-GigabitEthernet0/0/1]port trunk allow-pass vlan 1 2 3
[LSW1-GigabitEthernet0/0/1]quit
```

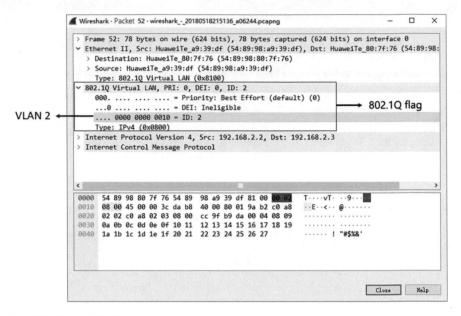

Fig. 7.30 Tagged VLAN frame structure

```
[LSW1]interface GigabitEthernet0/0/2
[LSW1-GigabitEthernet0/0/2]port link-type trunk
[LSW1-GigabitEthernet0/0/2]port trunk allow-pass vlan 1 2 3
[LSW1-GigabitEthernet0/0/2]quit
```

By capturing the trunk link frames, as shown in Fig. 7.30, you can see that the trunk link frames of the Huawei switch inserts VLAN tag between data link layer and network layer, using IEEE 802.1Q frame format. The VLAN ID is represented in 12 bits, and it takes the value between 0 and 4095. Since 0 and 4095 are reserved for protocols, the valid value range of VLAN ID is between 1 to 4094. The frame shown in Fig. 7.30 is a VLAN 2 frame.

7.3.7   Configure MAC Address-Based VLANs

MAC address-based VLAN classification is suitable for scenarios where mobile devices are connected to the enterprise network through the network cable. For example, enterprise employees use laptops in different offices to access the enterprise network through the network cable. No matter which port of the switch the laptop is connected to, the switch will assign it to the designated VLAN.

As shown in Fig. 7.31, ports GE1/0/1 of SwitchA and SwitchB are connected to two conference rooms, and Laptop1 and Laptop2 are laptops for conferences, which can be used in both conference rooms. Laptop1 and Laptop2 belongs to two

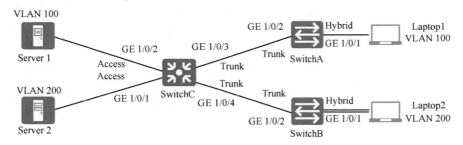

Fig. 7.31 MAC address-based VLAN

departments that are isolated by VLAN 100 and VLAN 200. Now it is required that whichever conference room the two laptops are used in, they can access only their own department's server, that is, Server1 and Server2, The MAC addresses of Laptop1 and Laptop2 are 0001-00ef-00c0 and 0001-00ef-00c1, respectively.

First, create VLANs on SwitchA and SwitchB, and configure trunk port and hybrid port. Then, classify VLANs on SwitchA and SwitchB based on MAC addresses. Finally, create VLANs on SwitchC and configure trunk and access ports to ensure that laptops can access the server.

1. Configure SwitchA. The configuration of SwitchB is similar to that of SwitchA, so it will not be repeated.

```
<HUAWEI> system-view
[HUAWEI] sysname SwitchA
[SwitchA] vlan batch 100 200            --Create VLAN 100 and VLAN 200
[SwitchA] interface gigabitethernet 1/0/2
[SwitchA-GigabitEthernet1/0/2] port link-type trunk  -- Trunk ports
are recommended for ports connecting between switches; the default port
type is not trunk; it needs to be manually configured as trunk
[SwitchA-GigabitEthernet1/0/2] port trunk allow-pass vlan 100 200  --
Allow VLAN 100 and VLAN 200 frames to pass through
[SwitchA-GigabitEthernet1/0/2] quit
[SwitchA] vlan 100
[SwitchA-vlan100] mac-vlan mac-address 0001-00ef-00c0 --Messages
whose MAC address is 0001-00ef-00c0 are forwarded in VLAN 100
[SwitchA-vlan100] quit
[SwitchA] vlan 200
[SwitchA-vlan200] mac-vlan mac-address 0001-00ef-00c1  -- Messages
whose MAC address is 0001-00ef-00c1 are forwarded in VLAN 200
[SwitchA-vlan200] quit
[SwitchA] interface gigabitethernet1/0/1
[SwitchA-GigabitEthernet1/0/1] port link-type hybrid  --MAC-based
VLAN classification can only be applied to hybrid ports; for V200R005C00
and later versions, the default port type is not hybrid, and it needs to be
manually configured
[SwitchA-GigabitEthernet1/0/1] port hybrid untagged vlan 100 200  --
For messages with VLAN 100 and VLAN 200, strip the VLAN tag
[SwitchA-GigabitEthernet1/0/1] mac-vlan enable --Can enable the
```

```
MAC-VLAN function of the port
 [SwitchA-GigabitEthernet1/0/1] quit
```

2. Check the configuration result. Execute the display mac-vlan mac-address all command in any view to view the configuration of MAC address-based VLAN classification.

```
[SwitchA] display mac-vlan mac-address all
----------------------------------------------------
MAC Address        MASK          VLAN  Priority
----------------------------------------------------
0001-00ef-00c0 ffff-ffff-ffff 100   0
0001-00ef-00c1 ffff-ffff-ffff 200   0
Total MAC VLAN address count: 2
```

3. Configure SwitchC. The configurations of GE1/0/3 and GE1/0/4 are the same, and configure them as trunk ports, allowing frames of VLAN 100 and VLAN 200 to pass through, so it is not repeated here. Port GE1/0/2 is the same as GE1/0/1, configured as access port, so it is not repeated here.

```
<HUAWEI> system-view
[HUAWEI] sysname SwitchC
[SwitchC] vlan batch 100 200   --Create VLAN 100 and VLAN 200
[SwitchC] interface gigabitethernet1/0/3
[SwitchC-GigabitEthernet1/0/3] port link-type trunk
[SwitchC-GigabitEthernet1/0/3] port trunk allow-pass vlan 100 200 --
Allow VLAN 100 and VLAN 200 frames to pass through
[SwitchC-GigabitEthernet1/0/3] quit
[SwitchC] interface gigabitethernet 1/0/2
[SwitchC-GigabitEthernet1/0/2] port link-type access
[SwitchC-GigabitEthernet1/0/2] port default vlan 100
[SwitchC-GigabitEthernet1/0/2] quit
```

7.4   Implement Inter-VLAN Routing

7.4.1   Why Is Implementing Inter-VLAN Routing Needed

VLANs isolate the Layer 2 broadcast domain, and thus isolate any traffic between individual VLANs, so traffic between different VLANs cannot directly cross the VLAN borders. Communication of devices in different VLANs requires the forwarding of messages from one VLAN to another through a Layer 3 device (router or Layer 3 switch). Layer 3 switches are capable of functions of VLAN classification, Layer 2 switching within VLANs, and inter-VLAN routing.

7.4.2   Implement Inter-VLAN Routing Through Routers

Multiple VLANs are created on the switch, and inter-VLAN communication can be enabled using a router. As shown in Fig. 7.32, two switches are connected using trunk links to create three VLANs. The router's ports, F0, F1, and F2, connect the access ports of the three VLANs, and the router forwards packets between the VLANs. A physical link of the router is figuratively called an "arm", and the computer gateways in VLAN 1, VLAN 2, and VLAN 3 are the addresses of the router's Port F0, F1, and F2, respectively. Figure 7.32 shows the use of a multi-armed router for inter-VLAN routing, and also shows how Computer A in VLAN 1 communicates with Computer L in VLAN 3. Pay attention to the VLAN tags of frames on the passing link. Think about the path of the frames and the VLAN tags as frames pass through each link when Computer H sends data to Computer L.

Connect the router's ports to the access ports of VLANs. A VLAN requires one physical port of the router, so that when adding VLANs you have to take into consideration whether the router's ports are sufficient. You can also connect the physical port of the router to the trunk port of the switch, as shown in Fig. 7.33, and divide the physical port of the router into multiple sub-interfaces, each of which corresponds to a VLAN. And then you can set the IP address of the sub-interface as the gateway of the corresponding VLAN, so one physical port is sufficient for inter-VLAN routing, which is using a one-armed router for inter-VLAN routing. Figure 7.33 shows the link the packet passes through when Computer A in VLAN 1 sends a packet to Computer L in VLAN 3.

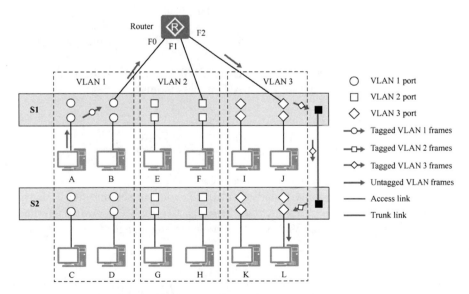

Fig. 7.32 Implement inter-VLAN routing with a multi-armed router

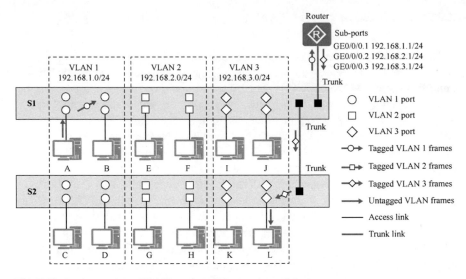

Fig. 7.33 Implement inter-VLAN routing with a one-armed router

7.4.3   Implement Inter-VLAN Routing Through a One-Armed Router

As shown in Fig. 7.34, the three VLANs across the switch have been created, and a router is connected to the LSW1 switch to realize inter-VLAN communication. You need to configure GE0/0/3 of Switch LSW1 as a trunk port to allow VLAN 1, VLAN 2 and VLAN 3 frames to pass. Configure the physical interface GE0/0/0 of router AR1 as the gateway for VLAN 1, configure the sub-interface GE0 /0/0.2 as the gateway for VLAN 2, and configure sub-interface GE0/0/0.3 as the gateway for VLAN 3.

Configure LSW1's interface GigabitEthernet0/0/3 connecting the router as a trunk interface to allow frames of all VLANs to pass thorugh.

```
[LSW1] interface GigabitEthernet0/0/3
[LSW1-GigabitEthernet0/0/3] port link-type trunk
[LSW1-GigabitEthernet0/0/3] port trunk allow-pass vlan all
```

All ports of the switch have a port-based VLAN ID (PVID), and the trunk port is no exception. By displaying GigabitEthernet0/0/3, you can see that the PVID of GigabitEthernet0/0/3 is 1. This interface removes the VLAN tag when sending VLAN 1 frames and adds the VLAN 1 tag when receiving untagged VLAN frames.

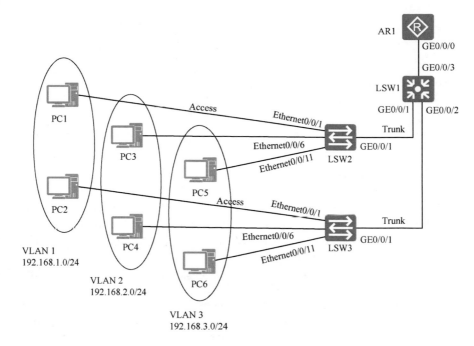

Fig. 7.34 Implement inter-VLAN routing by using a one-armed router

When sending frames to and receiving frames from other VLANs, the VLAN tags of the frames remain unchanged.

```
[LSW1]display interface GigabitEthernet0/0/3
GigabitEthernet 0/0/3current state : UP
Line protocol current state : UP
Description:
Switch Port, PVID :   1, TPID : 8100(Hex), The Maximum Frame Length
is 9216   --PVID is 1
```

Configure GE0/0/0 and the sub-interfaces of router AR1. Since the interface PVID of the switch connected to the router is VLAN 1, then this physical port is designated as a gateway for VLAN 1 and receives untagged VLAN frames. By adding a number after the physical port, it becomes a sub-interface. The sub-interface number is not necessarily the same as the VLAN number, but to make it easier to memorize, here the sub-interface number and VLAN number are usually set to be the same.

```
[AR1]interface GigabitEthernet0/0/0                      --Configure the
physical interface as the gateway of VLAN 1
  [AR1-GigabitEthernet0/0/0]ip address 192.168.1.1 24
  [AR1-GigabitEthernet0/0/0]quit
  [AR1]interface GigabitEthernet0/0/0.2          --Enter the
```

```
sub-interface
  [AR1-GigabitEthernet0/0/0.2]ip address 192.168.2.1 24
  [AR1-GigabitEthernet0/0/0.2]dot1q termination vid 2     --Specify
the VLAN corresponding to the sub-interface
  [AR1-GigabitEthernet0/0/0.2]arp broadcast enable        --Enable ARP
broadcast
  [AR1-GigabitEthernet0/0/0.2]quit
  [AR1]interface GigabitEthernet0/0/0.3
  [AR1-GigabitEthernet0/0/0.3]ip address 192.168.3.1 24
  [AR1-GigabitEthernet0/0/0.3]dot1q termination vid 3     --Specify
the VLAN corresponding to the sub-interface
  [AR1-GigabitEthernet0/0/0.3]arp broadcast enable
  [AR1-GigabitEthernet0/0/0.3]quit
```

The arp broadcast enable command is used to enable the ARP broadcast function of a sub-interface. The undo arp broadcast enable command is adopted to disable the ARP broadcast function of a sub-interface. By default, the ARP broadcast function of the sub-interface is not enabled.

If the arp broadcast enable command is not configured for the sub-interface, then the system will directly discard the IP message. At this time, the routes of this sub-interface can be regarded as black hole routes (black hole routes are routes that direct all irrelevant routes into them, so that the routes have no return). If the arp broadcast enable command is configured for the sub-interface, then the system will construct tagged ARP broadcast messages and then send them out from this sub-interface.

7.4.4   Implement Inter-VLAN Routing Through Layer 3 Switching

Layer 3 switching is a network technology that introduces a routing module into the switch, thereby replacing the traditional router so as to combine switching with routing. It improves the processing of IP routing by simplifying the IP forwarding process and using dedicated ASIC chips for hardware forwarding, so that most of the messages can be processed in hardware, and only a limited number of messages need to be forwarded by software. In this way, the forwarding performance of the whole system can be improved by a thousand times, and the cost of the devices of similar performance can also be significantly reduced.

If a switch is capable of Layer 3 switching, is it a switch or a router? This may be difficult for many readers to understand. You can think of a Layer 3 switch as a combination of a virtual router and a switch. There are several VLANs on the switch, and the virtual router has several virtual interfaces (Vlanif) connecting these VLANs.

As shown in Fig. 7.35, VLAN 1 and VLAN 2 are created on the Layer 3 switch, and the virtual router has two virtual interfaces Vlanif 1 and Vlanif 2, which are

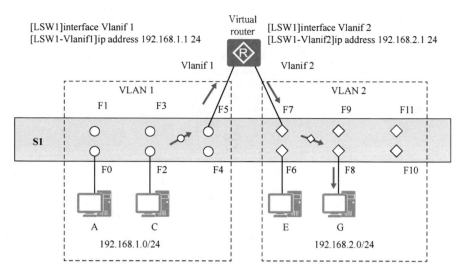

Fig. 7.35 Layer 3 switch equivalence diagram

equivalent to accessing an interface of VLAN 1 and an interface of VLAN 2, respectively. In the figure, interface F5 connects Vlanif 1, and interface F7 connects Vlanif 2. Figure 7.35 is purely for visual display; the virtual router is invisible, nor does it occupy the physical interface of the switch or the Vlanif interface for connection. All we can do is to configure the IP address and subnet mask for the virtual interface and make it a gateway of the VLAN so that computers in different VLANs can communicate with each other.

The experiment in 7.3.6 only configures VLANs across switches. Now we continue the experiment in 7.3.6 to implement inter-VLAN routing using a Layer 3 switch. In this example, LSW1 is a Layer 3 switch, and the LSW1 switch is configured to implement VLAN 1, VLAN 2, and VLAN 3 routing.

```
[LSW1] interface Vlanif 1
[LSW1-Vlanif1] ip address 192.168.1.1 24
[LSW1-Vlanif1] quit
[LSW1] interface Vlanif 2
[LSW1-Vlanif2] ip address 192.168.2.1 24
[LSW1-Vlanif2] quit
[LSW1] interface Vlanif 3
[LSW1-Vlanif3] ip address 192.168.3.1 24
[LSW1-Vlanif3] quit
```

Enter "display ip interface brief" to display the IP address information and the states Vlanif interface.

```
<LSW1>display ip interface brief
*down: administratively down
^down: standby
```

```
(1) : loopback
(s) : spoofing
The number of interface that is UP in Physical is 4
The number of interface that is DOWN in Physical is 1
The number of interface that is UP in Protocol is 4
The number of interface that is DOWN in Protocol is 1
Interface              IP Address/Mask   Physical   Protocol
MEth0/0/1                 unassigned       down       down
NULL0                     unassigned       up         up(s)
Vlanif1                192.168.1.1/24      up         up
Vlanif2                192.168.2.1/24      up         up
Vlanif3                192.168.3.1/24      up         up
```

7.5   Exercises

1. Which of the following descriptions of VLANs is incorrect ( )?

   A. VLANs divide the switch into multiple logically independent switches
   B. Trunk links can provide a common channel for communication of multiple VLANs
   C. VLANs expand the collision domain because they contain multiple switches
   D. A VLAN can span across switches

2. As shown in Fig. 7.36, when Host A communicates with Host C, the trunk link between SWA and SWB passes untagged VLAN frames, but when Host B communicates with Host D, the trunk link between SWA and SWB passes data frames with VLAN tag of 20.
   According to the above information, which of the following descriptions is correct ( ).

   A. Interface G0/0/2 on SWA does not allow VLAN 10 to pass
   B. The PVID of interface G0/0/2 on SWA is 10
   C. The PVID of interface G0/0/2 on SWA is 20
   D. The PVID of interface G0/0/2 on SWA is 1

Fig. 7.36 Communication
illustration (1)

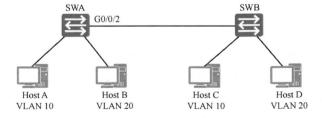

Fig. 7.37 Communication
illustration (2)

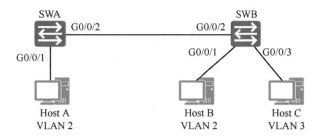

3. Which of the following descriptions of the forwarding state in Spanning Tree Protocol is incorrect ( )?

A. An interface in forwarding state can receive BPDU messages
B. An interface in forwarding state does not learn the source MAC addresses of messages
C. An interface in forwarding state can forward data packets
D. An interface in forwarding state can send BPDU messages

4. As shown in Fig. 7.37, the ports connecting the switch and the host are all access ports. The PVID of G 0/0/1 of SWA is 2, the PVID of G0/0/1 of SWB is 2, and the PVID of G0/0/3 of SWB is 3. G0/0/2 of SWA is a trunk port with a PVID of 2 and allows all VLANs to pass through. G0/0/2 of SWB is a trunk port with a PVID of 3 and allows all VLANs to pass.

If the IP addresses of hosts A, B and C are in the same network segment, then which of the following descriptions is correct ( )?

A. Host A can only communicate with Host B
B. Host A can only communicate with Host C
C. Host A can communicate with both Host B and Host C
D. Host A can neither communicate with Host B nor with Host C

5. When using a one-armed router to enable inter-VLAN communication, the common practice is to use sub-interfaces instead of directly using physical interfaces because ( ).

A. Physical interfaces cannot encapsulate 802.1Q
B. Sub-interface has a faster forwarding speed
C. Sub-interfaces can save physical interfaces
D. Sub-interfaces can be configured as access or trunk interfaces

6. The number of VLANs that can be created by using the "vlan batch 10 20" command and "vlan batch 10 to 20" command is ( ), respectively.

A. 2 and 2
B. 11 and 11

    C. 11 and 2

    D. 2 and 11

7. (Multi-selection) On the switch, which VLANs can be deleted by using the undo command? ( )

    A. VLAN 1

    B. VLAN 2

    C. VLAN 1024

    D. VLAN 4096

8. As shown in Fig. 7.38, two hosts communicate between VLANs through a one-armed router. When the sub-interface G0/0/1.2 of RTA receives a data frame Host B sends to Host A, which of the following operations will RTA perform? ( )

    A. RTA forwards the data frame directly through sub-interface G0/0/1.1

    B. RTA deletes the VLAN tag of 20 and sends the data frame out through interface G0/0/1.1

    C. RTA first removes the VLAN tag of 20, then adds a VLAN tag of 10 and sends the data frame out through the interface G0/0/1.1

    D. RTA will discard the data frame

9. Which of the following descriptions of VLAN configuration is correct ( )?

    A. VLAN 1 can be deleted from the switch

    B. VLAN 1 can be configured as Voice VLAN

    C. All trunk ports allow VLAN 1 data frames to pass thoguh by default

    D. Users can configure to use VLAN 4095

Fig. 7.38 Communication
illustration (3)

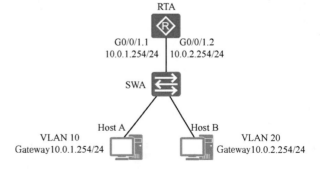

10. A switch receives a tagged VLAN data frame, but the destination MAC address of the frame is not found in the MAC address table. Which of the following descriptions is correct ( )?

   A. The switch broadcasts the frame to all interfaces
   B. The switch broadcasts the frame to all interfaces (except the receiving interface) in the VLAN where the frame is located
   C. The switch broadcasts the frame to all access interfaces
   D. The switch discards the frame

11. What does the port trunk allow-pass vlan all command do? ( )

   A. It allows data frames of all VLANs to pass through the port
   B. The peer port connected to the port must be configured with "port trunk permit vlan all" at the same time
   C. The connected peer device can dynamically determine which VLAN IDs are allowed to pass through
   D. If the port default vlan 3 command is configured for the connected remote device, the VLAN 3 between the two devices is not connected

12. Which of the following descriptions of the trunk port and the access port is correct ( )?

   A. Access port can only send untagged frames
   B. Access port can only send tagged frames
   C. Trunk port can only send untagged frames
   D. Trunk port can only send tagged frames

13. When an access port sends a message, it will ( ).

   A. Send a tagged message
   B. Strip the VLAN information of the message and send the message
   C. Add the VLAN information of the message and send message
   D. Add the PVID information of the port and then send the message

14. A switch port belongs to VLAN 5, and after deleting the port from VLAN 5, which VLAN does the port belong to?

   A. VLAN 0
   B. VLAN 1
   C. VLAN 1023
   D. VLAN 1024

Chapter 8
Advanced Ethernet Switching Technologies

Switch networking is often designed with a network architecture of dual aggregation layers and dual core layers to avoid single point of failure (e.g., network outage due to equipment damage). In this case, physical loops are formed. Once loops are formed, broadcast storms and MAC address flapping are generated in the network. Spanning tree protocol can prevent the formation of loops by blocking switch interfaces.

Networks formed using switches can configure multiple links into a single logical link to achieve traffic load balance and link redundancy, so as to save equipment costs. This is the link aggregation technology.

In certain network topologies, smart link can replace Spanning Tree Protocol (STP). Using Huawei's smart link private protocol, it is able to achieve fast (millisecond) link switching. Configuring monitor link on the upstream switch can support smart link in a satisfying way.

8.1 Spanning Tree Protocol

8.1.1 Loop Problem of Switch Networking

As shown in Fig. 8.1, enterprises form a LAN with Layer 2 architecture, and the access layer switch connects the aggregation layer switch. If the aggregation layer switch fails, the two access layer switches will not be able access each other, which is a single point of failure. For businesses of some enterprises and organizations, long-time network interruption caused by equipment failure is unacceptable. In order to avoid single point of failure of the aggregation layer switch, two aggregation layer switches are usually deployed during the networking, as shown in Fig. 8.2. When aggregation layer switch 1 fails, two switches in the access layer can communicate through aggregation layer switch 2.

© The Author(s) 2023
Huawei Technologies Co., Ltd., *Data Communications and Network Technologies*,
https://doi.org/10.1007/978-981-19-3029-4_8

Fig. 8.1 Single aggregation
layer network

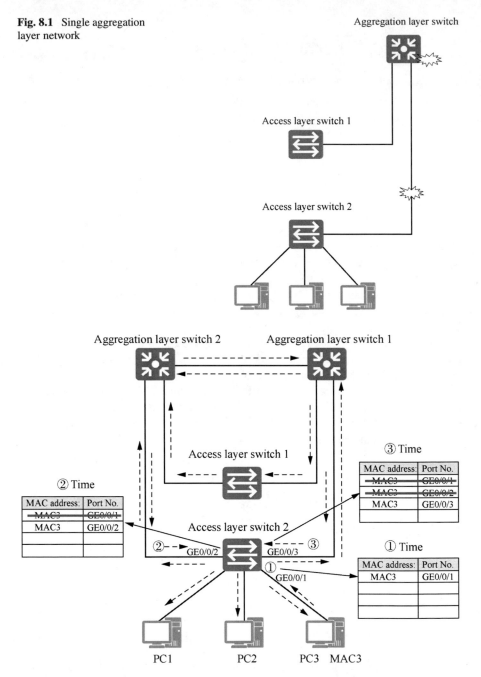

Fig. 8.2 Dual aggregation layer network

In this way, the network formed by the switches will then form a loop. As shown in Fig. 8.2, if Computer PC3 in the network sends a broadcast frame, the switch floods when it receives the broadcast frame, so the broadcast frame will continue to be forwarded in the loop, thus occupying the bandwidth of the switch port and consuming the resources of the switch. Computers in the network will keep receiving the frame repeatedly, and are unable to receive frames for normal communication. This is called a broadcast storm.

For a network formed by a switch, if there is a loop, there will also be a rapid flapping in the switch MAC address table. As shown in Fig. 8.2. At Time ①, port GE0/0/1 of access layer switch 2 receives a broadcast frame from PC3 and adds a mapping entry of MAC3 and Port GE0/0/1 to the MAC address table. The broadcast frame is sent out from GE0/0/3 and GE0/0/2 of access layer switch 2. At Time ②, GE0/0/2 of access layer switch 2 receives the broadcast frame from aggregation layer switch 2 and changes the port corresponding to MAC3 in the MAC address table to GE0/0/2. At Time ③, port GE0/0/3 of access layer switch 2 receives the broadcast frame from aggregation layer switch 1 and changes the port corresponding to MAC3 in the MAC address table to GE0/0/3. In this way, the contents of the table entry about the MAC address of PC3 in the MAC address table of access layer switch 2 will change endlessly and rapidly, which is MAC address flapping. Similarly, the MAC address table of access layer switch 1 and aggregation layer switches 1 and 2 will also experience the rapid flapping. The rapid flapping of the MAC address table will consume a lot of processing resources of the switch and may even cause the switch to breakdown.

This requires the switch to be able to effectively solve loops. Switches use the spanning tree protocol to prevent loops, and the Spanning Tree Protocol blocks loops by blocking ports.

8.1.2 Overview of the Spanning Tree Protocol

Spanning Tree Protocol can be applied to the establishment of tree topologies in computer networks, and its main function is to prevent redundant links from forming loops in switch networks. Spanning Tree Protocol is suitable for all vendors' network devices, which vary in configuration from vendor to vendor, but are consistent in principle and application effect.

By passing Bridge Protocol Data Units (BPDUs) among switches, the Spanning Tree algorithm is used to elect a root bridge, a root port, and a designated port to ultimately form a tree-structured network. Among them, the root port and designated port are in the forwarding state, while other ports are disabled. If the network topology is changed, the spanning tree topology will be regenerated. The existence of Spanning Tree Protocol meets core and aggregation layer networks' requirement for redundant links for network, and solves the "broadcast storm" problem and MAC address flapping problem caused by physical loops formed by redundant links.

Spanning Tree Protocol has the following three versions, and we can configure the version for Huawei switches, that is, specify the mode of Spanning Tree.

- Spanning Tree Protocol: Spanning Tree Protocol (STP) here refers to a version of Spanning Tree Protocol, which is a data link layer protocol defined in IEEE 802.1D. If the switch runs the Spanning Tree Protocol in STP mode, all traffic will take the same path regardless of how many VLANs are in the switch.
- Rapid Spanning Tree Protocol: in an STP network, if a switch is added or removed, or the bridge priority of a switch is changed, or a link fails, it is possible that the STP protocol will reselect the root bridge, reselect root ports for non-root bridges, and reselect the designated port for each link. Those ports that are in a blocking state may become forwarding ports. The process continues for tens of seconds (also known as convergence time), during which network disruptions may occur. To shorten the convergence time, IEEE 802.1w defines Rapid Spanning Tree Protocol (RSTP). This protocol has been improved a lot on the basis of STP to significantly reduce the convergence time to typically only a few seconds. STP is now rarely used in networks in reality and has been replaced by RSTP. One of the most important improvements of RSTP is that there are only three port states: discarding, learning and forwarding.
- Multiple Spanning Tree Protocol: both STP and RSTP have the same defect, that is, all VLANs in the LAN share one spanning tree, and the link will not carry any traffic once it is blocked, resulting in wasted bandwidth. Multiple Spanning Tree Protocol (MSTP) is a new type of spanning tree protocol defined in IEEE 802.1S. MSTP introduces the concepts of "Instance" and "Region". The so-called "instance" is a collection of multiple VLANs, and bundling multiple VLANs into a single instance is conducive to saving communication cost and resource usage. The topology of each instance of MSTP is calculated independently, and load balance can be achieved by these instances. When the protocol is used, multiple VLANs with the same topology can be mapped to an instance, and the forwarding state of these VLANs on ports will depend on the forwarding state of the corresponding instance in MSTP.

Huawei switch Spanning Tree Protocol uses MSTP mode by default, and this book will demonstrate how to change it to RSTP mode. Before illustrating the Spanning Tree Protocol, we also need to understand four basic terms, namely, bridge, bridge MAC address, bridge ID (BID), and port ID (PID).

1. Bridge

Due to performance limitations and other factors, early switches generally have only two forwarding ports (if the switch has more ports, its forwarding speed will be so slow that the receiver cannot receive), so then the switch is often called a "network bridge", or "bridge" for short. In IEEE terminology, the term "bridge" has been used to this day, but it does not specifically refer to switches with only two forwarding ports, but refers to switches with any number of ports in general. At present, "bridge" and "switch" are completely mixed, and they are also mixed in this book.

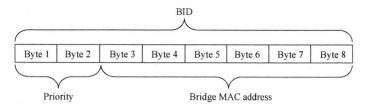

Fig. 8.3 BID composition

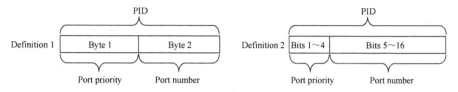

Fig. 8.4 PID composition

2. Bridge MAC address

A bridge has multiple forwarding ports, and each port has a MAC address. Usually, we take the MAC address of the port with the smallest port number as the MAC address of the whole bridge.

3. Bridge ID

As shown in Fig. 8.3, the bridge ID of a bridge (switch) consists of two parts. The first two bytes are the bridge priority, and the next six bytes are the bridge MAC address. The value of the bridge priority can be set manually, and the default value is 32,768.

4. Port ID

There are various ways to define the port ID of a port of a bridge (switch), two of which are given in Fig. 8.4. In the first definition, the port ID consists of two bytes, the first byte being the port priority of the port, and the second byte the port number. In the second definition, the port ID consists of 16 bits, the first four bits being the port priority of the port and the next 12 bits the port number. The value of the port priority can be set manually. The PID definition method used by different equipment vendors may vary. The PID of Huawei switches uses the first definition.

8.1.3   Basic Concepts and Working Principles of the Spanning Tree Protocol

The basic principle of Spanning Tree Protocol is that in a switch network with physical loops, the switch automatically generates a network topology without loops by running the STP protocol.

The task of STP is to find all links in the network and close all redundant links to prevent network loops. To this end, STP first needs to elect a root bridge (root

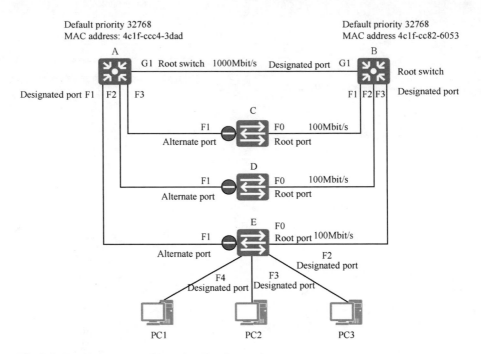

Fig. 8.5 Working process of Spanning Tree Protocol

switch), which is responsible for deciding the network topology. Once all switches agree to elect a switch as the root bridge, the remaining switches must select a unique root port. STP must also select a designated port for ports at both ends of each link connecting two switches (a network cable is a link), and the ports that are neither the root nor designated ports become the alternate ports, which do not forward frames of computer communication, thus preventing loops.

Next, the network topology shown in Fig. 8.5 is taken as an example to explain the working process of Spanning Tree Protocol. It is divided into four steps: electing the root bridge; selecting the root port (RP) for non-root bridges; selecting a designated port (DP) for the ports at both ends of each link; and blocking alternate ports (AP).

1. Elect the root bridge

   The root bridge is the root node of the STP tree. To generate an STP tree, a root bridge must first be identified. The root bridge is the logical center of the entire switch network, but not necessarily its physical center. When the network topology changes, the root bridge may also change.

   Switches running the STP protocol (shortened as STP switches) exchange STP protocol frames with each other, and the load data of these protocol frames are called bridge protocol data units (BPDUs). Although BPDU is the load data of STP protocol frames, it is not a network layer data unit; the generator, receiver, and processor of BPDU is STP switch itself, rather than the end computer. BPDU contains all the information related to STP protocol, and BID is one of them.

After the STP switches are first started, they all consider themselves as the root bridge and declare themselves as the root bridge in the BPDUs sent to other switches. When a switch receives BPDUs from other devices in the network, it compares the BID of the root bridge specified in the BPDU with its own BID. Switches continuously exchange BPDUs with each other while comparing BIDs until finally electing a switch with the smallest BID as the root bridge.

The network shown in Fig. 8.5 has five switches, A, B, C, D and E. The one with the smallest BID will be elected as the root bridge.

By default, BPDUs are sent every 2 s. In this example, Switch A and Switch B have the same priority, and the MAC address of Switch B is 4c1f-cc82-6053, which is smaller than that of Switch A, 4c1f-ccc4-3dad, so Switch B is more likely to be elected as the root bridge. In addition, you can specify the preferred switch to become the root bridge and alternate switches by changing the priority of switches. Usually, we designate in advance the switch with better performance and closer to the network center as the root bridge. In this example, it is clearly the optimal choice to make Switch B the preferred switch for the root bridge and Switch A the alternate switch.

2. Select the root port

Once the root bridge is determined, any other switches that do not become the root bridge are referred to as non-root bridges. A non-root bridge may have more than one port connected to the network. In order to ensure that the working path from a non-root bridge to the root bridge is optimal and unique, it is necessary to identify a "root port" from the ports of non-root bridges, and the root port functions as the port for message interaction between non-root bridges and the root bridge.

The first criterion for the election of the root port is the root path cost (RPC), which is used by the STP protocol as an important basis for determining the root port. The smaller the RPC, the more likely the port is selected. When the RPC is the same, the BIDs of the uplink switches are compared, that is, the BIDs of the BPDUs received by each port of the switch are compared, and the one with smaller value is more likely to be elected; when the BIDs of the uplink switches are the same, the PIDs of the local switches are compared, that is, the respective PIDs of each port of the local switches are compared, and the port with smaller value is more likely to be elected. There can be at most one root port on a non-root bridge device.

The Spanning Tree Protocol uses the root path cost as an important basis for determining the root port. In a network running the STP protocol, we refer the cumulative path cost of a switch's port to the root bridge (i.e., the sum of the path costs of all the links from that port to the root bridge) as the root path cost (RPC) of that port. The path cost of a link is related to the port bandwidth, and the larger the port bandwidth, the smaller the path cost. The correspondence between port bandwidth and path cost can be found in Table 8.1.

Table 8.1 Correspondence between port bandwidth and path cost

Port bandwidth	Path cost (IEEE 802.1t standard)
10 Mbit/s	2,000,000
100 Mbit/s	200,000
1000 Mbit/s	20,000
10 Gbit/s	2000

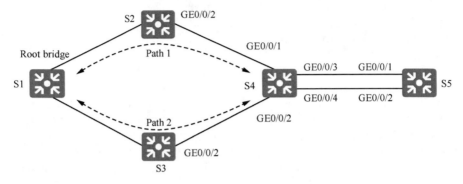

Fig. 8.6 Determine the root port

In Fig. 8.5, after identifying Switch B as the root bridge, and Switch A, C, D and E the non-root bridges, each non-root bridge has to choose the port closest to the root bridge (with the least cumulative cost) as the root port. Port G1 of Switch A and port F0 of Switch C, D and E in Fig. 8.5 become the root ports of these switches.

As shown in Fig. 8.6, S1 is the root bridge. Assuming that the costs of Path 1 and Path 2 are the same, then S4 will compare the bridge IDs of uplink devices S2 and S3. If S2's bridge ID is smaller than S3's, S4 will identify its G0/0/1 as its root port; if S3's bridge ID is smaller than S2's, S4 will identify its G0/0/2 as its root port.

For S5, assuming that the RPC of its port GE0/0/1 is the same as that of port GE0/0/2, since the uplink device of both ports is S4, S5 will also compare the PIDs of S4's ports GE0/0/3 and GE0/0/4. If the PID of S4's port GE0/0/3 is smaller than that of GE0/0/4, S5 will identify its GE0/0/1 as the root port. And if the PID of S4's port GE0/0/4 is smaller than that of GE0/0/3, then S5 will specify its GE0/0/2 as the root port.

3. Select the designated port

The root port ensures a unique and optimal working path between the switch and the root bridge. To prevent working loops, a designated port should also be determined for the ports connected to both ends of the network cable connecting the switch. The designated port is also determined by comparing RPCs, and the port with smaller RPC becomes the designated port; if their RPCs are the same, then BIDs are compared; if the BIDs are the same, PIDs of the devices are then compared, etc.; the one with smaller value becomes the designated port.

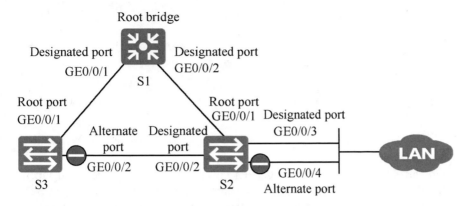

Fig. 8.7 Determine the designated port

As shown in Fig. 8.7, assume that S1 has been elected as the root bridge and that the costs of each link are equal. Obviously, the RPC of S3's port GE0/0/1 is smaller than that of S3's port GE0/0/2, so S3 identifies its port GE0/0/1 as its own root port. Similarly, the RPC of S2's port GE0/0/1 is smaller than that of S2's port GE0/0/2, so S2 identifies its port GE0/0/1 as its own root port.

For the network segment between S3's GE0/0/2 and S2's GE0/0/2, the RPC of S3's GE0/0/2 port is equal to that of S2's GE0/0/2 port, so it is necessary to compare S3's BID with S2's BID. Assuming that S2's BID is smaller than S3's BID, then S2's GE0/0/2 port will be determined as the designated port for the link between S3's GE0/0/2 and S2's GE0/0/2.

For network segment LAN, if LAN is a network formed with a hum, the hub is equivalent to network cables and does not participate in spanning tree. The only switch connected to LAN is S2. In this case, it is necessary to compare the PID of S2's port GE0/0/3 with the PID of port GE0/0/4. Assuming that the PID of port GE0/0/3 is smaller than that of port GE0/0/4, then S2's port GE0/0/3 will be determined as the designated port of the network segment LAN.

In the network shown in Fig. 8.5, since the connection bandwidth between Switch A and B is 1000 Mbit/s, then ports F1, F2, and F3 of Switch A have smaller RPCs than port F1 of Switch C, D and E. Therefore, ports F1, F2, and F3 of Switch A become designated ports. All ports of the root bridge are designated ports, and Switch E's ports F2, F3, and F4 connected to the computer are designated ports.

4. Block alternate ports

After determining the root port and the designated port, the remaining ports are the non-designated ports and non-root ports, which are collectively referred to as alternate ports. STP will logically block these alternate ports. Logical block means that these alternate ports are unable to forward frames generated and sent by the end computer, which are also known as user data frames. However, alternate ports can receive and process STP protocol frames, while the root and designated ports can both send and receive STP protocol frames and forward user data frames.

As shown in Figs. 8.5 and 8.7, once alternate ports are logically blocked, the STP tree (loop-free working topology) generation process is complete.

8.1.4   STP Message Types

The basic principle of STP: the topology of the network is determined by passing a special protocol message, the bridge protocol data unit (BPDU), between switches. STP protocol frames use the IEEE 802.3 encapsulation format, and their load data is called BPDUs. STP switches build and maintain STP trees by exchanging STP protocol frames, and rebuild new STP trees when the physical topology of the network changes. The STP protocol frames are generated, sent, received, and processed by the STP switch. STP protocol frames are a type of multicast frames whose multicast address is 01-80-c2-00-00-00.

There are two types of BPDUs: configuration BPDU and TCN (Topology Change Notification) BPDU. The former is used to calculate the loop-free spanning tree, and the latter is used to shorten the refresh time of MAC table entries (from the default 300 s to 15 s) when the Layer 2 network topology changes.

During the initial formation of the STP tree, each STP switch actively generates and sends configuration BPDUs at a regular interval (2 s by default). When the STP tree is formed and stabilized, only the root bridge actively generates and sends configuration BPDUs at a regular interval (2 s by default, which is called Hello Time and can be modified on the root switch). Accordingly, the non-root switch periodically receives configuration BPDUs from its own root port and is immediately triggered to generate its own configuration BPDUs, which are sent out from its own designated port. In the process, it seems that the configuration BPDUs sent by the root bridge "pass through" the other switches hop by hop.

If a link in the network fails, resulting in a change in the working topology, the switch at the point of failure can directly sense the change through the port state, but the other switches cannot directly sense the change. At this time, the switch at the point of failure keeps sending TCN BPDUs to the upstream switch through its root port with the Hello Time as the cycle until it receives an acknowledgment configuration BPDU from the upstream switch, and its TCA (Topology Change Acknowledgment) flag is set to 1. After receiving the TCN BPDU, on the one hand, the upstream switch will reply to the acknowledgment configuration BPDU through its designated port, and on the other hand, it will keep sending a TCN BPDU to its upstream switch through its root port with the Hello Time as the cycle. This process will be repeated until the root bridge receives the TCN BPDU. After receiving the TCN BPDU, the root bridge will send a configuration BPDU with a TC (Topology Change) flag location of 1 to advertise all switches that the network topology has changed. Figure 8.8 illustrates this process.

After receiving the configuration BPDU with TC flag location of 1, the switch realizes that the network topology has changed, which indicates that the content of

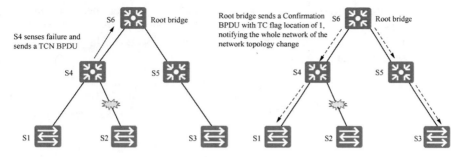

Fig. 8.8 Network topology change advertisement process

its own MAC address table is probably no longer correct. Then the switch will shorten the aging period of its own MAC address table (which is 300 s by default) to the length of Forward Delay (which is 15 s by default) to accelerate the aging of the original address table entries.

8.1.5 Port States of Spanning Tree

For a bridge or switch running STP, the port state will shift between the following five states.

1. Blocking: a blocked port is unable to forward frames, and can only listens for BPDUs. Blocking state is set to prevent the use of paths with loops. By default, all ports are in blocking state when the switch is powered up.
2. Listening: all switch ports listen for BPDUs so as to make sure no loops are generated on the network before transmitting data frames. Ports in the listening state are ready to forward data frames before the MAC address table is formed.
3. Learning: the switch port listens for BPDUs and learns all paths in the switch network. Ports in the learning state form a MAC address table, but cannot forward data frames. The forward delay is the time taken to transform the port from the listening state to the learning state, which is set to 15 s by default and can be viewed by executing the display spanning-tree command.
4. Forwarding: on the bridge ports, the port in the forwarding state sends and receives all data frames. If the interface is still the designated port or the root port at the end of the learning state, it enters the forwarding state.
5. Disabled: administratively speaking, an interface in the disabled state cannot forward frames or form STP. In the disabled state, the port is essentially non-functional.

   In most cases, switch ports are in the blocking or forwarding state. A forwarding port is the port with the lowest cost to the root bridge, but if the network topology changes (perhaps a link fails, or someone adds a new switch), the ports on the switch will be in the listening or learning state.

As mentioned earlier, blocking ports is a strategy to prevent network loops. Once the switch has decided on the optimal path to the root bridge, all other ports will be in the blocking state. The blocked ports can still receive BPDUs, but they cannot send any frames.

8.1.6   View and Configure STP

Set up an enterprise LAN with three switches, S1, S2 and S3, and the network topology is shown in Fig. 8.9. The operations below will enable the following functions.

1. Enable STP.
2. Determine the root bridge.
3. Check the port states.
4. Configure the STP mode as RSTP.
5. Specify S2 as the root bridge and S1 as the alternate root bridge.

Display the spanning tree operation states on S1.

```
[S1]display stp    --Display the configuration of STP
-------[CIST Global Info][Mode MSTP]-------          --Global
configuration, and the default STP mode is MSTP
  CIST Bridge        :32768.4c1f-cc82-6053           --Bridge ID of
```

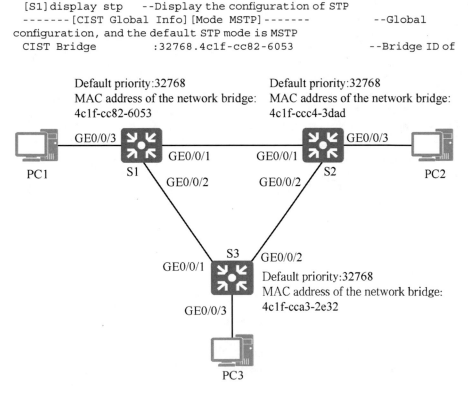

Fig. 8.9 Spanning tree experimental network topology

```
Switch, and 32768 is the priority
  Config Times        :Hello 2s MaxAge 20s FwDly 15s MaxHop 20
  Active Times        :Hello 2s MaxAge 20s FwDly 15s MaxHop 20
  CIST Root/ERPC      :32768.4c1f-cc82-6053 / 0        --Root bridge ID,
and S1 is the root bridge
  CIST RegRoot/IRPC   :32768.4c1f-cc82-6053 / 0
  CIST RootPortId     :0.0
  BPDU-Protection     :Disabled
  TC or TCN received  :7
  TC count per hello  :0
  STP Converge Mode   :Normal
  Time since last TC  :0 days 0h:3m:23s
  Number of TC        :8
  Last TC occurred    :GigabitEthernet0/0/1
  ----[Port1(GigabitEthernet0/0/1)][FORWARDING]----  --Port
GigabitEthernet 0/0/1 is in forwarding state
  Port Protocol       :Enabled
  Port Role           :Designated Port   --Designated port
  Port Priority       :128                        --Port priority, and the
default value is 128
  Port Cost(Dot1T )   :Config=auto / Active=20000
  Designated Bridge/Port   :32768.4c1f-cc82-6053 / 128.1
  Port Edged          :Config=default / Active=disabled
  Point-to-point      :Config=auto / Active=true
  Transit Limit       :147 packets/hello-time
  Protection Type     :None
  Port STP Mode       :MSTP
  Port Protocol Type  :Config=auto / Active=dot1s
  BPDU Encapsulation  :Config=stp / Active=stp
  PortTimes           :Hello 2s MaxAge 20s FwDly 15s RemHop 20
  TC or TCN send      :1
  TC or TCN received  :0
  BPDU Sent           :96
    TCN: 0, Config: 0, RST: 0, MST: 96
  BPDU Received       :1
    TCN: 0, Config: 0, RST: 0, MST: 1
    ......
```

Enter "display stp brief" to display STP port state.

```
[S1]display stp brief
  MSTID  Port                   Role  STP State   Protection
    0    GigabitEthernet0/0/1   DESI  FORWARDING  NONE       --
Designated port, forwarding state
    0    GigabitEthernet0/0/2   DESI  FORWARDING  NONE       --
Designated port, forwarding state
    0    GigabitEthernet0/0/3   DESI  FORWARDING  NONE       --
Designated port, forwarding state
```

All ports on the root switch are designated ports, among which GigabitEthernet0/0/3 is connected to the computer and will also participate in the spanning tree protocol.

Note: ① if there is no loop between the switches, you can enter "stp disable" to disable the spanning tree protocol, so that the switch will be powered on and the ports will enter the forwarding state soon, and there will be no spanning tree process.

```
[S1] stp disable
```

② Enter "stp enable" to enable spanning tree protocol, which is enabled by default on Huawei switches.

```
[S1] stp enable
```

The following commands can be used to view the STP modes supported by Huawei switches and configure the STP mode as RSTP.

```
[S1] stp mode ?              --View the STP modes supported
  mstp  Multiple Spanning Tree Protocol (MSTP) mode
  rstp  Rapid Spanning Tree Protocol (RSTP) mode
  stp   Spanning Tree Protocol (STP) mode
[S1] stp mode rstp          --Set the STD mode as RSTP
```

Although STP automatically elects the root bridge, usually, the network administrator will pre-designate the switch with better performance and closer to the network center as the root bridge. You can designate the root bridge and the alternate root bridge by changing the priority of the switches.

The following changes the priority of Switch S2 to make it a preferred choice for the root bridge, and changes the priority of S1 to make it the alternate root bridge.

```
[S2] stp priority ?   --View the value range of priority
  INTEGER<0-61440>  Bridge priority, in steps of 4096  --Value range
of priority, which is multiples of 4096
[S2] stp priority 0                       --Set the priority to 0
[S1] stp priority 4096                    --Set the priority to 4096
```

You can also use the following command to set the priority of S2 to 0.

```
[S2] stp root primary
```

You can also use the following command to set the priority of S1 to 4096.

```
[S1] stp root secondary
```

View the configuration information of STP on S2 and observe the mode of Spanning Tree Protocol, the root bridge ID and its priority.

```
[S2]display stp
-------[CIST Global Info][Mode RSTP]-------          --The STP mode is
RSTP
 CIST Bridge          :0    .4c1f-ccc4-3dad          --Root bridge ID, and
the priority is 0
 Config Times         :Hello 2s MaxAge 20s FwDly 15s MaxHop 20
 Active Times         :Hello 2s MaxAge 20s FwDly 15s MaxHop 20
 CIST Root/ERPC       :0    .4c1f-ccc4-3dad / 0
 CIST RegRoot/IRPC    :0    .4c1f-ccc4-3dad / 0
 ...
```

View the STP bried on S3, from which you can see the role and state of the ports.

```
<S3>display stp brief
 MSTID  Port                      Role    STP State       Protection
    0    GigabitEthernet0/0/1     ALTE    DISCARDING            NONE
    0    GigabitEthernet0/0/2     ROOT    FORWARDING            NONE
    0    GigabitEthernet0/0/3     DESI    FORWARDING            NONE
```

You can see that GigabitEthernet0/0/1 is an alternate (ALTE) port in discarding state. GigabitEthernet0/0/2 is a root port in forwarding state. GigabitEthernet 0/0/3 is a designated (DESI) port in forwarding state.

Note: ROOT means the port is a root port; ALTE is the abbreviation of the word Alternative, and the port is an alternate port; DESI is the abbreviation of the word Designation, and the port is a designated port.

The following operation disables port GigabitEthernet 0/0/3 of the switch. You can see that the initial state of the port is discarding, and 15 s later, the port enters the learning state, and only after 30 s does it finally enter the forwarding state.

```
[S3]display stp brief
 MSTID  Port                      Role    STP State       Protection
    0    GigabitEthernet0/0/1     ALTE    DISCARDING         NONE
    0    GigabitEthernet0/0/2     ROOT    FORWARDING         NONE
    0   GigabitEthernet0/0/3    DESI   FORWARDING    NONE    --In
forwarding state
 [S3]interface GigabitEthernet 0/0/3
 [S3-GigabitEthernet0/0/3]shutdown                           --
Shutdown port
 [S3-GigabitEthernet0/0/3]undo shutdown                      --
Enable port
 <S3>display stp brief
 MSTID  Port                      Role    STP State       Protection
    0    GigabitEthernet0/0/1     ALTE    DISCARDING         NONE
    0    GigabitEthernet0/0/2     ROOT    FORWARDING         NONE
    0   GigabitEthernet0/0/3    DESI   DISCARDING    NONE    --
Initial state
```

8.2   Link Aggregation

8.2.1   Basic Concepts of Link Aggregation

First, let's clarify some common concepts. Readers may often hear such concepts as standard Ethernet port, fast Ethernet (FE) port, 100 Gigabit port, Gigabit Ethernet (GE) port, and 10 Gigabit port. So, what exactly do these concepts mean?

In fact, these concepts are related to the specifications of Ethernet technology, especially to the bandwidth specifications of Ethernet ports. When IEEE develops specifications on the information transmission rate of Ethernet, the rate is almost always incremented by a factor of 10. At present, the standardized Ethernet port bandwidths are 10 Mbit/s, 100 Mbit/s, 1000 Mbit/s (1 Gbit/s), 10 Gbit/s and 100 Gbit/s. Increasing it by 10 times can not only well match the development of microelectronics and optical technology, but also control the confusing nature about the specifications on Ethernet information transmission rate. Imagine if the IEEE launches a specification of information transmission rates of 415 Mbit/ today and another one of 624 Mbit/s tomorrow. The manufacturers of Ethernet network interface cards must be suffering. And, when it comes to actually building Ethernet, the issue of matching the bandwidth of the ports at both ends of the Ethernet link can be a mess.

The concept of an Ethernet link corresponds to the concept of an Ethernet port. For example, if the ports at both ends of a link are GE ports, the link is called a GE link; if the ports at both ends of a link are FE ports, the link is called a FE link; and so on.

Now we are going to introduce what is link aggregation technology. Figure 8.10 illustrates the network structure of a company, where the access layer switches and aggregation layer switches are connected using GE links. If you intend to increase the connection bandwidth of the access layer switches and aggregation layer switches, theoretically, you can add another GE link, but the Spanning Tree Protocol will block a port of one of the links.

When devices at both ends of a link need to bundle multiple links into one logical link to increase the bandwidth of the link, Ethernet link aggregation (Eth-Trunk) technology is used. Eth-Trunk is also known as Link Aggregation, Link Trunking, and Link Bonding. It is important to note that the link aggregation technologies mentioned here are all for Ethernet links.

A link aggregation port can be used as an ordinary Ethernet port, and its difference with the ordinary Ethernet port is that when forwarding data, the link aggregation port (logical port) needs to select one or more ports from the member ports (physical ports) for data forwarding so as to achieve traffic load balance and link redundancy. As shown in Fig. 8.11, if a 2000 Mbit/s aggregation link built by two 1000 Mbit/s links is enough to meet the requirements, there is no need to purchase equipment for 10,000 Mbit/s interfaces.

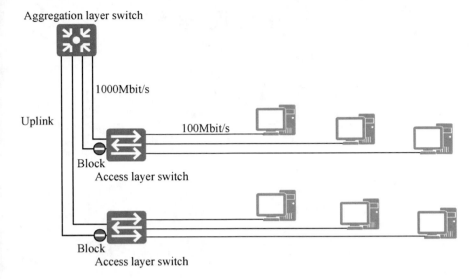

Fig. 8.10 Block a port of one of the links of the multi-uplink STP

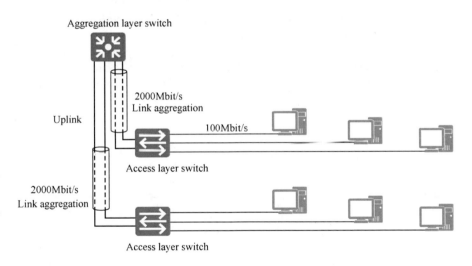

Fig. 8.11 Link aggregation

8.2.2 Application Scenarios of Link Aggregation Technology

In the example mentioned in the previous section, we applied the link aggregation technology between two switches. In fact, link aggregation technology can also be applied between switches and routers, between routers, between switches and servers, between routers and servers, and between servers, as shown in Fig. 8.12. Note that, in theory, link aggregation is also possible to be used on personal

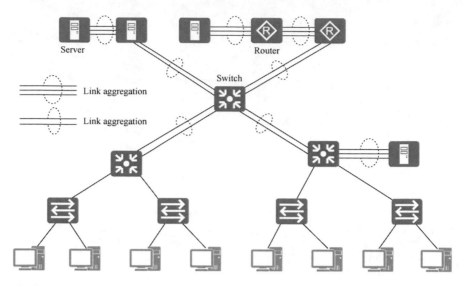

Fig. 8.12 Application scenarios of link aggregation technology

computers (PCs), but no one will actually implement it due to factors such as costs. In addition, from the perspective of principle, a server is nothing but a high-performance computer. From the point of view of network applications, the server is imperative, so it is necessary to ensure that the connection between the server and other devices is highly reliable. Therefore, link aggregation technology is often required on servers.

8.2.3   Basic Principles of Link Aggregation

As shown in Fig. 8.13, Switch A and Switch B are connected by three physical links, which are configured as an aggregation link. In each switch, there is an aggregated port at each end of the aggregation link, and each aggregation port has a queue of frames to be sent and a queue to be received. The following is an example of how an aggregation link can enable traffic load balance by sending frames from Computer A to Computer C.

The process of Computer A sending three frames to Computer C over the aggregation link as follows: ① Computer A sends three frames to Computer C, that is, I, Love, You. ② These three frames go to the frame sending queue at the aggregation port of Switch A. ③ Then the frames from the sending queue are distributed to the three physical ports through the frame distributor. ④ The frames received by the three physical ports go to receiving queue at the aggregation port of Switch B. ⑤ Then the frames from the receiving queue are sent to the port connected to Computer C. In this way, frames pass through all three ports, making full use of the bandwidth of all three links. This is the basic principle of link aggregation, which

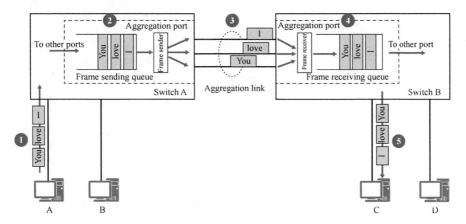

Fig. 8.13 The process of sending and receiving frames on an aggregation link

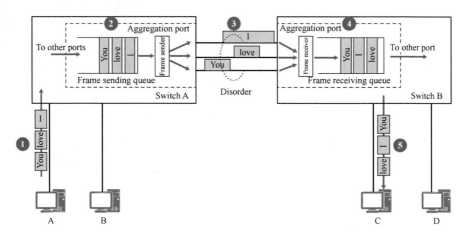

Fig. 8.14 Harmful disorder

is in fact "traffic sharing". In addition, if a member link of the aggregation link fails and goes down, the total traffic of the aggregation link will continue to be shared among the other member links.

The link aggregation technology seems to be simple but it is not. One of the main problems that link aggregation technology needs to face is the "disorder".

As shown in Fig. 8.14, frames in the sending queue of Switch A go through different physical links and their order may change when they reach Switch B. Some frames are longer and some are shorter, resulting in the following situation: frame "I" is sent before frame "love", but at the receiving end, frame "love" is shorter and is received first, so the order in the receiving queue becomes "love", "I", "you"; Computer C receives frames in the order of "love" "I" "you", and is unable to receive them in order, and this disorder is a harmful disorder.

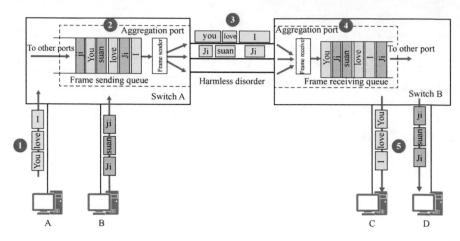

Fig. 8.15 Harmless disorder

The problem of harmful disorder can be solved by having all frames arriving at the same destination MAC address by the same physical link in the aggregation link. As shown in Fig. 8.15, frames to Computer C (frames whose destination MAC address is the MAC address of Computer C) are sent to Switch B through the link on the top, and frames to Computer D are sent to Switch B through the link in the middle. Although there is also disorder on the aggregation link, the frames reaching Computer C are in the correct order, and the frames to Computer D are in the correct order as well. This kind of disorder is called a harmless disorder. In this case, load balance is not guaranteed for multiple physical links of the aggregation link. As shown in Fig. 8.15, there is no traffic on the physical link at the bottom.

8.2.4 Modes of Link Aggregation

In order to make the link aggregation port work properly, it is required that all peer ports of member ports of local link aggregation ports belong to the same device end and have joined the same link aggregation port.

Similar to setting the port bandwidth, there are two ways to establish link aggregation: manual configuration and dynamic negotiation by both parties. In the context of Huawei Eth-trunk, the former is called Manual Mode, while the latter is named as LACP Mode according to the negotiation protocol, Link Aggregation Control Protocol.

1. Manual mode

Manual mode means that the administrator creates an Eth-trunk on a device and then adds multiple ports connected to the same switch to this Eth-trunk according to their needs, and then performs the corresponding operations on the peer switch. With Eth-trunk configured in manual mode, devices will not

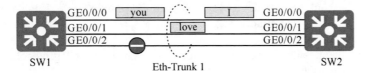

Fig. 8.16 In manual mode, whether the port is working properly can only be determined by its physical state

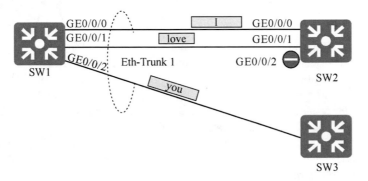

Fig. 8.17 In manual mode, Eth-trunk error connection results in abnormal communication

exchange information with each other for establishing Eth-trunk. Instead, they will only bundle links according to the administrator's configuration, and then send data through the bundled link by load balance.

Establishing Eth-Trunk by manual mode is inflexible. It can only determine whether the port is working properly by its physical state, and is unable to detect misconfigurations or incorrect links. If one of the links in a manually-configured Eth-trunk fails, then both devices can detect this and stop using that failed link and continue to use the normal link to send data. Although a portion of the bandwidth is unavailable due to the link failure, the effectiveness of the communication is still ensured, as shown in Fig. 8.16.

As shown in Fig. 8.17, the administrator mistakenly connects port GE0/0/2 of switch SW1 in Fig. 8.16 to switch SW3. SW1 will not know that the port is connected to other switch and still use port GE0/0/2 for load balance, so obviously frame "you" cannot be sent to SW2, thus resulting in abnormal communication. If LACP mode is used, SW1 and SW2 will automatically negotiate by exchanging LACP protocol frames to ensure that the peer is a member port of the same device and of the same aggregation port.

2. LACP mode

LACP mode is a link aggregation mode using LACP protocol. Devices interact with each other through link aggregation control protocol data unit (LACPDU), and the protocol negotiation ensures that the peer is a member port of the same device and the same aggregation port. It is not complicated to configure Eth-Trunk using LACP mode. The administrator only needs to first create Eth-Trunk ports on devices at both ends, then configure this Eth-Trunk port as LACP mode, and finally add the physical ports to be bundled into this Eth-Trunk.

If low-end devices of older generation do not support LACP protocol, manual mode can be used.

8.2.5   Load-Balance Mode

Eth-Trunk supports load balance based on the IP address or MAC address of the message. Different modes (locally valid, and effective for outbound messages) can be configured to share the data flow among different member ports.

Common load-balance modes are: source IP address, destination IP address, source MAC address, destination MAC address, source and destination IP address, as well as source and destination MAC address. In the actual service, users need to configure the appropriate load-balance mode according to the characteristics of service traffic. If a certain parameter in the service traffic changes frequently (that is, the number is large), you should select a load-balance mode with a higher load balance degree regarding this parameter.

If the IP address of the message changes more frequently, then a load-balance mode based on the source IP address, destination IP address or source and destination IP address is more conducive to reasonably balancing the traffic load among physical links.

If the MAC address of the message changes more frequently and the IP address is relatively fixed, then the load-balance mode based on source MAC address, destination MAC address or source and destination MAC address is more conducive to reasonably balancing traffic load among physical links.

If the load-balance mode selected does not match the actual service characteristics, it may lead to uneven traffic sharing, that is, some member links are heavily loaded while the rest of the member links are idle. For example, if source MAC address mode is selected in a scenario where the source IP address of the message changes frequently but the source MAC address is fixed, all traffics will be shared on a single member link.

Let's look at an example: as shown in Fig. 8.18, computers in Area A access a server in Area B. There are a lot of computers in Area A and a lot of source MAC addresses. The link aggregation port on SW1 is configured to use the load-balance mode based on source MAC address, so that the traffic of computers in Area A accessing the server in Area B will be shared relatively evenly among three physical links. Then link aggregation port on SW2 cannot be configured to use the load-balance mode based on source MAC address. If you do, there will be only one source MAC address (one server), and all traffic to Area A will go through only one physical link. For traffic from Area B to Area A, since there are a lot of destination MAC addresses, and SW2 is configured to use the load-balance mode based on destination MAC address. In this way, the traffic sent by the server to the computers in Area A is shared comparatively evenly over three physical links.

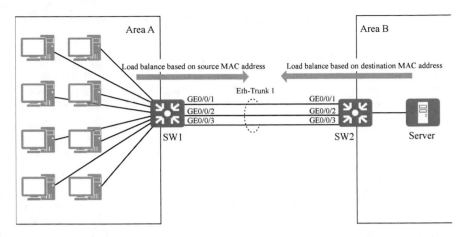

Fig. 8.18 Load-balance mode based on source MAC address and destination MAC address

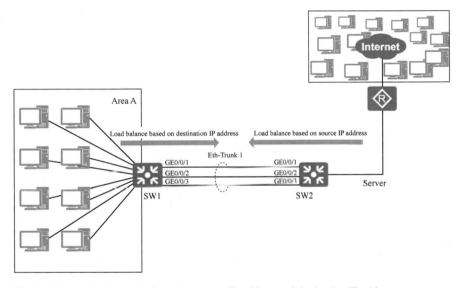

Fig. 8.19 Load-balance mode based on source IP address and destination IP address

Figures 8.18 and 8.19 are similar, and both have Area A. Computers in Area A need to access the Internet through the link aggregation port. How to choose the load-balance mode for the link aggregation ports of two switches SW1 and SW2?

Computers in Area A access the Internet, and there are more computers in the Internet than in Area A. In other words, for the traffic of computers in Area A accessing the Internet, the parameter of destination IP address is the largest, so the load-balance mode based on destination IP address is configured for the link aggregation port of SW1, and the load-balance mode based on source IP address is configured for the link aggregation port of SW2.

8.2.6   An Example of Link Aggregation Configuration

Port bandwidths, duplex modes, and VLAN configurations of the physical ports joining the link aggregation port must be the same. The ports must all be access ports or all be trunk ports. If they are access ports, the default VLAN must be the same, and if they all trunk ports, then the PVID and the allowed VLAN of the port must be the same.

As shown in Fig. 8.20, three links connected to GE0/0/1, GE0/0/2, GE0/0/3 of switch SW1 and GE0/0/1, GE0/0/2, GE0/0/3 of switch SW2 are configured as one aggregation link. The load-balance mode is based on the source MAC address.

Create interface Eth-Trunk 1 on SW1, and the interface number should be the same as that of SW2. Configure the working mode of interface Eth-Trunk 1 as manual mode, add interfaces from GE0/0/1 to GE0/0/3 to interface Eth-Trunk 1, and configure Eth-Trunk 1 as a trunk link to allow all VLANs to pass through.

```
[SW1] interface Eth-Trunk 1
[SW1-Eth-Trunk1] mode ?                      --View working mode supported by
aggregation link
 lacp-static   Static working mode
 manual     Manual working mode
[SW1-Eth-Trunk1] mode manual load-balance         --Configure link
aggregation mode as manual mode
[SW1-Eth-Trunk1] trunkport GigabitEthernet 0/0/1 to 0/0/3
[SW1-Eth-Trunk1] load-balance ?              --View load-balance modes
supported
 dst-ip    According to destination IP hash arithmetic
 dst-mac    According to destination MAC hash arithmetic
 src-dst-ip  According to source/destination IP hash arithmetic
 src-dst-mac According to source/destination MAC hash arithmetic
 src-ip    According to source IP hash arithmetic
 src-mac    According to source MAC hash arithmetic
[SW1-Eth-Trunk1] load-balance src-mac         --Configure load-balance
mode based on source MAC address
[SW1-Eth-Trunk1] port link-type trunk
```

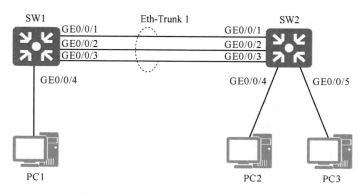

Fig. 8.20 Eth-Trunk configuration illustration

```
[SW1-Eth-Trunk1]port trunk allow-pass vlan all
[SW1-Eth-Trunk1]quit
```

Create interface Eth-Trunk 1 on SW2, and the interface number should be the same as that of SW1. Configure the working mode of interface Eth-Trunk 1 as manual mode, add interfaces from GE0/0/1 to GE0/0/3 to interface Eth-Trunk 1, and configure Eth-Trunk 1 as a trunk link to allow all VLANs to pass through.

```
[SW2]interface Eth-Trunk 1
[SW2-Eth-Trunk1]mode manual load-balance
[SW2-Eth-Trunk1]trunkport GigabitEthernet 0/0/1 to 0/0/3
[SW2-Eth-Trunk1]load-balance src-mac
[SW2-Eth-Trunk1]port link-type trunk
[SW2-Eth-Trunk1]port trunk allow-pass vlan all
[SW2-Eth-Trunk1]quit
```

Enter "display eth-trunk 1" to view the configuration information of Eth-Trunk 1.

```
[SW1]display eth-trunk 1
Eth-Trunk1's state information is:
WorkingMode: NORMAL      Hash arithmetic: According to SA
Least Active-linknumber: 1 Max Bandwidth-affected-linknumber: 8
Operate status: up      Number Of Up Port In Trunk: 3
--------------------------------------------------------------
PortName            Status    Weight
GigabitEthernet0/0/1      Up      1
GigabitEthernet0/0/2      Up      1
GigabitEthernet0/0/3      Up      1
```

In the above echo message, "WorkingMode:NORMAL" indicates that the link aggregation mode of interface Eth-Trunk 1 is NORMAL, that is, manual mode. "Least Active-linknumber:1" means that the lower limit threshold of the member links in Up state is 1. The minimum number of active interfaces is set to ensure the minimum bandwidth. When the bandwidth is too small, some services that have high demand for link bandwidth will be abnormal. In this situation, the Eth-Trunk is cut off, and the service is switched to other paths through the high reliability of the network itself, so as to ensure the normal operation of the service. "Operate status: up" indicates that the status of Eth-Trunk 1 interface is "Up". From the information in the bottom lines, you can see that Eth-Trunk 1 contains three member ports, GigabitEthernet0/0/1, GigabitEthernet0/0/2, and GigabitEthernet0/0/3.

8.3   Smart Link

Smart Link private protocol of Huawei can replace the STP protocol in certain scenarios and can achieve fast (millisecond-level) link switching.

8.3.1 Basic Principles of Smart Link

As shown in Fig. 8.21, access layer switch S4 has N user terminals connected to it, and S4 is connected to aggregation layer switches S2 and S3 via Link2-4 and Link 3-4, respectively. S2 and S3 are connected to core layer switch S1 via Link1-2 and Link1-3, respectively, and S1 is connected to the Internet via a router. To eliminate working loops, STP protocol is run on each switch. Assuming that the links in the STP tree contain Link1-2, Link1-3, and Link2-4, then when Link2-4 is disconnected, Link3-4 joins the STP tree, thus ensuring the connectivity of the network.

The convergence of Spanning Tree Protocol is relatively slow, which usually takes seconds. If some links in the network are high-speed links, a large amount of data will be lost when STP switches links. If some services sensitive to packet loss are run in the user terminal, then these services will be seriously impacted.

To address the above problems, Huawei has designed and implemented a private protocol called Smart Link, whose main role is to replace the STP protocol in certain scenarios and enable fast (millisecond-level) link switching. A Smart Link group consists of two interfaces, one of which is the master interface and the other is the slave interface. Under normal conditions, only the master interface is active for forwarding, while the slave interface is blocked and in standby (inactive) state. When the master interface fails, the Smart Link group automatically blocks the master

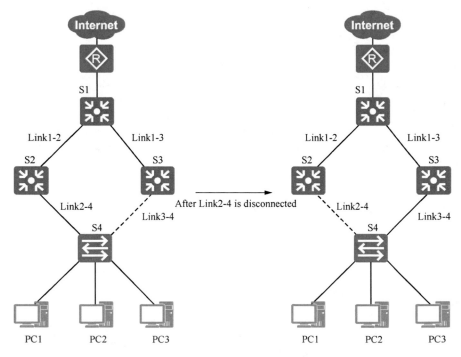

Fig. 8.21 Eliminate working loops using STP

interface and immediately switches the state of the slave interface from inactive to active. Smart Link technology is commonly used in dual uplink networking environments.

As shown in Fig. 8.22, a Smart Link group is configured on switch S4, with GE1/0/1 as its master interface and GE1/0/2 as its slave interface. Under normal circumstances, master interface GE1/0/1 is active for forwarding and the slave interface GE1/0/2 in the standby state, so the links that are really working are Link1-3, Link1-2, and Link2-4, while Link3-4 is in the interrupted state, which prevents the loops. If master interface GE1/0/1 suddenly fails, or if master interface GE1/0/1 senses Link2-4 is interrupted, then the Smart Link group immediately sets master interface GE1/0/1 to the blocking state, while switching slave interface GE1/0/2 from the standby state to the forwarding state. In this way, the links that are really working immediately become Link1-3, Link1-2, and Link3-4, while Link2-4 is in the interrupted state. In this way, the network connectivity is ensured, and meanwhile loops are prevented. Note that the Link protocol is mutually exclusive with the STP protocol, so there is no STP running in the network shown in Fig. 8.22.

From the above description, we can see that Smart Link technology works in a very simple way. However, the real situation may not be as simple as we think. Next, an example will be used to illustrate the main problems that Smart Link technology needs to solve.

Fig. 8.22 Basic principle of Smart Link

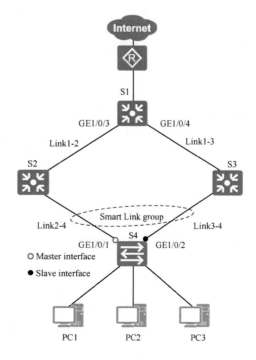

Fig. 8.23 Situation at
moment *t*

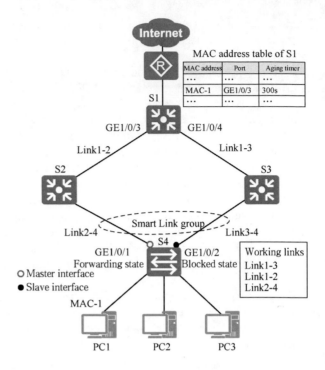

As shown in Fig. 8.23, a Smart Link group is configured on switch S4 with
GE1/0/1 as its master interface and GE1/0/2 its slave interface. The network is
currently in a normal working state, i.e., Link3-4 is interrupted and Link1-3,
Link1-2 and Link2-4 are all working. In addition, we assume that the MAC address
of PC1's network interface is MAC-1.

Suppose that at moment *t*, PC1 sends a frame to the Internet, then this frame must
pass through Link2-4 and Link1-2 and then enter S1 from port GE1/0/3 of switch S1,
and then S1 will forward this frame to the router. According to the MAC address
learning mechanism of the switch, at moment *t* (ignoring the time this frame takes to
move from PC1 to S1), the table entry about MAC-1 on S1 will become: the
corresponding interface is GE1/0/3 and the value of aging timer (countdown
timer) is 300 s (the default value).

Then, as shown in Fig. 8.24, we assume that at moment *t* + 5 s, Link2-4 is
interrupted, and master interface GE1/0/1 of S4 is immediately blocked, and slave
interface GE1/0/2 is immediately switched to the forwarding state. The working
links at this time become Link1-3, Link1-2, Link3-4. Meanwhile, the table entry
about MAC-1 on S1 will become: the corresponding interface is GE1/0/3 and the
value of aging timer is 295 s.

Now, let's assume that the time has transitioned from 5 s to 10 s, and let's assume
that PC1 has not sent any frames outward during this period, so there is still a table
entry about MAC-1 in the MAC address table on S1, in which the interface
corresponding to MAC-1 is still GE1/0/3, but the aging timer value has changed

Fig. 8.24 Situation at
moment $t + 5$ s

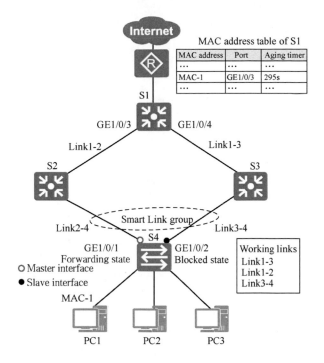

to 290 s, as shown in Fig. 8.25. For moment $t + 10$s, we assume that S1 receives a frame with the destination MAC address MAC-1 from the router. Obviously, after querying its own MAC address table, S1 will forward this frame out of its interface GE1/0/3 instead of its interface GE1/0/4. However, we know that Link2-4 is interrupted at this point, so the frame cannot be delivered to PC1, which results in a frame loss that we hate to see. In an extreme case, suppose that PC1 has not sent any frames during the period from $t + 10$s to $t + 300$ s, that is, the interface corresponding to MAC-1 in the MAC address table on S1 has always been GE1/0/3, then all frames sent by the router to S1 with MAC-1 as the destination MAC address during this period will be lost.

How does Smart Link avoid the above-mentioned frame loss? To address this problem, Smart Link defines a protocol frame called a flush frame, whose destination MAC address is a multicast MAC address 01-0f-e2-00-00-04. The main purpose of a flush frame is to notify the switch concerned to immediately clear the error table entry in the MAC address table.

As shown in Fig. 8.26, assume that the time reverts to moment $t + 5$ s. At this moment, Link2-4 is interrupted, and master interface GE1/0/1 of S4 is immediately blocked, while slave interface GE1/0/2 is immediately switched to the forwarding state. At this point the working links become Link1-3, Link1-2, Link3-4. Meanwhile, the table entry about MAC-1 on S1 reads: the corresponding interface is GE1/0/3 and the value of aging timer is 295 s. Now, with the Smart Link protocol, S4 immediately sends a flush frame through its slave interface GE1/0/2. After

Fig. 8.25 Situation at moment $t + 10$s

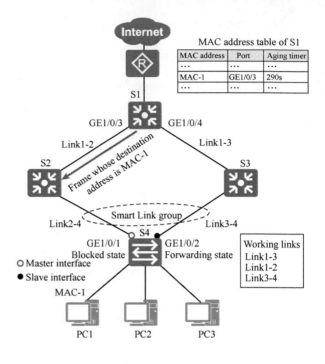

Fig. 8.26 Return to moment $t + 5$ s

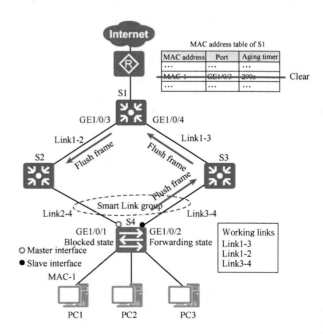

receiving the flush frame and analyzing it, S1 immediately clears the table entry about MAC-1 in its MAC address table. The structure of the flush frame and the control information it carries are not described here.

Next, assume that the time again progresses from moment $t + 5$ s to moment $t + 10$s, and assume that PC1 has not sent any frames during this time, so there will be no table entry about MAC-1 in the MAC address table of S1, as shown in Fig. 8.27. At moment $t + 10$s, we assume that S1 receives a frame from the router with a destination MAC address of MAC-1. Obviously, S1 cannot find a table entry about MAC-1 in its own MAC address table, so it floods this frame out of its interfaces GE1/0/3 and GE1/0/4. Clearly, the frame with MAC-1 as its destination MAC address going out from S1's interface GE1/0/3 cannot reach PC1 (because Link2-4 is interrupted), but the frame with MAC-1 as its destination MAC address going out from GE1/0/4 will go through Link1-3 and Link3-4 and reach PC1, thus avoiding frame loss.

As we can see from the previous examples, flush frames play a critical role in the Smart Link protocol. In order to control the communication and scope of flush frames, Smart Link specifically defines a VLAN for flush frames, called the control VLAN. Flush frames must carry the control VLAN tag before they are sent. If a device needs to receive and process flush frames, it must be configured accordingly so it can receive, identify, and process frames with control VLAN tags. If a device is not configured as described above, it will directly discard the frames with control VLAN tags when it receives them.

Fig. 8.27 Return to moment $t + 10$s

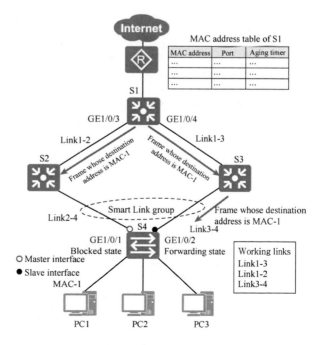

Finally, let's briefly introduce the restore function of Smart Link. Under normal circumstances, the master interface of Smart Link is active while the slave interface is inactive. When the master interface is down, it will switch to inactive state and the slave interface will switch to active state. However, after the master interface is back up, Smart Link will not automatically switch the state of the master interface back to active and that of slave interface to inactive. If we need to restore the state of the master interface to active and the state of the slave interface to inactive, we must configure the restore function of Smart Link in advance. In addition, when configuring the link restore function, we also need to configure a parameter called "wait to restore time", and its default value is 60 s. In other words, although the master interface is back up (the main link is reconnected), it has to wait for a period of time (which is the so-called wait to restore time) before performing the restore action. This is because although the main interface is back up, its working state may not be stable, and it may even subject to flashes. Therefore, the restore operation should not be performed immediately.

8.3.2   An Example of Smart Link Configuration

As shown in Fig. 8.28, S1, S2, S3 and S4 form a loop. We need to configure interfaces GE0/0/1 and GE0/0/2 in a Smart Link group on S4, and make GE0/0/1 the master interface and GE0/0/2 the slave interface.

1. Configuration roadmap

    (a) Create a Smart Link group, add the corresponding interface to the Smart Link group, and specify the interface role.
    (b) Enable the flush frame sending function.
    (c) Enable the flush frame receiving function.
    (d) Enable the Smart Link restore function.
    (e) Enable the Smart Link function.

2. Configuration steps

    Since Smart Link protocol is mutually exclusive with STP protocol, you need to disable the STP function by entering the corresponding interface view and use the stp disable command before configuring Smart Link.

```
[S4] interface GigabitEthernet 0/0/1
[S4-GigabitEthernet0/0/1] stp disable
[S4-GigabitEthernet0/0/1] quit
[S4] interface GigabitEthernet 0/0/2
[S4-GigabitEthernet0/0/2] stp disable
[S4-GigabitEthernet0/0/2] quit
```

Fig. 8.28 Smart Link
configuration example

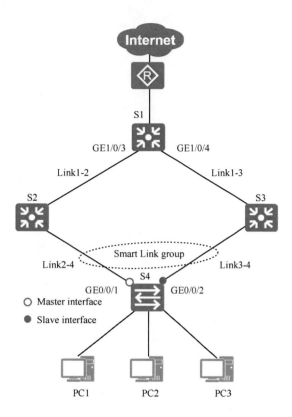

Next, create Smart Link group 1 on S4, and use the port command to configure GE0/0/1 as the master interface of Smart Link group 1 and GE0/0/2 as the slave interface, enable Smat Link, and set the wait to restore time to 30 s.

```
[S4] smart-link group 1
[S4-smlk-group1] port GigabitEthernet 0/0/1 master
[S4-smlk-group1] port GigabitEthernet 0/0/2 slave
[S4-smlk-group1] restore enable          --Enable restore
[S4-smlk-group1] smart-link enable
[S4-smlk-group1] timer wtr 30            --Set wait to restore time
```

Then, use the flush send command to enable Smart Link group 1 to send flush frames, with 10 as the control VLAN tag and "Huawei" as the password.

```
[S4-smlk-group1] flush send control-vlan 10 password simple huawei
```

Use the smart-link flush receive command on S1, S2 and S3 to specify that their interfaces GE0/0/1 and GE0/0/2 can receive and process flush frames carrying control VLAN 10.

Execute the following commands on S2.

```
 [S2] interface GigabitEthernet 0/0/1
 [S2-GigabitEthernet0/0/1] smart-link flush receive control-vlan
10 password simple huawei
 [S2-GigabitEthernet0/0/1] quit
 [S2] interface GigabitEthernet 0/0/2
 [S2-GigabitEthernet0/0/2] smart-link flush receive control-vlan
10 password simple huawei
 [S2-GigabitEthernet0/0/2] quit
```

Execute the following commands on S1.

```
 [S1] interface GigabitEthernet 0/0/1
 [S1-GigabitEthernet0/0/1] smart-link flush receive control-vlan
10 password simple huawei
 [S1-GigabitEthernet0/0/1] quit
 [S1] interface GigabitEthernet 0/0/2
 [S1-GigabitEthernet0/0/2] smart-link flush receive control-vlan
10 password simple huawei
 [S1-GigabitEthernet0/0/2] quit
```

Execute the following commands on S3.

```
 [S3] interface GigabitEthernet 0/0/0
 [S3-GigabitEthernet0/0/1] smart-link flush receive control-vlan
10 password simple huawei
 [S3-GigabitEthernet0/0/1] quit
 [S3] interface GigabitEthernet 0/0/2
 [S3-GigabitEthernet0/0/2] smart-link flush receive control-vlan
10 password simple huawei
 [S3-GigabitEthernet0/0/2] quit
```

Enter "display smart-link group 1" to view the information related to the Smart Link of S4.

```
 <S4>display smart-link group 1
 Smart Link group 1 information :
  Smart Link group was enabled
  Wtr-time is: 30 sec.
  There is no Load-Balance
  There is no protected-vlan reference-instance
  DeviceID: 4c1f-cc88-31fe Control-vlan ID: 10
  Member        Role  State  Flush Count Last-Flush-Time

----------------------------------------------------------
  GigabitEthernet0/0/1  Master Active  0     0000/00/00 00:00:00 UTC
+00 :00
  GigabitEthernet0/0/2  Slave Inactive 0     0000/00/00 00:00:00 UTC
+00 :00
```

You can see that Smart Link group 1 is enabled, GigabitEthernet0/0/1 is active as the master interface, GigabitEthernet0/0/2 is inactive as the slave interface, the ID of the control VLAN is 10, and the wait to restore time is 30 s.

8.4   Monitor Link

8.4.1   Basic Principles of Monitor Link

As shown in Fig. 8.29, a Smart Link group is configured on Switch S4, with GE1/0/1 as the master interface and GE1/0/2 the slave interface. GE1/0/1 is active and GE1/0/2 inactive. If now interface GE1/0/1 of S2 fails, resulting in the interruption of Link1-2, then what will be the consequence? Obviously, it is impossible for S4 to sense the failure of S2's interface GE1/0/1, so as a result all frames from S4's master interface GE1/0/1 will be lost.

To address the above problem, Huawei has designed and implemented a private protocol called Monitor Link, which is mainly used in conjunction with Smart Link in certain scenarios to prevent frame loss.

In Fig. 8.29, we can configure a Monitor Link group on S2. This Monitor Link group contains two interfaces: interface GE1/0/1, which functions as an uplink interface, and interface GE1/0/2, which functions as a downlink interface. The

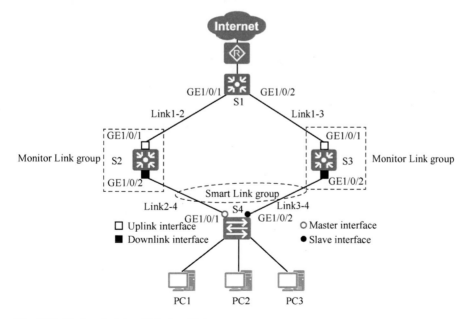

Fig. 8.29   Basic principle of Monitor Link

working principle of Monitor Link is that: a Monitor Link group consists of one uplink interface and several downlink interfaces; if the uplink interface fails to work properly for various reasons, the state of all of its downlink interfaces must be immediately turned to "Down". In other words, there is a linkage mechanism between the uplink interface and the downlink interfaces, and the working state of the downlink interfaces should be consistent with that of the uplink interface.

Let's take another look at Fig. 8.29. Under normal conditions, the links in working state are Link2-4, Link1-2 and Link1-3. If interface GE1/0/1 of S2 fails, because of the Monitor Link protocol, the state of interface GE1/0/2 of S2 will be immediately turned to "Down". In this way, interface GE1/0/1 of S4 cannot work properly. Therefore, Smart Link of S4 then immediately switches the state of its slave interface GE1/0/2 from inactive to active. Thus, the links in working state become Link1-3 and Link3-4, and the network connectivity is still ensured.

Similarly, to further strengthen the reliability of the network, we can also configure a Monitor Link group on S3, so that interface GE1/0/2 of S3 can be linked with interface GE1/0/1.

Let's take a look at a more complicated case. As shown in Fig. 8.30, a Smart Link group is configured on S1, S2, and S3, and a Monitor Link group is configured on S2 and S3, respectively. Note that for the Monitor Link group on S2, the entire Smart Link group on S2 is considered its uplink interface, and the state of its downlink interface will be turned to "Down" only if both interfaces of that Smart Link group

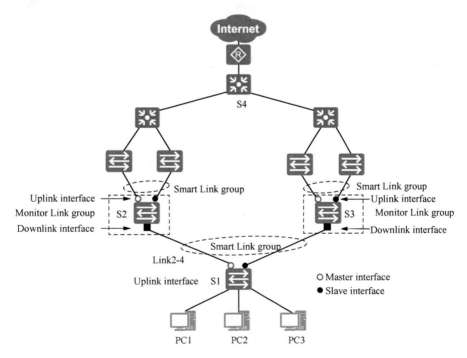

Fig. 8.30 Monitor Link and Smart Link in a complex situation

are not working properly. The situation is the same for S3, so it will not be repeated here.

In Fig. 8.30, if S2's master interface fails, its slave interface is immediately switched to the working state, and at this time, the Monitor Link group on S2 does not have a linkage effect. If both the master and slave interfaces of S2 fail, then the state of the downlink interface of S2 is turned to "Down", which triggers the Smart Link group on S1 to perform switching action. This example shows us that a flexible and clever combination of Smart Link and Monitor Link technology can often be used to better satisfy the special needs in complex networking situations.

When the uplink interface of a Monitor Link group does not work properly, all its downlink interfaces will be "down" as a result. If the uplink interface recovers, its downlink interface will also be automatically turned back to "up", which is the restore function of Monitor Link. Similar to the Smart Link case, we can also configure a suitable wait to restore time for the Monitor Link.

8.4.2   An Example of Monitor Link Configuration

As shown in Fig. 8.31, a Smart Link group has been configured on S2 and S4, and we now need to configure a Monitor Link group on S2 and S3.

1. Configuration roadmap

    (a) Create a Monitor Link group on S2 and S3, and add the corresponding uplink and downlink ports.
    (b) Configure the recover time of the Monitor Link group on S2 and S3.

2. Configuration steps

    Create Monitor Link group 1 on S2, add the already created Smart Link group 1 as the uplink port to Monitor Link group 1, and add port GE2/0/1 as the downlink interface to Monitor Link group 1.

```
[S2] monitor-link group 1
[S2-mtlk-group1] smart-link group 1 uplink
[S2-mtlk-group1] port GigabitEthernet 0/0/1 downlink ?
 INTEGER<1-24> Downlink's index, ranging from integer 1 to 24    --
Support up to 24 downlink ports
 <cr>
 [S2-mtlk-group1] port GigabitEthernet 2/0/1 downlink 1    --Specify
the downlink port as 1
```

Create Monitor Link group 2 on S3, add port GE1/0/1 as the uplink port to Monitor Link group 2, and add port GE2/0/1 as the downlink port to Monitor Link group 2.

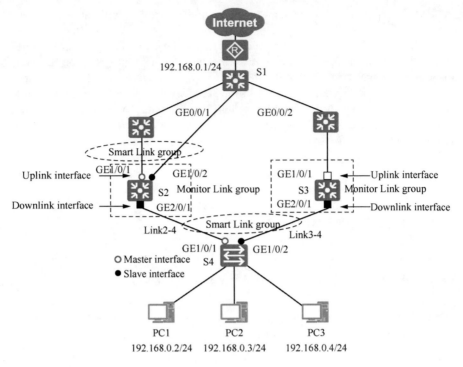

Fig. 8.31 Monitor Link configuration illustration

```
[S3Jmonitor-link group 2
[S3-mtlk-group2]port GigabitEthernet 1/0/1 uplink
[S3-mtlk-group2] port GigabitEthernet 2/0/1 downlink 1
```

Then, configure the recover time on S2 and S3. Use the timer recover-time command to set the recover time for the Monitor Link group to 10 s.

```
[S2-mtlk-group1]timer recover-time 10
[S3-mtlk-group2]timer recover-time 10
```

Now, we need to confirm the configuration made, that is, use the display smart-link group all command to view the information of all Smart Link groups and the display monitor-link group all command to view the information of all Monitor Link groups.

8.5 Alternatives to STP and Current Networking Recommendations

Four alternatives to STP are listed below.

1. Link aggregation refers to aggregating multiple physical interfaces together to form a logical interface for the load balance of outgoing and ingoing traffic on each member interface. The switch decides through which member interface packets are sent to the peer switch based on the interface load balance policy configured by the users. When the switch detects a link failure on one of the member interfaces, it stops sending packets on this interface and recalculates to decide which interface among the remaining links shall send the packets according to the load balance policy. The failed interface will resume the role of sending and receiving packets once it recovers. Link aggregation is an imperative technology in increasing link bandwidth, achieving link transmission resilience and link redundancy. Aggregation enables multiple links to be treated as one, which prevents loops.

2. Smart Link is a solution tailored for dual uplink networking. If a Smart Link group is created on a device, then two uplink interfaces are added to the group. One of the interfaces is designated as the master interface and the other as the slave interface. By default, only the master interface is active and it forwards traffic normally, while the slave interface is blocked so the Layer 2 loop is broken. When the Smart interface fails or its directly connected link fails, Smart Link will immediately sense the change, and can switchover in milliseconds. The slave interface instantly changes to an active state, and starts sending and receiving service traffic. Smart Link is easy to configure and can switch in a fast speed. However, due to the limitation of its working mechanism, this technology is only applicable to specific networking scenarios.

3. iStack/CSS. iStack is the stacking technology of Huawei box switches. The so-called stacking technology refers to the technology that multiple physical switches are connected through specific cables and configured accordingly so they logically become one device. And the concept of Cluster Switch System (CSS) is similar to iStack, except that it targets Huawei frame switches. When a Layer 2 loop is formed, the loop has to be broken by blocking the interface, but stacking/clustering is different. Stacking/clustering can connect the switches using stacking cables and then form a stacking system. After the establishment is complete, the two switches become one and are logically one switch.

4. A scenario without Layer 2 loop. The Layer 2 loop in the network is manually broken to circumvent the application of spanning tree.

8.6 Exercises

1. Which of the following descriptions of the forwarding state in the Spanning Tree Protocol is incorrect ( ).

   A. The port in forwarding state can receive BPDU messages
   B. The port in forwarding state does not learn the source MAC address of the message
   C. The port in forwarding state can forward data packets
   D. The port in forwarding state can send BPDU messages

2. The following information is the port state information displayed on a switch running STP. Based on this information, which of the following descriptions is correct ( ).

   ```
   <S3>display stp brief
   MSTID  Port                    Role   STP State        Protection
     0    GigabitEthernet0/0/1    ALTE   DISCARDING            NONE
     0    GigabitEthernet0/0/2    ROOT   FORWARDING            NONE
     0    GigabitEthernet0/0/3    DESI   FORWARDING            NONE
   ```

   A. This may be the only switch in this network
   B. This switch is the root switch in the network
   C. This switch is a non-root switch in the network
   D. This switch must be connected to three other switches

3. When there are redundant paths in a Layer 2 switch network, what method can be used to prevent loops and improve the reliability of the network? ( )

   A. Spanning Tree Protocol
   B. Horizontal Partitioning
   C. Route Poisoning
   D. Trigger Update

4. A user reports that the files are transferred in an extremely low speed in the network, and the administrator finds some duplicate frames in the network using Wireshark packet capture tool. Which of the following descriptions of the possible causes or solutions is correct ( ).

   A. The switch floods the data frame when it cannot find the destination MAC address of the frame in the MAC address table
   B. The switching equipment in the network must be upgraded
   C. There are loops in the network at Layer 2
   D. No VLANs are configured in the network

Fig. 8.32 Communication illustration

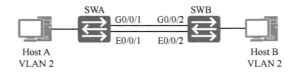

Host A
VLAN 2

Host B
VLAN 2

5. (Multi-selection) What is the role of link aggregation? ( )

   A. Increase bandwidth
   B. Enable load balance
   C. Increase network reliability
   D. Facilitate data analyzing

6. How to ensure that a switch becomes the root switch of the entire network? ( )

   A. Configure an IP address for the switch that is lower than that of other switches
   B. Set the root path cost of the switch to the lowest value
   C. Configure a priority lower than the other switches for the switch
   D. Configure a MAC address lower than the other switches for the switch

7. The port cost calculated by STP has a certain relationship with the port bandwidth, that is, greater bandwidth leads to ( ) cost.

   A. Smaller
   B. Greater
   C. Consistent
   D. Unsure

8. As shown in Fig. 8.32, by default, the network administrator wants to manually aggregate the two physical links between SWA and SWB using Eth-Trunk, and which of the following descriptions is correct ( ).

   A. After aggregation, it can work normally
   B. They can be aggregated, but after aggregation, only Interface G can send and receive data
   C. They can be aggregated, but after aggregation, only Interface E can send and receive data
   D. They cannot be aggregated

Chapter 9
ACL and AAA

With the rapid development of network, network security and network quality of service issues become increasingly prominent. Access Control List (ACL) is a technology closely related to it.

ACL can control network access behavior, prevent network attacks and improve network bandwidth utilization by accurately identifying the message flow in the network and working in conjunction with other technologies, thus effectively guaranteeing a secure network environment and reliable network service quality.

For any network, user management is one of the basic security management requirements, and AAA (Authentication, Authorization, Accounting) is a management framework that provides a security mechanism to authorize some users to access specified resources and record their operation behaviors. It is widely used for its good scalability as well as convenient centralized management of user information. AAA can be implemented by various protocols, and in practice, the most commonly used one is Remote Authentication Dial-in User Service (RADIUS).

In this chapter, we will introduce the basic principles and basic roles of ACL, its different types and characteristics, its basic composition and matching order, the usage of wildcard masks and ACL-related configuration, the basic concepts of AAA, the implementation methods of AAA, the basic configuration of AAA and common AAA application scenarios.

9.1 Working Principles of ACL

9.1.1 Overview of ACL

ACL is an extensively used network technology, and its basic principles are extremely simple. A network device configured with an ACL matches messages passing through the device according to pre-defined message matching rules, and then processes the matched messages as is predetermined. These matching rules and

Huawei Technologies Co., Ltd., *Data Communications and Network Technologies*,
https://doi.org/10.1007/978-981-19-3029-4_9

corresponding processing actions are set according to the specific network requirements. The different processing actions and the diverse matching rules allow ACLs to be effective in a variety of ways.

ACL technology is always associated with technologies such as firewall, routing policy, QoS, and traffic filter. In this book, we only briefly introduce the basic knowledge about ACL from the perspective of traffic control. In addition, it should be noted that different network equipment vendors differ in the details of how ACL is implemented. The description of ACL technology in this book is for the ACL technology implemented in Huawei network equipment.

9.1.2   Composition of ACL

As shown in Fig. 9.1, an ACL is composed of several "deny I permit" statements, each of which is a rule of ACL. The deny or permit in each statement is the processing action corresponding to the rule. In particular, it should be noted that ACL technology is always used in combination with other technologies, so for different technologies combined, "permit" and "deny" have different meanings and functions. For example, when ACL technology is used in conjunction with traffic filter technology, permit means "permit passage" and deny means "deny passage".

After receiving a message, a device configured with the ACL will match the message against the rules in the ACL one by one. If the message cannot match current rule, it will continue to be matched against next rule. Once the message

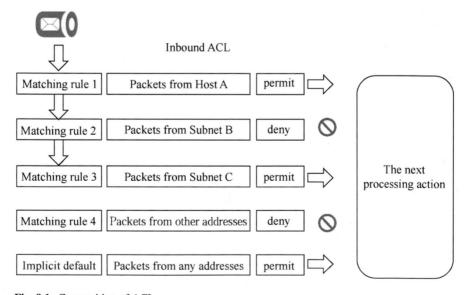

Fig. 9.1 Composition of ACL

matches a rule, the device will perform the processing action ("permit" or "deny") defined in the rule on the message, and stop matching the massage against subsequent rules. If the message cannot match any of the rules of ACL, the device "permits" the message. The last implicit default rule of ACL in Huawei router is to allow any address to pass. You can add a rule at the end of the ACL to deny packets from any address. In this way, the implicit default rule will never work.

Each rule in an ACL has a corresponding number, called the "rule-id". By default, messages are always matched against the rules from the smallest to largest rule-id. And by default, the device will automatically assign a number to each rule during the creation of the ACL. If the step length of the rule-id is set to be 10 (Note: the default value of the step length of rule-id is 5), the rule-ids will be automatically assigned as 10, 20, 30, 40... If the step length of the rule-id is set to 2, the rule-ids will be automatically assigned as 2, 4, 6, 8... The step length indicates the interval between adjacent rule-ids. In fact, the interval exists to facilitate the insertion of a new rule between two adjacent rules.

9.1.3 Classification of ACLs

ACLs are classified into different types according to their characteristics, namely basic ACLs, advanced ACLs, Layer 2 ACLs, and user-defined ACLs, among which basic ACL and advanced ACL are the more widely used. When configuring ACL on network devices, each ACL needs to be assigned a number, called ACL number. The number range of basic ACL is from 2000–2999, that of advanced ACL is 3000–3999, that of Layer 2 ACL is 4000–4999, and that of user-defined ACL is 5000–5999. When configuring ACL, the type of ACL should be consistent with the corresponding number range.

Basic ACLs can only define rules based on the source IP address, message fragmentation tag and time period information of IP messages. The structure of the command to configure a basic ACL rule is as follows.

```
rule [rule-id] {deny | permit } [ source { source-address source-
wildcard | any } | logging | time-range time-name ]
```

The following is the explanation of each component of the command.

rule: indicates that this is a rule.

rule-id: is the number of this rule.

deny I permit: an either-or option, which indicates the processing action associated with this rule.

source: indicates the source IP address information.

source-address: indicates the specific source IP address.

source-wildcard: indicates a wildcard mask corresponding to the *source-address*. The combination of *source-wildcard* and *source-address* can determine an IP addresses set.

any: indicates that the source IP address can be any address.

logging: indicates that IP messages matching this rule are required to be logged.

time-range *time-name*: indicates that the time period for the rule to take effect is *time-name*, and the specific usage is not described here.

Advanced ACL can define rules based on information such as source IP address, destination IP address, protocol field, priority, length, source port number of TCP messages, destination port number of TCP messages, source port number of UDP messages and destination port number of UDP messages. The functions of basic ACL are only a subset of the functions of advanced ACL, and advanced ACL can define rules that are more precise, complex, and flexible than basic ACL.

The configuration of rules in advanced ACLs is much more complicated than that of rules in basic ACLs, and the format of configuration commands varies depending on the types of load data of IP messages. For example, for different types of messages such as ICMP messages, TCP messages, and UDP messages, the format of the corresponding configuration commands also varies. The following is a simplified format of the configuration command for all IP messages.

```
rule [rule-id] { deny | permit } ip [destination { destination-address
destination-wildcard | any }] [ source { source-address source-wildcard
| any }]
```

9.1.4   Wildcard-Mask

When a wildcard-mask is combined with an IP address, it represents a set of IP addresses. A wildcard-mask is a 32-bit value that indicates which bits of an IP address need to be strictly matched and which do not. Wildcard-masks are usually represented in a dotted decimal form similar to subnet masks, but have a completely different meaning from subnet masks.

When a wildcard-mask is converted to binary, "0" means "match", and "1" means "ignore". As shown in Fig. 9.2, the wildcard-mask of 192.168.1.0 is 0.0.0.255, indicating that the network segment is 192.168.1.0/24.

Use the following command to create ACL 2000, and add four rules. The bolded part after each rule is a wildcard-mask.

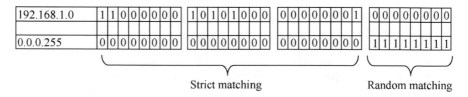

Fig. 9.2 Wildcard-mask

```
[AR1]acl 2000
[AR1-acl-basic-2000]rule 5  deny     source 10.1.1.1      0.0.0.0
[AR1-acl-basic-2000]rule 10 permit   source 192.168.1.0   0.0.0.255
[AR1-acl-basic-2000]rule 15 permit   source 172.16.0.0
0.0.255.255
[AR1-acl-basic-2000]rule 20 deny     source 0.0.0.0
255.255.255.255
[AR1-acl-basic-2000]quit
```

rule 5: denies the passage of messages whose source IP address is 10.1.1.1. Because the wildcard-mask is all 0s, every bit must be strictly matched. Therefore, the matching host IP address is 10.1.1.1.

rule 10: allows the passage of messages whose source address is network segment address 192.168.1.0/24. The wildcard-mask is written in binary as 0.0.0.11111111, and the last 8 bits are all 1s, which means to ignore. Therefore, the last 8 bits of 192.168.1.xxxx can be any value, thus matching the network segment 192.168.1.0/24.

rule 15: allows passages of messages with whose source address is network segment address 172.16.0.0/16. The wildcard is written in binary as 0.0.111111111.11111111, and the last 16 bits are all 1s, which means to ignore. Therefore, the last 16 bits of 172.16.xxxxxxxxx.xxxxxxxxx can be any value, thus matching network segment 172.16.0.0/16.

rule 20: denies the passage of messages whose source address is network segment address 0.0.0.0/0, which is equivalent to denying all network segments. The wildcard-mask is written in binary as 11111111.11111111.11111111.11111111, and all 32 bits are 1s, which means to ignore them all. Therefore, the 32 bits of xxxxxxxxxx.xxxxxxxxx.xxxxxxxxx.xxxxxxxxx can be any value, thus matching network segment 0.0.0.0/0.

The "1" or "0" in the wildcard-mask can be non-consecutive.

When using wildcard-masks to match an odd IP address in the network segment 192.168.1.0/24, such as 192.168.1.1, 192.168.1.3 and 192.168.1.5., how to write the wildcard-mask?

As shown in Fig. 9.3, by writing the last part of the odd IP address in binary, you can see the that the last bit of all odd IP addresses is 1, so it shall be strictly matched, and the answer is "192.168.1.1 0.0.0.254 (0.0.0.11111110)".

Think about it. When using a wildcard-mask to match an even IP address in network segment 192.168.1.0/24, such as 192.168.1.0, 192.168.1.2, and 192.168.1.4, 192.168.1.6, how to write the wildcard-mask?

The answer is "192.168.1.0 0.0.0.254". If readers do not understand, they can write the even address into binary, and then write the wildcard-mask.

There are also two special wildcard-masks. When matching wildcard-mask of all 0s to an IP address, it means to match a certain IP address. When matching wildcard-mask of all 1s to addresses 0.0.0.0, it means match all addresses.

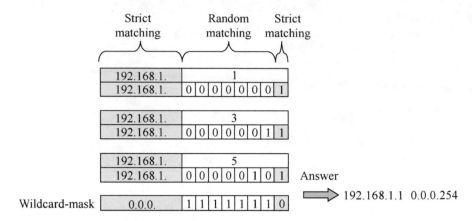

Fig. 9.3   The 0s and 1s in wildcard-mask can be discontinuous

9.1.5   ACL Design Roadmap

When using ACLs to control network traffic, the first thing to consider is whether to use basic ACL or advanced ACL. If the control is based only on the source IP address of the packet, then basic ACL is used. And if the control is based on the source IP address, destination IP address, protocol and destination port of the packet, then advanced ACL is used. Then you should consider which direction of which port of which router to control. Once all of these are determined, you can determine which IP addresses are the source and which are the destination in the ACL rules.

Before creating ACL rules, the order of the rules in the ACL also needs to be determined. If the address ranges in each rule do not overlap, the order of rule-ids is irrelevant; if the addresses used in multiple rules overlap, the rules with smaller address blocks should be put in the front and those with larger address blocks should be put in the back.

Only one ACL can be bound to each direction in the outbound and inbound directions of each port of the router, and one ACL can be bound to multiple ports.

Figure 9.4 shows an example to control solely the access from the intranet to the Internet, which is a control based on source IP address, so the basic ACL is sufficient. Intranet computers have to pass through two routers, R1 and R2, to access Internet, which requires consideration of which router to control and which port to bind to. If you create an ACL on router R1, you should bind it to the outbound direction of GE0/0/1 of router R1 and check the application of the ACL at the exit. In this example, ACL is created on router R2 and is bound to the inbound direction of GE0/0/0 of router R2.

You can see that there are four matching rules in the ACL in Fig. 9.4. The last implicit default rule of the ACL in Huawei routers is to allow any address to pass, and the matching rule 4 created in this example is to deny any address to pass, then the implicit default rule will never be used. This is because the rules in the ACL are

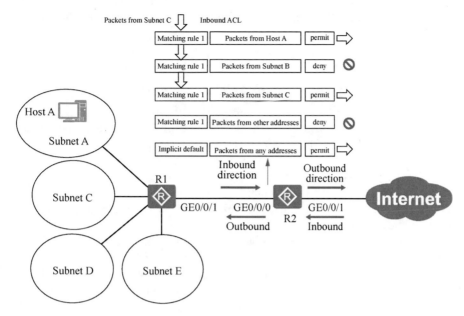

Fig. 9.4   ACL example

matched from the smallest to largest, and once it is successfully matched, it will not be matched against subsequent rules.

In this example, the source address in rule 2 contains the Host A in rule 1, that is, the addresses in the rules overlap, as shown in Fig. 9.4. This requires the rule for Host A to precede the rule for Subnet B. If the order is reversed, the rule for Host A will not have a chance to be matched.

The created ACL should be bound to the port and the direction should be specified. The direction is viewed from the router's point of view. Entering the router through the port is the inbound direction, and leaving the router through the port is the outbound direction. In this example, the defined ACL is bound to port GE0/0/0 of router R2, which is the inbound direction, and to port GE0/0/1 port of router R2, which is the outbound direction.

The packet from Subnet C in Fig. 9.4 comes in through GE0/0/0 of router R2. It compares rule 1 and rule 2 in order and finally matches rule 3, and the processing action is to permit. Subnet E is not explicitly specified in the rule, but it will match rule 4, and the processing action is to deny, so that the implicit default rule will not be used.

Let's think about it. Is it OK to bind this ACL to the outbound direction of GE 0/0/1 of router R2? Is it OK to bind it to the inbound direction of GE0/0/1 of router R2?

Answer: it can be bound to the outbound direction of GE0/0/1 of R2, but it cannot be bound to the inbound direction of GE0/0/1 of R2, because all source addresses are intranet addresses when the rule is created, and the access from intranet to Internet is controlled.

9.1.6   Implementation of Basic ACL Configuration

The following is an example of an enterprise network, which is used to introduce the implementation of basic ACLs.

Packet filtering is performed at a mandatory destination (a port of a router) based on the path of packets from the source network to the destination network. Before creating an ACL, you need to determine which direction of which port of which router along the path to perform packet filtering on in order to determine the source address in the ACL rule.

As shown in Fig. 9.5, an enterprise intranet has three network segments. VLAN 10 is the finance department server, VLAN 20 is the engineering department network segment, VLAN 30 is the finance department network segment, and the enterprise router AR1 is connected to the Internet. Now you need to create an ACL on AR1 to achieve the following functions.

- Traffic whose source IP address is a private address cannot enter the enterprise network from the Internet.
- The finance department server can only be accessed by the computers in the finance department.

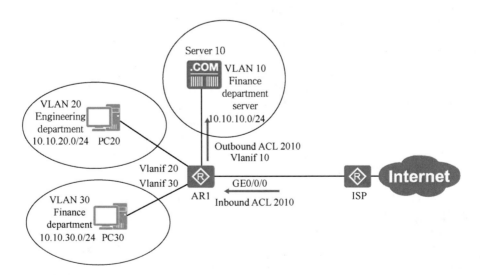

Fig. 9.5 Enterprise network

First you need to determine the two ACLs to be created, one bound to the inbound direction of port GE0/0/0 of router AR1 and the other bound to the outbound direction of port Vlanif 10 of AR1.

Create two basic ACLs on AR1: ACL 2000 and ACL 2010.

```
[RA1] acl ?
INTEGER<2000-2999> Basic access-list (add to current using rules)  --
Basic ACL number range
  INTEGER<3000-3999> Advanced access-list (add to current using rules)
--Advanced ACL number range
  INTEGER<4000-4999> Specify a L2 acl group
  ipv6         ACL IPv6
  name          Specify a named ACL
  number        Specify a numbered ACL
[AR1] acl 2000       --Create ACL
[AR1-acl-basic-2000] rule deny source 10.0.0.0 0.255.255.255
[AR1-acl-basic-2000] rule deny source 172.16.0.0 0.15.255.255
[AR1-acl-basic-2000] rule deny source 192.168.0.0 0.0.255.255
[AR1-acl-basic-2000] quit
[AR1] acl 2010
[AR1-acl-basic-2010] rule permit source 10.10.30.0 0.0.0.255
[AR1-acl-basic-2010] rule 20 deny source any          --Specify rule-
id
[AR1-acl-basic-2010] quit
```

Enter "display acl all" to view all ACLs, and enter "display acl 2000" to view ACL 2000.

```
[AR1] display acl all
Total quantity of nonempty ACL number is 2
Basic ACL 2000, 3 rules
Acl's step is 5
 rule 5 deny source 10.0.0.0 0.255.255.255
 rule 10 deny source 172.16.0.0 0.15.255.255
 rule 15 deny source 192.168.0.0 0.0.255.255
Basic ACL 2010, 2 rules
Acl's step is 5
 rule 5 permit source 10.10.30.0 0.0.0.255
 rule 20 deny
```

Bind the created ACL to the interface.

```
[AR1] interface GigabitEthernet 0/0/0
[AR1-GigabitEthernet0/0/0] traffic-filter inbound acl 2000   --Inbound
[AR1-GigabitEthernet0/0/0] quit
[AR1] interface Vlanif 1
[AR1-Vlanif1] quit
[AR1] interface Vlanif 10
[AR1-Vlanif10] traffic-filter outbound acl 2010        -Outbound
[AR1-Vlanif10] quit
```

After the ACL is defined, you can also edit it to delete some of its rules or insert the rules in the specified location.

Now modify ACL 2000 to delete rule 10 and add a rule to allow network segment 10.30.30.0/24 to pass through. Think about it. Where should this rule be placed?

```
[RA1]acl 2000
[RA1-acl-basic-2000]undo rule 10    --删除rule 10
[RA1-acl-basic-2000]rule 2 permit source 10.30.30.0 0.0.0.255   --
Insert rule 2 with a number less than 5
[RA1-acl-basic-2000]rule 15 permit source 192.168.0.0 0.0.255.255
--Modify rule 15 to permit
[AR1-acl-basic-2000]display this
[V200R003C00]
#
acl number 2000
 rule 2 permit source 10.30.30.0 0.0.0.255
 rule 5 deny source 10.0.0.0 0.255.255.255
 rule 15 permit source 192.168.0.0 0.0.255.255
#
return
```

Deleting the ACL does not automatically remove the binding to the interface, and the ACL bound to the interface needs to be deleted.

```
[RA1]undo acl 2000                          --Delete ACL
[RA1]interface GigabitEthernet 0/0/0
[AR1-GigabitEthernet0/0/0]display this
[V200R003C00]
#
interface GigabitEthernet0/0/0
 ip address 20.1.1.1 255.255.255.0
 traffic-filter inbound acl 2000              --ACL 2000 is still bound to
the inbound interface
#
return
[AR1-GigabitEthernet0/0/0]undo traffic-filter inbound        --Delete
inbound binding
```

9.1.7 Implementation of Advanced ACL Configuration

As shown in Fig. 9.6, an advanced ACL is required to be created on router AR1 to enable the following functions.

- Permit the engineering department to access the Internet.
- Permit the finance department to access the Internet, but it is only allowed to access websites as well as send and receive emails.

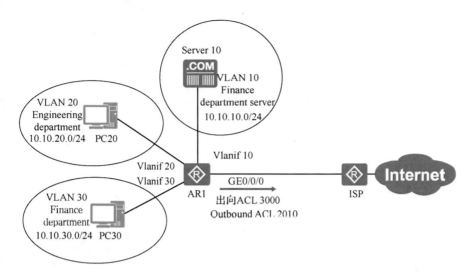

Fig. 9.6 Application of advanced ACL

- Permit the finance department to use the ping command to test whether the network to the Internet is unobstructed.
- Deny the finance department server to access the Internet.

The traffic control in this case is based on the source IP address, destination IP address, protocol and port number of the packet, so an advanced ACL is needed. Create an advanced ACL on AR1 and bind this ACL to the outbound direction of interface GE 0/0/0 of AR1.

Permit the finance department to access the Internet websites. Accessing the website requires domain name resolution, which uses DNS protocol, and the DNS protocol uses Port 53 of UDP. The HTTP protocol and HTTPS protocol are used to access websites, and the former uses TCP port 80, while the latter uses TCP port 443.

To avoid the impact of the basic ACLs previously created on this operation, delete all ACLs first, and then unbind the ACLs bound to Vlanif 10 and GE0/0/0.

```
[AR1] undo acl all                    --Delete all ACLs previously created
[AR1] interface Vlanif 10
[AR1-Vlanif10] undo traffic-filter outbound      --Delete the binding to
the interface
```

To create advanced ACLs on AR1, the destination port shall be specified when creating rules based on TCP and UDP.

```
[AR1] acl 3000                    --Create advanced ACL
[AR1-acl-adv-3000] rule 5 permit ?        --View available protocols
<1-255>  Protocol number
gre    GRE tunneling(47)
icmp   Internet Control Message Protocol(1)
```

```
igmp    Internet Group Management Protocol(2)
ip    Any IP protocol            --IP protocols include TCP, UDP and ICMP
ipinip  IP in IP tunneling(4)
ospf   OSPF routing protocol(89)
tcp    Transmission Control Protocol (6)
udp    User Datagram Protocol (17)
[AR1-acl-adv-3000]rule 5 permit ip source 10.10.20.0 0.0.0.255
destination any
[AR1-acl-adv-3000]rule 10 permit udp source 10.10.30.0 0.0.0.255
destination any ?
                         --View available parameters
destination-port    Specify destination port
dscp             Specify dscp
fragment            Check fragment packet
none-first-fragment  Check the subsequence fragment packet
......
[AR1-acl-adv-3000]rule 10 permit udp source 10.10.30.0 0.0.0.255
destination any destination-port ?          --Specify the destination
port to be greater, smaller than or equal to a given port number or in a
port range
eq   Equal to given port number
gt   Greater than given port number
lt   Less than given port number
range  Between two port numbers
[AR1-acl-adv-3000]rule 10 permit udp source 10.10.30.0 0.0.0.255
destination any destination-port eq ?          --You can specify port
number or access layer protocol name
<0-65535>   Port number
biff     Mail notify (512)
bootpc    Bootstrap Protocol Client (68)
bootps    Bootstrap Protocol Server (67)
discard   Discard (9)
dns       Domain Name Service (53)
dnsix     DNSIX Security Attribute Token Map (90)
echo      Echo (7)
......
[AR1-acl-adv-3000]rule 10 permit udp source 10.10.30.0 0.0.0.255
destination any destination-port eq dns
[AR1-acl-adv-3000]rule 15 permit tcp source 10.10.30.0 0.0.0.255
destination-port eq www
[AR1-acl-adv-3000]rule 20 permit tcp source 10.10.30.0 0.0.0.255
destination-port eq 443
[AR1-acl-adv-3000]rule 25 permit icmp source 10.10.30.0 0.0.0.255
[AR1-acl-adv-3000]rule 30 deny ip
[AR1-acl-adv-3000]quit
```

Bind the ACL to the interface.

```
[AR1] interface GigabitEthernet 0/0/0
[AR1-GigabitEthernet0/0/0] traffic-filter outbound acl 3000
```

9.2 AAA

Network devices or operating systems are usually accessed by multiple users. Different access authority can be set for different users. Accesses of users shall also be tracked for security.

To login to an operating system or network device, users need to enter their account name and password to verify their identity. This process is called authentication. The process of granting different authorities to different users is called authorization. For security purposes, access or changes to system resources after a user logs in can be recorded, which is a process called accounting. These three independent security functions are collectively called AAA. Accounting is not discussed in this book.

9.2.1 Working Modes of AAA

A network device can use two modes perform authentication, authorization, and accounting on users who initiate administrative access. One mode is done locally, as shown in Fig. 9.7, that is, the network device authenticates and authorizes the user through the username and password information in its own local database.

The other mode is done through an external AAA server. When a user initiates administrative access to the network device, the network device sends query information to the AAA server located at the specified address, so that the AAA server can determine whether to allow this user to access and what authority this user has, etc., as shown in Fig. 9.8.

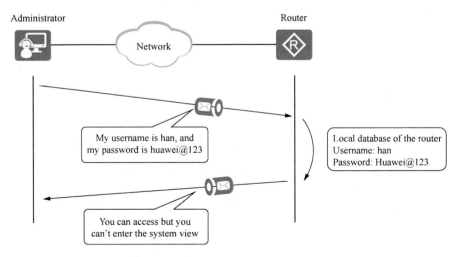

Fig. 9.7 Illustration of how local AAA works

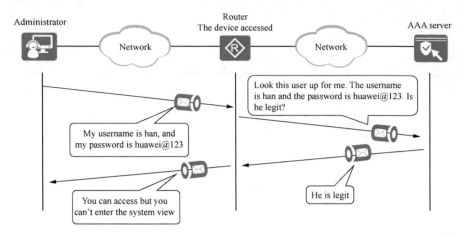

Fig. 9.8 Illustration of how AAA works using an AAA server

Fig. 9.9 Login
authentication using AAA
local authentication

Compared with performing AAA operations locally on the device, AAA services can be provided centrally for network devices via AAA servers. The most obvious advantage of this approach is scalability. Therefore, in medium- to large-scale networks, relying on AAA servers to centrally provide AAA services, as shown in Fig. 9.8, is more common. In this environment, the standard for communication between managed devices and AAA servers needs to be defined. RADIUS protocol is the standard protocol for communication between managed devices and AAA servers, with the AAA server being the RADIUS server and the router being the RADIUS client.

This book will not explain in detail how the AAA server performs AAA or the RADIUS protocol.

9.2.2   Configuration of AAA

This section explains configuring AAA local authentication for Huawei routers. When using Telnet to remotely login to a Huawei router, you can use password authentication, and there is no way to set different authorities for different users using password authentication. To improve security and grant different access authorities to different users, it is necessary to use AAA for local authentication when using Telnet to login. The network environment used in this case is shown in Fig. 9.9.

In this environment, to enable AAA local authentication for Telnet on router AR1, users can only successfully login to AR1 via Telnet if they have entered the correct username and password.

On a Huawei network device, there is a default authentication-scheme named default, which cannot be deleted by the administrator but can be modified. In the default authentication-scheme, the default authentication mode is local authentication, which means that the router will use the local database to authenticate the user's login behavior. In this case, we directly use the default authentication-scheme and leave the default authentication mode "local" unchanged.

Check the default AAA configuration information on AR1.

```
[AR1] aaa
[AR1-aaa] display this
[V200R003C00]
#
aaa
 authentication-scheme default
 authorization-scheme default
 accounting-scheme default
 domain default
 domain default_admin
 local-user admin password cipher %$%$K8m.Nt84DZ}e#<0`8bmE3Uw}%$%$
 local-user admin service-type http
#
return
[AR1-aaa]
```

Enter AAA view using the aaa comment, and then the display this command is used in the AAA view. With this command, you are able to view the configuration commands in the current view. In the output of the display this command, we focus on authentication-scheme default and domain default_admin.

- authentication-scheme default: this is the default authentication scheme. If you enter "authentication-scheme default" in AAA view, you can enter the default authentication scheme view and modify the parameters in "default". In the default authentication scheme view, the administrator can use the authentication-mode local command to set the local authentication mode. Since this is the default authentication mode, even if the administrator enters this command, the setting is not visible in the configuration.

```
[AR1-aaa] authentication-scheme default
[AR1-aaa-authen-default] authentication-mode ?   -- View
authentication modes supported
 hwtacacs HWTACACS
 local    Local
 none     None
 radius   RADIUS
[AR1-aaa-authen-default] authentication-mode local
```

- domain default_admin: this is the default administrator domain "default_admin", which is the domain of the user logging in to the device via HTTP, SSH, Telnet, Terminal or FTP. If you enter "domain default_admin" in the AAA view, you can enter the "default_admin" domain view and modify the parameters in this domain.

```
[AR1-aaa]domain default_admin
[AR1-aaa-domain-default_admin]?
aaa-domain-default_admin view commands:
 accounting-scheme    Configure accounting scheme
 arp-ping             ARP-ping
 authentication-scheme Configure authentication scheme
 authorization-scheme  Configure authorization scheme
 backup              Backup information
 ......
```

Users logging in to the device via Telnet belong to the "default_admin" domain that uses the default authentication-scheme. The default authentication-scheme in turn sets the default local authentication mode. In this nested configuration, if the administer wants to protect Telnet through AAA local authentication, there is no need to make any change. Thus, the next step is to create the local user that will login via Telnet.

The following commands creates two users, user1 and user2, on router AR1. When creating user1, the administrator specifies the username (user1) and password (huawei111), and sets the access service type of user1 to "telnet". When creating user2, in addition to specifying the username (user2) and password (huawei222) and setting the access service type of user 2 to "telnet", the administrator also specifies user2's privilege level to be 15, which is the highest level. The administrator does not specify a privilege level for user1, so user1 has the default level of 0, the lowest one.

```
 [AR1]aaa
 [AR1-aaa]local-user user1 password cipher huawei111
 Info: Add a new user.
 [AR1-aaa]local-user user1 service-type telnet
 [AR1-aaa]local-user user2 privilege level 15 password cipher
huawei222
 Info: Add a new user.
 [AR1-aaa]local-user user2 service-type telnet
```

Finally, the administrator also needs to configure the VTY user interface and set its authentication mode to AAA.

```
 [AR1]user-interface vty 0 4
 [AR1-ui-vty0-4]authentication-mode aaa
 [AR1-ui-vty0-4]quit
```

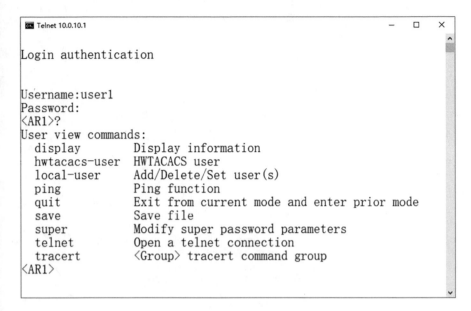

Fig. 9.10 Login test using user1

Apply the account user1, Telnet and router AR1 on a Windows system. After a successful login, by entering a question mark, you can query the commands that are currently available, and then you will find that the commands listed are very limited because user1's level is 0. Figure 9.10 shows the commands available after user1 logs in.

As shown in Fig. 9.11, after logging in with user2 and entering the question mark to query the commands that can be used currently, it is found that user2 can use a lot of commands because its privilege level is 15, which is the highest level, meaning that user2 can use all commands.

By using the display local-user command, you can view the locally configured user information of the device.

```
[AR1] display local-user
- - - - - - - - - - - - - - - - - - - - - - - - - - - - - - - - - - - - - - - - - - -
User-name              State    AuthMask   AdminLevel
- - - - - - - - - - - - - - - - - - - - - - - - - - - - - - - - - - - - - - - - - - -
admin              A      H          -
user1              A      T          -
user2              A      T         15
- - - - - - - - - - - - - - - - - - - - - - - - - - - - - - - - - - - - - - - - - - -
Total 3 user(s)
[AR1]
```

In the above output, if the state is A, the user is active, and of the state is B, the user is blocked. AuthMask indicates the access type of local users. The access type

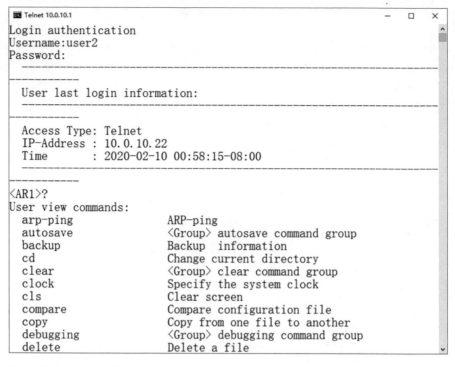

Fig. 9.11 Login test with user2

of admin is H (HTTP), the access type of user1 and user2 is T (Telnet), and there are other access types such as S(SSH) and F(FTP). AdminLevel represents the user level of the local user, and from here you can also see that the level of user2 is 15.

The display local-user user name *user name* command allows you to view the information of a particular user, and next let's view the information of user2.

```
[AR1] display local-user user name user2
The contents of local user(s):
Password      : ****************
State         : active
Service-type-mask : T
Privilege level  : 15
Ftp-directory    : -
Access-limit     : -
Accessed-num     : 0
Idle-timeout     : -
User-group       : -
```

9.3   Exercises

1. Regarding the correspondence between access control list number and type, which of the following descriptions is correct ( ).

    A. The number range of basic access control list is from 1000 to 2999
    B. The number range of advanced access control list is from 3000 to 4000
    C. The number range of Layer 2 access control list is from 4000 to 4999
    D. The number range of port-based access control list is from 1000 to 2000

2. Complete the following ACL configuration on router RTA. Which of the following descriptions is correct ( ).

    ```
    [RTA] acl 2001
    [RTA-acl-basic-2001] rule 20 permit source 20.1.1.0 0.0.0.255
    [RTA-acl-basic-2001] rule 10 deny source 20.1.1.0 0.0.0.255
    ```

    A. The VRP system will automatically adjust the sequence number of the first rule to 5 based on the configuration order
    B. The VRP system will not adjust the sequence number, but will first match the first configured rule "20.1.1.0 0.0.0.255"
    C. The configuration is incorrect, as the sequence number of rules must be configured from the smallest to largest
    D. The VRP system will match the second rule "deny source 20.1.1.0 0.0.0.255" first according to the sequence number

3. (Multi-selection) Each rule in the ACL has a corresponding rule-id to indicate the matching order. In the configuration shown below, which of the descriptions of the numbers of two rules is correct ( )?

    ```
    [RTA] acl 2002
    [RTA-acl-basic-2002] rule permit source 20.1.1.10
    [RTA-acl-base-2002] rule permit source 30.1.1.10
    ```

    A. The sequence number of the first rule is 1
    B. The sequence number of the first rule is 5
    C. The sequence number of the second rule is 2
    D. The sequence number of the second rule is 10

4. As shown in Fig. 9.12, the network administrator wants to forbid Host A to access WebServer, but does not restrict its access to other servers, then which of the following ACLs of RTA can meet the demand ( ).

Fig. 9.12 Question 4

Host A   RTA   WebServer

GE0/0/0

10.1.1.1/24   202.100.1.12/24

A. rule deny tcp source 10.1.1.10 destination 202.100.1.12 0.0.0.0 destination-port eq. 21
B. rule deny tcp source 10.1.1.10 destination 202.100.1.12 0.0.0.0 destination-port eq. 80
C. rule deny udp source 10.1.1.10 destination 202.100.1.12 0.0.0.0 destination-port eq. 21
D. rule deny udp source 10.1.1.10 destination 202.100.1.12 0.0.0.0 destination-port eq. 80

5. The following ACL configuration is used on an AR2220 router to filter packets, and which of the following descriptions is correct ( ).

```
[RTA] acl 2001
[RTA-acl-basic-2001] rule permit source 10.0.1.0 0.0.0.255
[RTA-acl-basic-2001] rule deny source 10.0.1.0 0.0.0.255
```

A. Packets on network segment 10.0.1.0/24 will be denied
B. Packets on network segment 10.0.1.0/24 will be permitted
C. The ACL is incorrectly configured
D. All of the above choices are incorrect

6. (Multi-selection) As shown in Fig. 9.13, the network administrator uses ACL 2000 to filter packets on router RTA, then which of the following descriptions is correct ( ).

A. RTA forwards packets from Host A
B. RTA discards packets from Host A
C. RTA forwards packets from Host B
D. RTA discards packets from Host B

7. (Multi-selection) When using the following ACL to match routing entries in router RTA, which of the following entries will be matched? ( )

```
[RTA] acl 2002
[RTA-acl-basic-2002] rule deny source 172.16.1.1 0.0.0.0
[RTA-acl-basic-2002] rule deny source 172.16.0.0 0.0.255.255
```

A. 172.16.1.1/32
B. 172.16.1.0/24

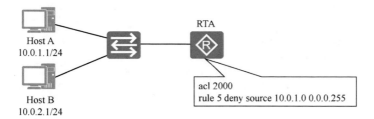

Fig. 9.13 Question 6

C. 192.17.0.0/24
D. 172.18.0.0/16

8. Which of the following parameters cannot be used for the advanced access control list? ( )

A. Physical port
B. Destination port number
C. Protocol number
D. Time range

9. (Multi-selection) When logging in to the router by Telnet, which authentication methods can be selected? ( )

A. AAA local authentication
B. No authentication
C. Password authentication
D. MD5 cipher authentication

10. (Multi-selection) At present, the company has a network administrator, and the AR2200 in the company's network can perform remote management by directly entering the password through Telnet. After the arrival of two new network administrators, the company wants to assign all the administrators their own usernames and passwords, as well as different privilege levels. So how should this be done? ( )

A. When configuring each administrator's account, different privilege levels need to be configured
B. The user authentication mode configured by Telnet must use the AAA mode
C. Configure three usernames and their corresponding passwords in the AAA view
D. Each administrator uses a different public IP address of the device when running Telnet commands

11. The AAA protocol is a RADIUS protocol. This statement is ( ).

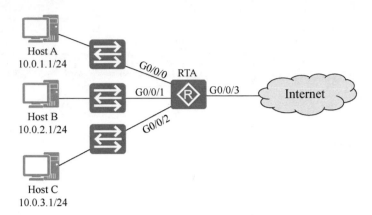

Fig. 9.14 Topology

    A. Correct
    B. Incorrect

12. As shown in Fig. 9.14, create an ACL on router RTA to deny 10.0.1.0/24, 10.0.2.0/24 and 10.0.3.0/24 to access each other and allow these three network segments to access the Internet. Determine whether a basic ACL or an advanced ACL should be used, and the location and direction of the ACL binding. Create the ACL and bind it to the appropriate interface.

Chapter 10
Network Address Translation Technologies

With the development of the Internet and the increase of network applications, the limited IPv4 public addresses have become a bottleneck restricting the network development. Enterprise intranets usually use private IP addresses, and the Internet uses public IP addresses. Network Address Translation (NAT) technology is required for computers using private addresses to access the Internet (public network).

NAT technology is mainly used to enable hosts of intranet to access extranet. On the one hand, NAT alleviates the shortage of IPv4 addresses; and on the other hand, NAT technology makes it impossible for the extranet to directly communicate with the intranet that uses private addresses, which enhances the security of the intranet.

NAT is divided into static NAT, dynamic NAT, Network Address and Port Translation (NAPT), easy IP and NAT server. When the intranet of an enterprise actively accesses the extranet, it usually uses static NAT, dynamic NAT, NAPT and easy IP. If the server of an enterprise is deployed in the enterprise intranet (private network) and you intend to allow computers on the Internet to access the intranet server, you need to configure NAT server on the router connected to the Internet.

10.1 Public Addresses and Private Addresses

As the number of Internet users grows, public IP address resources become increasingly scarce. At the same time, IPv4 public addresses are distributed unevenly, which leads to a serious shortage of available public IPv4 addresses in some areas. To address this problem, it is essential to use transition technologies to solve the shortage of public IPv4 addresses.

Public network refers to the Internet, and public IP addresses refer to the globally unified and planned IP addresses on the Internet. Address blocks of network segments cannot overlap. Routers on the Internet are able to forward packets whose destination addresses are public addresses.

Huawei Technologies Co., Ltd., *Data Communications and Network Technologies*, https://doi.org/10.1007/978-981-19-3029-4_10

Fig. 10.1 Private addresses

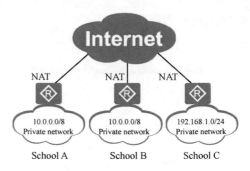

In the IP address space, each of the three types of addresses, A, B and C, retains a portion of the addresses as private addresses, and private addresses cannot appear on the public network, but can only be used in the intranet. Routers in the Internet do not have routes to private addresses.

The range of private addresses reserved for Class A, B, and C addresses are as follows.

Class A addresses: 10.0.0.0 to 10.255.255.255.

Class B addresses: 172.16.0.0 to 172.31.255.255.

Class C addresses: 192.168.0.0 to 192.168.255.255.

The intranets of enterprises or schools can choose appropriate private addresses segment according to the number of computers and the size of the network. Networks of small enterprises or homes can choose the reserved Class C private addresses, and networks for medium and large enterprises can choose the reserved Class B or Class A private addresses. As shown in Fig. 10.1, School A chooses 10.0.0.0/8 as its intranet address, and School B also chooses 10.0.0.0/8 as its intranet address. Anyway, the networks of these two schools do not need to communicate with each other now and do not intend to access each other in the future, so it does not matter if they use the same network segment or overlapping addresses. If the networks of School A and School B need to communicate with each other in the future, they cannot use overlapping addresses so both schools will need to replan their intranet addresses.

The enterprise intranet uses private addresses, which reduces the use of public addresses. NAT is typically used in border routers, such as the company's router that connects the Internet. NAT has the following typical advantages.

- By using NAPT technology, an enterprise private network can use a public address when accessing the Internet, which saves public IP addresses.
- When ISP is changed, intranet address does not have to be changed, which makes the Internet connection more flexible.
- The private network is not directly accessible on the Internet, which improves the security of the intranet.

However, NAT also has the following disadvantages.

- Configuring NAT or NAPT on the router requires modifying the network layer and transport layer of the packet, as well as keeping and recording the port address translation correspondence in the router, which generates a longer switching delay compared to routing packets, and consumes more resources in the router.
- A private address is used to access the Internet, and the source address is replaced with a public address. If a student from a school posts a message on a forum, the forum can only record that the IP address of the poster is the public address of the school, and there is no way to track which intranet address it is, which means that end-to-end IP tracking is not possible.
- The public network cannot access the private computers, and port mapping is required if access is needed.
- Certain applications cannot run in a NAT network, for example, IPSec does not allow intermediate packets to be modified.

10.2 NAT Types

NAT can be divided into five types: static NAT, dynamic NAT, NAPT, easy IP, and NAT server.

10.2.1 Static NAT

Static NAT is configured on the router connecting to the private network and the public network. Each private address has a corresponding and fixed public address, that is, a one-to-one mapping from a private address to a public address, and this type of NAT does not save public IP addresses.

Static NAT supports two-way inter-access. When the private address accesses the Internet, it will be converted to the corresponding public address by the outbound device's NAT translation. At the same time, when the extranet accesses the intranet, the public address (destination address) carried in its message is also converted into the corresponding private address by the NAT device.

As shown in Fig. 10.2, static mapping is configured on router R1, and the source IP address is replaced with public address 12.2.2.2 when intranet 192.168.1.2 accesses the Internet, and the source IP address is replaced with public address 12.2.2.3 when intranet 192.168.1.3 accesses the Internet. Figure 10.2 shows the source and destination addresses of the packets on the intranet when PC1 and PC2 access the Web server, and the source and destination addresses of the packet after it is sent to the Internet; it also displays the source and destination addresses on the

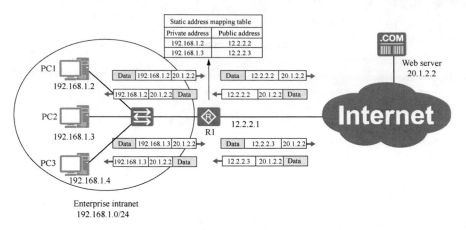

Fig. 10.2 Static NAT illustration

Internet of the packet sent by the Web server to PC1 and PC2, as well as the source and destination addresses after it enters the intranet.

PC3 cannot access the Internet because there is no public address specified on router R1 to replace IP address 192.168.1.4. With static NAT configured, computers on the Internet can access PC1 on the intranet by accessing 12.2.2.2 and PC2 on the intranet by accessing 12.2.2.3.

10.2.2   Dynamic NAT

Static NAT strictly enforces one-to-one address mapping, so the corresponding public address will be in use even if the intranet host is offline or does not send data for a long time. To avoid address waste, dynamic NAT introduces the concept of address pool, which is formed by all available public addresses.

When an internal host accesses the extranet, it is temporarily assigned an unused address in the address pool and the address is marked as "In Use". When the host no longer accesses the extranet, the assigned address is recycled and remarked "Not Use".

Dynamic NAT is configured on the router that connects the private and public networks, creating a public address (address segment) pool on the router, using ACLs to define which addresses need to be translated, and not specifying which public address to replace which private address. When an intranet computer accesses the Internet, the router randomly selects an unused public address from the public address pool to replace the source address. Dynamic NAT only allows the intranet to actively access the Internet, while computers on the Internet is not allowed to actively access computers on the intranet by public address. This is different from static NAT.

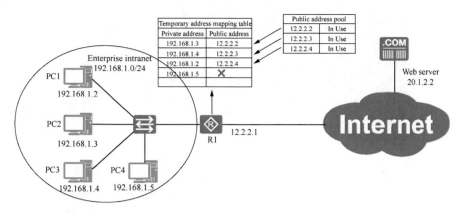

Fig. 10.3 Dynamic NAT

As shown in Fig. 10.3, there are four computers in the intranet, and three public IP addresses in the public address pool, so only three computers in the intranet are allowed to access the Internet. Then which computer can access the Internet in the end depends on which is online first. PC4 in the figure has no public address available so it cannot access the Internet.

10.2.3   NAPT

With dynamic NAT, a public address is still mapped to a private address, which cannot improve the utilization of the public address. In contrast, when NAPT selects addresses from the address pool for address translation, it not only translates IP addresses but also port numbers, thus realizing a one-to-many mapping from public to private addresses so as to effectively improve the utilization of public addresses.

If the number of public addresses used for NAT is less than that of computers on the intranet, the intranet computers use the IP addresses in the public address pool to access the Internet, and the outbound packets have to replace the source IP address and source port. There is a table in the router for recording address-port translation, as shown in Fig. 10.4.

Source ports (public ports in Fig. 10.4) are uniformly assigned by routers and will not be duplicated. When router R1 receives the returned packet, it can determine which computer in the intranet the packets should be given to based on the destination port. This is network address port translation (NAPT), and the application of NAPT can save public addresses.

NAPT only allows computers on the intranet to initiate access to the Internet, but computers in the Internet cannot initiate communication to computers on the intranet, which makes the intranet invisible to the Internet.

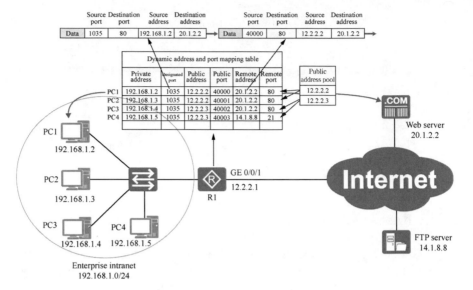

Fig. 10.4 Illustration of network address port translation

10.2.4   Easy IP

Easy IP implements the same principle as NAPT, translating IP addresses and transport layer ports at the same time. The difference is that easy IP does not have the concept of address pools and it uses port addresses as the public addresses for NAT translation.

Easy IP is suitable for scenarios where fixed public addresses are not available. For example, network egresses using DHCP and PPPoE dial-up to obtain addresses can directly use the dynamic addresses obtained for translation.

As shown in Fig. 10.5, easy IP does not need to establish a public IP address pool, because it only uses one public address, which is the IP address of interface GE 0/0/1 of router R1. Easy IP also creates and maintains a dynamic address and port mapping table, and binds the public IP address in this table to be the IP address of interface GE 0/0/1. If the IP address of interface GE 0/0/1 of R1 is changed, the public IP address in this table will be automatically changed accordingly. The IP address of interface GE 0/0/1 can be manually configured or dynamically assigned.

In other aspects, easy IP is exactly the same as NAPT, so it is not repeated here.

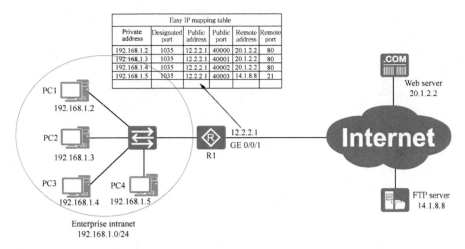

Fig. 10.5 Easy IP

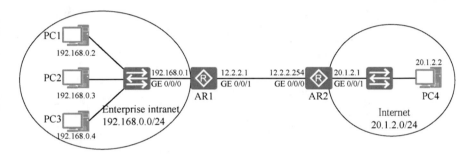

Fig. 10.6 Configure static NAT

10.3 Implementation of NAT

As shown in Fig. 10.6, the private address of the enterprise intranet is 192.168.0.0/
24, and the router AR1 is connected to the Internet with a default route pointing to
the address of interface GE 0/0/0 of AR2, which represents the ISP's router on the
Internet and the router has no route to the private network. The ISP assigns three
public addresses to the enterprise, 12.2.2.1, 12.2.2.2, and 12.2.2.3, among which
12.2.2.1 is assigned to AR1's interface GE 0/0/1.

Now it is required to configure static NAT on router AR1, and the IP address that
PC1 uses to access the Internet is replaced with 12.2.2.2, while the IP address of PC2
to access the Internet is replaced by 12.2.2.3. Address 12.2.2.1 has been assigned to
AR1's interface GE 0/0/1, so this address can no longer be used for static mapping.

Before configuring static NAT, computers on the intranet cannot access computers on the Internet. Think about why that is. Is it because the packets cannot reach

the destination address, or that the response packets sent by the computers on the
Internet cannot be returned to the intranet?

There are two ways to configure static NAT: configuring it in the interface view
and configuring it in the global view.

Here is an example of configuring static NAT on AR1 in the interface view.

```
[AR1]interface GigabitEthernet 0/0/1
[AR1-GigabitEthernet0/0/1]nat static global 12.2.2.2 inside
192.168.0.2
[AR1-GigabitEthernet0/0/1]nat static global 12.2.2.3 inside
192.168.0.3
```

Here is an example of configuring static NAT mapping on AR1 in the system
view.

```
[AR1]nat static global 12.2.2.2 inside 192.168.0.2
[AR1]nat static global 12.2.2.3 inside 192.168.0.3
[AR1]interface GigabitEthernet 0/0/1
[AR1-GigabitEthernet0/0/1]nat static enable    --Enable static NAT in
the interface view
```

View static NAT mapping in AR1.

```
<AR1>display nat static
Static Nat Information:
Interface  : GigabitEthernet0/0/1
  Global IP/Port      : 12.2.2.2/----
  Inside IP/Port      : 192.168.0.2/----
  Protocol : ----
  VPN instance-name  : ----
  Acl number          : ----
  Netmask  : 255.255.255.255
  Description : ----
  Global IP/Port      : 12.2.2.3/----
  Inside IP/Port      : 192.168.0.3/----
  Protocol : ----
  VPN instance-name  : ----
  Acl number          : ----
  Netmask  : 255.255.255.255
  Description : ----
 Total :    2
```

After the configuration is complete, PC1 and PC2 can ping 20.1.2.2. PC3 cannot
ping the IP address of computers on the Internet. PC4 on the Internet can access PC1
on the intranet through the address 12.2.2.2 and access PC2 on the intranet through
the address 12.2.2.3.

After the test is complete, delete the static NAT settings. For the static NAT
configured in the interface view, enter the following commands to delete the
configuration.

```
[AR1-GigabitEthernet0/0/1]undo nat static global 12.2.2.2 inside
192.168.0.2
[AR1-GigabitEthernet0/0/1]undo nat static global 12.2.2.3 inside
192.168.0.3
```

For the static NAT configured in system view, enter the following commands to delete the configuration.

```
[AR1]undo nat static global 12.2.2.2 inside 192.168.0.2
[AR1]undo nat static global 12.2.2.3 inside 192.168.0.3
[AR1]interface GigabitEthernet 0/0/1
[AR1-GigabitEthernet0/0/1]undo nat static enable
```

10.4   Implementation of NAPT

In this section, the network environment is shown in Fig. 10.6. The ISP assigns public addresses 12.2.2.1, 12.2.2.2 and 12.2.2.3 to the enterprise. 12.2.2.1 is assigned to interface GE 0/0/1 of router AR1, while the other two public addresses 12.2.2.2 and 12.2.2.3 are given to the intranet computers for NAPT.

Create a public address pool on router AR1.

```
[AR1]nat address-group 1 ?                          --Specify the
number of public address pool as 1
  IP_ADDR<X.X.X.X>  Start address
  [AR1]nat address-group 1 12.2.2.2 12.2.2.3        --Specify
start address and end address
```

If there are multiple network segments on the enterprise intranet, perhaps only certain network segments are permitted to access the Internet. Define the intranet segments that are allowed to access the Internet through NAPT according to the definition of ACL. In this case, there is only one network segment on the intranet.

```
[AR1]acl 2000
[AR1-acl-basic-2000]rule 5 permit source 192.168.0.0 0.0.0.255
[AR1-acl-basic-2000]rule deny
[AR1-acl-basic-2000]quit
```

Configure NAPT for interface GigabitEthernet 0/0/1 connected to the Internet on AR1.

```
[AR1]interface GigabitEthernet 0/0/1
[AR1-GigabitEthernet0/0/1]nat outbound 2000 address-group 1 ? -
Specify the public address pool to use
  no-pat  Not use PAT                    --If it has no-pat, it is dynamic
NAT
  <cr>    Please press ENTER to execute command
```

```
[AR1-GigabitEthernet0/0/1]nat outbound 2000 address-group 1  --If
it does not have no-pat, it is NAPT
```

Ping PC4 on the Internet on PC1, PC2, and PC3 to test if the network is connected.

10.5   Implementation of Easy IP

As shown in Fig. 10.7, the enterprise intranet uses private address 192.168.0.0/24, and the ISP only assigns the enterprise one public address, 12.2.2.1/24. Configure NAPT on AR1 to allow computers on the intranet to use the public address of interface GE 0/0/1 of router AR1 for address translation so as to access the Internet.

If there are multiple network segments on the enterprise intranet, perhaps only certain network segments are permitted to access the Internet. Define the intranet segments allowed to access the Internet through NAPT according to the definition of ACL. In this case, there is only one network segment on the intranet.

```
[AR1]acl 2000
[AR1-acl-basic-2000]rule 5 permit source 192.168.0.0 0.0.0.255
[AR1-acl-basic-2000]rule deny
[AR1-acl-basic-2000]quit
```

Configure NAPT for interface GigabitEthernet 0/0/1 connected to the Internet on AR1.

```
[AR1]interface GigabitEthernet 0/0/1
[AR1-GigabitEthernet0/0/1]nat outbound 2000     --Specify the ACL
that allows NAPT
```

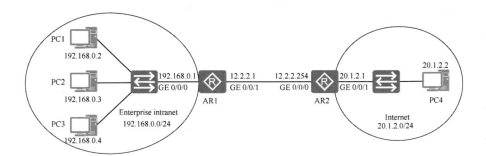

Fig. 10.7 Use an extranet interface address for NAPT

10.6 NAT Server

10.6.1 Application Scenarios of NAT Server

When a server in the private network needs to provide service to the public network, NAT server needs to be configured on the router to specify a one-to-one mapping between [public address: port] and [private address: port] to map the intranet server to the public network. The public host accesses [public address: port] so as to access the intranet server.

As shown in Fig. 10.8, Router RA connects the intranet to the Internet, planning to allow computers on the Internet to access the intranet Web server's website. To enable the above function, you need to configure a NAT server on Router RA, which is essentially adding a static NAT mapping to the NAT mapping table to map port 80 of the TCP protocol to Port 80 of the intranet Web server.

In Fig. 10.8, a packet from PC4 on the Internet accesses TCP port 80 at address 12.2.2.8. After receiving the packet, Router RA looks up the NAT mapping table, finds the corresponding [private address: port] based on the [public address: port] information, then translates the destination address and port of the IP address data message, and sends the packet to the intranet Web server on the intranet.

Router RA receives the packet returned to PC4 from the Web server, and then sends the packet to PC4 after translating the source IP address and port according to the NAT mapping table.

10.6.2 Implementation of NAT Server

As shown in Fig. 10.9, a company's intranet uses network segment 192.168.0.0/24 and is connected to the Internet via router AR1 whose public IP address is 12.2.2.1. The Web server in the company's intranet needs to be accessible for computers on the Internet, and the employees of the company's IT department have to use remote

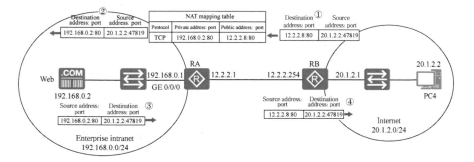

Fig. 10.8 NAT server

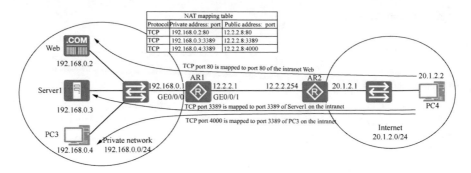

Fig. 10.9 Configure NAT server

desktop to connect to Server1 and PC3 of the enterprise intranet after they return home from work.

The HTTP protocol is used to access the website. This protocol uses TCP port 80 by default, and maps TCP port 80 of 12.2.2.8 to TCP port 80 of 192.168.0.2 on the intranet.

The remote desktop uses the RDP protocol. This protocol uses TCP port 3389 by default, and maps TCP port 3389 of 12.2.2.8 to TCP port 3389 of 192.168.0.3 on the intranet.

TCP port 3389 has been mapped to Server1 on the intranet, so when you use remote desktop to connect to PC3, you can no longer use port 3389, but can map TCP port 4000 of 12.2.2.8 to port 3389 of 192.168.0.4 on the intranet. By accessing TCP port 4000 of 12.2.2.8, you can access the remote desktop (port 3389) of PC3.

Configure easy IP on interface GE 0/0/1 of router AR1, and the source address of packets of intranet accessing the Internet is replaced by the public address of this interface. This example configures NAT server and uses another public address 12.2.2.8 as the NATServer address to allow Internet access to the Web server, Server1 and PC3's remote desktop on the intranet.

Map the address of interface GigabitEthernet 0/0/1 of AR1 from TCP port 80 to port 80 of address 192.168.0.2 on the intranet.

```
[AR1-GigabitEthernet0/0/1] nat server protocol tcp global 12.2.2.8 ?
  <0-65535>  Global port of NAT          --It can be followed by port
number
  ftp        File Transfer Protocol (21)
  pop3       Post Office Protocol v3 (110)
  smtp       Simple Mail Transport Protocol (25)
  telnet     Telnet (23)
  www        World Wide Web (HTTP, 80)      --www is equivalent to port 80
  [AR1-GigabitEthernet0/0/1] nat server protocol tcp global 12.2.2.8
www inside 192.168.0.2 www
 Warning:The port 80 is well-known port. If you continue it may cause
function failure.
 Are you sure to continue? [Y/N] :y
```

Map the address of interface GigabitEthernet 0/0/1 on AR1 from TCP port 3389 o port 3389 of address 192.168.0.3 on the intranet.

```
[AR1-GigabitEthernet0/0/1]nat server protocol tcp global 12.2.2.8
3389 inside 192.168. 0.3 3389
```

Map the address of interface GigabitEthernet 0/0/1 on AR1 from TCP port 4000 to port 3389 of address 192.168.0.4 on the intranet.

```
[AR1-GigabitEthernet0/0/1]nat server protocol tcp global 12.2.2.8
4000 inside 192.168. 0.4 3389
```

View the NAT Server configuration of interface GigabitEthernet 0/0/1 on AR1.

```
<AR1>display nat server interface GigabitEthernet 0/0/1

Nat Server Information:
Interface  : GigabitEthernet0/0/1
  Global IP/Port      : 12.2.2.8/80(www)
  Inside IP/Port      : 192.168.0.2/80(www)
  Protocol : 6(tcp)
  VPN instance-name  : ----
  Acl number         : ----
  Description : ----
  Global IP/Port      : 12.2.2.8/3389
  Inside IP/Port      : 192.168.0.3/3389
  Protocol : 6(tcp)
  VPN instance-name  : ----
  Acl number         : ----
  Description : ----
  Global IP/Port      : 12.2.2.8/4000
  Inside IP/Port      : 192.168.0.4/3389
  Protocol : 6(tcp)
  VPN instance-name  : ----
  Acl number         : ----
  Description : ----
Total :    3
```

10.7 Exercises

1. As shown in Fig. 10.10, which NAT translation mode should be configured on router R1 so that Host A can access public networks and public network users can also actively access Host A? ( )

   A. Static NAT
   B. Dynamic NAT

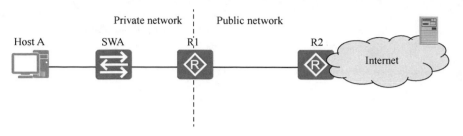

Fig. 10.10 Communication illustration (1)

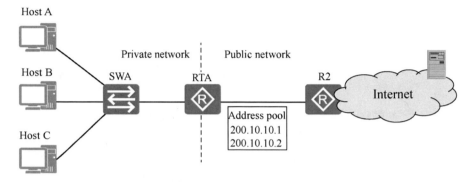

Fig. 10.11 Communication illustration (2)

    C. Easy IP
    D. NAPT

2. As shown in Fig. 10.11, RTA uses NAT technology and defines an address pool
   to enable many-to-many non-NAPT address translation so that private network
   hosts can access public networks. Suppose there are only two public IP addresses
   in the address pool that have been assigned to Host A and B, and address
   translation has been done. Then if Host C also wants to access public networks,
   which of the following descriptions is correct ( )

    A. RTA assigns the first public address to Host C, and Host A is kicked offline
    B. RTA assigns the last public address to Host C, and Host B is kicked offline
    C. Host C cannot be assigned a public address and cannot access the public
        network
    D. All hosts take turns to use the public address and all can access the public
        network

3. (Multi-selection) Which of the following descriptions of NAT is correct ( )

   A. NAT's full name is Network Address Translation
   B. NAT is usually used to translate between private addresses and public addresses
   C. When a host on an intranet using a private address accesses an external public network, NAT is not used
   D. NAT technology has made great contribution to solving the problem of IP address shortage

4. If a company has 50 private IP addresses in its network, the network administrator uses NAT technology to access the public network, and the company has only one public address available, then which of the following NAT translation methods meets the requirements? ( )

   A. Static translation
   B. Dynamic translation
   C. Easy IP
   D. NAPT

5. NAPT allows multiple private IP addresses to be mapped to the same public IP address through different port numbers, then which of the following descriptions of the port numbers of NAPT is correct ( )

   A. You must manually configure the correspondence between the port number and the private address
   B. Only the range of port numbers needs to be configured
   C. There is no need to do any configuration regarding the port number
   D. The port number needs to be assigned using ACLs

6. Which of the following option is the necessary technology to enable a host whose IP address is 10.0.0.1 to access the Internet ( )

   A. Dynamic routing
   B. NAT
   C. Import-route
   D. Static routing

7. As shown in Fig. 10.12, the following static NAT command is run on router R1. When the PC accesses the Internet, the destination address in the packet does not change. Is this statement correct? ( )

   A. Correct
   B. Incorrect

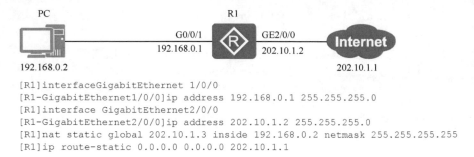

```
[R1]interfaceGigabitEthernet 1/0/0
[R1-GigabitEthernet1/0/0]ip address 192.168.0.1 255.255.255.0
[R1]interface GigabitEthernet2/0/0
[R1-GigabitEthernet2/0/0]ip address 202.10.1.2 255.255.255.0
[R1]nat static global 202.10.1.3 inside 192.168.0.2 netmask 255.255.255.255
[R1]ip route-static 0.0.0.0 0.0.0.0 202.10.1.1
```

Fig. 10.12 Static NAT configuration

8. When NAT uses dynamic address pools, the addresses in the pool can be reused, i.e., the same IP is mapped to multiple intranet IPs at the same time. Is this statement correct? ( )

   A. Correct
   B. Incorrect

Chapter 11
DHCP

Network parameters such as IP addresses, subnet masks, gateways and DNSs are required for computers and mobile devices to access the network. There are two ways to configure IP addresses: static address assignment and dynamic address assignment.

Static address assignment requires manually inputting network parameters. Ordinary users' lack of understanding on network parameters often leads to misconfiguration, so that the network cannot be accessed normally; and address conflicts caused by arbitrary IP address configuration are frequent. Wireless networks providing Internet access in public places such as hotels and restaurants, as well as 4G and 5G access for cell phones, are all temporary access, and the most convenient way is to automatically configure IP addresses and other parameters for the accessing device.

This chapter introduces the working principles of DHCP, and configures Huawei routers as DHCP servers to configure dynamic addresses for computers and mobile devices in the network.

11.1   Application Scenarios of Static Addresses and Dynamic Addresses

There are two ways to configure IP addresses for computers: the first is to manually specify configuration information such as IP addresses, subnet masks, gateways and DNS, and the IP addresses obtained in this way are called static addresses; the second is to use a DHCP server to specify configuration information IP addresses, subnet masks, gateways and DNSs for computers, and the addresses obtained in this way are called dynamic addresses.

1. The problems of manual configuration of network parameters

   (a) Many parameters are difficult to understand. For ordinary users, it is most desirable that they are able to access the Internet simply by connecting the network cable or connect to Wi-Fi without any other settings needed. If ordinary users are required to configure IP addresses, subnet masks, gateways, DNSs and other parameters in order to access the Internet, each time the network administrator also needs to provide an unused IP address.

   (b) High workload. If there are a large number of computers in the enterprise network, manual configuration by the network administrator is a massive workload and repetitive work, as the network administrator needs to plan the IP addresses in advance and assign them to individuals.

   (c) Low utilization rate. Each person in the enterprise network uses a fixed IP address, leading to low utilization rate of IP address.

   Some addresses may be in a long-term unused state. For example, if a Mr. Zhang goes on a business trip for a month, the IP address assigned to his computer will not be used for a long time. Meanwhile, new IP addresses need to be assigned to new employees.

   (d) Poor flexibility. Due to the emergence of WLAN, the terminal location is no longer fixed, so when the wireless terminal moves to an area covered by another wireless network, the IP address may need to be reconfigured.

2. Application scenario of static addresses

   (a) Computers do not often change their location in the network. For example, in school server rooms, the location of desktop computers is fixed, so static addresses are usually used. And to make it easier for student to access resources, IP addresses are also set according to certain rules, such as setting the IP address of the computer in the first row of the fourth column to 192.168.0.14, and the IP address of the computer in the third row of the second column to 192.168.0.32.

   (b) Enterprise servers also use fixed IP addresses (static addresses), which is to facilitate users to use IP addresses to access the server. For example, enterprise Web servers, FTP servers, domain controllers, file servers and DNS servers usually use static addresses.

3. Application scenario of dynamic addresses

   (a) Computers in the network are not fixed. For example, for the School of Software, each classroom belongs to a network segment: the network of Class 202 is network segment 10.7.202.0/24, the network of Class 204 is network segment 10.7.204.0/24. When students move from Class 202 to Class 204, the IP addresses of their laptops will have to be changed. If you ask the students to change the IP address (static address) by themselves, and the address configured may have already been used by other students' laptops. Manually assigning addresses to mobile devices is troublesome, and moreover, the assigned addresses are prone to conflict with the others. If a DHCP server is used to uniformly assign addresses, no conflicts will arise.

(b) For devices connected via Wi-Fi, usually, their addresses are also automatically assigned by a DHCP server. Accessing the network via Wi-Fi is supposed to be convenient, and it would be inconvenient if you have to set the IP address, subnet mask, gateway and DNS before you can access the Internet after connecting to Wi-Fi.

11.2 Working Principles of DHCP

11.2.1 Basic Concepts of DHCP

In order to solve the shortcomings of traditional static manual configuration method, Dynamic Host Configuration Protocol (DHCP) came into being. It can dynamically assign IP addresses to hosts. DHCP adopts C/S (Client/Server) architecture, and hosts only need to set the mode to obtain an IP address automatically from the server, so that the network can be directly used once it is connected to the network.

As shown in Fig. 11.1, the DHCP client can be a wireless mobile device, a laptop or a desktop computer. As long as the mode is set to obtain an IP address automatically (which is the default mode), the device becomes an DHCP client. The DHCP server can be a Windows server, Linux server, or Huawei Layer 3 device and router. DHCP client sends a DHCP request, and DHCP server receives the request and provides the client with an available address and parameters such as subnet mask, gateway and DNS.

DHCP has the following advantages.

1. Unified management. IP addresses are obtained from the address pool of DHCP server, and the server will record and maintain the usage status of IP addresses,

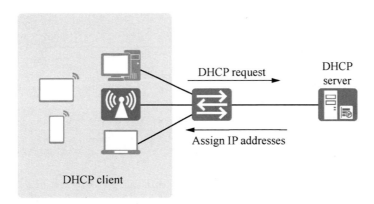

Fig. 11.1 DHCP working illustration

such as which IP addresses have been used and which addresses have not been used, so as to uniformly assign and manage IP addresses.
2. Address lease period. DHCP introduces the concept of lease period. For the assigned IP address, if the terminal has not renewed the lease after the lease period expires, the server will conclude that the terminal no longer needs the IP address and will take the address back, and this IP address can be assigned to other terminals.

11.2.2   Working Process of DHCP

1. When a DHCP client needs to obtain a new IP address

    (a) It is the first time for the client computer to obtain an IP address from the DHCP server.
    (b) The IP address originally rented by the client computer has been taken back by the DHCP server and rented to other computers, so the client needs to rent a new IP address from the DHCP server.
    (c) The client releases the original IP address rented and requests a new one.
    (d) The client computer has changed its network interface card.
    (e) The client computer has moved to another network segment.

2. Types of DHCP packets
   In the above five cases, DHCP client and DHCP server will communicate with each other through the following four types of packets, and the working process of DHCP is shown in Fig. 11.2.

    (a) DHCP Discover.
        The DHCP client discovers available DHCP servers by broadcasting a DHCP Discover packet to the network.

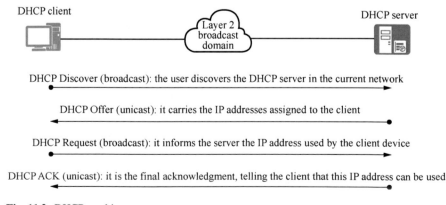

Fig. 11.2   DHCP working process

The computer that sets the IP address to automatic mode is the DHCP client. It has no idea who is the DHCP server in the network and has no address. DHCP client sends a broadcast packet to request the address, and all devices in the network can receive the request. The source IP address of the broadcast packet is 0.0.0.0 and the destination IP address is 255.255.255.255.

(b) DHCP Offer.

The DHCP server answers the client's request by broadcasting a DHCP Offer packet to the network.

When a DHCP server receives a DHCP Discover packet broadcasted by a DHCP client, all DHCP servers in the network will broadcast a DHCP Offer packet to the network. The so-called DHCP Offer packet is the information used by the DHCP server to provide IP address to the DHCP client.

(c) DHCP Request.

The DHCP client broadcasts a DHCP Request packet to the network to select IP addresses offered by multiple servers.

After receiving a DHCP Offer packet from a server, the DHCP client broadcasts a DHCP Request packet to the network to accept the assignment. The DHCP Request packet contains the identification of the DHCP server that provides the lease for the client, so that other DHCP servers will revoke the assignment to this client after receiving this packet and the IP addresses that should have been assigned are withdrawn for responding to the lease request from other clients.

(d) DHCP ACK (DHCP Acknowledgement)

The selected DHCP server broadcasts a DHCP ACK packet to the network to confirm the client's selection.

After the DHCP server receives the DHCP Request packet broadcasted by the client, it then broadcasts a DHCP ACK packet to the network. The so-called DHCP ACK packet is the information sent by the DHCP server to the DHCP client to confirm the successful generation of the IP address lease. This information contains the valid lease of the IP address and other IP configuration information.

After the DHCP client receives the DHCP ACK information, the process of obtaining an IP address is complete and this IP address can be used to communicate with other computers in the network.

Think about it: why doesn't the DHCP client directly use the IP address after receiving the DHCP Offer, but send a DHCP Request to inform the server?

The broadcasted DHCP Request message informs other DHCP servers in the network that the client has selected an IP address assigned by a server, so as to ensure that other servers can retrieve the IP address assigned to the client through unicast DHCP Offer.

11.2.3   Lease Renewal

Before the lease expires, the DHCP client needs to renew the address lease assigned to it from the server.

1. Two methods of lease renewal.

   (a) Automatic renewal.

       DHCP automatically renew its lease. as soon as 50 percent of the lease duration has expired, A DHCP client automatically attempts to renew its lease, as shown in Fig. 11.3.

   (b) Manual renewal.

       If you need to update the DHCP configuration information immediately, you can manually renew an IP address lease. For example, if we want the DHCP client to immediately get the address of a newly installed router from the DHCP server, you simply need to renew the lease on the client side.

       You can directly execute the: ipconfig /renew command at the command prompt of the client.

2. The process of automatic renewal

   The DHCP client renews its lease periodically according to the set time to ensure that it is using the latest configuration information. When the lease expires and the client still has not renewed its address lease, the DHCP client will lose the address lease and start a DHCP lease generation process. The DHCP lease renewal process is as follows.

   (a) When 50% of the lease duration has expired, the client sends a request to the DHCP server, asking to renew and extend the current lease. The client sends a request directly to the DHCP server and can re-send it up to 3 times, at 4 s, 8 s and 16 s respectively.

   (b) If a server responds a DHCP Offer message to renew the client's current lease, the client renews the lease with the information provided by the server and continues to work.

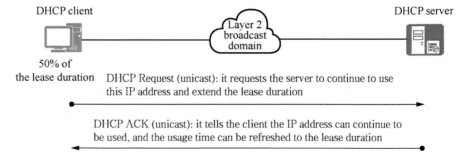

Fig. 11.3   DHCP lease renewal

If the client does not get a response from the original server half way through its lease duration, the client broadcasts a DHCP Request at 87.5% of the lease term, and any DHCP server can respond. This process is called rebinding.

(c) If the lease is terminated and there is no connection to the server, the client must immediately stop using its leased IP address. The client then performs the same process as during its initial startup to obtain a new IP address lease.

11.3 DHCP Service Configuration

As shown in Fig. 11.4, a company has three departments; the network of the sales department uses network segment 192.168.1.0/24, the network of the marketing department uses network segment 192.168.2.0/24, and the network of the R&D department uses network segment 172.16.5.0/24. Now you have to configure router AR1 as a DHCP server to assign IP addresses to the computers in these three departments.

Create an address pool vlan1 for the sales department on AR1, vlan1 is the name of the address pool, and the name can be specified as you like.

```
[AR1]dhcp enable                        --Enable the global DHCP service
[AR1]ip pool vlan1                      --Create an address pool for VLAN 1
[AR1-ip-pool-vlan1]network 192.168.1.0 mask 24   --Specify the
network segment of the address pool
[AR1-ip-pool-vlan1]gateway-list 192.168.1.1      --Specify the
gateway of the address pool
[AR1-ip-pool-vlan1]dns-list 8.8.8.8              --Specify the DNS server
[AR1-ip-pool-vlan1]dns-list 222.222.222.222      --Specify the second
```

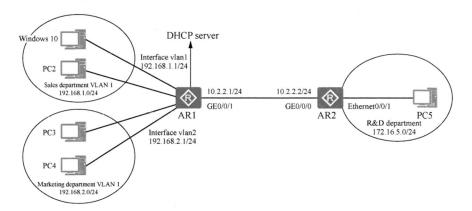

Fig. 11.4 DHCP network topology

```
DNS server
  [AR1-ip-pool-vlan1] lease day 0 hour 8 minute 0     --Address lease, the
time the client is allowed to use
  [AR1-ip-pool-vlan1] excluded-ip-address 192.168.1.1 192.168.1.10
--Specify the excluded address range
  Error:The gateway cannot be excluded.                --Gateway cannot be
excluded
  [AR1-ip-pool-vlan1] excluded-ip-address 192.168.1.2 192.168.1.10
--Specify the excluded address range
  [AR1-ip-pool-vlan1] excluded-ip-address 192.168.1.50 192.168.1.60
--Specify the excluded address range
  [AR1-ip-pool-vlan1] display this              --Display the address
pool configuration
  [V200R003C00]
  #
  ip pool vlan1
  gateway-list 192.168.1.1
  network 192.168.1.0 mask 255.255.255.0
  excluded-ip-address 192.168.1.2 192.168.1.10
  excluded-ip-address 192.168.1.50 192.168.1.60
  lease day 0 hour 8 minute 0
  dns-list 8.8.8.8 222.222.222.222
  #
  Return
```

Configure the Vlanif 1 interface to select addresses from the global address pool. The vlan1 address pool created above is a global address pool.

```
[AR1] interface Vlanif 1
[AR1-Vlanif1] dhcp select global
```

A network segment is only able to create one address pool. If some addresses in the network segment are already occupied, they shall be excluded from the pool to avoid conflicts between the addresses assigned by the DHCP and other computers. The IP address and other configuration information assigned to the client by DHCP has a time limit (lease duration). If computers in the network changes frequently, the lease duration should be set shorter; and if the computers in the network are relatively stable, the lease duration should be set longer. Students in the School of Software are likely to change classrooms every two hours for lectures, so the lease duration can be set to 2 hours. Normally, the client will automatically find the DHCP server to renew the lease after half of the lease duration expires. If the duration expires and the client does not find the DHCP server to renew the lease, the DHCP server assumes the client is no longer in the network and its IP address will be retrieved and can be assigned to other computers later.

Create an address pool for the marketing department.

```
[AR1] ip pool vlan2
[AR1-ip-pool-vlan2] network 192.168.2.0 mask 24
[AR1-ip-pool-vlan2] gateway-list 192.168.2.1
```

```
[AR1-ip-pool-vlan2] dns-list 114.114.114.114
[AR1-ip-pool-vlan2] lease day 0 hour 2 minute 0
[AR1-ip-pool-vlan2] quit
```

Configure interface Vlanif 2 to select addresses from the global address pool.

```
[AR1] interface Vlanif 2
[AR1-Vlanif2] dhcp select global
```

Enter "display ip pool" to display the defined address pool.

```
<AR1>display ip pool
----------------------------------------------------------------
  Pool-name       : vlan1
  Pool-No         : 0
  Position        : Local      Status      : Unlocked
  Gateway-0        : 192.168.1.1
  Mask           : 255.255.255.0
  VPN instance    : --
----------------------------------------------------------------
  Pool-name       : vlan2
  Pool-No         : 1
  Position        : Local      Status      : Unlocked
  Gateway-0        : 192.168.2.1
  Mask           : 255.255.255.0
  VPN instance    : --
  IP address Statistic
   Total         :506
   Used          :4      Idle      :482
   Expired       :0      Conflict  :0      Disable  :20
```

Run the packet capture tool on Windows 10 and set the mode to obtain an IP address automatically to obtain IP addresses so that the packets the DHCP client uses to request an IP address can be captured. As shown in Fig. 11.5, you can see the four packets interacting between DHCP client and DHCP server, which is the working process of DHCP protocol.

Enter "display ip pool name vlan1 used" to display the address lease usage of address pool vlan1. The two addresses that have been assigned to the computers are highlighted in bold below.

```
<AR1>display ip pool name vlan1 used
  Pool-name       : vlan1
  Pool-No         : 0
  Lease           : 0 Days 8 Hours 0 Minutes
  Domain-name     : -
  DNS-server0     : 8.8.8.8
  DNS-server1     : 222.222.222.222
  NBNS-server0    : -
  Netbios-type    : -
  Position        : Local           Status        : Unlocked
```

```
Gateway-0     : 192.168.1.1
Mask          : 255.255.255.0
VPN instance  : --
--------------------------------------------------------------------
      Start          End      Total  Used   Idle(Expired)   Conflict
Disable
--------------------------------------------------------------------
    192.168.1.1  192.168.1.254   253     2       231(0)            0
20
--------------------------------------------------------------------
  Network section :
--------------------------------------------------------------------
  Index       IP              MAC            Lease    Status
--------------------------------------------------------------------
    252   192.168.1.253   5489-9851-4a95     335     Used    --Lease,
with client MAC address
    253   192.168.1.254   5489-9831-72f6     344     Used    --Lease,
with client MAC address
--------------------------------------------------------------------
```

11.4   Assign Addresses to Directly Connected Network Segments Using Interface Address Pool

The above operation configures the Huawei router as a DHCP server, creates an address pool for one network segment, and also assigns a network segment and subnet mask to the address pool. If the router assigns addresses for directly connected network segments, it is not necessary to create address pools. As the

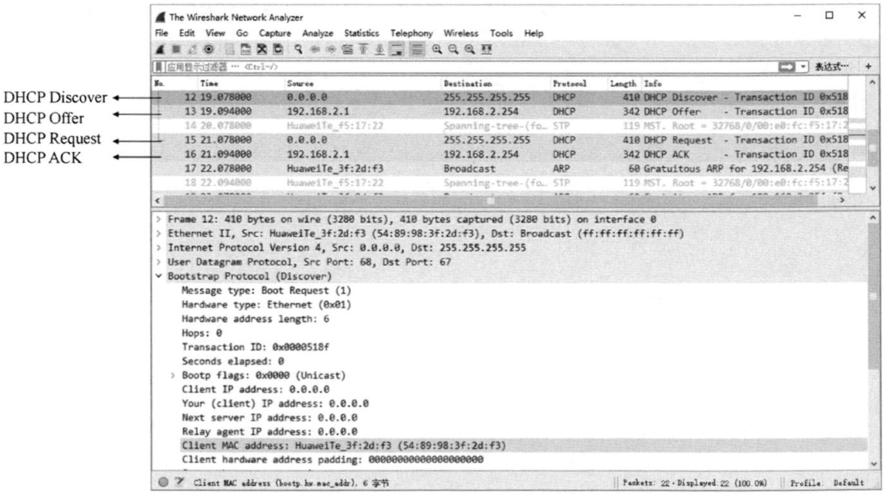

Fig. 11.5 The working process of DHCP protocol

Fig. 11.6 Topology for assigning addresses to directly connected network segments using interface address pools

router port has been configured with address and subnet mask, you can use the network segment where the port is located as the network segment and subnet mask for the address pool.

As shown in Fig. 11.6, router AR1 is connected to two network segments 192.168.1.0/24 and 192.168.2.0/24. It is required to configure router AR1 to assign IP addresses to these two network segments.

Configure the addresses of interfaces GigabitEthernet 0/0/0 and GigabitEthernet 0/0/1 for AR1.

```
[AR1]interface GigabitEthernet 0/0/0
[AR1-GigabitEthernet0/0/0]ip address 192.168.1.1 24
[AR1-GigabitEthernet0/0/0]quit
[AR1]interface GigabitEthernet 0/0/1
[AR1-GigabitEthernet0/0/1]ip address 192.168.2.1 24
[AR1-GigabitEthernet0/0/1]
```

Enable DHCP service and configure interface GigabitEthernet 0/0/0 to select addresses from the interface address pool.

```
[AR1]dhcp enable                             --Enable global DHCP
service
[AR1]interface GigabitEthernet 0/0/0
[AR1-GigabitEthernet0/0/0]dhcp select interface    --Select an
address from the interface address pool
[AR1-GigabitEthernet0/0/0]dhcp server dns-list 114.114.114.114
[AR1-GigabitEthernet0/0/0]dhcp server ?            --You can view all
configurations
  dns-list             Configure DNS servers
  domain-name          Configure domain name
  excluded-ip-address  Mark disable IP addresses
  ......
  lease                Configure the lease of the IP pool
[AR1-GigabitEthernet0/0/0]dhcp server excluded-ip-address
192.168.1.2 192.168.1.20     --Exclude the address
```

Configure interface GigabitEthernet 0/0/1 to select addresses from the interface address pool.

```
[AR1]interface GigabitEthernet 0/0/1
[AR1-GigabitEthernet0/0/1]dhcp select interface
[AR1-GigabitEthernet0/0/1]dhcp server dns-list 8.8.8.8
[AR1-GigabitEthernet0/0/1]dhcp server lease day 0 hour 4 minute 0
```

11.5 DHCP Relay

11.5.1 Principles of DHCP Relay

The previous part talks about DHCP server assigning IP addresses to directly connected network segments. DHCP server can also assign IP addresses to non-directly connected network segments. As shown in Fig. 11.7, AR1 is configured as a DHCP server to assign IP addresses to the R&D department. This requires enabling DHCP relay on interface Vlanif 1 of router AR2.

The principles of DHCP relay are explained below.

1. When the DHCP client starts and performs DHCP initialization, it sends a DHCP Discover request message in the local network.
2. If a DHCP server exists in the local network, DHCP configuration can be directly performed without DHCP relay.
3. If there is no DHCP server in the local network, after receiving the broadcast message, the network device with DHCP relay function connected to this local network will process it appropriately and forward it to the DHCP server on the other network specified. As shown in Fig. 11.7, the DHCP relay forwards the DHCP request packet whose destination address is the IP address of the DHCP server, and the source address is the IP address of interface Vlanif 1 of AR2. DHCP is able to determine which network segment this request is from based on the source address.

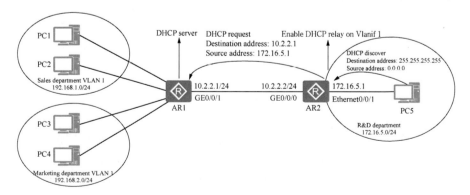

Fig. 11.7 DHCP relay illustration

4. DHCP server configures correspondingly according to the information provided by DHCP client, and sends the configuration information to DHCP client through DHCP relay to complete the dynamic configuration of DHCP client.

In fact, several interaction processes like this are required from the beginning to the final completion of the configuration. The DHCP relay device modifies the corresponding fields in the DHCP message, changes the DHCP broadcast packets to unicast packets, and is responsible for the conversion between the server and the client.

11.5.2   *Configure DHCP Relay for Cross-Network Segment Address Assignment*

According to Fig. 11.7, the network environment is set up and the address pool remoteNet is created on router AR1 so as to assign addresses to the computers in the R&D department. The network of the R&D department is not directly connected to router AR1. The router isolates broadcasts, so AR1 cannot receive the DHCP discovery packets sent by the computers in the R&D department. This requires configuring interface Vlanif 1 of router AR2 to enable the DHCP relay function, which converts the received DHCP discovery packets into directed DHCP discovery packets with a destination address of 10.2.2.1 and a source address of 172.16.5.1, which is the address of the interface Vlanif 1. Once router AR1 receives such a packet, it knows that this is a request from network segment 172.16.5.0/24, so it selects an IP address from the address pool remoteNet for PC5. The prerequisite for completing this experiment is to ensure that these networks are unimpeded.

The following creates the address pool remoteNet on AR1 for the network of the R&D department. Gateways must be set for the address pool of the remote network segment.

```
[AR1]ip pool remoteNet
[AR1-ip-pool-remoteNet]network 172.16.5.0 mask 24
[AR1-ip-pool-remoteNet]gateway-list 172.16.5.1          --Gateway
must be set
[AR1-ip-pool-remoteNet]dns-list 8.8.8.8
[AR1-ip-pool-remoteNet]lease day 0 hour 2 minute 0
[AR1-ip-pool-remoteNet]quit
```

Configure interface GE0/0/1 of AR1 to select an address from the global address pool.

```
[AR1]interface GigabitEthernet 0/0/1
[AR1-GigabitEthernet0/0/1]dhcp select global
[AR1-GigabitEthernet0/0/1]quit
```

Enable the DHCP function on router AR2, configure interface Vlanif 1 of router AR2, enable the DHCP relay function, and specify the address of the DHCP server.

```
[AR2]dhcp enable                    --Enable DHCP
[AR2]interface Vlanif 1
[AR2-Vlanif1]dhcp select relay              --Enable DHCP relay on the
interface
[AR2-Vlanif1]dhcp relay server-ip 10.2.2.1    --Specify the address
of the DHCP server
```

Set the address of PC5 to be dynamically assigned by DHCP, enter "ipconfig" to check the obtained IP address and verify the cross-network segment assignment. If it is unsuccessful, check the routing table on routers AR1 and AR2 to make sure the network is unobstructed for DHCP to assign IP addresses across network segments.

```
PC>ipconfig
Link local IPv6 address...........: fe80::5689:98ff:fe61:65d
IPv6 address.....................: :: / 128
IPv6 gateway.....................: ::
IPv4 address.....................: 172.16.5.254
Subnet mask......................: 255.255.255.0
Gateway..........................: 172.16.5.1
Physical address.................: 54-89-98-61-06-5D
DNS server.......................: 8.8.8.8
```

11.6 Exercises

1. (Multi-selection) After deploying a DHCP server in the network, the administrator finds that some hosts obtain addresses that are not specified by the DHCP server. What are the possible reasons for this? ( )

   A. There is a more efficient DHCP server in the network
   B. Some hosts cannot communicate with the DHCP server normally, and the client system of these hosts automatically generates addresses in the range of 169.254.0.0
   C. Some hosts cannot communicate with the DHCP server normally, and the client system of these hosts automatically generates addresses in the range of 127.254.0.0
   D. The address pool of the DHCP server has been fully assigned

2. When the administrator configures the DHCP server, which of the following commands configures the shortest lease duration? ( )

   A. DHCP select
   B. Lease day 1

    C. Lease 24
    D. Lease 0

3. When the host reboots after obtaining an IP address from DHCP server A, which of the following messages will be sent to DHCP server A? ( )

    A. DHCP Discover
    B. DHCP Request
    C. DHCP Offer
    D. DHCP ACK

4. As shown in Fig. 11.8, which configuration needs to be done on Router RB to enable DHCP service on Router RA and create an address pool for network segment 192.168.3.0/24 so that PC2 can obtain an IP address from Router RA? ( )

    A. [RB]dhcp enable
        [RB]interface GigabitEthernet 0/0/0
          [RB-GigabitEthernet 0/0/0]dhcp select global
    B. [RB]dhcp enable
        [RB]interface GigabitEthernet 0/0/0
          [RB-GigabitEthernet 0/0/0]dhcp select relay
          [RB-GigabitEthernet 0/0/0]dhcp relay server-ip 192.168.2.1
    C. [RB]dhcp enable
        [RB]interface GigabitEthernet 0/0/1
          [RB-GigabitEthernet 0/0/0]dhcp select relay
          [RB-GigabitEthernet 0/0/0]dhcp relay server-ip 192.168.2.1
    D. [RB]interface GigabitEthernet 0/0/0
          [RB-GigabitEthernet 0/0/0]dhcp select relay
          [RB-GigabitEthernet 0/0/0]dhcp relay server-ip 192.168.2.1

5. (Multi-selection) What are the advantages of using DHCP to assign IP addresses? ( )

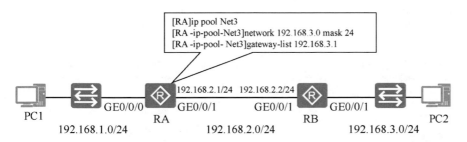

Fig. 11.8 Communication illustration

   A. IP addresses can be reused
   B. IP address conflicts can be avoided
   C. The workload is huge and it is difficult to manage
   D. When the configuration information changes (such as DNS), only the administrator needs to modify it on the DHCP server, which is convenient for unified management

6. What kind of DHCP message does a DHCP client send when it wants to leave the network? ( )

   A. DHCP Discover
   B. DHCP Release
   C. DHCP Request
   D. DHCP ACK

7. The priority of DHCP protocol interface address pool is higher than that of global address pool. This statement is ( ).

   A. Correct
   B. Incorrect

Chapter 12
WLAN Technologies

Wired LAN using wired cable or optical fiber as transmission medium is widely used, but wired transmission medium is subject to high laying cost, fixed the location and poor mobility. With the increasing demand for the portability and mobility of network, traditional wired network can no longer meet the demand, and Wireless Local Area Network (WLAN) technology comes into being.

At present, WLAN has become an economic and efficient way to access the network.

This chapter first introduces the development history of WLAN at different stages, then elaborates the concepts related to WLAN technology and the working principles of common networking architectures, and finally explains the basic configuration of common WLAN networking architectures and the future development trends of WLAN technologies.

12.1 Overview of WLAN

12.1.1 What Is WLAN

WLAN, that is Wireless LAN, is a wireless local area network built by wireless technology. WLAN in a broad sense refers to a network formed by replacing part or all of the transmission media in a wired LAN with wireless signals such as radio waves, lasers and infrared rays. Note: the wireless technology referred to here not only includes Wi-Fi, but also infrared rays, Bluetooth, ZigBee, etc.

Through WLAN technology, users can easily access wireless network and move freely within the area covered by wireless network, so that they are free from the bondage of wired network, as shown in Fig. 12.1.

According to the application scope, wireless network can be divided into Wireless Personal Area Network (WPAN), Wireless Local Area Network (WLAN),

© The Author(s) 2023
Huawei Technologies Co., Ltd., *Data Communications and Network Technologies*,
https://doi.org/10.1007/978-981-19-3029-4_12

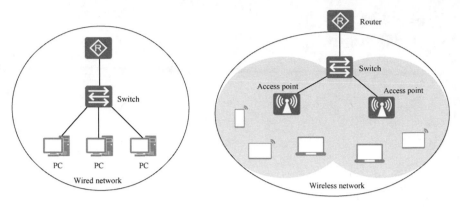

Fig. 12.1 Wired network and wireless network

Wireless Metropolitan Area Network (WMAN) and Wireless Wide Area Network (WWAN).

- The common technologies of WPAN include Bluetooth, ZigBee, NFC, HomeRF, and UWB.
- The common technologies of WLAN include Wi-Fi. (WPAN related technologies are also used in WLAN.)
- The common technologies of WMAN include WiMax.
- The common technologies for WWAN include GSM, CDMA, WCDMA, TD-SCDMA, LTE, and 5G.

WLAN has the following main advantages over current wired broadband networks.

- The network is used freely. Any free space can be connected to the network, not limited by the cable or port location. It is especially suitable for office buildings, airport terminals, resorts, business hotels, stadiums, coffee shops, etc.
- The network is deployed flexibly. When wiring is difficult, such as in subways and for highway traffic monitoring, the use of WLAN for wireless network coverage eliminates or reduces complicated network wiring, and it is simple to implement, low cost, and has excellent scalability.

The WLAN introduced in this section specifically refers to the wireless LAN based on 802.11 standard series that utilizes WI-Fi technologies to use high frequency signals (such as 2.4 GHz or 5 GHz) as the transmission medium.

12.1.2 WLAN Standards and Wi-Fi Evolution

IEEE 802.11 is the current standard of wireless LAN. It is a wireless network communication standard defined by the International Institute of Electrical and Electronic Engineers (IEEE).

Wi-Fi in the context of wireless LANs means "wireless fidelity", which is essentially a commercial certification and also a wireless networking technology. Wi-Fi is a trademark of wireless network communication technology owned by the Wi-Fi Alliance to improve interoperability of wireless network products based on the IEEE 802.11 standard. As the two systems are closely related, Wi-Fi is often used as a synonymous term for the IEEE 802.11 standard.

The various versions of the IEEE 802.11 standard and Wi-Fi are shown in Table 12.1.

The IEEE 802.11 standard focuses on the lower two layers of the TCP/IP peer-to-peer model. The data link layer is mainly responsible for channel access, addressing, data frame checksum, error detection, security mechanisms, etc. And the physical layer is mainly responsible for the transmission of bitstreams in the air interface, e.g., specifying the frequency band to be used.

The first version of IEEE 802.11 was published in 1997. Since then, more complementary standards based on IEEE 802.11 have been gradually defined, among which the widely known standards are the ones that have influenced the intergenerational evolution of Wi-Fi, such as 802.11b, 802.11a, 802.11g, 802.11n and 802.11ac.

When the IEEE 802.11ax standard was introduced, the Wi-Fi Alliance simplified the name of the new Wi-Fi specification to Wi-Fi 6, and the mainstream IEEE 802.11ac was renamed Wi-Fi 5, IEEE 802.11n was renamed Wi-Fi 4, and so on for the other versions.

12.1.3 Development of Wi-Fi in Office Scenarios

The development of Wi-Fi in office scenarios has gone through the following three stages.

1. Primary mobile office era when wireless connection is a complement to wired connection.

   The application of WaveLAN technology can be considered as the earliest prototype of enterprise WLAN. Wi-Fi was born in this period, and the early Wi-Fi technology was mainly used in IOT devices like "wireless radios", but with the introduction of 802.11a/b/g standards, the advantages of wireless connection became increasingly obvious. Businesses and consumers began to recognize the potential of Wi-Fi technology, and wireless hotspots began to appear in coffee shops, airports, and hotels.

   This is the first stage of WLAN application, the main purpose of which was to solve the problem of "wireless access", and the core value was to get rid of the constraints of wires so as to enable the devices to move freely within a certain range, and cover the area uncovered by the wired network using wireless network. However, WLAN at this stage did not pose clear requirements for security, capacity and roaming, and the form of access point (AP) is still a single access

Table 12.1 IEEE 802.11 standard and various versions of Wi-Fi

Frequency	2.4 GHz	2.4 GHz	2.4 GHz &5 GHz	2.4 GHz & 5 GHz	5 GHz	5 GHz	2.4 GHz & 5 GHz
Speed	2 Mbit/s	11 Mbit/s	54 Mbit/s	300 Mbit/s	1300 Mbit/s	6.9 Gbit/s	9.6 Gbit/s
IEEE 802.11 standard	802.11	802.11b	802.11a, 802.11g	802.11n	802.11ac wave1	802.11ac wave2	802.11ax
Wi-Fi version	Wi-Fi 1	Wi-Fi 2	Wi-Fi 3	Wi-Fi 4	Wi-Fi 5	Wi-Fi 5	Wi-Fi 6

point, which is used for single-point network coverage. Usually, the AP of single access point architecture is called FAT AP.

2. Wireless office era when wired and wireless connection was integrated.

With the further popularization of wireless devices, WLAN evolved from being a mere supplement to wired networks to being as indispensable as wired networks, thus entering the second phase.

In this stage, WLAN, as part of the network, also needs to provide network access for enterprise visitors.

In office scenarios, there are a large number of large bandwidth services such as video and voice services, which imposes a greater demand for WLAN bandwidth. Since 2012, the 802.11ac standard has matured and made many improvements on the operating frequency band, channel bandwidth, modulation and coding methods. Compared with the previous Wi-Fi standards, it has higher throughput rate, less interference, and allows more users to access.

3. All-wireless office era with wireless connection as the center.

At present, WLAN has entered the third phase, where wired networks are completely replaced by wireless networks in office environments. The office area is fully covered by Wi-Fi, and the office cubicles are no longer equipped with wired network ports, making the office environment more open and intelligent.

In the future, large-bandwidth services such as cloud desktop office, intelligent and simulated meeting, and 4K video will migrate from wired to wireless networks, while new technologies such as VR/AR will be deployed directly based on wireless networks. New application scenarios put forward higher requirements for the design and planning of WLAN.

In 2018, the new generation Wi-Fi standard Wi-Fi 6 (named as 802.11ax by IEEE, and it is named as Wi-Fi 6 by Wi-Fi Alliance) was released, which is another major milestone in the history of Wi-Fi development. The core value of Wi-Fi 6 is the further expansion of capacity, leading wireless communication into the 10Gbit/s era. Multi-user concurrent performance is improved by four times, allowing the network to maintain excellent service capability despite high density access and heavy service load.

12.2   WLAN Devices and Networking

12.2.1   Introduction to WLAN Devices

Huawei wireless LAN products come in a variety of forms, covering various application scenarios such as indoor-outdoor, home, and enterprise, providing fast, secure and reliable wireless network connections, as shown in Fig. 12.2.

WLAN products for home include Wi-Fi routers for home, which enable wireless Internet access by converting wired network signals into wireless signals to be received by computers, cell phones, and other devices at home.

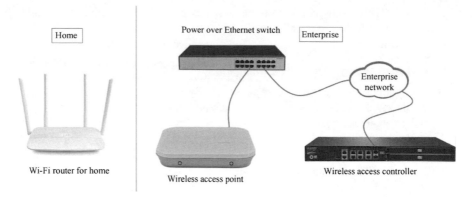

Fig. 12.2 Home wireless devices and enterprise wireless devices

WLAN products for enterprise include wireless access points (APs), wireless access controllers (ACs), Power over Ethernet (PoE) switches, and stations (SATs). Wireless access points and wireless access controllers have been introduced in Chap. 1 and will not be repeated here. The following is a brief introduction to PoE switches and stations.

PoE refers to power over Ethernet, also known as Power over LAN (PoL) or Active Ethernet. PoE allows electrical power to be transmitted to terminal devices over the lines that transmit data or over idle lines. In WLAN networks, power can be supplied to AP devices through PoE switches.

Stations refer to terminal devices that support 802.11 standard, such as computers with wireless network interface cards, and WLAN-enabled cell phones.

12.2.2 Basic WLAN Networking Architecture

WLAN network architecture is divided into two parts, the wired side and wireless side, as shown in Fig. 12.3. The wired side is the network from the AP uplink to the Internet, which uses Ethernet protocol. And the wireless side is the network from STA to AP, which uses 802.11 standard.

The WLAN network architecture for wireless access is a centralized architecture. It has evolved from the initial FAT AP architecture to an AC+FIT AP architecture.

1. FAT AP architecture.

    This architecture can complete the functions of wireless user access, encryption of service data and forwarding of service data messages without using special devices for centralized control. Therefore, it is also called autonomous network architecture. It is suitable for wireless coverage at home. If the WLAN coverage area increases and more users access the network, the number of FAT APs to be deployed will also increase. However, the FAT APs work independently and

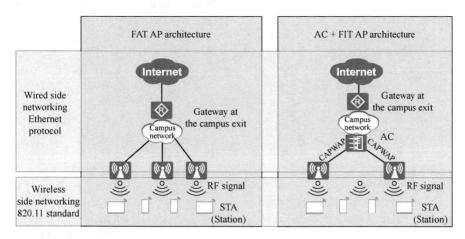

Fig. 12.3 WLAN networking architecture

there is no unified control device, so it is troublesome to manage and maintain these FAT APs.

2. AC + FIT AP architecture.

In this architecture, the AC is responsible for WLAN access control, forwarding and statistics, configuration monitoring of APs, roaming management, network management agent of APs and security control. FIT APs are responsible for 802.11 message encryption and decryption, 802.11 physical layer functions, and being managed by the AC. This architecture has various features and requires network operation and maintenance personnel to be skillful. It is suitable for wireless coverage in medium and large enterprises.

In this book, we mainly use AC+FIT AP architecture as an example to explain.

12.2.3   Agile Distributed AP Architecture

Over the past 5 years, the number of access terminals in Wi-Fi networks has increased by 10 times, the amount of data traffic carried has increased by four times, and meanwhile, 70% of data transmission occurs indoors. Although numerous new WLAN products and protocols have been introduced in recent years, the problem of weak indoor coverage has not been properly addressed. The main reason for this is the formation of blind spots after the signal goes through the wall in traditional installation solutions. When deployed in large hotels or advanced school dormitories with a large number of rooms, more than thousands of APs need to be deployed, which increases the management difficulty.

To fundamentally solve this problem, a change in wireless network architecture is key. Huawei has introduced an agile distributed Wi-Fi solution, as shown in Fig. 12.4, which changes the traditional AC+FIT AP architecture from a Layer 2 architecture to a Layer 3 distributed architecture of AC + central AP+ remote

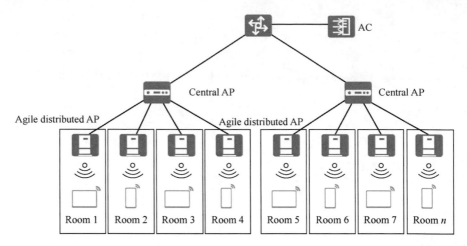

Fig. 12.4 Agile distributed AP architecture

radio frequency units (RF units). Among them, the central AP uniformly processes the service, configuration and roaming functions to improve performance and save management nodes; meanwhile, the distributed architecture sends RF units into rooms through network cable to achieve signal coverage free of dead ends, increasing the user capacity of each room from 32 to 80 and the bandwidth of each user from 10 Mbit/s to 20 Mbit/s; moreover, RF units are only responsible for wireless access and data forwarding, which improves the performance by 20% compared to traditional APs.

Agile distributed Wi-Fi solution solves the multi-room signal coverage problem in hotels or dormitories and the management problem caused by a large number of APs through distributed coverage.

12.2.4 Concepts of Wired Networking

The concepts involved in wired networking include CAPWAP protocol, AP-AC networking method and AC connection method.

1. CAPWAP protocol

   In order to meet the requirements of large-scale networking, a unified management of multiple APs in the network is necessary, so IETF established the Control and Provisioning of Wireless Access Points Protocol (CAPWAP) working group, and finally developed CAPWAP protocol. The protocol defines a specific method for AC for the management and service configuration of APs: CAPWAP tunnels will first be established between AC and APs, and then AC will centrally manage and control APs through the CAPWAP tunnel, as shown in Fig. 12.5.

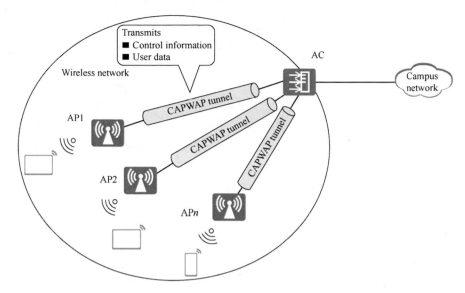

Fig. 12.5 CAPWAP Tunnel

The following lists the functions of CAPWAP tunnels.

- State maintenance between APs and the AC.
- The AC manages and distributes service configuration to APs through CAPWAP tunnels.
- When tunnel mode forwarding is used, APs forward the data sent by the STA to interact with the AC through CAPWAP tunnels.

  CAPWAP is an application layer protocol based on UDP for transmission. The CAPWAP protocol transmits two types of messages at the transport layer.

- Service data traffic, which encapsulates and forwards wireless data frames.
- Management traffic, which manages the management messages exchanged between APs and the AC.

  CAPWAP data and control messages are sent based on different UDP ports. The traffic management port is UDP port 5246 and the service data traffic port is UDP port 5247.

2. AP-AC networking methods

The networking between APs and the AC is divided into Layer 2 and Layer 3 networking, as shown in Fig. 12.6.

Layer 2 networking means that the network between AP and AC is a directly connected network or Layer 2 network. Layer 2 networking AP enable an AP to be immediately applicable once it is plugged in and on line through Layer 2 broadcast or DHCP process. Layer 2 networking is relatively simple. It is suitable for simple temporary networking, and the networking configuration is relatively fast, but it is inappropriate for large networking architecture.

Fig. 12.6 AP-AC
networking method

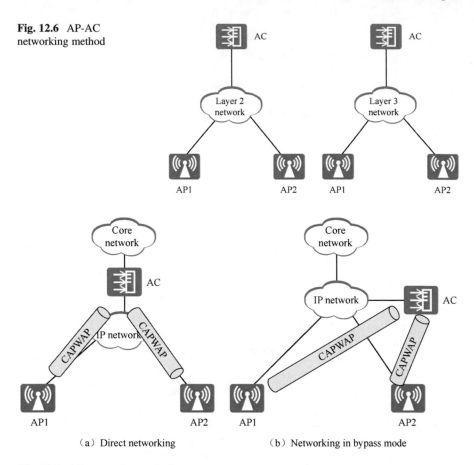

（a）Direct networking   （b）Networking in bypass mode

Fig. 12.7 AC connection method

Layer 3 networking means that the network between AP and AC is a Layer 3 network. APs cannot discover the AC directly. It needs to discover the AC dynamically through DHCP or DNS, or to be configured with static IPs. In the actual networking, one AC can connect dozens or even hundreds of APs, and the network is generally complex. For example, in an enterprise network, APs can be placed in offices, conference rooms, waiting rooms, etc., while the AC can be placed in the company server room. In this way, the network between AP and AC is a complex Layer 3 network. Therefore, in large networks, Layer 3 networks are generally used.

3. AC connection method

The AC connection method is divided into direct networking and networking in bypass mode, as shown in Fig. 12.7.

In direct networking, AC is deployed in the user's forwarding path, and the traffic of directly connected user needs to pass through the AC, which consume the forwarding capacity of AC, posing relatively high requirements for AC's throughput and data processing capacity. If the AC has poor performance, it may become the bottleneck of the entire wireless network bandwidth. However, with this way of networking, the network architecture is clear and the networking is simple to implement.

In networking in bypass mode, the AC is deployed in the direct network between the AP and the uplink network, and are no longer directly connected to the APs. APs' service data can reach the uplink network directly without going through the AC.

As in the actual networking, most of the wireless network is not planned at an early stage, and the wireless network coverage is mostly extended in the existing network at a later stage, so it is easier to expand the network by using the network in bypass mode, which only needs to put the AC in the existing network, such as on the aggregation layer switch, to manage terminal APs. Therefore, this networking method is more used.

In the bypass-mode network, the AC is only able to manage APs, and the management traffic is encapsulated in the CAPWAP tunnel and transmitted. Data service traffic can be forwarded through the CAPWAP data tunnel via AC, or directly forwarded without AC. For the latter, wireless user service traffic passes the aggregation layer switch and is transmitted to the upper layer network by the aggregation layer switch.

12.2.5 Concepts of Wireless Networking

1. Wireless communication system

In wireless communication system, the information can be image, text, sound and so on. As shown in Fig. 12.8, the information needs to be firstly converted into digital signal that is convenient for circuit calculation and processing by source coding, and then it is transmitted after being converted into radio wave by channel coding and modulation. The receiver receives it and then demodulates and decodes it to get the information.

Some concepts involved in wireless communication are introduced below.

Source coding: the process of converting the most primitive information into a digital signal through corresponding coding.

Channel coding: a technology for error correction and error detection of information, which can improve the reliability of channel transmission. Information is prone to be disturbed by noises during wireless transmission, resulting in

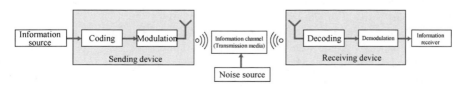

Fig. 12.8 Wireless communication system

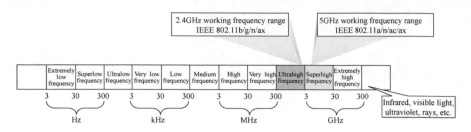

Fig. 12.9 Wireless electromagnetic wave spectrum

errors in the received information. The introduction of channel coding can maximize the recovery of information and reduce the error rate of the receiving device.

Modulation: digital signal is superimposed on the high-frequency signal generated by the high-frequency oscillator circuit so that it can be converted into radio waves and transmitted through the antenna. The superimposition is the process of modulation.

Information channel: the channel to transmit information, and a wireless channel is radio waves in space.

Air interface: refers to the interface used by a wireless channel. Transmitting and receiving devices use the interface to be connected to the channel. For wireless communication, the interface is invisible, and is connected to invisible space.

2. Wireless electromagnetic wave

Wireless electromagnetic waves are electromagnetic waves with frequencies between 3 Hz and 300 GHz. They are also known as radio frequency waves, or RF, radio for short, as shown in Fig. 12.9. Radio technology converts sound signals or other signals and uses wireless electromagnetic waves to communicate.

In Fig. 12.9, the specific descriptions about each frequency band are as follows.

Extremely low frequency (3–30 Hz): submarine communication or direct conversion to sound.

Superlow frequency (30–300 Hz): direct conversion to sound or AC transmission system (50–60 Hz).

Ultralow frequency (300 Hz–3 kHz): mine communication or direct conversion to sound.

Very low frequency (3–30 kHz): direct conversion to sound, ultrasound, geophysical research.

Low frequency (30–300 kHz): international broadcasting.

Medium frequency (300 kHz–3 MHz): amplitude modulation (AM) broadcasting, maritime and aviation communications.

High frequency (3–30 MHz): shortwave, civilian radio.

Very high frequency (30–300 MHz): frequency modulation (FM) broadcasting, TV broadcasting, aviation communication.

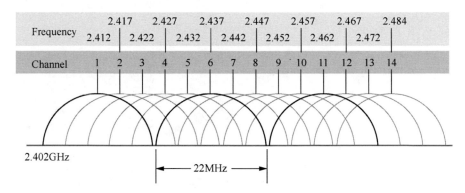

Fig. 12.10 Division of the 2.4GHz channel

Ultrahigh frequency (300 MHz–3 GHz): TV broadcasting, wireless telephone communication, wireless network, microwave oven.

Superhigh frequency (3–30 GHz): wireless network, radar.

Extremely high frequency (30–300 GHz): radio astronomy, remote sensing, human body scanning security checker.

Above 300 GHz: infrared, visible light, ultraviolet, rays, etc.

WLAN technology is to transmit information in space through wireless electromagnetic waves. The currently used frequency bands are 2.4 GHz band (2.4–2.4835 GHz) and 5 GHz band (5.15–5.35 GHz, 5.725–5.85 GHz).

3. Wireless information channel

An information channel is a channel for transmitting information, and the wireless information channel is the wireless electromagnetic wave in space. Wireless electromagnetic waves are everywhere. If the spectrum resources are used arbitrarily, it will result in interferences, so the wireless communication protocol should not only define the frequency band allowed, but also precisely divide the frequency band, and each frequency range is an information channel.

Wireless networks (routers, AP hotspots, computer wireless network interface cards) can operate in multiple channels. Various wireless network devices within the wireless signal coverage area are suggested to use different information channels to avoid interference between signals.

Figure 12.10 shows the information channel division in the 2.4 GHz (=2400 MHz) band. There are actually 14 information channels in total, and the 14th channel is marked in the figure, but this channel is often not used. The center frequency of the channel is given in the figure. The effective width of each channel is 20 MHz, and there is also a 2 MHz mandatory isolation band (similar to an isolation band on a highway). For example, for Channel 1 whose center frequency is 2412 MHz, the frequency range is 2401 to 2423 MHz.

The current mainstream wireless Wi-Fi network devices generally support 13 channels regardless of whether they are 802.11b/g standard or 802.11b/g/n standard. Although their center frequencies are different, they will have some overlap with each other due to certain frequency ranges they occupy. The

Fig. 12.11 BSS

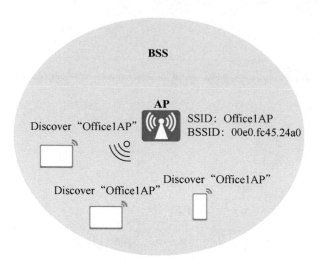

frequency ranges of these 13 channels are given in Fig. 12.10. Knowing the frequency bands in which these 13 channels are located helps us understand what is meant by the three nonoverlapping channels people usually talk about.

From Fig. 12.10, it is easy to see that channels 1, 6 and 11 (marked in dark color) do not overlap with each other at all, which is often referred to as the three nonoverlapping channels. Each channel has 20 MHz bandwidth. It is also easy to see from the figure how the spectrums of other channels overlap with each other. In addition, apart from channels 1, 6 and 11, a group of channels that do not interfere with each other, there are other three groups of channels that do not interfere with each other, channels 2, 7 and 12, channels 3, 8 and 13, and channels 4, 9 and 14.

In WLAN, the working state of APs is affected by the surrounding environment. For example, when there are overlapping frequency bands in the working channels of neighboring APs, the excessive power of one AP will cause signal interference to the neighboring APs.

Through the RF tuning function, the channel and power of APs can be dynamically adjusted, so that the channel and power of APs managed by the same AC can be kept relatively balanced to ensure that APs work in the optimal state.

4. BSS/BSSID/SSID

Basic Service Set (BSS) is the range covered by an AP, which is the basic service unit of a wireless network, usually consisting of an AP and several STAs. BSS is the basic structure of network 802.11, as shown in Fig. 12.11. Due to the sharing nature of wireless media, messages sent and received in the BSS need to have the Basic Service Set Identifier (BSSID).

The terminal needs to discover and find an AP through the identifier of the AP, which is the BSSID. BSSID is the data link layer MAC address of the AP. In

Fig. 12.12 SSIDs
discovered

order to distinguish the BSSs, it is required that each BSS has a unique BSSID, so the MAC address of the AP is used to ensure its uniqueness.

If multiple BSSs are deployed in a space, the terminal will discover multiple BSSIDs, and it only need to select the BSSID to join. But it is the user who makes the selection. To make the AP's identity easier to identify, a string is used as the AP's name. This string is the Service Set Identifier (SSID), which is used instead of the BSSID.

SSID is the identifier of the wireless network and is used to distinguish different wireless networks. APs can send SSIDs to facilitate wireless device selection and access. For example, when searching for an accessible wireless network on a laptop, the network name displayed is the SSID, as shown in Fig. 12.12.

5. VAP

In early days, an AP only supported one BSS, so if you want to deploy multiple BSSs in the same space, multiple APs are needed, which not only increases the cost, but also occupies the channel resources. To improve this situation, APs nowadays usually support the creation of multiple virtual access points (VAPs).

Multiple virtual APs can be created on a physical entity AP, and each virtual AP created is a VAP, and each VAP provides the same function as the physical AP. As shown in Fig. 12.13, each VAP corresponds to a BSS, so that one AP can provide multiple BSSs, thus setting different SSIDs and different access passwords for these BSSs, as well as specifying different service VLANs. In this way, different wireless access services can be provided for different user groups. For example, the computer accessing the wireless network through VAP1 is in VLAN 10, which does not allow access to the Internet, while the computer accessing the

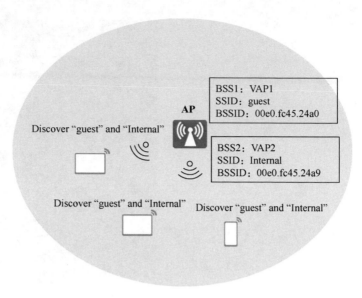

Fig. 12.13   VAP

wireless network through VAP2 is in VLNA 20, which allows access to the Internet.

VAP simplifies the deployment of WLAN, but it does not mean that the more the VAPs the better. It is necessary to plan according to the actual demand. Blindly increasing the number of VAPs not only makes it time-consuming for users to find the SSID, but also makes the AP configuration more complicated. VAP is not equivalent to a real AP, and all VAPs share the software and hardware resources of this AP, and all VAP users share the same channel resources, so the capacity of the AP is constant and does not increase exponentially with the number of VAPs.

6. ESS

In order to meet the actual service demand, the coverage of BSS needs to be extended. If users are supposed to not feel the change in SSID when moving from one BSS to another, this can be achieved by Extend Service Set (ESS), as shown in Fig. 12.14.

ESS is a larger virtual BSS composed of multiple BSSs with the same SSID. Users can move and roam freely within the ESS with their terminals, and they can be considered to be using the same WLAN no matter where they move to.

STA moves between the coverage of different APs belonging to the same ESS and keeps the user service uninterrupted, which we call WLAN roaming.

The biggest advantage of WLAN network is that STAs are not affected by physical media, so they can move around within the WLAN coverage and keep the service uninterrupted. There are multiple AP devices in the same ESS. When an STA moves from one AP coverage area to another AP coverage area, the

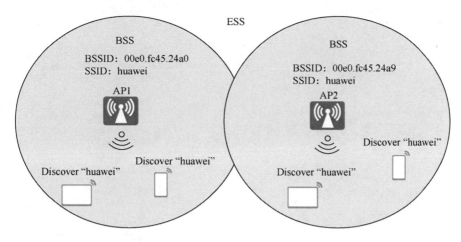

Fig. 12.14 ESS

WLAN roaming technology can be applied to smoothly switch the STA user services.

12.3   Working Principles of WLAN

12.3.1   Working Process of WLAN

In the AC+FIT AP networking architecture, APs are managed uniformly by the AC, so all configurations are performed on the AC. The working process of WLAN is divided into four phases, as shown in Fig. 12.15.

12.3.2   APs Go Online Process

Only after fit APs go online that the AC can centrally manage and control the APs as well as deliver services. The process of AP going online is as follows.

1. Pre-configuration on the AC
   To ensure that APs can go online, the AC needs to pre-configure the following.

   (a) Configure network interworking: configure a DHCP server to assign IP addresses to APs and STAs, or you can configure the AC device as a DHCP server. Configure network interworking between APs and the DHCP server and between APs and the AC.
   (b) Create AP groups: each AP will join and can only join one AP group, and the AP group is usually used for common configuration of multiple APs.

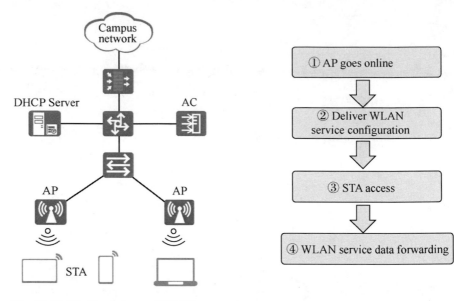

Fig. 12.15 Working process of WLAN

(c) Configure the country and area code (regulatory domain profile) of the AC: the regulatory domain profile provides configurations such as AP's country and area code, tuning channel set and tuning bandwidth.

(d) Configure the source interface or source address (to establish a tunnel with the AP): each AC must uniquely specify an IP address, VLANIF interface, or Loopback interface, and the APs attached to this AC device learn this IP address or the IP address configured for this interface for communication between the AC and the APs. This IP address or interface is called the source address or source interface. Only by specifying a unique source interface or source address for each AC can an AP establish a CAPWAP tunnel with the AC. The device supports using VLANIF interface or loopback interface as the source interface and the IP address of the VLANIF interface or the loopback interface as the source address.

(e) Configure automatic upgrade when the AP goes online (optional): automatic upgrade means that the AP automatically compares its own version with the version of the AP configured on the AC or SFTP or FTP server during the process of going online. If they are not the same, the AP will be upgraded, and then the AP will automatically restart and go online again.

(f) Add an AP device (configure AP authentication mode): that is, configure AP authentication mode and the AP goes online. There are three ways to add APs: importing APs offline, auto-discovering APs and manually confirming the APs in the unauthenticated list.

Fig. 12.16 AP
discovers AC

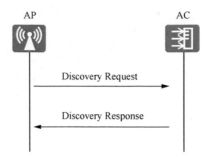

2. AP obtains IP address

AP must obtain an IP address before it can communicate to the AC and the WLAN can work normally. There are two ways for AP to obtain the IP address: one is static mode, and you need to login to the AP device to manually configure IP address; the other is DHCP mode, and by configuring DHCP server, AP can act as a DHCP client to request an IP address from the DHCP server.

You can deploy a Windows server or Linux server as a dedicated DHCP server to assign IP addresses to APs, or use DHCP service of the AC to assign IP addresses to APs, or use devices in the network, such as Layer 3 switches or routers, to assign IP addresses to APs.

3. AP discovers ab AC and establishes CAPWAP tunnel with it

The AP finds an available AC by sending Discovery Request messages. There are two ways for the AP to discover an AC.

(a) Static mode: the static address list of the AC is pre-configured on the AP. The static IP address list of the AC is pre-configured on the AP, and when the AP goes online, as shown in Fig. 12.16, the AP sends Discovery Request unicast messages to all ACs with IP addresses corresponding to the pre-configured list, and then the AP selects an AC to start establishing the CAPWAP tunnel by receiving the Discovery Response messages from the AC.

(b) Dynamic mode: it is divided into DHCP mode, DNS mode and broadcast mode. This chapter mainly introduces DHCP mode and broadcast mode.

- The process of AP discovering AC through DHCP method.

    In order for AP to discover AC by configuring DHCP server, the DHCP response message must carry Option 43 and Option 43 carries the IP address list of the AC. The Option 43 of DHCP essentially informs AP of the IP address of AC and lets it find AC for registration.

    Huawei devices such as switches, routers, and ACs are configured with Option 43 when they are used as DHCP servers.

    Take the IP address 192.168.22.1 of the AC as an example, the configuration command on the DHCP server is option 43 sub-option 3 hex 3139322E3136382E32322E31 or option 43 sub-option 3 ascii 192.168.22.1.

In the commands above, sub-option 3 is a fixed value representing the sub-option type; hex 3139322E3136382E32322E31 and ascii 192.168.22.1 are the HEX (hexadecimal) format and ASCII format of the AC's address 192.168.22.1, respectively.

When more than one AC is involved, and multiple IP addresses need to be filled for Option, IP addresses should also be spaced by ",". The comma "," corresponds to the ASCII value of 2C. For example, the IP addresses of the two ACs are 192.168.22.1 and 192.168.22.2, then the DHCP server configuration command is option 43 sub-option 3 hex 3139322E3136382E3130302E322C3139322E31, 36382E3130302E33 or option 43 sub-option 3 ascii 192.168.22.1,192.168.22.2.

After the AP obtains the IP address of the AC through the DHCP service, it learns which ACs are available by the AC discovery mechanism and decides to establish a CAPWAP connection with the best AC.

The AP starts the discovery mechanism of CAPWAP protocol and sends a discovery request message in the form of unicast or broadcast to try to be associated with the AC. After receiving the Discovery Request from the AP, the AC sends a unicast Discovery Response to the AP, and the AP can determine which AC to establish a session with based on the priority of the AC in the Discover Response or the number of current APs on the AC.

- The process of AP discovering ACs by broadcasting.

After the AP starts, if both DHCP and DNS modes cannot obtain the IP of the AC or the AP does not receive a response after sending a discovery request message, the AP starts the broadcast discovery process and sends a discovery request message as a broadcast packet.

The AC that receives the discovery request message checks whether the AP has access to the local machine (authorized MAC address or serial number), and returns a response if it does. If the AP does not have the access, the AC rejects the request.

The broadcast discovery method is only applicable to the network scenario where the network between AC and AP is a Layer 2 reachable network.

The AP discovers the AC and establishes a CAPWAP tunnel, which consists of a data channel and a control channel and is used to maintain the state between the AP and the AC.

The CAPWAP data channel is used to centralize the service data messages received by the AP to the AC for forwarding. In the meantime, by option, the data channel can be encrypted with Datagram Transport Layer Security (DTLS), and after enabling the DTLS encryption function, all CAPWAP data messages will be encrypted and decrypted by DTLS.

The control channel is used for the exchange of management messages between the AP and the AC. In the meantime, you can also choose to encrypt the control channel with DTLS. After enabling DTLS encryption, all CAPWAP control messages will be encrypted by DTLS.

Fig. 12.17 AP joins AC

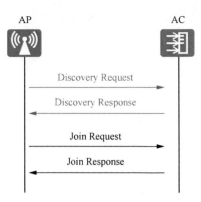

4. AP access control

    After the AP finds the AC, it will send a Join Request, and when the AC receives the message from the AP, it will authenticate the AP's legality. If the authentication is approved, the AC will add the corresponding AP device and respond to the Join Request message, as shown in Fig. 12.17.

    The AC supports the following three types of authentication methods for APs.

(a) MAC authentication.
(b) Serial number (SN) authentication.
(c) No authentication.

      There are the following three ways to add APs on AC.

- Offline import of AP: pre-configure the MAC address and SN of the AP. When the AP is connected to the AC, if the AC finds that the AP matches the MAC address of the pre-configured AP and SN, the AC starts to establish a connection with the AP.
- Auto-discovery of AP: if the authentication mode of AP is configured as no authentication, or if the authentication mode of AP is configured as MAC or SN authentication and AP is added to the AP whitelist, then when the AP is connected to the AC, the AP will be automatically discovered by AC and go online normally.
- Manual confirmation of the AP in the unauthenticated list: when the authentication mode of the AP is configured as MAC or SN authentication, but the AP is not imported offline and is not in the set AP whitelist, this AP will be recorded in the unauthenticated AP list. It needs to be manually confirmed by the user before this AP can go online normally.

5. Version upgrade of AP

    The AP determines whether the current system software version is consistent with the one specified on the AC according to the parameters in the received Join

Fig. 12.18 Version
upgrade request and
response

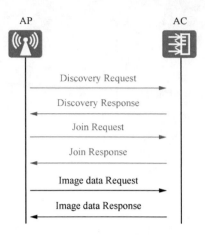

Response message. If inconsistent, the AP requests the software version by
sending an Image Data Request message, and then upgrades the version, which
includes AC mode, FTP mode and SFTP mode. The AP restarts after the software
version is updated and repeats the previous three steps, as shown in Fig. 12.18.

There are two ways to upgrade the AP on the AC: auto upgrade and timed
upgrade.

Auto upgrade is mainly used in scenarios where the AP is not yet online in the
AC. Usually, the auto upgrade parameters when the AP goes online are configured first, and then the AP access is configured. The AP will automatically
upgrade during the online process afterwards. If the AP is already online, after
configuring the auto upgrade parameters, the AP will also be automatically
upgraded if it is triggered to restart in any way. However, compared to the auto
upgrade, using the online upgrade mode can shorten the service interruption time.
There are three upgrade modes, which are illustrated below.

(a) The AC mode: the upgrade version is downloaded from the AC when the AP
    is upgraded, which is applicable to the scenario when there are only a
    few APs.
(b) The FTP mode: the upgrade version is downloaded from the FTP server when
    the AP is upgraded, which is appropriate to the file transfer scenarios with low
    network security requirement and the data is transmitted in plain text. It is not
    secure.
(c) The SFTP mode: the upgrade version is downloaded from the SFTP server
    when the AP is upgraded, which is suitable for scenarios with high network
    security requirements, and the transmission data is strictly encrypted, offering
    integrity protection for online upgrading.

    Timed upgrade is mainly used for scenarios where the AP is already online
    in the AC and has carried WLAN services. Usually, the upgrade is designated
    to commence at a time when network traffic is low.

6. CAPWAP tunnel maintenance

The data channel maintenance detects the connectivity status of the data channel by interacting Keepalive (UDP port 5247) messages between the AP and the AC.

The control channel maintenance detects the connectivity status of the control tunnel by interacting by Echo (UDP port number 5246) messages between the AP and the AC.

12.3.3   Deliver WLAN Service Configuration

The AC sends a Configuration Update Request message to the AP, which responds with a Configuration Update Response message, and the AC then sends the AP's service configuration information to the AP, as shown in Fig. 12.19.

After the AP comes online, it will actively send a Configuration Status Request message to the AC, which contains the existing configuration of the AP. When the existing configuration of the AP does not meet the requirements of the AC, the AC notifies the AP via a Configuration Status Response.

Note	After APs come online, they will first actively obtain the current configuration from AC, and then the AC will centrally manage APs and deliver service configuration.

1. Configuration profile

There are a large number of APs in the WLAN network, and in order to simplify the configuration steps of APs, APs can be added to an AP group, and can be uniformly set with the same configuration through the AP group. However, each AP that has different parameter configuration from other APs is not

Fig. 12.19 Configuration update request and response

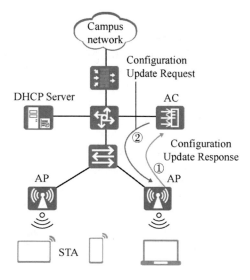

Fig. 12.20 Profiles
referenced by APs or AP
groups

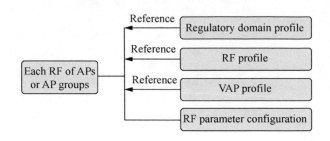

suitable for unified configuration through the AP group. Such personalized parameters can be configured directly in each AP. Each AP joins and can only join in one AP group when it comes online. When the AP obtains the AP group configuration and personalized AP configuration from the AC, the AP configuration is preferred.

Both AP groups and APs are able to reference regulatory domain profiles, RF profiles, VAP profiles, as shown in Fig. 12.20, and some of these profiles can reference other profiles, which are collectively referred to as WLAN profiles.

(a) Regulatory domain profile.

One of the most important parameters of the regulatory domain profile is the configuration of country and area codes. Country and area codes are used to identify the country where the RF of AP is located. Different country and area codes specify the RF characteristics of different APs, including the AP's transmit power, and the channels supported. Country and area codes are configured so that the RF characteristics of APs can comply with the legal requirements of different countries or areas.

By configuring the tuning channel set, you can specify the range of dynamic adjustment of the AP channel when configuring the RF tuning function, while avoiding the radar channel and the terminal unsupported channel.

(b) RF profile.

According to the actual network environment, the parameters of RF are adjusted and optimized, so that the AP has the RF capability to meet the actual demand and improve the signal quality of WLAN network. After the parameters in the RF profile are sent to the AP, only the parameters supported by the AP will take effect on the AP.

The configurable parameters include RF type, RF rate, the multicast sending rate of RF wireless messages, and the cycle AP uses to send beacon frames.

(c) VAP profile.

When configuring the parameters in the VAP profile, and then referencing the VAP profile in the AP group or AP, the VAP will be generated on the AP and provide wireless access service for the STA. By configuring the

Fig. 12.21 VAP
parameters to be configured
and profiles referenced

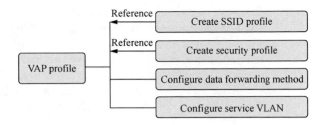

parameters in the VAP profile, AP manages can provide different wireless services to the STA.

In the VAP profile, other profiles can also be used, such as the SSID profile, security profile, traffic profile.

(d) RF parameter configuration.

The AP radio frequency needs to be configured with different basic radio frequency parameters according to the actual WLAN network environment in order to achieve better performance of the AP radio frequency.

In WLAN networks, when there are overlapping frequency bands in the working channels of neighboring APs, it is easy to generate signal interference that affect the working status of APs. To avoid signal interference, improve the working state of the AP, and enhance the quality of WLAN network, you can manually configure the neighboring APs to work on non-overlapping channels.

According to the demand of the actual network environment, the transmit power of RF and antenna gain are configured so that the strength of the RF signals can meet the actual network demand and the signal quality of WLAN network can be improved.

In actual application scenarios, two APs may be tens of meters to tens of kilometers apart, and because of the different distance between APs, the time to wait for the ACK messages when transmitting data between APs also differs. By adjusting the appropriate timeout parameters, the efficiency of data transmission between APs can be improved.

2. VAP Profile

VAP profile should reference the SSID profile, security profile, as well as configure data forwarding and service VLAN, as shown in Fig. 12.21.

(a) SSID profile.

The SSID profile is primarily used to configure the SSID name of the WLAN network, and other functions can also be configured, mainly including the following functions.

• Hide SSID: when users create a wireless network, they can configure to hide the name of the wireless network in order to protect the security of the network. In this way, only wireless users who know the network name can connect to this wireless network.

- Maximum number of users that can be successfully associated with a single VAP: the more users are connected to a single VAP, the less average network resources each user can use. To ensure the users' Internet experience, you can configure a reasonable maximum number of users that can access the network according to the actual network conditions.
- Automatically hide SSID when the number of users reaches the maximum: after configuring this function, when the number of users accessing the WLAN network reaches the maximum, SSID will be hidden and new users will not be able to find the SSID.

(b) Security profile.

Configuring WLAN security policy can authenticate wireless terminals and encrypt users' messages to protect the security of WLAN network and users.

The WLAN security policy supports open authentication, WEP, WPA/WPA2-PSK, WPA/WPA2-802.1X, etc. You can select one of them in the security profile for configuration.

(c) Data forwarding method.

The control message is forwarded through the control channel of CAPWAP, and users can use two data forwarding modes, that is tunnel forwarding (also known as "centralized forwarding") and direct forwarding (also known as "local forwarding"). This will be introduced in detail in later sections.

(d) Service VLAN.

Due to the flexible access to the WLAN wireless network, STAs may centrally access the same WLAN wireless network at a certain location (such as the entrance to an office area or the entrance to a stadium) and then roam to other wireless network environments covered by the AP.

When the service VLAN is configured as a single VLAN, IP address resources easily become insufficient in the area with a large number of STAs accessed, while the IP address resources in other areas are wasted.

When the service VLAN is configured as a VLAN pool, multiple VLANs can be added to the VLAN pool, and then one SSID is able to simultaneously support multiple service VLANs by configuring the VLAN pool as the service VLAN of the VAP. Newly connected STAs are dynamically assigned to each VLAN in the VLAN pool, reducing the number of STAs in a single VLAN and narrowing the broadcast domain; at the same time, each VLAN is assigned IP addresses as evenly as possible, so fewer IP addresses are wasted.

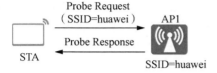

Active scanning with a probe containing
a designated SSID, used for STA
to access designated wireless network

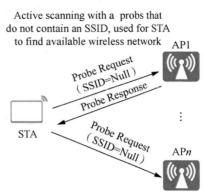

Active scanning with a probs that
do not contain an SSID, used for STA
to find available wireless network

Fig. 12.22 Active scanning

12.3.4 STA Access

Once the CAPWAP tunnel is established, users can access the wireless network. The STA access process is divided into six phases: scanning, link authentication, association, access authentication, STA address assignment (DHCP), and user authentication.

1. Scanning

  STA can periodically search for nearby wireless networks by active scanning to obtain information about the surrounding wireless networks. According to whether the Probe Request frame carries an SSID, active scanning can be divided into two types, as shown in Fig. 12.22.

  (a) Active scanning with a probe containing a specified SSID.

    This method is applicable when the STA uses active scanning to access the specified wireless network. The client sends a Probe Request containing the specified SSID, and the STA sends a Probe Request frame in each channel in turn to find an AP with the same SSID as the STA. Only the AP that can provide the specified SSID wireless service receives the Probe Request and then replies with a Probe Response.

  (b) Active scanning with probes that do not contain an SSID.

    This method is also suitable when the STA uses active scanning to fine whether there is an available wireless network. The client sends a broadcast Probe Request, and the client periodically sends Probe Request frames to scan for wireless networks in its supported information list. After receiving the Probe Request frame, the AP responds with a Probe Response frame advertising available wireless networks.

    STA also supports passive scanning for wireless networks. Passive scanning means that the client discovers nearby wireless networks by listening to the Beacon frames (which contain information such as SSID, and support rate) periodically sent by the AP. By default, the AP sends Beacon frames with a cycle of 100 TUs (1 TU = 1024 us).

2. Link authentication

WLAN technology uses wireless RF signals as the transmission media for service data, and this open channel makes it easy for attackers to eavesdrop and tamper with the service data transmitted in the wireless channel, so security has become an important factor hindering the development of WLAN technology.

WLAN security provides security policies such as Wired Equivalent Privacy (WEP), Wi-Fi Network Protected Access (WPA), and WPA2. Each security policy contains a set of security mechanisms, including the link authentication method when the wireless link is established, the user access authentication method when the wireless user goes online, and the data encryption method when the wireless user transmits data services.

To ensure the security of the wireless link, AP needs to authenticate the STA in the access process. The 802.11 link defines two authentication mechanisms: open system authentication and shared key authentication.

Open system authentication means no authentication, and any STA can be authenticated successfully.

Shared key authentication means that STA and AP are pre-configured with the same shared key and the key configurations of both sides need to be verified to see whether they are the same. If they the same, then the authentication is successful, otherwise the authentication fails.

3. Association

After completing link authentication, STA will continue to initiate link service negotiation, and the specific negotiation is realized through the Association message. The process of terminal association is essentially a process of link service negotiation, which includes the supported rate, channel, etc.

4. Access authentication

Access authentication is to distinguish users and restrict their access rights before they access the network. Compared with link authentication, access authentication is more secure, mainly including PSK authentication and 802.1X authentication.

5. STA address assignment

STA obtains its own IP address, which is a prerequisite for STA to go online normally. If the STA obtains IP address through DHCP, it can use an AC device or aggregation layer switch as a DHCP server to assign IP address for STA. Generally, the aggregation layer switch is used as the DHCP server.

6. User authentication

User authentication is an "end-to-end" security structure, including 802.1X authentication, MAC authentication and Portal authentication. Portal authentication is also known as Web authentication, and the Portal authentication site is generally called a portal. When users access the Internet, they must be authenticated in the portal, and only after the authentication is passed can they use the network resources. This authentication usually requires WeChat login or cell phone SMS to verify the user' identity. Because WeChat or cell phone numbers are registered with real names, the information of the user accessing the network can be recorded and the specific person can be traced in case of a security incident.

12.3.5 WLAN Service Data Forwarding

The data in CAPWAP includes control messages (management messages) and data messages. Control messages are forwarded through the control channel of CAPWAP. Users can use two data forwarding modes, that is tunnel forwarding (also known as "centralized forwarding") and direct forwarding (also known as "local forwarding").

Tunnel forwarding mode means that after the user's data message arrives at the AP, it needs to be encapsulated by the CAPWAP data tunnel and sent to the AC, which then forwards it to the upper layer network, as shown in Fig. 12.23a.

Direct forwarding mode means that after the user's data message arrives at the AP, it is directly forwarded to the upper layer network without being encapsulated in the CAPWAP, as shown in Fig. 12.23b.

The advantage of tunnel forwarding is that the AC centrally forwards data messages so it is secure and convenient for centralized management and control; the disadvantage is that the service data must be forwarded by the AC, so the

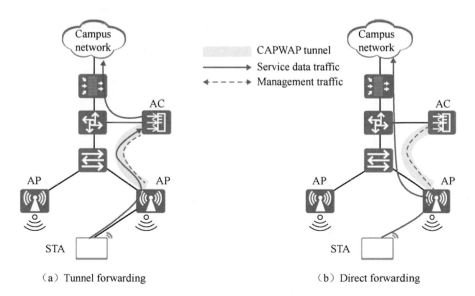

(a) Tunnel forwarding   (b) Direct forwarding

Fig. 12.23 Tunnel forwarding and direct forwarding

message forwarding efficiency is lower than that of direct forwarding, putting the AC under great pressure.

The advantage of direct forwarding is that data messages do not need to be forwarded by the AC, so the message forwarding efficiency is higher, and the pressure on AC is alleviated; the disadvantage is that it is inconvenient for centralized management and control of the service.

12.4   Case: Layer 2 Networking Tunnel Forwarding in Bypass Mode

Service requirements: enterprise users can access the network through WLAN to meet the most basic needs of mobile office.

The networking requirements are as follows.

1. AC networking mode: Layer 2 networking in by pass mode
2. DHCP deployment mode: AC functions as a DHCP server to assign IP addresses to APs and STAs.

   Service data forwarding mode: tunnel forwarding.

   Figure 12.24 draws the physical topology and logical topology. Because it is tunnel forwarding, the service VLAN data of two offices are sent to the AC through CAPWAP tunnel, so it is equivalent to two VLANs connected to the AC. The logical topology is drawn in the right side of Fig. 12.24.

   You can see that AC is equivalent to a router connected to VLAN 100, VLAN 101 and VLAN 102. In order for these three VLANs to access the upstream network, it is also necessary to create a VLAN 110 on AC and SW1. The VLAN is created to connect AC and SW1, so this VLAN is called an interconnection VLAN. A VLAN 111 needs to be created for the connection of SW1 and the

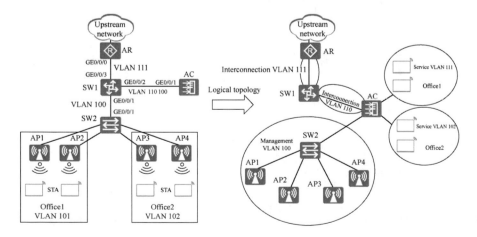

Fig. 12.24   Network topology

Table 12.2 Address planning

Data	Configuration
AP management VLAN	VLAN 100
Office1 service VLAN	VLAN 101
Office2 service VLAN	VLAN 102
SW1和AC interconnection VLAN	VLAN 110
SW1 and AR interconnection VLAN	VLAN 111
Network segment VLAN 100	192.168.100.0/24
Network segment VLAN 101	192.168.101.0/24
Network segment VLAN 102	192.168.102.0/24
Network segment VLAN 110	192.168.110.0/24
Network segment VLAN 111	192.168.111.0/24
DHCP server	AC functions as a DHCP server to assign IP addresses to APs and STAs
IP address of the source interface of the AC	Vlanif 100:192.168.100.1/24

upstream router AR. With the logical topology on the right, it is clear how to add routes to each device. The connection between SW1 and SW2 only needs to transmit frames of VLAN 100, so interface GE0/0/1 of SW1 is configured as an access interface and is designated to VLAN 100. The connection between SW1 and AC needs to transmit frames of VLAN 110 and VLAN 100, so it needs to be configured as trunk interface.

The address planning and profile configuration are shown in Tables 12.2 and 12.3.

The configuration roadmap is as follows.

(a) Configure network interworking of the AC, APs, and other network devices.
(b) Configure APs to go online.
(c) Create an AP group, and all APs that need the same configuration are added to the AP group for unified configuration.
(d) Configure the system parameters of the AC, including the country and area codes, and the source interface for communication between the AC and the AP.
(e) Configure the authentication method of AP going online and import AP offline so that AP can go online normally.
(f) Configure the WLAN service parameters so that the STA can access WLAN network.

Table 12.3 Profile configuration

AP group	Name: ap-Office1. Referenced profiles: VAP profile VAP-Office1, and regulatory domain profile default
	Name: ap-Office2. Referenced profiles:VAP profile VAP-Office2, regulatory domain profile default
Regulatory domain profile	Name: default
	Country code: CN
SSID profile	Name: SSID-Office1
	SSID name: AP-Office1
	Name: SSID-Office2
	SSID name: AP-Office2
Security profile	Name: Sec-Office1
	Security policy: WPA-WPA2+PSK
	Password: a1234567
	Name: Sec-Office2
	Security policy: WPA-WPA2+PSK
	Password: b1234567
VAP profile	Name: VAP-Office1
	Forwarding mode: tunnel forwarding
	Service VLAN: VLAN 101
	Referenced profiles: SSID-Office1 and security profile Sec-Office1
	Name: VAP-Office2
	Forwarding mode: tunnel forwarding
	Service VLAN: VLAN 102
	Referenced profiles: SSID-Office2 and security profile Sec-Office2

12.4.1   Configure Network Interworking

Before configuring the WLAN, the network interworking of AP, AC and nearby network devices need to be configured. Figure 12.25 is the logical topology. The interface address is set with reference to the address planned in the figure, and routes are added to router AR and SW1 to make the network smooth.

Create VLAN 100, VLAN 101, VLAN 102 and VLAN 110 on the AC. Configure addresses for interface Vlanif so that it functions as a gateway for these network segments. Meanwhile, add a default route to the address of interface Vlanif 110 of SW1. Add routes to network segments VLAN 100, VLAN 101, and VLAN 102 on SW1, with the next hop to the address of interface Vlanif 110 on the AC.

Configure the DHCP service on the AC to assign addresses to VLAN 100, VLAN 101, and VLAN 102.

The configuration on the AR is as follows.

```
[AR] interface GigabitEthernet 0/0/0
[AR-GigabitEthernet0/0/0] ip address 192.168.111.2 24
[AR-GigabitEthernet0/0/0] quit
[AR] ip route-static 192.168.0.0 16 192.168.111.1
```

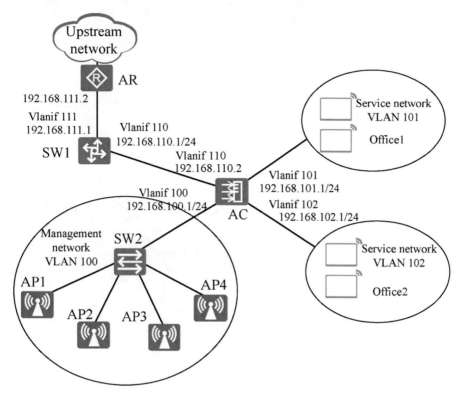

Fig. 12.25 Logical topology

The configuration on SW1 is as follows.

```
[SW1] vlan batch 100 110 111
[SW1] interface Vlanif 111
[SW1-Vlanif111] ip address 192.168.111.1 24
[SW1-Vlanif111] quit
[SW1] interface Vlanif 110
[SW1-Vlanif110] ip address 192.168.110.1 24
[SW1-Vlanif110] quit
[SW1] interface GigabitEthernet 0/0/3
[SW1-GigabitEthernet0/0/3] port link-type access
[SW1-GigabitEthernet0/0/3] port default vlan 111
[SW1-GigabitEthernet0/0/3] quit
[SW1] interface GigabitEthernet 0/0/2
[SW1-GigabitEthernet0/0/2] port link-type trunk
[SW1-GigabitEthernet0/0/2] port trunk allow-pass vlan 110 100
[SW1-GigabitEthernet0/0/2] quit
[SW1] interface GigabitEthernet 0/0/1
[SW1-GigabitEthernet0/0/1] port link-type access
[SW1-GigabitEthernet0/0/1] port default vlan 100
```

```
[SW1-GigabitEthernet0/0/1] quit
[SW1] ip route-static 192.168.100.0 24 192.168.110.2
[SW1] ip route-static 192.168.101.0 24 192.168.110.2
[SW1] ip route-static 192.168.102.0 24 192.168.110.2
```

The configuration on the AC is as follows.

```
[AC] vlan batch 100 101 102 110
[AC] interface Vlanif 100
[AC-Vlanif100] ip address 192.168.100.1 24
[AC-Vlanif100] interface Vlanif 101
[AC-Vlanif101] ip address 192.168.101.1 24
[AC-Vlanif101] interface Vlanif 102
[AC-Vlanif102] ip address 192.168.102.1 24
[AC-Vlanif102] interface Vlanif 110
[AC-Vlanif110] ip address 192.168.110.2 24
[AC] interface GigabitEthernet 0/0/1
[AC-GigabitEthernet0/0/1] port link-type trunk
[AC-GigabitEthernet0/0/1] port trunk allow-pass vlan 110 100
[AC] ip route-static 0.0.0.0 0 192.168.110.1
```

Configure the DHCP service.

```
[AC] dhcp enable
[AC] interface Vlanif 100
[AC-Vlanif100] dhcp select interface
[AC-Vlanif100] interface Vlanif 101
[AC-Vlanif101] dhcp select interface
[AC-Vlanif101] interface Vlanif 102
[AC-Vlanif102] dhcp select interface
```

Enter "display ip interface brief" in the AP to display the automatically obtained IP address.

```
[Huawei] display ip interface brief
Interface            IP Address/Mask    Physical  Protocol
Vlanif1              192.168.100.123/24  up        up
```

12.4.2   Configure the APs to Go On Line

Create a regulatory domain profile on the AC, create an AP group, apply the regulatory domain profile to the AP group, configure the interface or source address of the AC, and specify to add the AP to the AP group.

Create a regulatory domain profile. Since all WLAN-related configurations need to be done in the WLAN view, the administrator needs to first enter the WLAN view via the wlan command.

Use the regulatory-domain-profile name *profile-name* command in the WLAN view to create a regulatory domain profile and enter the view of this profile. In the regulatory domain profile, the administrator can set parameters such as country and area code, optimized channel and bandwidth. The following operation creates a regulatory domain profile, default, specifying the country and area code as cn.

```
[AC]wlan
[AC-wlan-view]regulatory-domain-profile name default
[AC-wlan-regulate-domain-default]country-code cn
[AC-wlan-regulate-domain-default]quit
[AC-wlan-view]
```

Next, use the WLAN view command ap-group name group-name to create AP groups named ap-Office1 and ap-Office2, and then enter the configuration view of the AP group and apply the regulatory domain profile here. When changing the regulatory domain profile applied to the AP group, the system will prompt a warning message and ask the administrator for confirmation. If the administrator wants to confirm the change, enter "y" and press the Enter key and then the change takes effect.

```
[AC-wlan-view]ap-group name ap-Office1
[AC-wlan-ap-group-ap-Office1]regulatory-domain-profile default
 Warning:Modifying the country code will clear channel,power and
antenna gain configurations of the radio and reset the AP.Continue?
[Y/N]:y
[AC-wlan-ap-group-ap-Office1]quit
[AC-wlan-view]ap-group name ap-Office2
[AC-wlan-ap-group-ap-Office2]regulatory-domain-profile default
 Warning:Modifying the country code will clear channel,power and
antenna gain configurations of the radio and reset the AP.Continue?
[Y/N]:y
[AC-wlan-ap-group-ap-Office2]quit
```

Configure the source interface of the AC. Establish a CAPWAP tunnel of AP and the address of interface Vlanif 100.

```
[AC]capwap source interface Vlanif 100
```

Import the AP offline to the AC, and the following configuration adds the AP to the AP group via MAC address authentication.

```
[AC-wlan-view]ap auth-mode ?       --View the identity authentication
modes supported
  mac-auth MAC authenticated mode, default authenticated mode
  no-auth  No authenticated mode
  sn-auth  SN authenticated mode
[AC-wlan-view]ap auth-mode mac-auth   --Specify to use MAC address
authentication
```

```
[AC-wlan-view]ap-id 1 ap-mac 00e0-fcc4-15a0
[AC-wlan-ap-1]ap-name ap1
[AC-wlan-ap-1]ap-group ap-Office1
Warning: This operation may cause AP reset. If the country code changes,
it will clear channel, power and antenna gain configurations of the radio,
Whether to continue? [Y/N]:y
 Info: This operation may take a few seconds. Please wait for a moment..
done.
[AC-wlan-ap-1]quit
[AC-wlan-view]ap-id 2 ap-mac 00e0-fcb1-02b0
[AC-wlan-ap-2]ap-name ap2
[AC-wlan-ap-2]ap-group ap-Office1
Warning: This operation may cause AP reset. If the country code changes,
it will clear channel, power and antenna gain configurations of the radio,
Whether to continue? [Y/N]:y
[AC-wlan-ap-2]quit
[AC-wlan-view]ap-id 3 ap-mac 00e0-fc33-5190
[AC-wlan-ap-3]ap-name ap3
[AC-wlan-ap-3]ap-group ap-Office2
Warning: This operation may cause AP reset. If the country code changes,
it will clear channel, power and antenna gain configurations of the radio,
Whether to continue? [Y/N]:y
 Info: This operation may take a few seconds. Please wait for a moment..
done.
[AC-wlan-ap-3]quit
[AC-wlan-view]ap-id 4 ap-mac 00e0-fcaf-5610
[AC-wlan-ap-4]ap-name ap4
[AC-wlan-ap-4]ap-group ap-Office2
Warning: This operation may cause AP reset. If the country code changes,
it will clear channel, power and antenna gain configurations of the radio,
Whether to continue? [Y/N]:y
 Info: This operation may take a few seconds. Please wait for a moment..
done.
[AC-wlan-ap-4]quit
```

After bringing the AP online, execute the display ap all command on the AC to check the status of the AP. When you see the "State" field of the AP is "nor", it means the AP has been successfully online on the AC and it is in a normal state.

```
[AC]display ap all
 Info: This operation may take a few seconds. Please wait for a moment.
done.
Total AP information:
nor : normal     [4]
-----------------------------------------------------------------
ID  MAC          Name Group IP          Type     State  STA Uptime
-----------------------------------------------------------------
 1  00e0-fcc4-15a0 ap1 ap-Office1 192.168.100.123   AP2050DN  nor   0
14M:48S
. 2  00e0-fcb1-02b0 ap2 ap-Office1 192.168.100.20    AP2050DN  nor   0
12M:4S
 3  00e0-fc33-5190 ap3 ap-Office2 192.168.100.11    AP2050DN  nor   0
```

```
10M:5S
 4   00e0-fcaf-5610 ap4 ap-Office2 192.168.100.144    AP2050DN    nor    0
20S
 ---------------------------------------------------------------
 Total: 4
```

The output information of the display ap command is explained as follows.

- ID: AP ID.
- MAC: AP MAC address.
- Name: AP name.
- Group: the name of the AP group to which the AP belongs.
- IP: IP address of the AP. In NAT scenario, the AP is on the private network and the AC is on the public network. This value is the private IP address of the AP.
- Type: the AP type.
- State: the AP state.

    - normal: the normal state of the AP, meaning that the AP is successfully online on the AC.
    - commit-failed: the WLAN service configuration fails to deliver after the AP is online.
    - download: AP is being upgraded.
    - fault: AP fails to go online.
    - idle: the initial state before the AP and AC establish connection.

- STA: the number of end users connected on the AP.
- Uptime: the length of time the AP has been online.
- ExtraInfo: extra information. P indicates that the device is under powered.

12.4.3 Configure WLAN Service Parameters

The administrator needs to configure service parameters related to the WLAN on the AC, which include SSID profiles, security profiles, and VAP profiles.

1. Configure SSID profiles.

    Since the SSIDs of the two offices are different, two SSID profiles need to be created.

```
[AC-wlan-view] ssid-profile name ssid-Office1
[AC-wlan-ssid-prof-ssid-Office1] ssid AP-Office1
[AC-wlan-ssid-prof-ssid-Office1] quit
[AC-wlan-view] ssid-profile name ssid-Office2
[AC-wlan-ssid-prof-ssid-Office1] ssid AP-Office2
[AC-wlan-ssid-prof-ssid-Office1] quit
```

The administrator first enters the WLAN view using the wlan command, then creates an SSID profile named ssid-office1 using the ssid-profile name profile-name command, and enters the configuration view of this SSID profile. The length of SSID profile names is between 1 to 35 characters and names are not case-sensitive. In the SSID profile, the administrator can also configure other parameters, such as those related to QoS.

2. Configure the security profile.

Two offices have different passwords for connecting to the AP, so two security profiles need to be created.

```
[AC-wlan-view] security-profile name Sec-Office1
[AC-wlan-sec-prof-Sec-Office1] security wpa-wpa2 psk pass-phrase
a1234567 aes
[AC-wlan-sec-prof-Sec-Office1] quit
[AC-wlan-view] security-profile name Sec-Office2
[AC-wlan-sec-prof-Sec-Office2] security wpa-wpa2 psk pass-phrase
b1234567 aes
[AC-wlan-sec-prof-Sec-Office2] quit
```

In this example, the administrator created two security profiles, Sec-Office1 and Sec-Office2, on the AC. The length of the SSID profile name is between 1 to 35 characters and names are not case-sensitive. In the security profile view, the administrator sets the WPA2 + PSK + AES security policy and specifies the passwords as a1234567 and b1234567. The full syntax of this command is security {wpa I wpa2 I wpa-wap2} psk {pass-phrase I hex} key -value {aes I tkip I aes -tkip}. In this example, the administrator has chosen WPA2 as the authentication mode and AES the encryption mode. The length of the password that can be configured is between 8 to 63 characters. When setting the password, it is recommended that the administrator use a combination of upper- and lower-case letters, numbers and special characters to create a strong password.

3. Configure VAP profiles.

VAP is short for Virtual AP, and by configuring multiple VAP profiles the delivering configurations in these VAP templates to the AP, the administrator can provide differentiated services for mobile access devices.

In this example, the wireless networks of Office1 and Office2 have different service VLANs and different authentication passwords, so two VAP profiles need to be created. In the VAP profile, set the data forwarding mode to tunnel forwarding, specify the service VLAN, and apply the SSID profile and security profile created previously.

```
[AC-wlan-view] vap-profile name vap-Office1
[AC-wlan-vap-prof-vap-Office1] forward-mode tunnel
[AC-wlan-vap-prof-vap-Office1] service-vlan vlan-id 101
[AC-wlan-vap-prof-vap-Office1] ssid-profile ssid-Office1
[AC-wlan-vap-prof-vap-Office1] security-profile Sec-Office1
[AC-wlan-vap-prof-vap-Office1] quit
```

```
[AC-wlan-view] vap-profile name vap-Office2
[AC-wlan-vap-prof-vap-Office2] forward-mode tunnel
[AC-wlan-vap-prof-vap-Office2] service-vlan vlan-id 102
[AC-wlan-vap-prof-vap-Office2] ssid-profile ssid-Office2
[AC-wlan-vap-prof-vap-Office2] security-profile Sec-Office2
[AC-wlan-vap-prof-vap-Office2] quit
```

The administrator uses the vap-profile name *profile-name* command in WLAN view to create two VAP profiles named vap-office1 and vap-office2, and enters the configuration view of this VAP profile. The length of VAP profile names is between 1 to 35 characters and names are not case-sensitive.

In the VAP profile view, the administrator first sets the forwarding mode to tunnel forwarding by using the forward-mode tunnel command. Then the service-vlan vlan-id 101 command is used to specify the service VLAN as 101, the ssid-profile ssid-office1 command is used to apply the SSID profile, and the security-profile sec-office1 command is used to apply the security profile.

4. Apply the VAP profiles to the AP group

The administrator needs to apply the configured VAP profiles to the AP groups before the AC can distribute the configuration of the VAP profiles to the APs so that the APs can work. Both RF0 and RF1 on the APs use the VAP profiles.

```
[AC-wlan-view] ap-group name ap-Office1
[AC-wlan-ap-group-ap-Office1] vap-profile vap-Office1 wlan 1 radio 0
[AC-wlan-ap-group-ap-Office1] vap-profile vap-Office1 wlan 1 radio 1
[AC-wlan-ap-group-ap-Office1] quit
[AC-wlan-view] ap-group name ap-Office2
[AC-wlan-ap-group-ap-Office2] vap-profile vap-Office2 wlan 2 radio 0
[AC-wlan-ap-group-ap-Office2] vap-profile vap-Office2 wlan 2 radio 1
[AC-wlan-ap-group-ap-Office2] quit
[AC-wlan-view]
```

The administrator first enters the WLAN view using the wlan command, and then enters AP group ap-group-office1 view using the ap-group name ap-group-office1 command. In the AP group view, the administrator uses the vap-profile command to bind the specified VAP profile to the specified RF. The full syntax of this command is vap-profile profile-name wlan wlan-id {radio {radio-id | all}}. The parameter profile-name is the name of the previously created VAP profile; the parameter wlan-id is the ID of the VAP in the AC, a maximum of 16 VAPs can be created in an AC, the value range of VAP ID is between 1 to 16, and ID 1 and 2 are used in this example; the parameter radio-id is the RF ID, and the AP in this example supports zero to one RF: RF 0 and RF 1, where RF 0 is the 2.4GHz RF and RF 1 is the 5GHz RF.

The WLAN service configuration will be automatically delivered to APs by the AC, and the administrator can use the display vap all command to check whether the VAP has been successfully created on all AP-supported RFs. The entry, AP name, shows the AP name configured by the administrator, and the

RfID indicates the RF ID. When the Status is ON, it means that the VAP has been successfully created on the AP's RF ID 1.

```
[AC]display vap all
Info: This operation may take a few seconds, please wait.
WID : WLAN ID
----------------------------------------------------------------
AP ID AP name RfID WID BSSID        Status Auth type   STA    SSID
-------
  1    ap1    0   1   00E0-FCC4-15A0 ON    WPA/WPA2-PSK 1   AP-Office1
  1    ap1    1   1   00E0-FCC4-15B0 ON    WPA/WPA2-PSK 0   AP-Office1
  2    ap2    0   1   00E0-FCB1-02B0 ON    WPA/WPA2-PSK 0   AP-Office1
  2    ap2    1   1   00E0-FCB1-02C0 ON    WPA/WPA2-PSK 0   AP-Office1
  3    ap3    0   2   00E0-FC33-5190 ON    WPA/WPA2-PSK 0   AP-Office2
  3    ap3    1   2   00E0-FC33-51A0 ON    WPA/WPA2-PSK 0   AP-Office2
  4    ap4    0   2   00E0-FCAF-5610 ON    WPA/WPA2-PSK 1   AP-Office2
  4    ap4    1   2   00E0-FCAF-5620 ON    WPA/WPA2-PSK 0   AP-Office2
----------------------------------------------------------------
Total: 8
```

The administrator uses the display vap ssid AP-Office1 command to check if the VAP has been successfully created on the AP-supported RF whose "ssid" is AP-Office1.

```
[AC]display vap ssid AP-Office1
Info: This operation may take a few seconds, please wait.
WID : WLAN ID
----------------------------------------------------------------
AP ID AP name  RfID WID BSSID        Status   Auth type STA   SSID
-------
  1    ap1     0   1   00E0-FCC4-15A0 ON    WPA/WPA2-PSK 1   AP-Office1
  1    ap1     1   1   00E0-FCC4-15B0 ON    WPA/WPA2-PSK 0   AP-Office1
  2    ap2     0   1   00E0-FCB1-02B0 ON    WPA/WPA2-PSK 0   AP-Office1
  2    ap2     1   1   00E0-FCB1-02C0 ON    WPA/WPA2-PSK 0   AP-Office1
----------------------------------------------------------------
Total: 4
```

Enter "display station all" to view the connected mobile devices.

```
[AC]display station all
Rf/WLAN: Radio ID/WLAN ID
Rx/Tx: link receive rate/link transmit rate(Mbps)
----------------------------------------------------------------
STA MAC  AP ID Ap name Rf/WLAN Band Type Rx/Tx RSSI VLAN IP address SSID
----------------------------------------------------------------
 5489-9895-16a0 1 ap1     0/1   2.4G - -/-   -  101 192.168.101.218
AP-Office1
 5489-98ab-4629 4 ap4     0/1   2.4G - -/-   -  102 192.168.102.73
AP-Office2
----------------------------------------------------------------
 Total: 2 2.4G: 2 5G: 0
```

In the above output information, STA MAC is the MAC address of the mobile device, AP ID is the ID of the AP, Ap name is the name of the AP, VLAN is the service VLAN to which it belongs, and IP address is the IP address the client obtains. You can see that some mobile devices are in VLAN 101 and some are in VLAN 102, and they all obtain the IP addresses of the corresponding VLANs.

12.5 Development Trends of WLAN Technologies

Wi-Fi has become a ubiquitous technology in today's world, providing wireless connections for billions of devices, and is also the favorable choice for more and more users to access the Internet. There is a trend that Wi-Fi is going to gradually replace wired access. To accommodate new service applications and reduce the bandwidth gap with wired networks, each generation of the 802.11 standard has been developed to significantly increase its rate.

With the emergence of various video conferences, wireless interactive VR, mobile teaching and other services applications, the number of Wi-Fi access terminals keeps growing. The development of IT is allowing more and more smart home devices to access Wi-Fi networks. Therefore, Wi-Fi networks still need to continuously improve its rate, and meanwhile consider whether more terminals can be connected so as to adapt to the expanding number of client devices and accommodate users' experience needs of different applications.

The next generation of Wi-Fi needs to address the problem of reduced efficiency of the entire Wi-Fi network due to the increasing number of terminals connected, and the IEEE 802.11 working group has already started to deal with this challenge as early as 2014. The 802.11ax standard will introduce technologies such as Orthogonal Frequency Division Multiple Access (OFDMA), Multi-User Multiple-Input Multiple-Output (MU-MIMO), and 1024-QAM high-order modulation, so as to solve the problem of network capacity and transmission rate in terms of spectrum resource utilization and multi-user access. The goal is to increase the average user throughput by at least four times compared to today's Wi-Fi 5 in a dense user environment and increase the number of concurrent users by more than three times, hence Wi-Fi 6 (802.11ax) is also known as High efficiency WLAN (HEW).

As Wi-Fi standards evolve, the Wi-Fi Alliance has renamed Wi-Fi using numeric sequences in order to make it easy for Wi-Fi users and device manufacturers to understand standards of the Wi-Fi their devices are connected to or support. On the other hand, the next-generation naming approach was also chosen to highlight the significant advancements in Wi-Fi technology, which offers a host of new features, including greater throughput, faster speeds, more concurrent connections supported, etc. On September 16, 2019, the Wi-Fi 6 certification program was announced to certify devices using the next-generation 802.11ax standard wireless communication technology.

As with each previous release of a new 802.11 standard, 802.11ax will be compatible with the previous 802.11ac/n/g/a/b standards, and older terminals can seamlessly access 802.11ax networks in the same way.

802.11ax was originally designed to suit high-density wireless access and high-capacity wireless services, such as outdoor large public places, high-density venues, high-density wireless indoor offices and electronic classrooms.

In these scenarios, client devices accessing the Wi-Fi networks will register a tremendous growth. In addition, the voice and video traffic that is also increasing has an impact on Wi-Fi networks. We all know that 4K video streaming (bandwidth requirement of 50 Mbit/s per person), voice streaming (time latency of less than 30 ms), VR streaming (bandwidth requirement of 75 Mbit/s per person, time latency of less than 15 ms) are very sensitive to bandwidth and time latency. Transmission latency caused by network congestion or retransmission will have a huge impact on users' experience. Though the existing Wi-Fi 5 (802.11ac) network is able to provide large bandwidth capability, as more users access the network, throughput performance hits a bottleneck. In contrast, the Wi-Fi 6 (802.11ax) network make these services more reliable through technologies such as OFDMA, UL MU-MIMO, and 1024-QAM. Only can it support more clients to access, but it can also balance the bandwidth per user. For example, in an electronic classroom, previously, if the lecture is convened in a large class with more than 100 students, transmitting video or uplink and downlink interactions are facing comparatively huge challenge, but the 802.11ax network can easily handle the scenario.

12.6   Exercises

1. What are the advantages of direct networking and networking in bypass mode?
2. (Multi-selection) What are the ways for fit APs to discover ACs? ( )

   A. Static discovery
   B. DHCP dynamic discovery
   C. FTP dynamic discovery
   D. DNS dynamic discovery

3. Which of the following standards organizations is for WLAN device authentication to achieve WLAN technology interoperability? ( )

   A. Wi-Fi Alliance
   B. IEEE
   C. IETF
   D. FCC

4. The CAPWAP protocol is a WLAN standard proposed by the IEEE standards organization in April 2009 for communication between ACs and Fit APs. Is this statement correct? ( )

A. Correct

B. Incorrect

5. What is the number of channels supported by China in the 2.4 GHz band? ( )

   A. 11
   B. 13
   C. 3
   D. 5

6. (Multi-selection) What are the WLAN working bands? ( )

   A. 2 GHz
   B. 5 GHz
   C. 5.4 GHz
   D. 2.4 GHz

7. Which of the following standards is a wireless LAN standard originally developed by IEEE? ( )

   A. IEEE 802.11
   B. IEEE 802.10
   C. IEEE 802.12
   D. IEEE 802.16

8. Huawei's AP products can only support the configuration of one SSID. Is this statement correct? ( )

   A. Correct
   B. Incorrect

9. What is the full name of SSID? ( )

   A. Basic service set
   B. Basic service area
   C. Extended service set
   D. Service set identifier

10. The infrastructure mode network consisting of multiple APs and the distributed systems connecting them is also called ( ).

    A. Basic service set
    B. Basic service area
    C. Extended service set
    D. Extended service area

11. The VLAN used as the AP to establish the CAPWAP tunnel with the AC is ( ).

    A. Management VLAN
    B. Service VLAN
    C. User VLAN
    D. Authentication VLAN

12. (Multi-selection) To configure the authentication mode of the AP, the authenti-
    cation modes supported by the AP are ( ).

    A. mac-auth
    B. sn-auth
    C. no-auth
    D. mac-sn-auth

13. When the AC uses networking in bypass mode, if the data is forwarded directly,
    the data flow _____ the AC; if the data is forwarded in tunnels, the data flow
    the AC. ( )

    A. does not pass, passes
    B. does not pass, does not pass
    C. passes, passes
    D. passes, does not pass

14. When an AC has only one interface to the aggregation layer switch, and user
    traffic goes out of the public network directly through the aggregation layer
    switch without flowing through the AC, then the networking mode should be ( )
    at this time.

    A. bypass mode + tunnel forwarding
    B. bypass mode + direct forwarding
    C. Direct connection mode + tunnel forwarding
    D. Direct connection mode + direct forwarding

Chapter 13
IPv6

In the 1980s, the IETF (Internet Engineering Task Force) released RFC791, i.e., IPv4 protocol, marking the formal standardization of IPv4. In the decades that followed, the IPv4 protocol became one of the most dominant protocols. Countless people have developed applications based on IPv4 and made various additions and enhancements to this protocol, assisting the IPv4 in supporting the thriving Internet of today.

However, as the Internet grows larger and larger, and technologies such as 5G and the Internet of Things develop merge, IPv4 is facing daunting challenges. Therefore, it is imperative to replace IPv4 with IPv6.

IPv6 is a set of specifications designed by the IETF and is an upgraded version of IPv4. It is the second generation of standard network layer protocols, also known as IPng (IP next generation). The most significant difference between IPv6 and IPv4 is that the length of IP address is upgraded from 32 bits to 128 bits.

13.1 Overview of IPv6

13.1.1 The Dilemma Faced by IPv4

On February 3, 2011, IANA (Internet Assigned Numbers Authority) announced that its last 4.68 million IPv4 addresses would be distributed equally among the five RIRs (Regional Internet Registry) worldwide. After that, IANA had no more IPv4 addresses to assign. As shown in Fig. 13.1, the IPv4 addresses of these five organizations have now been assigned as well.

IANA is the organization responsible for the assignment of Internet IP address numbers around the world. IANA assigns some IPv4 addresses to RIRs at the continental level, and each RIR then allocates addresses within its jurisdiction. The five major RIRs include:

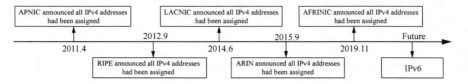

Fig. 13.1 Assignment of the final IPv4 addresses

- RIPE (Reseaux IP Europeans), which serves Europe, the Middle East, and Central Asia;
- LACNIC (Latin American and Caribbean Internet Address Registry), which serves Central and South America and the Caribbean.
- ARIN (American Registry for Internet Numbers), which serves North America and parts of the Caribbean.
- AFRINIC (African Network Information Centre), which serves the African region.
- APNIC (Asia Pacific Network Information Centre), which serves the Asia and Pacific region.

IPv4 has proven to be a very successful protocol, and it has withstood the test of the Internet's development from a network formed by a small number of computers to the current interconnection of hundreds of millions of computers. Nevertheless, the protocol was designed decades ago based on the size of the network at that time. Now it seems that the designers of IPv4 have underestimated and under-anticipated the Internet. With the continuous expansion of the Internet and the introduction of new applications, the limitations of IPv4 have become increasingly prominent.

The rapid expansion of the Internet was not anticipated by the designers of IPv4. Especially in the last decade, the Internet has exploded in size, reaching millions of households and making it indispensable to people's daily lives. Since the assignment of IPv4 addresses is based on the principle of "first-come, first-served and need-oriented assignment", the development of the Internet is extremely uneven in countries around the world or regions in each country. This will inevitably result in a large number of IP address resources being concentrated in certain developed countries or certain developed regions in a certain country. Because of the rapid development and uneven distribution, the IP address spaces are depleted as a result.

In the 1990s, the IETF introduced technologies such as NAT (Network Address Translation) and CIDR (Classless Inter Domain Routing) to delay the point at which IPv4 addresses will be exhausted. However, these transition solutions can only slow down the rate of IPv4 address depletion, but not solve the problem from its root. In addition, the requirements for security, quality of service (QoS), and easy configuration also suggest that at this time a new protocol is in need to fundamentally solve the problems currently faced by IPv4.

13.1.2 Advantages of IPv6

Compared with IPv4, IPv6 has the following advantages.

- Virtually unlimited address space: this is the most obvious advantage compared to IPv4. IPv6 addresses consist of 128 bits, which is about 2×10^{96} times the address capacity of IPv4. This makes it possible for a vast ocean of terminals to be online at the same time as well as for unified addressing management. It also provides strong support for interconnection of everything.
- Hierarchical address structure: because of the virtually unlimited address space, IPv6 is divided into various address segments according to the application scenarios during address planning. It also strictly requires the continuity of unicast IPv6 address segments to facilitate IPv6 route aggregation and reduce the size of IPv6 address tables.
- Plug-and-play: any computer or terminal must have a clear IP address to access network resources and transmit data. The traditional way to assign IP addresses is manual obtaining IP addresses or automatically obtaining IP addresses by DHCP. In addition to the above two ways, IPv6 also supports SLAAC (StateLess Address AutoConfiguration).
- End-to-end network integrity: IPv4 networks that use NAT technology on a large scale fundamentally undermine the integrity of end-to-end connection. With IPv6, NAT network devices will no longer be needed, and Internet behavior management and network supervision will become simple.
- Enhanced security: IPSec (Internet Protocol security) was originally designed for IPv6, so protocol messages based on IPv6 (routing protocols, neighbor discovery, etc.) can be encrypted end-to-end, but currently this feature is not widely used. IPv6 data message security is basically the same as IPv4 + IPSec.
- Strong scalability: the IPv6 extension headers are not part of the network layer headers, but they are inserted between the IPv6 base headers and the payload when it is necessary to assist IPv6 in encryption, mobility, optimal path selection, QoS, etc., and to improve the efficiency of forwarding messages.
- Improved mobility: when a user moves from one network segment to another, a traditional network generates "triangular routing", but in a IPv6 network, the communication of such mobile devices will no longer go through the original "triangular routing", but be directly routed and forwarded, which reduces the cost of traffic forwarding and improves network performance and reliability.
- QoS is further enhanced: IPv6 retains all the QoS attributes of IPv4, and additionally defines a 20 Byte flow label field that can be used by applications or terminals, and allocates specific resources for particular services and data flows. Currently, this mechanism is not fully developed and applied.

Figure 13.2 shows a comparison of the TCP/IPv4 protocol stack and the TCP/IPv6 protocol stack.

As can be seen from the figure, the TCP/IPv4 protocol stack implements the same functions as the TCP/IPv6 protocol stack, except that the network layer has changed.

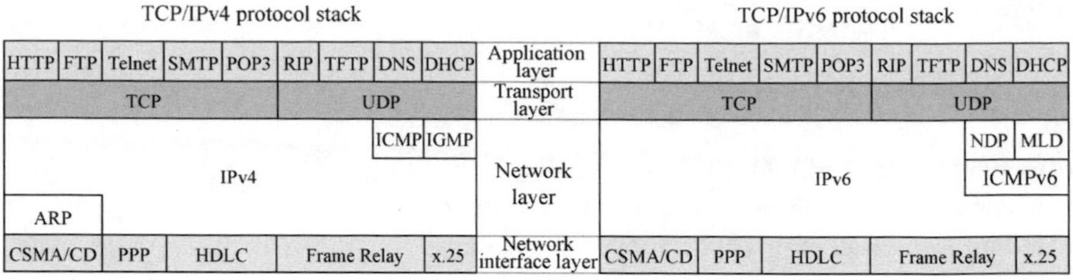

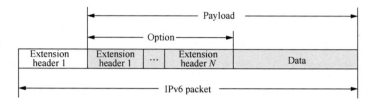

Fig. 13.2 IPv4 protocol stack and IPv6 protocol stack

Fig. 13.3 Base and extension headers

The network layer of the TCP/IPv6 protocol stack does not have the ARP protocol and IGMP protocol, and the functions of the ICMP protocol have been greatly extended. The functions of the ARP protocol in the IPv4 stack and the multicast group membership management functions of the IGMP protocol are also embedded in the ICMPv6, that is, the Neighbor Discovery Protocol (NDP) and Multicast Listener Discovery (MLD) protocols, respectively.

The functions of the core protocols of IPv6 network layer are as follows.

- Internet Control Message Protocol version IPv6 (ICMPv6): ICMPv6 replaces ICMP and is used to test whether the network is running smoothly and to report errors and other information to help users determine network failures.
- Neighbor Discovery Protocol (NDP): NDP replaces ARP and is used to manage interactions between neighboring IPv6 nodes, including automatic address configuration and the resolution of the next IPv6 address to a MAC address.
- Multicast Listener Discovery (MLD) protocol: MLD replaces IGMP and is used to manage the identity of IPv6 multicast group members.

13.1.3 IPv6 Base Headers

IPv6 packets are allowed to have zero or more extension headers after the base header, followed by data, as shown in Fig. 13.3. Note, however, that none of the extension headers are part of the IPv6 packet header. The combination of all the extension headers and data is called the payload or net load of the packet.

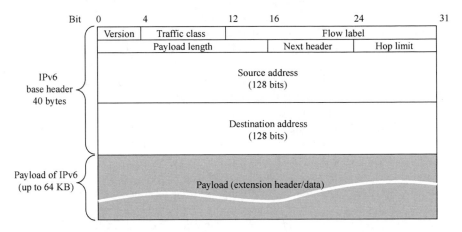

Fig. 13.4 IPv6 base header

Figure 13.4 shows the base header of IPv6. Following the base header is the payload, which includes the transport layer data and possible optional extensions.

Compared to IPv4, IPv6 has made the following alterations to some of the fields in headers.

- The "header length" field has been removed because the header length is fixed (40 bytes).
- The "service type" field has been removed because the priority and flow label fields are used in combination to implement the function of the "service type" field.
- The "total length" field has been replaced by the "payload length" field.
- The "identification", "flag", and "fragment offset" fields are removed as these functions are already included in the fragmentation extension header.
- The TTL field is renamed to "Hop Limit" field, but their functions are the same (the name is now more consistent with the function).
- The "protocol" field is replaced by the "next header" field.
- The "checksum" field has been removed, which speeds up the processing of packets by the router. Error checking is implemented by the data link layer and the transport layer. At the data link layer, erroneous frames are discarded if they are detected. At the transport layer, when using UDP, user packets are discarded if errors are detected; when using TCP, message segments are retransmitted if errors are detected until they are correctly delivered to the destination process.
- The "option" field is eliminated and the "option" function is implemented by an extension header.

By eliminating unnecessary functions from the header, the number of fields in the IPv6 base header is reduced to eight (although the length of the base header is doubled).

The following explains the role of each field in the IPv6 basic prefix.

- Version number: four bits long; the value is 6 for IPv6.
- Traffic class: eight bits long, equivalent to the QoS field in IPv4, which indicates the class or priority of IPv6 packets and is mainly used for QoS.
- Flow label: 20 bits long. It is a new field in IPv6 that is used to distinguish real-time traffic. Different flow labels + source address can uniquely identify a data flow, and intermediate network devices can distinguish data flows more efficiently based on this information.
- Payload length: 16 bits long. Payload is the rest of the packet (i.e., extension headers and upper layer protocol data unit) that immediately follows the IPv6 base header.
- Next header: eight bits long. This field defines the type of the first extension header (if present) immediately following the IPv6 base header, or the protocol type in the upper-layer protocol data unit (similar to the Protocol field in IPv4).
- Hop limit: eight bits long, similar to the Time to Live field in IPv4. This field defines the maximum number of hops that an IP packet can take. Every time a router forwards a packet, it decrements the value of this field by 1, and if the value reaches zero, the packet is discarded.
- Source address: 128 bits long, indicating the address of the sender.
- Destination address: 128 bits long, indicating the address of the receiver.

13.1.4   IPv6 Extension Headers

If IPv4 packets use options in their header, these options must be checked by every router along the packet's path, which slows down the router's packet processing speed. However, in practice, many of these options do not need to be checked by the routers along the path (because there is no need to use the information of these options).

IPv6 puts the function of "options" of the original IPv4 header in the extension headers, and leaves the extension headers to be processed by the computers at the source and destination of the path, while the routers along the packets' path do not process these extension headers (with the exception of one header, that is the hop-by-hop options header). In this way, the processing efficiency of the routers is significantly improved. The following six extension headers are defined in RFC 2460, and when more than one extension header is used in the same IPv6 message, the extension headers must appear in the following order.

Hop-by-hop options header: it is mainly used to specify sending parameters for each hop on the transmission path, and each intermediate node on the transmission path has to read and process this field.

Destination options header: it carries some information that only the destination node will process.

Routing header: it is used by the IPv6 source nodes to force packets to go through specific devices.

Table 13.1 Header values corresponding to extension headers

Extension header	Next header value
Hop-by-hop options header	0
Destination options header	60
Routing header	43
Fragment header	44
Authentication header	51
Encapsulating Security Payload header	50
No next header	59

Fragment header: the message needs to be sent in fragments when its length exceeds the Maximum Transmission Unit (MTU), and in IPv6, the fragment header is used for fragmentation sending.

Authentication header: this header is used by IPsec to provide authentication, data integrity, and replay protection.

Encapsulating Security Payload header: this header is used by IPsec mainly to provide authentication, data integrity and replay protection and confidentiality of IPv6 packets.

The "next header" field of the IPv6 base header can be used to indicate which protocol at which layer the data following the base header should be delivered to. For example, 6 indicates that it should be delivered to TCP at the transport layer, 17 means that it should be delivered to UDP at the transport layer, and 58 indicates that it should be delivered to ICMPv6 at the network layer.

Table 13.1 shows the values of the "next header" for all extension headers defined in the specification.

Each extension header consists of several fields that vary in length. However, the first field of all extension headers is an 8-bit "next header" field. The value of this field indicates the field following the extension header. As shown in Fig. 13.5, IPv6 extension headers include routing headers, fragment headers, and TCP headers.

13.2 IPv6 Addressing

13.2.1 Overview of IPv6 Address

A 128-bit IPv6 address allows for more address hierarchies, a wider address assignment space, and automatic address configuration. The virtually unlimited address space is the biggest advantage of IPv6, as shown in Table 13.2.

As shown in Fig. 13.6, an IPv6 address consists of a 128-bit binary number that identifies an interface or a group of interfaces. An IPv6 address is typically written as xxxx:xxxx:xxxx:xxxx:xxxx:xxxx:xxxx:xxxx, where xxxx is four hexadecimal digits, equivalent to a 16-bit binary number; the eight groups of xxxx together make up a 128-bit IPv6 address. An IPv6 address is composed of an IPv6 network prefix

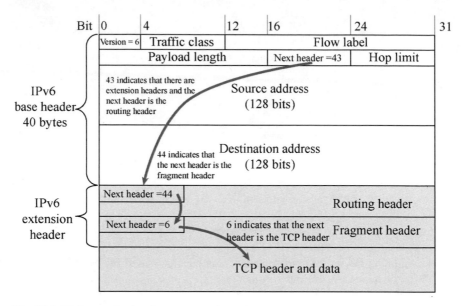

Fig. 13.5 IPv6 extension header

Table 13.2 Comparison of the numbers of IPv4 and IPv6 addresses

Version	Length	Number of addresses
IPv4	32 bits	4,294,967,296
IPv6	128 bits	340,282,366,920,938,463,374,607,431,768,211,456

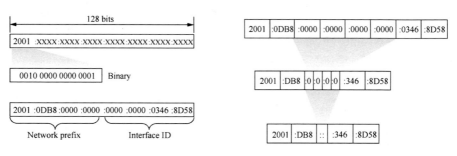

Fig. 13.6 IPv6 address composition

and an interface identify. The former is used to identify the IPv6 network and the latter the interface.

An IPv6 address is 128 bits long, so it can be inconvenient to write. In addition, due to the huge address space of IPv6 addresses, the address will often contain multiple zeros. To this end, IPv6 provides compression methods to simplify the address writing, as shown in the following compression rules.

Fig. 13.7 Simplified IPv6
address representation

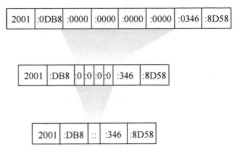

- The starting zeros in every 16 bits can be omitted.
- Two or more consecutive groups of zeros contained in an address can be replaced with a double colon "::". Note that the double colon can only be used once in an IPv6 address; otherwise, the device cannot determine the number of zeros in each segment when it restores the compressed address to 128 bits, as shown in Fig. 13.7.

This example shows how to use compression rules for a simplified representation of IPv6 addresses.

IPv6 addresses are divided into IPv6 network prefixes and interface identifiers, and subnet masks are identified using the prefix length. The representation is like this: IPv6 address/prefix length, where "prefix length" is a decimal number indicating how many starting bits of the address are the address prefix. For example, F00D:4598:7304:6540:FEDC:BA98:7654:3210 has a 64-bit address prefix, which can be expressed as F00D:4598:7304: 6540:FEDC:BA98:7654:3210/64, and its network segment is F00D:4598:7304:6540::/ 64.

13.2.2 Classification of IPv6 Addresses

According to the network prefix of IPv6 addresses, IPv6 addresses can be classified into unicast addresses, multicast addresses and anycast addresses, as shown in Fig. 13.8. Unicast addresses are further divided into global unicast addresses, unique

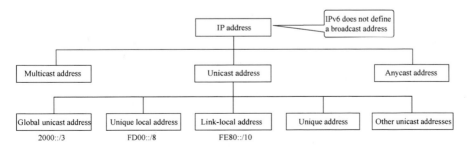

Fig. 13.8 IPv6 address classification

local addresses, link-local addresses, unique addresses, and other unicast addresses. IPv6 does not define a broadcast address. In IPv6 networks, all broadcast scenarios will be replaced by IPv6 multicast.

13.2.3 Unicast Addresses

1. Composition of unicast address

    A unicast address is an address used for point-to-point communication that identifies only one interface, and the network is responsible for transmitting packets sent to the unicast address to this interface.

    An IPv6 unicast address can be divided into the following two parts, as shown in Fig. 13.9.

    Network prefix: n bits, equivalent to the network ID in an IPv4 address.

    Interface identifier: $(128-n)$ bits, equivalent to the computer ID in an IPv4 address.

    Common IPv6 unicast addresses include global unicast address (GUA), unique local address (ULA), link-local address (LLA), etc. The network prefix and interface identifier must be 64 bits.

2. Global unicast address

    Global unicast address is also known as aggregatable global unicast address. This type of address is globally unique and is used for computers that need to access Internet, which is tantamount to the public address of IPv4.

    Usually, both the network address and the interface identifier of GUA are 64 bits long, as shown in Fig. 13.10.

    IPv6 global unicast addresses are assigned as follows: top-level aggregators (TLAs) (large ISP or address management institutions) get the bulk address. TLAs are responsible for assigning addresses to the next-level aggregators (NLAs) (small and medium-sized ISPs), and NLAs then assign addresses to site-level address aggregators (SLAs) (subnets) and network users.

    If needed, a global unicast address can be requested from the carrier or directly from the IPv6 address authority in your region.

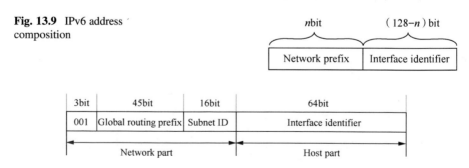

Fig. 13.9 IPv6 address composition

Fig. 13.10 Global unicast address structure

- Global routing prefix: it is assigned by the provider to an organization, and is usually at least 45 bits long.
- Subnet ID: an organization subdivides the network according to its network requirements.
- Interface ID: it is used to identify (the interface of) a device.

3. Unique local address

A unique local address is an IPv6 private address that can only be used on the intranet. This address space is not routable in the IPv6 public network so the public network cannot be directly accessed. As shown in Fig. 13.11, the unique local address uses the FC00::/7 address block, and only the FD00::/8 address segment is currently in use, with FC00::/8 reserved for future expansion. The unique local address is only valid in a limited range, but it also has a globally unique prefix (although it is randomly generated, conflicts are unlikely to occur).

4. Link-local address

There is a type of address in IPv6 called a link-local address, which is used for communications between IPv6 computers on the same subnet. This type of address can be used for auto-configuration, neighbor discovery, and nodes on links without routers. The valid range of a link-local address is the local link, as shown in Fig. 13.12, with a prefix of FE80::/10. If packets are supposed to be sent to devices on a single link, and for protocols that do not want packets to go outside the range of the link, a link-local address can be used. When a unicast IPv6 address is configured, a link-local address is automatically configured on the interface. A link-local address can coexist with a routable IPv6 address.

The interface identifier of an IPv6 address is 64 bits long and is used to identify the interface on the link. Among the many usages of the interface identifier, the most common one is to append it to the prefix of the link-local address to form the link-local address of the interface or; in stateless autoconfiguration, to append it to the prefix of the acquired IPv6 global unicast address to form the global unicast address of the interface.

5. Interface identifier generation method for unicast address

8bit	40bit	16bit	64bit
1111 1101	Global ID	Subnet ID	Interface identifier

Fig. 13.11 Unique local address

10bit	54bit	16bit	64bit
1111 1101 10	0	Subnet ID	Interface identifier
	Fixed to be 0		

Fig. 13.12 Valid range of link-local addresses

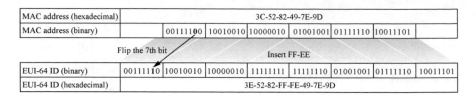

Fig. 13.13 EUI-64 specification

The IPv6 unicast address interface identifier can be generated in three ways.

- Manual configuration.
- Automatic generation by the system.
- Generated through the IEEE EUI-64 (64-bit Extended Unique Identifier) specification.

The generation through EUI-64 specification is most commonly used. The specification converts the MAC address of an interface into an IPv6 interface identifier. The IEEE EUI-64 specification inserts FF-FE into the MAC address and flips the seventh bit of the MAC address to form a 64-bit network interface identifier for IPv64 addresses, as shown in Fig. 13.13.

This method of generating IPv6 address interface identifier from MAC address reduces the configuration workload. Especially when stateless address autoconfiguration is used, only an IPv6 prefix needs to be obtained to form an IPv6 address with the interface identifier.

The biggest disadvantage of using this approach is that those with malicious intention can deduce the Layer 2 MAC address from the Layer 3 IPv6 address.

13.2.4   Multicast Addresses

1. Composition of multicast addresses
   Similar as IPv4 multicast, an IPv6 multicast address can identify multiple interfaces and is generally used in a "one-to-many" communication scenario.

   A multicast address is equivalent to the channel of a radio station. A radio station sends a signal on a specific channel, and radios that are tuned to that channel will receive the program of that radio station, while radios that are not tuned to that channel will ignore the signal.

   As shown in Fig. 13.14, a multicast source sends a multicast stream using a multicast address, and computers that intend to receive the multicast information need to join the multicast group, that is, bind their network interface cards to the multicast IP address and generate corresponding multicast MAC addresses. All interfaces that join the multicast can receive and process multicast packets, while computers that are not bound to the multicast address ignore the multicast information.

Fig. 13.14 Multicast illustration

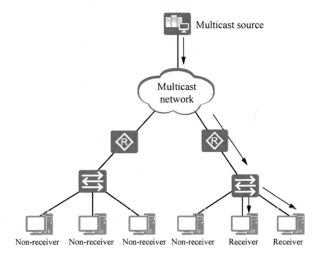

8bit   4bit   4bit   80bit   32bit

| 11111111 | Flags | Scope | Reserved(has to be 0) | Gruop ID |

Fig. 13.15 Composition of Multicast Addresses

Table 13.3 Multicast scope

Scope value	Scope
0	Reserved
1	Interface-local scope; it spans only a single interface and is useful only for loopback transmission of multicast
2	Link-local scope, i.e., FF02::1
5	Site-local scope
8	Organization-local scope
E	Global scope
F	Reserved

The multicast address starts with 11111111 (i.e., ff), as shown in Fig. 13.15.

Flags: it indicates permanent or temporary multicast group. 0000 indicates permanently assigned or well known; and 0001 indicates temporary.

Scope: it indicates the scope of multicast, as shown in Table 13.3.

Group ID: the multicast group ID.

Reserved: 80 bits long, and it must be 0.

2. Solicited-node multicast address

When a node has a unicast or anycast address, it will generate a solicited-node multicast address and join the multicast group. This address is mainly used for

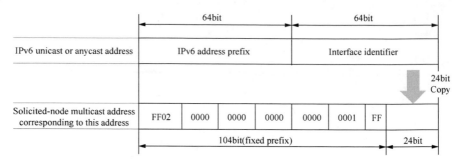

Fig. 13.16 Composition of solicited-node multicast address

neighbor discovery mechanism and duplicate address detection. The valid range of the solicited-node multicast address is the local link range.

As shown in Fig. 13.16, the first 104 bits of the solicited-node multicast address are fixed with the prefix FF02:0000:0000: 0000:0000:0001:FFxx:xxxx/ 104, or abbreviated to FF02::1:FFxx:xxxx/104. A solicited-node multicast address is formed by taking the low-order 24 bits of an IPv6 address and appending those bits to the back.

For example, the solicited-node multicast address for IPv6 address 2001::1234:5678/64 is FF02::1:FF34:5678/104, where FF02::1:FF is a 104-bit fixed part.

On the local link, the solicited-node multicast address contains only one interface. Once the IPv6 address of an access point is known, the solicited-node multicast address can be calculated.

The role of the solicited-node multicast address is as follows.

- There is no ARP in IPv6. ICMP replaces the function of ARP and the solicited-node multicast address is used by the node to obtain the link layer addresses of neighboring nodes on the same local link.
- For Duplicate Address Detection (DAD). Before a node configure an address as its own IPv6 address using stateless autoconfiguration, it uses DAD to verify whether the address has been in use on other local links.

Since only the destination node listens to this solicited-node multicast address, the multicast message can be received by the destination node without influencing the network performance of other non-destination nodes.

13.2.5 Anycast Addresses

An anycast address identifies a set of interfaces and differs from a multicast address in the method of sending packets. Packets sent to an anycast address are not distributed to all members of the group, but are sent to the "nearest" interface identified by the address.

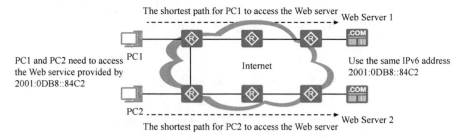

Fig. 13.17 Role of anycast addresses

As shown in Fig. 13.17, Web Server 1 and Web Server 2 are assigned the same IPv6 address, 2001:0DB8::84C2. Then this unicast address becomes an anycast address. PC1 and PC2 need to access the Web service by sending a request to address 2001:0DB8::84C2. PC1 and PC2 will then access the Web server closest to them (with the lowest routing cost, i.e., the shortest path).

The anycast process involves an initiator of an anycast message and one or more responders.

- The initiator of an anycast message is usually the host requesting a service (e.g., a Web service).
- An anycast address is the same as a unicast address in terms of format. The only difference is that a single device can send messages to multiple devices with the same address.

The application of anycast addresses in a network has the following advantages.

- Service redundancy. For example, users can access the same service (e.g., Web services) through multiple servers that use the same address. These servers are all responders to the anycast messages. If the anycast addresses is not used for communication, then when one of the servers fails, the user needs to obtain the address of another server to re-establish the communication. If an anycast address is used, then when one server fails, the initiator of the anycast message can automatically communicate with another server using the same address, thus achieving service redundancy.
- Provision of better-quality services. For example, a company deploys one server providing the same Web service in Province A and in Province B. Based on routing optimization rules, when accessing the Web services provided by the company, users in Province A will give priority to the server deployed in Province A, thus increasing the access speed and reducing access latency so as to tremendously improve the user experience.

Anycast addresses are assigned from the unicast address space, using any format of unicast addresses. Thus, syntactically, there is no difference between an anycast address and a unicast address. When a unicast address is assigned to more than one interface, it is converted to an anycast address. The node assigned with an anycast address must be explicitly configured to know it is an anycast address.

13.2.6   Common IPv6 Address Types and Ranges

The common IPv6 address types and ranges are listed in Table 13.4.

Now a small number of global unicast addresses have been assigned by IANA (a division of ICANN, the Internet Corporation for Assigned Names and Numbers). Unicast addresses are in the format 2000::/3 and represent any reachable address on the public IP network. IANA is responsible for assigning addresses in this address range to multiple Regional Internet Registries (RIRs), who are responsible for assigning addresses in five regions worldwide. The following address scopes have been assigned: 2400::/12 (APNIC), 2600::/12 (ARIN), 2800::/12 (LACNIC), 2A00::/12 (RIPE), and 2C00::/12 (AFRINIC). They will use a single address prefix to identify all addresses in a given region.

Address space is also reserved in the 2000::/3 address range for document examples, such as 2001:0DB8::/32.

Link-local addresses can only be used for communication between nodes in the same network segment. IPv6 messages with a link-local address as the source or destination address are not forwarded by the router to other links. The prefix of link-local addresses is FE80::/10. Computers that use IPv6 for communication will have both a link-local address and a global unicast address.

The prefix of multicast addresses is FF00::/8. Most of the addresses in the multicast address range are reserved for specific multicast groups. Like IPv4, IPv6 multicast addresses also support routing protocols. There are no broadcast addresses in IPv6, and replacing broadcast addresses with multicast addresses ensures that messages are sent only to specific multicast groups and not to arbitrary terminals in the IPv6 network.

0:0:0:0:0:0:0:0/128 is equal to ::/128, which is the equivalent address of 0.0.0.0 in IPv4 and represents an unspecified address in IPv6.

0:0:0:0:0:0:0:1 is equal to ::1, which is the equivalent address of 127.0.0.1 in IPv4 and represents the local loopback address.

Table 13.4 Common IPv6 address types and ranges

Address range	Address type
2000::/3	Global unicast address
2001:0DB8::/32	Reserved address
FE80::/10	Link-local address
FF00::/8	Multicast address
::/128	Unspecified address
::1/128	Loopback address

13.3　IPv6 Address Configuration

13.3.1　IPv6 Addresses for Computers and Routers

Computers and router interfaces that are configured or enabled with IPv6 addresses will automatically join multicast-specific multicast addresses, as shown in Fig. 13.18.

Multicast address of all nodes: FF02:0:0:0:0:0:0:1.
Multicast address of all routers: FF02:0:0:0:0:0:0:2.
Multicast address of solicited nodes: FF02:0:0:0:0:0:1:FFXX:XXXX.
Multicast address of all OSPF routers: FF02:0:0:0:0:0:0:5.
Multicast address of all OSPF DR routers: FF02:0:0:0:0:0:0:6.
Multicast address of all RIP routers: FF02:0:0:0:0:0:0:9.

As you can see in Fig. 13.18, both the computer and the router interface generate two "solicited-node multicast addresses", which are generated by the link-local address of the interface and the global unicast address assigned by the administrator, respectively.

13.3.2　Service Process of IPv6 Unicast Address

A computer or router has to go through three stages: address configuration, duplicate address detection and address resolution before sending IPv6 messages. As shown in Fig. 13.19, Neighbor Discovery Protocol (NDP) plays an important role in this. You can see from the figure that NDP is used in stateless autoconfiguration, stateful address configuration, duplicate address detection and address resolution.

The following process is needed from the IP address configuration to forwarding.

1. Global unicast address and link-local address are the most common IPv6 unicast addresses on an interface, and multiple IPv6 addresses can be configured for an interface. The global unicast address configuration can be either manually

Fig. 13.18 IPv6 interface addresses and the specific multicast groups joined

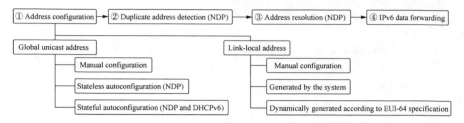

Fig. 13.19 The process of configuring IPv6 addresses on an interface

configured static IPv6 address, stateless autoconfiguration, or stateful autoconfiguration. Link-local addresses are usually generated dynamically by the system according to the EUI-64 specification and are rarely configured manually.

2. DAD is similar to the free ARP detection in IPv4, which is used to detect whether the current address conflicts with IPv6 addresses of other interfaces.
3. Address resolution is similar to ARP request in IPv4, which forms a mapping relationship between IPv6 address and data link layer address (usually MAC address) through ICMPv6 messages.
4. After IPv6 is configured, IPv6 data can be forwarded using this address.

13.3.3   Neighbor Discovery Protocol

The Neighbor Discovery Protocol (NDP), as a fundamental protocol for IPv6, provides address autoconfiguration, duplicate address detection (DAD), address resolution and other functions, as shown in Fig. 13.20.

1. Stateless autoconfiguration is a highlight of IPv6, which enables IPv6 computers to access the IPv6 network conveniently. Plug-and-play is made possible without the need to manually configure redundant IPv6 addresses or deploy application servers (such as DHCP servers) to distribute addresses for computers. The stateless autoconfiguration mechanism uses the Router Solicitation (RS) and Router Advertisement (RA) messages of ICMPv6. Through the stateless autoconfiguration mechanism, the nodes on the link can automatically obtain IPv6 global unicast addresses.

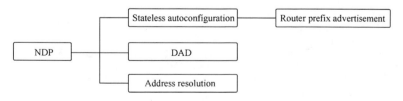

Fig. 13.20 NDP functions

Table 13.5 ICMPv6 messages used by NDP

ICMPv6 type	Message name
133	Router Solicitation (RS)
134	Router Advertisement (RA)
135	Neighbor Solicitation (NS)
136	Neighbor Advertisement (NA)

Table 13.6 Types of messages used for address resolution, prefix advertisement and DAD

Mechanism	RS133	RA134	NS135	NA136
Address resolution			√	√
Prefix advertisement	√	√		
DAD			√	√

2. Duplicate address detection uses ICMPv6 NS and ICMPv6 NA messages to ensure that there are no identical unicast addresses in the network. All interfaces are required to do DAD before using a unicast address.
3. Address resolution is a method to determine the link layer address of the destination node. The address resolution function in NDP not only replaces the original ARP in IPv4, but also uses neighbor unreachability detection to maintain reachability status information between neighbor nodes. The address resolution process uses two types of ICMPv6 messages: Neighbor Solicitation (NS) and Neighbor Advertisement (NA). Neighbors in this case refer to all nodes attached to the same link.

   NDP uses ICMPv6 messages, and the NDP protocol is encapsulated in ICMPv6 and uses type fields to identify the different messages of NDP. Table 13.5 lists the type fields used by various messages of NDP.

   Table 13.6 lists the message types used for address resolution, prefix advertisement, and DAD. Address resolution uses NS135 and NA136 packets, prefix advertisement uses RS133 and RA134 packets, and DAD uses NS135 and NA136 packets.

13.3.4   Configuration Methods of IPv6 Address

Computers using IPv6 for communication can either manually specify a static address or be set to automatically obtain an IPv6 address, as shown in Fig. 13.21. There are two ways of autoconfiguration, namely stateless autoconfiguration and stateful autoconfiguration.

13.3.5   Two Autoconfiguration Methods of IPv6 Address

IPv6 supports two types of address autoconfiguration, that is stateful and stateless autoconfiguration, and the method of automatically obtaining addresses by the

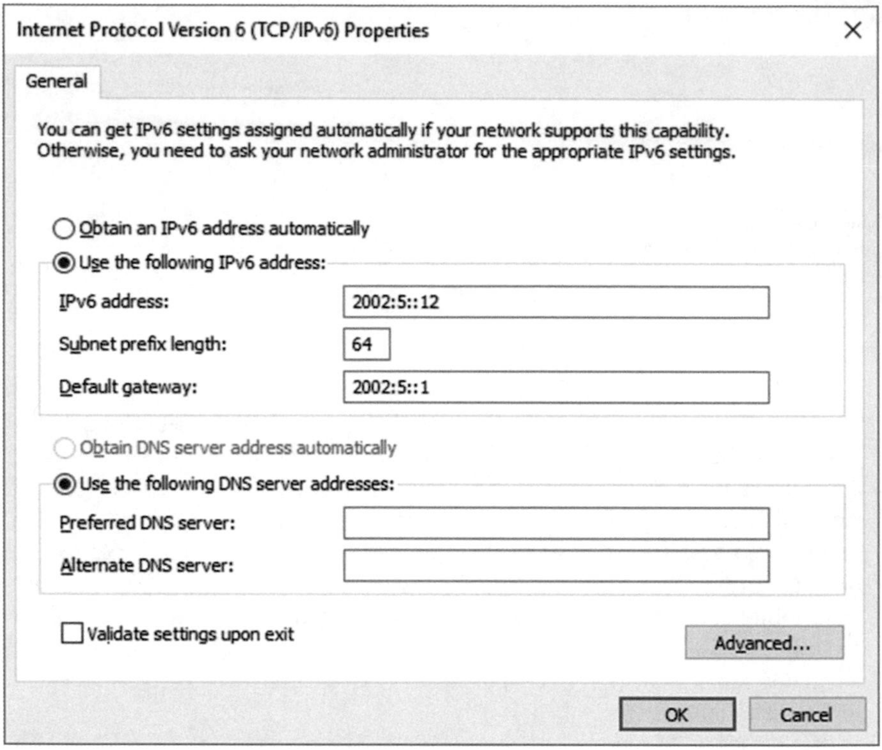

Fig. 13.21 Static IPv6 address and obtain IPv6 address automatically

terminal is controlled by the M-flag (Managed Address Configuration Flag) and O-flag (Other Stateful Configuration Flag) in the RA message advertised by the router interface.

The M field is the Managed Address Configuration flag. When $M = 0$, it identifies stateless address assignment, and clients can obtain IPv6 addresses through stateless protocols (such as ND). When $M = 1$, it identifies a stateful address assignment and the client can obtain an IPv6 address through a stateful protocol (e.g., DHCPv6).

The O field is Other Configurations. When $O = 0$, it means that the client can obtain configuration information other than addresses through stateless protocols (such as ND). When $O = 1$, it means that the client can obtain configuration information other than addresses, such as DNS, SIP server and other information, through stateful protocols (e.g., DHCPv6).

The protocol specifies that it is only meaningful if $M = 1$ and $O = 1$; and if $M = 0$ and $O = 1$, it has no meaning.

The following describes the stateless address autoconfiguration process. In RA, $M = 0$ and $O = 0$.

Stateless autoconfiguration of NDP consists of two phases: the configuration of link-local addresses and configuration of global unicast addresses. When an interface

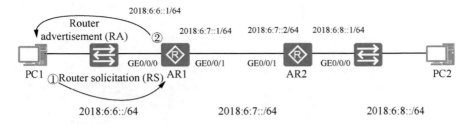

Fig. 13.22 IPv6 stateless autoconfiguration illustration

is enabled, the computer first generates a link-local address for the interface based on the local prefix FE80::/64 and the EUI-64 interface identifier. If an address conflict occurs in the subsequent DAD, the local-link address must be manually configured for the interface, or the interface will be unavailable.

The following is an example of IPv6 stateless autoconfiguration for computer PC1 in Fig. 13.22 to explain the steps of IPv6 stateless autoconfiguration.

1. After configuring the link-local address, computer node PC1 sends an RS message to solicit routing prefix information.
2. After receiving the RS message, the router sends a unicast RA message carrying prefix information for stateless address autoconfiguration with an M flag of 0 and an O flag of 0. Meanwhile, the router also periodically sends a multicast RA message.
3. After receiving the RA message, PC1 generates a temporary global unicast address based on the routing prefix information and configuration information. At the same time, DAD is started and NS messages are sent to verify the uniqueness of the temporary address, which is in a temporary state at this time.
4. After other nodes on the link receive the NS message from DAD, if no node uses the address, the message will be discarded, otherwise an NA message will be generated to respond to NS.
5. If PC1 does not receive the NA message from DAD, it means that the address is globally unique, then the temporary address is used to initialize the interface, and the address enters the valid state.

The key to stateless address configuration is that the router does not care at all about the state of the computer, such as whether it is online, so it is called stateless configuration. Stateless address configuration is mostly used for scenarios where terminals such as the Internet of Things are used, and the terminal does not require parameters other than addresses.

Figure 13.23 shows an example of f IPv6 stateful autoconfiguration (DHCPv6) for computer PC1 to explain the steps of IPv6 stateful autoconfiguration.

1. PC1 sends a router request (RS).
2. Router AR sends a router advertisement (RA). There are two flag bits in the RA message. The M flag bit is 1, which tells PC1 it can get the complete 128-bit IPv6 address from DHCPv6 server. The O flag bit is 1, which tells PC1 it can get other

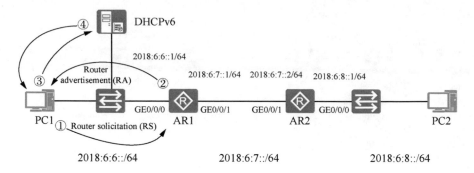

Fig. 13.23 Stateful autoconfiguration illustration

configurations such as DNS from DHCPv6 server. If both flag bits are 0, it is stateless autoconfiguration and no DHCPv6 server is needed.

3. PC1 sends a DHCPv6 solicitation message. The solicitation message is actually a multicast message, and the destination address is ff02::1:2, which is the multicast address of all DHCPv6 servers and relay agents.

4. DHCPv6 server provides IPv6 address and other configurations for PC1. In addition, the DHCPv6 server will record the assignment of this address (which is why it is called stateful autoconfiguration).

Stateful address configuration requires a DHCPv6 server to be configured in the network, and is mostly used for address configuration of wired terminals within a company to facilitate address management.

13.4   Implement IPv6 Address Autoconfiguration

13.4.1   Implement IPv6 Address Stateless Autoconfiguration

The experimental environment is shown in Fig. 13.24. There are three IPv6 networks, and you need to configure the IPv6 addresses of the interfaces of routers AR1 and AR2 with reference to the addresses marked in the topology. Set the IPv6 address of Windows 10 to automatically obtain the IPv6 address for stateless autoconfiguration.

The configuration of router AR1 is as follows.

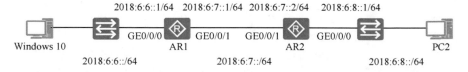

Fig. 13.24 Experimental topology diagram of stateless autoconfiguration of IPv6 addresses

```
   [AR1]ipv6                                        --Globally enable the IPv6
support
   [AR1]interface GigabitEthernet 0/0/0
   [AR1-GigabitEthernet0/0/0]ipv6 enable                        --Enable IPv6
support on the interface
   [AR1-GigabitEthernet0/0/0]ipv6 address 2018:6:6::1 64   --Add an
IPv6 address
   [AR1-GigabitEthernet0/0/0]ipv6 address auto link-local  -Configure
auto generation of link-local address
   [AR1-GigabitEthernet0/0/0]undo ipv6 nd ra halt           --Allow the
interface to send the RA message, and by default, the RA message is not
sent
   [AR1-GigabitEthernet0/0/0]quit
   [AR1]display ipv6 interface GigabitEthernet 0/0/0        --View the
IPv6 address of the interface
   GigabitEthernet0/0/0 current state : UP
   IPv6 protocol current state : UP
   IPv6 is enabled, link-local address is FE80::2E0:FCFF:FE29:31F0  --
Link-local address
   Global unicast address(es):
   2018:6:6::1, subnet is 2018:6:6::/64                  --Global unicast
address
   Joined group address(es):                     --Multicast address bound
   FF02::1:FF00:1
   FF02::2                                 --Multicast address bound to the
router
   FF02::1                                 --Multicast address bound to the
router enabled with IPv6
   FF02::1:FF29:31F0            --Solicitated-node multicast address
   MTU is 1500 bytes
   ND DAD is enabled, number of DAD attempts: 1    --ND network
discovery, number of duplicate address detections
   ......
   ND router advertisement max interval 600 seconds, min interval 200
seconds
   ND router advertisements live for 1800 seconds
   ND router advertisements hop-limit 64
   ND default router preference medium
   Hosts use stateless autoconfig for addresses    --Hosts use stateless
autoconfiguration
```

In Windows 10, you can set the mode to obtain IPv6 address automatically. By opening the command prompt and typing in "ipconfig /all", you can see the IPv6 address generated by stateless autoconfiguration, and also the link-local address (called local connection IPv6 address on Windows), and the IPv6 gateway is the link-local address of the router interface, as shown in Fig. 13.25 shows.

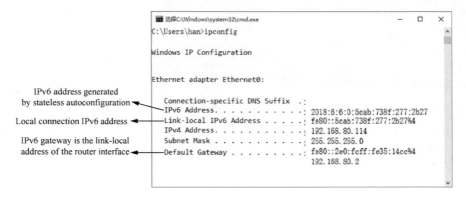

Fig. 13.25   IPv6 address generated by stateless auto-configuration

13.4.2   Packet Capture Analysis of RA and RS Packets

IPv6 addresses support stateless address autoconfiguration, which allows computers to obtain IPv6 prefixes and automatically generate interface IDs without using auxiliary protocols such as DHCP. Route discovery is the basis of IPv6 address autoconfiguration, and is mainly implemented through RA and RS packets.

Each router periodically sends RA messages carrying network configuration parameters in multicast mode so that computers and other routers on the Layer 2 network can learn about its existence. The value of the Type field of RA messages is 134.

A computer can actively send RS messages after it is connected to the network. RA messages are sent periodically by the router, but if a computer wants to receive an RA message as soon as possible, it can actively send an RS message to the router. After the router on the network receives the RS message, it immediately responds a unicast RA message to the corresponding computer, informing the computer of the default router and related configuration parameters of the network segment. The value of the Type field of the RS message is 133.

In order for the packet capture tool to capture the RS messages sent by the IPv6 autoconfiguration and the RA messages responded by the router, first run the packet capture tool on Windows, then assign a static IPv6 address to IPv6 on Windows 10, and then select "Obtain IPv6 address automatically" so that the computer will send RS messages and the router will respond to RA messages.

As shown in Fig. 13.26, in the packets captured by the packet capture tool, enter "icmpv6.type == 133" in the "Display filters" box, and the 22nd packet shown is a router solicitation (RS) packet sent by Windows 10, using ICMPv6 protocol, and the type field is 133. You can see the destination address is multicast address ff02::2, representing all router interfaces enabled with IPv6 in the network, and the source address is the link-local address of Windows 10.

Enter :icmpv6.type == 134″ in the "Display filters" box. The 60th packet displayed is a router advertisement (RA) packet sent by a router with the multicast

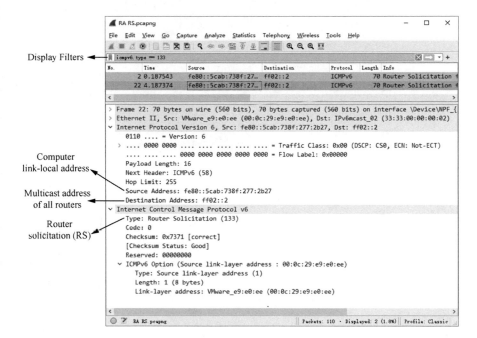

Fig. 13.26 RS packet

address ff02::1 as its destination address (representing all IPv6-enabled interfaces in the network). It uses the ICMPv6 protocol, and the type field is 134. You can see that the M flag bit is 0 and the O flag bit is 0, telling Windows 10 to use stateless autoconfiguration with a network prefix of 2018:6:6::, as shown in Fig. 13.27.

View the IPv6 configuration on Windows 10, as shown in Fig. 13.28. Open the command prompt, type in "netsh", type in "interface ipv6", and then type in "show interface" to view the index of "Ethernet0", and you can see it is 4. Then enter show interface "4" and you can see the configuration parameters related to IPv6. The "Managed Address Configuration" is "disabled", which means no IPv6 address is obtained from DHCPv6 server; and the "Other Stateful Configuration" is "disabled", which means other parameters such as DNS are not obtained from the DHCPv6 server, i.e., stateless autoconfiguration.

13.4.3   Implement IPv6 Address Stateful Autoconfiguration

You can use DHCPv6 to assign IPv6 addresses and configure other settings such as DNS for computers.

The following describes the IPv6 stateful address autoconfiguration with the network environment shown in Fig. 13.29. Configure router AR1 as the DHCPv6 server, and configure interface GE 0/0/0. Both the M flag bit and the O flag bit in

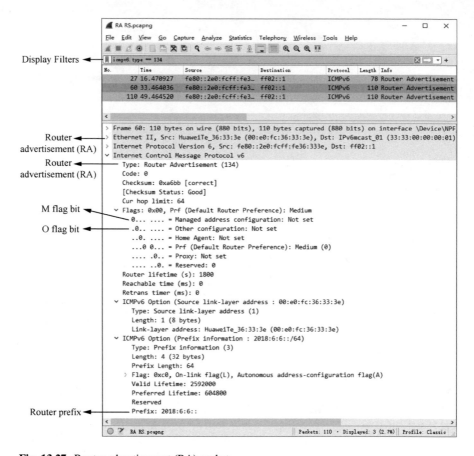

Fig. 13.27   Router advertisement (RA) packet

router advertisement message are 1. Windows 10 will obtain IPv6 addresses from
DHCPv6.

```
[AR1]ipv6                          --Enable IPv6
[AR1]dhcp enable                        --Enable DHCP
[AR1]dhcpv6 duid ?                  --Method to generate the unique
DHCP ID
   ll   DUID-LL
   llt  DUID-LLT
[AR1]dhcpv6 duid llt               --Use llt method to generate the
unique DHCP ID
[AR1]display dhcpv6 duid              --Display the unique DHCP ID
 The device's DHCPv6 unique identifier: 0001000122AB384A00E0FC2931F0
[AR1]dhcpv6 pool localnet          --Create an IPv6 address pool
named localnet
[AR1-dhcpv6-pool-localnet]address prefix 2018:6:6::/64     --Address
prefix
[AR1-dhcpv6-pool-localnet]excluded-address 2018:6:6::1     --
```

Fig. 13.28 View IPv6 configuration

```
Administrator: Command Prompt - netsh                              –  □  ×
C:\Users\han>netsh
netsh>interface ipv6
netsh interface ipv6>show interface

Idx     Met       MTU        State              Name
---  ---------  ----------  -----------  ---------------------------
  1      50   4294967295   connected    Loopback Pseudo-Interface 1
  5      50         1280   disconnected isatap.{3E7B0E5E-613C-4FC8-8
0F3-1EBC9DDA6CB4}
  4      10         1500   connected    Ethernet0


netsh interface ipv6>show interface "4"

Interface Ethernet0 Parameters
----------------------------------------------------------------
IfLuid                               : ethernet_32769
IfIndex                              : 4
State                                : connected
Metric                               : 10
Link MTU                             : 1500 bytes
Reachable Time                       : 42500 ms
Base Reachable Time                  : 30000 ms
Retransmission Interval              : 1000 ms
DAD Transmits                        : 1
Site Prefix Length                   : 64
Site Id                              : 1
Forwarding                           : disabled
Advertising                          : disabled
Neighbor Discovery                   : enabled
Neighbor Unreachability Detection    : enabled
Router Discovery                     : enabled
Managed Address Configuration        : disabled
Other Stateful Configuration         : disabled
Weak Host Sends                      : disabled
Weak Host Receives                   : disabled
Use Automatic Metric                 : enabled
Ignore Default Routes                : disabled
Advertised Router Lifetime           : 1800 seconds
Advertise Default Route              : disabled
Current Hop Limit                    : 64
Force ARPND Wake up patterns         : disabled
Directed MAC Wake up patterns        : disabled
ECN capability                       : application

netsh interface ipv6>_
```

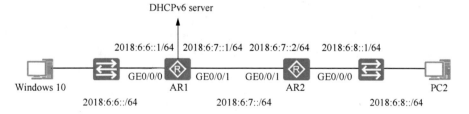

DHCPv6 server

2018:6:6::1/64 2018:6:7::1/64 2018:6:7::2/64 2018:6:8::1/64

GE0/0/0   AR1   GE0/0/1   GE0/0/1   AR2   GE0/0/0

Windows 10   PC2

2018:6:6::/64   2018:6:7::/64   2018:6:8::/64

Fig. 13.29 Network topology with stateful autoconfiguration

```
Excluded address
  [AR1-dhcpv6-pool-localnet]dns-domain-name huawei.com        --Domain
name suffix
  [AR1-dhcpv6-pool-localnet]dns-server 2018:6:6::2000          --DNS
server
  [AR1-dhcpv6-pool-localnet]quit
```

View the configured DHCPv6 address pool.

```
<AR1>display dhcpv6 pool
DHCPv6 pool: localnet
 Address prefix: 2018:6:6::/64
  Lifetime valid 172800 seconds, preferred 86400 seconds
  2 in use, 0 conflicts
 Excluded-address 2018:6:6::1
 1 excluded addresses
 Information refresh time: 86400
 DNS server address: 2018:6:6::2000
 Domain name: 91xueit.com
 Conflict-address expire-time: 172800
 Active normal clients: 2
```

Configure interface GE 0/0/0 of router AR1.

```
[AR1]interface GigabitEthernet 0/0/0
[AR1-GigabitEthernet0/0/0]ipv6 enable
[AR1-GigabitEthernet0/0/0]dhcpv6 server localnet      --Specify to
choose addresses from the address pool localnet
 [AR1-GigabitEthernet0/0/0]undo ipv6 nd ra halt      --Allow to send RA
messages
 [AR1-GigabitEthernet0/0/0]ipv6 nd autoconfig managed-address-flag
--M flag bit is 1
 [AR1-GigabitEthernet0/0/0]ipv6 nd autoconfig other-flag           --O
flag bit is 1
 [AR1-GigabitEthernet0/0/0]quit
```

In order to allow the packet capture tool to capture the RS messages automatically configured and sent by IPv6 and the RA messages responded by the router, first assign a static IPv6 address to IPv6 on Windows 10 and then select "Obtain IPv6 address automatically", so that the computer will send RS messages and the router will respond with RA messages. Find the router advertisement (RA) message from the packet capture tool, as shown in Fig. 13.30, and you can see that the value of the M flag bit and the O flag bit are both 1; the router prefix is also advertised, but the computer will still obtain the IPv6 address and other settings from the DHCPv6 server.

Open a command prompt in Windows 10, as shown in Fig. 13.31. By typing in "ipconfig /all", you can see the IPv6 configuration obtained from DHCPv6 as well as the DNS suffix search list "huawei.com" obtained from DHCPv6, DNS, and lease duration.

As shown in Fig. 13.32, enter "show interface "4"", and you can see that both the "managed address configuration" and the "other stateful configuration" are also "enabled".

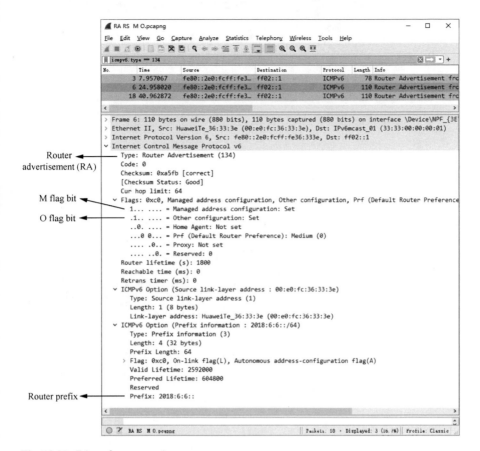

Router advertisement (RA)

M flag bit

O flag bit

Router prefix

Fig. 13.30 RA packet captured

13.5 IPv6 Routing

The condition for a smooth IPv6 network is the same as IPv4, that is, the network is only unobstructed if packets can be sent and returned. For networks that are not directly connected, static routes need to be manually added or dynamic routing protocols need to be used to learn routes to each network.

The dynamic routing protocols that support IPv6 also require new versions. OSPFv3 (OSPF version 3) supports IPv6 while OSPFv2 (OSPF version 2) supports IPv4.

The following will demonstrate the configuration of static routes for IPv6 and the configuration of OSPFv3, the dynamic routing protocol that supports IPv6.

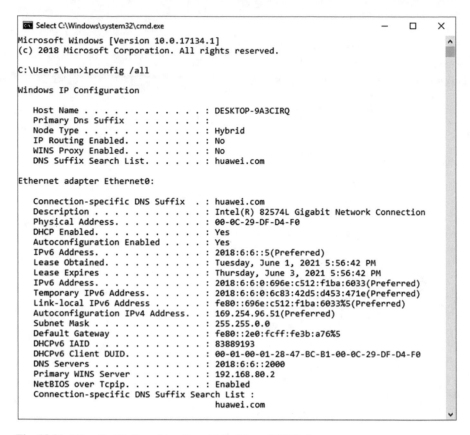

Fig. 13.31 View the IPv6 configuration obtained from DHCPv6

13.5.1 IPv6 Static Routing

As shown in Fig. 13.33, there are three IPv6 network segments and two routers in the network. Please refer to the addresses marked in the figure to configure the IPv6 addresses of the router interfaces. Add static routes to AR1 and AR2 to enable these three networks to communicate with each other.

Enable IPv6 on AR1, configure the interface to enable IPv6, and configure the IPv6 address of the interface, and add a route to network segment 2018:6:8::/64.

```
[AR1]ipv6
[AR1]interface GigabitEthernet 0/0/0
[AR1-GigabitEthernet0/0/0]ipv6 enable
[AR1-GigabitEthernet0/0/0]ipv6 address 2018:6:6::1 64
[AR1-GigabitEthernet0/0/0]undo ipv6 nd ra halt
[AR1-GigabitEthernet0/0/0]quit
[AR1]interface GigabitEthernet 0/0/1
[AR1-GigabitEthernet0/0/1]ipv6 enable
```

Fig. 13.32 IPv6 state

2018:6:6::1/64   2018:6:7::1/64   2018:6:7::2/64   2018:6:8::1/64

PC1   GE0/0/0   AR1   GE0/0/1   GE0/0/1   AR2   GE0/0/0   PC2

2018:6:6::/64   2018:6:7::/64   2018.6.8::/64

Fig. 13.33 Network topology for static routing

```
[AR1-GigabitEthernet0/0/1]ipv6 address 2018:6:7::1 64
[AR1-GigabitEthernet0/0/1]quit
```

Add a static route to the network segment 2018:6:8::/64.

```
[AR1]ipv6 route-static 2018:6:8:: 64 2018:6:7::2
```

Display the IPv6 static route.

```
[AR1]display ipv6 routing-table protocol static
Public Routing Table : Static
Summary Count : 1
Static Routing Table's Status : < Active >
Summary Count : 1
 Destination  : 2018:6:8::   PrefixLength : 64
 NextHop   : 2018:6:7::2  Preference   : 60
 Cost   : 0 Protocol   : Static
 RelayNextHop : ::   TunnelID  : 0x0
 Interface  : GigabitEthernet0/0/1 Flags  : RD

 Static Routing Table's Status : < Inactive >
 Summary Count : 0
```

Display the IPv6 routing table.

```
[AR1]display ipv6 routing-table
```

Enable IPv6 on AR2, configure the interface to enable IPv6, configure the IPv6 address of the interface, and add a route to network segment 2018:6:6::/64.

```
[AR2]ipv6
[AR2]interface GigabitEthernet 0/0/1
[AR2-GigabitEthernet0/0/1]ipv6 enable
[AR2-GigabitEthernet0/0/1]ipv6 address 2018:6:7::2 64
[AR2-GigabitEthernet0/0/1]quit
[AR2]interface GigabitEthernet 0/0/0
[AR2-GigabitEthernet0/0/0]ipv6 enable
[AR2-GigabitEthernet0/0/0]ipv6 address 2018:6:8::1 64
[AR2-GigabitEthernet0/0/0]quit
[AR2]ipv6 route-static 2018:6:6:: 64 2018:6:7::1
```

Test if the network 2018:6:8::1 is working on AR1.

```
<AR1>ping ipv6 2018:6:8::1
 PING 2018:6:8::1 : 56  data bytes, press CTRL_C to break
  Reply from 2018:6:8::1 bytes=56 Sequence=4 hop limit=64  time = 20
ms
  Reply from 2018:6:8::1 bytes=56 Sequence=5 hop limit=64  time = 20
ms
  Reply from 2018:6:8::1 bytes=56 Sequence=5 hop limit=64  time = 20
ms
  Reply from 2018:6:8::1 bytes=56 Sequence=4 hop limit=64  time = 20
ms
  Reply from 2018:6:8::1 bytes=56 Sequence=5 hop limit=64  time = 20
ms

 --- 2018:6:8::1 ping statistics ---
 5 packet(s) transmitted
 5 packet(s) received
```

```
0.00% packet loss
round-trip min/avg/max = 10/32/80 ms
```

Delete the IPv6 static route.

```
[AR1] undo ipv6 route-static 2018:6:8:: 64
[AR2] undo ipv6 route-static 2018:6:6:: 64
```

13.5.2   OSPFv3

The new version of OSPF has many similarities to OSPF in IPv4.

The basic concept of OSPFv3 is the same as that of OSPFv2. It is still a link-state routing protocol, and OSPFv3 can divide an entire network or autonomous system into areas, thus making the network hierarchical.

In OSPFv2, the router ID (RID) is determined by the largest IP address assigned to the router (which can also be manually assigned). In OSPFv3, the RID, area ID and link state ID need to be assigned. The link state ID is still a 32-bit value, but can no longer be found using IP addresses because IPv6 addresses are 128-bit. The router ID of OSPFv3 must be manually assigned.

OSPFv3 routers use the link-local address as the source address for sending messages and use multicast traffic to send update and response messages. For OSPF routers, the address is FF02::5, and for designated OSPF routers, the address is FF02::6. These new addresses are tantamount to multicast addresses 224.0.0.5 and 224.0.0.6 used by OSPFv2. A router can learn the link-local addresses of all other routers connected to this link and use these link-local addresses as the next hop addresses for forwarding messages.

The following illustrates the process of configuring OSPFv3. As shown in Fig. 13.34, the router interface addresses in the network have been configured, and now you need to configure OSPFv3 on routers AR1 and AR2.

The configuration on AR1 is as follows.

```
[AR1] ospfv3 1                          --Enable OSPFv3, and specify
process ID
[AR1-ospfv3-1] router-id 1.1.1.1        --Specify a router-id,
which must be a unique one
[AR1-ospfv3-1] quit
[AR1] interface GigabitEthernet 0/0/0
```

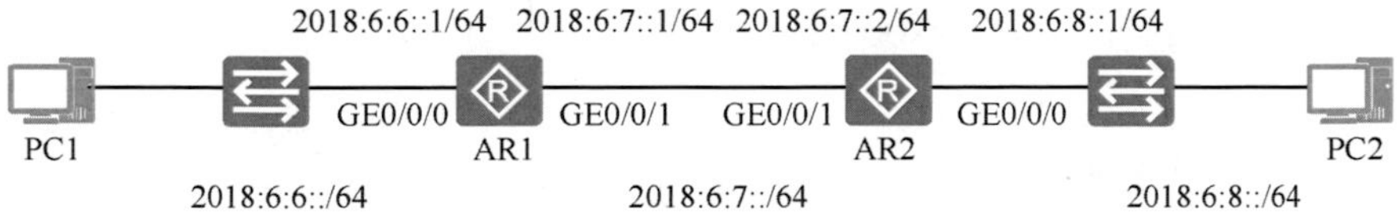

Fig. 13.34 Configure OSPFv3

```
[AR1-GigabitEthernet0/0/0]ospfv3 1 area 0        --Enable OSPFv3 on the
router and specify an area ID
 [AR1-GigabitEthernet0/0/0]quit
 [AR1]interface GigabitEthernet 0/0/1
 [AR1-GigabitEthernet0/0/1]ospfv3 1 area 0
 [AR1-GigabitEthernet0/0/1]quit
```

The configuration on AR2 is as follows.

```
[AR2]ospfv3 1                                --Enable OSPFv3, and specify
a process ID
 [AR2-ospfv3-1]router-id 1.1.1.2
 [AR2-ospfv3-1]quit
 [AR2]interface GigabitEthernet 0/0/0
 [AR2-GigabitEthernet0/0/0]ospfv3 1 area 0
 [AR2-GigabitEthernet0/0/0]quit
 [AR2]interface GigabitEthernet 0/0/1
 [AR2-GigabitEthernet0/0/1]ospfv3 1 area 0
 [AR2-GigabitEthernet0/0/1]quit
```

View routes learned via OSPFv3.

```
[AR1]display ipv6 routing-table protocol ospfv3
Public Routing Table : OSPFv3
Summary Count : 3
OSPFv3 Routing Table's Status : < Active >
Summary Count : 1
 Destination   : 2018:6:8::   PrefixLength : 64
 NextHop   : FE80::2E0:FCFF:FE1E:7774 Preference   : 10
 Cost   : 2 Protocol   : OSPFv3
 RelayNextHop : ::                               TunnelID    : 0x0
 Interface    : GigabitEthernet0/0/1             Flags       : D
......
```

13.6   Exercises

1. (Multi-selection) Which of the following abbreviations is correct for IPv6 address 2031:0000:72C:0000:0000:09E0:839A:130B? ( )

   A. 2031:0:720C:0:0:0:9E0:839A:130B
   B. 2031:0:720C:0:0:0:9E:839A:130B
   C. 2031::720C::9E:839A:130B
   D. 2031:0:720C::9E0:839A:130B

2. (Multi-selection) Which of the following IPv6 addresses can be manually configured on a router interface? ( )

  A. fe80:13dc::1/64

  B. ff00:8a3c::9b/64

  C. ::1/128

  D. 2001:12e3:1b02::21/64

3. (Multi-selection) Which of the following descriptions of IPv6 is correct ( )?

  A. An IPv6 address is 64 bits long

  B. An IPv6 address is 128 bits long

  C. IPv6 address stateful configuration uses DHCP server to assign addresses and configure other settings

  D. IPv6 address stateless configuration uses DHCPv6 server to assign addresses and configure other settings

4. Which of the following types of addresses does not belong to IPv6 addresses? ( )

  A. Unicast address

  B. Multicast address

  C. Broadcast address

  D. Anycast address

5. Which of the following options is the address prefix for link-local addresses? ( )

  A. 2001::/10

  B. fe80::/10

  C. feC0::/10

  D. 2002::/10

6. Which of the following commands is used to add an IPv6 default route? ( )

  A. [AR1]ipv6 route-static :: 0 2018:6:7::2

  B. [AR1]ipv6 route-static ::1 0 2018:6:7::2

  C. [AR1]ipv6 route-static :: 64 2018:6:7::2

  D. [AR1]ipv6 route-static :: 128 2018:6:7::2

7. What are the protocols of the IPv6 network layer? ( )

  A. ICMPv6, IPv6, ARP, ND

  B. ICMPv6, IPv6, MLD, ND

  C. ICMPv6, IPv6, ARP, IGMPv6

  D. ICMPv6, IPv6, MLD, ARP

8. Which of the following forms of DUIDs can be configured when DHCPv6 is configured in a VRP system? ( )

  A. DUID-LL

  B. DUID-LLT

  C. DUID-EN

  D. DUID-LLC

9. DHCPv6 messages need to be carried by which of the following protocol messages? ( )

  A. FTP
  B. TCP
  C. UDP
  D. HTTP

10. (Multi-selection) Which of the following statements about IPv6 address configuration is correct ( )?

  A. IPv6 addresses can only be configured manually.
  B. IPv6 supports address configuration in the form of DHCPv6
  C. IPv6 addresses support stateless autoconfiguration
  D. IPv6 addresses support autoconfiguration in various ways

11. 2001::12:1 corresponds to solicitated-node multicast address FF02::1:FF12:1.( )

  A. Correct
  B. Incorrect

Chapter 14
WAN Fundamentals

With the accelerated economic globalization and digital transformation, enterprises are expanding in scale and more and more branches are established in different geographical areas. The network of each branch office is considered as a Local Area Network (LAN), and communication between headquarters and branch offices needs to span a certain geographical area. Therefore, enterprises need to connect these geographically dispersed branch offices through Wide Area Network (WAN) so as to improve their business.

The development of WAN technology is accompanied by the continuous upgrade of bandwidth. The WAN protocol X.25 that emerged in the earlier stage could only provide 64 kbit/s bandwidth, while the subsequent Digital Data Network (DDN), Frame Relay (FR) and Asynchronous Transfer Mode (ATM) further increased the bandwidth to 10 Gbit/s, and it is finally developed to the current IP-based WAN of 10 Gbit/s or even higher bandwidth.

The WAN uses GSMA/CD protocol, and there are many protocols for WAN links, such as High-Level Data Link Control (HDLC) protocol, Point-to-Point Protocol (PPP), X.25, Frame Relay. PPP is a typical protocol used for point to point WAN links, and is the protocol used by routers to connect to WANs.

CSMA/CD protocol does not support the authentication of access devices. PPP supports the authentication of devices that access the network and assigns IP addresses to access devices. If the Ethernet switch is made to be able to authenticate users of the access devices and assign IP addresses to those devices, then the PPPoE (PPP over Ethernet) protocol is required. A router can act as a PPPoE server or a PPPoE client, and a Windows system can also function as a PPPoE client to set up a dial-up connection to the PPPoE server.

Huawei Technologies Co., Ltd., *Data Communications and Network Technologies*,
https://doi.org/10.1007/978-981-19-3029-4_14

14.1   Overview of WAN

WAN normally covers a large geographical distance, ranging from a few kilometers to several thousands of kilometers. Meanwhile, it can provide long-distance communication, connect multiple cities or countries, or even span several continents to form an international long-distance network. A LAN is usually connected to the WAN as an end-user of the WAN. As shown in Fig. 14.1, a company has three LANs in Beijing, Shanghai and Shenzhen, which are interconnected through the network of a telecom carrier that provides WAN connection for the enterprise.

LANs are usually set up, managed and maintained by enterprises themselves by purchasing network equipment such as routers and switches. WAN, the other hand, is typically set up, managed and maintained by telecom department or telecom company, and provides communication-oriented paid services to the whole society, whose traffic will be recorded and billed. For example, home users accessing the Internet through dial up or through optical fibers is one of the applications of WAN.

As shown in Fig. 14.2, LAN1 (Ethernet) and LAN2 (Ethernet2) are connected through WAN links. In the figure, the interface on the router that connects to the WAN is the Serial interface. There are several standards of Serial interfaces, and the figure shows two kinds of interfaces, "asynchronous interface and synchronous interfaces" and "non-channelized E1/T1 WAN interface".

As shown in Fig. 14.2, WAN links can have different protocols. The serial link between routers AR1 and AR2 uses the high-level data link control protocol, that

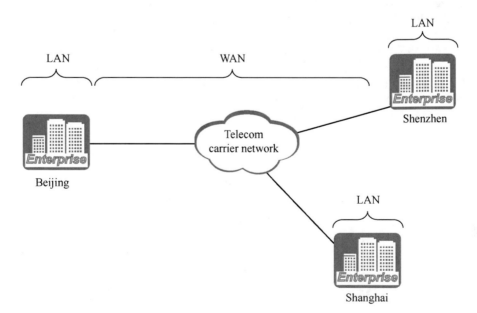

Fig. 14.1 LAN and WAN illustration

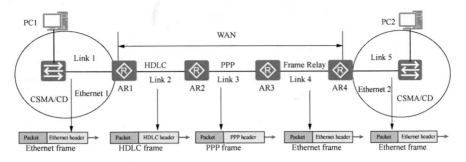

Fig. 14.2 WAN illustration

between AR2 and AR3 uses the point to point protocol, and AR3 and AR4 that are connected by the frame relay switch use the frame relay protocol.

As can be seen in Fig. 14.2, different links can use different data link layer protocols. Each data link layer protocol defines the corresponding data link layer encapsulation (frame format), and data packets passing through different links have to be encapsulated into different frames. The diagram shows the whole process of sending packets from PC1 to PC2. First, the packets are encapsulated into Ethernet frames when they pass through Ethernet1. They are encapsulated into HDLC frames when they are transmitted on the link between AR1 and AR2, encapsulated into PPP frames on the link between AR2 and AR3, encapsulated into relay frames on the link between AR3 and AR4, and encapsulated into Ethernet frames when they are sent from AR4 to PC2.

This chapter focuses on two protocols, PPP and PPPoE, and analyzes the process of PPP link establishment.

14.2 Principles and Configuration of PPP

14.2.1 Overview of PPP

PPP is a common WAN data link layer protocol, mainly used for point to point data transmission over a full-duplex link. The predecessors of PPP are Serial Line Internet Protocol (SLIP) and CSLIP (Compressed SLIP), which are basically out of use now. However, since its introduction in the 1990s, PPP has been widely used and is now the most universally used data link layer protocol for Internet access.

PPP provides Password Authentication Protocol (PAP), Challenge Handshake Authentication Protocol (CHAP) and Link Control Protocol (LCP) for the negotiation of various link layer parameters, such as maximum receive unit (MRU), authentication mode and magic number. It also provides various Network Control Protocols (NCPs), such as IP Control Protocol (IPCP), for the negotiation of various network layer parameters so as to better support the network layer protocols.

PPP can be combined with ADSL, Cable Modem, LAN and other technologies to enable various types of broadband access. PPP has good scalability. For example, it can be extended to PPPoE when it is needed to carry PPP on Ethernet links. The most commonly used broadband access method in homes is PPPoE. This is a technology that uses Ethernet resources and runs PPP on Ethernet to authenticate users when they access networks. PPP is responsible for establishing a communication link between the user and the carrier's access server.

CMSA/CD protocol works on Ethernet interfaces and Ethernet links, while PPP works on serial interfaces and serial links. There are various types of serial interfaces, such as EIA RS-232-C interface, EIARS-422 interface, EIARS-423 interface and ITU-T V.35 interface. These are common serial interfaces and can support PPP. In fact, any serial interface that can support full-duplex communication supports PPP. In addition, PPP does not have any special rules for the information transmission rate of serial interfaces, but only requires serial interfaces to have consistent rate at both ends of the serial link. This chapter collectively refers to the serial interfaces that support and run PPP as PPP interfaces.

14.2.2   PPP Frame Format

The data frame encapsulation format of PPP is shown in Fig. 14.3. Its header has five bytes, of which the Flag field is a one-byte start frame delimiter (0x7E); the Address field is one byte; the Control field is one byte; and the two-byte Protocol field is used to indicate what protocol the information part. Its footer has three bytes, two of which are the frame check sequence while the other one is the end frame delimiter (0x7E). Its information part does not exceed 1500 bytes.

The encapsulation of PPP is largely based on the HDLC protocol specification, and PPP uses the exact flag fields and the frame check sequence (FCS) fields from the HDLC protocol encapsulation. In addition, many fields in PPP data frames have fixed values. Given that PPP is purely a protocol applied in a point to point environment, where messages sent by any party are only received and processed by a designated other party, the existence of the address field is no longer necessary,

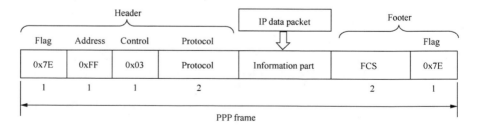

Fig. 14.3 PPP frame format

so the value of the PPP address field is specified as all 1s, indicating all interfaces on this link. Finally, the value of the PPP Control field is also explicitly fixed at 0x03.

There are also some differences between the encapsulation of PPP and HDLC protocols, for example, PPP adds a protocol field to the encapsulation field.

14.2.3 Three Stages of PPP Negotiation

A link using PPP needs to go through a three-stage negotiation process before it can communicate: link layer negotiation, authentication negotiation (optional) and network layer negotiation.

1. Link layer negotiation. Link parameters are negotiated through Link Control Protocol (LCP) messages to establish link-layer connections. Link parameter negotiation can be used to determine different parameters, such as maximum receive unit, authentication mode and magic number. Parameters that are not negotiated use the default operation.
2. Authentication negotiation (optional). Authentication is performed through the authentication mode negotiated at the link layer. If one party needs to authenticate, the other party is required to show their account and password. The most common authentication protocols include Password Authentication Protocol (PAP) and Challenge Handshake Authentication Protocol (CHAP). PAP and CHAP are typically applied on links that use PPP and they provide secure authentication.
3. Network layer negotiation. The configuration parameters of network layer protocols are negotiated through NCP. NCP is not a specific protocol, but refers to a series of protocols in PPP that control different network layer transport protocols. Each type of different network layer protocols has a corresponding NCP, for example, IPv4 protocol corresponds to IPCP, IPv6 protocol corresponds to IPv6CP, IPX protocol corresponds to IPXCP, AppleTalk protocol corresponds to ATCP, etc. Taking IPCP as an example, the configuration parameters to be negotiated include whether the PPP and IP headers of the message are compressed, what algorithm is used for the compression and the IPv4 address of the PPP interface.

14.2.4 PPP Working Process

The basic PPP working process consists of five phases: Link Dead, Link Establishment, Authentication, Network Layer Protocol, and Link Termination.

1. Before communication, the link is Dead. When the two communicating devices establish a PPP link, they first enter the link establishment phase.

2. Link layer negotiation is performed during the link establishment phase. Parameters such as the maximum receive unit of both communicating parties, authentication mode and magic number are negotiated. After successful negotiation, the link turns opened, indicating that a lower-layer link has been established.
3. If authentication is configured, the two devices enter the authentication phase. Otherwise, the devices will go directly to the network layer protocol phase.
4. In the authentication phase, the link will be authenticated according to the authentication mode negotiated in the link establishment phase. There are two authentication modes: PAP and CHAP. If the authentication is successful, the devices enter the network layer protocol phase, otherwise they enter the link termination phase. The link is removed, and the LCP turns Down.
5. In the network layer protocol phase, the PPP link will perform an NCP negotiation. The NCP negotiation is used to select and configure a network layer protocol and to negotiate network layer parameters.
6. In the link termination phase, the two devices enter the Dead phase after all resources are released. The connection may be interrupted at any time during the PPP operation, for example, the physical link is disconnected, the PPP authentication fails, the negotiation timer expires, or the administrator closes the connection through configuration, and after the interruption, the link enters the link termination phase.

The following is a detailed description of the three phases of PPP working process: link establishment phase, authentication phase and network layer protocol phase.

1. Link establishment phase

The first phase of the basic PPP working process is the link dead phase. In this phase, the physical layer function of the PPP interface has not yet entered the normal state. Only when the physical layer functions of both the local interface and the peer interface enter the normal state, PPP can enter the next working phase, i.e., the link establishment phase. In this phase, the local interface and the peer interface will send PPP frames carrying LCP messages to each other.

The LCP message format is shown in Fig. 14.4.

The Protocol field is used to indicate the protocol message type encapsulated by PPP. 0xC021 represents LCP messages, 0xC023 represents PAP messages, and 0xC223 represents CHAP messages. When the Protocol field is 0xC021, there is a Code field to identify the different types of LCP messages.

The information part contains the contents of the specified protocol in the Protocol field, and the maximum length of this field is called Maximum Receive Unit (MRU), whose default value is 1500. When the Protocol field is 0xC021, the structure of the information part is as follows.

- The Identifier field is used to match and respond to the request and it takes up one byte.
- The value of the Length field is the total number of bytes of the LCP message.
- The Data field carries various configuration parameters, such as the TLV (Type, Length, Value).

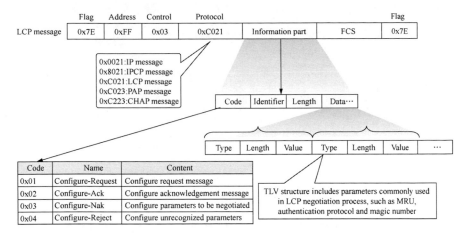

Fig. 14.4 LCP message format

Some common configuration parameters carried by LCP messages are MRU, authentication protocol and magic number.

- On the Versatile Routing Platform (VRP), the MRU parameter is expressed using the maximum transmission unit (MTU) value configured on the interface.
- The common PPP authentication protocols are PAP and CHAP. Different authentication modes can be used at the two ends of a PPP link to authenticate the peer, but the authenticatee must support the authentication protocol required by the authenticator and properly configure the authentication information such as username and password.
- LCP uses magic numbers to detect routing loops and other anomalies. A magic number is a randomly generated number, and the random generation mechanism needs to ensure that it is almost impossible to generate same magic numbers at both ends.

As shown in Fig. 14.5, RA and RB are connected using a serial link and running PPP. After the physical layer link becomes available, RA and RB use LCP to negotiate link parameters. The following steps describe the process of link parameter negotiation between RA and RB.

- RA first sends a Configure-Request message that contains the link layer parameters configured on RA.
- After receiving this Configure-Request message, RB responds with a Configure-Ack message to the RA if it can recognize and accept all the parameters in this message. In this example, RB cannot receive the MRU value so it sends a Configure-Nak message to RA containing the link layer parameters that cannot be received and the values (or value range) that RB can receive. In this example, the Configure-Nak message contains the MRU parameters that cannot be received and the value of MRU that can be received, which is 1500.

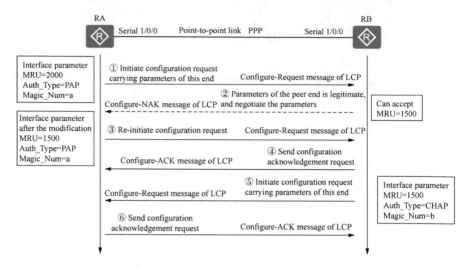

Fig. 14.5 LCP negotiation process

- After receiving the Configure-Nak message, RA reselects the other locally configured parameters according to the link layer parameters in this message and sends a new Configure-Request message.
- After receiving the Configure-Request message, RB responds with a Configure-Ack message to RA if it can identify and receive all parameters in this message.
- Similarly, RB needs to send a Configure-Request message to RA, carrying its interface parameters.
- Use RA to check if the parameters of RB are acceptable. If they are all acceptable, a configuration acknowledgement message will be sent.

If RA does not receive the Configure-Ack message or Configure-Nak message, it will resend the Configure-Request message every 3 s. If it sends the Configure-Request message 10 times in a row but does not receive the Configure-Ack message, it will consider RB unavailable and stops sending Configure-Request messages.

2. Authentication phase

After the link is successfully established, the authentication negotiation (optional) will be carried out. There are two modes of authentication negotiation: PAP and CHAP. In this example, RA requires the authentication mode to be PAP in the LCP negotiation parameters, so RA is the authenticator and RB is the authenticatee. The PAP authentication protocol is a two-way handshake protocol, and its password will be transmitted in plain text on the link, as shown in Fig. 14.6.

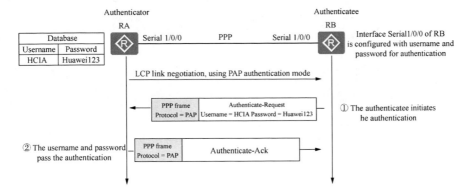

Fig. 14.6 PAP authentication

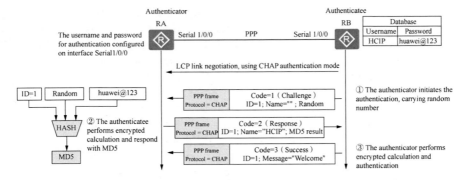

Fig. 14.7 CHAP authentication

- The authenticatee sends the configured username and password to the authenticator in plain text by the Authenticate-Request message.
- After receiving the username and password sent by the authenticatee, the authenticator checks whether the username and password match based on the locally configured username and password database. If they match, it responds with an Authenticate-Request message, indicating successful authentication; otherwise, it responds with an Authenticate-Nak message, indicating that the authentication is failed.

  In this example, after LCP negotiation is completed, RB requires RA to use CHAP mode for authentication. Both sides of the CHAP authentication perform the three-way handshaking, and the negotiation message is encrypted and then transmitted on the link. The process is shown in Fig. 14.7.
- The authenticator RA initiates the authentication request and sends the authenticatee RB a Challenge message, which contains a random number (Random) and ID (the sequence number of this authentication).
- After receiving the Challenge message, the authenticated RB performs an encryption operation using the MD5 formula (ID + random

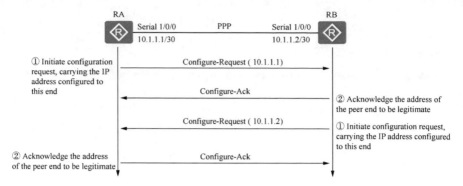

Fig. 14.8 Static IP address negotiation

number + password), which means that the ID, random number and password
are concatenated into a string, and then MD5 is performed on this string to get
a 16-byte digest information, which is then encapsulated with the CHAP
username configured on the interface in the Response message and sent back
to the authenticator RA.
- After receiving the Response message from the authenticatee RB, the authenticator RA finds the local corresponding password information according to
the username in it. After getting the password information, it performs an
encryption operation in the same way as the authenticatee's encryption operation, and then compares the digest information obtained from the encryption
operation with the digest information encapsulated in the Response message.
If the information is the same, the authentication is successful; if not, the
authentication fails.

When using CHAP authentication mode, the password of the authenticatee
is encrypted before transmission, which significantly improves the security.

When using encryption algorithms, MD5 (in digital signature scenarios and
password encryption) encryption algorithm is less secure and is subject to
security risks. Within the range of encryption algorithms supported by the
protocol, it is recommended to use more secure encryption algorithms, such as
AES/RSA (2043 bits or more)/SHA2/ HMAC-SHA2.

3. Network layer protocol stage

After the PPP authentication, both parties enter the network layer protocol
phase to negotiate the format and type of packets to be transmitted over the data
link, and establish and configure different network layer protocols. Take the
common IPCP protocol as an example. IPCP protocol is divided into static IP
address negotiation and dynamic IP address negotiation.

Static IP address negotiation requires manual configuration of IP addresses on
both ends of the link. The process of static IP address negotiation is shown in
Fig. 14.8.

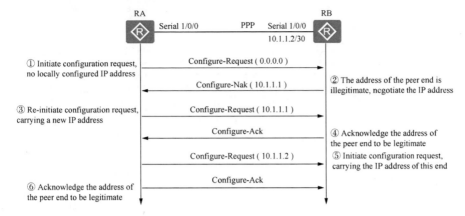

Fig. 14.9 Dynamic IP address negotiation

- Each end sends a Configure-Request message, which contains the locally configured IP address.
- After each end receives the Configure-Request message from the other end, it checks the IP address in it. If the IP address is a legitimate unicast IP address and is different from the locally configured IP address (no IP address conflict), it is considered that the peer end be able to use the IP address and a Configure-Ack message is sent to the peer end.

  Dynamic IP address negotiation supports the configuration of IP addresses for the peer at one end of the PPP link. The process of a dynamic IP address negotiation is shown in Fig. 14.9.
- RA sends RB a Configure-Request message, which contains an IP address 0.0.0.0, indicating that it requests an IP address from the peer.
- After receiving the above Configure-Request message, RB considers that the IP address 0.0.0.0 in the message is illegitimate and responds with a new IP address 10.1.1.1 using Configure-Nak.
- After receiving this Configure-Nak message, RA updates the local IP address and resends a Configure-Request message with the new IP address 10.1.1.1.
- After receiving the Configure-Request message, RB considers the IP address in the message to be legitimate and responds with a Configure-Ack message.
- In the meantime, RB also sends a Configure-Request message to RA to request the use of address 10.1.1.12.
- If RA considers this address legitimate, it responds with a Configure-Ack message.

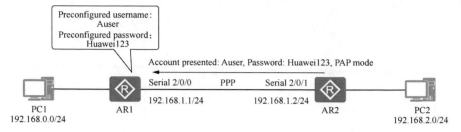

Fig. 14.10 Configure PPP: PAP mode for authentication

14.2.5   Configure PPP: PAP Mode for Authentication

Configure routers AR1 and AR2 in the network according to Fig. 14.10 for the following functions.

- Configure PPP as the data link layer protocol on the link between AR1 and AR2.
- Create a user and password on AR1 for PPP authentication.
- Configure the PPP authentication mode as PAP on interface Serial 2/0/0 of AR1.
- Configure the account and password presented to router AR1 on interface Serial 2/0/1 of AR2.

From the figure, you can see that interface Serial 2/0/0 of router AR1 is configured to use PPP for the data link layer, and the Huawei router serial interface also uses PPP by default. By the following operation, you can check the data link layer protocols supported by the serial interface, and the same interface can be specified to use different data link layer protocols.

```
[AR1]interface Serial 2/0/0
[AR1-Serial2/0/0]link-protocol ?    --View data link layer protocols
supported by the serial interface
  fr   Select FR as line protocol
  hdlc Enable HDLC protocol
  lapb LAPB(X.25 level 2 protocol)
  ppp  Point-to-Point protocol
  sdlc SDLC(Synchronous Data Line Control) protocol
  x25  X.25 protocol
[AR1-Serial2/0/0]link-protocol ppp    --Specify PPP as the data link
layer protocol
```

Check the state of interface Serial 2/0/0 of router AR1. The returned message shows the physical layer state is UP, indicating that the interfaces at both ends are properly connected, and the data link layer state is UP, indicating that the protocols at both ends are consistent.

```
<AR1>display interface Serial 2/0/0
Serial2/0/0 current state : UP            --Physical layer state is UP
Line protocol current state : UP         --Data link layer state is UP
 Description:HUAWEI, AR Series, Serial2/0/0 Interface
 Route Port,The Maximum Transmit Unit is 1500, Hold timer is 10(sec)
 Internet Address is 192.168.1.1/24
Link layer protocol is PPP               --Data link layer protocol is
PPP
 LCP reqsent
 ......
```

Create a user for PPP authentication on AR1.

```
[AR1]aaa
[AR1-aaa]local-user Auser password cipher Huawei123   --Create user
Auser with the password Huawei123
[AR1-aaa]local-user Auser service-type ppp            --Specify Auser
for PPP authentication
[AR1-aaa]quit
```

Configure the interface Serial 2/0/0 of AR1; PPP requires authentication to connect, and the authentication mode is PAP.

```
[AR1]interface Serial 2/0/0
[AR1-Serial2/0/0]ppp authentication-mode ?          --View PPP
authentication mode
 chap  Enable CHAP authentication                 --Password secure
transmission
 pap   Enable PAP authentication                 --Password plain text
transmission
[AR1-Serial2/0/0]ppp authentication-mode pap      --PAP
authentication is required
```

If you want to remove the PPP authentication of this interface, the following commands shall be executed.

```
[AR1-Serial2/0/0]undo ppp authentication-mode pap
```

Configure interface Serial 2/0/1 of router AR2 to use PPP at the data link layer, and specify the account and password to present to AR1.

```
[AR2]interface Serial 2/0/1
[AR2-Serial2/0/1]link-protocol ppp
[AR2-Serial2/0/1]ppp pap local-user Auser password cipher
Huawei123
```

Note	The "[AR2-Serial2/0/1] ppp authentication-mode pap" is not executed on interface Serial 2/0/1 of AR2, and AR1 does not need to present the account and password when connecting to AR2 using PPP.

14.2.6 Configure PPP: CHAP Mode for Authentication

The previous configuration only allows AR1 to authenticate AR2, now you need to configure to allow AR2 to authenticate AR1. Create user Buser on AR2 with password huawei@123. Configure interface Serial 2/0/1 of AR2 to use PPP and require authentication using the authentication mode CHAP. Configure interface Serial 2/0/0 of AR1 to present the account and password, as shown in Fig. 14.11.

Create a user for PPP authentication on AR2. Configure interface Serial 2/0/1 and PPP requires authentication for connection.

```
[AR2]aaa
[AR2-aaa]local-user Buser password cipher huawei@123
[AR2-aaa]local-user Buser service-type ppp
[AR2-aaa]quit
[AR2]interface Serial 2/0/1
[AR2-Serial2/0/1]ppp authentication-mode chap        --
Authentication is required for connection
[AR2-Serial2/0/1]quit
```

The configuration on AR1 is as follows. First specify the account to be used for PPP authentication and then the password.

```
[AR1]interface Serial 2/0/0
[AR1-Serial2/0/0]ppp chap user Buser                  --Account
[AR1-Serial2/0/0]ppp chap password cipher huawei@123  --Password
[AR1-Serial2/0/0]quit
```

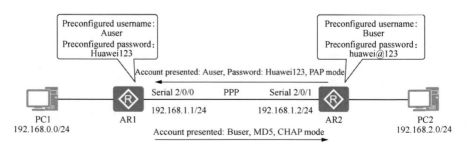

Fig. 14.11 Configure PPP: CHAP mode for authentication

14.2.7 Packet Capture Analysis for PPP Link Establishment Process

After completing the configuration in Sect. 14.2.5, the PPP frames of the point to point link can be captured, as shown in Fig. 14.12. It can be seen from the figure that frames 1 to 5 are sent in the link establishment phase using PPP LCP, frames 6 to 7 are sent in the authentication phase using PPP PAP, and frames 8 to 11 are sent in the network layer protocol phase using PPP IPCP. After three phases of establishing the PPP link, IP packets can be sent. Frames 12 to 18 in Fig. 14.12 are encapsulated IP packets.

The process of PPP link establishment is analyzed below by observing the captured frames PPP uses to establish the connection. The numbers describing the frames below are based on the sequence numbers of the frames captured in Fig. 14.12.

As shown in Fig. 14.13, Frame 2 is a configuration request frame sent by router AR1 during the link establishment phase, with Link Control Protocol as the Protocol and Configuration Request as the Code. The three interface parameters are as follows: the maximum receive unit is 1500, the Authentication Protocol is Password Authentication Protocol, and the magic number is 0x328c2356, which is randomly generated by AR1.

After receiving the configuration request frame from AR1, AR2 first identifies and accepts these three parameters, and then sends a configuration acknowledgment frame (Frame 3) to AR1. Note that the magic number of Frame 3 is the same as that of Frame 2, so that Frame 3 is ensured to be the configuration acknowledgement frame of Frame 2. We can also see that the configuration acknowledgement frame contains all the parameters of the configuration request frame.

As shown in Fig. 14.14, Frame 4 is the configuration request frame sent by AR2 to AR1, which has only two parameters to negotiate with AR1: the maximum receive unit and the magic number. Frame 5 is a configuration acknowledgement frame sent by AR1 to RA2, which indicates that it can recognize and accept these two parameters. Note that the magic numbers in Frame 4 and 5 are also identical.

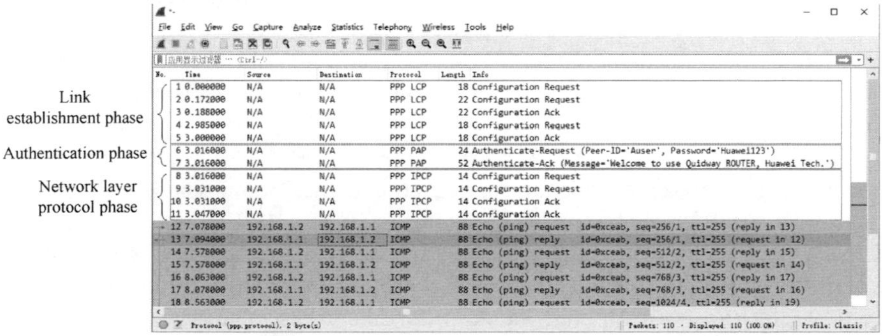

Fig. 14.12 Three phases of PPP link establishment

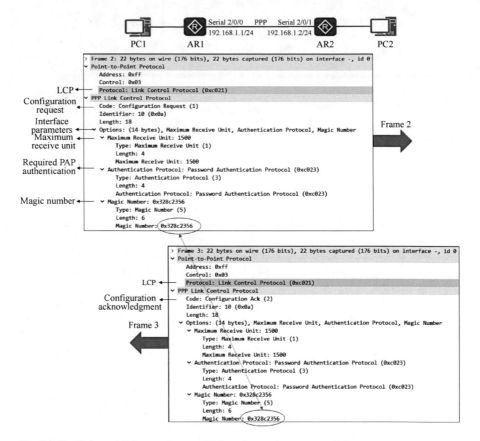

Fig. 14.13 Link establishment phase: AR1 interface parameter negotiation

In the link establishment phase, AR1 enters the authentication phase by requesting PAP authentication. As shown in Fig. 14.15, Frame 6 is the authentication request sent by AR2 to AR1. The Protocol is Password Authentication Protocol, and the Data part contains the username Auser and the password Huawei123. The figure shows that the account and password are transmitted in plain text. After receiving the authentication request, AR1 starts to verify the username and password, and if they pass the authentication, it sends an authentication acknowledgment frame (Frame 7).

What follows the authentication phase is the network layer protocol phase. As shown in Fig. 14.16, Frame 8 is the configuration request frame sent by AR1. Note that the Protocol is Internet Protocol Control Protocol (IPCP) and the Options includes the IP address of interface Serial 2/0/0 of AR1. Frame 9 is a configuration request frame sent by AR1. Note that the Protocol is Internet Protocol Control Protocol (IPCP) and the Options includes the IP address of interface Serial 2/0/1 of AR 2.

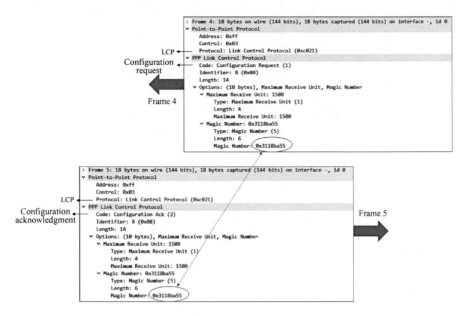

Fig. 14.14   Link establishment phase: AR2 interface parameter negotiation

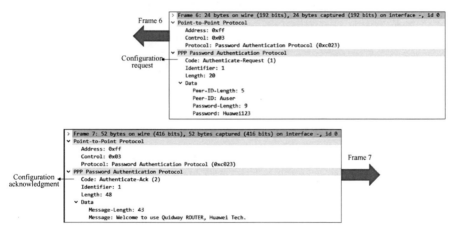

Fig. 14.15   Authentication phase: AR1 authenticates AR2

After receiving the configuration request sent in the network protocol phase, you have to determine whether the IP address presented by the other party conflicts with your own IP address and whether it is in the same network segment. If the address is legitimate, a configuration acknowledgment is sent to the other party, as shown in Fig. 14.17, Frame 10 is the configuration acknowledgment sent by AR2 to AR1, and Frame 11 is the configuration acknowledgment sent by AR1 to AR2.

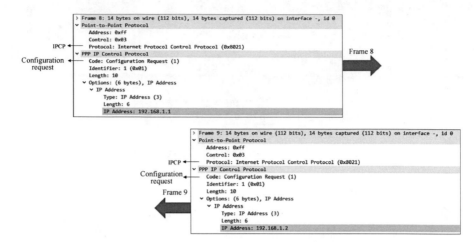

Fig. 14.16   Network protocol phase: send configuration request

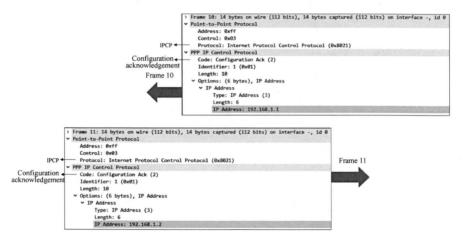

Fig. 14.17   Network protocol phase: send configuration acknowledgement

14.3   PPPoE

14.3.1   Overview of PPPoE

Now let's first take a look at a typical networking scenario for home users to access
the Internet. As shown in Fig. 14.18, a PC and a Home Gateway (HG) form a home
network. In this home network, the end PC is typically connected to the HG through
a common standard Ethernet link or Fast Ethernet link. HG1 is the egress gateway
for Home Network 1. In order to use the already laid telephone link for communication, HG1 uses Asymmetric Digital Subscriber Line (ADSL) technology to mod-
ulate the Ethernet data frames ready for outbound transmission into a physical signal

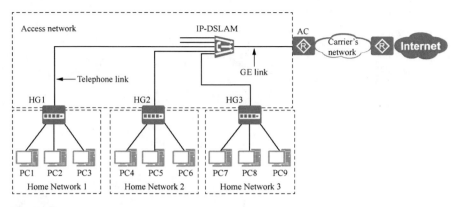

Fig. 14.18 A networking scenario for home users to access the Internet.

suitable for transmission over the telephone link before they are sent. The network carrier's IP-DSLAM (IP Digital Subscriber Line Multiplexer) equipment will receive the ADSL signals from different HGs, demodulates the Ethernet data frame information in them, and sends these Ethernet data frames over a GE (Gigabit Ethernet) link to a device named AC (Access Concentrator). From a data link layer perspective, an IP-DSLAM device is a normal Layer 2 Ethernet aggregation switch.

The network carrier is responsible for charging home users for Internet access and other access controls. However, the Ethernet data frame forwarded by the IP-DSLAM to the AC is unable to indicate whether it is sent from gateway HG-1 or HG-2. Furthermore, there is no field in the frame structure carrying information such as the "user name" and "password". If the carrier cannot distinguish the data traffic from different home users, it cannot perform management and control actions such as billing. Therefore, in Fig. 14.18, the AC device must identify the home users corresponding to these frames based on the Ethernet data frames received, and authenticate the different home users by usernames and passwords. This makes it possible for the carrier to perform management and control actions such as billing for the home user's Internet activity.

PPP itself is capable of authentication in the form of username and password. However, PPP is only applicable to the point-to-point network. In Fig. 14.18, the Ethernet formed by different HGs and ACs is a Multi-Access Network, and PPP cannot be directly applied to such a network. In order to apply PPP to Ethernet (Multi-Access Network), a protocol called PPPoE (PPP over Ethernet) has been created.

PPPoE is essentially a protocol that allows the creation of point to point tunnels between two Ethernet interfaces in an Ethernet broadcast domain (all interfaces that a broadcast frame can reach are a Layer 2 broadcast domain; usually, a network formed by a switch is a broadcast domain, and a VLAN is a broadcast domain if it is created). It describes how to encapsulate PPP frames in Ethernet data frames. From the perspective of PPPoE, the access network address in Fig. 14.18 can be simplified to the network shown in Fig. 14.19.

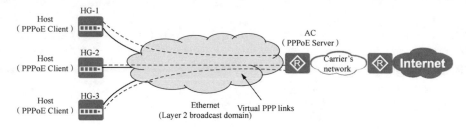

Fig. 14.19 View the access network from the perspective of PPPoE

By using the PPPoE protocol, each home user's HG can establish a virtual PPP link (a PPP link in the logical sense) with the AC, that is, the HG and the AC are able to interact with PPP frames. However, these PPP frames are not passed on the real physical PPP link, but are encapsulated in the Ethernet data frames that are exchanged between the HG and the AC and pass along with these Ethernet data frames on the Ethernet link.

Figure 14.19 shows the basic architecture of the PPPoE protocol. The PPPoE protocol uses the Client/Server model. In the standard terminology of the PPPoE protocol, the device running the PPPoE Client program is called Host, and the device running the PPPoE Server program is called AC. The home gateway's router HG in Fig. 14.19 is the Host, and the carrier's router is the AC.

14.3.2   PPPoE Message Format

PPP does not support Ethernet environment, so the Ethernet network adapter (network interface card) can only encapsulate data into Ethernet data frame format, but not into PPP frame format. Therefore, people come up with a solution: to encapsulate the encapsulated PPP data frames into another layer of Ethernet data frames, and then put this nested Ethernet data frame with PPP data frames into Ethernet for transmission. In this way, when the carrier's device receives the Ethernet data frame, it will first obtain the encapsulated PPP data frame by decapsulating it, and then process the data frame according to the protocol encapsulated inside the PPP data frame.

Figure 14.20 shows the format of a PPPoE message. If the value of the Type field of the Ethernet data frame is 0x8863 or 0x8864, it means that the load data of this Ethernet data frame is a PPPoE message.

The PPPoE message is divided into two parts, PPPoE header and PPPoE payload. In the PPPoE header, the value of VER field (Version field) is always 0x1, the value of Type field is always 0x1, the Code field can be used to represent different types of PPPoE messages, the Session-ID field can be used to distinguish different PPPoE sessions, and the Length field can be used to indicate the length of the whole PPPoE message. The PPP frame is in the PPPoE Payload.

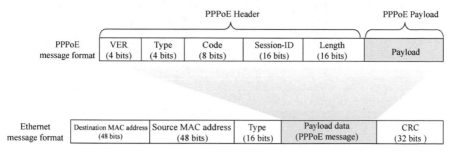

Fig. 14.20 PPPoE message format

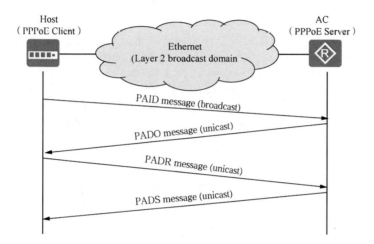

Fig. 14.21 Discovery phase of PPPoE

14.3.3   Working Process of PPPoE

The working process of PPPoE is divided into two different phases: Discovery phase and PPP Session phase.

1. Discovery phase

   As shown in Fig. 14.21, during the discovery phase of PPPoE, four different types of PPPoE messages are exchanged between the Host and the AC, that is PADI (PPPoE Active Discovery Initiation) message (the value of the Code field in the PPPoE header is 0x09), PPPoE Active Discovery Offer) message (the value of the Code field in the PPPoE header is 0x07), PADR (PPPoE Active Discovery Request) message (the value of the Code field in the PPPoE header is 0x19), and PADS (PPPoE Active Discovery Session-confirmation) message (the value of the Code field in the PPPoE header is 0x65).

   First, the Host sends a PADI message as a broadcast message (see Fig. 14.22), aiming to find an AC in the network and telling the AC the information about the type of services it wishes to obtain. The Payload of the PADI message contains

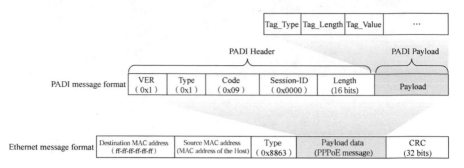

Fig. 14.22   PADI message format

several Tag fields in the form of Type-Length-Value, which represent the various types of service information that the Host wants to obtain. Note that the value of the Session-ID field in the PADI message is 0.

After receiving a PADI message, AC compares the service requested in the PADI message with the services it can provide. If the AC is able to provide the service requested by the Host, it replies with a unicast PADO message; if not, it does not respond at all.

If there are multiple ACs in the network, the Host may receive PADO messages from different ACs in response. Normally, Host will select the AC corresponding to the first received PADO message as its own PPPoE Server and send a unicast PADR message to this AC. The value of the Session-ID field in the PADR message is still 0.

After receiving the PADR message, the AC determines a PPPoE Session-ID and includes this PPPoE Session-ID in the unicast PADS message sent to the Host. The value of the Session-ID field in the PADS message is 0xXXXX, which is the PPPoE Session_ID.

The Host receives the PADS message and is informed of the PPPoE Session-ID, marking the successful establishment of a PPPoE Session between the Host and the AC. Next, the Host and the AC can enter the PPP Session phase.

2. PPP Session Phase

In the PPP Session phase, the interaction between the Host and the AC is still conducted by Ethernet data frames, but these Ethernet data frames carry PPP frames. Figure 14.23 shows the contents of the Ethernet data frames exchanged between the Host and the AC during the PPP Session phase. The value of the Type field of the Ethernet data frame is 0x8864 (Note: in the Discovery phase, the value of the Type field of the Ethernet data frame is always 0x8863), indicating that the payload data of the Ethernet data frame is a PPPoE message. The value of the Code field in the PPPoE message is 0x00 and that of the Session-ID field remains the value determined at the Discovery phase. Now we can finally see that the Payload of the PPPoE message at this point is a PPP frame! However, it is important to note that the Payload of the PPPoE message is not a complete PPP frame as we are previously familiar with, but only the Protocol and Information

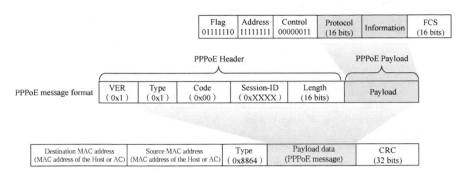

Fig. 14.23 Ethernet data frame carrying a PPP frame

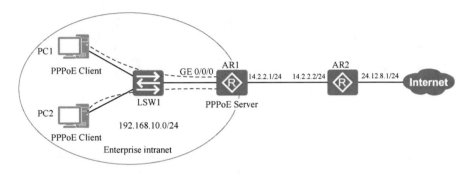

Fig. 14.24 PPPoE experimental network topology

fields of the PPP frame. This is because the other fields of the PPP frame are no longer necessary on this virtual PPP link.

We can see that through the intermediary of the PPPoE protocol, the PPP frames can be interacted between the Host and the AC at the PPP phase. Through the interaction of PPP frames, the Host and AC can go through the Link Establishment phase, Authentication phase and Network Layer Protocol phase of PPP, and finally realize the PPP function.

14.3.4   Configure Windows PPPoE Dial-Up Access

As shown in Fig. 14.24, PC1 and PC2 are two computers in an enterprise intranet, which are connected to router AR1 through switch LSW1, and then they are connected to the internet through AR1. For security reasons, computers in the enterprise intranet must verify the user's identity before being allowed to access the Internet. The experiment below configures router AR1 as a PPPoE Server and create a dial-up account and password for each user in the enterprise. As the PPPoE Clients, PC1 and PC2 need to establish a PPPoE dial-up connection, and users can only get a legal address to access the Internet after their identity is verified.

First configure router AR1 as the PPPoE server, and create accounts and passwords for PC1 and PC2 for PPP dial-up.

```
[AR1]aaa
[AR1-aaa]local-user hanligang password cipher huawei@123
[AR1-aaa]local-user lishengchun password cipher Huawei123
[AR1-aaa]local-user hanligang service-type ppp
[AR1-aaa]local-user lishengchun service-type ppp
[AR1-aaa]quit
```

Create an address pool. If the PPPoE dial-up is successful, you need to assign IP addresses to computers that need dial up.

```
[AR1]ip pool PPPoE1
[AR1-ip-pool-PPPoE1]network 192.168.10.0 mask 24
[AR1-ip-pool-PPPoE1]quit
```

Create an interface virtual template which can be bound to multiple physical interfaces

```
[AR1]interface Virtual-Template ?
  <0-1023>  Virtual template interface number
[AR1]interface Virtual-Template 1
[AR1-Virtual-Template1]remote address pool PPPoE1    --The address
pool this virtual interface assigns to the PPPoE Client
[AR1-Virtual-Template1]ip address 192.168.10.100 24  --The IP
address this virtual interface assigns
[AR1-Virtual-Template1]ppp ipcp dns 8.8.8.8 114.114.114.114   --
Assign master and slave DNS servers for PPPoE Client
[AR1-Virtual-Template1]quit
```

Bind the virtual interface template to interface GigabitEthernet 0/0/0 which does not require an IP address.

```
[AR1]interface GigabitEthernet 0/0/0
[AR1-GigabitEthernet0/0/0]undo ip address            --Remove the
configured IP address
[AR1-GigabitEthernet0/0/0]pppoe-server bind virtual-template 1
--Bind the virtual interface template to this interface
[AR1-GigabitEthernet0/0/0]quit
```

A virtual interface template can be bound to multiple physical interfaces of the PPPoE Server.

As shown in Fig. 14.25, router AR1 has two Ethernet interfaces connected to two Ethernet networks. Computers in these two Ethernet networks need PPPoE dial-up Internet access, and the addresses assigned to them belong to network segment 192.168.10.0/24, so that the virtual interface template can be bound to these two physical interfaces.

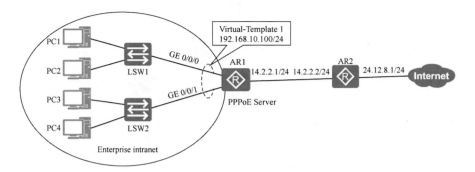

Fig. 14.25 Topology for binding a virtual interface template to a physical interface

To set up Windows PPPoE dial-up Internet access, you need to configure your Windows computer as a PPPoE client, that is, to create a PPPoE dial-up connection on your Windows operating system.

1. Log in to Windows 10, open "Network and Sharing Center", and click "Set up a new connection or network".
2. In the "Choose a connection option" dialog box that appears, tick the "Connect to the Internet" option, and then click "Next".
3. In the "How you want to connect" dialog box that appears, click "Broadband (PPPoE)".
4. In the "Type the information from your Internet Service Provider (ISP)" dialog box that appears, type the username, password, and connection name, and then click "Connect", as shown in Fig. 14.26.
5. After dialing in, type "ipconfig /all" at the command prompt to view the IP address and DNS obtained from the dial-up.

```
C:\Users\win10>ipconfig /all
Windows IP Configuration
  Host name  . . . . . . . . . . . . . : win10-PC
  Primary DNS Suffix . . . . . . . . . . :
  Node Type  . . . . . . . . . . . . : Hybrid
  IP Routing Enabled . . . . . . . . . : No
  WINS Proxy enabled . . . . . . . . . : No
PPP adaptor to Internet:     --PPPoE dial up to obtain IP address and DNS
  Connection-specific DNS Suffix . . . . . . . :
  Description. . . . . . . . . . . . . . : toInternet
  Physical Address. . . . . . . . . . . . . :
  DHCP Enabled . . . . . . . . . . . : No
  Autoconfiguration Enabled. . . . . . . . . . : Yes
  IPv4 address . . . . . . . . . . . . : 192.168.10.254(Preferred)
  Subnet Mast  . . . . . . . . . . . . : 255.255.255.255 – Subnet mask
obtained by PPPoE dial up is 255.255.255.255
  Default Gateway. . . . . . . . . . . . . . : 0.0.0.0
  DNS Server  . . . . . . . . . . . . : 8.8.8.8
                              114.114.114.114
  NetBIOS over TCPIP  . . . . . . . : Disabled
```

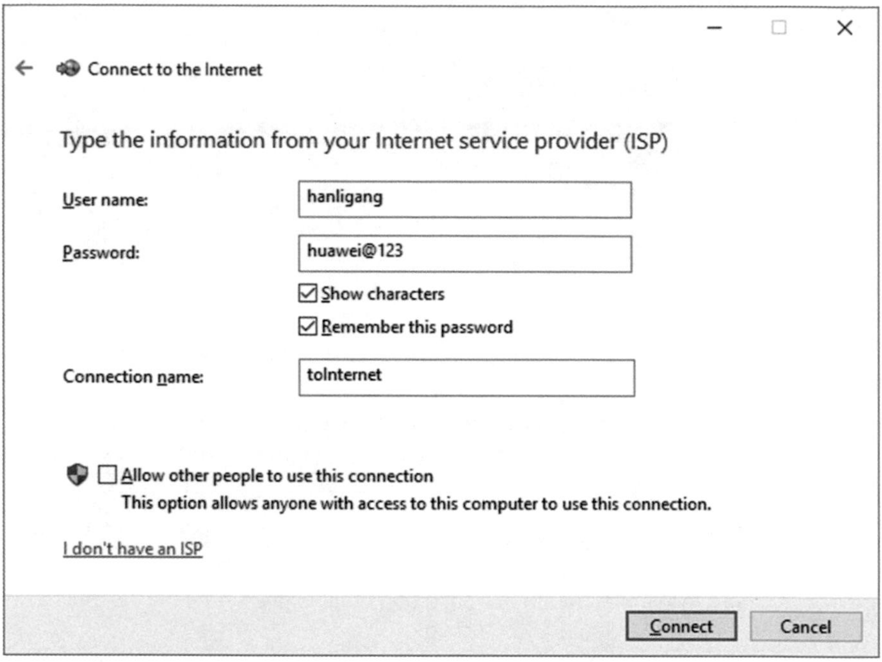

Fig. 14.26 Enter the PPPoE dial-up user name and password

On router AR1, you can see which PPPoE clients are dialing in, as well as the MAC address of the PPPoE client, that is, the RemMAC.

```
<AR1>display pppoe-server session all
SID Intf          State OIntf    RemMAC        LocMAC
 1 Virtual-Template1:0   UP   GE0/0/0   000c.2920.c578  00e0.
fc4d.3146
```

After establishing a PPPoE dial-up connection, packet capture analysis can be used to analyze the frame format of PPPoE packets. Run the packet capture tool on Windows 10 to start capturing packets and ping 24.12.8.1. As shown in Fig. 14.27, observe the 411th packet. The PPPoE Payload encapsulates the PPPoE header, and then encapsulates it into the Ethernet data frame with the type field 0x8864. In the PPPoE header encapsulation, it can be seen that the Session-ID is 0x0001.

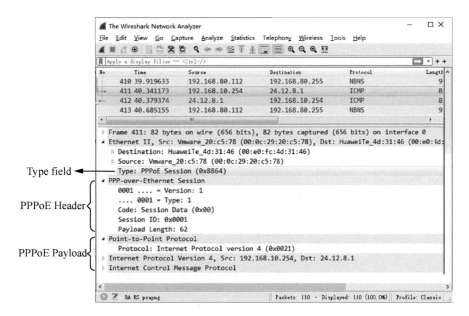

Fig. 14.27 View the frame format of PPPoE packet

14.4 Exercises

1. (Multi-selection) Which of the following operations are necessary when configuring the PPP authentication mode as PAP? ( )

    A. Add the username and password of the authenticatee to the local user list of the authenticator
    B. Configure the encapsulation type of the interface connected to the peer device as PPP
    C. Set the authentication mode of PPP to CHAP
    D. Configure the username and password sent by the authenticatee to the authenticator

2. When configuring encapsulation PPP on the serial interface of Huawei router, the command you need to enter in the interface view is ( ).

    A. link-protocol ppp
    B. encapsulation ppp
    C. enable ppp
    D. address ppp

3. Two routers are connected via serial interface and the data link layer protocol is PPP. If you want to improve security by configuring PPP authentication on both routers, which of the following PPP authentications is more secure? ( )

    A. CHAP
    B. PAP
    C. MD5
    D. SSH

4. In a multipoint access network like Ethernet, the PPPoE server can establish a PPP connection to many PPPoE clients through a single Ethernet interface, so the PPPoE server must establish a unique session identifier for each PPP session to distinguish between the different connections. What parameter does PPPoE use to establish the session identifier? ( )

    A. MAC address
    B. IP address and MAC address
    C. MAC address and PPP-ID
    D. MAC address and Session-ID

5. What does the ip address ppp-negotiate command do? ( )

    A. To enable the function of requesting the peer for IP addresses
    B. To enable the function of receiving IP address request from the remote end
    C. To enable the static IP address assignment
    D. All of the above options are incorrect

6. (Multi-selection) Which of the following descriptions of PPP is correct ( ).

    A. PPP supports bundling multiple physical links into one logical link to increase the bandwidth
    B. PPP supports plain text and cipher text authentication
    C. PPP has poor scalability and cannot be deployed on Ethernet links
    D. For physical layers, PPP supports asynchronous and synchronous links
    E. PPP supports various network layer protocols, such as IPCP and IPXCP

7. The PPPoE client sends PADI messages to the Server, and the Server responds with PADO messages. What is the frame of the PADO message? ( )

    A. Multicast
    B. Broadcast
    C. Unicast
    D. Anycast

8. (Multi-selection) Which of the following protocols is PPP composed of? ( )

    A. Authentication protocol
    B. NCP
    C. LCP
    D. PPPoE

9. If the authenticatee sends the wrong username and password to the authenticator during the PPP authentication process, which type of the message will the authenticator send to the authenticatee? ( )

    A. Authenticate-Reject
    B. Authenticate-Ack
    C. Authenticate-Nak
    D. Authenticate-Reply

10. Which level of the encapsulation format in the OSI reference model is defined by PPP? ( )

    A. Network layer
    B. Data link layer
    C. Presentation layer
    D. Application layer

11. Which of the following statements about PPP configuration and deployment is correct ( ).

    A. PPP does not support two-way authentication
    B. PPP cannot modify the keepalive time
    C. PPP cannot be used to assign IP addresses
    D. PPP supports both CHAP and PAP authentication modes

12. (Multi-selection) Which of the following advantages does PPP have? ( )

    A. PPP supports the negotiation of link layer parameters
    B. PPP supports the negotiation of network layer parameters
    C. PPP supports both synchronous and asynchronous transmission
    D. PPP supports authentication

Chapter 15
Typical Networking Architectures for Campus Networks and Case Practice

When readers study on campus, work in a company, or shop at the mall, they may notice that these places are all covered by networks. Through these networks, one can access internal school resources, use internal devices of the company such as printers, or access the Internet to browse news and information. These networks are classified as campus networks and are usually built by the companies or organizations themselves. Campus networks not only enhance the operational efficiency of enterprises, but also provide network access services to the outside world.

This chapter will introduce the definition of campus network, explain the typical networking architecture of campus network, analyze the planning and design methods of small campus network, deployment and implementation methods, as well as the basic work required for operation, maintenance and optimization. At the end of this chapter, a network engineering project will be created based on enterprise requirements.

15.1 Basic Concepts of Campus Networks

15.1.1 What Is a Campus Network?

A campus network is a local area network that connects people and things in a limited area, and usually has only one management body. If there are multiple management bodies, it will be considered as multiple campus networks.

A campus network can be large or small in size, ranging from smaller ones such as a small home office (SOHO) and wireless coverage in a coffee shop, to larger ones like networks for a campus, corporate campus, park and shopping center. The scale of the campus is limited, and the general size of large campuses, such as college campuses and industrial parks, is generally within a few square kilometers. Within this range, we can use LAN technology to build a network. A "campus" larger than

Huawei Technologies Co., Ltd., *Data Communications and Network Technologies*, https://doi.org/10.1007/978-981-19-3029-4_15

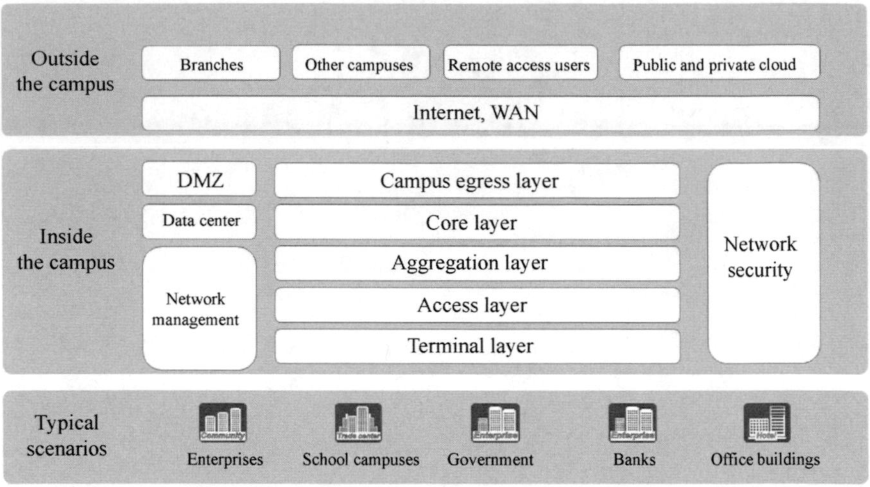

Fig. 15.1 Campus network

this is usually regarded as a "metropolitan area" and needs to use WAN technology, and the corresponding network will be regarded as a MAN.

As shown in Fig. 15.1, campus networks can be used in enterprises, school campuses, government, banks and office buildings. Inside the campus network is usually a hierarchical and regional design, which is the modular design we usually refer to. Hierarchical design by the location of devices in the network can divide the network devices into terminal layer (wireless devices such as computers and cell phones are in the terminal layer), access layer, aggregation layer and core layer. According to the functions achieved, network is divided into network management, network security, Demilitarized Zone (DMZ) and data center zone. The area connecting the outside of the campus is the campus egress layer, which connects other branches, other campuses, remote access users and private and public clouds via Internet and WAN (Wide Area Network).

Typical LAN technologies used in the campus network include Ethernet technology (wired) following the IEEE 802.3 standard and Wi-Fi technology (wireless) following the IEEE 802.11 standard.

15.1.2   Typical Architecture of Campus Network

Campus networks generally follow the principles of hierarchical, regional and modular design. According to the number of end users or network elements (including routers, switches, wireless ACs, APs and other devices), campus networks can be divided into small campus networks, medium campus networks, and large campus networks. Figure 15.2 shows the typical architecture of a campus network.

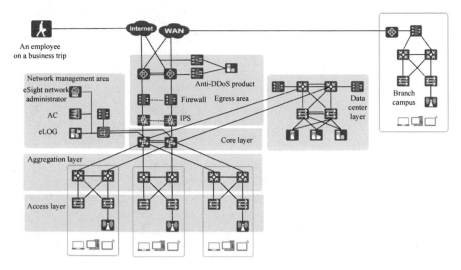

Fig. 15.2 Typical campus network architecture

1. The core layer is the backbone of the campus network and the core of data exchange in the campus. It connects various components of the campus network, such as the aggregation layer, data center, egress area and network management area.
2. The aggregation layer is in the middle level of the campus network, performing the function of data aggregation or exchange, and providing some key basic network functions, such as routing, QoS (Quality of Service) and security.
3. The access layer provides end users with campus network access services and is the border of the campus network.
4. The egress area is the border separating the internal campus network from the external network, and is used to realize internal users' access to the public network as well as the external users' access to the internal network. Generally, a large number of network security devices are deployed in this area to defend against attacks from external networks, such as IPS (Intrusion Prevention System), Anti-DDOS (traffic cleaning) devices and Firewall.
5. The data center area is the area where servers and application systems are deployed to provide data and application services for internal and external users.
6. Network management area is the area where network management system is deployed, including SDN controller, wireless controller, eLOG (log server), etc. It manages and monitors the whole campus network.

1. Small campus network architecture

   Small campus networks are mostly used in scenarios where there are a small number of access users, generally supporting a few to dozens of users. The network is built to enable the access to internal resources. It only covers a single location, and is not hierarchical, with simple networking requirements. The architecture of small campus network is shown in Fig. 15.3.

Fig. 15.3 Small campus
network architecture

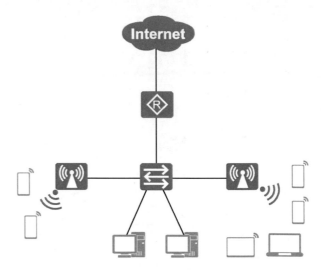

2. Medium campus network architecture

The number of end users of medium campus network is generally between 200 and 2000, and the number of network devices is generally between 25 and 100, which can support several hundreds to thousands of users to access. For medium networks, the concept of dividing areas by function is introduced, which is the modular design, but there are relatively few functional modules. Areas are generally flexibly divided according to business needs.

The medium campus network is used in the most scenarios, and its functional modules are shown in Fig. 15.4. It generally adopts a Layer 3 network structure – core layer, aggregation layer, and access layer, and it is divided into two functional areas– the data center and egress layer. The data center is usually deployed with enterprise servers, such as Web sites of the intranet, office systems and database servers. The egress layer is connected to the Internet and the core layer, and usually deploys firewalls to control the traffic from the intranet to the Internet. In the meantime, it prevents attackers on the Internet from invading the intranet. In addition, the network address is also translated at the egress layer.

3. Large campus network architecture

A large campus network may be a network covering multiple buildings, or a network connecting multiple campuses within a city via WAN. It generally provides access services, such as allowing traveling users to access the company's internal network through technologies such as VPN.

A large network has the following features: wide coverage, large number of users, complex network requirements, full functional modules and rich network hierarchy. The architecture of large campus network is shown in Fig. 15.5. The functional modules of the headquarters campus are access layer, aggregation layer, core layer, egress layer, data center and network management area. At the egress layer, cloud data centers and branch campuses can be connected via

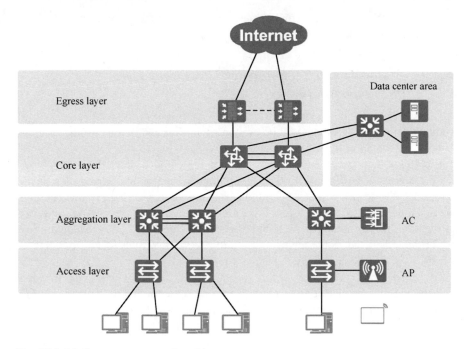

Fig. 15.4 Medium campus network architecture

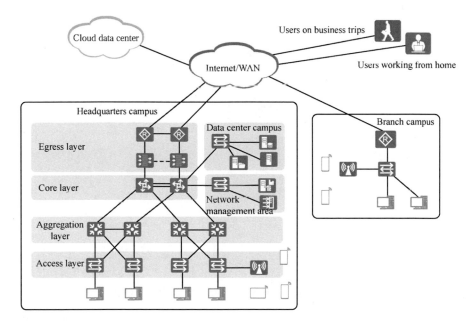

Fig. 15.5 Large campus network architecture

Internet or WAN, and users on business trips and users working from home can access the network of the headquarters campus via Internet.

15.1.3   Protocols and Technologies Commonly Used in Campus Networks

Protocols or technologies that will be used in each layer and module of the campus network are shown in Fig. 15.6.

The technologies used in the core layer of the campus network are stacking, OSPF, static routing and ACL. The technologies used at the aggregation layer include DHCP, stacking, link aggregation, spanning tree, OSPF and static routing. The technologies used at the access layer are VLAN, spanning tree, AAA and link aggregation. The technologies used in the egress area are NAT, OSPF, static routing and PPPoE. And the technologies used in the network management area include SNMP.

To be specific, core layer switches, aggregation layer switches, egress area firewalls and routers all need to be configured with static routing or dynamic routing to enable network connections between the intranets and to access the Internet. Among them, the router in the egress area connected to the Internet is configured with NAT or NAPT to enable the intranet to access the Internet, and NAT Server can also be configured so that computers in the Internet can access the servers on the intranet. The link in the egress area connecting the ISP is usually a WAN link and may also use PPPoE or PPP protocol. The aggregation layer switches and access layer switches use Spanning Tree Protocol to prevent loops. Inter-VLAN routing is usually implemented on aggregation layer switches, and aggregation layer switches

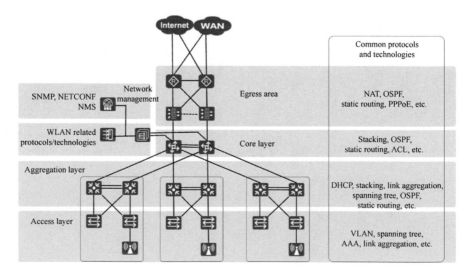

Fig. 15.6 Protocols or technologies commonly used in campus networks

use DHCP to assign IP addresses to computers in the VLANs. The FIT APs of the campus network are configured on the AC through WLAN-related protocols. And devices in the network is managed and monitored on the network management server via SNMP protocol or NETCONF protocol.

15.2 Lifecycle of a Campus Network

Generally speaking, the life cycle of a campus network includes at least the whole process of planning and programming, deployment and implementation, operation and maintenance, and network optimization of the network system. The life cycle of a campus network is a cyclic iterative process, and each cyclic iteration is driven by changes in network application requirements. Each cycle of change is centered on four phases: planning and programming, deployment and implementation, operation and maintenance, and network optimization.

1. Planning and design.

   Network planning and design is the starting point of a project. Perfect and detailed planning will lay a solid foundation for the specific subsequent work of the project. The work in this phase includes determining the physical topology of the network, the logical topology, technologies and protocols to be used, etc.

2. Deployment and implementation.

   Project implementation is where engineers deliver the specific operation of the project. Systematic management and efficient processes are the fundamental elements to ensure the successful implementation of the project. The work in this phase includes equipment installation, stand-alone commissioning, interconnection testing, cutover and grid connection, etc.

3. Operation and maintenance.

   To ensure the normal operation of network functions and thus support the successful provision of user services, daily maintenance and troubleshooting of the network are required. The work in this phase includes daily maintenance, software and configuration backup, centralized network management monitoring, software upgrade, etc.

4. Network optimization.

   The user's business is constantly evolving, so the user's demand for network functions will change accordingly. When the existing network fails to meet the business needs, or when the network reveals certain hidden problems during the operation, network optimization is required to address the problems. The work in this phase includes improving the security of the network and enhancing the experience of network users.

15.3   Hands-On Practice of Campus Network Projects

15.3.1   Network Requirements

A company (with about 200 employees) plans to create a new campus network due to business development needs, and the network requirements are as follows.

1. It can meet the current business needs of the company.
2. The network has a simple topology and is easy to maintain.
3. It provides wired access for employees to use in their offices and Wi-Fi service for visitors.
4. Simple network traffic management.
5. A certain level of security is ensured.

15.3.2   Planning and Design of Small Campus Networks

The planning and design of small and medium campus networks in this case need to take into consideration the following elements.

1. The design of networking plan, including equipment selection, physical topology and equipment naming.
2. Basic service design, including VLAN design and planning, IP address design and planning, IP address assignment method, and routing design.
3. WLAN design, including WLAN networking design, WLAN data forwarding mode design.
4. Network reliability design.
5. Layer 2 loop avoidance design.
6. Egress NAT design.
7. Security design, including traffic control, DHCP security and network management security.
8. Operation, maintenance management design, including the management using traditional equipment, and management based on the iMaster NCE platform.

1. The design of networking plan

    After taking into consideration the budget, business requirements and other factors, the physical layer topology in this case is designed as shown in Fig. 15.7. The devices can be named according to a uniform method that is easy to remember and scalable. For example, the access layer switches are named Acc-S1, Acc-S2, Acc-S3, etc., and the aggregation layer switches are named Agg-S1, Agg-S2, etc. The selection of interfaces for interconnecting devices should meet the bandwidth requirements.

    Note: Acc is the abbreviation of Access, which represents the access layer device; and Agg is the abbreviation of Aggregation, which represents the aggregation layer device.

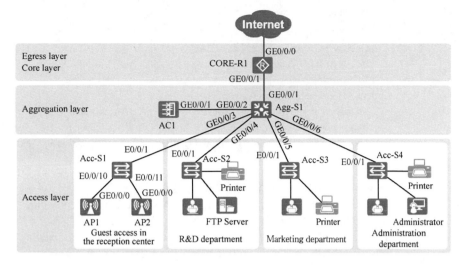

Fig. 15.7   Network topology

The entire network adopts a Layer 3 architecture. The access layer switch is S3700, which provides 100-gigabit network access for employees' PCs, printers and other terminals. The aggregation layer switch is an S5700, which serves as the gateway to the Layer 2 network. The core and egress layers are combined into one, and the router is AR2240, which functions as the egress of the whole campus network.

2. Basic service design

(a) Design and planning of VLAN.
The design of VLANs is recommended as follows.

- VLAN numbers are recommended to be assigned consecutively to ensure the reasonable use of VLAN resources.
- VLAN division needs to distinguish between service VLAN, management VLAN and interconnection VLAN.
- VLANs can be divided based on interfaces.
- Service VLAN design can divide VLANs by geographical area, by logical area, by personnel structure and by service type.
- Management VLANs are mostly used for remote management of network devices, and it is necessary to configure IP addresses, subnet masks and default routes for the devices to be managed. It is recommended that all switches belonging to the same Layer 2 network use the same management VLAN, with the managed address in the same network segment. Usually, Layer 2 switches use the VLANIF interface address as the managed address.
The VLAN planning for this case is as follows (see Table 15.1).

Table 15.1 VLAN planning for this case

VLAN number	VLAN description	VLAN category
1	Guest VLAN/service VLAN of WLAN	Service VLAN
2	VLAN of R&D department	
3	VLAN of marketing department	
4	VLAN of administration department	
100	Management VLAN of Layer 2 devices	Management VLAN
101	Management VLAN of WLAN	
102	Interconnection VLAN of Agg-S1 and CORE-R1	Interconnection VLAN

- Management VLANs for Layer 2 devices are reserved.
- Based on the personnel structure, the VLANs are divided into guest VLAN, R&D VLAN, marketing VLAN and administration VLAN.
- Considering that Layer 3 switches need to be connected to routing through VLANIF, it is necessary to reserve interconnection VLANs.
- The VLANs required to establish CAPWAP tunnel between AP and AC are reserved.

(b) Design and planning of IP addresses.

The service IP address is the address allocated to servers, hosts, wireless devices, etc. The design and planning principles of the service IP address are as follows.

- Gateway IP address is recommended to uniformly use the last or the first available address of this network segment, for example, for network segment 192.168.80.0/24, the address of the gateway is 192.168.80.254 or 192.168.80.1, so as to avoid conflict with the computer addresses of the network segment as far as possible.
- The IP address range planning of each service VLAN should ensure that the IP address of each type of service terminal is continuous and aggregatable, which is convenient for routing aggregation.
- It is recommended to use an IP address segment with a 24-bit mask.
- Switches use VLANIF interfaces to configure the managed addresses, and it is recommended that all switches use the same network segment for their managed addresses.
- It is recommended that network device interconnection IP addresses use IP addresses with 30-bit masks and core devices use IP addresses with smaller addresses.

When planning network segments and gateway addresses for each type of services, the number of access clients should be taken into account and sufficient IP addresses should be reserved. Table 15.2 lists the addresses, subnets and gateways of each network segment in this case.

Table 15.2 IP address planning for each network segment

IP network segment/mask	Gateway address	Network segment description	VLAN belonged	VLAN category
192.168.1.0/24	192.168.1.254	Network segment of wireless access guests; the gateway is in Agg-S1	VLAN 1	Service VLAN
192.168.2.0/24	192.168.2.254	Network segment of R&D department; the gateway is in Agg-S1	VLAN 2	
192.168.3.0/24	192.168.3.254	Network segment of marketing department; the gateway is in Agg-S1	VLAN 3	
192.168.4.0/24	192.168.4.254	Network segment of administration department; the gateway is in Agg-S	VLAN 4	
192.168.100.0/24	192.168.100.254	Network segment of Layer 2 device management; the gateway is in Agg-S1	VLAN 100	Management VLAN
192.168.101.0/24		Management network segment of WLAN	VLAN 101	
192.168.102.0/30		Interconnection network segment of Agg-S1 and CORE-R1	VLAN 102	Interconnection VLAN
1.1.1.1/32		Loopback interface address on CORE-R1, used for managing IPs		

(c) IP address assignment method.

Dynamic IP address assignment or static IP address assignment can be adopted to assign IP addresses. In small and medium campus networks, the specific assignment principles of IP addresses are as follows.

IP addresses of WAN interfaces are assigned by the carriers, such as through static IP addressing and dynamic IP addressing (DHCP or PPPoE method). For IP addresses of WAN interfaces, communication with the carrier is required in advance in order to obtain them.

For servers and special terminal devices (such as punch-card machines, printers, IP video monitoring devices, etc.), it is recommended to use static IP address binding to assign them.

For user terminal devices (such as PCs in user's offices, IP phones, etc.), their IP addresses are recommended to be dynamically assigned through DHCP by deploying a DHCP server on the gateway device in a unified manner.

The IP address assignment method in this case is shown in Table 15.3. The WAN interface connected to the Internet can use PPPoE to obtain IP address. All terminals (office computers and devices that wirelessly access the network) can obtain IP addresses by DHCP. Servers and printers will be

Table 15.3 Address assignment methods

IP network segment/interface	Assignment method	Description of assignment method
192.168.1.0/24	DHCP	Assigned by gateway Agg-S1; fixed IP addresses assigned to fixed devices such as servers and printers
192.168.2.0/24		
192.168.3.0/24		
192.168.4.0/24		
192.168.100.0/24	Static	Device management IPs; static configuration
192.168.101.0/24	DHCP	AC addresses static assignment: AP addresses are assigned by Agg-S1
192.168.102.0/30	Static	Interconnection Ips; static configuration
CORE-R1的GE0/0/0	PPPoE	IP addresses assigned by carriers

assigned fixed IP addresses. IP addresses of all network devices can be configured by a static method (except APs).

(d) Route design.

The route design of small and medium campus network includes the internal route design and the campus egress route design.

The internal route design must meet communication requirements of devices and terminals on the campus network and enable communication with the external network. As the network of small and medium campus is relatively small and the network structure is comparatively simple, the internal route design is not complicated. By default, AP devices generate a default route after IP addresses are assigned by DHCP. Switches and gateway devices can meet the demand through static routes without deploying complex routing protocols.

The route design of the campus egress is mainly required to meet the demand of the internal users of the campus to access the Internet and WAN, and it is recommended to configure static default routes on the egress devices.

In this case, the routes on devices Agg-S1 and CORE-R1 are shown in Fig. 15.8. Add a default route in device Agg-S1 to address 192.168.102.1 of interface GE0/0/1 of router CORE-R1. Add a default route in router CORE-R1 to IP address 22.1.2.1 of interface GE0/0/0 of router ISP-R1., and another static route to the intranet, which summarizes the intranet into a network segment 192.168.0.0/16, with the next hop pointing to IP address 192.168.102.2 of interface VLANIF 102 of device Agg-S1.

3. WLAN Design

(a) WLAN networking design.

According to the IP addresses of AC and AP, and whether the data traffic passes through AC, the network can be divided into directly connected Layer 2 network, Layer 2 network in bypass mode, directly connected Layer

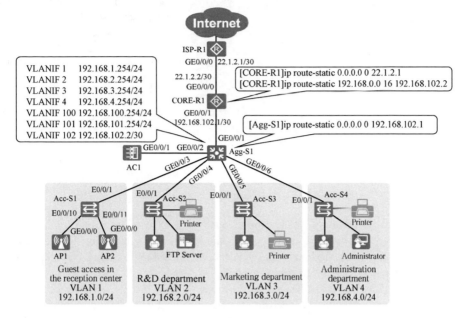

Fig. 15.8 Interface address and routing configuration

Fig. 15.9 Layer 2 networking in bypass mode

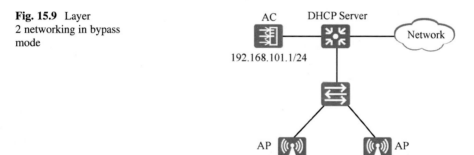

3 network, and Layer 3 network in bypass mode. As shown in Fig. 15.9, this case adopts the Layer 2 networking in bypass mode.

(b) WLAN data forwarding mode design.

The data in WLAN includes control messages and data messages. Control messages are forwarded through CAPWAP tunnel, while data messages are forwarded by tunnel forwarding and direct forwarding. This case uses the direct forwarding, as shown in Fig. 15.10.

(c) Other designs.

In addition to planning the networking and data forwarding methods, the following designs are also necessary.

Fig. 15.10 Direct
forwarding

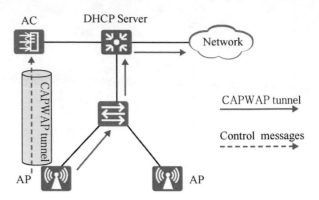

Network coverage design: the area covered by wireless network shall be designed and planned to ensure that the signal strength within the covered area can meet the requirements of users and solve the problem of co-channel interference between neighboring APs.

Network capacity design: the number of APs for the network shall be designed and deployed according to data such as the bandwidth requirements of wireless terminals, the number of terminals, concurrent volume and single AP performance to ensure that the wireless network performance can meet the Internet service needs of all terminals.

AP layout design: based on the network coverage design, the actual layout location of the AP, layout method and power supply alignment principle will be revised and confirmed according to the actual situation.

In addition, WLAN security design and roaming design are also vital, which are not listed in this chapter.

There are many items and contents to be configured when configuring WLAN. Before configuring WLAN, it is necessary to clarify the configuration options and contents. Table 15.4 shows the WLAN configuration items and configuration contents in this case. In the process of configuration, the configuration items should be configured with reference to the configuration content to avoid errors.

4. Network reliability design

The access layer and aggregation layer in this case both use a switch for networking. The reliability of switch networking is divided into port-level reliability and device-level reliability.

(a) Port-level reliability. Using Ethernet link aggregation technology can enhance the reliability between the access switch and the aggregation switch, and also increase the link bandwidth. As shown in Fig. 15.11, link aggregation is implemented between AC1 and Agg-S1, between AP1 and Acc-S1, and between the access layer switch and the aggregation layer switch.

Table 15.4 WLAN configuration items and configuration contents

Configuration item	Configuration content
AP management VLAN	VLAN 101
STA service VLAN	VLAN 1
DHCP server	Agg-S1 assigns addresses for APs and STAs as a DHCP server; the default gateway of STA is 192.168.1.254
AP address pool	192.168.101.2 – 192.168.101.253/24
STA address pool	192.168.1.1 – 192.168.1.253/24
AC source interface IP address	VLANIF 101:192.168.101.1/24
AP group	Name: ap-group1
	Referenced profile: VAP profile WLAN-Guest, regulatory domain profile default
regulatory domain profile	Name: default
	Country code: CN
SSID profile	Name: WLAN-Guest
	SSID name: WLAN-Guest
Security profile	Name: WLAN-Guest
	Security policy: WPA-WPA2 + PSK + AES
	Password: WLAN@Guest123
VAP profile	Name: WLAN-Guest
	Forwarding mode: direct forwarding
	Service VLAN:VLAN 1
	Referenced profile: SSID profile WLAN-Guest, security profile WLAN-Guest

(b) Device-level reliability. This can be achieved by using dual aggregation layers and dual layers, as shown in Fig. 15.12. You can also use iStack or CSS technology, which is not introduced in this case.

In this case, port-level reliability is chosen. Compared with device-level reliability, this scheme uses fewer devices and can save network cost.

5. Layer 2 loop avoidance design

According to the reliability design, this case chooses the port-level reliability design scheme. Redundant links are not introduced to the current network segment, and there is no loop, as shown in Fig. 15.13. However, it is possible for office workers to connect two switches by mistake and form a loop. To prevent the loops caused by the maloperation of office workers, the switches can be configured to use spanning tree technology. The Rapid Spanning Tree Protocol (RSTP) is adopted, and in the meantime, it is recommended to manually configure Agg-S1 as the root bridge.

6. Egress NAT design

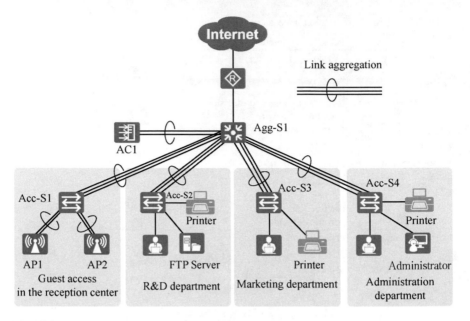

Fig. 15.11 Port-level reliability

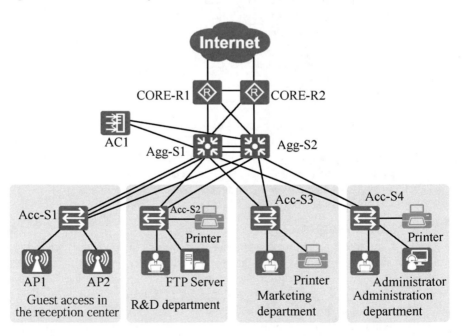

Fig. 15.12 Device-level reliability

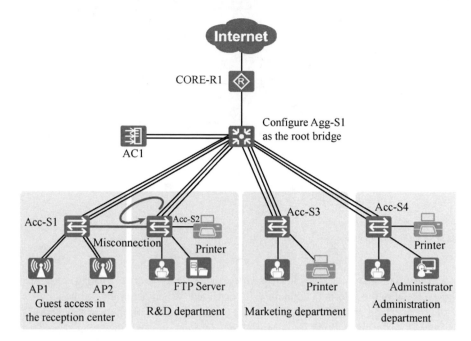

Fig. 15.13 Loop avoidance

The intranet of the campus network usually uses private addresses, and network address translation (NAT) is needed for the intranet computers to access the Internet. The router connected to the Internet usually has a public address and is configured with NAT. NAT includes static NAT, dynamic NAT, NAPT, easy IP and NAT server, and the appropriate type of NAT can be selected according to the actual situation.

Static NAT is suitable for the scenario where there are a lot of static public IP addresses and the intranet computers need to use a fixed public address to access the Internet. In this scenario, computers on the Internet can also use the public address to directly access the corresponding private address.

An address pool is a concept for dynamic NAT, and the available addresses in the public address pool are chosen to enable the intranet computers to access the Internet. In this scenario, the intranet can initiate an access to the Internet, while the Internet is unable to initiate an access to the intranet through the public address. A public address can only translate the address for one computer on the intranet.

NAPT is suitable for scenarios where there are a limited number of IP addresses in the public address pool. If there are more computers on the intranet than the addresses in the public address pool, NAPT should be configured to save public network IP addresses and improve the utilization of public network IP addresses.

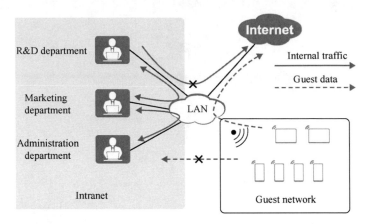

Fig. 15.14   Traffic control

Easy IP is appropriate for scenarios where the address of the interface connected to the Internet is dynamically obtained. When using the public address of the interface as NAPT, there is no need to configure a public address pool.

NAT server is suitable for scenarios where computers on the intranet need to provide services to computers on the Internet. With NAT server configured, computers on the Internet can access specific services on the intranet, such as Web services on the intranet, through the public address of the router.

In this case, it is recommended to choose easy IP for egress NAT, and the NAT server does not need to be configured.

7. Security design

The security design in this case involves traffic control, DHCP security and network management security, which can be enabled by using routers and switches.

(a) Traffic control.

As shown in Fig. 15.14, the computers in R&D department, marketing department and administration department are allowed to access each other, but not the Internet. Computers in the guest network can access the Internet, but not the internal campus network. We can use traffic-policy, traffic-filter and other technologies to control the traffic and allow the guest network to access the Internet by configuring NAPT. Configuring NAPT requires creating ACLs and defining the network segments that are allowed to access the Internet. In this case, only two rules need to be added to the ACL, one is to allow the guest traffic to pass and the other is to deny other traffic to pass. Then configure Easy IP at the router egress.

Fig. 15.15 DHCP security

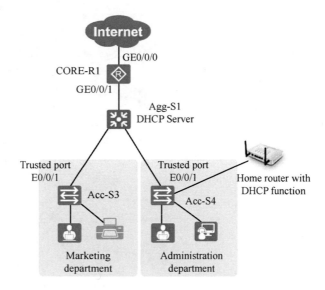

```
[CORE-R1]acl 2000
[CORE-R1-acl-basic-2000]rule 5 permit source 192.168.1.0 0.0.0.255
[CORE-R1-acl-basic-2000]rule 10 deny
[CORE-R1-GigabitEthernet0/0/0]nat outbound 2000
```

(b) DHCP security.

In campus networks, it is a common situation that employees connect to DHCP wireless router without permission, so that the intranet addresses become a mess, which results in address conflict and inability to access the Internet. At this time, DHCP Snooping can be adopted in the access layer switch to prevent this situation and ensure DHCP security.

As shown in Fig. 15.15, to prevent the computers in the administration department from obtaining IP addresses from the home router, DHCP Snooping is enabled on the Acc-S4 switch and E0/0/1 is set as the Trusted port. so that DHCP requests sent by computers will only be sent to interface E0/0/1.

```
[Acc-S4]dhcp enable
[Acc-S4]dhcp snooping enable
[Acc-S4]vlan 4
[Acc-S4-vlan4]dhcp snooping enable
[Acc-S4-vlan4]quit
[Acc-S4]interface Ethernet 0/0/1
[Acc-S4-Ethernet0/0/1]dhcp snooping trusted
```

(c) Network management security.

When using Telnet, Web or other methods for network management of the device, only fixed users (computers with fixed IP addresses) can be allowed to

Fig. 15.16 Traditional
device management

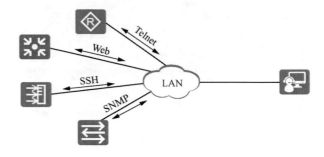

Fig. 15.17 iMaster NCE
platform management.

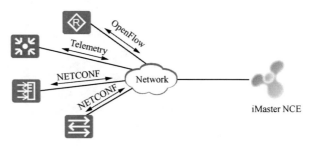

login for network management through ACL technology. For centralized network management [the administrator can get the working status of all the
managed devices in time through the operation port of a management terminal
program, and can configure all the managed devices through this port. Simple
Network Management Protocol (SNMP) defines the standard for the management communication between the management terminal and the network
devices]. SNMPv3 adds authentication and encryption processing, which can
significantly improve the security of network management.

8. Operation, maintenance and management design
      The operation, maintenance and management of small and medium campus
network can be managed by traditional devices or on the iMaster NCE platform.
Traditional device management is chosen in this case.

(a) Management by traditional devices.
          If the network administrator and the device IP are reachable, the device can
      be managed through Telnet, Web and SSH, as shown in Fig. 15.16. When
      there are many network devices, SNMP protocol-based unified network
      management software can be deployed for network operation, maintenance
      and management.
(b) Management based on iMaster NCE platform.
          In addition to management by traditional devices based on SNMP, Huawei
      iMaster NCE platform can also be adopted for network operation, mainte-
      nance and management so as to achieve "autopilot" of the network. As shown
      in Fig. 15.17, on iMaster NCE platform, network devices can be managed
      through OpenFlow, NETCONF and Telemetry protocols.

15.3.3 Deployment and Implementation of Small Campus Networks

In the deployment and implementation phase, a list of configuration contents is required before configuring the network devices, and then the devices are configured with reference to the list. After the configuration is completed, testing is performed to ensure that the configuration can achieve the designed functionality.

1. Network configuration

   (a) Configure the port.
       After physical lines between the network devices are connected, you need to configure the link aggregation between the access layer switches and aggregation layer switches and add the port description. To avoid configuration errors, first, information including the link aggregation interface (Eth-Trunk) number, link aggregation mode, port members of the link aggregation port and link aggregation port description required for each switch shall be organized in the table. The Eth-Trunk ports that need to be created on the switch in this case and what needs to be configured are shown in Tables 15.5 and 15.6.
   (b) Configure VLANs.
       In this case, VLANs are created based on the personnel structure. Four service VLANs, two management VLANs and one interconnection VLAN need to be created for three departments and guests (see Table 15.1). After creating the port-based VLANs on the switch, you also need to configure the

Table 15.5 Configure ports

Device	Port	Configuration content
Acc-S1	Eth-trunk 1	Mode: LACP-static
		Trunkport: GE0/0/1, GE0/0/2, GE0/0/3
		Description: to Agg-S1's eth-trunk 1
	E0/0/10	Description: to AP1
	E0/0/11	Description: to AP2
Acc-S2	Eth-trunk 2	Mode: LACP-static
		Trunkport: GE0/0/1, GE0/0/2, GE0/0/3
		Description: to Agg-S1's eth-trunk 2
Acc-S3	Eth-trunk 3	Mode: LACP-static
		Trunkport: GE0/0/1, GE0/0/2, GE0/0/3
		Description: to Agg-S1's eth-trunk 3
Acc-S4	Eth-trunk 4	Mode: LACP-static
		Trunkport: GE0/0/1, GE0/0/2, GE0/0/3
		Description: to Agg-S1's eth-trunk 4
AC1	GE0/0/1	Description: to Agg-S1's GE0/0/2
CORE-R1	GE0/0/1	Description: to Agg-S1's GE0/0/1

Table 15.6 Configure ports

Device	Port	Configuration content
Agg-S1	Eth-trunk 1	Mode: LACP-static
		Trunkport: GE0/0/3, GE0/0/7, GE0/0/8
		Description: to Acc-S1's eth-trunk 1
	Eth-trunk 2	Mode: LACP-static
		Trunkport: GE0/0/4, GE0/0/9, GE0/0/10
		Description: to Acc-S2's eth-trunk 2
	Eth-trunk 3	Mode: LACP-static
		Trunkport: GE0/0/5, GE0/0/11, GE0/0/12
		Description: to Acc-S3's eth-trunk 3
	Eth-trunk 4	Mode: LACP-static
		Trunkport: GE0/0/6, GE0/0/13, GE0/0/14
		Description: to Agg-S1's eth-trunk 4
	GE0/0/1	Description: to CORE-R1's GE0/0/1
	GE0/0/2	Description: to AC1's GE0/0/1

Table 15.7 Port types and configuration contents

Device	Port	Type	Configuration content
Acc-S1	Eth-trunk 1	Trunk	PVID:100
			Allow-pass VLAN 1, 100, 101
	E0/0/10		PVID: 101
	E0/0/11		Allow-pass VLAN 1, 101
Acc-S2	Eth-trunk 2	Trunk	PVID: 100
			Allow-pass VLAN 2, 100
	Other interfaces	Access	Default VLAN 2
Acc-S3	Eth-trunk 3	Trunk	PVID: 100
			Allow-pass VLAN 3, 100
	Other interfaces	Access	Default VLAN 3
Acc-S4	Eth-trunk 4	Trunk	PVID: 100
			Allow-pass VLAN 4, 100
	Other interfaces	Access	Default VLAN 4

port type and the VLAN to which the access port belongs, and configure the PVID of the trunk port and the VLANs allowed to pass through.

In order to avoid errors in the configuration process, the information that needs to be configured can be listed in advance in tables. Tables 15.7 and 15.8 show the types of each port and the content that needs to be configured. As it can be seen from the table, we have configured the Eth-Trunk port type as Trunk, the same PVID is specified, and only the necessary VLANs are allowed to pass through the trunk.

(c) Configure static addresses.

The addresses of the management ports of access layer switch and aggregation layer switch, and the ports of aggregation layer switch Agg-S1 and

Table 15.8 Port types and configuration contents

Device	Port	Type	Configuration content
Acc-S1	Eth-trunk 1	Trunk	PVID:100
			Allow-pass VLAN 1, 100, 101
	Eth-trunk 2	Trunk	PVID:100
			Allow-pass VLAN 2, 100
	Eth-trunk 3	Trunk	PVID:100
			Allow-pass VLAN 3, 100
	Eth-trunk 4	Trunk	PVID:100
			Allow-pass VLAN 4, 100
	GE0/0/2	Access	Default VLAN 101
	GE0/0/1	Access	Default VLAN 102
AC1	GE0/0/1	Access	Default VLAN 101

Table 15.9 IP address configuration

Device	Port	Address/mask
Agg-S1	VLANIF 1	192.168.1.254/24
	VLANIF 2	192.168.2.254/24
	VLANIF 3	192.168.3.254/24
	VLANIF 4	192.168.4.254/24
	VLANIF 100	192.168.100.254/24
	VLANIF 101	192.168.101.254/24
	VLANIF 102	192.168.102.2/30
CORE-R1	GE0/0/1	192.168.102.1/30
	GE0/0/0	PPPoE自动获取
	Loopback 0	1.1.1.1/32
Agg-S1	VLANIF 100	192.168.100.1/24
Agg-S2	VLANIF 100	192.168.100.2/24
Agg-S3	VLANIF 100	192.168.100.3/24
Agg-S4	VLANIF 100	192.168.100.4/24
AC1	VLANIF 101	192.168.1.101/24

core layer router CORE-R1 are also statically configured. To avoid errors in the configuration, the address of each port needs to be planned in advance. The details of the IP address configuration of routers and switches in this case are shown in Table 15.9. As it can be seen from the table, inter-VLAN routing is enabled by the aggregation layer switch Agg-S1, and the address configured for port VLANIF corresponds to the last address of the VLAN.

(d) Configure DHCP.

Terminals and APs use DHCP to obtain addresses. In this case, Agg-S1, the aggregation layer switch, is configured as a DHCP server to assign addresses to computers in the VLANS of R&D department, marketing department, and administration department as well as for guests, and also to assign addresses to APs in the management VLAN of the WLAN. Therefore, four address pools need to be created on Agg-S1. Gateways and DNS have to

Table 15.10 IP address assignment methods

Network segment	Other parameters	Note
192.168.1.0/24	Gateway:192.168.1.254	Agg-S1 is the DHCP Server
	DNS:192.168.1.254	
192.168.2.0/24	Gateway:192.168.2.254	Agg-S1is the DHCP Server
	DNS:192.168.2.254	Assign fixed addresses to Printer (1) and FTP
192.168.3.0/24	Gateway:192.168.3.254	Agg-S1 is the DHCP Server
	DNS:192.168.3.254	Assign fixed addresses to Printer (2)
192.168.4.0/24	Gateway:192.168.4.254	Agg-S1 is the DHCP Server
	DNS:192.168.4.254	Assign fixed addresses to Printer (3) and the network administrator
192.168.101.0/ 24		Agg-S1 is the DHCP Server
		Do not assign the address taken by the AC (192.168.101.1)

be assigned to each address pool, and the lease duration needs to be specified based on the time the terminal stays after accessing the network. If a fixed address needs to be assigned to a specific device, the IP address and MAC address need to be bound. If there are addresses in the address pool that have already been taken, they will be excluded. In this case, the IP address taken by the AC needs to be excluded from the management VLAN of the WLAN.

The IP address pools created on Agg-S1, the gateway and DNS of each address pool, the excluded addresses and the bound addresses in this case also need to be planned and sorted in advance. The details can be found in Table 15.10.

(e) Configure routing.

This case uses static routing. In order to allow administrators to access the access layer switch and AC1 across network segments, it is necessary to configure default routes on the access layer switch and AC1. On the aggregation layer switch, you only need to add a default route to the core layer router CORE-R1, and on CORE-R1, you need to add a route to the intranet and then add a default route to the Internet. The configuration details can be found in Table 15.11.

(f) Network management configuration.

Telnet remote management is applied in this case, and the authentication mode is AAA. On the managed device, you need to create users, set passwords and configure to allow users for Telnet login. In addition, user privilege levels are set. The configuration details can be found in Table 15.12.

(g) Configure the network egress.

In this case, the port of the core layer router CORE-R1 connecting to the Internet uses PPPoE dial-up to obtain the public address. The public address obtained by each dial-up is not fixed, so easy IP should be selected for NAT. See Table 15.13 for configuration details.

(h) Configure the WLAN.

Table 15.11   Routing configuration

Device	Route configuration	Note
Acc-S1	0.0.0.0	To enable network administrators to access Layer 2 switch across network segments
Acc-S2	0 192.168.100.254	
Acc-S3		
Acc-S4		
AC1	0.0.0.00 192.168.101.254	To enable network administrators to access AC1 across network segments
Agg-S1	0.0.0.00 192.168.102.1	The route that matches the traffic accessing the Internet
CORE-R1	192.168.0.0 16 192.168.102.2	The route added by the core router to the intranet, which is an aggregated route
	Default route	To the interface of the extranet

Table 15.12   Network management method

Device	Management mode	Authentication mode	Note
Acc-S1	Telnet	Local AAA	The username and password should be complex and inconsistent, and need to be written down
Acc-S2			
Acc-S3			
Acc-S4			
CORE-R1			
AC1			
AP1	Centralized control and management by the AC		
AP2			

Table 15.13   Network egress configuration

Device	Port	Access more	NAT mode	Note
CORE-R1	GE0/0/0	PPPoE	Easy IP	User name: PPPoEUser123
				Password: Huawei@123

You only need follow the WLAN design and planning content to configure.

(i) Configure network security.

Network security in this case involves three aspects: traffic control, network management security and DHCP security. We can use different security measures in different devices. Traffic control can be enabled by creating basic ACLs and advanced ACLs on the core layer router CORE-R1. Network security management requires creating ACLs on each managed device to allow only specified IP addresses to remotely manage, and creating different

Table 15.14 Network security configuration

Module	Related technologies	Configuration content
Traffic control	Traffic-Policy	• Configure an advanced ACL to block traffic whose source address is 192.168.1.0/24 and destination address is the intranet service segment and allow other traffic to pass. Configure Traffic-filter to introduce this ACL and apply it on the interface.
	NAT	•
	ACL	Configure a basic ACL to allow only the traffic of 192.168.1.0/24 to pass and reference it to the NAT function on the network egress
Network management security	AAA	Configure a basic ACL to allow only addresses whose source is the administrator's IP address and wildcard mask is 0, and reference it to the VTY port of all managed devices
	ACL	
DHCP security	DHCP Snooping	Enable DHCP Snooping on all access switches, and configure the uplink port as Trusted port

users and setting strict privilege levels for different operators. DHCP security needs to be configured on the access layer switch, and the configured uplink port is the Trusted port. See Table 15.14 for the configuration details.

2. Network testing

After the network is configured, connectivity test, high reliability capability test and service performance test should be conducted.

(a) The connectivity test includes basic link interconnection test, Layer 2 interconnection test, and Layer 3 interconnection test.
(b) High reliability test includes loop avoidance function test and path switching test.
(c) Service performance testing includes service traffic testing and access control testing.

15.3.4   Operation and Maintenance of Small Campus Networks

After the project goes online and runs, it enters the operation and maintenance phase of the network.

Network device operation and maintenance is a daily preventive work. It refers to the regular inspection and maintenance of the equipment in the normal operation of the equipment in order to timely detect and eliminate defects or hidden dangers to maintain the health of the equipment, so that the system can operate safely, stably and reliably for a long time.

1. Environmental requirements of the server room

Under normal circumstances, the temperature of the long-term working environment of the server room should be kept between 0 °C and 45 °C, and the temperature of the short-term working environment should be between −5 °C and 55 °C. If the temperature of the server room fails to meet the requirements in the long term, the maintenance personnel should consider overhauling or replacing the air-conditioning system of the server room, checking the cooling situation of air conditioners, the switch situation, etc. The air-conditioning refrigeration should function normally and the switch should be in good contact.

Under normal circumstances, the relative humidity (RH) of the long-term working environment of the server room should be kept between 10% RH and 95% RH, and the relative humidity of short-term working environment should be between 5% RH and 95% RH. If the relative humidity of the server room becomes excessive, the maintenance personnel should consider installing dehumidification equipment for the server room; if the server room is too dry, the maintenance personnel should consider installing humidification equipment for the server room.

2. Network equipment hardware maintenance requirements

(a) The cleaning condition.

All equipment should be clean and tidy, with no obvious dust attached. Equipment shells, the inside of the equipment, and the inside of the rack have to be equipped with a dust net. Pay attention to the cleaning condition of the dust net of the cabinet, which should be timely cleaned or replaced, so as not to affect ventilation and heat dissipation of cabinet door and fan frame.

(b) Heat dissipation condition.

When the equipment is working normally, it is required to keep the fan running (except during the cleaning of the fan). Turning off the fan without permission will cause the temperature of the equipment to rise and may damage the single board. It is not allowed to place sundris on the equipment shelves at the vents, and the fan's dust net should be cleaned on a regular basis.

(c) Cable laying.

Power cables and service cables are required to be laid separately. Power cables and service cables should be placed in a neat and orderly manner.

(d) Cable labeling.

Pay attention to the cable labels inside the cabinet, which are required to be clear and accurate, and in line with the specifications.

(e) Equipment appearance.

Observe whether the equipment is complete, and whether the free slot is protected by a dummy panel.

3. Network equipment alarms and data configuration maintenance requirements

  (a) Alarm information.

     Under normal circumstances, there should be no alarm information. If there is an alarm, it needs to be records, and serious alarms need to be immediately analyzed and dealt with.

  (b) Log information.

     Under normal circumstances, there should not be excessive duplicate information in the logs. If there is, it must be immediately analyzed and dealt with.

  (c) CPU occupancy status.

     Under normal circumstances, the CPU occupancy should be less than 80%. If the CPU occupancy rate is too high for a long time, the device should be checked and the cause analyzed.

  (d) Memory occupancy.

     Under normal circumstances, the occupancy rate of memory should be lower than 80%. If the occupancy rate is too high for a long time, the equipment should be checked and the cause determined.

  (e) Interface traffic.

     Compare the current traffic with the interface bandwidth. If the utilization rate exceeds 80% of the port bandwidth, it needs to be recorded and confirmed. Check whether there are error statistics in the inbound and outbound directions of the interface, focusing on the growth of error statistics.

  (f) Interface and link status.

     The status of interfaces and links in use is UP, and that of unused interfaces is SHUTDOWN.

  (g) Debug switch.

     Check whether the switch of the current debugging information "debugging" is off. Under normal operating conditions, all switches of all debugging information are off.

  (h) Configuration file.

     Check whether the current configuration information and the saved configuration information are consistent. The configuration being run needs to be the same as the configuration saved.

  (i) Remaining capacity of Flash.

     All the files in Flash must be useful, otherwise the delete/unreserved command should be executed to delete them.

  (j) Administration level user control.

     The system must set a password for the administration level user, and the password is required to be set in the cipher text format and longer than six digits.

  (k) Telnet login control.

     Telnet users must be authenticated. The password must be in cipher text format and cannot be too simple.

(l) Telnet and serial login.

Telnet and serial login are tested to ensure that users can login by both of the two methods.

(m) Change the user password.

For system security, the user password of the device must be changed on a regular basis. Moreover, the password must be set in the cipher text format and longer than six digits. The password is recommended to be updated every quarter.

(n) Interface configuration.

Check the status and the configuration of the interface. The interface whose status is DOWN (except SHUTDOWN) is not allowed to have configuration, and the interface whose status is UP must have configuration.

(o) Interface description.

All activated interfaces are described using the specification. If there is no corresponding specification, it is recommended that the interface description specification be: Local device name_Local port number - >Peer device name_Peer port number_Port rate.

(p) Interface mode.

Execute the display interface command to check the configuration of the interface. The local interface mode (including rate and duplex mode) must be consistent with the peer interface mode. The actual operating mode (Trunk or Access) of the local interface must be the same as that of the peer interface.

(q) System time.

Execute the display clock command to query the system date and time. The time should be consistent with the actual local time (the time difference is no more than 5 min).

15.3.5   Network Optimization of Small Campus Networks

If there are changes in network requirements, a suitable optimization plan needs to be formulated with the actual situation taken into consideration. For example, in this case, the control and security requirements for guests accessing the Internet in the reception center have increased, and bandwidth restrictions are imposed on each guest accessing the Internet, so it is necessary to deploy firewall devices at the egress layer to set security policies and bandwidth restriction policies. Another example is that the number of guests in the reception center has increased, and the performance of the core layer device CORE-R1 is not satisfied, so it is necessary to upgrade the device.

Through network optimization, the overall security and reliability of the network can be improved to better support the development of enterprise services. Common optimization solutions include, but are not limited to, the following.

- Device performance optimization, for example, upgrading hardware devices, replacing existing devices with higher performance devices, and updating the software versions of the devices.
- Network infrastructure optimization, for example, network architecture optimization and routing protocol adjustment. Other examples of network architecture optimization include the shift from single-link to dual-link Internet access, and the adjustment of WLAN data forwarding method from direct forwarding to tunnel forwarding. Moreover, changing the static routes to dynamic routes on the intranet is a routing protocol adjustment.
- Service quality optimization, for example, reserving higher bandwidth for specific guests to the Internet, or prioritizing traffic forwarding for voice and video services.

15.4   Exercises

1. What is the complete life cycle of a campus network?
2. What is the role of managed addresses?

Chapter 16
Network Management, Operation and Maintenance

As the scale of network grows larger and larger, and the variety of devices in the network becomes increasingly diverse, how to effectively manage the growingly complex network to provide high-quality network services has become a daunting challenge for network management.

There are various means for network management, operation and maintenance, and this chapter mainly explains how to use the network management system to unify the management and monitoring of devices in the enterprise network. The chapter introduces not only the working principles and configuration of the SNMP protocol, but also the working principle of the NTP protocol, as well as how to configure network devices to synchronize clocks using the NTP protocol.

16.1 Overview of Network Management, Operation and Maintenance

The OSI reference model defines five major functional models of network management.

- Configuration management. Configuration management is responsible for monitoring the configuration information of the network, so that network administrators can generate, query, modify the operating parameters and conditions of hardware and software, and can configurate related services.
- Performance management. Performance management takes network performance as a guideline to ensure that the network can provide reliable and continuous communication capabilities while using fewer network resources and reducing time latency.
- Fault management. The primary goal of fault management is to ensure that the network is always available and that faults are repaired as soon as possible when they occur.

© The Author(s) 2023
Huawei Technologies Co., Ltd., *Data Communications and Network Technologies*,
https://doi.org/10.1007/978-981-19-3029-4_16

- Security management. Security management protects the network and system from unauthorized access and security attacks.
- Billing management. Billing monitoring is mainly used to track and control the use of network resources by users and store the relevant information in the operation log database to provide a basis for billing.

There are only two means of network device management: one is to manage the device by connecting to the dedicated management interface of the network device (such as Console, MiniUSB) and using the virtual terminal software (such as SecureCRT); and the other is to launch Telnet/SSH remote management access to network devices by using the interface used for data transmission. Both of these management methods require administrators to establish connections and perform management on a device-by-device basis. This type of management method is appropriate for newly created projects or projects whose network is changed, because at this time the technicians proactively carry out all operations on each network device and the purpose of the operations is quite clear. However, this method is not suitable for administrators to manage and maintain the entire network on a daily basis. One of the key reasons is that technicians cannot predict on which component of which device network failures and network attacks will occur.

For example, a network deploys standby devices and corresponding high-availability technologies at certain critical points in the hope that the network will provide users with uninterrupted communication services 24/7. However, when the primary device breaks down, the smooth switchover of the forwarding device from the primary device (and link) to the standby device (and link) goes unnoticed by any user. The administrator is also unaware that the network has failed, and he certainly will not login to the primary device that has crashed and check for faults that could have caused the shutdown, much less repair or replace this device accordingly. Thus, the first time the administrator realizes that the primary device has failed is when the user complains to him about the disruption of network communication (caused by the breakdown of the backup device). In other words, redundant devices are unable to optimally improve the network availability.

The above example shows that in a network, a complex system containing a large number of devices, it is often inadequate to initiate management access on a device-by-device basis. Even if there are only a few common errors in the network, as long as the network is large enough, using the device management approach described earlier to troubleshoot them is akin to a blindfolded man trying to understand an elephant solely by touch. Therefore, managing the network requires a more macro management approach than managing network devices on a device-by-device basis.

For such complex systems, the most ideal management approach is for administrators to be able to access the working status of all managed devices in a timely manner through the operation interface of a management program, and to be able to configure all managed devices through this interface. The Simple Network Management Protocol (SNMP) defines the standard for the management communication performed by the management end and the network devices.

16.2 Principles and Configuration of SNMP

The following explains the SNMP principles and configures Huawei devices as SNMP agents.

16.2.1 Overview of SNMP Protocol

There are various types of network devices, and the management interfaces (such as command line interfaces) of different devices provided by different vendors vary, which makes network management increasingly complicated. To address this problem, SNMP came into existence. As a standard protocol for network management widely used in TCP/IP networks, SNMP provides a uniform interface that enables unified management among different types and vendors of network devices.

SNMP protocol is divided into three versions: SNMPv1, SNMPv2c and SNMPv3.

SNMPv1 is the original version of the SNMP protocol and provides minimal network management functions. SNMPv1 is based on community name authentication and is less secure, but returns messages with fewer error codes.

SNMPv2c also uses community name authentication. It introduces GetBulk and Inform operations on top of SNMPv1, supporting more standard error code messages and more data types (e.g., Counter64, Counter32).

SNMPv3 is enhanced mainly in the aspect of security, providing USM (User Security Module) based authentication encryption and VACM (View-based Access Control Model) based access control. The operations supported by SNMPv3 are the same as those supported by SNMPv2c.

16.2.2 Components of SNMP System

As shown in Fig. 16.1, the SNMP system consists of four components, namely, Network Management System (NMS), SNMP Agent, Management Information Base (MIB), and Managed Object.

The composition of SNMP system is shown in Fig. 16.1. Each managed device contains SNMP Agent, MIB and multiple managed objects. NMS interacts with the SNMP Agent running on the managed device, and the SNMP Agent operates on the MIB of the device to complete the NMS commands.

1. NMS is the administrator in the network, a system running on the NMS server that uses SNMP protocol to manage and monitor network devices. NMS can send requests to the SNMP agents on the device to query and modify the values of one or several specific parameters. The NMS can receive SNMP Traps (SNMP Traps

Fig. 16.1 SNMP system
composition

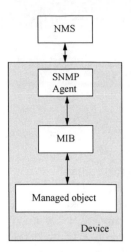

will be introduced in detail in 16.2.5) actively sent by the SNMP agent on the
device to be informed of the current status of the managed device.

2. SNMP agent is an agent process in the managed device, which is used to maintain
   the information data of the managed device, respond to the requests from NMS,
   and report the management data to the NMS that sends the request. After
   receiving the request information from NMS, the SNMP agent completes the
   corresponding command through MIB database and submits the operation result
   to the NMS. When the device fails or other events occur, the device sends SNMP
   traps to the NMS through SNMP Agent and reports to it the current status change
   of the device.

3. MIB is a database that stores the variables maintained by the managed device.
   These variables are a series of attributes of the managed device, such as the name,
   status, access rights and data type of the managed device. MIB can also be
   regarded as an interface between the NMS and the SNMP agent, through which
   the NMS can query and set the variables maintained by the managed device.

4. Each device may contain multiple managed objects, which can be a hardware in
   the device or a collection of parameters configured on the hardware and software
   (such as routing protocol).

The MIB stores data in a tree structure, as shown in Fig. 16.2. The nodes of the tree
represent managed objects, and we can identify it with a path starting from the root,
which is called OID (Object IDentifier). For example, the OID of system object is
1.3.6.1.2.1.1, and the OID of interfaces object is 1.3.6.1.2.1.2.

A subtree can also be identified by the OID of the root node of that subtree, e.g.,
for a subtree with private as the root node, its OID is the OID of the object "private",
i.e., 1.3.6.1.4.

The MIB view is a subset of the MIB, and the user can configure the MIB view to
restrict the MIB managed objects that the NMS can access. The user can configure
the subtree (or node) within the MIB view as exclude or include, where "exclude"

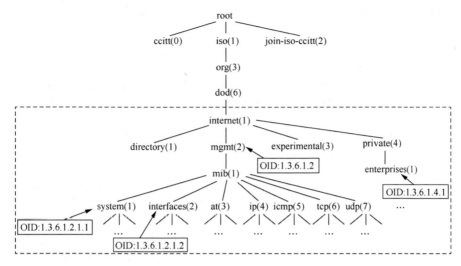

Fig. 16.2 OID tree structure

Fig. 16.3 SNMP query

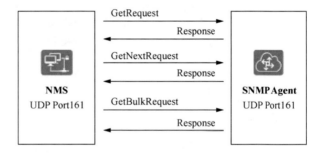

means that the current view excludes all nodes of the MIB subtree, and "include" means that the current view includes all nodes of the MIB subtree.

16.2.3 SNMP Queries

SNMP query means that NMS voluntarily send query request to the SNMP agent, and after receiving the query request, the SNMP agent completes the corresponding instruction through MIB table and feeds the result to the NMS, as shown in Fig. 16.3.

There are three types of SNMP query operation: Get, GetNext and GetBulk. Version SNMPv1 does not support GetBulk operation.

- Get: NMS uses this operation to get one or more parameter values from the SNMP agent.
- GetNext: the NMS uses this operation to get the next parameter value for one or more parameters from the SNMP agent.

- GetBulk: this operation is based on GetNext, and is equivalent to performing multiple GetNext operations in succession. The number of times the managed device performs the GetNext operation during one GetBulk message interaction can be configured on the NMS.

The working principles of SNMP query operation of different versions are basically the same, the only difference being that authentication and encryption processing are added in version SNMPv3. The following uses the Get operation of version SNMPv2c as an example to introduce the working principles of SNMP query operation.

Assuming that the NMS wants to get the value of node sysContact of the managed device MIB, and the readable community name used is "public". The specific process is as follows.

1. NMS: it sends a Get request message to the SNMP agent. The settings of the fields in the message are as follows: the version number is the SNMP version used; the community name is "public"; the PDU type in the Protocol Data Unit (PDU) is Get, and the binding variable is filled with the MIB node name sysContact.
2. SNMP Agent: it first authenticates the version number and community name carried in the request message; after successful authentication, the SNMP agent will query the sysContact node in MIB according to the request, get the value of sysContact and encapsulate it into the PDU in the response message, and send the response message to the NMS; if the query is unsuccessful, the SNMP agent will send an error response to the NMS.

16.2.4   SNMP Setting

The SNMP setting means that NMS voluntarily sends a request to the SNMP agent to perform Set operation on the device. After receiving the Set request, the SNMP agent completes the corresponding instruction through the MIB table and feeds the result to NMS, as shown in Fig. 16.4.

The SNMP setting has only one Set operation, which can be used by the NMS to set one or more parameter values in the SNMP agent.

Fig. 16.4 SNMP set

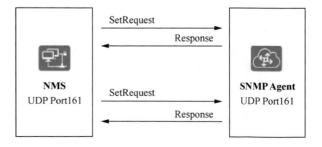

The working principles of SNMP Set operation of different versions are basically the same, the only difference being that authentication and encryption processing are added in version SNMPv3. The following uses the SNMP Set operation in version SNMPv3 as an example to introduce the working principles of SNMP Set operation.

Assuming that the NMS wants to set the value of node sysName of the managed device MIB to HUAWEI, the detailed process is as follows.

1. NMS: it sends a Set request message without security parameters to the SNMP agent to get the information about SNMP managed device engine.
2. SNMP agent: it responds to the request from NMS and feeds the requested parameters to NMSs.
3. NMS: it again sends the Set request to the SNMP agent, and the settings of the fields in the message are as follows

   • Version: SNMPv3.
   • Message header data: specify the authentication and encryption mode to be used.
   • Security parameters: the NMS calculates the authentication parameters and encryption parameters by the configured algorithm, and fills these parameters and the obtained security parameters into the corresponding fields.
   • PDU: the obtained Context EngineID and Context Name are filled into the corresponding fields, the PDU type is configured as Set, the binding variable is filled with the MIB node name sysName and HUAWEI, the value to be set, and the PDU is encrypted using the configured encryption algorithm.

4. SNMP agent: first, the version number and community name carried in the message are authenticated. After successful authentication, the SNMP agent sets the nodes in the management information database MIB corresponding to the management variables according to the request, and sends a response message to the NMS after successful setting. If the setting is unsuccessful, the agent will send an error response to the NMS.

16.2.5 SNMP Traps

SNMP traps means that the SNMP agent voluntarily report alarms or events generated by the device to the NMS so that the network administrator can be timely informed of the current operation status of the device.

There are two ways for the SNMP agent to report SNMP traps: Trap and Inform. Version SNMPv1 does not support Inform. The difference between Trap and Inform is that after the SNMP agent sends an alarm or event to NMS via Inform, the NMS needs to reply InformResponse for acknowledgement; when SNMP agent sends a Trap message to the NMS, the NMS does not send an acknowledgment message to the SNMP agent, as shown in Fig. 16.5.

1. Working principles of the trap operation

Fig. 16.5 SNMP traps

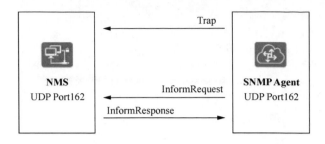

Trap operation does not belong to the basic operation of NMS on the managed device. Instead, it is the spontaneous behavior of the managed device. When the managed device reaches the condition to trigger an alarm, it will send a trap message to the NMS through the SNMP agent to inform it of the abnormal situation of the device so that the network administrator can deal with the abnormality in time. For example, the SNMP agent sends a trap of warmStart to the NMS after the warm start of the managed device.

This kind of trap message is restricted. The SNMP agent reports to the management process only when the module of the device reaches the its predefined alarm trigger conditions. The advantage of this approach is that a trap message is sent only when a serious event occurs, which reduces the traffic generated by message interactions.

2. How the inform operation works

The inform operation is also the active behavior of a managed device sending alarms to the NMS. Unlike the trap operation, after the managed device sends an inform message, the NMS is required to receive and acknowledge the message. If the managed device does not receive an acknowledgement message, the following processing is performed.

(a) Save the alarm or event temporarily in the inform cache.
(b) Repeat the alarm or event until the NMS acknowledges the receipt of the alarm or event, or the number of transmissions reaches the maximum number of retransmissions.
(c) Generate the corresponding alarm or event log on the managed device.

It can be seen from above that using the inform operation will take up more system resources.

16.2.6   Configure SNMP

When the network construction of an enterprise or organization is completed, the whole network project will proceed to the operation and maintenance phase. In larger networks, the more network devices are involved in the work, the greater the

Fig. 16.6 Enable the management of AR1 via SNMPv2c on NMS

NMS
192.168.56.12/24

AR1
192.168.56.14/24

maintenance workload of interfaces, cables, dynamic routing protocols and other information, and the difficulty of the operation and maintenance will increase accordingly. Generally speaking, for a large network, there will be a team responsible for the "network management system". They are shouldering a major responsibility, as they are the first to find the problems in the network when problems arise. In order to enable a team of two or three people to take up this heavy responsibility, administrators can reduce their workload by enabling the SNMP agent function on network devices and deploying NMS in the network in advance during the implementation of network projects.

This section demonstrates how to enable the SNMP agent function on a Huawei router. The SNMP version configured in this section is SNMPv2c, which is commonly used at present. With the exemplary topology in Fig. 16.6, the following part talks about enabling the SNMPv2c agent function on AR1 and managing it on the NMS.

As shown in Fig. 16.6, AR1 and NMS belong to the same IP subnet. The network is designed in this way to simplify the experimental environment so as to highlight the focus of the experiment. We only focus on the factors related to the SNMP configuration and ignore the IP routing. However, in practice, the NMS and the managed device often belong to different IP subnets, and the administrator needs to ensure that the IP communication with the managed device is enabled before configuring the SNMP agent function. In this case, the administrator wants to enable this specified NMS to communicate with AR1 (and other managed devices) via SNMPv2c.

To restrict one or more NMSs from using SNMP to manage network devices, the administrator can allow the IP address (or subnet) of the NMS in the basic access control list (ACL) and deny other IP addresses. When applying an ACL on a device with SNMP agent enabled, the IP address allowed in the ACL is the IP address of the NMS, and there is no need to consider the directionality of the ACL. Next the administrator will apply it in the configuration command of SNMP agent.

```
[AR1]acl 2000
[AR1-acl-basic-2000]rule permit source 192.168.56.12 0.0.0.0
[AR1-acl-basic-2000]rule deny source any
```

The following shows the configuration commands to enable the SNMP agent function on AR1.

```
[AR1]snmp-agent                         --Enable snmp-agent
[AR1]snmp-agent sys-info version v1 v2c           --Specify the snmp
version
```

```
  [AR1] snmp-agent sys-info contact hanligang@huawei.com     --Specify
the contact, optional configuration
  [AR1] snmp-agent sys-info location Office101          --Specify the device
location, optional configuration
  [AR1] snmp-agent community read public acl 2000         --Specify the
readable community name
  [AR1] snmp-agent community write private acl 2000         --Specify the
writable community name
  [AR1] snmp-agent target-host trap-hostname windows10 address
192.168.80.112 udp-port 161 trap-paramsname public         --Specify
snmp-agent to send trap messages to NMS
```

The first command is to enable snmp-agent. The SNMP agent function is enabled by default, so it is not actually necessary to enter the first command.

The second command configures the SNMP version supported by the Huawei router. The SNMP agent function is enabled by default for all SNMP versions, and this command changes the SNMP version supported to v1 and v2c.

The third command specifies the administrator information of this device.

The fourth command specifies the location information of this device.

The fifth command associates several configuration elements together, and these elements can be better clarified in the full command method: **snmp-agent community {read | write}** *community-name* **acl** *acl-number*. We can easily identify from the bold keywords that main purpose of this command is to define the read and write of the community name, and also to restrict the use of this community name. In this case, an ACL is used to restrict the NMS (NMSs) that can use this community name. The ACL 2000 created above is applied to the SNMP service module here. The readable community name set by the administrator in this command is "public", which meets the complexity requirement for writing a community name: it contains at least six characters and consists of at least two types of characters (lowercase letters, uppercase letters, numbers, and special characters other than blank spaces). After the community name is successfully configured, it is saved in the router's configuration in cipher text.

The sixth command sets the writable community name as "private".

The seventh command sets the NMS to which the device can send trap messages.

16.3   Principles and Configuration of NTP

16.3.1   Overview of NTP Protocol

As the network topology becomes increasingly complex, it will become important to synchronize the clocks of devices within the entire network. If we solely rely on the administrator to manually modify the system clock, we will face huge workload, and meanwhile, the accuracy of the clock cannot be guaranteed. Network Time Protocol

(NTP) emerged to address the problem of synchronizing system clocks of devices in the network.

NTP is mainly used when all device clocks in the network need to be consistent.

- Network management: when analyzing the log information and debugging information collected from different routers, the time needs to be used as a reference basis.
- Billing system: all device clocks are required to be consistent.
- Multiple systems collaborating on the same complex event: to ensure the correct execution sequence, multiple systems must refer to the same clock.
- Incremental backups between backup servers and clients: it is required that the clocks of backup servers and all clients should be synchronized.
- System time: some applications need to know when users logged into the system and when files were modified.

NTP is an application layer protocol of the TCP/IP stack. NTP is mostly used to synchronize clocks of a series of distributed NTP time serversand clients.

NTP evolved from time protocols and ICMP timestamp messages with special design in terms of accuracy and robustness. There are five versions of NTP: NTPv0, NTPv1, NTPv2, NTPv3 and NTPv4. The latest version, NTPv4, provides support for IPv6 based on NTPv3 with enhanced security and backward compatibility with NTPv3. NTP uses UDP as the transport layer protocol, whose public port number is 123.

NTP defines two different types of messages, synchronization messages and control messages. In most cases, NTP devices will use the client-server communication model to communicate with each other, while the server and the client will often send these two types of messages in the form of unicast. This NTP communication model is called unicast client-server mode. Moreover, NTP also defines four other modes including peer-to-peer model (called P2P mode) and client-server model that uses broadcast communication (broadcast mode). When an NTP device receives an NTP message, it can use the Mode field in this NTP message encapsulation to determine the mode used by the sender and the type of this message (whether it is a synchronization message or a control message).

Basically, all current mainstream network devices, such as ACs, APs, firewalls, routers, switches and servers, can be used as NTP clients, and some of them can also be used as NTP time servers.

16.3.2 Basic Principles of NTP

Figure 16.7 is an example of system clock synchronization based on the NTP protocol. As shown in Fig. 16.7, the NTP client and the NTP time server are connected, both of which have their own independent system clocks. Now the clock of the NTP client has to be synchronized with the clock of the NTP time server. This suction introduces the basic principles of NTP under the assumption that

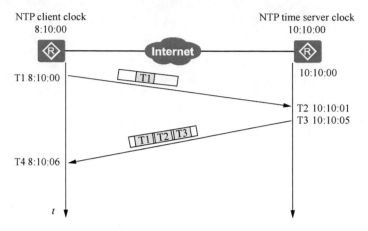

NTP client clock   NTP time server clock
    8:10:00   10:10:00

Fig. 16.7 NTP protocol clock synchronization process

the system clock accuracy of the NTP client and the NTP time server is 0, i.e., they are perfectly accurate.

The methods for setting parameters and synchronization are as follows.

1. Before synchronizing the system clocks of the NTP client and NTP time server, set the clock of NTP client to Ta and the clock of NTP time server to Tb.
2. The clock of the NTP client is to be synchronized with the clock of the NTP time server.
3. The principle described here is performed in a scenario where the system clock accuracy of the NTP client and the NTP time server is 0, i.e., they are perfectly accurate.

The system clock synchronization process is as follows.

1. The NTP client sends an NTP request message to the NTP time server at time T1, which carries the timestamp T1 when it leaves the NTP client.
2. The NTP request message arrives at the NTP time server, and the current time of the NTP time server is T2. After processing, the NTP time server sends an NTP response message at T3. The response message carries the timestamp T1 when it leaves the NTP client, the timestamp T2 when it arrives at the NTP time server, and the timestamp T3 when it leaves the NTP time server.
3. The NTP client receives the response message at T4.

Through the above NTP message interaction, the NTP client can obtain four time parameters, that is T1, T2, T3 and T4. Since the clocks of the NTP client and the NTP time server are perfectly accurate, we can calculate the time offset between the NTP client and the NTP time server, which is the time offset that the NTP client needs to adjust, by the following formula.

• Calculate the time Delay required for an NTP message to be sent from the NTP client to the NTP time server, where equal round-trip time is assumed.

$$\text{Delay} = [(T4 - T1) - (T3 - T2)]/2$$

- Calculate the time Offset between the NTP client and the NTP time server.

Take T4 as an example. At T4, the message sent by the NTP time server is received by the NTP client when the server's time is already T3 + Delay, then the time Offset can satisfy the following formula.

$$T4 + \text{Offset} = T3 + \text{Delay}.$$

After organizing the equation, we can get.

$$\text{Offset} = T3 + \text{Delay} - T4 = T3 + [(T4 - T1) - (T3 - T2)]/2 - T4$$
$$= [(T2 - T1) + (T3 - T4)]/2.$$

The NTP client adjusts its own clock according to the calculated Offset to synchronize its clock with the NTP time server.

16.3.3 NTP Network Architecture

The following concepts exist in the network architecture of NTP.

- Synchronization subnet: as shown in Fig. 16.8, a synchronization subnet can be formed by the master time server, secondary time server, PC client and the transmission path interconnected between them.

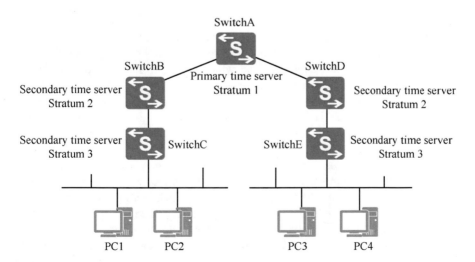

Fig. 16.8 NTP network structure

- Master time server: it can be directly synchronized to a standard reference clock via cable or radio, which is usually a radio clock or a global positioning system, etc.
- Secondary time server: it is synchronized to the master time server or other secondary servers in the network. The secondary time server can transmit time information to other hosts inside the LAN through NTP.
- Stratum: stratum is a grading standard for clock synchronization, which represents the accuracy of a clock. The value range of stratum is between 1 and 16. The smaller the value, the higher the accuracy, where 1 means the highest clock accuracy while 16 means it is not synchronized.

Under normal circumstances, the primary and secondary time servers in the synchronization subnet exhibit a hierarchical master-slave structure. In this hierarchical structure, the master time server is located at the root, while the secondary time servers approach the leaf nodes. The larger the stratum, the less the accuracy. The accuracy reduced depends on the network path and the stability of the local clock.

16.3.4   Working Modes of NTP

NTP has several operating modes for time synchronization, and users can choose the appropriate operating mode according to their needs.

- Unicast server/client mode.
- Peer mode.
- Broadcast mode.
- Multicast mode.

This section focuses on the unicast server/client mode. First, we need to explain the client and server here.

Client: a host running in client mode (referred to as a client) sends periodic messages to the server with the Mode field set to 3 (client mode). The client is usually a workstation inside the network, which is synchronized according to the other party's clock, but does not modify that clock.

Server: a host running in server mode (referred to as a server) can receive and respond to messages with the Mode field set to 4 (server mode). The server is usually a time server within the network that provides synchronization information to the client, but does not modify its own clock.

The unicast server/client mode operates at a higher stratum of the synchronization subnet. This mode requires to know the IP address of the server in advance, and the working process of the unicast server/client mode is as shown in Fig. 16.9.

The client sends NTP messages to the server at restart and in a regular basis after restart. After receiving the message from the client, the server first exchanges the destination IP address and destination port number of the message with its source IP address and source port number, respectively, and then fills in the required

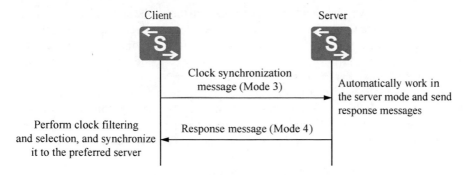

Fig. 16.9 NTP unicast server/client mode

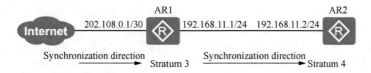

Fig. 16.10 NTP configuration environment

information and sends the message to the client. The server does not need to keep any status information, and the client can freely manage the time interval for sending messages according to the local situation.

16.3.5 Configure NTP

There are many time servers on the Internet, for example, Alibaba Cloud provides seven NTP time servers, i.e., Internet time synchronization servers. Their domain names are as follows.

```
ntp1.aliyun.com
ntp2.aliyun.com
ntp3.aliyun.com
ntp4.aliyun.com
ntp5.aliyun.com
ntp6.aliyun.com
ntp7.aliyun.com
```

The following is a simple experiment to demonstrate how to configure the NTP protocol on a Huawei network device. Figure 16.10 shows the configuration environment for the experiment.

In the network environment shown in Fig. 16.10, AR1 is connected to the Internet as the gateway router of the enterprise and has applied for public network IP address 202.108.0.1/30 through the ISP. AR1 uses the unicast client-server mode of NTP to synchronize with Alibaba cloud time server through the public network. Meanwhile, as the clock source (NTP time server) inside the enterprise network, it still uses the unicast client-server mode of NTP, synchronizing with the time of other network devices in the enterprise. For other network devices in the enterprise, only one router, AR2, is given in this case, and it is used as the NTP client.

In the unicast client-server mode, the clock information can only be synchronized by the client with the server, and the server will not actively synchronize with the client. For a device like AR1 that also needs to function as a local network NTP time server, only after its own clock has been synchronized can it act as an NTP time server to synchronize other devices; and also, only when the server's stratum is smaller than the client's, the client will synchronize with it.

When using the unicast client-server mode of NTP, the administrator needs to configure the master clock in the NTP time server, which requires the use of the system view command ntp-service refclock-master [ip-address] [strtum]. The administrator also needs to use the system view command ntp-service unicast-server ip-address on the NTP client to specify the IP address of the NTP time server to enable the client to synchronize with the server.

In order to configure the synchronization with Alibaba cloud time server on AR1, in this case, ntp1.aliyun.com is chosen as the time server, whose address is 120.25.115.20. Make sure that AR1 has been configured with the interface address and route, and can access the Internet.

```
[AR1]ntp-service unicast-server 120.25.115.20
[AR1]ntp-service refclock-master
```

In the above, "ntp-service unicast-server 120.25.115.20" is a system view command to specify the IP address of the NTP time server in the unicast client-server mode of NTP. In this case, AR1 wants to synchronize the clock with Alibaba cloud time server, so the IP address is set to 120.25.115.20.

The command "ntp-service refclock-master" is a system view command to configure the master clock on the NTP time server. In this case, AR1 not only acts as an NTP client to synchronize clock information from Alibaba cloud time server, but also functions as an NTP time server in the enterprise to provide clock information to other network devices in the enterprise, so the administrator can use this command to set the local clock of the router as the master clock. In this command you can also set the number of stratums. In this case AR1 gets the clock information through an external clock source, so here we do not have to manually specify the stratum information.

Check the NTP status on AR1.

```
<AR1>display ntp-service status
clock status: synchronized
clock stratum: 3
reference clock ID: 120.25.115.20
nominal frequency: 100.0000 Hz
actual frequency: 100.0000 Hz
```

```
clock precision: 2^17
clock offset: -28799204.0460 ms
root delay: 111.35 ms
root dispersion: 7.22 ms
peer dispersion: 1.02 ms
reference time: 11:10:10.292 UTC Mar 19 2020(E21DD192.4AD86EC1)
```

The "display ntp-service status" command enables you to view the NTP status on the router. From the above commands, we can see that the clock status on AR1 is synchronized (clock status:synchronized), the stratum is 3 (clock stratum:3), and the reference clock ID is 120.25.115.20, which is the NTP time server manually specified by the administrator.

Since AR1' own clock has been synchronized, it already has the prerequisites to become an NTP time server. Then configure its NTP client AR2.

```
[AR2]ntp-service unicast-server 192.168.11.1
```

Check the NTP status on AR2.

```
[AR2]display ntp-service status
clock status: synchronized
clock stratum: 4
reference clock ID: 192.168.11.1
nominal frequency: 100.0000 Hz
actual frequency: 100.0000 Hz
clock precision: 2^17
clock offset: 28799747.5500 ms
root delay: 332.64 ms
root dispersion: 0.65 ms
peer dispersion: 304.50 ms
reference time: 22:30:56.086 UTC Mar 19 2020(E21E7120.16096787)
[AR2]
```

As you can see from the above code, the clock status on AR2 is synchronized (clock status:synchronized), the stratum increment is 4 (clock statum:4), and the reference clock ID is 192.168.11.1.

On the router, the administrator can also use the display ntp-service session command to view the status statistics of the NTP session. In an environment of the unicast client-server mode of NTP, all NTP sessions are manually added.

```
[AR2]display ntp-service sessions
     source        reference      stra reach poll now offset delay disper

********************************************************************
  [12345]192.168.11.1   120.25.115.20   3  63  64  -  -8h 111.0  1.0
note: 1 source(master),2 source(peer),3 selected,4 candidate,5
configured, 6 vpn-instance
```

The output of the display ntp-service sessions command shows that there is one NTP session on AR2. The source of this NTP session is 192.168.11.1, the reference clock is 120.25.115.20, and the stratum is 3.

16.4   Exercises

1. Which of the following SNMP messages is sent from the agent on the managed device to the NMS? ( )

   A. Get NextRequest
   B. Get Request
   C. Set Request
   D. Response

2. Which of the following versions of SNMP protocol supports the encryption feature? ( )

   A. SNMPv2c
   B. SNMPv3
   C. SNMPv2
   D. SNMPv1

3. The management station manages network devices through the SNMP protocol. Which SNMP message will the network management station receive when an exception occurs in the managed device? ( )

   A. Get Response message
   B. Trap message
   C. Set Request message
   D. Get Request message

4. In the SNMP protocol, which port number does the agent process use to send alarm messages to the NMS? ( )

   A. 163
   B. 161
   C. 162
   D. 164

5. The following ACLs are applied in the SNMP. Which of the following statements is incorrect ( )?

```
acl number 2000
rule 5 permit source 192.168.1.2 0
rule 10 permit source 192.168.1.3 0
rule 15 permit source 192.168.1.4 0
```

A. The device whose IP address is 192.168.1.5 can use the SNMP service
B. The device whose IP address is 192.168.1.3 can use the SNMP service
C. The device whose IP address is 192.168.1.4 can use the SNMP service
D. The device whose IP address is 192.168.1.2 can use the SNMP service

6. SNMP messages are carried by the TCP. ( )

   A. Correct
   B. Incorrect

7. Illustrate the five major functions of network management defined by OSI.
8. Which four parts does the SNMP system consist of?

Chapter 17
SDN and NFV

The open ecology of the computing industry has brought about the booming development of many fields such as general-purpose hardware, operating systems, virtualization, middleware, cloud computing and software applications. The networking industry is also seeking to change and evolve, with Software Defined Networking (SDN) and Network Functional Virtualization (NFV) being two concepts in the limelight.

This chapter is designed to help engineers understand the concepts of SDN and NFV, the SDN network architecture and NFV key technologies and the history of architecture development. Meanwhile, it is also a brief introduction to Huawei SDN solutions and NFV solutions.

17.1 Overview of Traditional Networks

17.1.1 Traditional Networks and Their Distributed Control Architectures

Traditional network (classical IP network) is a distributed, peer-to-peer control network. As shown in Fig. 17.1, each device in the network has a separate management plane, control plane, and forwarding plane. The control plane of the devices interacts with routing protocols peer-to-peer and then independently generates the forwarding plane to guide the forwarding of messages.

- The management plane mainly includes the device management system and the service management system. The device management system is responsible for managing network topology, device interfaces and device characteristics, and can also deliver configuration scripts to devices. The service management system is responsible for managing services, such as service performance monitoring and service alarm management.

© The Author(s) 2023
Huawei Technologies Co., Ltd., *Data Communications and Network Technologies*,
https://doi.org/10.1007/978-981-19-3029-4_17

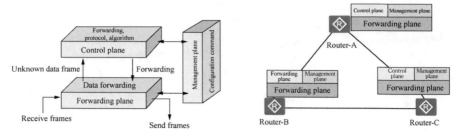

Fig. 17.1 Distributed control architecture of traditional network

- The control plane is responsible for network control, and its main function is protocol processing and computation. For example, routing protocols are used for the calculation of routing information and the generation of routing tables.
- The forwarding plane refers to the device forwarding and processing the user services according to the instructions generated by the control plane. For example, the router forwards the received packets from the corresponding outbound interface according to the routing table generated by the routing protocol.

The following takes a switch as an example to introduce the management plane, control plane and forwarding plane.

- Switch management plane: the management plane provides functions such as operation status monitoring, environment monitoring, log and alarm information processing, system loading and system upgrade. The management plane of the switch is for network managers to manage devices using TELNET, SSH, SNMP, etc., and to support, understand and execute managers' setting commands for various network protocols of network devices. The management plane must pre-set the parameters related to various protocols in the control plane and support intervention in the operation of the control plane when it is necessary.
- Switch control plane: the control plane provides protocol processing, service processing, routing operations, forwarding control, service scheduling, traffic statistics, system security and other functions. The control plane of the switch can control and manage the operations of all network protocols. It offers various network information and forwarding query table entries required before the data is processed and forwarded.
- Switch forwarding plane: the forwarding plane provides high-speed, unblocked data channels to enable the service exchange function between various service modules. The basic task of the switch is to process and forward various types of data on different ports of the switch. Various specific data processing and forwarding processes such as L2/L3/ACL/QoS/multicast/security protection all belong to the tasks performed by the switch forwarding plane.

Traditional networks use a distributed control architecture. Distributed control here means that in traditional IP networks, the control plane for protocol computation and the forwarding plane for message forwarding are located in the same device. After the routing calculation and topology change, each device has to re-calculate the routes, which is called the distributed control process. In traditional IP networks, each device independently collects network information and computes, and is concerned only with its own routing. The disadvantage of this model architecture is the lack of uniformity in the computation of paths by all devices.

The advantage of the traditional network is the decoupling of devices from the protocol, better compatibility between vendors, and the network convergence guaranteed by protocols in case of failures.

17.1.2 Problems Faced by Traditional Networks

1. The network is prone to congestion
   Calculating the forwarding path based on constant bandwidth is prone to network congestion, and the solution is to calculate the forwarding path based on real-time bandwidth. For example, when router C sends a message to router D, Link C-D is the shortest forwarding path. When the service traffic between router C and router D starts to exceed the bandwidth and packet loss occurs, the algorithm will still choose the shortest path for forwarding though other links are available. A global consideration will reveal that the optimal forwarding path at this time should be C-A-D, as shown in Fig. 17.2.
2. Network technology is too complex
   Traditional networks have a lot of protocols. If you want to become a network technology expert, you need to read about 2500 documents of Request for Comment (RFC) related to network equipment. If you read one per day, it would take up to 6 years, and that is only 1/3 of the entire RFC, and the number is still growing.

   There are also countless configuration commands of traditional network. If you want to become a know-all of the devices of a certain manufacturer, you need to master over 10,000 network configuration command lines, and the number is still increasing.
3. Network fault positioning and diagnosis are difficult

Fig. 17.2 Network congestion

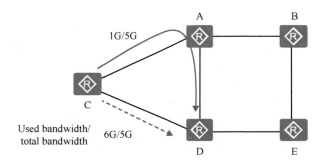

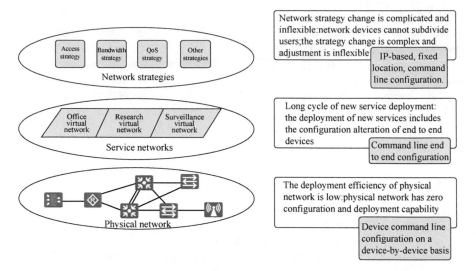

Fig. 17.3 Traditional network service deployment

In traditional operations and maintenance, network faults rely on manual identification, manual positioning and manual diagnosis, making it hard to discover faults. According to the statistics of the Data Center, it takes an average of 76 min to locate a fault, and more than 85% of the faults are found only after complaints. Traditional operation and maintenance cannot effectively and proactively identify and analyze problems.

Traditional operation and maintenance only monitor equipment indicators and lacks correlation analysis of users and network, so sometimes the indicators are normal but users have poor experience.

4. The deployment speed of network services is too slow

Traditional network service deployment is slow and inflexible, as shown in Fig. 17.3.

The goal of network service deployment: network policy enables service free mobility, which is irrelevant to the physical location. New services are rapidly deployed, and the physical network supports zero-configuration deployment, so that plug-and-play can be enabled for devices.

17.2   SDN and OpenFlow Protocol

17.2.1   Concept of SDN

SDN (Software Defined Network) is a new innovative network architecture proposed by Clean Slate Research Group at Stanford University in 2006. SDN proposes three features: separation of transfer and control, centralized control and open programming interfaces. The core concept of SDN is to enable centralized control

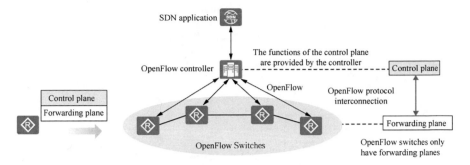

Fig. 17.4 SDN architecture

of the control plane by separating the control plane of the network devices from the forwarding plane so as to provide good support for the innovation of network applications. The SDN architecture is shown in Fig. 17.4.

For the past 30 years, traditional networks have always been fully distributed and have made distinctive achievements, satisfying the needs of a variety of uses. Today, in order to better meet users' needs SDN is trying to get rid of the hardware limitations on the network architecture so that the network can be modified like installing and upgrading software to facilitate the rapid deployment of more applications (Apps) to the network. If you think of the existing network as a cell phone, the goal of SDN is to make an Android system for the network world.

The essence of SDN is to make the network resemble software and enhance the network programmability. SDN is a reconfiguration of the network architecture, rather than a new feature or function. We cannot simply equate SDN with the separation of forwarding and control or OpenFlow protocol. Separation of control and forwarding and separation of management and control are only a means to meet the SDN, and the OpenFlow protocol is only a protocol to meet the SDN.

17.2.2 OpenFlow Protocol

SDN network adopts OpenFlow protocol, which is based on the flow table to forward traffic. The flow table is generally calculated by OpenFlow controller and then distributed to the switch. The OpenFLow switch forwards traffic by querying the flow table. The flow table is variable in length and has all kinds of matching rules and forwarding rules. A network device has multiple flow tables, as shown in Fig. 17.5.

The matching principle of the flow table is that for the existing "table0-table255", the matching priority starts from Table0. Within the same table, it is matched according to the priorities, and the one with higher priority is matched first.

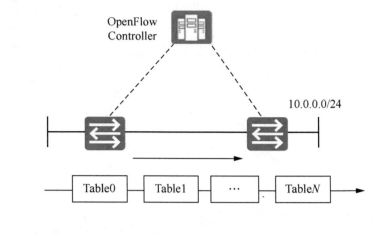

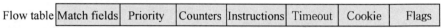

Flow table	Match fields	Priority	Counters	Instructions	Timeout	Cookie	Flags

Fig. 17.5 Flow tables in a network device

OpenFlow is a southbound interface protocol between a controller and a switch. It defines three types of messages, controller-to-switch, asynchronous and symmetric messages, each of which contains additional subtypes.

1. Controller-to-switch: this message is sent by the controller to manage the switch and query information about the switch.
   The controller-to-switch message have the following subtypes.

   - Features message: after an SSL/TCP session is established, the controller sends a features message to the switch requesting information about the switch, and the switch must respond with the features it supports, including basic information such as the interface name, interface MAC address and the rate supported by the interface.
   - Configuration message: the controller can set or query the state of the switch.
   - Modify-State message: the controller can send this message to the switch to manage the state of the switch, i.e., add, delete, change the flow table, and set the interface properties of the switch.
   - Read-State message: the controller can use this message to collect statistical information on the switch.
   - Send-Packet message: the controller can send this message to a specific interface of the switch.

2. Asynchronous: this message is initiated by the switch. When the state of the switch changes, this message is sent to tell the controller about the change in state. The asynchronous message has the following subtypes.

   - Packet-in message: the switch sends a packet-in message to the controller when there is no matching table entry in the flow table or when it matches "send to Controller".
   - Packet-out message: it is a response message from the controller.
   - Flow-Removed message: when a table entry is added to the switch, a timeout period is set. When the timeout expires, the entry is removed. This is when the switch sends a flow-removed message to the controller; the switch also sends this message to the controller when an entry is to be deleted from the flow table.
   - Port-status message: this message can be used to notify the controller when a data path interface is added, deleted or modified.

3. Symmetric: this message has no fixed initiator and can be initiated by the switch or controller, for example, the Hello, Echo, Error messages.

   - Hello message: when an OpenFlow connection is established, the controller and switch will immediately send an OFPT_HELLO message to the other side, and the version field in this message is populated with the highest version number of the OpenFlow protocol supported by the sender; after receiving the message, the receiver will calculate the protocol version number, i.e., choose the smaller one of the version numbers of the sender and the receiver; if the receiver supports this version, it continues to process the connection and the connection is successful; otherwise, the receiver responds with an OFPT_ERROR message with the type field populated with ofp_error_type. OFPET_HELLO_FAILED.
   - Echo message: either switch and controller can initiate an Echo request message, but the receiver must respond with an Echo reply message. This message measures latency and the connectivity between controller and switch, i.e., the heartbeat message.
   - Error messages: when the switch wants to notify the controller of a problem or error, it sends an Error message to the controller.

More and more complete message types can be viewed on the official ONF website.

17.2.3 Introduction to FlowTable

OpenFlow switches, that is, switches that support the OpenFlow protocol, are based on FlowTables to forward messages. Each flow table entry consists of match fields, priority, counters, instructions, timeout, cookie and flags, as shown in Fig. 17.6. The two key elements of forwarding are match fields and instructions.

| Match fields | Priority | Counters | Instructions | Timeout | Cookie | Flags |

Flow table fields can be customized, such as the match fields in this example

Ingress Port	Ether Source	Ether Dst	Ether Type	VLAN ID	VLAN Priority	IP Src	IP Dst	TCP Src Port	TCP Dst Port
3	MAC1	MAC2	0x8100	10	7	IP1	IP2	5321	8080

Fig. 17.6 Composition of stream flow entries

1. Match fields consist of flow table fields, and the fields are matching rules, which can be customized.
2. Instructions are used to describe the processing after matching.

   • Match Fields: the flow table entry match fields (OpenFlow version 1.5.1 supports 45 optional match fields) can match inbound interfaces, physical inbound interfaces, inter-flow table data, Layer 2 message headers, Layer 3 message headers, Layer 4 port numbers and other message fields.
   • Priority: the priority of flow table entries defines the matching order of flow table items, and the entry with higher priority is matched first.
   • Counters: the counters of flow table entries can count how many messages and bytes can be matched to the flow table entry.
   • Instructions: the instructions set of flow table entries defines the instructions to be performed by the messages matching the flow table entry. When a message matches a flow table entry, the instructions set contained in each flow table entry is executed. These instructions affect the message, the instructions set, and the pipeline flow.
   • Timeouts: the timeouts of flow table entries include idle time and hard time.

     – Idle Time: after the idle time timeout, the flow table entry will be deleted if no message matches it.
     – Hard Time: after the hard time timeout, the flow table entry will be deleted regardless of whether there are messages matching it.

   • Cookie: it is the identifier of the flow table entry delivered by the controller.
   • Flags: this field changes the management of the flow entry.

17.2.4 SDN Network Architecture

SDN is a reconfiguration of the traditional network architecture from the original distributed control network architecture to the centralized control network architecture (Fig. 17.7).

Fig. 17.7 SND network architecture

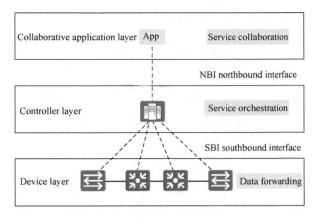

1. The collaborative application layer mainly includes various upper layer applications to meet user needs. Typical collaborative application layer applications include OSS, OpenStack, etc. OSS is responsible for service collaboration of the whole network, and OpenStack cloud platform is generally used in data centers, responsible for service collaboration of network, computing and storage. There are other collaborative application layer applications. For example, users want to deploy a security App, and this App does not care about the specific deployment location of the device and only calls the northbound interface of the controller, like Block (source IP, Dest IP), and then the controller will give instructions to each network device, and the instructions will vary according to the southbound protocol.
2. The entity at the controller layer is the SDN controller, which is also the most central part of the SDN network architecture. The controller layer is the brain of the SDN system, and its core function is to implement network service orchestration.
3. Network devices in the device layer can receive commands from the controller and perform device forwarding.
4. Northbound interface (NBI) is the interface of the controller connected to the collaborative application layer, mainly RESTful. RESTful is a network application design style and development approach based on HTTP, and can be defined using XML format or JSON format.
5. Southbound interface (SBI) is the protocol for the controller to interact with devices, which includes NETCONF, SNMP, OpenFlow, OVSDB, etc.

17.3   Overview of NFV

17.3.1   Concepts of NFV

In recent years, IT technologies such as virtualization and cloud computing have flourished, and traditional applications are gradually cloud-based and deployed on private, public or hybrid clouds in a software-based manner.

Network Function Virtualization (NFV) builds a Data Center Network (DCN) by integrating many different types of network devices (such as Servers, Switches and Storage), forms a Virtual Machine (VM) through virtualization technology, and then deploys traditional Communications Technology (CT) services to the VM.

When we talk about VNF (Virtualized Network Function), we usually refer to tasks carried out after the virtualization of carrier IMS (IP Multi-Media Sub-System, a generic term for various network entities in a communication network), CPE (Customer Premise Equipment), and other traditional network elements (network elements, including servers, storage, switches, and network services)., including servers, storage, switches and routers). After the hardware generalization, the traditional network elements are no longer embedded hardware and software products, but are mounted on the general hardware as pure software, i.e., NFV Infrastructure (NFVI).

The evolution of the NFV concept is as follows.

In October 2012, 13 major carriers (AT&T, Verizon, VDF, DT, T-Mobile, BT, Telefonica, etc.) released the first version of the NFV white paper at the SDN and OpenFlow World Congress, and established the ISG (Industry Specification Group) to promote the requirements definition and system architecture formulation for network virtualization.

In 2013, the NFV ISG (Industry Specification Group) of the European Telecommunications Standards Institute (ETSI) conducted the first phase of research and developed related standards. It mainly defines the requirements and architecture of network function virtualization and sorts out the standardization process of different interfaces.

In 2015, the NFV research entered the second phase. The main goal of this phase of research is to build an interoperable NFV ecosystem, promote broader industry participation, and ensure that the requirements defined in the first phase are met. In the meantime, it also clarifies related standards such as NFV and SDN, as well as collaborative relationship of open-source projects, etc. The second phase of NFV research is divided into five working groups: IFA (Interface and Architecture), EVE (Evolution and Ecosystem), REL (Reliability), SEC (Security) and TST (Testing, Experimentation and Open Source). These working groups mainly discuss the documentation framework of deliverables and delivery plans.

The ETSI NFV standards organization cooperated with the Linux Foundation to launch the open-source project OPNFV (aiming to provide an integrated, open reference platform) to bring together the industry's superior resources and actively build the NFV industrial ecology. 2015 saw the release of the first version of OPNFV, which further promoted the commercial deployment of NFV.

17.3.2   Value of NFV

NFV is proposed by carriers to solve the problems of overelaborate hardware, complex deployment, operation and maintenance, and difficulties in service innovation of telecommunications. While reconfiguring telecom networks, the NFV brings the following values to carriers.

1. Shortened service launch time.

   In a network with NFV architecture, adding new service nodes becomes exceptionally simple. No more complex work surveys and hardware installation processes are required. For service deployment, you need to apply virtualized resources (computing, storage, network, etc.) and load the software, making network deployment much easier. At the same time, if you need to update the service logic, you only need to update the software or load new service modules to complete the service orchestration, so business innovation becomes simpler.

2. Reduced network construction cost

   First, the virtualized network elements can be merged into general devices to obtain economies of scale. Second, the network resource utility and efficiency are increased to reduce the networking cost. NFV adopts cloud computing technology to build a unified resource pool using generalized hardware, and dynamically allocate resources according to the actual needs of the services so as to share resources and improve resource utilization and efficiency. For example, it solves the resource utilization problem caused by the tidal effect of services through automatic capacity expansion and reduction.

3. Improved network operation and maintenance efficiency

   Automated centralized management can improve operational efficiency and reduce operation and maintenance costs. Some of the examples are the automation of centralized management of hardware units in data centers, the automation of application lifecycle management based on MANO (Management and Orchestration), and the network automation based on NFV/SDN collaboration.

4. The building of an open ecosystem

   The traditional telecom network is a closed system because of its proprietary hardware and software model. On the other hand, the telecom network under NFV architecture, based on the standard hardware platform and virtualized software architecture, is easier to open the platform and interfaces to introduce third-party developers, so that carriers can build an open ecosystem with third-party partners.

17.3.3   Key Technologies for NFV

On the road to NFV, virtualization is the foundation and cloudization is the key.

1. Virtualization

In traditional telecom networks, individual network elements are implemented by dedicated hardware. The problem with this approach is that, on the one hand, building a network requires a lot of interoperability testing and installation and configuration of different hardware, which is time-consuming and laborious. On the other hand, service innovation is dependent on the hardware vendors, which usually takes a long time and is thus difficult to meet the carrier's demand for service innovation.

In this context, carriers want to introduce the virtualization model, which make network elements resemble software so that they can be run on a general infrastructure (including general servers, storage, switches, etc.). Virtualization has the characteristics of partitioning, isolation and encapsulation, and is independent relative to hardware, so it can well meet the needs of NFV, as shown in Fig. 17.8.

By using general hardware, firstly, carriers can reduce the cost of procuring dedicated hardware; secondly, service software can be developed rapidly and iteratively, which also allows operators to quickly innovate their services and enhance their competitiveness; and finally, this also empowers operators to enter the cloud computing market.

2. Cloudization

Cloudization is the process of migrating existing services to a cloud computing platform. As defined by the National Institute of Standards and Technology,

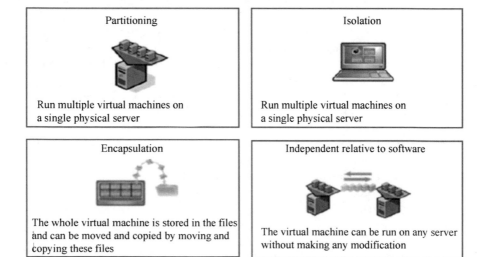

Fig. 17.8 Virtualization characteristics

cloud computing is a model for enabling ubiquitous, convenient, on-demand network access to a shared pool of configurable computing resources (e.g., networks, servers, storage, applications and services) that can be rapidly provisioned and released with minimal management effort or service provider interaction.

Cloud computing services should have the following characteristics.

- On-demand self-service: cloud computing enables on-demand self-service of IT resources, so that resources can be requested and released without the intervention of IT administrators.
- Extensive network access: the network can be accessed anywhere, anytime as long as there is a network.
- Resource pooling: resources in the resource pool, including network, server, storage and other resources, are available to users.
- Fast resilient scaling: resources can be quickly provisioned and released. Resources can be used upon request and reclaimed immediately upon release.
- Measurable service: billing function. The basis for the billing is that the resources used are measurable. For example, the number of CPUs, occupied storage space, and bandwidth of the network are combined for billing based on hours of use.

The cloudization of network functions in carrier networks mainly takes advantage of both resource pooling and fast resilient scaling.

17.3.4   NFV Architecture

The NFV architecture is divided into functional modules such as NFVI, VNF and MANO, and also supports the existing OSS/BSS (Operation Support System/Business Support System) functional modules, as shown in Fig. 17.9.

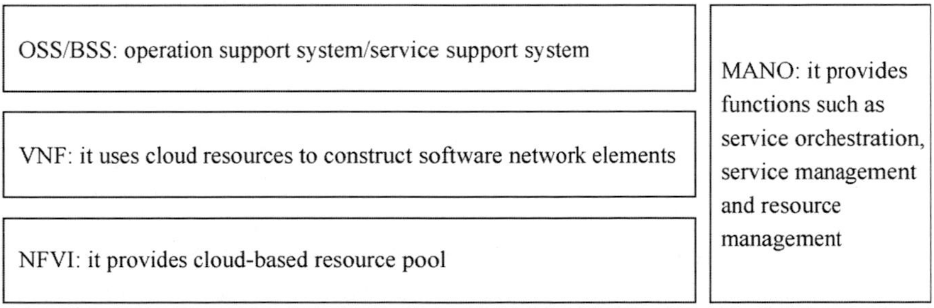

OSS/BSS: operation support system/service support system

VNF: it uses cloud resources to construct software network elements

NFVI: it provides cloud-based resource pool

MANO: it provides functions such as service orchestration, service management and resource management

Fig. 17.9 NFV architecture

1. OSS/BSS: it is the management functional module of the service provider, which is not a functional component within the NFV framework. However, MANO and network elements need to provide interface support to OSS/BSS.
2. VNF: it refers to the virtual machine and the service network elements, network function software and others deployed on the virtual machine. VNF can also be understood as an App of various different network functions, which is the software implementation of the carrier's traditional network elements (IMS, EPC, BRAS, CPE, etc.).
3. NFVI: NFV infrastructure contains a hardware layer and a virtualization layer, which provides the operating environment for VNFs. It is also referred to as COTS and CloudOS in the industry.

   - COTS (Commercial Off-The-Shelf), or general hardware, emphasizes easy availability and versatility. For example, Huawei FusionServer series hardware servers.
   - CloudOS: platform software for cloud-based devices, which can be regarded as an operating system for the telecom industry. CloudOS provides the ability to virtualize hardware devices, which can turn physical computing, storage and network resources into virtual resources to be used by upper-layer software. For example, Huawei cloud operating system Fusion Sphere.

4. MANO: the introduction of MANO is to solve the problem of delivering network services in the NFV multi-CT/IT vendor environment, including vertically opening up the management layers and quickly adapting to and interconnecting new network elements from new vendors. The MANO includes three parts, namely, NFVO (Network Functions Virtualization Orchestrator, which orchestrates and manages the entire NFV infrastructure, software resources and network services), VNFM (Virtualized Network Function Manager, which is responsible for the lifecycle management of VNFs, such as instantiation, configuration and shutdown), VIM (Virtualized Infrastructure Manager, which is responsible for resource management of NFVI and usually runs in the corresponding infrastructure site; its main functions include resource discovery, management and allocation of virtual resources, fault handling, etc.).

   The solutions of each functional module of NFV architecture can be provided by different vendors, which increases the complexity of system integration while improving system developability.

17.3.5   Huawei NFV Solutions

In Huawei's NFV solution (see Fig. 17.10), Huawei CloudStack can provide some functions of NFNI: computing can be provided by FusionCompute, the storage can be provided by FusionStorage, and network can be provided by FusionNetwork.

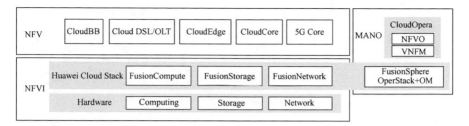

Fig. 17.10 Huawei NFV solution

FusionNetwork is not a specific product, but a generic term for network virtualization or software-defined network functional modules. Huawei CloudStack is capable of comprehensive virtualization of computing, storage and network resources, and can unify the management, monitoring and optimization of physical hardware virtualization resources.

Huawei VNF solutions include CloudBB, Cloud DSL/OLT, CloudEdge, CloudCore and 5G Core, which correspond to virtualization solutions for virtual network elements carried by different kinds of core networks. Huawei provides comprehensive cloud-based solutions for carriers' wireless networks, bearer networks, transmission networks, access networks, core networks and so on. [Note: DSL is a digital subscriber line; and OLT is an optical line terminal.

17.4 Exercises

1. What is the relationship between SDN and NFV?
2. What is the relationship between SDN and NFV in Huawei solution?

Chapter 18
Network Programming and Automation

New protocols, technologies, delivery, and operation and maintenance models continue to emerge in the field of network engineering. Traditional networks are challenged by new connectivity needs such as cloud computing and artificial intelligence. Meanwhile, enterprises are also constantly seeking convenience, flexibility and resiliency in their business. Against this backdrop, network automation is becoming increasingly imperative.

Network programming and automation aim to simplify network engineers' network configuration, management, monitoring, operations and other tasks, and improve the efficiency of their deployment, operation and maintenance. This chapter is designed to guide network engineers through an initial understanding of how to use Python programming to enable network automation.

18.1 Introduction to Network Programming and Automation

The following are some classic network operation and maintenance scenarios that you may have encountered in your work.

1. Device upgrade: there are thousands of network devices in the network, and you need to upgrade the devices in a regular basis and in bulk.
2. Configuration audits: enterprises need to conduct configuration audits on devices, for example, requiring all devices to be enabled with STelnet function and all Ethernet switches to be configured with Spanning Tree security. You need to quickly identify devices that do not meet the requirements.
3. Configuration changes: because of the network security requirements, the accounts and passwords of devices need to be changed every 3 months. You need to delete the original accounts and create new ones on thousands of network devices.

© The Author(s) 2023
Huawei Technologies Co., Ltd., *Data Communications and Network Technologies*,
https://doi.org/10.1007/978-981-19-3029-4_18

Traditional network operation and maintenance require network engineers to manually login to the network devices, manually view and execute configuration commands, and screen the configuration results with their bare eyes. This working method that heavily relies on "humans" is an enduring and inefficient operation process, and the operation process is not audited.

Network automation, that is, using tools for automatic network deployment, operation and maintenance, can gradually reduce the reliance on "humans". This can be a desirable solution to the traditional network operation and maintenance problems. There are also many open-source tools for network automation, such as Ansible, SaltStack, Puppet, and Chef.

From the perspective of building network engineering capabilities, it is more recommended that engineers have programming skills that focus on network programming. Network programming, in a broad sense, is the development of programs to send and receive information over the network. The main task of network programming is to assemble the information on the sending end through a defined protocol, and to parse the packets according to the specified protocols at the receiving end to extract the corresponding information for communication purposes. The most important work in the process is packet assembly, packet filtering, packet capture and packet analysis, and of course some processing is needed at the end. We may come into contact with five parts, that is, code, development tools, database, server setup and web design.

In recent years, with the rise of network automation technology, the abilities to program, of which Python is a major one, become a new skill requirement for network engineers. Automation scripts written in Python can perform repetitive, time-consuming and regular operations excellently.

What can network automation do? One of the most intuitive examples is the automated configuration of devices. We can break this process into two steps: writing a configuration file and writing Python code to push the configuration file to the device. This approach is easier for network engineers who are new to network programming and automation to understand. This chapter focuses on how this approach enables network automation. As shown in Fig. 18.1, first, write the script using command lines, and then pass it to the device to run via Telnet/SSH.

18.2   Overview of Programming Languages

A computer programming language is the most important tool for programming. It is a language with certain syntax rules that a computer can accept and process. Since the birth of computers, computer languages have gone through several stages, including machine languages, assembly languages and high-level languages.

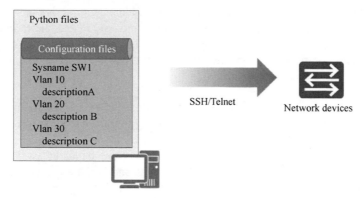

Fig. 18.1 Write a Python script to pass the configuration to the device for automated configuration

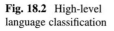

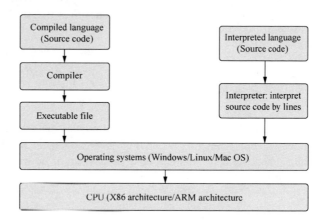

18.2.1 Classification of High-Level Programming Languages

According to whether the language needs to be compiled before execution, high-level languages can be classified into compiled languages that require compilation, and interpreted languages that do not need compilation, as shown in Fig. 18.2.

1. Compiled language

   Compiled languages have separate compilation and execution processes. Before a program is executed, a compilation process is needed to compile the source code into a binary file of machine language. The executable programs generated by compiled languages do not need recompilation to run and they directly use the compiled results, which makes them more efficient. However, executable programs are platform-specific and cannot be executed in other platforms. C, C++ and Go languages are typical compiled languages.

   Figure 18.3 shows the process of compiled language from source code to program: the source code needs to be compiled into machine instructions by compiler and assembler, and then the machine language program is generated by link library functions of the linker. The machine language program has to match the instruction set of the CPU, and is loaded into memory by the loader when it is run. Then the CPU executes the instructions. The source code of a compiled language is compiled and converted into a format that the computer can execute, such as .exe, .dll, and .ocx.

2. Interpreted languages

Interpreted languages do not require prior compilation, and the source code is directly interpreted into machine code, so the program can be run as long as the platform provides the corresponding interpreter. Interpreted languages require the source code to be interpreted into machine code and executed every time the program is run, which is inefficient. Both Python and Perl are typical interpreted languages.

Figure 18.4 shows the process of interpreted languages from source code to program: the source code file (Python file) is converted into a byte code file (.pyc file) by an interpreter and then run on a Python virtual machine (Python VM, PVM).

18.2.2 Computing Technology Stack and Program Execution Process

As mentioned earlier, programming languages can be classified as machine languages, assembly languages and high-level languages. Machine languages consist of binary machine code that can be directly recognized by computers. Since machine language is obscure and difficult to understand, people have made a simple

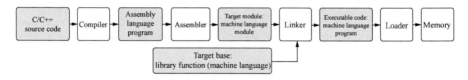

Fig. 18.3 The process of compiling a language from source code to program

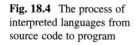

Fig. 18.4 The process of interpreted languages from source code to program

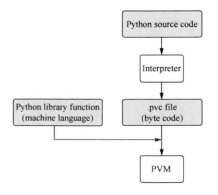

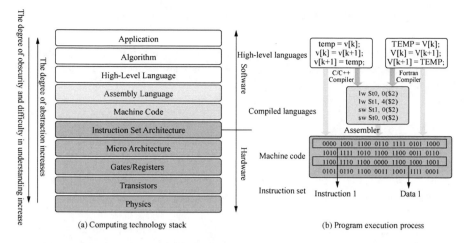

Fig. 18.5 Computing technology stack and program execution process

encapsulation of hardware instructions consisting of 0s and 1s to make them easier to be recognized and memorized by programmers (e.g., MOV, ADD), which is the assembly language. Both of these languages are low-level languages, while languages such as C, C++, Java, Python, Pascal, Lisp, Prolog and Fortran are high-level languages.

Among all programming languages, only the source programs written in machine language can be directly understood and executed by computers; programs written in other programming languages must first be "translated" into machine language programs that computers can recognize using language processing programs.

Figure 18.5 illustrates the computational technology stack and the program execution process.

In the computing stack shown in Fig. 18.5a, we can see the bottom layer of hardware, consisting of physics and transistors for implementing gate circuits and registers, which then constitute the CPU micro architecture, whose instruction set is the interface of the hardware and the software. Applications use the instructions defined in the instruction set to drive the hardware to perform the computation. Applications are usually developed using high-level languages such as C, C++, Java, Go and Python.

In the execution of a program shown in Fig. 18.5b, the high-level language first needs to be compiled into assembly language and then converted into binary machine code by the assembler according to the CPU instruction set. A program exists on a disk in the form of a stack of binary machine code consisting of instructions and data, which is also commonly referred to as a binary file.

18.3   Python Language

Python is a high-level object-oriented programming language. Programs written in Python language are cross-platform, and Python can be seen everywhere from clients, servers to Webs and mobile.

18.3.1   What Is Python

Python is an object-oriented interpreted computer programming language invented by Dutchman Guido van Rossum in 1989, and the first publicly available version of Python was released in 1991.

Python is a purely free software, whose source code and interpreter are under the GPL (GNU General Public License) protocol. Its syntax is clean and clear, with the mandatory use of White Space as a statement indent as one of its features.

Python has a rich and powerful library. It is often referred to as a glue language that can easily integrate various modules made in other languages (especially C/C++). A common application scenario is to use Python to quickly generate a prototype of a program (and sometimes even the final interface of the program) and then rewrite parts of it that have special requirements in a more appropriate programming language. For example, a graphics rendering module in a 3D game with particularly high-performance requirements can be rewritten in C/C++ and then wrapped into an extended class library that Python can call. It is important to note that you may need to consider platform issues when using extended class libraries, and some libraries may not provide cross-platform implementations.

Although Python source code files (.py) can be directly executed using Python commands, Python does not actually interpret Python source code straightly; instead, Python source code is compiled to generate Python byte code (the extensions of byte code files are generally .pyc), which is then executed by the Python Virtual Machine (PVM). The Python here is an interpreted language, meaning that it interprets the Python byte code, rather than the Python source code. The basic idea of this mechanism is the same as Java and .NET.

Although Python also has its own virtual machine, unlike the virtual machines of Java or .NET, the Python virtual machine here is a more advanced virtual machine. The "advanced" here is unlike the advanced in the usual sense, and it does not mean the Python virtual machine is more powerful than Java or .NET virtual machines. Instead, it means that Python virtual machine is farther away from the real machine than Java or .NET. Or, you could say that the Python virtual machine is a more abstract virtual machine.

The execution of the Python program source code is shown in Fig. 18.6.

1. Install Python and the runtime environment on the operating system.
2. Write the Python source code.

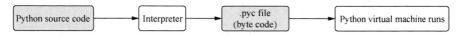

Fig. 18.6 Python source code execution process

3. The interpreter runs Python source code and interprets it to generate a .pyc file (byte code).
4. The Python virtual machine converts the byte code into the machine language.
5. The hardware executes the machine language.

18.3.2 Application Areas of Python

Python is a cross-platform programming language, and in theory, it can run on any operating system platform. The current common operating system platforms are Windows, Mac OS X and Linux.

Python is easy to learn, has various third-party libraries and a fast operation speed, so it has an exceptionally wide range of applications. Python's areas of application mainly include the following.

- Linux/Unix operations and maintenance.
- Command-line program development.
- GUI program development (PyQt, Kivy, etc.).
- Web program development (Django and other frameworks).
- Mobile App development (PyQt, Kivy, etc.).
- Server program development (based on protocols such as Socket)
- Web crawlers (data sources for search engines, deep learning, etc.)
- Data analysis.
- Deep learning.
- Scientific computing.

Although not all of Python's application areas are listed here, these listed areas alone cover the vast majority of the development scenarios. Readers who have used Mac OS X or Linux will find that the Python interpreter is already built into these two operating systems, which means that Python programs can be run directly on Mac OS X and Linux. Therefore, many operations and maintenance engineers are accustomed to using Python for many automated operations. For the currently popular deep learning, Python has become its first language. Therefore, from all angles, whether you are a student, a programmer, a data analyst or a scientist, you cannot live without Python. Python has become the world language of programming languages.

This chapter focuses on how to use Python for network programming and to manage network devices.

18.3.3   How Python Code Works

Python can run codes in two ways: interactive mode and scripted mode.

Programming in the interactive mode (i.e., interactive programming) does not require the creation of a script file, and code can be written by the interactive mode of the Python interpreter. Figure 18.7 illustrates the process of interactive programming on a Windows system. [Note: in Fig. 18.7, Print( ) is a built-in Python function that serves to output the contents in the parentheses.]

Code written in the scripted mode of programming (i.e., scripted programming) can be run on a variety of Python interpreters or integrated development environments. For example, IDLE, Atom, Visual Studio, Pycharm, and Anaconda that come with Python. A typical script-based programming process is shown in Fig. 18.8. First, write a Python script using Notepad software, save the script file and change its extension to .py, and then execute the script file in the Python interpreter.

```
                  Select the command prompt  -  python                    —   □   ×
                 d:\python>
                 d:\python>python
                 Python 3.8.3 (tags/v3.8.3:6f8c832, May 13 2020, 22:37:
                 02) [MSC v.1924 64 bit (AMD64)] on win32
                 Type "help", "copyright", "credits" or "license" for m
                 ore information.
1.Input    ←    >>> print("hello world")
2.Output  ←    hello world
3.Input    ←    >>> a = 1
4.Input    ←    >>> b = 2
5.Input    ←    >>> print(a+b)
6.Output  ←    3
                 >>> ▮
```

Fig. 18.7   The interactive programming process

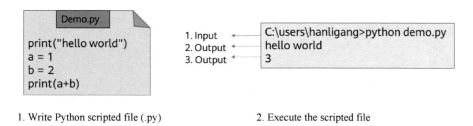

Demo.py

```
print("hello world")
a = 1
b = 2
print(a+b)
```

1. Input   ←   C:\users\hanligang>python demo.py
2. Output ←   hello world
3. Output ←   3

1. Write Python scripted file (.py)   2. Execute the scripted file

Fig. 18.8   The scripted programming process

18.3.4   *Coding Specifications of Python*

Coding specifications are the naming rules, code indentation, code and statement splitting and so on that should be followed when writing code in Python. Good coding specifications help improve the readability of code and make it easier to maintain and modify.

1. Suggestions for the use of semicolons, blank lines, parentheses and spaces.

Semicolons: Python programs allow semicolons at the end of lines, but it is not suggested to use semicolons to isolate statements. It is recommended that each statement occupy a separate line. If there are multiple statements on a line, they can be separated by semicolons.

Blank lines: blank lines can be used to separate different functions or statement blocks so as to distinguish between two pieces of code and improve the readability of the code.

Parentheses: parentheses can be used to continue long statements, and unnecessary brackets are generally eliminated.

Spaces: it is not recommended to use spaces within the parentheses. You can decide whether to add spaces on both sides of an operator according to your personal habits.

2. Identifier naming conventions.

Python identifiers are commonly used to represent the names of constants, variables, functions, and other objects. Identifiers usually consist of letters, numbers and underlines, but they cannot begin with a number. Identifiers are case-sensitive and do not allow renaming. If an identifier does not conform to the naming convention, the compiler will output a SyntaxError error message when it runs the code. As shown in Fig. 18.9, the fifth identifier starts with a number, which is an incorrect identifier.

3. Code indentation.

When writing conditional and looping statements in Python, you need to use the concept of code blocks. A code block is a set of statements that are executed when certain conditions are met. In Python programs, code indentation can be used to delimit a code block. If a code block contains two or more statements, they must have the same amount of indentation, and the Python language uses code indentation and colons to distinguish between levels of code. For Python, code indentation is a syntax rule.

1. Value assignment	--	User_ID = 10	print (User_ID)
2. Value assignment	--	User_id = 20	print (user_id)
3. String value assignment	--	User_Name = 'Richard'	print (User_Name)
4. Value assignment	--	Count = 1 + 1	pinrt (Count)
5. Error identifier	--	4_passwd = "Huawei"	print (4_passwd)

Fig. 18.9 Identifier naming specification

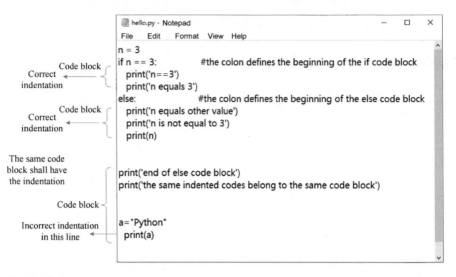

Fig. 18.10 Code blocks and indentations

When writing code, it is recommended to use four spaces for indentation. If the wrong indentation is used in the code, an IndentationError message will be returned when the program is run. The judgment statements shown in Fig. 18.10 list the beginning and end of code blocks, as well as examples of correct and incorrect indentation. The if line and the else line in the figure belong to the same code block and have the same indentation. The last line print (a) belongs to the same block as the if and else lines, so the indentation should be the same.

4. Use comments

Comments are explanatory notes added to the program that can enhance the readability of the program. As shown in Fig. 18.11, in Python programs, comments are divided into single-line comments and multi-line comments. Single-line comments begin with # and end at the end of the line. Multi-line comments can contain multiple lines of contents that are contained within a pair of triple quotes ("'…'" or """…""").

5. The structure of code file.

A complete Python source code file generally contains an interpreter and encoding format declarations, documentation strings, module imports and runtime code.

If you need to call classes from the standard library or other third-party libraries in your program, you need to first use the "import" or "from … import" statement to import the relevant module. The import statement is always located at the top of the file after the module comment or documentation string. Figure 18.12 is an example of the structure of a source code file.

- The interpreter declaration is used to specify the path to the compiler that runs this file (the compiler is installed via a non-default path or there are multiple

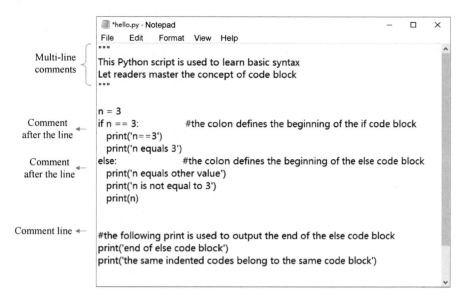

Fig. 18.11 Comments

Fig. 18.12 Structure of
source code file

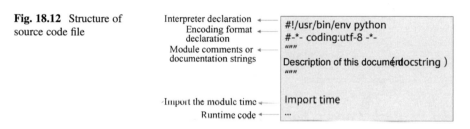

Python compilers). The interpreter declaration in the first line of this example
can be omitted on Windows operating systems.

- The encoding format declaration is used to specify the encoding type used by
  this program and to read the source code in the specified encoding type.
  Python 2 uses ASCII encoding by default (Chinese is not supported), and
  Python 3 supports UTF-8 encoding by default (Chinese is supported).
- The documentation string serves as a general introduction to the program's
  functionality.
- The module import section imports the time module, which is a built-in Python
  module that provides functions for handling time-related issues.

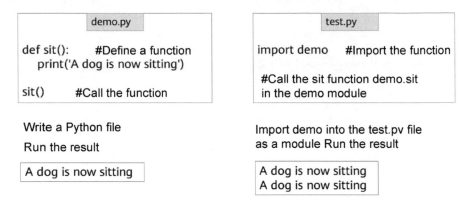

Fig. 18.13 Functions and modules

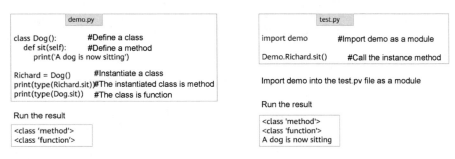

Fig. 18.14 Classes and methods

18.3.5   Basic Concepts of Python

1. Data types of Python

   The most basic data types in Python are boolean (True/False), integers, floating-point numbers and strings, and all data in Python (boolean, integers, floating point numbers, strings and even large data structures, functions and programs) exists as objects. This makes the Python language extremely uniform.

2. Functions and modules of Python

   A function is an organized, reusable piece of code that improves the modularity and code utilization of a program. Functions can be defined using the keyword def.

   A module is a saved Python file that can be composed of functions or classes. The only difference between a module and a regular Python program is that they serve different purposes. Modules can be called by other programs and therefore usually do not have a main function. The definition and call of functions and the import and call of modules are shown in Fig. 18.13.

3. Classes and methods of Python

A class is a description of a collection that has the same properties and methods. Classes can be defined using the keyword class. The functions of an instantiated class are called methods. When defining methods, the class must carry the keyword self and it represents the created class instance itself. Figure 18.14 illustrates how a defining class and instantiable class call the instance.

18.4 Manage Network Devices with Python

18.4.1 Introduction to Telnet

Telnet defines the Network Virtual Terminal (NVT). It describes a standard representation of data and command sequences transmitted over the Internet, thus shielding differences across platforms and operating systems, such as different commands for line breaks on different platforms. In order to distinguish Telnet commands from ordinary data, Telnet uses escape sequences. Each escape sequence consists of two bytes. The first byte is 0xFF, called IAC (Interpret as Command, which is an escape character indicating that the byte following the character is the command code); and the second byte is the code of the command to be executed. Telnet can be used on Windows or Linux systems to remotely configure network devices such as Huawei routers and switches.

The telnetlib is a module in the Python standard library. It provides a class telnetlib.Telnet that implements the functions of Telnet. Table 18.1 shows the

Table 18.1 Methods of telnetlib module

Methods	Functions
Telnet.open(host,port = 0 [, timeout])	Connect to a host. The optional second argument is the port number, which defaults to the standard Telnet port (23). The optional timeout parameter specifies a timeout in seconds for blocking operations like the connection attempt (if not specified, the global default timeout setting will be used).
Telnet.read_until(expected, timeout = None)	Read until a given byte string (b") expected is encountered or until timeout seconds have passed. When no match is found, return whatever is available instead, possibly empty bytes. Raise EOFError if the connection is closed and no cooked data is available.
Telnet.read_all( )	Read all data until EOF as bytes; block until connection closed.
Telnet.read_very_eager( )	Read everything that can be without blocking in I/O (eager), return the byte string Raise EOFError if connection closed and no cooked data available.
Telnet.write(buffer)	Write a byte string to the socket, doubling any IAC characters. This can block if the connection is blocked. May raise OSError if the connection is closed.
Telnet.close( )	Close the connection.

methods defined by the telnetlib module, where different functions can be enabled by calling different methods of the Telnet class of the telnetlib module.

18.4.2   Manage Huawei Routers with Telnet

This case will show how to import the telnetlib module using Python script file, how to configure Huawei router via Telnet and how to change the device name, create VLAN, and set the interface IP address of a Huawei router.

1. First, configure the interface IP address of the Huawei router.

```
Enter system view, return user view with Ctrl+Z.
[Huawei] interface GigabitEthernet 0/0/0
[Huawei-GigabitEthernet0/0/0] ip address 192.168.80.99 24
[Huawei-GigabitEthernet0/0/0] quit
```

2. Configure the router to allow Telnet.

```
[Huawei] user-interface vty 0 4
[Huawei-ui-vty0-4] authentication-mode password
Please configure the login password (maximum length 16) : huawei@123
[Huawei-ui-vty0-4] user privilege level 15
[Huawei-ui-vty0-4] quit
```

3. Use Telnet to login to the router on Windows, and observe the interaction process.

```
C:\Users\hanlg>telnet 192.168.80.99
Login authentication
Password:
<Huawei>system-view
Enter system view, return user view with Ctrl+Z.
[Huawei] quit
```

4. Based on the Telnet interaction in the previous step, write a Python script to read the Telnet output using the telnetlib module, and then enter the Telnet command to configure the network device.

```
import telnetlib                    #Import telnetlib module
host = '192.168.80.99'              #Specify the IP address to login to the
device
password = 'huawei@123'            #Specify the password to login to the
device
tn = telnetlib.Telnet(host)         #Login to the device via Telnet
tn.read_until(b'Password:')         #Read until the echo message (the
message returned by the device) is "Password:"
```

```
   tn.write(password.encode('ascii')+b'\n')    #Enter the password of
code ASCII and enter a new line
   #Enter the system view, and change the device name
   tn.read_until(b'<Huawei>')              #Output and read until the message
"<Huawei>"
   tn.write(b'system-view'+b'\n')            #Enter the command system and
enter a new line
   tn.read_until(b'[Huawei]')             #Output and read until the message
"[Huawei]"
   tn.write(b'sysname R1'+b'\n')             #Change the router name to R1
   tn.read_until(b'[R1]')                #Read until the echo message "[R1]"
   #Create VLAN 2
   tn.write(b'vlan 2'+b'\n')               #Enter the command to create vlan 2
   tn.read_until(b'vlan2]')               #Output and read until the message
"vlan2]"
   tn.write(b'quit'+b'\n')               #Enter the command to exit the vlan2
view
   tn.read_until(b'[R1]')                #Output and read until the message
"[R1]"
   #Enter the interface view, and configure the interface IP address
   tn.write(b'interface GigabitEthernet 0/0/1'+b'\n')   #Enter the
command and enter the interface configuration mode
   tn.read_until(b'1]')                 #Output and read until the message "1]"
   tn.write(b'ip address 10.1.1.1 24'+b'\n')    #Enter the command to
configure the interface IP address and subnet mask
   tn.read_until(b'1]')                 #Output and read until the message "1]"
   tn.close()                     #Close the Telnet connection
```

The encode() and decode() functions of Python are used to encode and decode strings in the specified way. In this case, password.encode(' ascii') means to convert the string huawei@123 to ASCII. Here the encoding format follows the official requirements of the telnetlib module.

Python prefixes the string with a b, such as b'string', to convert the string to bytes. In this case, b'Password:' indicates that the string Password: is converted to a byte-type string. The encoding format here follows the official requirements of the telnetlib module.

18.5 Exercises

1. Python is a compiled language. ( )

   A. Correct
   B. Incorrect

2. Briefly describe the naming specification for Python identifiers.

Index

A

AAA authentication, 83, 84, 88, 89

Access control list (ACL), vii, 307–328, 337, 338, 476, 488, 490, 496, 509, 510, 522

Access link, 243, 244

Access point (AP), 8, 9, 270, 363, 365–371, 373–389, 391, 392, 394–401, 403, 404, 418, 480, 482, 484, 485

Accounting, 208, 307, 319

Acknowledgement number, 42–44, 46, 48, 50

Address pool, 76, 332–334, 337, 342, 344, 347, 351–360, 432, 464, 485, 487, 488, 493, 494

Address resolution, 421–423

Address resolution protocol (ARP), 51, 59–64, 67, 69, 70, 224, 228, 258, 408, 418, 422, 423, 439

Advanced ACL, 309, 310, 312, 316–318, 328, 495, 496

Anycast addresses, 413, 417–420, 439

Application layer, 15, 18–21, 23–37, 39–41, 50, 51, 67, 68, 70, 74, 90, 369, 469, 511, 529

Authentication, 8, 9, 24, 31, 83–85, 87, 89, 91, 92, 108, 110, 220, 307, 319–322, 327, 378, 381, 386–389, 391, 395, 398, 402–404, 411, 441, 443, 445–450, 452–457, 459, 463, 467–469, 490, 494, 495, 503, 506, 507

Authentication header, 411

Authentication negotiation, 445, 448

Authorization, 307, 319

Autonomous system (AS), 194–196, 206, 207, 210, 437

B

Backbone router, 206

Backup designated router (BDR), 193, 195, 202–205

Basic ACL, 309, 310, 312, 314–317, 328, 495, 496

Basic service set (BSS), 374–376, 403, 533, 534

Basic service set identifier (BSSID), 374, 375

Broadcast, 6, 38, 59, 61, 62, 64, 69, 70, 118, 127–129, 151, 202–204, 221, 222, 224, 228, 231, 234, 237, 239, 240, 243, 258, 263, 267, 349, 351, 356, 357, 369, 379, 380, 387, 414, 459, 461, 468, 511, 514

Broadcast address, 39, 60, 64, 127, 129, 135, 137, 138, 141, 144, 151, 414, 420, 439

Broadcast domain, 6, 156, 224, 225, 237–240, 254, 386, 459

Broadcast MAC address, 226, 228

Broadcast storm, 265, 267

Bus ethernet, 222

Bus network, 2, 3, 224

C

Challenge Handshake Authentication Protocol (CHAP), 443, 445–450, 454, 467–469

Channel division, 373

Checksum, 45, 55, 57, 363, 409

Class A address, 126, 330

Class B address, 127, 198, 330

Class C address, 127, 134, 142, 147, 148, 198, 330

Class D address, 127, 128

© The Author(s) 2023
Huawei Technologies Co. , Ltd., *Data Communications and Network Technologies*,
https://doi.org/10.1007/978-981-19-3029-4

Printed in the United States
by Baker & Taylor Publisher Services